T0189159

Communications
in Computer and Information Science 2010

Rationale

The CCIS series is devoted to the publication of proceedings of computer science conferences. Its aim is to efficiently disseminate original research results in informatics in printed and electronic form. While the focus is on publication of peer-reviewed full papers presenting mature work, inclusion of reviewed short papers reporting on work in progress is welcome, too. Besides globally relevant meetings with internationally representative program committees guaranteeing a strict peer-reviewing and paper selection process, conferences run by societies or of high regional or national relevance are also considered for publication.

Topics

The topical scope of CCIS spans the entire spectrum of informatics ranging from foundational topics in the theory of computing to information and communications science and technology and a broad variety of interdisciplinary application fields.

Information for Volume Editors and Authors

Publication in CCIS is free of charge. No royalties are paid, however, we offer registered conference participants temporary free access to the online version of the conference proceedings on SpringerLink (http://link.springer.com) by means of an http referrer from the conference website and/or a number of complimentary printed copies, as specified in the official acceptance email of the event.

CCIS proceedings can be published in time for distribution at conferences or as postproceedings, and delivered in the form of printed books and/or electronically as USBs and/or e-content licenses for accessing proceedings at SpringerLink. Furthermore, CCIS proceedings are included in the CCIS electronic book series hosted in the SpringerLink digital library at http://link.springer.com/bookseries/7899. Conferences publishing in CCIS are allowed to use Online Conference Service (OCS) for managing the whole proceedings lifecycle (from submission and reviewing to preparing for publication) free of charge.

Publication process

The language of publication is exclusively English. Authors publishing in CCIS have to sign the Springer CCIS copyright transfer form, however, they are free to use their material published in CCIS for substantially changed, more elaborate subsequent publications elsewhere. For the preparation of the camera-ready papers/files, authors have to strictly adhere to the Springer CCIS Authors' Instructions and are strongly encouraged to use the CCIS LaTeX style files or templates.

Abstracting/Indexing

CCIS is abstracted/indexed in DBLP, Google Scholar, EI-Compendex, Mathematical Reviews, SCImago, Scopus. CCIS volumes are also submitted for the inclusion in ISI Proceedings.

How to start

To start the evaluation of your proposal for inclusion in the CCIS series, please send an e-mail to ccis@springer.com.

Harkeerat Kaur · Vinit Jakhetiya · Puneet Goyal ·
Pritee Khanna · Balasubramanian Raman ·
Sanjeev Kumar
Editors

Computer Vision and Image Processing

8th International Conference, CVIP 2023
Jammu, India, November 3–5, 2023
Revised Selected Papers, Part II

 Springer

Editors
Harkeerat Kaur
Indian Institute of Technology
Jammu, India

Vinit Jakhetiya
Indian Institute of Technology
Jammu, India

Puneet Goyal
Indian Institute of Technology
Ropar, India

Pritee Khanna
Indian Institute of Information Technology
Jabalpur, India

Balasubramanian Raman
Indian Institute of Technology
Roorkee, Uttarakhand, India

Sanjeev Kumar
Indian Institute of Technology
Roorkee, Uttarakhand, India

ISSN 1865-0929   ISSN 1865-0937 (electronic)
Communications in Computer and Information Science
ISBN 978-3-031-58173-1   ISBN 978-3-031-58174-8 (eBook)
https://doi.org/10.1007/978-3-031-58174-8

This Springer imprint is published by the registered company Springer Nature Switzerland AG
The registered company address is: Gewerbestrasse 11, 6330 Cham, Switzerland

If disposing of this product, please recycle the paper.

Preface

The 8th International Conference on Computer Vision & Image Processing (CVIP 2023), a premier annual conference focused on Computer Vision and Image Processing, was held during November 3–5, 2023 at Indian Institute of Technology Jammu (IIT Jammu), India. CVIP provides a great platform for students, academics, researchers and industry persons. Previous editions of CVIP were held at VNIT Nagpur (CVIP 2022), IIT Ropar (CVIP 2021), IIIT Allahabad (CVIP 2020), MNIT Jaipur (CVIP 2019), IIIT Jabalpur (CVIP 2018), and IIT Roorkee (CVIP 2017 and CVIP 2016). All editions of CVIP have been endorsed by the International Association for Pattern Recognition (IAPR).

This year we had paper submissions in two rounds. We received a total of 467 submissions, out of which 140 were accepted. CVIP 2023 set a benchmark as receiving the highest number of submissions in CVIP history till now. Submissions were received from almost all premier Indian institutions including IIT Kharagpur, IIT Guwahati, IIT Roorkee, IIT Delhi, IIT Bombay, IIT Kanpur, IIT Patna, IIT Goa, IIT Tirupati, IIT Varanasi, IIT Ropar, IIT Pallakad, IISC, ISI, IIIT Allahabad, IIIT Delhi, IIIT Gwalior, IIIT Jabalpur, IIIT Kanchipuram, and various NITs (Calicut, Warangal, Silchar, Delhi, Agartala) and various internationally renowned institutes such as Norwegian University of Science and Technology, Trinity College Dublin, NTU Singapore, New York University, etc. spanning over 10 different countries. A single-blind review policy was used with a minimum of three reviews per manuscript to decide acceptance or rejection. The selected papers cover various important and emerging aspects of image processing, computer vision applications and advance deep learning and machine learning techniques in the domain. The selected publications also address various practical and life-touching scenarios in the domain.

The technical program committee was led by Puneet Goyal, Pritee Khanna, Aparajita Ojha, Santosh Kumar Vipparthi (IIT Guwahati), Deepak Mishra (IIST Trivandrum), Ananda S. Chowdhury (Jadavpur University), Gaurav Bhatanagar (IIT Jodhpur), Deep Gupta (VNIT Nagpur), Ranjeet Kumar Rout (NIT Srinagar), Nidhi Goel (IGDTUW, Delhi), Rama Krishna Sai Gorthi (IIT Tirupati), Shiv Ram Dubey (IIIT Allahabad), Arvind Selwal (Central University Jammu) and Jagadeesh Kakarla (IIIT Kanchipuram). Apart from their roles as TPC members, their significant contribution along with IIT Jammu faculty members Karan Nathwani, Badri S. Subudhi, Yamuna Prasad, Ambika Shah, Gaurav Varshney, Shaifu Gupta, Samaresh Bera, Quleen Bijral, and Subhasis Bhattacharjee under the mentorship of Manoj Singh Gaur (General Chair and Director IIT Jammu) led to successful completion of the event.

CVIP 2023 was an incredible concoction of Academia, Industry and Entrepreneurship. Keynotes talks were delivered by Santanu Chaudhury (IIT Jodhpur), D. Ram Rajak (ISRO), Amal Chaturvedi (Roche), Tsachy Weissman (Stanford University), and Isao Echizen (University of Tokyo). For the first time in CVIP history a special session on Women in Computer Vision with keynote talks was given by Sushmita Mitra (ISI

Kolkata), Devi Parikh (Georgia Tech) and Geetha Manjunath (Niramai Health analytics), who have distinguished themselves in top research and entrepreneurial positions. The practical and real-life aspects of computer vision were demonstrated in special stalls set up by UNITY AR/VR, Niramai Health Analytics (a breast cancer detection device using AI and image processing), Asterbyte (emotion detection) and a special stall by IHUB Drishti (IIT Jodhpur). A challenge was also organized, Automatic Detection and Classification of Bleeding and Non-Bleeding frames in Wireless Capsule Endoscopy, with over 150 participants who took this challenge. Several technical workshops were also organized by Mathworks and UNITY AR/VR and a special tutorial on Learned Image Compression was delivered by Pulkit Tandon (Grancia) and Animesh Chaturvedi (Amazon).

CVIP 2023 presented high-quality research works with innovative ideas. To acknowledge and promote the spirit of research and participation, five different awards were announced: IAPR Best Paper Award, IAPR Best Student Paper, CVIP 2023 Best Paper Award, CVIP 2023 Best Student Paper Award and CVIP 2023 Best Poster Award. Three prizes were awarded to the challenge winners who secured first, second and third positions. Moreover, to celebrate outstanding work the committee nominated Umapada Pal, ISI Kolkata, for the CVIP 2023 Lifetime Achievement Award for his remarkable research in the field of Image Processing and Computer Vision. Also 75 travel grants were offered to partially support the travel of various participants who travelled to Jammu from near and far places.

We wish the CVIP conference series a grand success as the baton is passed to IIIT Kanchipuram for CVIP 2024 in high spirits!

November 2023

Harkeerat Kaur
Vinit Jakhetiya
Puneet Goyal
Pritee Khanna
Balasubramanian Raman
Sanjeev Kumar

Organization

Patron

B. B. Chaudhuri   ISI Kolkata, India

General Chairs

Manoj Singh Gaur   IIT Jammu, India
Santanu Choudhary   IIT Jodhpur, India
Isao Echizen   National Institute of Informatics, Japan

General Co-chairs

R. Balasubramanian   IIT Roorkee, India
Pritee Khanna   IIITDM Jabalpur, India
Yudong Zhang   University of Leicester, UK

Conference Chairs

Harkeerat Kaur   IIT Jammu, India
Vinit Jakhetiya   IIT Jammu, India
Puneet Goyal   IIT Ropar, India
Deep Gupta   VNIT Nagpur, India
Aparajita Ojha   IIITDM Jabalpur, India

Conference Co-chairs

Sanjeev Malik   IIT Roorkee, India
Partha Pritam Roy   IIT Roorkee, India
Naoufel Werghi   Khalifa University, UAE

Conference Conveners

Gaurav Bhatnagar	IIT Jodhpur, India
Subrahmanyam Murala	IIT Ropar, India
Satish K. Singh	IIIT Allahabad, India
Shiv Ram Dubey	IIIT Allahabad, India
Santosh Vipparthi	IIT Guwahati, India

Publicity Chairs

Jagadeesh Kakarla	IIITDM Kancheepuram, India
Arvind Selwal	Central University Jammu, India
Gaurav Varshney	IIT Jammu, India

Local Organization Committee

Yamuna Prasad	IIT Jammu, India
Shaifu Gupta	IIT Jammu, India
Badri Subudhi	IIT Jammu, India
Karan Nathwani	IIT Jammu, India
Samaresh Bera	IIT Jammu, India
Ambika Prasad Shah	IIT Jammu, India
Subhasis Bhattacharjee	IIT Jammu, India

Technical Program Committee

M. K. Bajpai	IIITDM Jabalpur, India
Deepak Mishra	IIST Trivandrum, India
Ananda S. Chowdhury	Jadavpur University, India
Rama Krishna Sai Gorthi	IIT Tirupati, India
M. V. Joshi	DA-IICT, India
Priyanka Singh	DA-IICT India
Ayan Seal	IIITDM Jabalpur, India
Abhinav Dhall	IIT Ropar, India
Durgesh Singh	IIITDM Jabalpur, India
Shreelekha Pandey	Thapar University, India
Nidhi Gupta	NIT Kurukshetra, India
Amal Chaturvedi	Roche, USA
Pulkit Tandon	Grancia, USA

Debashis Sen	IIT Kharagpur, India
M. Tanveer	IIT Indore, India
Surya Prakash	IIT Indore, India
Deepak Mishra	IIT Jodhpur, India
Basant Kumar	MNNIT Allahabad, India
Shubham Chandak	Amazon, USA
Ajay Mittal	UIET, Panjab University, India
Sumam David S.	NITK Surathkal, India
Shitala Prasad	IIT Goa, India
Anuj Mahajan	SMVDU Jammu, India
Mahesh R. Panicker	IIT Palakkad, India
Indukala Naladala	Apple Inc., India
Pankaj Pratap Singh	CIT Kokrajhar, India
Vishwas Rathi	NIT Kurukshetra, India

International Advisory Committee

Iman Behesti	University of Manitoba, Canada
Anil K. Jain	Michigan State University, USA
Kiran Raja	Nanyang Technological University, Singapore
Raghavendra Ramachandra	NTNU, Norway
Ondrej Krejcar	University of Hradec Kralove, Czech Republic
Bharat Biswal	New Jersey Institute of Technology, USA
Fabio Dell'Acqua	University of Pavia, Italy
K. P. Subbalakshmi	Stevens Institute of Technology, USA
Waleed H. Abdulla	University of Auckland, New Zealand
Yasushi Yamaguchi	University of Tokyo, Japan
Petia Radeva	Universitat de Barcelona, Spain
R. Venkatesh Babu	IISC Bangalore, India
Sharath Chandra Guntuku	University of Pennsylvania, USA
Shou Li	Case Western Reserve, University, USA
Gaurav Sharma	University of Rochester, USA
Rangaraj M. Rangayyan	University of Calgary, Canada
Yongmin Li	Brunel University London, UK
Phalguni Gupta	IIT Kanpur, India

Reviewers

Aashish Kumar	IIT Jammu, India
Abhimanyu Sahu	Motilal Nehru National Institute of Technology, India
Abhishek Singh Sambyal	Indian Institute of Technology Ropar, India
Aditi Palit	Indian Institute of Technology Tirupati, India
Ajay Mittal	Panjab University, India
Ajeet Verma	IIT Jammu, India
Amardeep Gupta	Amity University, India
Ambreen Sabha	Central University of Jammu, India
Amit Bhati	Indian Institute of Information Technology, Design and Manufacturing, Jabalpur, India
Amit Kumar	Indian Institute of Information Technology Kota, India
Amit Vishwakarma	Indian Institute of Information Technology, Design and Manufacturing, Jabalpur, India
Amitesh Rajput	Birla Institute of Technology & Science, Pilani, India
Angshuman Paul	Indian Institute of Technology Jodhpur, India
Anjali Gautam	Indian Institute of Technology Jodhpur, India
Ankit Bhurane	Visvesvaraya National Institute of Technology, India
Ankit Jain	National Institute of Technology Kurukshetra, India
Anuj Mahajan	Shri Mata Vaishno Devi University, India
Anuj Rai	Indian Institute of Technology Indore, India
Aravinda P. N.	Indian Institute of Technology Kharagpur, India
Arif Ahmed Sekh	XIM University, India
Arijit De	Jadavpur University, India
Arindam Sikdar	Jadavpur University, India
Arnav Bhavsar	IIT Mandi, India
Aroof Aimen	Indian Institute Of Technology Ropar, India
Arun Kumar Sivapuram	Indian Institute of Technology Tirupati, India
Ashish Gupta	Thapar University, India
Ashish Mishra	Indian Institute of Technology Madras, India
Ashish Phophalia	Indian Institute of Information Technology Vadodara, India
Ashish Tripathi	Malaviya National Institute of Technology Jaipur, India
Ashutosh Kulkarni	Indian Institute of Technology Ropar, India
Bala Venkateswarlu Isunuri	IIITDM, India

Basant Kumar	Motilal Nehru National Institute of Technology, India
Bharat Singh	Indian Institute of Information Technology Ranchi, India
Bhaskar Mukhoty	Mohamed bin Zayed University of Artificial Intelligence, UAE
Bhavana Singh	Maulana Azad National Institute of Technology Bhopal, India
Bhukya Krishna Priya	IIITDM Kancheepuram, India
Bindu Avadhani	IIITDM Kancheepuram, India
Bindu Avadhani	Amrita Vishwa Vidyapeetham, India
Chandranath Adak	Indian Institute of Technology Patna, India
Chinmaya Panigrahy	Thapar University, India
Debasis Samanta	Indian Institute of Technology Kharagpur, India
Deebha Mumtaz	IIT Jammu, India
Deep Gupta	Visvesvaraya National Institute of Technology, India
Deepak Mishra	Indian Institute of Space Science and Technology, India
Deepak Ranjan Nayak	Malaviya National Institute of Technology Jaipur, India
Deval Verma	Bennett University, India
Jagadeesh Kakarla	IIITDM Kancheepuram, India
Krishan Kumar	National Institute of Technology Kurukshetra, India
Mukesh Kumar	Indian Institute of Technology Patna, India
Palak Mahajan	Central University of Jammu, India
Rahul Nijhawan	Thapar University, India
Shiwangi Mishra	Asterbyte Software Systems Ltd., India
Soubhagya Barpanda	Vellore Institute of Technology, India
Arvind Selwal	Central University of Jammu, India
B. Surendiran	National Institute of Technology Puducherry, India
Chandra Prakash	National Institute of Technology Delhi, India
Debanjan Sadhya	Atal Bihari Vajpayee - Indian Institute of Information Technology & Management, India
Irshad Ahmad Ansari	Atal Bihari Vajpayee - Indian Institute of Information Technology & Management, India
Kirti Raj Bhatele	Rustamji Institute of Technology, India
Mohammed Javed	Indian Institute of Information Technology Allahabad, India
Parveen Kumar	National Institute of Technology Kurukshetra, India

Soumendu Chakraborty	Indian Institute of Information Technology Lucknow, India
Tusar Kanti Mishra	Manipal Institute of Technology, Manipal Academy of Higher Education, India
Vikram Pudi	Indian Institute of Technology Tirupati, India
Vishwas Rathi	Thapar University, India
Ayan Seal	IIITDM Jabalpur, India
Durgesh Singh	IIITDM Jabalpur, India
Gaurav Bhatnagar	Indian Institute of Technology Jodhpur, India
Gian Luca Foresti	University of Udine, Italy
Gorthi Rama Krishna Sai Subrahmanyam	Indian Institute Of Technology Tirupati, India
Gourav Siddhad	IIT Roorkee, India
Gulshan Sharma	Indian Institute of Technology Ropar, India
Gurinder Singh	Cleveland State University, USA
Gyan Singh Yadav	IIIT Kota, India
Hadia Kawoosa	Indian Institute of Technology Ropar, India
Harkeerat Kaur	Indian Institute of Technology Jammu, India
Indukala Naladala	Apple Co., USA
Ishrat Nazeer	National Institute of Technology Srinagar, India
Jagannath Sethi	Jadavpur University, India
Jasdeep Singh	Indian Institute of Technology Ropar, India
Jayant Mahawar	Indian Institute of Technology Jodhpur, India
Joohi Chauhan	Indian Institute of Technology Ropar, India
Joy Dhar	Indian Institute of Technology Ropar, India
Kailash Kalare	Motilal Nehru National Institute of Technology Allahabad, India
Kanchan Kashyap	VIT Bhopal University, India
Kanishka Tyagi	UHV Technologies Inc., USA
Kapil Rana	Indian Institute of Technology Ropar, India
Karan Nathwani	Indian Institute of Technology Jammu, India
Katta Ranjith	Indian Institute of Technology Ropar, India
Komuravelli Prashanth	Indian Institute of Technology Tirupati, India
Krishan Sharma	Scaledge India Pvt. Ltd., India
Krishna Kumar Mohbey	Central University of Rajasthan, India
Krishna Sumanth Vengala	Indian Institute of Technology Tirupati, India
Kushall Singh	Malaviya National Institute of Technology Jaipur, India
K. V. Sridhar	National Institute of Technology Warangal, India
Lalit Kane	MIT World Peace University, India
Mahapara Khurshid	IIT Jodhpur, India
Mahendra Gurve	Indian Institute of Technology Jammu, India

Mahesh Raveendranatha Panicker	Indian Institute of Technology Palakkad, India
Manisha Sawant	Visvesvaraya National Institute of Technology Nagpur, India
Manjunath Joshi	Dhirubhai Ambani Institute of Information and Communication Technology, India
Manoj Kumar	GLA University, India
Massimo Tistarelli	University of Sassari, Italy
Mayank Sharma	IIT Jammu, India
Meghna Kapoor	Indian Institute of Technology Jammu, India
Mohit Dua	National Institute of Technology Kurukshetra, India
Monika Khandelwal	National Institute of Technology Srinagar, India
Monika Mathur	IGDTUW, India
Monu Verma	University of Miami, USA
Mrinal Kanti Bhowmik	Tripura University, India
Muhammad Kanroo	Indian Institute of Technology Ropar, India
Mukesh Mann	Indian Institute of Information Technology Sonepat, India
Muzammil Khan	Maulana Azad National Institute of Technology, India
Nand Yadav	Indian Institute of Information Technology Allahabad, India
Neeru Rathee	MSIT, India
Neha Gour	Indian Institute of Information Technology, Design and Manufacturing, Jabalpur, India
Nidhi Goel	IGDTUW, India
Nidhi Gupta	National Institute of Technology Kurukshetra, India
Nikita Yadav	Maulana Azad National Institute of Technology, India
Nirmala Murali	IIST, India
Nitigya Sambyal	Thapar University, India
Nitin Kumar	Punjab Engineering College Chandigarh, India
Nitin Kumar	National Institute of Technology Uttarakhand, India
Nitish Kumar Mahala	Maulana Azad National Institute of Technology, India
Palak H.	Delhi Technological University, India
Palak Verma	IIT Jammu, India
Pankaj Kumar Sa	National Institute of Technology Rourkela, India
Pankaj P. Singh	Central Institute of Technology Kokrajhar, India
Partha Pratim Das	Indian Institute of Technology Kharagpur, India

Pisharody Harikrishnan Gopalakrishnan	Indian Institute of Technology Palakkad, India
Poonam Kainthura	University of Petroleum and Energy Studies, India
Poornima Thakur	Indian Institute of Information Technology, Design and Manufacturing, Jabalpur, India
Pournami P. N.	National Institute of Technology Calicut, India
Prashant Patil	Deakin University, India
Prashant Patil	Indian Institute of Technology Ropar, India
Pritee Khanna	Indian Institute of Information Technology, Design and Manufacturing, Jabalpur, India
Priyanka Kokil	Indian Institute of Information Technology, Design and Manufacturing, Jabalpur, India
Priyanka Mishra	Indian Institute of Technology Ropar, India
Protyay Dey	Indian Institute of Technology Ropar, India
Puneet Goyal	Indian Institute of Technology Ropar, India
Pushpendra Kumar	Maulana Azad National Institute of Technology Bhopal, India
R. Malmathanraj	NIT Tiruchirappalli, India
Rahul Raman	IIITDM Kancheepuram, India
Rakesh Sanodiya	Indian Institute of Information Technology Sri City, India
Ram Padhy	IIITDM Kancheepuram, India
Ramesh Kumar Mohapatra	National Institute of Technology Rourkela, India
Rameswar Panda	MIT-IBM Watson AI Lab, USA
Randheer Bagi	Thapar University, India
Ranjeet Rout	National Institute of Technology Srinagar, India
Raqib Khan	Indian Institute of Technology, India
Ravi Shanker	Indian Institute of Information Technology Ranchi, India
Ridhi Arora	IIT Roorkee, India
Rishabh Shukla	Indian Institute of Technology Jammu, India
Rohit Kumar	The Captury, Germany
Rukhmini Bandyopadhyay	University of Texas MD Anderson Cancer Center, India
S. N. Tazi	RTU, India
S. H. Shabbeer Basha	Indian Institute of Information Technology Sri City, India
Sachin Kansal	Thapar Institute of Engineering Technology, India
Sadbhawna	Indian Institute of Technology Jammu, India
Sadbhawna Thakur	Indian Institute of Technology Jammu, India
Samir Jain	IIITDM Jabalpur, India
Samridhi Singh	NIT Hamirpur, India
Sandeep Kumar	National Institute of Technology Delhi, India

Sania Bano	Indian Institute of Technology Ropar, India
Sanjay Kuanar	GIET University, India
Sankar Behera	Indian Institute of Technology Jammu, India
Santosh Vipparthi	Indian Institute of Technology Ropar, India
Santosh Mishra	Indian Institute of Technology Patna, India
Saquib Mazhar	IIT Guwahati, India
Sevakram Kumbhare	Jadavpur University, India
Shanti Chandra	Indian Institute of Information Technology Allahabad, India
Shehla Rafiq	Islamic University of Science & Technology, India
Shitala Prasad	NTU, Singapore
Shiv Ram Dubey	Indian Institute of Information Technology Allahabad, India
Shounak Chakraborty	Indian Institute of Information Technology Design and Manufacturing Kurnool, India
Shree Prakash	IIITDM Kancheepuram, India
Shruti Phutke	Indian Institute of Technology Ropar, India
Shubham Chandak	Amazon, USA
Snehasis Mukherjee	Shiv Nadar University, India
Soumi Dhar	NIT Silchar, India
Sree Rama Vamsidhar S.	Indian Institute of Technology Tirupati, India
Subin Sahayam	Shiv Nadar University, India
Sukrit Gupta	Hasso Plattner Institute, Germany
Sumam David S.	National Institute of Technology Karnataka, India
Surabhi Narayan	PES University, India
Surbhi Madan	Indian Institute of Technology Ropar, India
Surinder Singh	Central University of Jammu, India
Sushanta Sahu	Jadavpur University
Swalpa Kumar Roy	Alipurduar Government Engineering and Management College, India
Tajamul Ashraf	Indian Institute of Technology Delhi, India
Tanisha Gupta	Central University of Jammu, India
Tasneem Ahmed	Integral University Lucknow, India
Usma Bhat	Indian Institute of Technology Ropar, India
Vaishnavi Ravi	Indian Institute of Technology Tirupati, India
Vinayak Nageli	DRDO, India
Vipin Kamble	Visvesvaraya National Institute of Technology Nagpur, India
Vishal Satpute	VNIT Nagpur, India
Vishnu Srinivasa Murthy Yarlagadda	Manipal Institute of Technology Bengaluru, India

Vivekraj K.   Indian Institute of Information Technology
                                   Dharwad, India
Watanabe Osamu   Takushoku University, Japan
Ximi Hoque   Indian Institute of Technology Ropar, India

Contents – Part II

Robustness of ConvNet to High-Frequency Image Corruptions

Arnab Banerjee[✉]

Zoom Video Communications India Pvt. Ltd, Mumbai, India
arnab.banerjee@zoom.us

Abstract. Image processing techniques such as blurring, JPEG compression are applied to natural images to meet different objectives. Additionally, corruptions such as Gaussian and shot noise appear on images due to digital fluctuations. Unfortunately, standard vision models tend to perform quite poorly under such unavoidable corruptions, *i.e.*, these models are not robust to the distribution shifts induced by these corruptions at test time. The standard approach for overcoming this issue for a known corruption is by augmenting the training data with images perturbed using the corruption of interest. Motivated by settings where the corruption might not be known during training, Gaussian noise is used as an augmentation strategy to gain robustness to high-frequency corruptions. In this paper, we try to understand its properties from a Fourier lens. However, we show that Gaussian augmentation fails to maintain robustness to few high-frequency corruptions at high severity levels. Analyzing the Fourier signature of those corruptions reveal a change in behavior - at high severity they corrupt low frequencies as well. A Gaussian-trained model loses its performance due to this change. Current augmentation strategies for low-frequency corruptions are discussed at the end.

Keywords: Fourier transform · synthetic corruptions · deep learning · data augmentation

1 Introduction

As deep neural networks (DNN) find usage in multiple application domains, there is a growing need for these models to handle out-of-distribution data. For example, an autonomous vehicle must learn to handle novel road or lighting conditions; a UAV must learn to navigate in novel weather conditions; on-device voice recognition must work well with untested accents, and so on.

A lot of research over the last decade has shown that in spite of their success, DNN models can be surprisingly "brittle". Starting with the work of Szegedy et al. [17], several works have shown a drastic reduction in the effectiveness of trained neural network models when fed with out-of-distribution data [8,14,16,18]. While

---

A part of this work done as a graduate student at University of Utah, USA.

© The Author(s), under exclusive license to Springer Nature Switzerland AG 2024
H. Kaur et al. (Eds.): CVIP 2023, CCIS 2010, pp. 1–12, 2024.
https://doi.org/10.1007/978-3-031-58174-8_1

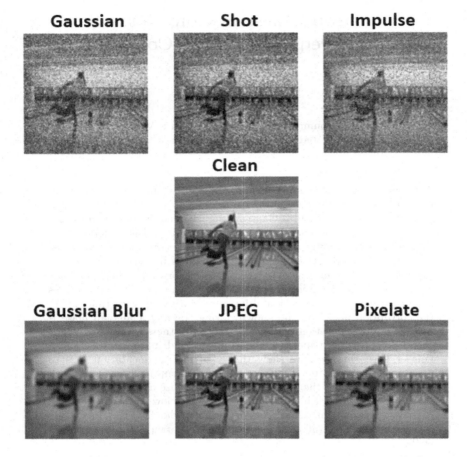

Fig. 1. Visualization of different corruptions on an example from SUN397 [20] dataset.

achieving robustness to natural distribution shifts presents an unique challenge, one may still hope that DNN models be made robust to synthetic distribution shifts/corruptions. Examples of such corruptions include blurring, JPEG compression [19] (performed automatically on many edge devices), digital noise and so on.

An effective way to deal with synthetic corruptions is to train a model via data augmentation. For example, to make a model robust to the shift introduced by JPEG compression, we simply train the model on clean images as well as JPEG compressed images with the original class labels. Augmentations like Gaussian blur, rotations, etc. are now a standard part of the training pipeline [13,23].

While the augmentation approach has been quite successful, it has a key limitation: the final model can only be expected to be robust to the *given corruption* (i.e., the one used for augmentation). But in practice, we may hope for a more general augmentation strategy which increases the robustness of the model over most commonly encountered corruptions [3,9,10,22]. In this paper, we focus on an important subset of such corruptions: high-frequency corruptions. The high-frequency corruptions studied in this paper are digital noises comprising of Gaussian, Shot, and Impulse noise. The other corruptions considered here are Gaussian Blur, JPEG compression and pixelation. These three corruption show up as image processing artifacts. Figure 1 provides a visual example of these corruptions on an image from SUN397 [20] dataset.

Following [22], we generate the Fourier signature of clean images and the above corruptions. The signatures are shown in Fig. 2. Note that the zero-frequency component is shifted to the center of the spectrum. Clean images have high Fourier intensities in low frequencies with comparative lesser Fourier information in the higher frequencies. The first three corruptions (digital corruptions) add noise uniformly and independently across the spectrum resulting in higher Fourier intensities in high-frequency regions relative to natural images. The other corruptions are designed to remove high frequencies from natural images indicated by the presence of red&yellow regions.

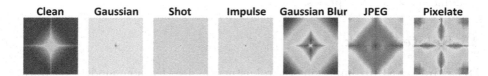

Fig. 2. Fourier signatures of different high frequency corruptions on SUN397 dataset. Given an image X and $C(X)$ being its corrupted version, the Fourier *signature* of the corruption C (with respect to the given dataset) is defined as $\mathcal{F}(C) = \mathbb{E}[\mathcal{F}(C(X) - X)]$ where the expectation is over an image drawn from the dataset, and $\mathcal{F}$ is the standard 2-dimensional DFT. In our case, the quantity $\mathcal{F}(C)$ is estimated by averaging the effect of C at severity level 3 over all test images of SUN397 dataset. Here the zero-frequency component is shifted to the center of the spectrum. Reddish (darker) regions indicate higher Fourier intensities. The intensities should not be compared between different corruptions. (Color figure online)

A simple yet effecting way of dealing with such type of corruptions is Gaussian noise data augmentation. In this method, Gaussian Noise is added to the augmentation pipeline while training a model. This makes models robust to other high-frequency corruptions. This method shows better accuracy on high frequency corruptions than a complex augmentation strategy like AutoAugment [22]. Additionally, this method is used as a baseline for the entire suite of synthetic corruptions [11,15,22]. In this paper, we analyze the robustness of a Gaussian-noise trained model to the distribution shift induced by the other corruptions. However, contrary to other works where model robustness is measured by averaging its performance over all the considered severity levels, we focus on each severity levels separately and estimate the model's robustness at those levels.

Outline and Results

1. Firstly we analyze the Fourier signature (spectrum) of Gaussian noise at different severity levels to understand the frequency changes induced by it on clean images at each severity level. Similarly, we study the Fourier signature of the other corruptions. Shot and impulse noise shows signatures similar to Gaussian. However, an important observation was that the other high-frequency corruptions do not behave like Gaussian noise. They gradually start affecting lower frequencies at higher severity levels.
2. Secondly, we estimate the fraction of high frequency energy induced by these corruptions across different severity levels. Gaussian noise and other digital noises maintain a high fraction of high frequency energy whereas other corruptions show a gradual decrease in high frequency energy as their severity increases. It confirms that those corruptions induces high amount of low frequency changes at higher severity levels.
3. Estimate the robustness of a Gaussian-trained model by testing its performance on the other corruptions. Our experiments show that the performance of the model is directly related to the fraction of high frequency energy induced by the corruptions.

2   Related Work

Distribution Shift: Improving the robustness of deep learning models to covariate shifts encountered during test time is a challenging task. In the existing literature, two kind of shifts are studied: Synthetic corruptions and natural data shift. [8] introduced a set of common synthetic corruptions and provided benchmark datasets. Notable among them are ImageNet-C and CIFAR-10-C. Adversarial examples [4,14,17] are examples of corruption that have been extensively studied by carefully formulating synthetic test images. Measuring robustness to natural shifts in datasets has also been studied recently by [12,16,18]. The authors of those works empirically observe that most existing models and training algorithms are not robust to natural shift in data at test time.

Robustness Towards Distribution Shift: One approach towards increasing robustness was to introduce larger models coupled with data augmentation [7,8,21]. [2] observes that augmentations like Gaussian noise or adversarial noise tend to achieve robustness to some corruptions while degrading on others. Subsequently, [22] discussed the role of frequency statistics to understand the above trade-off. More complicated augmentation strategies have been developed to improve robustness across the entire suite of corruptions [1,10]. Few methods relying on self-supervised learning have been found to improve robustness [9,21]. [18] observed larger and diverse datasets help in improving generalization/ robustness towards natural data shift.

3 Gaussian Noise Augmentation: Fourier Properties and Its Robustness

This section analyses the Fourier properties of Gaussian noise. Additionally, we evaluate the robustness of a Gaussian trained model to the distribution shift induced by the other corruptions. For our experiments, different *severity* levels labeled 1 (lowest level) to 5 (highest level) are considered for each corruption. Lower severity levels correspond to less corrupted (higher quality/close to original) images while higher severity levels correspond to higher amount of corruptions on the image. The severity values for each of the corruptions have been chosen to align with the severity values used for creating ImageNet-C [8]. The associated severity values are shown in Table 1.

Table 1. Severity levels of High-Frequency corruptions

Corruption	Parameter	Level 1	Level 2	Level 3	Level 4	Level 5
Gaussian	Standard deviation	.08	.12	0.18	0.26	0.38
Shot	Mean Intensity	60	25	12	5	3
Impulse	Amount	.03	.06	.09	0.17	0.27
JPEG	Quality factor	25	18	15	10	7
Gaussian Blur	Standard deviation	1	2	3	4	6
Pixelate	Downsample	0.6	0.5	0.4	0.3	0.25

In our experiments, we consider the SUN397 [20] dataset. The SUN397 dataset contains 108,754 images of 397 categories (classes), used in the Scene UNderstanding (SUN) benchmark. The number of images varies across categories, but there are at least 100 images per category. Each image in this dataset has resolution comparable to ImageNet's. This dataset is generally used to fine-tune pre-trained models, serving as an important benchmark for a model's transfer learning performance. Recent vision models have been able to achieve accuracy of about 80% on this dataset [5]. For our experiments, the dataset was randomly split into train/test with a ratio of 0.7/0.3. A pre-trained ResNet-50 [6] model, a standard vision model publicly available on Torchvision, was finetuned with SUN397's training data. However, any other latest vision model like ResNet-18 should also suffice.

Figure 3 shows a high level diagram of the training and the inference process. During training (finetuning), Gaussian noise was introduced along with the other standard data augmentations on training images. In this operation, i.i.d Gaussian noise $\mathcal{N}(0, \sigma_t^2)$ is added to every pixel in an image in the training batch, where σ_t is chosen uniformly at random from $[0, \sigma]$. Note that different images in the batch would be corrupted with different values of σ_t. The probability of applying this operation on each image was set to 40%. For SUN397 dataset, the value of σ was chosen to be 0.4 so that the model gets trained on all severity levels (values) of Gaussian noise. At inference time, the other high frequency corruptions are introduced to images of the test set and classified using the trained model.

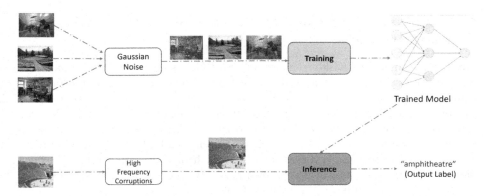

Fig. 3. Block diagram of the training and inference process of Gaussian-trained model. Note that the image for the trained model is a simplified representation of a ConvNet.

3.1 Fourier Signature Across Severity Levels

Though Fig. 2 showed the Fourier signature of Gaussian noise corruption at severity 3 only, it is also equally important to understand how this corruption behaves at increasing severity levels. Any change in its behavior may make a model non-robust unless specifically trained for those changes. Figure 4 shows the Fourier signature of Gaussian noise at all the five severity levels. It is evident that Gaussian noise remain uniformly spread across all frequencies. The increase in magnitude of the corruption is indicated by the change in color. Therefore, Gaussian noise, being an additive noise, is able to continually introduce more high frequency changes relative to the high frequency information present in clean images.

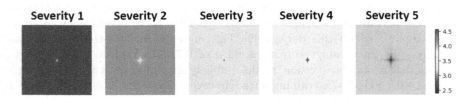

Fig. 4. Fourier signatures of Gaussian noise across all the 5 severity levels on SUN397 dataset (Color figure online)

Consequently, a model trained with Gaussian noise becomes invariant to high frequency information as it is never able to rely on high frequency information present in the images due to the added Gaussian noise. Instead, the model learns to use low frequency information to make its judgement making it robust to other high frequency corruptions at test time.

3.2 High Frequency Information in Gaussian Noise

The extent to which a particular corruption changes the high frequencies in clean images can be estimated by the fraction of high frequency energy induced by it. A high-frequency corruption should consistently maintain a significantly high fraction of energy in the higher frequencies across all severity levels. Given a clean image X and its corrupted version $C_s(X)$ where C_s is the corruption at severity level s, the fraction of high frequency energy induced by C_s can be given by $f = \frac{\|H(C_s(X)-X)\|_F^2}{\|C_s(X)-X\|_F^2}$. The $\|.\|_F$ is the Frobenius norm of a matrix and H is a square shaped high-pass filter of size 56.

Figure 5 shows the fraction of high-frequency energy for Gaussian noise. From the figure, it is evident that Gaussian noise introduces corruptions in the higher frequencies of the Fourier spectrum. Increasing the severity of Gaussian noise does not change its behavior. We discuss the high frequency information for other corruptions in Sect. 4.

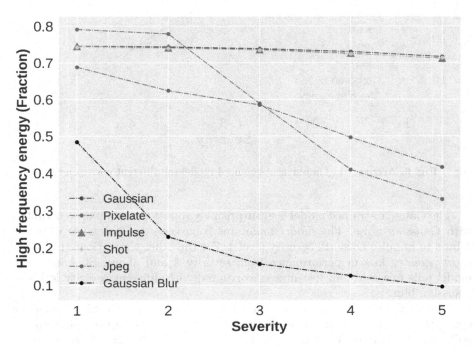

Fig. 5. Fraction of high frequency energy for different corruptions at increasing severity levels

3.3 Model Performance on Other Corruptions

Figure 6 shows the top - 1 classification accuracy of the Gaussian-trained model on the test data of SUN397 dataset. Each test image is corrupted with the other high-frequency corruptions at the defined severity levels and evaluated by the model. The horizontal line represents the accuracy of the model on clean/uncorrupted test images.

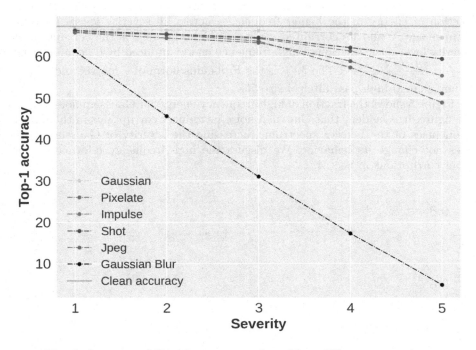

Fig. 6. Accuracy of Gaussian augmented model on different corruptions

The Gaussian-trained model is unsurprisingly robust to test images corrupted with Gaussian noise. The model maintains robustness to shot noise while its robust to impulse noise till severity level 4. For the other corruptions the model shows greater loss in performance from severity 3 and above. Strikingly, the model fails miserably on test images corrupted with different severity levels of Gaussian blur.

Summarily, though all the above corruptions are considered high frequency corruptions, a model trained to remain invariant to high-frequency corruption still fails to maintain robustness on few of them. Notably the corruptions on which the model lose performance introduce high-frequency changes by systematically removing high-frequency information from clean images. On the other hand, the corruptions on which the model perform well mostly add to the high-frequency information in clean images. In the next section, we shall analyze the Fourier signature of the remaining corruptions and try to understand the reason for the decline in performance.

4   High Frequency Corruptions Impacts Lower Frequencies

4.1   Fourier Signature of Other High-Frequency Corruptions:

Similar to Fig. 4, the Fourier signature of the other corruptions (across all severity levels) is shown in Fig. 7. Observe that the range of Fourier intensities vary among the corruptions. For example, JPEG compression's Fourier intensities are much lower than others.

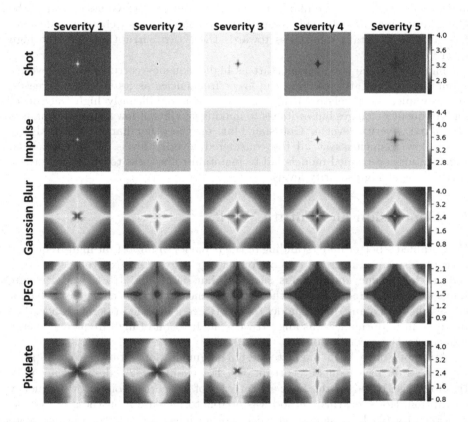

Fig. 7. Fourier signature of other corruptions across all severity levels (Color figure online)

Figure 7 clearly shows shot and impulse noise continue to affect the high frequencies uniformly albeit with a stronger intensity as the severity increases. However a noticeable change in behavior is observed for the other corruptions: Gaussian blur, pixelate and JPEG compression. They gradually start affecting the lower frequencies as their severity level increases. The center (low frequency) regions of the Fourier signatures for these corruptions shows a significant reduction in blue color at severity level 5 when compared to severity level 1. Additionally, the regions of high magnitude (red regions) moves towards the center as the severity level increases indicating that these corruptions gradually affects the lower frequencies more.

4.2   High Frequency Energy of Other High-Frequency Corruptions:

Figure 5 shows the high frequency energy for other corruptions. As shot noise and impulse noise show similar high frequency statistics as Gaussian noise, the Gaussian-trained model is able to ignore these high frequency changes and therefore able to maintain robustness towards these two corruptions even at high severity levels.

The other three corruptions start as high-frequency corruptions at severity 1 but gradually starts affecting the lower frequencies as its severity increases. For example, the pixelate corruption starts at a significantly high fraction of high frequency changes but switches to making significant low frequency changes at around severity level 4. Gaussian blur, on the other hand, almost always affects low frequencies at all the considered severity levels. As evident from Fig. 6, Gaussian-trained models fail to maintain robustness towards these three corruptions at high severity levels.

5   Conclusion and Future Work

We obtained a better understanding of the behavior of important high-frequency corruptions using the useful tool of Fourier signatures. Our experiments showed that high-frequency corruptions such as Gaussian Blur, JPEG and Pixelate impact the lower frequencies as their severity increases. This change in behavior causes the Gaussian-trained model to experience a decline in performance. The decrease in performance was aligned with the fraction of high frequency energy induced by these corruptions.

Attempts have been made to design augmentation strategies to improve robustness on low-frequency corruptions. For example, [22] designed an additive fog noise based on the Fourier statistics of fog corruption, a low-frequency corruption. However, this method was unable to increase robustness to fog corruption. [15] tried augmentation with another low-frequency corruption - contrast. Even though an increase was observed on few low-frequency corruptions such as brightness, fog but it resulted in reduced accuracy on Gaussian Blur. This shows that the benefits of low frequency augmentation are not yet fully understood and thus realizing a general low frequency augmentation should be a topic of active research. Similarly, appropriate low-frequency augmentation strategies needs to be developed for the corruptions which change behavior at high severity levels such as those we discussed in this paper.

References

1. Cubuk, E.D., Zoph, B., Mané, D., Vasudevan, V., Le, Q.V.: Autoaugment: learning augmentation policies from data. CoRR **abs/1805.09501** (2018). http://arxiv.org/abs/1805.09501
2. Ford, N., Gilmer, J., Carlini, N., Cubuk, D.: Adversarial examples are a natural consequence of test error in noise. arXiv preprint arXiv:1901.10513 (2019)
3. Geirhos, R., Rubisch, P., Michaelis, C., Bethge, M., Wichmann, F.A., Brendel, W.: ImageNet-trained CNNs are biased towards texture; increasing shape bias improves accuracy and robustness. arXiv preprint arXiv:1811.12231 (2018)
4. Goodfellow, I.J., Shlens, J., Szegedy, C.: Explaining and harnessing adversarial examples. In: Bengio, Y., LeCun, Y. (eds.) 3rd International Conference on Learning Representations, ICLR 2015, San Diego, CA, USA, May 7–9, 2015, Conference Track Proceedings (2015). http://arxiv.org/abs/1412.6572
5. Goyal, P., et al.: Vision models are more robust and fair when pretrained on uncurated images without supervision. arXiv preprint arXiv:2202.08360 (2022)
6. He, K., Zhang, X., Ren, S., Sun, J.: Deep residual learning for image recognition. In: Proceedings of the IEEE Conference on Computer Vision and Pattern Recognition, pp. 770–778 (2016)
7. Hendrycks, D., et al.: The many faces of robustness: a critical analysis of out-of-distribution generalization. In: Proceedings of the IEEE/CVF International Conference on Computer Vision, pp. 8340–8349 (2021)
8. Hendrycks, D., Dietterich, T.G.: Benchmarking neural network robustness to common corruptions and perturbations. In: 7th International Conference on Learning Representations, ICLR 2019, New Orleans, LA, USA, May 6–9, 2019. OpenReview.net (2019). https://openreview.net/forum?id=HJz6tiCqYm
9. Hendrycks, D., Mazeika, M., Kadavath, S., Song, D.: Using self-supervised learning can improve model robustness and uncertainty. In: Advances in Neural Information Processing Systems, vol. 32 (2019)
10. Hendrycks, D., Mu, N., Cubuk, E.D., Zoph, B., Gilmer, J., Lakshminarayanan, B.: AugMix: a simple data processing method to improve robustness and uncertainty. In: 8th International Conference on Learning Representations, ICLR 2020, Addis Ababa, Ethiopia, April 26–30, 2020. OpenReview.net (2020). https://openreview.net/forum?id=S1gmrxHFvB
11. Kireev, K., Andriushchenko, M., Flammarion, N.: On the effectiveness of adversarial training against common corruptions. In: Uncertainty in Artificial Intelligence, pp. 1012–1021. PMLR (2022)
12. Koh, P.W., et al.: WILDS: A benchmark of in-the-wild distribution shifts. In: Meila, M., Zhang, T. (eds.) Proceedings of the 38th International Conference on Machine Learning, ICML 2021, 18–24 July 2021, Virtual Event. Proceedings of Machine Learning Research, vol. 139, pp. 5637–5664. PMLR (2021). http://proceedings.mlr.press/v139/koh21a.html
13. Krizhevsky, A., Sutskever, I., Hinton, G.E.: ImageNet classification with deep convolutional neural networks. In: Advances in Neural Information Processing Systems, vol. 25 (2012)
14. Madry, A., Makelov, A., Schmidt, L., Tsipras, D., Vladu, A.: Towards deep learning models resistant to adversarial attacks. In: 6th International Conference on Learning Representations, ICLR 2018, Vancouver, BC, Canada, April 30 – May 3, 2018, Conference Track Proceedings. OpenReview.net (2018). https://openreview.net/forum?id=rJzIBfZAb

15. Saikia, T., Schmid, C., Brox, T.: Improving robustness against common corruptions with frequency biased models. In: 2021 IEEE/CVF International Conference on Computer Vision, ICCV 2021, Montreal, QC, Canada, October 10–17, 2021, pp. 10191–10200. IEEE (2021). https://doi.org/10.1109/ICCV48922.2021.01005

16. Santurkar, S., Tsipras, D., Madry, A.: BREEDS: benchmarks for subpopulation shift. In: 9th International Conference on Learning Representations, ICLR 2021, Virtual Event, Austria, May 3–7, 2021. OpenReview.net (2021). https://openreview.net/forum?id=mQPBmvyAuk

17. Szegedy, C., et al.: Intriguing properties of neural networks. In: Bengio, Y., LeCun, Y. (eds.) 2nd International Conference on Learning Representations, ICLR 2014, Banff, AB, Canada, April 14–16, 2014, Conference Track Proceedings (2014). http://arxiv.org/abs/1312.6199

18. Taori, R., Dave, A., Shankar, V., Carlini, N., Recht, B., Schmidt, L.: Measuring robustness to natural distribution shifts in image classification. In: Larochelle, H., Ranzato, M., Hadsell, R., Balcan, M., Lin, H. (eds.) Advances in Neural Information Processing Systems 33: Annual Conference on Neural Information Processing Systems 2020, NeurIPS 2020, December 6–12, 2020, virtual (2020). https://proceedings.neurips.cc/paper/2020/hash/d8330f857a17c53d217014ee776bfd50-Abstract.html

19. Wallace, G.K.: The jpeg still picture compression standard. IEEE Trans. Consum. Electron. **38**(1), xviii–xxxiv (1992)

20. Xiao, J., Hays, J., Ehinger, K.A., Oliva, A., Torralba, A.: Sun database: large-scale scene recognition from abbey to zoo. In: 2010 IEEE Computer Society Conference on Computer Vision and Pattern Recognition, pp. 3485–3492. IEEE (2010)

21. Xie, Q., Luong, M.T., Hovy, E., Le, Q.V.: Self-training with noisy student improves ImageNet classification. In: Proceedings of the IEEE/CVF Conference on Computer Vision and Pattern Recognition, pp. 10687–10698 (2020)

22. Yin, D., Lopes, R.G., Shlens, J., Cubuk, E.D., Gilmer, J.: A Fourier perspective on model robustness in computer vision. In: Wallach, H.M., Larochelle, H., Beygelzimer, A., d'Alché-Buc, F., Fox, E.B., Garnett, R. (eds.) Advances in Neural Information Processing Systems 32: Annual Conference on Neural Information Processing Systems 2019, NeurIPS 2019, December 8–14, 2019, Vancouver, BC, Canada, pp. 13255–13265 (2019). https://proceedings.neurips.cc/paper/2019/hash/b05b57f6add810d3b7490866d74c0053-Abstract.html

23. Zbontar, J., Jing, L., Misra, I., LeCun, Y., Deny, S.: Barlow twins: self-supervised learning via redundancy reduction. In: Meila, M., Zhang, T. (eds.) Proceedings of the 38th International Conference on Machine Learning, ICML 2021, 18–24 July 2021, Virtual Event. Proceedings of Machine Learning Research, vol. 139, pp. 12310–12320. PMLR (2021). http://proceedings.mlr.press/v139/zbontar21a.html

Automated Detection of Cracks in Asphalt Pavement Images Using Texture Descriptors and Machine Learning Classifier

R. Rakshitha[1(✉)], S. Srinath[1], N. Vinay Kumar[2], S. Rashmi[1], and B. V. Poornima[1]

[1] JSS Science and Technology University, Mysuru, India
rakshitha.r@jssstuniv.in
[2] Bangalore, India

Abstract. The cracks play a major role in deteriorating the transportation infrastructure. The maintenance of the pavement is done by the early diagnosis of crack. The manual approaches for evaluating a pavement is done by the experts which consumes more time and the occasionally produces subjective results. Hence an 2D digital road image is analyzed to detect the crack automatically. The proposed work focuses on the pre-processing the image, extracting the texture feature and classification using LGBM classifier. The texture descriptor explored here are Grey-level Co-occurrence matrix (GLCM), Local binary pattern (LBP), Gabor filter and their respective combinations for extracting the features on the non-overlapping image blocks (80 × 80 pixels) and a Light Gradient Boosting Machine (LGBM) algorithm to classify the image block containing a crack or not and then localizing the cracks. The experimentation was performed on the four standard dataset like Road Damage Dataset (RDD)-2018, Road Damage Dataset (RDD)-2019, Road Damage Dataset (RDD)-2020 and Road Damage Dataset (RDD)-2022 considering the different locations and uneven illumination condition. From the study it is figured out that Co-occurrence matrix of the LBP image with Light Gradient Boosting Machine (LGBM) Classifier gave good accuracy results. The accuracy for RDD-2018, RDD-2019, RDD 2020 and RDD 2022 dataset are 0.7707, 0.6778, 0.6227 and 0.6051 respectively. This proposed framework was successfully in identifying and localizing the cracks in a irregular texture background or uneven illumination in the pavement image based on the conventional machine learning approach which helps in the easy maintenance of the pavement.

Keywords: Crack detection · texture descriptor · Machine learning · LGBM

1 Introduction

The roads facilitate human transportation and exchange of goods. Due to increase in the heavy road traffic causes deterioration of roads, hence the early pavement maintenance is essential for the safety of the public. The resource required to maintain or repair

---

N. Vinay Kumar—Freelance Researcher.

H. Kaur et al. (Eds.): CVIP 2023, CCIS 2010, pp. 13–24, 2024.
https://doi.org/10.1007/978-3-031-58174-8_2

the road will be less compared to reconstruction of the road and hence it brings socio-economic benefit. The crack identification was done manually by the experts by being physically present. But this manual approach consumes lot of time, and experts will be put into more hazardous situations and subjectivity. In order to address the drawbacks of manual approach, the automatic recognition of cracks are developed. The automated crack detection examines the 2D digital images for localization of cracks in images.

The pavement crack detection has the subject of research by many researchers ranging from image processing to machine learning techniques, including deep learning techniques, have been presented [1]. The crack detection is complex when structure of crack is a non-uniform texture and under different illumination conditions. A crack in the image is able to identify by considering the variations in the edge characteristics, grey-scale values, the small gradient and grey-scale variation compared to image background.

Due to the advancement of machine learning (ML) and deep learning (DL) techniques there is great improvement in the automated crack detection algorithms. Several Machine learning methods are used to detect the cracks by learning the features. The Conventional Machine learning techniques requires the feature extraction stage to represent the patterns of data, and is given as input for classification algorithm to predict the new data. The crack detection task is done by both supervised and unsupervised learning techniques. The texture feature extractors are preferred because the texture feature of the road and the crack damage type are different.

Majority of recent works for crack detection are concentrating on the deep learning techniques. Deep learning a part of machine learning will learn features automatically from the data, does not require any feature extraction stage [2]. The proposed work illustrates the texture feature extraction techniques like GLCM, LBP, Gabor filter in association with machine learning classifier LGBM to detect the road cracks automatically to get the accurate detection of cracks in images. The experimentation was done to observe the performance of traditional machine learning approach for detection of crack damage type.

The remaining of the paper is organized as follows. In Sect. 2, the related work using conventional machine learning approaches (non-deep learning-based approaches) for locating the crack is discussed. In Sect. 3, the dataset and methods are presented. In Sect. 4, the Experimental results with discussion are presented. In Sect. 5 the proposed method is presented.

2 Related Work

The techniques to highlight the crack present in the image as reported in literature are based on the image processing techniques. The crack is exposed to the influence of noise caused due to the shadows, stains etc. The crack detection based on image processing approach involves 3 groups namely threshold segmentation, edge detection, region-growing. The threshold segmentation approach, the pixel intensity threshold value is used to select the pixel that belongs to the crack, the various thresholding algorithms such as Otsu threshold, adaptive iterative threshold segmentation [3–6] are employed. The drawback of these methods are they are performed on individual pixels. The edge detection method uses edge detection operators including Sobel operator, Canny operator [7], Gabor filters were used for the pavement crack detection problem [8, 9] to identify the edges of the road crack. These methods fails to perform well in complex topology. The region growing technique [10, 11] forms the region with the pixels with similar characteristics. These methods will fail if the initial seed point is not selected appropriately.

The Supervised learning techniques the pavement images are first divided into many sub-blocks and each of the block are manually labelled and trained the classifier to classify the block having crack. The feature extractors are applied to the sub-blocks and feature descriptors that provide information of crack is necessary to improve the detection accuracy of the classifier. The important distinctive feature that identifies the crack block from non-crack block are texture features [12], standard deviation and mean parameters [13]. The traditional classifier [14–18] such as KNN (K-Nearest Neighbour), RBF (Radial Basis Function), Random Forest, Bayesian DataFusion and artificial neural networks (ANNs) for crack detection with acceptable accuracy of 80 -90% and these methods are trained and tested with different datasets of varying sizes.

In recent times, deep learning methods are proposed for crack detection. The convolutional neural networks (CNN) [19–22] and its variations networks such as Alexnet [23], VGG-net, and ResNet are implemented to classify crack images. The Crack-pot method [24] combination of traditional image processing techniques and deep learning to detect potholes and cracks in the road. In [] large-scale road damage dataset (RDD-2018) that is openly available has been used to train a real-time road damage detection model based on SDD. The models such as YOLO [25] (Alfarrarjeh et al. 2018), Faster R-CNN [26] (Kluger et al. 2018), Faster R-CNN with ResNet- 152 [27] (Wang et al. 2018a), Ensemble models with Faster R-CNN and SSD [28] (Wang et al. 2018b), and RetinaNet [29] (Angulo et al.) further improves the detection performance. The progressive growing-generative adversarial networks (PG-GANs) with Poisson mixing is trained with RDD-2018 to create new training data (RDD-2019) in order to increase the accuracy of road damage detection [30]. The [31] (Arya et al. 2020, 2021b) have recently suggested a transfer learning (TL)-based road damage detection model such as EfficientDet-D7 has been used in [32] Naddaf-Sh et al. (2020), YOLO CSPDarknet53 [33] (Mandal et al. 2020), YOLO network [34] (Du et al. 2021) to identify asphalt pavement distress that takes various countries into account.

The present work proposes the model based on the conventional machine learning methods which rely on discriminative and representative hand-crafted features. These algorithms requires less computational resources for training and deployment compared to deep neural networks.

From the literature, it is reported that crack detection in varying textures and shadows or uneven light illumination conditions causes the significant challenge. The proposed work sees the pavement surface as some texture surface and detects the crack as in homogeneities occurring in the texture. The combination of texture descriptors along with the machine learning classifier was implemented to detect the crack.

The presented work has two contributions are:

- The work has presented to verify the appropriate feature extractor to separate crack and non-crack region for automatic road condition monitoring.

- The machine learning model has been built to classify the road images captured from different locations with different lightening condition are considered for finding the efficiency of the algorithm based on the features extracted.

3 Materials and Methods

Dataset
The experiment was performed initially on Road Damage Dataset-2018 (RDD-2018) called as Dataset A comprises of 9,053 road images with resolution of 600x600 pixels with 15,435 annotations. The data was collected from seven local regions of Japan like Ichihara city, Chiba city, Sumida ward, Nagakute city, Adachi ward, Muroran city, and Numazu city) by setting the smartphone on the dashboard of the car moving with a speed 40 km/h. The results are obtained by training with the training dataset of the particular locality and tested with the test images of the same locality respectively. The additional details of the dataset is available in [35].

The second dataset for the experiment considered was Road Damage Dataset-2019 (RDD 2019) called as Dataset B comprises 13,133 road images with 30,989 annotations with resolution of 600 × 600 pixels from local regions of Japan. The PG-GAN was trained on the images of RDD-2018 to increase the training dataset. The additional details of the dataset is available in [30].

The third dataset considered was Road Damage Dataset-2020 (RDD 2020) called as Dataset C comprises of 26,336 road images with 31,000 annotations from regions of India, Japan, and the Czech Republic. The training set contains 10,506 images of Japan country, 2829 images of Czech Republic country with resolution of 600 × 600 pixels and 7706 images from India country with 720 × 720 pixels. The Dataset contains test1 and test2 folder contains 1313 and 1314 images from Japan, 969 and 990 images from India, 349 and 360 images from the Czech Republic respectively. The images of India country are resized into standard size of 600 × 600 pixels. The additional details of the dataset is available in [36].

The fourth dataset considered was Road Damage Dataset-2022 (RDD 2022) called as Dataset D comprises of 47,420 images with 55,000 instance of damage type with four types of road damages. The additional details of the dataset is available in [37].

Pre-processing Method
The image will be pre-processed first to determine the Region of Interest (RoI), In this study the ROI is the road region in the image where the crack damage is located, hence the following steps are followed to extract the road region, hence significant local features around the road region are considered to reduce the computation cost in terms of storage space, and time. The local features from the road ROI region are extracted to classify the damage type of road. The resulting size of ROI varies dynamically depending upon on the region of the gray color in the image.

The following steps are followed to extract the road region from the given image of various locations of different countries.

- The RGB image is converted to HSV color space, the HSV color codes for dark_gray and light_gray are in the range of (0,0,0) to (140,140,140).

- The mask is created in the range of dark_gray and light_gray and bitwise AND operation is performed between the image and mask, then the grey colour region is segmented from the image.
- Then, apply threshold algorithm called THRESH_BINARY and THRESH_OTSU algorithm.
- After thresholding the image find the contours with the maximum area. Then get bounding rectangle co-ordinate values of x, y, w, h and crop the original image (Fig. 1).

| (a) | (b) | (c) | (d) |

Fig. 1. (a) & (c) are the pavement image, (b) & (d) are corresponding ROI road region.

After obtaining the road region as ROI from the image, the sliding widow protocol is applied to divide the ROI into non-overlapping patches. The image is partitioned into the patches Each patch is of size 64 × 64 (pixel) and 80 × 80 (pixel) was experimented and then based on the accuracy of the detection, the patch size of 80x80 pixels was considered. When the block size is smaller, then there is a increase of false positive crack detections, whereas with larger block size, the small cracks will vanish in the computation of statistical features. On an average each ROI of the image forms around 56 overlapping patches approximately and co-ordinate values along with image filename is saved.

The training patches are created by comparing with the ground truth co-ordinates value, if the patches falling inside the ground truth bounding box co-ordinate value then the patch is placed in the crack folder and the patch whose co-ordinate values outside the ground truth bounding box are placed in the Non-crack folder (Fig. 2).

| (a) | (b) |

Fig. 2. (a) Positive data (crack) (b) Negative data (Non-crack)

Feature Extraction and Classifier

The texture descriptor indicates the variation in the intensity level. The crack pixel are found to have low intensity than the neighboring region pixels, this variation in intensity level helps to separate the crack and non-crack pixel. The Gray Level Co-Occurrence Matrix (GLCM), LBP, Gabor filter are the texture feature extractor experimented in this study to calculate the texture descriptor.

Gray Level Co-Occurrence Matrix (GLCM)

GLCM is proposed by 1973 by Haralick [38]. GLCM feature extraction extracts the value of texture features from the grayscale image patch. GLCM is a matrix of size n x n with grayscale value in the range of 0 to 255, It is a matrix that counts the number of times pairs of pixels with specific values and spatial relationship exists in a image. The GLCM matrix is computed using a distance of 1, 3, 5 pixel and an angle of 0, 45, 90 in radians. We adopt 5 descriptors for texture measurements. The Energy(E), correlation (Co), dissimilarity (D), homogeneity(H), contrast (C) texture features from GLCM matrix.

Local Binary Pattern (LBP)

LBP was proposed in 1994 by Ojala et al. [39]. In our work we calculate the LBP value by considering the distance as 1 pixel with 8 pixel's circular neighbourhood. LBP code describes the local texture pattern, it returns a matrix of LBP codes where each code represents the binary pattern. The resulting matrix is converted into 1D array by computing mean in each row and column, It results in a LBP texture features of the input patch.

Gabor Filter

A Gabor filter was proposed by Dennis Gabor [40]. A Gabor kernel is a linear filter that is useful for texture analysis, edge detection, and feature extraction in images. In our work the Gabor filter creates a filter of size 5x5 size, sigma values of (1,3,5,7) as standard deviation of the Gaussian envelope, the theta value is 45 degrees orientation, lamba value is (0, np.pi, np.pi/4) which is wavelength of sinusoidal factor, gamma is aspect ratio value of (0.05, 0.5), phi is the phase offset value of 0, ktype is the datatype of the kernel considered was cv2.CV_32F. The resulting values are concatenated together to form the feature vector.

Calculate Co-Occurrence Matrix on LBP Image

The LBP image is found and then the co-occurrence matrix which represent the proability that a pair of gray levels (i,j) occurs at a distance of d along the direction θ in an image is calculated on the LBP image. Hence the co-occurrence matrix calculating for LBP image contains more information. Therefore find the GLCM matrix property values such as the Energy(E), correlation (Co), dissimilarity (D), homogeneity(H), contrast (C) are concatenated and used as descriptors for texture measurements.

Applying the Gabor Filter on LBP Image

The LBP image is found by applying LBP feature extractor. Then, the Gabor Filter calculates the texture features by convolving the LBP image with Gabor filter bank along different orientation and frequencies.

Light Gradient Boosting Machine (LGBM) Classifier

In 2017, Guolin Ke, et al. [41] introduced the Light Gradient Boosting Machine (LGBM), a high-performance ensemble machine learning algorithm. The proposed method uses

LGBM parameters as learning_rate of 0.05, boosting_type is dart objective is multi-class, metric is multi_logloss, num_leaves is 100 max_depth of 10 num_class is 4. The training was performed for 100 iterations. The LGBM classifier performs the feature classification more faster with higher accuracy when compared the XGBoost, SVM and Random Forest classifier.

4   Overview of the Framework

The target object for detection is road cracks. The automated road crack detection is done in sequence using supervised machine learning and texture features.

The procedure of training and applying the trained model to test the test images is described below:

- The Pre-processing activity is performed for the collection of road crack images, the result is the ROI of the images. The ROI of the images are divided into Non-over lapping patches of size 80×80 pixels by applying Sliding Window protocol and mark the crack and Non-crack patch of the set of images.
- For each crack and Non-crack patch compute the texture features and accordingly label the features values as crack and Non-crack.
- The labelled data is given for training to the supervised Machine learning algorithm LGBM, and model is validated by test images.
- The test images are pre-processed and divided into patches similar to training set and features are given input to the trained model.
- The model predicts the patch as crack or Non-crack.
- Once all the patches are labelled as crack and Non-crack,

  a. The input patch labelled as crack are located on the input image by drawing the rectangular bounding box.
  b. The input patch labelled as Non-crack, then the image is crack free.

5   Results and Discussion

The performance evaluation of the application of textures features for crack detection are illustrated in this section. The results are showed for Dataset A where the dataset is split into the training set and test set in the ratio of 80 and 20. Since the dataset has imbalance class distribution the Stratified sampling is done to increase the accuracy. The patches of the pre-processed images were given as input to the feature extraction methods GLCM, LBP, Gabor Filter, Co-Occurrence Matrix on LBP Image, Gabor Filter on LBP Image (Table 1).

Table 1. Performance of the various feature extractors given to the LGBM classifier.

Feature Extractor	Accuracy
Gray-Level Co-occurrence Matrix (GLCM)	0.7346
Local Binary Pattern (LBP)	0.7056
Gabor Filter	0.6821
Combination of GLCM and LBP	0.7564
Combination of GLCM and Gabor filter	0.7162
Combination of LBP and Gabor filter	0.7032
Finding of GLCM matrix of LBP image	**0.7707**
Applying Gabor Filter on LBP Image	0.7267

The Co-occurrence Matrix on LBP Image which resulted in highest accuracy is given to LGBM classifier along with Stratified 5-fold cross-validation. The detection accuracy considering the average of all 5-folds, has increased the performance by 3 to 4% overall. The overall evaluation precision, recall, F1-score are 0.7730,0.7690,0.7754 are respectively (Fig. 3).

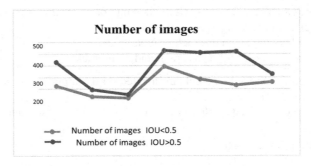

Fig. 3. Graph showing number of images having IOU value above 0.5.

The metrics called Intersection Over Union (IOU) is calculated to evaluate the performance of the crack detection model. The numerator is area of intersection and denominator is area over union between the predicted bounding box co-ordinate values and ground truth co-ordinate values. The IOU score of about 0.5 and above is considered as a good prediction (Fig. 4).

☐ Ground truth prediction   ▭ Model prediction

Fig. 4. The Sample of images with crack prediction are shown

5.1 State of Art Comparison

The results compared with existing machine learning approaches following the same train and test data split is presented in Table 2. The proposed approach performs better in terms of accuracy but requires more time than other existing methods.

Table 2. Results of the proposed model on the other datasets.

Dataset	Method	Accuracy	Inference time (sec)
Dataset A	Hiroya Maeda,2018	0.77	1.5
	Proposed Work	**0.7707**	**4.67**
Dataset B	Hiroya Maeda,2020	0.64	1.5
	Proposed Work	**0.6778**	**5.02**
	Vinuta Hegde, 2020	0.67	0.66
	Keval Doshi,2020	0.62	0.63
Dataset C	Rahul Vishwakarma,2020	0.53	0.54
	Sadra Naddaf-Sh, 2020	0.52	0.59
	Vishal Mandal,2020	0.58	0.57
	Proposed Work	**0.6227**	**0.60**
Dataset D	**Proposed Work**	**0.6051**	**0.67**

This model involves the patch of the image, hence this method is time consuming to extract the texture features and give it to the classifier but the consideration of texture features is an added advantage as it increased the accuracy of the model. The parallel execution of the feature extraction would try to reduce the time required for the execution.

6 Conclusion

This manuscript depicts the application of texture features for the classification of crack damage type. The 5 Gy-level Co-occurrence matrix features, Local Binary Pattern, Gabor Filter are the texture features considered for the crack and non-crack region classification. The proposed work is extracting the texture features from the image patch and projecting the patch's location in the image by drawing a bounding box. The pavement images were captured from different locations and various illumination conditions are considered to analyze the performance. The model exhibits an accuracy of 0.7707 for Dataset A, 0.6778 for Dataset B, 0.6227 for Dataset C and 0.6051 for Dataset D. Around 70% of the predicted bounding box gave Intersection Over Union (IOU) value more than 0.5. In recent years, higher accuracy is witnessed in Deep learning frameworks but very few reports on the implementation the traditional Machine learning based on texture features. The Co-occurrence Matrix on LBP Image feature extractor showed the highest accuracy. This study can be extended by finding the severity of the crack damage.

References

1. Cao, W., Liu, Q., He, Z.: Review of pavement defect detection methods. IEEE Access **8**, 14531–14544 (2020). https://doi.org/10.1109/aCCESS.2020.2966881
2. Hsieh, Y.-A., Tsai, Y.J., Asce, M.: Machine learning for crack detection: review and model performance comparison (2020). https://doi.org/10.1061/(ASCE)
3. Zhu, S., Xia, X., Zhang, Q., Belloulata, K.: An image segmentation algorithm in image processing based on threshold segmentation. In: Proceedings - International Conference on Signal Image Technologies and Internet Based Systems, SITIS 2007, pp. 673–678 (2007). https://doi.org/10.1109/SITIS.2007.116
4. Li, P., Wang, C., Li, S., Feng, B.: Research on crack detection method of airport runway based on twice-threshold segmentation. In: Proceedings - 5th International Conference on Instrumentation and Measurement, Computer, Communication, and Control, IMCCC 2015, Institute of Electrical and Electronics Engineers Inc., pp. 1716–1720, February 2016. https://doi.org/10.1109/IMCCC.2015.364
5. Wang, S., Tang, W.: Pavement Crack segmentation algorithm based on local optimal threshold of cracks density distribution (2011)
6. Oliveira, H., Correia, P.L.: Automatic road crack segmentation using entropy and image dynamic thresholding Segmentation Quality Evaluation View project Políticas deSaúde View project (2009). https://www.researchgate.net/publication/242091397
7. Ayenu-Prah, A., Attoh-Okine, N.: Evaluating pavement cracks with bidimensional empirical mode decomposition. EURASIP J. Adv. Sig. Process. **2008**(1), 1–7 (2008). https://doi.org/10.1155/2008/861701
8. Zalama, E., Gómez-García-Bermejo, J., Medina, R., Llamas, J.: Road crack detection using visual features extracted by Gabor filters. Comput.-Aided Civil Infrastruct. Eng. **29**(5), 342–358 (2014). https://doi.org/10.1111/mice.12042
9. Institute of Electrical and Electronics Engineers: 2013 16th International IEEE Conference on Intelligent Transportation Systems - (ITSC) : Intelligent Transportation Systems for All Modes, 6–9 October 2013, Kurhaus, The Hague, The Netherlands (2013)
10. Zhou, Y., Wang, F., Meghanathan, N., Huang, Y.: Seed-based approach for automated crack detection from pavement images. Transp. Res. Rec. **2589**, 162–171 (2016). https://doi.org/10.3141/2589-18

11. Li, Q., Zou, Q., Zhang, D., Mao, Q.: FoSA: F* Seed-growing approach for crack-line detection from pavement images. Image Vis. Comput. **29**(12), 861–872 (2011). https://doi.org/10.1016/j.imavis.2011.10.003

12. Cord, A., Chambon, S.: Automatic road defect detection by textural pattern recognition based on AdaBoost. Comput.-Aided Civil Infrastruct. Eng. **27**(4), 244–259 (2012). https://doi.org/10.1111/j.1467-8667.2011.00736.x

13. Oliveira, H., Correia, P.L.: Automatic road crack detection and characteriza-tion. IEEE Trans. Intell. Transp. Syst. **14**(1), 155–168 (2013). https://doi.org/10.1109/TITS.2012.2208630

14. Institute of Electrical and Electronics Engineers: ICIP 2014 : 2014 IEEE International Conference on Image Processing (ICIP) took place 27–30 October 2014, Paris, France (2014)

15. Sun, X., Huang, J., Liu, W., Xu, M.: Pavement crack characteristic detection based on sparse representation. EURASIP J. Adv. Signal Process. **1**, 2012 (2012). https://doi.org/10.1186/1687-6180-2012-191

16. Gavilán, M., et al.: Adaptive road crack detection system by pavement classification. Sensors **11**(10), 9628–9657 (2011). https://doi.org/10.3390/s111009628

17. Shi, Y., Cui, L., Qi, Z., Meng, F., Chen, Z.: Automatic road crack detection using random structured forests. IEEE Trans. Intell. Transp. Syst. **17**(12), 3434–3445 (2016). https://doi.org/10.1109/TITS.2016.2552248

18. Hassan, N., Mathavan, S., Kamal, K.: Road crack detection using the particle filter, pp. 1–6. https://doi.org/10.23919/IConAC.2017.8082050

19. Xu, G., Ma, J., Liu, F., Niu, X.: Automatic recognition of pavement surface crack based on BP neural network. In: Proceedings of the 2008 International Conference on Computer and Electrical Engineering, ICCEE 2008, pp. 19–22 (2008). https://doi.org/10.1109/ICCEE.2008.9

20. Li, L.I.: Automatic pavement crack recognition based on BP neural network. PROMET – Traffic Transp. **26** (2014). https://doi.org/10.7307/ptt.v26i1.1477

21. Zhang, L., Yang, F., Zhang, Y.D., Zhu, Y.J.: Road crack detection using deep convolutional neural network (2016)

22. Nhat-Duc, H., Nguyen, Q.L., Tran, V.D.: Automatic recognition of asphalt pavement cracks using metaheuristic optimized edge detection algorithms and convolution neural network. Autom. Constr. **94**, 203–213 (2018). https://doi.org/10.1016/j.autcon.2018.07.008

23. Rajadurai, R.S., Kang, S.T.: Automated vision-based crack detection on concrete surfaces using deep learning. Appl. Sci. (Switz.) **11**(11) (2021). https://doi.org/10.3390/app11115229

24. Anand, S., Gupta, S., Darbari, V., Kohli, S.: Crack-pot: autonomous road crack and pothole detection, September 2018. http://arxiv.org/abs/1810.05107

25. Abe, N., Institute of Electrical and Electronics Engineers, IEEE Computer Society: In: IEEE International Conference on Big Data : Proceedings , 10–13 December 2018, Seattle, WA, USA (2018). http://cci.drexel.edu/bigdata/bigdata2018/index

26. Kluger, F., et al.: Region-based cycle-consistent data augmentation for object detection, pp. 5205–5211 (2018). https://doi.org/10.1109/BigData.2018.8622318

27. Wang, W., Wu, B., Yang, S., Wang, Z.: Road damage detection and classification with faster R-CNN (2018). https://github.com/zhezheey/tf-faster-rcnn-rddc

28. Wang, Y.J., Ding, M., Kan, S., Zhang, S., Lu, C.: Deep Proposal and detection networks for road damage detection and classification (2018). https://github.com/shichao/DPDN_for_Road_Damage_Detection_and_Classification

29. Ochoa-Ruiz, G.: Road damage detection acquisition system based on deep neural networks for physical asset management. https://www.researchgate.net/publication/335926180

30. Maeda, H., Kashiyama, T., Sekimoto, Y., Seto, T., Omata, H.: Generative adversarial network for road damage detection. Comput.-Aided Civil Infrastruct. Eng. **36**(1), 47–60 (2021). https://doi.org/10.1111/mice.12561

31. Arya, D., et al.: Deep learning-based road damage detection and classification for multiple countries. Autom. Constr. **132** (2021). https://doi.org/10.1016/j.autcon.2021.103935
32. Naddaf-Sh, S., Naddaf-Sh, M.M., Kashani, A.R., Zargarzadeh, H.: An efficient and scalable deep learning approach for road damage detection, November 2020. http://arxiv.org/abs/2011.09577
33. Mandal, V., Mussah, A.R., Adu-Gyamfi, Y.: Deep Learning Frameworks for Pavement Distress Classification: A Comparative Analysis (2020)
34. Du, Y., Pan, N., Xu, Z., Deng, F., Shen, Y., Kang, H.: Pavement distress detection and classification based on YOLO network. Int. J. Pavement Eng. **22**(13), 1659–1672 (2021). https://doi.org/10.1080/10298436.2020.1714047
35. Maeda, H., Sekimoto, Y., Seto, T., Kashiyama, T., Omata, H.: Road damage detection and classification using deep neural networks with smartphone images. Comput.-Aided Civil Infrastruct. Eng. **33**(12), 1127–1141 (2018). https://doi.org/10.1111/mice.12387
36. Arya, D., Maeda, H., Ghosh, S.K., Toshniwal, D., Sekimoto, Y.: RDD2020: an annotated image dataset for automatic road damage detection using deep learning. Data Brief **36** (2021). https://doi.org/10.1016/j.dib.2021.107133
37. Arya, D., Maeda, H., Ghosh, S.K., Toshniwal, D., Sekimoto, Y.: RDD2022: multi-national image dataset for automatic Road Damage Detection Background and Summary. https://crddc2022.sekilab.global/
38. Haralick, R.M., Shanmugam, K., Dinstein, I.H.: Textural features for image classification. IEEE Trans. Syst. Man Cybern. **SMC-3**, 610–621 (1973)
39. Ojala, T., Pietikhen, M., Harwood, D.: Performance evaluation of texture measures with classification based on Kullback discrimination of distributions (1994)
40. Derpanis, K.G.: Gabor filters (2007)
41. Ke, G., et al.: LightGBM: A Highly Efficient Gradient Boosting Decision Tree. https://github.com/Microsoft/LightGBM
42. Hegde, V., Trivedi, D., Alfarrarjeh, A., Deepak, A., Ho Kim, S., Shahabi, C.: Yet another deep learning approach for road damage detection using ensemble learning. In: 2020 IEEE International Conference on Big Data (Big Data), Atlanta, GA,USA, pp. 5553- 5558 (2020). https://doi.org/10.1109/BigData50022.2020.9377833
43. Doshi, K., Yilmaz, Y.: Road damage detection using deep ensemble learning, October 2020. http://arxiv.org/abs/2011.00728
44. Naddaf-Sh, S., Naddaf-Sh, M.M., Kashani, A.R., Zargarzadeh, H.: An efficient and scalable deep learning approach for road damage detection, November 2020. http://arxiv.org/abs/2011.09577
45. Vishwakarma, R., Vennelakanti, R.: CNN Model & Tuning for Global Road Damage Detection. In: 2020 IEEE International Conference on Big Data (Big Data), Atlanta, GA,USA, pp. 5609–5615 (2020). https://doi.org/10.1109/BigData50022.2020.9377902

Automated BBPS Scoring in Colonoscopy: A Comparative Analysis of Pre-trained Deep Learning Architectures

Tanisha Singh[1], Palak Handa[2], and Nidhi Goel[1($\boxtimes$)]

[1] Department of ECE, IGDTUW, Delhi, India
tanisha083btece21@igdtuw.ac.in, nidhi.iitr1@gmail.com
[2] Department of ECE, DTU, Delhi, India

Abstract. Presently, an effective computer-aided system to assess the quality of bowel preparation in colonoscopy is lacking. The present work focuses on the development of automated Boston Bowel Preparation Scale (BBPS) segmental score-based classification for an accurate assessment of the quality of bowel preparation in colonoscopy. Five different deep learning architectures, namely ResNet-50, ResNet-101, MobileNet-V2, Xception, and Inception-V3, were applied to benchmark the existing dataset in this research area. A comparative analysis has been shown using various evaluation metrics, test set analysis, and interpretability plots. The results indicate that ResNet-50 achieved the highest performance, with 100% AUC, 100% F1 score, and 100% accuracy on the training data, and 96.67% AUC, 93.89% F1 score, and 93.89% accuracy on the validation data. ResNet-101, MobileNet-V2, and Xception also delivered robust results, while Inception-V3 lagged behind. The findings demonstrate the effectiveness of deep learning architectures in the automatic assessment of bowel cleanliness in colonoscopy procedures.

Keywords: Boston scoring · Transfer learning · Colonoscopy · Performance analysis

1 Introduction

Colorectal cancer (CRC) is the third most common and second most lethal cancer in the world [1]. Colonoscopy is considered the gold standard for colon cancer screening and diagnosing colonic mucosal diseases [2]. The diagnostic accuracy of a colonoscopy is dependent on meticulous visualization of the colonic mucosa, which is directly related to the quality of bowel preparation [3]. Moreover, quality indicators for colonoscopy, such as cecal intubation and adequate bowel preparation have been linked to increased Adenoma Detection Rate (ADR) and reduced risk of Post-Colonoscopy Colorectal Cancer (PCCRC) [4,5]. Despite the guidelines issued by gastrointestinal societies for optimal bowel preparation, the incidence of inadequate bowel preparation remains significantly high, estimated to be

H. Kaur et al. (Eds.): CVIP 2023, CCIS 2010, pp. 25–36, 2024.
https://doi.org/10.1007/978-3-031-58174-8_3

around 20–25% [6]. Inadequate bowel preparation can reduce the effectiveness of colonoscopy, resulting in incomplete visualization of the colorectal mucosa, higher lesion miss rates (about 22–48%), procedural difficulties, extended operation duration, shortened repeat-procedure interval time, and a 12–22% increase in procedure costs [7]. Therefore, an accurate assessment of bowel preparation quality becomes imperative.

Several known scales such as the Aronchick Scale, Ottawa Scale, Harfield Cleansing Scale, the Chicago Scale, and the Boston Bowel Preparation Scale (BBPS) have been proposed for an accurate assessment of bowel preparation [8–11]. BBPS has been found to be the most validated scoring system with proven consistent inter-observer and intra-observer agreement [12]. However, the subjective nature of bowel cleanliness assessments creates grading inconsistencies among practitioners [13,14], and the documentation of bowel preparation scores varies widely, with some reports as low as 20% across different physicians and centers [15]. This variability underscores a pressing need for a standardized, objective, and automated system. Such a system would not only enhance the accuracy of colonoscopy but also streamline the process, ensuring optimal patient outcomes and efficient resource utilization. This research aims to bridge this gap by leveraging advanced computational techniques to enhance the quality and consistency of colonoscopy evaluations.

There have been several attempts to create automated systems for the assessment of bowel preparation quality. Initially, techniques such as Logistic Regression (LR), Random Forest (RF) algorithms, and Logistic Model Trees (LMT) integrated with Global Features (GF) and Transfer Learning (TL) were deployed for predicting preparation inadequacy [16–18]. Support Vector Machines (SVM) and Convolutional Neural Network (CNN) models found applications in the analysis of Colon Capsule Endoscopy (CCE) videos [18,19]. With the recent development of more sophisticated models, Deep CNNs (DCNN) were used in this research area [20,21].

The primary objective of this work is to develop an automated BBPS segmental score-based classification for an accurate assessment of the quality of bowel preparation in colonoscopy. For this we evaluate five distinct TL architectures on the Nerthus dataset, which is used for classifying colonoscopy images based on a four-point BBPS segmental score, as outlined in Table 1. To carry out an exhaustive comparison between five existing Deep Learning architectures: Inception version three (Inception-V3), Mobile Network version two (MobileNet-V2), Residual Network (ResNet-101), ResNet-50, and Xception have been trained and evaluated to benchmark the existing dataset. Various machine learning metrics and parameters such as accuracy, F1-score, Area Under the Curve (AUC), loss, recall, precision on training and validation data, and the confusion matrix for evaluating the est set were used to report the efficacy of the aforementioned architectures. Artificial Intelligence (AI) interpretability tools, namely, Gradient-weighted Class Activation Mapping (GradCAM), Shapley Additive Explanations (SHAP), and Local Interpretable Model-agnostic Explanations (LIME) plots were utilized to facilitate the understanding and interpretation of the model's decision-making process.

The structure of the present work is as follows: Sect. 2 presents a review of the relevant existing research in this domain. Section 3 details the materials and methodologies employed. Sects. 4 and 5 highlight the achieved outcomes and provide a comparative assessment of performance. These are followed by concluding remarks and future prospects.

2   Related Works

Efficient assessment of bowel cleanliness before and during colonoscopy procedure is vital in clinical practice, as it significantly impacts the adenoma detection rate, a key indicator of CRC risk [22]. This section presents a review of recent works employing Machine Learning (ML) and Deep Learning (DL) techniques.

Low et al. [19] used a DCNN with DenseNet architecture to develop an automated method for detecting the Appendiceal Orifice (AO) during colonoscopy, irrespective of bowel preparation quality. Later Low et al. [20] developed DCNN using Dense Network (DenseNet-169) architecture to objectively assess bowel preparation adequacy and scoring. The DCNN achieved high accuracy of 91% for BBPS sub-classification and 98% for determining adequacy. A notable limitation of the author's approach stems from the class imbalance present in their dataset. Despite their efforts to mitigate this through weighted sampling, the algorithm's performance remained less than optimal for BBPS sub-classification. Wang et al. [21] used DL and the U-Net convolutional network architecture to develop an automatic segmentation method for evaluating colon preparation. The method achieved a high overlap area (94.7% ± 0.67%) with manual segmentation. Kurlander et al. [16] used LR and RF algorithms to predict inadequate bowel preparation in colonoscopy patients. Both methods showed modest predictive power, highlighting the need for more research on additional predictors and alternative ML approaches. The CNN achieved 94% accuracy and an area under the receiver operating curve of 0.98. Buijs et al. [18] developed an SVM-based ML model and a pixel analysis model to classify bowel cleansing quality in CCE videos. The SVM model outperformed the pixel analysis model. Pogorelov et al. [17] presented Nerthus, Bowel Preparation Quality Video Dataset, and explored classification methods using GF, CNNs, and TL. GF with LMT performed best, while DL showed potential but had lower performance due to inadequate parameter tuning and limited training epochs.

The above-cited research works have certain limitations. Most of them have not made use of open source datasets, which helps in generalized comparison of the achieved results in different works. Although some of the works have shown promising results, their performance can still be improved, as demonstrated by the success of DL approaches. Our work adds to the current literature by benchmarking the Nerthus dataset, the sole public dataset for bowel preparation quality assessment using advanced deep learning. While the Hyper-Kvasir dataset [23] is also public, it only covers BBPS 0–1 and BBPS 2–3 classes, limiting its utility for four-score classification. This work lays the groundwork for later developing a novel model for fully automated BBPS scoring.

3   Materials and Method

3.1   Dataset Preparation

The present work has utilized a publicly available dataset called the Nerthus [17]. It is a collection of video data with varied bowel cleanliness levels as shown in Table 1. This dataset contains a total of 21 videos, all recorded in the left portion of the large bowel, accounting for an overall total of 5,525 frames. These frames are categorized into four classes, each representing a unique BBPS score (0–3), indicating varying degrees of bowel preparation quality (Table 1). The original distribution of the dataset consisted of 500 images corresponding to a BBPS segmental score of 0, 2700 images with a score of 1, 975 images with a score of 2, and 1350 images associated with a score of 3.

For effective DL architecture training, the dataset was manually divided into three segments - training, testing, and validation, which is detailed in Table 2. To enhance data diversity and augment the data volume for model training, on-the-fly augmentation techniques were implemented on the training and validation sets. These techniques included Random Rotate, Transpose, hue saturation value, and horizontal flip. All the colonoscopy video frames were of 720 × 576 dimensions.

Figure 1(a) details a visual representation of the AI pipeline workflow, illustrating images from the dataset along with GradCAM, LIME, and SHAP interpretability plots.

3.2   Interpretability of Deep Learning Architectures

DL architectures are often criticized for their black-box nature, making it difficult to interpret their predictions [18]. To address this challenge, the present work employed LIME, SHAP, and GradCAM methods to generate interpretable images as shown in Fig. 1(b). These plots helped in providing insights into the decision-making process of the DL architectures. LIME creates a locally linear approximation of the model's behavior, enabling the identification of relevant features for a specific prediction. SHAP values offer a unified measure of feature importance by attributing a value to each feature based on its contribution to the prediction. GradCAM generates visual explanations by highlighting regions in the input image that are most relevant to the predicted class.

3.3   Transfer Learning Architecture Used in Bench-Marking

TL enables the use of pre-trained CNN models as feature extractors, improving classification performance with limited training data. The present work evaluated and compared the performance of five TL architectures, namely Inception-V3, MobileNet-V2, ResNet-50, ResNet-101, and Xception. The selection of these architectures was influenced by their proven efficacy in other medical imaging tasks and the intricacy of the classification dataset at hand.

Table 1. Description of score points used to define the degrees of bowel cleanliness on the Boston bowel preparation scale [24, 25].

Score	Description
0	Unprepared colon segment with mucosa not seen because of solid stool that cannot be cleared
1	Portion of the mucosa of the colon segment is seen, but other areas of the colon segment are not well seen due to staining, residual stool, and/or opaque liquid
2	Minor amount of residual staining, small fragments of stool, and/or opaque liquid, but mucosa of colon segment is seen well
3	Entire mucosa of colon segment seen well, with no residual staining, small fragments of stool, or opaque liquid

Table 2. Distribution of dataset in the training, validation, and test folders.

Type of data	BBPS 0	BBPS 1	BBPS 2	BBPS 3	Total
Training data	400	2600	875	1250	5125
Validation data	50	50	50	50	200
Test data	50	50	50	50	200

Inception-V3 Inception-V3 is an extended network of the well-known Google Network (GoogLeNet) [26], which has obtained good classification performance in a variety of biomedical applications by utilizing TL [27]. The Inception-V3 network contains 6 convolutional layers, 2 pooling layers, and 3 inception modules with 22 million trainable parameters, allowing for multi-scale feature extraction and complex pattern recognition in images.

MobileNet-V2 MobileNetV2, a CNN architecture, introduces a bottleneck depth-separable convolution with residuals. It comprises an initial convolution layer followed by 19 residual bottleneck layers, with consistent expansion rates across the network. MobileNetV2 optimizes robustness with ReLU6 non-linearity and fine-tunes performance via hyper-parameters, leading to efficient computational cost and parameter usage.

ResNet-101 ResNet-101 is a DL architecture with 101 layers. It introduces residual learning with identity shortcuts to address the degradation problem. With 33 residual blocks, it achieves higher model capacity for complex learning tasks while maintaining computational efficiency.

ResNet-50 Residual Network-50 introduced in 2015 [28] is a CNN architecture composed of 50 layers, 48 of which are convolutional layers, with a MaxPool and average pool layer. It implements residual connections, which facilitate the learning of residual functions. This helps in mitigating the vanishing gradient problem and enhancing model performance, convergence rate, and parameter efficiency.

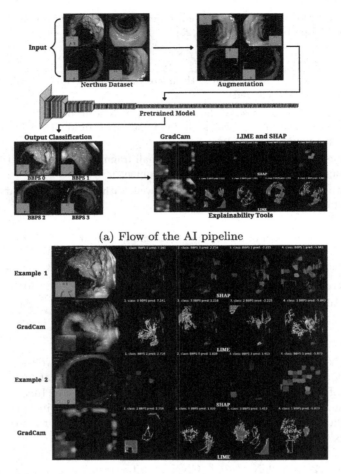

(a) Flow of the AI pipeline

(b) Examples of interpretable images generated using GradCAM, SHAP and LIME methods.

Fig. 1. Overview of the AI pipeline and examples of interpretable images produced by GradCAM, SHAP, and LIME methods

Xception The Xception network, or 'Extreme Inception', is a CNN architecture based on depthwise separable convolutions, comprising 36 convolutional layers within 14 modules. Its unique design allows it to efficiently decouple cross-channel and spatial correlations, enhancing computational efficiency and robustness.

4   Results and Discussion

In this section, the results of the classification task using five different DL models: Inception-V3, ResNet-50, ResNet-101, MobileNet-v2, and Xception is detailed.

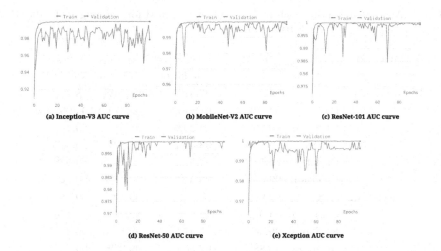

Fig. 2. AUC graphs v/s epochs for Inception-V3, MobileNet-V2, ResNet-101, ResNet-50 and Xception architectures.

An overview of the experimental setup, including the hardware and software used, as well as the training parameters and performance metrics in subsection A has been provided. In subsection B, we delve into a detailed analysis of the performance of each model, along with a discussion of the observed differences in their performance and the potential reasons behind it.

4.1   Experimental Setup

The experiments were conducted using Python scripts in Jupyter notebooks on a 40GB A100 DGX NVIDIA workstation with a pre-installed Ubuntu Linux-based system. The training dataset was batch-processed with a batch size of 16 images per epoch. To ensure reproducible results, a fixed seed was used to generate tensors. The backbone layers of the transfer learning architectures were kept frozen during training, and the top layers consisted of a flattened layer followed by a dense layer, a dropout layer, a batch normalization layer, and a final dense layer with Softmax activation for multi-class classification. The models were compiled using an SGD optimizer with a learning rate of 3e-4, a momentum of 0.8, and no Nesterov acceleration. The loss function used was categorical cross-entropy, and the performance metrics included AUC, accuracy, recall, precision, and F1 score. The prediction performance was assessed on a test set of 200 images, for which the labels were only provided during the prediction stage.

4.2   Performance Evaluation

In this work, five deep learning architectures were employed, and their performances were comparatively evaluated based on metrics such as AUC, loss, F1

Table 3. Average and last epoch metrics values obtained for training and validation data using different transfer learning architectures.

Architecture	Metric	Last Epoch Training	Last Epoch Validation	Average Training	Average Validation
Inception-V3	AUC	99.99%	97.87%	98.84%	98.29%
	Loss	0.0102	0.2813	0.0374	0.3058
	F1 Score	99.55%	93.39%	98.58%	89.47%
	Accuracy	99.61%	93.50%	98.82%	90.05%
	Recall	99.55%	93.50%	98.64%	89.54%
	Precision	99.64%	93.50%	99.01%	90.72%
MobileNet-V2	AUC	99.99%	99.85%	99.92%	99.58%
	Loss	0.0042	0.0859	0.0221	0.1146
	F1 Score	99.86%	97.47%	99.10%	96.21%
	Accuracy	99.88%	97.50%	99.33%	96.35%
	Recall	99.88%	96.49%	99.24%	95.87%
	Precision	99.90%	97.47%	99.45%	96.79%
ResNet-101	AUC	99.99%	99.96%	99.97%	99.93%
	Loss	0.0109	0.0512	0.0127	0.0650
	F1 Score	99.70%	98.01%	99.61%	97.50%
	Accuracy	99.70%	98.00%	99.67%	96.93%
	Recall	99.70%	98.00%	99.21%	96.73%
	Precision	99.74%	98.49%	99.47%	97.63%
ResNet-50	AUC	99.98%	99.99%	99.45%	99.81%
	Loss	0.0120	0.0180	0.0162	0.0826
	F1 Score	99.69%	100%	99.47%	96.76%
	Accuracy	100%	99.67%	99.24%	96.90%
	Recall	99.61%	100%	98.73%	96.83%
	Precision	99.72%	100%	99.15%	97.05%
Xception	AUC	99.99%	99.63%	99.93%	97.54%
	Loss	0.0101	0.0464	0.0248	0.0924
	F1 Score	99.65%	98.49%	99.16%	97.53%
	Accuracy	99.70%	98.50%	99.28%	97.54%
	Recall	99.61%	97.50%	98.81%	97.82%
	Precision	99.67%	97.50%	99.14%	98.00%

score, accuracy, recall, and precision. The results of these evaluations are detailed in Table 3. Additionally, Fig. 2 provides a graphical representation of the AUC plotted against the training epochs for each model. The models were also evaluated using a test set, and the resulting confusion matrices are provided in Fig. 3.

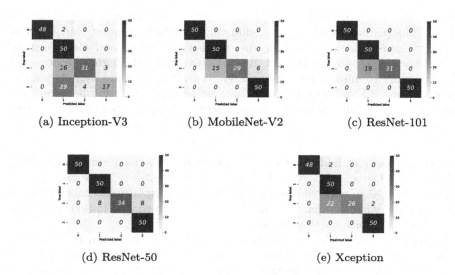

(a) Inception-V3   (b) MobileNet-V2   (c) ResNet-101

(d) ResNet-50   (e) Xception

Fig. 3. Confusion Matrix

Inception-V3 achieved a high training AUC but showed a noticeable drop in the validation AUC to 97.87%. This discrepancy, combined with a relatively high validation loss of 0.2813, suggests potential overfitting. The recall and precision values for the validation set were both 93.50% for Inception-V3, which is significantly lower than other models, showing that Inception-V3 might have a reduced capacity to generalize well on unseen data. On the test set, Inception-V3 achieved an accuracy of 73%, the lowest among the models, with 54 missed classifications, primarily in classes 2 and 3. This indicates a need for further optimization to enhance the model's performance.

MobileNet-V2 outperformed Inception-V3 with a higher validation AUC of 99.85% and a commendable accuracy of 97.50%. The recall and precision values for the validation set were 96.49% and 97.47%, respectively. On the test set, MobileNet-V2 achieved an accuracy of 89.5%, with 21 missed classifications. For class 2, there were 15 FNs (False Negative), indicating that the model had difficulty correctly identifying this class. The 6 FNs for class 3 suggest some misclassifications, but they are considerably fewer than Inception-V3.

ResNet-101 showcased a strong performance with a validation AUC of 99.96% and an accuracy of 98.00%. The recall and precision values for the validation set were 98.00% and 98.49%, respectively. On the test set, ResNet-101 achieved an accuracy of 90%, with 19 FN classifications in class 2, indicating that even this deep architecture faced challenges in distinguishing this class.

ResNet-50 stood out with an impressive AUC of 99.99% and an accuracy of 99.67%. The perfect recall and precision values of 100% suggest that ResNet-50 was the most adept at handling the imbalanced dataset and distinguishing between the classes. On the test set, ResNet-50 achieved the highest accuracy of 92%, with only 16 missed classifications. For class 2, while there were 8 FNs, the model also had 8 FPs (False Positive), suggesting some confusion between class 2 and class 3. Overall, the model demonstrated a balanced performance across all classes and making it the most promising choice for this specific dataset.

Xception achieved a high validation AUC of 99.63% and an accuracy of 98.50%, with recall and precision values of 97.50%. On the test set, Xception achieved an accuracy of 87%, with 26 missed classifications, primarily in classes 2 and 3. These metrics, when compared to ResNet-50, indicate that Xception might not be the optimal choice for this dataset.

In summary, all models demonstrated proficient classification for classes 0, 1, and 3. However, consistent challenges arose in distinguishing class 2 across every architecture. This underscores the intrinsic complexity of the dataset, as even manual examination found it challenging to differentiate certain images of class 2 from classes 1 and 3. While the classification model has demonstrated high accuracy, further research is needed to optimize the top-performing architectures and explore techniques to better address the class imbalance problem.

5   Conclusion

In this work, five DL architectures were evaluated for the computer-aided assessment of bowel preparation quality in colonoscopy images. The results showed that ResNet-50 achieved the highest performance, followed by ResNet-101, MobileNet-V2, Xception, and Inception-V3. These findings highlight the potential of deep learning models in objectively assessing bowel cleanliness and optimizing colonoscopy procedures. Further research and development in this area could lead to the implementation of automated systems that improve diagnostic accuracy, reduce costs, and enhance patient care in colorectal cancer screening and surveillance. Future prospects include the development of a second dataset in this area and a novel model for fully automated BBPS scoring [29].

References

1. Erratum: global cancer statistics 2018: Globocan estimates of incidence and mortality worldwide for 36 cancers in 185 countries. CA Cancer J. Clin. **70**(4), 313–313 (2020)
2. K. Davidson, et al.: Screening for colorectal cancer: Us preventive services task force recommendation statement. JAMA J. Am. Med. Assoc. **325**, 1965–1977 (2021)
3. Hassan, C., et al.: Bowel preparation for colonoscopy: European society of gastrointestinal endoscopy (ESGE) guideline - update 2019. Endoscopy **51**, 775–794 (2019)

4. Tollivoro, T.A. et al.: Index colonoscopy-related risk factors for postcolonoscopy colorectal cancers. Gastrointest. Endosc. **89**(03), 168–176 (2019)
5. Baxter, N.N., et al.: Analysis of administrative data finds endoscopist quality measures associated with postcolonoscopy colorectal cancer. Gastroenterology **140**, 65–72 (2011)
6. Liu, Z., Zhang, M.M., Li, Y.Y., Li, L.X., Li, Y.Q.: Enhanced education for bowel preparation before colonoscopy: a state-of-the-art review. J. Dig. Dis. **18**(2), 84–91 (2017)
7. Lebwohl, B., Kastrinos, F., Glick, M., Rosenbaum, A., Wang, T., Neugut, A.: The impact of suboptimal bowel preparation on adenoma miss rates and the factors associated with early repeat colonoscopy. Gastrointest. Endosc. **73**, 1207–1214 (2011)
8. Calderwood, A.H., Jacobson, B.C.: Comprehensive validation of the Boston bowel preparation scale. Gastrointest. Endosc. **72**, 686–692 (2010)
9. Rostom, A., Jolicoeur, E.: Validation of a new scale for the assessment of bowel preparation quality. Gastrointest. Endosc. **59**, 482–486 (2004)
10. Halphen, M., Heresbach, D., Gruss, H.-J., Belsey, J.: Validation of the Harefield cleansing scale: a tool for the evaluation of bowel cleansing quality in both research and clinical practice. Gastrointest. Endosc. **78**, 03 (2013)
11. Gerard, D., Foster, D., Raiser, M., Holden, J., Karrison, T.: Validation of a new bowel preparation scale for measuring colon cleansing for colonoscopy: the Chicago bowel preparation scale. Clin. Transl. Gastroenterol. **4**, e43 (2013)
12. Parmar, R., Martel, M., Rostom, A., Barkun, A.N.: Validated scales for colon cleansing: a systematic review. Am. J. Gastroenterol. **111**, 197–204 (2016)
13. Kastenberg, D., Bertiger, G., Brogadir, S.: Bowel preparation quality scales for colonoscopy. World J. Gastroenterol. **24**, 2833–2843 (2018)
14. Handa, P., Goel, N., Indu, S.: Automatic intestinal content classification using transfer learning architectures. In: 2022 IEEE International Conference on Electronics, Computing and Communication Technologies (CONECCT), pp. 1–5. IEEE (2022)
15. Singh, H., Kaita, L., Taylor, G., Nugent, Z., Bernstein, C.: Practice and documentation of performance of colonoscopy in a central Canadian health region. Can. J. Gastroenterol. hepatol. **28**, 185–90 (2014)
16. Kurlander, J.E., et al.: Regression and random forest machine learning have limited performance in predicting bowel preparation in veteran population. Dig. Dis. Sci. **67**, 2827–2841 (2022)
17. Pogorelov, K., et al.: Nerthus: a bowel preparation quality video dataset (2017)
18. Mangotra, H., Goel, N., et al.: Effect of selection bias on automatic colonoscopy polyp detection. Biomed. Signal Process. Control **85**, 104915 (2023)
19. Buijs, M., et al.: Assessment of bowel cleansing quality in colon capsule endoscopy using machine learning: a pilot study. Endosc. Int. Open **6**, E1044–E1050 (2018)
20. Low, D.J., Hong, Z., Khan, R., Bansal, R., Gimpaya, N., Grover, S.C.: Automated detection of cecal intubation with variable bowel preparation using a deep convolutional neural network. Endosc. Int. Open 09, E1778–E1784 (2021)
21. Low, D., Hong, Z., Jugnundan, S., Mukherjee, A., Grover, S.: Automated detection of bowel preparation scoring and adequacy with deep convolutional neural networks. J. Can. Assoc. Gastroenterol. **5**, 04 (2022)
22. Wang, Y.-P., et al.: Use of u-net convolutional neural networks for automated segmentation of fecal material for objective evaluation of bowel preparation quality in colonoscopy. Diagnostics **12**, 613 (2022)

23. Borgli, H., et al.: Hyper-Kvasir: a comprehensive multi-class image and video dataset for gastrointestinal endoscopy (2019)

24. D. Corley, et al.: Adenoma detection rate and risk of colorectal cancer and death. N. Engl. J. Med. **370**, 1298–1306 (2014)

25. Lai, E., Calderwood, A., Doros, G., Fix, O., Jacobson, B.: The Boston bowel preparation scale: a valid and reliable instrument for colonoscopy-oriented research. Gastrointest. Endosc. **69**, 620–625 (2009)

26. Szegedy, C., et al.: Going deeper with convolutions. In: 2015 IEEE Conference on Computer Vision and Pattern Recognition (CVPR), pp. 1–9 (2015)

27. Morid, M.A., Borjali, A., Fiol, G.D.: A scoping review of transfer learning research on medical image analysis using ImageNet. Comput. Biol. Med. **128**, 104115 (2020)

28. He, K., Zhang, X., Ren, S., Sun, J.: Deep residual learning for image recognition. In: 2016 IEEE Conference on Computer Vision and Pattern Recognition (CVPR), pp. 770–778 (2015)

29. Masashi Misawa, M. et al.: Development of a computer-aided detection system for colonoscopy and a publicly accessible large colonoscopy video database (with video). Gastrointest. Endosco. 93, 960–967 (2021)

Image Dehazing Based on Online Distillation

R. S. Jaisurya and Snehasis Mukherjee[✉][iD]

Shiv Nadar Institute of Eminence, Delhi NCR, India
snehasis.mukherjee@snu.edu.in

Abstract. Advanced supervised single-image dehazing models require a large number of trainable parameters and a huge amount of training data, containing a paired set of hazy images and corresponding clear images. To address this, knowledge distillation paves the way for training a small student network with the help of a larger teacher network. We propose an online distillation network for image dehazing in which, the teacher is an autoencoder network with feature attention blocks, and the student is a smaller autoencoder with fewer feature attention blocks. Specifically, the proposed model trains both the heavy Teacher network and the compact student network at the same time, with the student network learning the weights of the intermediate layers from the teacher network. The results of the experiments conducted on both indoor and outdoor datasets, demonstrate a significant improvement in performance compared to the state-of-the-art models on the basis of both image quality and fewer model parameters.

Keywords: Single image dehazing · haze removal · knowledge distillation · image restoration · online distillation

1 Introduction

Image dehazing is a task to clear the haze of an image. Haze appears in an image due to particles suspended in the medium due to fog, during capturing the image. Traditional dehazing methods rely on various image priors based on the atmospheric scattering model, which does not always translate to real-world haze, resulting in degraded image quality. Deep learning has recently achieved great success in single-image dehazing, yielding good results in terms of image aesthetics, without requiring prior knowledge [9]. The success of deep learning models can be attributed to the ability to handle a huge number of model parameters and massive amounts of data. However, due to their high computational complexity and large storage requirements, the supervised deep models are difficult to deploy on devices with limited resources, such as mobile phones and embedded devices. Distillation of the knowledge learned by a bigger model transferred to a simpler model can be a key to reducing the model's complexity while maintaining its performance of the model.

© The Author(s), under exclusive license to Springer Nature Switzerland AG 2024
H. Kaur et al. (Eds.): CVIP 2023, CCIS 2010, pp. 37–48, 2024.
https://doi.org/10.1007/978-3-031-58174-8_4

Inspired by the success of knowledge distillation in model compression [7], we propose a knowledge distillation-based network for single-image dehazing. The proposed knowledge distillation technique requires a lightweight student network (auto-encoder network with a few feature attention blocks and deformable convolution blocks) that learns the mapping from a heavy teacher network (auto-encoder network with more feature attention blocks and deformable convolution blocks). Furthermore, we use a one-stage knowledge distillation strategy known as online knowledge distillation to avoid the lengthy training time required by the highly complex teacher network. In online distillation, Both the teacher and student network are trained concurrently. As a result, unlike traditional knowledge distillation, the proposed model does not require pretraining of the teacher network, making the entire knowledge distillation framework end-to-end trainable. Our major contributions can be summarized as follows:

1. We propose an online distillation model for single-image dehazing containing a compact student network that is end-to-end trainable.
2. We include a feature attention module in the proposed lightweight student network, to enhance the quality of the dehazed image.
3. We include a deformable convolution block to the student network to deal with the variation in haze intensity.

Next, we make a survey of the literature.

2   Literature Survey and Motivation

Image dehazing is an active area of interest to researchers in the image processing field [9]. Supervised image dehazing methods can be categorized into two classes: Model-based methods and End-to-end methods.

2.1   Model Based Methods

Model-based methods restore dehazed images using an atmospheric scattering model, emphasizing the estimation of atmospheric light and transmission maps [1,2,21]. Early model-based methods estimate the transmission map using statistical priors (e.g., dark channel prior [10]) derived from haze-free images, and then recover haze-free images using an atmospheric scattering model. Borkar et al. eliminated the additional airlight component present in the haze, using the Nearest Neighbor regularizer [1]. The recent model-based methods tend to estimate transmission maps and global atmospheric light using data-driven methods [8]. For example, MSCNN [21] and DehazeNet [2] construct an efficient CNN to estimate transmission maps and produce visually appealing results. Efforts have been made by applying vision transformers in dehazing images [22]. However, atmospheric light is still estimated using traditional methods, which reduces the performance of the models. AOD-Net [16] solves this problem by combining atmospheric light and transmission map into a parameter via a linear equation.

Model-based methods, however, suffer from color and illumination changes as the atmospheric scattering model is a simplified model that cannot completely replace the haze formation process.

2.2 End-to-End Methods

End-to-end methods establish a direct mapping between hazy and clear images rather than using an atmospheric scattering model [3,13,14,16]. Because of the large difference between the intensity distributions of the hazy and clear image domains, these methods frequently improve feature extraction ability by increasing network depths and scales. GridDehazeNet [18] constructs a deep multi-scale based on a grid architecture and improves the information flow of different scales to recover haze-free images. Efforts have been made by proposing generative models for haze removal (especially, GAN) [3,6,13,14]. In [16], an encoder-decoder architecture is proposed where a shallow transformer is included between the encoder and decoder. These methods often fail to preserve the minute texture and object information in the image. A feature attention mechanism can help to preserve minute information while dehazing the image. In [20], FFA-Net is proposed with novel feature attention modules, including pixel attention and channel attention, which increased the model's adaptability by efficiently preserving the minute information. Wu et al. [23] proposed ACER-Net, which uses contrastive regularization and an autoencoder-like dehazing network along with deformable convolution to produce haze-free images. The supervised image dehazing techniques yield good results but necessitate a large collection of hazy and corresponding haze-free images, which are challenging to obtain. Furthermore, supervised learning approaches are prone to be biased toward annotation errors. The knowledge distillation approach provides the opportunity to reduce the complexity of the model, thus enhancing the ability to learn with fewer samples.

2.3 Motivation

Knowledge distillation is widely used in recent image super-resolution tasks, with the goal of transferring useful information from a heavy network to a lightweight network designed to reduce parameters while maintaining performance. The majority of knowledge distillation methods are offline. Vanilla knowledge distillation [11] involves transferring knowledge from a pre-trained teacher model to a student model. The main advantage of offline methods is their simplicity and ease of implementation. Offline distillation methods are typically based on one-way knowledge transfer and a two-phase training procedure. However, the complex high-capacity teacher model with extensive training time cannot be avoided, whereas offline distillation training of the student model is usually efficient under the guidance of the teacher model. Furthermore, there is always a capacity gap between a large teacher and a small student, and the student relies heavily on the teacher.

To overcome the limitations of offline distillation, online distillation is proposed to improve the performance of the student model even further, particularly when a large-capacity high-performance teacher model is not available. In ShuffleNet [24], multiple neural networks are proposed to work collaboratively. During the training process, any network can be the student model and other models can be the teacher. In this case, both the teacher and the student model are updated concurrently, eliminating the need for a pre-trained teacher model, and the entire knowledge distillation framework is trainable from beginning to end. There have been very few efforts in the Dehazing domain to implement knowledge distillation. In [12] knowledge distillation is applied to heterogeneous task imitation, using a complex dehazing network to guide the training of a simple dehazing network and achieving the same dehazing performance. OKDNet [15] enhanced the idea of applying online distillation for image dehazing, alongwith a multi-scale attention mechanism. Inspired by the success of the online distillation models, we propose an online distillation network for single-image dehazing. Unlike OKDNet [15], the proposed method enhances the attention mechanism following [20]. Further, the proposed method has a simple transformer network embedded inside an encoder and a decoder, making the proposed model parameterless and robust. Next, we illustrate the proposed method.

3   Proposed Model

The proposed model aims to generate clear images from hazy images, even if the haze is inconsistent across the image while maintaining the texture and structural information of the image while dehazing. The Overall Structure of the proposed model is illustrated in Fig. 1.

3.1   Online Knowledge Distillation Network

The proposed Teacher model is an autoencoder-like network consisting of an encoder, a feature transformation module, and a decoder, similar to the generator architecture of [14]. Encoder employs a 4X downsampling operation for extracting the latent features with a downsampling module consisting of a convolution layer (7 × 7 kernel, stride 1) followed by Instance Normalization and ReLU Layer and two more downsampling modules with a convolution layer (3 × 3 kernel, stride 2), Instance Normalization and ReLU Layer. Next comes the Feature transformation module which translates the features from the input domain to the target domain. We use the highly effective Feature attention (FA) block from FFA-Net 6x times [20] for performing channel-wise and pixel-wise attention mechanisms along with an improved version of the Dynamic Feature Enhancement Module from ACER-Net [23] 2x times to preserve the spatially structured information. The student model contains a reduced number of Feature Attention blocks from six to two and a Dynamic Feature Enhancement module from two to one, which makes the student model much more compact. To implement Online knowledge distillation we calculate the loss between the intermediate feature between the student and teacher model as shown in Fig. 1, and train both models simultaneously.

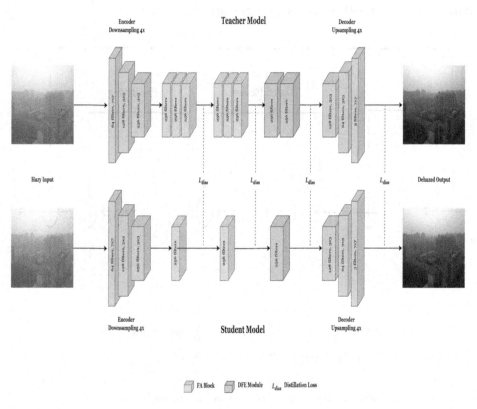

Fig. 1. Overview of the proposed Knowledge Distillation Network.

3.2   Feature Attention Module

Handling images with uneven haze distribution and weighted channel-wise features is challenging. Because most image-dehazing networks treat channel-wise and pixel-wise features equally. We use the FFA-net's [20] Feature Attention block, which consists of channel attention and a pixel attention block that treats various features and pixel regions differently, to deal with different types of feature information. The proposed feature attention module is shown in Fig. 2.

The Channel Attention (CA) block is concerned with how different channel features should be weighted differently depending on how much haze is distorting the visual information. The CA block creates a weight map of shape $C \times 1 \times 1$, which is used to assign weights adaptively, to incorporate the channel attention mechanism.

The Pixel Attention (PA) block, following the CA block, aims to deal with the uneven distribution of haze throughout the image by allowing the network to focus more on high-frequency and heavy haze regions of the image. Similar to the CA block, the PA block generates a weight map for each pixel with the dimensions $1 \times H \times W$ to be adaptively learned.

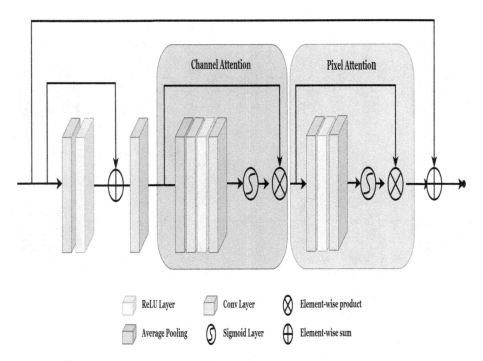

Fig. 2. Architecture of Feature Attention Module.

3.3 Dynamic Feature Enhancement

The spatially invariant convolutions often lead to generating images with corrupted textures and over-smoothing artifacts. To tackle this, we apply Dynamic Feature Enhancement (DFE) following ACER-net [23], to use the Deformable Convolution Network (DCN), to deal with corrupted image textures. Instead of using a fixed kernel, we use a DCN with grid points. Each grid point n is moved by a learnable offset $\Delta \mathbf{p}_n$, and the convolution is applied to the new grid points. First, N input features are subjected to regular convolution to produce an offset mask of $2N$ feature maps of offsets $\Delta\mathbf{p}_n$ (x-axis offset and y-axis offset). The generated offset mask is used by the DCN to perform convolution on values selected at various locations. Each location p_0 on the output feature map has a deformable convolution feature of the form $y(p_0)$.

$$y(p_0) = \sum_{p_n \in \mathcal{R}} w(p_n) \cdot x(p_0 + p_n + \Delta p_n). \tag{1}$$

We sample over the input feature map x using the regular grid $\mathcal{R}$, where p_n enumerates the location, and the sum of the sampled value is weighted by w.

3.4   Loss Functions

In our model for the overall loss function, we use the combination of L1 loss, perceptual loss, and distillation loss

$$L_{\text{loss}} = L_1 + L_{\text{per}} + L_{\text{diss}} \tag{2}$$

L1 Loss. We use L1 loss for network training rather than the L2 loss function because previous works demonstrated that pixel-to-pixel losses can quickly match the feature distribution between hazy images and clear images. Moreover, L2 loss is more sensitive to the outliers compared to L1 loss. As a result, employing L2 loss often causes a loss of minute texture information from the images while dehazing. Hence, we use L1 loss in our experiments.

$$L_1 = \|GT - J\|_1, \tag{3}$$

where GT is the ground truth clean image and J is the dehazed image produced by the proposed student model or the teacher model during training.

Perceptual Loss. We include Perceptual Loss for maintaining feature-wise consistency. We compute L1 loss on feature maps derived from the pre-trained VGG16's *2nd* and *5th* pooling layers ϕ_2 and ϕ_5, respectively.

$$\mathcal{L}_{\text{per}} = ||\phi_2(GT) - \phi_2(J)||_1 + ||\phi_5(GT) - \phi_5(J)||_1. \tag{4}$$

Distillation Loss. The teacher network guides the training of the student network by calculating the Distillation loss (L1 loss) between features from the teacher and student networks across four feature points, as shown in Fig. 1.

$$\mathcal{L}_{\text{diss}} = ||T_1 - S_1||_1 + ||T_2 - S_2||_1 + ||T_3 - S_3||_1 + ||T_4 - S_4||_1, \tag{5}$$

where T_n and S_n refers to the features extracted from the *nth* feature point of teacher and student networks, respectively.

4   Datasets and Implementation Details

We train and evaluate the proposed model on both indoor and outdoor datasets.
We first briefly describe the datasets used in this study for experiments, followed by the implementation details of the proposed method.

4.1   Datasets

For training the proposed model we use the Indoor Training Set (ITS) and Outdoor Training Set (OTS) of RESIDE Dataset [17]. The ITS Dataset contains 13990 synthetic indoor hazy images and the corresponding 1399 clear images. The OTS Dataset contains 70000 synthetic outdoor hazy images and corresponding 2061 clear images. We evaluate the proposed model on Synthetic Object Testing Set (SOTS) from RESIDE Dataset, which contains 500 indoor and outdoor hazy images.

4.2   Implementation Details

The proposed Model is implemented in PyTorch Framework on the Google Colab Platform. On both the RESIDE ITS and OTS datasets, the model is trained for 60000 iterations. We use the Adam optimizer (momentum = 0.5) with a learning rate of 0.0001 that decays to 0.00005 using cosine decay and a batch size of 1. As a pre-processing step before training, we use data augmentation by randomly cropping and scaling images to a resolution of 256×256. Subsequently, the test images are also rescaled to the same size, as well as the ground truth images, for testing with PSNR and SSIM measurements.

5   Results and Discussions

Table 1. Comparisons of the proposed method against the SOTA Models over RESIDE indoor and outdoor datasets

Method	Indoor (PSNR/SSIM)	Outdoor (PSNR/SSIM)	Parameters
DCP [10]	19.95/0.872	20.44/0.898	-
MSBDN [5]	32.67/0.983	23.16/0.936	28.7M
GridDehazeNet [18]	32.16/0.984	16.21/0.783	0.96M
FFA [20]	36.39/0.988	33.57/0.984	4.68M
PSD [4]	16.32/0.729	15.15/0.771	6.2M
Jaisurya et al. [13]	31.67/0.961	36.17/0.975	-
OKDNet [15]	30.86/0.982	23.26/0.938	2.58M
AMSFF-Net [19]	34.87/0.983	36.12/0.987	-
Ours (Teacher network)	37.14/0.985	36.72/0.987	10.2M
Ours (with KD)	**34.95/0.984**	**36.61/0.988**	**4.13M**

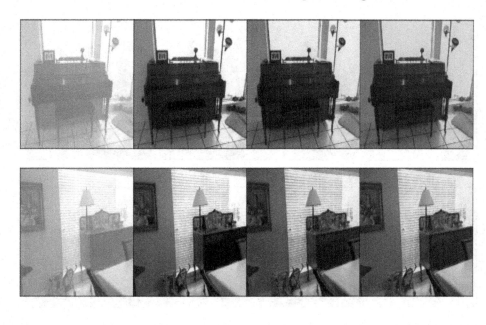

(a) Hazy Input   (b) Ground Truth   (c) Dehazed (Student with KD)   (d) Dehazed (Student w/o KD)

Fig. 3. Qualitative results over RESIDE Indoor dataset

In Table 1, we summarize the performance of our model compared to the SOTA models on RESIDE dataset, along with model parameter count comparison. We can observe that, the proposed method provides comparable results with the SOTA models, even with a much less number of parameters. Especially for outdoor datasets, the proposed model outperforms all the competing methods due to the dynamic feature enhancement mechanism. Moreover, the proposed method outperforms the existing online distillation model due to the feature attention mechanism embedded in the proposed method. The qualitative results of our model are shown in Figs. 3 and 4. We can see that our model removes most of the haze in both indoor and outdoor settings while retaining the minute structural information of the images. Especially for outdoor images the proposed student network performs very well. Further, the proposed student model can preserve the color information, as shown in the result images.

We conduct an ablation study to demonstrate the effectiveness of the proposed model. We use knowledge distillation to train the Student network. Following that, we train without knowledge distillation. The DFE module is then removed. Finally, we remove the FA module. We observe in Table 2 that each contribution to the proposed model improves the overall model's performance, particularly the inclusion of the FA module and knowledge distillation.

(a) Hazy Input   (b) Ground Truth   (c) Dehazed (Student with KD)   (d) Dehazed (Student w/o KD)

Fig. 4. Qualitative results over RESIDE Outdoor dataset

Table 2. Ablation study of the proposed model on ITS dataset.

Model	PSNR	SSIM
Student with KD	34.09	0.982
Student without KD	33.94	0.975
Student without KD and DFE	33.52	0.973
Student without KD, DFE and FA	32.54	0.973

6   Conclusion

We propose an end-to-end framework for single-image dehazing using online distillation. The proposed model could effectively reduce the model parameters while maintaining the performance on both indoor and outdoor images. Especially for outdoor images the proposed model outperforms the SOTA by a significant margin, due to the DFE module embedded in the proposed model. The proposed feature attention mechanism helps to preserve the minute texture information. Given the success of this effort of applying knowledge distillation approach for single-image dehazing, in the future, the proposed model can be experimented with a combination of online and self-distillation.

References

1. Borkar, K., Mukherjee, S.: Single image dehazing by approximating and eliminating the additional airlight component. Neurocomputing **400**, 294–308 (2020)
2. Cai, B., Xu, X., Jia, K., Qing, C., Tao, D.: DehazeNet: an end-to-end system for single image haze removal. IEEE Trans. Image Process. **25**(11), 5187–5198 (2016)
3. Chaitanya, B., Mukherjee, S.: Single image dehazing using improved cyclegan. J. Vis. Commun. Image Represent. **74**, 103014 (2021)
4. Chen, Z., Wang, Y., Yang, Y., Liu, D.: PSD: principled synthetic-to-real dehazing guided by physical priors. In: Proceedings of the IEEE/CVF Conference on Computer Vision and Pattern Recognition, pp. 7180–7189 (2021)
5. Dong, H., et al.: Multi-scale boosted dehazing network with dense feature fusion. In: Proceedings of the IEEE/CVF Conference on Computer Vision and Pattern Recognition, pp. 2157–2167 (2020)
6. Fu, M.: A Discrete Wavelet Transform GAN for NonHomogeneous Dehazing. Ph.D. thesis (2021)
7. Gou, J., Yu, B., Maybank, S.J., Tao, D.: Knowledge distillation: a survey. Int. J. Comput. Vis. **129**, 1789–1819 (2021)
8. Gui, J., et al.: A comprehensive survey and taxonomy on single image dehazing based on deep learning. ACM Comput. Surv. (2022). https://doi.org/10.1145/3576918
9. Gui, J., et al.: A comprehensive survey on image dehazing based on deep learning. In: IJCAI, pp. 4426–4433 (2021)
10. He, K., Sun, J., Tang, X.: Single image haze removal using dark channel prior. IEEE Trans. Pattern Anal. Mach. Intell. **33**(12), 2341–2353 (2010)
11. Hinton, G., Vinyals, O., Dean, J., et al.: Distilling the knowledge in a neural network, vol. 2, no. 7. arXiv preprint arXiv:1503.02531 (2015)
12. Hong, M., Xie, Y., Li, C., Qu, Y.: Distilling image dehazing with heterogeneous task imitation. In: Proceedings of the IEEE/CVF Conference on Computer Vision and Pattern Recognition, pp. 3462–3471 (2020)
13. Jaisurya, R.S., Mukherjee, S.: Attention-based single image dehazing using improved CycleGan. In: IJCNN (2022)
14. Jaisurya, R., Mukherjee, S.: AGLC-GAN: attention-based global-local cycle-consistent generative adversarial networks for unpaired single image dehazing. Image Vis. Comput. **140**, 104859 (2023)
15. Lan, Y., et al.: OKDNet: online knowledge distillation network for single image dehazing (2022)
16. Li, B., Peng, X., Wang, Z., Xu, J., Feng, D.: AOD-Net: all-in-one dehazing network. In: Proceedings of the IEEE International Conference on Computer Vision, pp. 4770–4778 (2017)
17. Li, B., et al.: Benchmarking single-image dehazing and beyond. IEEE Trans. Image Process. **28**(1), 492–505 (2018)
18. Liu, X., Ma, Y., Shi, Z., Chen, J.: GridDehazeNet: attention-based multi-scale network for image dehazing. In: Proceedings of the IEEE/CVF International Conference on Computer Vision, pp. 7314–7323 (2019)
19. Memon, S., Arain, R.H., Mallah, G.A.: AMSFF-Net: attention-based multi-stream feature fusion network for single image dehazing. J. Vis. Commun. Image Represent. **90**(2023) (2023)
20. Qin, X., Wang, Z., Bai, Y., Xie, X., Jia, H.: FFA-Net: feature fusion attention network for single image dehazing. In: Proceedings of the AAAI Conference on Artificial Intelligence, vol. 34, pp. 11908–11915 (2020)

21. Ren, W., Liu, S., Zhang, H., Pan, J., Cao, X., Yang, M.-H.: Single image dehazing via multi-scale convolutional neural networks. In: Leibe, B., Matas, J., Sebe, N., Welling, M. (eds.) ECCV 2016. LNCS, vol. 9906, pp. 154–169. Springer, Cham (2016). https://doi.org/10.1007/978-3-319-46475-6_10
22. Song, Y., He, Z., Qian, H., Du, X.: Vision transformers for single image dehazing. arXiv preprint arXiv:2204.03883 (2022)
23. Wu, H., et al.: Contrastive learning for compact single image dehazing. In: Proceedings of the IEEE/CVF Conference on Computer Vision and Pattern Recognition, pp. 10551–10560 (2021)
24. Zhang, X., Zhou, X., Lin, M., Sun, J.: ShuffleNet: an extremely efficient convolutional neural network for mobile devices. In: Proceedings of the IEEE Conference on Computer Vision and Pattern Recognition, pp. 6848–6856 (2018)

On the Application of Log Compression and Enhanced Denoising in Contrast Enhancement of Digital Radiography Images

M. S. Asif and Mahesh Raveendranatha Panicker[(✉)]

Center for Computational Imaging and Department of Electrical Engineering, Indian
Institute of Technology Palakkad, Palakkad, India
mahesh@iitpkd.ac.in
https://www.iitpkd.ac.in

Abstract. Digital radiography (DR) is becoming popular for the point
of care imaging in the recent past. To reduce the radiation exposure, controlled radiation based on as low as reasonably achievable (ALARA) principle is employed and this results in low contrast images. To address this
issue, post-processing algorithms such as the Multiscale Image Contrast
Amplification (MUSICA) algorithm can be used to enhance the contrast
of DR images even with a low radiation dose. In this study, a modification of the MUSICA algorithm is investigated to determine the potential
for further contrast improvement specifically for DR images. The conclusion is that combining log compression and its inverse at the appropriate
stage with a multi-stage MUSICA and denoising is very promising. The
proposed method resulted in an average of 66.5% increase in the mean
contrast-to-noise ratio (CNR) for the test images considered.

Keywords: Low Dose DR · Image enhancement · log compression ·
Multi-stage MUSICA

1 Introduction

One of the main issues with the digital radiography (DR) is the low contrast
of the images which will eventually affect the diagnostics adaptability. Multi
scale/frequency methods employing Laplacian pyramid and wavelets have been
quite relevant for increasing the contrast of DR images [1,2], where the former
has been shown to result in less artefacts compared to the latter [2].

The multiscale image contrast amplification (MUSICA) algorithm, based on
the laplacian pyramid concept, was introduced in [1] and pioneered by AGFA
healthcare [3]. In [4], a qualitative comparison between the second generation
MUSICA (MUSICA 2) and the third generation MUSICA (MUSICA 3) for various test images was presented, which depicts the importance of the algorithm

© The Author(s), under exclusive license to Springer Nature Switzerland AG 2024
H. Kaur et al. (Eds.): CVIP 2023, CCIS 2010, pp. 49–56, 2024.
https://doi.org/10.1007/978-3-031-58174-8_5

in the radiography world. Improvements in the non-linear function used in conventional MUSICA have also been proposed in the recent past [5].

In this work, a novel multi-stage MUSICA approach is introduced, capable of enhancing the contrast of the CT images much better than a single-stage MUSICA, with the aid of log compression and enhanced denoising. Though image enhancements by processing the image after taking log and then finally inverting the log has been done before [6], a multi-stage approach of MUSICA in the manner proposed here has not been explored before.

2   Proposed Approach

2.1   Review of MUSICA Algorithm

The original MUSICA algorithm [1] involves decomposing the input image into a multi-resolution pyramid, known as the Laplacian pyramid, that represents local details at all levels, where each layer of the pyramid is termed as a detail layer. The detail layer coefficients are subsequently transformed by employing a nonlinear function as in (1). The non-linear function has the property of increasing the magnitude of low amplitudes and decreasing the magnitude of high amplitudes of the detail coefficients. The modified detail coefficients are reconstructed back resulting in a contrast-enhanced image. Unlike contrast enhancement methods that use sliding neighborhood techniques which often lead to the production of artifacts near sudden signal changes, such as at the boundary between bone and soft tissue, this algorithm is not based on sliding neighborhoods which reduces the chances of external artifacts appearing at high contrast edges and is widely applied to DR images of chest, skull, spine, shoulder, pelvis, extremities and abdomen and finds application in non-destructive testing (NDT) industry also.

$$y(x) = \begin{cases} aM \frac{x}{x_c} \left(\frac{x_c}{M}\right)^p, & \text{if } |x| < x_c \\ aM \frac{x}{|x|} \left(\frac{|x|}{M}\right)^p, & \text{if } |x| > x_c \end{cases} \tag{1}$$
$$-M < x < M \text{ and } 0 < x_c \ll M$$

where x are the detail coefficient values, a is the global amplification factor (kept as 1 in this work), M are the upper bounds for the coefficient values. The key parameters which will affect the performance of the MUSICA algorithm are x_c and p, which represents the noise control threshold and the non-linearity in the output. The noise control threshold x_c if kept very low will amplify even granular details and hence increases the effective noise in the signal.

The non-linearity factor p is typically kept between 0.2 to 0.8 to achieve the desired result and higher the value less will be the non-linearity effect.

2.2   Proposed Approach Employing Log Compression and Enhanced Denoising

The proposed approach as shown in Fig. 1 consists of the MUSICA algorithm applied at multiple stages. The input image, normalized to the range [0, 1],

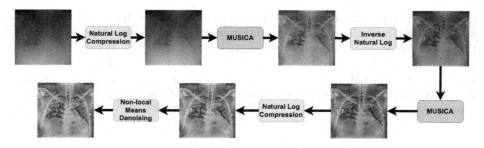

Fig. 1. Proposed framework which consists of applying MUSICA on a log compressed image followed by applying MUSICA on the enhanced inverselog image and non-local means denoising.

is pre-processed with $f(X)$ as in (2) (basically log compression) before doing contrast enhancement based on MUSICA. The choice of $ln(1 + X)$ over $ln(X)$ is due to the fact that the logarithm expression is undefined for $X = 0$.

$$f(X) = \ln(1 + X) \tag{2}$$

The purpose of $f(X)$ is to adjust the dynamic range of the input image such that the lower-intensity edges and the higher-intensity (dominating) edges are brought into the same range. After pre-processing the input image using log, the image is decomposed into aforementioned detail layers which are then modified using a nonlinear function (1) as described in [1]. The image is then reconstructed as in the typical MUSICA algorithm [1]. The dynamic range is brought back to the original dynamic range by employing (3) after the MUSICA stage.

$$f^{-1}(X) = e^X - 1 \tag{3}$$

After the MUSICA on the log compressed image, the MUSICA is again repeated on the normal scale. At the output of this stage, noise (details) may be significantly enhanced. To reduce the noise, log compression is again employed followed by the non-local means denoising algorithm [7]. This step is optional, where the degree of denoising can be controlled by changing the value of the hyperparameter h.

2.3 Evaluation Metrics - Contrast to Noise Ratio (CNR)

To evaluate the performance of the proposed approach, the contrast to noise ratio (CNR) is employed as in [8]. A CNR image is generated to quantify the contrast given for each coordinate (i, j) of the image to be evaluated as in (4).

$$CNR(i, j) = \frac{sdev_3(i, j)}{Noise_3} \tag{4}$$

where, $sdev_3(i, j)$ and $Noise_3$ denotes the standard deviation image in the third detail layer corresponding to the pixel location (i, j) and the reference noise level in that layer (computed by finding the pixel value corresponding to the maximum of the histogram of the standard deviation image, $sdev_3(i,j)$), respectively. The third detail layer is employed for the generation of the CNR image so that the contribution of the local noise can be reduced [8]. A 9×9 neighborhood window with a stride value of 1 was used for the calculation of the standard deviation image. A white region in the CNR image corresponds to a higher CNR at that specific region.

3   Results

In this work, a set of 10 DR images, corresponding to chest X-rays, were taken for the testing of the proposed algorithm from a publicly available dataset [9]. The CNR images using (4) were generated for the original image, conventional MUSICA, and the proposed framework. A comparison of the aforementioned CNR images for four of the test images is given in Fig. 2. Each row corresponds to a unique test image. For the first test image shown (Fig. 2(a)), the CNR image (Fig. 2(b)) appears to be dark, which implies a low contrast. When the same test image is processed using conventional MUSICA, the resultant CNR image (Fig. 2(c)) is brighter which shows improvement in contrast. The CNR image of the test image processed using the proposed approach appears to improve the CNR (Fig. 2(d)), implying a significant contrast increase. A similar trend is observed for other test images (Fig. 2(e)–(h), (i)–(l), (m)–(p)) as well.

The results of the proposed algorithm for four of the test images can be seen in Fig. 3. For the first test image (Fig. 3(a)), the conventional MUSICA algorithm results in a contrast-enhanced image as can be qualitatively observed in Fig. 3(b). For the same image, the proposed approach is observed to result in a better contrast enhanced image (Fig. 3(c)). A similar observation holds true for the other test images as in Fig. 3(d)–(f), (g)–(i) and (j)–(l). The number of levels of decomposition was chosen as 7 as it is stated to provide a clear separation between anatomical structures and diagnostic details [10]. The nonlinearity parameter p was taken as 0.5 at all the decomposition levels. The values for M and a chosen were both 1 and x_c was chosen as 0.01. A patch size of 7 and a search window size of 21 has been used while employing the non-local means denoising algorithm.

The proposed algorithm showed much better promise in enhancing the contrast of the original image than that of conventional MUSICA. The improvement in the CNR is further quantified in Fig. 4. The CNR images similar to as depicted in Fig. 2 was taken for all the 10 test images to obtain the box plot as shown in Fig. 4. The plot shows a consistent increase in the median CNR value across all the ten test images when processed using the proposed approach rather than when the conventional MUSICA algorithm is employed. It is also interesting to note that the standard deviation of the CNR is also much better for the proposed framework and this shows that the contrast ratio (highest to lowest contrast) is also higher for the proposed approach. The algorithm was implemented on an Intel(R) Core (TM) i5-8265U CPU (1.60 GHz) PC and takes an average of 23 s

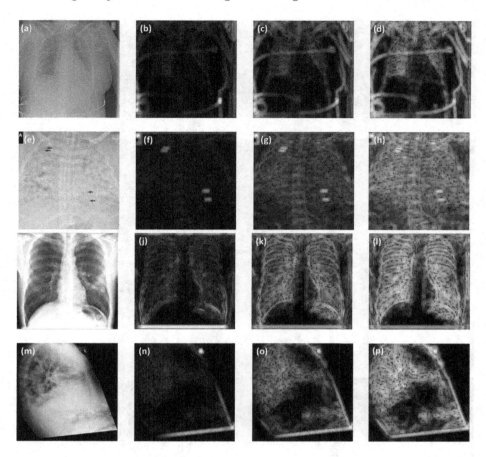

Fig. 2. Row-wise comparison among the original images (a, e, i, m) and the CNR images corresponding to the third detail layer for the original images (b, f, j, n), that of images processed using conventional MUSICA (c, g, k, o) and that of images processed using the proposed framework (d, h, l, p)

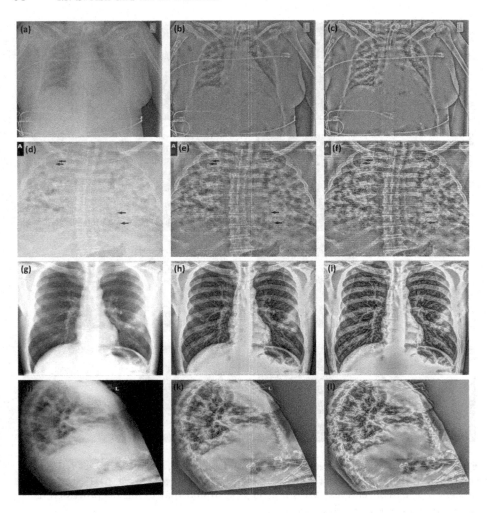

Fig. 3. Row-wise comparison among the original images (a, d, g, j), images processed using conventional MUSICA, (b, e, h, k) and that using the proposed framework (c, f, i, l)

of compute time for the 10 test images. The implementation of the proposed framework has been made open-source and is available at [11]. In the proposed approach, the parameters such as p and x_c have been assumed constant. The future work involves an accelerated optimization framework which will give the optimal values of the above parameters such that the CNR is maximized.

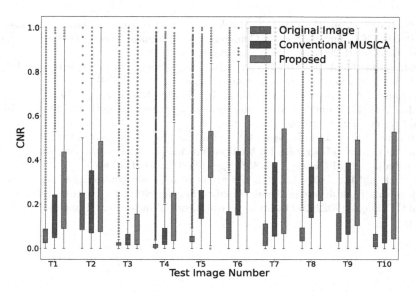

Fig. 4. A box plot for the CNR Image comparison among Original Image, Conventional MUSICA and the Proposed algorithm

4   Conclusions

A multi-stage MUSICA approach for enhancing the contrast of DR images has been proposed in this work. The proposed approach employs the MUSICA on both the log compressed image and the image at normal scale, along with non-local means based denoising. The results show that the proposed algorithm has enhanced the contrast of the input DR images, resulting in higher CNR values ($\sim$0.30 $\pm$ 0.20) compared to conventional MUSICA ($\sim$0.19 $\pm$ 0.15).

References

1. Vuylsteke, P., Schoeters, E.P.: Multiscale image contrast amplification (MUSICA). In: Medical Imaging 1994: Image Processing, vol. 2167, pp. 551–560. SPIE (1994)
2. Dippel, S., Stahl, M., Wiemker, R., Blaffert, T.: Multiscale contrast enhancement for radiographies: Laplacian pyramid versus fast wavelet transform. IEEE Trans. Med. Imaging **21**(4), 343–353 (2002)
3. Agfa-Gevaert. Agfa-musica (2022–2023). https://medimg.agfa.com/main/musica/
4. Notohamiprodjo, S., et al.: Advances in multiscale image processing and its effects on image quality in skeletal radiography. Sci. Rep. **12**(1), 4726 (2022)
5. Liu, M., Mei, S., Liu, P., Gasimov, Y., Cattani, C.: A new X-ray medical-image enhancement method based on multiscale Shannon–Cosine wavelet. Entropy **24**(12), 1754 (2022)
6. Zhang, M., Mou, X., Long, Y.: A novel contrast equalization method for chest radiograph. In: Medical Imaging 2006: Image Processing, vol. 6144, pp. 2146–2155. SPIE (2006)

7. Buades, A., Coll, B., Morel, J.-M.: A nonlocal algorithm for image denoising. In: 2005 IEEE Computer Society Conference on Computer Vision and Pattern Recognition (CVPR 2005), vol. 2, pp. 60–65. IEEE (2005)

8. Schaetzing, R.: Agfa's MUSICA2, taking image processing to the next level. http:// citeseerx.ist.psu.edu/viewdoc/summary?doi=10.1.1.129.6101

9. Cohen, J.P., Morrison, P., Dao, L., Roth, K., Duong, T.Q., Ghassemi, M.: COVID19 image data collection: prospective predictions are the future. arXiv:2006.11988 (2020)

10. Hoeppner, S., Maack, I., Neitzel, U., Stahl, M.: Equalized contrast display processing for digital radiography. In: Medical Imaging 2002: Visualization, Image-Guided Procedures, and Display, vol. 4681, pp. 617–625. SPIE (2002)

11. Panicker,M.R., Asif, M.S.: On the application of log compression and enhanced denoising in multi-stage signal amplification algorithm for contrast enhancement of CT images (2022–2023). https://github.com/WindRay123/ImageEnhancement. git

A Lightweight UNet with Inverted Residual Blocks for Diabetic Retinopathy Lesion Segmentation

Amit Bhati[1], Karan Choudhary[2], Samir Jain[1], Neha Gour[3], Pritee Khanna[1(✉)],
Aparajita Ojha[1], and Naoufel Werghi[3]

[1] PDPM Indian Institute of Information Technology, Design and Manufacturing, Jabalpur, India
pkhanna@iiitdmj.ac.in
[2] Indian Institute of Information Technology Vadodara - International Campus, Diu, India
[3] C2PS, Khalifa University, Abu Dhabi, UAE

Abstract. Diabetic Retinopathy (DR) is a progressive disease that significantly contributes to vision impairment and blindness. Its complex nature, characterized by subtle variations among different grades and the presence of numerous important small features, poses a considerable challenge for accurate recognition. Currently, the process of identifying DR relies heavily on the expertise of physicians, making it a time-consuming and labor-intensive task. However, automated detection of specific lesions plays a crucial role in visualizing, characterizing, and determining the severity of DR. Timely detection of DR in its early stages is vital for diagnosis and can potentially prevent blindness through appropriate treatment. Nonetheless, segmenting lesions in fundus imaging is a challenging task due to variations in lesion sizes, shapes, similarities, and limited contrast with other parts of the eye, leading to ambiguous results. In this work, a shallow UNet-based architecture with inverted residual skip connections is proposed to segment lesion parts of DR disease. Performance of the model is evaluated on Indian Diabetic Retinopathy Image Dataset (IDRiD) and DDR datasets. Results show that the proposed model is able to distinguish different kinds of DR lesion parts with a very less number of parameters (3.3 M).

Keywords: Diabetic Retinopathy · Lesion Segmentation · Lightweight Model · Inverted Residual Block · UNet

1 Introduction

Diabetic Retinopathy (DR) results from excess blood glucose damaging the blood vessels in the retina. It is a rapidly progressive disease that can eventually lead to blindness, if not cured at an early stage. It is possible to identify lesions and determine the severity of DR by analyzing fundus images. Lesions related to DR include microaneurysms (MA), haemorrhages (HH), soft exudates (SE), and hard exudates (HE). MA are small red dots that appear in the fundus images of DR patients because of swelling or dilation in tiny blood vessels inside the retina. HH are large red blotches that indicate bleeding in the retina due to MA rupture or injury. SE are irregular yellow-white spots, also called

H. Kaur et al. (Eds.): CVIP 2023, CCIS 2010, pp. 57–66, 2024.
https://doi.org/10.1007/978-3-031-58174-8_6

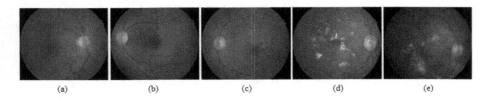

Fig. 1. Fundus images with DR severity (a) No DR, (b) Mild DR, (c) Moderate DR, (d) Severe DR, and (e) Proliferative DR [12,13].

cotton wool, that appear because of low blood flow and oxygen. SE usually cover less than a quarter of the optic disc and the back part of the fundus. HE are also yellow-white fatty deposits that leak from MA, but they are near the macula and have a clearer shape than SE.

Figure 1 showcases the progression of DR in fundus images. The progression of DR is typically categorized into four stages: mild non-proliferative, moderate non-proliferative, severe non-proliferative, and proliferative DR [2]. In the mild stage, microaneurysms occur in the retinal blood vessels. Microaneurysms are often unnoticed as they do not affect vision. The moderate stage involves multiple MA, HH, and venous beading, which impairs the blood flow to the retina. The retina shows visible changes as it does not get enough nourishment due to swollen blood vessels. In the third stage, severe non-proliferative DR, a significant portion of the blood vessels in the retina is blocked. In the severe decrease of the necessary blood flow to it, the retina sends signals to the body to grow new blood vessels. The most severe stage is proliferative DR, characterized by the development of fragile new blood vessels and scar tissue on the retinal surface, significantly increasing the risk of blood leakage and permanent vision loss.

Although DR can cause damage to the retina without exhibiting evident symptoms in its early stages, timely detection plays a crucial role in mitigating the risk of progression to advanced stages [8]. However, this task presents several challenges, including the small sizes of lesions, diverse lesion morphological structures, and similarities in color and texture between lesions and other structures like parts of the vascular tree. Currently, the detection of DR involves the manual assessment of retinal fundus images by well-trained physicians, who identify vascular abnormalities and structural changes after dilating the patient's retina. However, due to the subjective nature of manual DR screening methods, significant variability in results is observed among different physicians. Consequently, the development of automated techniques for diabetic retinopathy diagnosis becomes vital for addressing these challenges and ensuring consistent and reliable assessments.

The dual attention network proposed in this work captures contextual information for DR grading. The main contributions of this work are:

1. A lightweight UNet with inverted residual to extract DR lesion-specific contextual information.
2. Lesion-specific features are refined and passed to the decoder with inverted residual skip connections.

3. Experiments are performed on two clinically acquired benchmark datasets for multi-class DR lesion segmentation.

The paper is organized as follows. Section 2 describes related works in the area of DR lesions segmentation. Section 3 introduces the approach for residual connection based UNet. Datasets used in the model building and experimental setup are discussed in Sect. 4. Results are discussed in Sect. 5. Section 6 concludes the work with future directions.

2   Related Works

Detection of DR lesions in the early stage poses significant challenges due to their small size, which makes them hard to spot. Additionally, these lesions often have a similar color to the surrounding background, with different shapes further complicating their identification, adding to the difficulty in early detection of DR. Conventional automated DR detection systems relied on hand-crafted feature extraction and conventional machine learning algorithms for prediction. These approaches relied on manual feature extraction based on intensity, where MA and HE typically exhibit distinct intensity characteristics. Kaur and Mittal [10] employed a dynamic region-growing method to segment hard exudates by setting a threshold just below the intensity value of the reference background image. Similarly, Karkuzhali and Manimegalai [9] proposed a region-growing technique for haemorrhage segmentation, preceded by two pre-processing steps: median filtering for noise removal and uneven illumination, and Sobel operator for edge detection and gradient magnitude identification in DR images.

Imani et al. [7] pursued a similar approach based on thresholding, focusing solely on the intensity of lesions. In contrast, Van et al. [16] proposed a method to accelerate the training of Convolutional Neural Networks (CNNs) by increasing the probability of selecting false positive samples to improve the identification of HE lesions. Huang et al. [6] introduced a bounding box refining network that employed fine annotations along with corresponding coarse annotations to train a network for annotation refinement.

In recent years, modern deep learning algorithms, particularly Deep Convolutional Neural Networks (DCNNs), have achieved remarkable success in various computer vision problems [11]. DCNNs have demonstrated impressive performance in tasks such as classification and segmentation, prompting an exploration of their potential in lesion detection and segmentation for DR analysis. Sarhan et al. [15] proposed a two-stage deep learning approach for MA detection. In the first stage, a fully convolutional network was utilized to identify regions of interest (ROI). The second stage employed a CNN with triplet loss to further refine the MA detection from the ROI candidates. Adem et al. [1] employed circular Hough transformation to remove the optic disk (OD), followed by a CNN to determine the presence of exudates in the retinal image. Guo et al. [3] introduced a top-k loss and a bin loss to address class imbalances in exudate segmentation.

Instead of designing a more accurate segmentation model, Xie et al. [17] developed a comprehensive four-stage segmentation pipeline called Segmentation-Emendation-reSegmentation-Verification (SESV) to detect and refine MA. Yan et al. [18] proposed a framework that utilized both global image and local patch inputs for DR lesion segmentation. However, these individual approaches for each DR lesion type are deemed less efficient and have limited practical value. In a recent study, Huang et al. [5] proposed an innovative network that enhanced the interaction between lesions and vessels in UNet architecture by incorporating self-attention and cross-attention blocks. Despite this advancement, the study overlooked the potential influence of varying lesion scales on the segmentation performance. Similarly, Guo et al. [4] proposed a multi-scale based Fully Convolution Network (FCN). The model utilises multi-scale features to capture DR lesions of different shapes. Although the model can capture differently shaped lesion parts by using multi-scale features, high computation and memory resource requirements make it unsuitable to deploy in the resource constraint environment.

Recent research has emphasized simultaneous multi-lesion segmentation to improve efficiency and account for different lesion scales. However, challenges remain in achieving accurate segmentation results. In this work, a shallow UNet-based architecture utilizing Inverted Residual [14] Block connection is proposed, which is capable to extract DR lesion-specific parts efficiently with less memory footprint (3.3 M parameters). This approach makes the model suitable to deploy on resource constraints environment. To facilitate the training and experimentation with segmentation using DCNNs, comprehensive datasets called the Indian Diabetic Retinopathy Image Dataset (IDRiD) [13] and DDR [12] have been curated. IDRiD dataset enables researchers to test and evaluate the identification, localization, and segmentation of lesions and structures in fundus imaging. Notably, the IDRiD dataset is the only dataset providing pixel-level annotations for DR lesions and other retinal structures, offering valuable resources for algorithm development and evaluation.

3 Methodology

3.1 Pre-processing

Retinal images obtained from various cameras may exhibit disparities in terms of color, illumination, and contrast, impacting their backgrounds. To facilitate effective learning, these dissimilarities are normalized. Moreover, to preserve the aspect ratio of training images, crop, padding, and resize operations are employed. Additionally, data augmentation techniques, including Flip, Rotate, Crop, Zoom, and Alpha, are applied to address the class-imbalance issue present in the training dataset. In the case of RGB images, there is redundant information across the channels. To optimize computations, the green channel is chosen as the input to the model, as it contains the most relevant information compared to the other channels in the image.

3.2 Proposed Architecture

This section describes the architectural detail of the shallow U-Net network and inverted residual block (IRB). As shown in Fig. 2, the features extracted from each encoder layer are passed through the inverted residual block for feature re-calibration. These refined features are then forwarded to the corresponding decoder layer utilizing skip

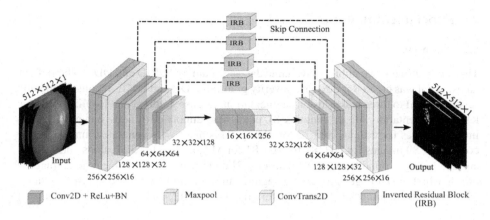

Fig. 2. Block diagram of the proposed UNet with inverted residual blocks for DR Lesion Segmentation.

connections. The decoder layer adds these feature maps with up-sampled feature maps obtained from its downstream decoder layer.

The encoder and decoder parts of the proposed architecture are implemented similarly to U-Net architecture for a fair comparison with state-of-the-art methods. However, the proposed model differs in the convolutional operation from the standard U-Net backbone. The standard 3×3 convolution of the U-Net backbone is replaced with a series of 3×3, 1×1 convolution, and 3×3 convolution block with added residual connection in IRB. A shallow 4-layer U-Net architecture is adopted for experimentation in this work. The upsampling layers of the decoder are replaced with transpose-convolutions to learn the pixel mapping corresponding to the features extracted by the encoder. Incorporating IRB layers ensures that most optimized features are received as input to the decoder.

The input of the IRB module is a low-dimensional feature map having k channels. Three distinct convolutional operations are performed in the IRB module. Initially, a 1×1 point-wise convolution is performed to extend the low-dimensional input feature map into a higher-dimensional space, followed by the ReLU activation function. Subsequently, a 3×3 depth-wise convolution is executed, followed by ReLU activation, resulting in spatial filtering of the higher-dimensional tensor. Finally, the spatially-filtered feature map is mapped back to a low-dimensional subspace using another point-wise convolution. As the projection step leads to some loss of information, a residual connection is introduced to facilitate increased information flow within the network to ensure gradient flow during the backpropagation process. The IRB block enhances features while maintaining minimal parameters, thereby making it memory and computationally-efficient. Experimental results demonstrate that a shallow U-Net with inverted residual blocks outperforms a larger, more complex U-Net architecture for lesion segmentation as discussed in the subsequent section.

4 Experimental Setup

4.1 Datasets

This study utilizes two publicly available datasets, namely IDRiD and DDR. The IDRiD dataset [13] was created for disease severity grading of DR and DME. It consists of subsets dedicated to three tasks: lesion segmentation, disease grading, and localization. The lesion segmentation subset contains 81 pixel-wise annotated fundus images, divided into 54 images for training and 27 for testing. This pixel-wise annotated image dataset consists of 80 images for HH, 81 for HE, 81 for MA, and 40 for SE lesions, along with corresponding ground truth. DDR dataset [12] comprises 12,522 color fundus images, out of which 757 images are having segmentation ground truth. The dataset contains 570 ground truth images for MA, 601 for HH, 486 for HE, and 239 for SE lesions.

4.2 Parameters Setting and Loss Function

The experiments of the proposed work are implemented on Python with Keras environment and TensorFlow backend. The models are trained and tested on NVidia DGX-A100 machine having AMD ROM 7742, 2.25 GHz 128 cores CPU with 512 GB memory size, and NVidia Tesla P100 40 GB GPU. The hyperparameters are chosen based on experimentation, and the initial learning rate is kept at 0.0001 with a decay rate of 0.00001 to handle the vanishing gradient issue. The batch size is kept at 8 based on empirical experimentation. The models are trained for 100 epochs with the DICE loss function defined in Eq. (1):

$$Loss(y, \hat{y}) = 1 - \frac{2|y \cap \hat{y}|}{|y| + |\hat{y}|} \tag{1}$$

Here y is the ground truth label and $\hat{y}$ represents the predicted label.

5 Results and Discussion

The proposed model is trained and validated on two publicly available datasets: IDRiD and DDR. The semantic segmentation model achieved state-of-the-art results on both of these datasets. The performance of the proposed models is evaluated using the area under the curve (AUC) and DICE score. The performance of the proposed U-Net models with and without adding residual blocks is summarized in Table 1. It can be observed that UNet with residual block performs better for DR lesion segmentation than vanilla shallow UNet architecture. The proposed model has proven to be highly reliable for comprehensive use. During both the training and validation phases, the DICE score is calculated. Clear and indisputable evidence of the reliability of the proposed segmentation approach is obtained by comparing AUC, loss, and DICE scores of the UNet with residual connection to the basic version of the shallow U-Net architecture. The UNet architecture with inverted residual blocks exhibits better performance and is utilized for further comparison.

The performance of the proposed residual block model is compared with state-of-the-art methods from the literature as shown in Table 2. The proposed model achieved

Table 1. Performance of DR lesions segmentation on backbone networks.

Dataset	Model	Lesions	Params	AUC	Loss	DICE
IDRID	Backbone Unet (without residual connections)	MA	3.1 M	47.43	0.471	47.54
		HH		87.64	0.274	65.08
		HE		69.61	0.389	49.01
		SE		72.33	0.318	52.83
	Backbone Unet (with residual connections)	MA	3.3 M	51.59	0.419	49.38
		HH		91.22	0.279	67.47
		HE		72.33	0.241	52.76
		SE		79.43	0.245	55.11
DDR	Backbone Unet (without residual connections)	MA	3.1 M	9.47	0.403	8.16
		HH		52.89	0.230	56.01
		HE		41.83	0.349	40.77
		SE		30.09	0.401	29.92
	Backbone Unet (with residual connections)	MA	3.3 M	11.80	0.371	10.51
		HH		61.96	0.179	59.84
		HE		43.74	0.265	42.79
		SE		33.07	0.362	31.7

Table 2. Comparison with state-of-the-art methods on AUC for DR lesion segmentation.

Dataset	Model	Parameters	MA	HH	HE	SE
IDRiD	Yan et al. 2019 [18]	56.13 M	**52.5**	88.90	70.30	67.9
	Guo et al. 2020 [3]	36.3 M	46.27	79.45	67.34	71.13
	Xie et al. 2020 [17]	42.65 M	50.99	–	–	–
	Huang et al. 2022 [5]	48.03 M	48.97	90.24	68.8	75.02
	Guo et al. 2023 [4]	33.85 M	49.75	89.61	68.84	75.63
	Proposed Method	**3.3 M**	51.59	**91.22**	**72.33**	**79.43**
DDR	Guo et al. 2020 [3]	36.3 M	10.52	55.46	35.86	26.48
	Huang et al. 2022 [5]	48.03 M	11.76	56.71	36.56	29.43
	Guo et al. 2023 [4]	33.85 M	**11.94**	60.14	36.52	30.94
	Proposed Method	**3.3 M**	11.80	**61.96**	**43.74**	**33.07**

51.59%, 91.22%, 72.33%, and 79.43% AUC for MA, HH, HE, and SE on the IDRiD dataset. The AUC for the model implemented on the DDR dataset achieved 11.80%, 61.96%, 43.74%, and 33.07% values for MA, HH, HE, and SE lesion classes. The model performed better than other methods from the literature for HE, HH, and SE classes. Table 2 shows that the proposed model underperforms for MA in comparison to models proposed by Yan et al. [18] for the IDRiD dataset and Guo et al. [4] for the DDR dataset. However, it can be seen that the performance of the proposed model is comparable with these works with fewer parameters and computations.

64   A. Bhati et al.

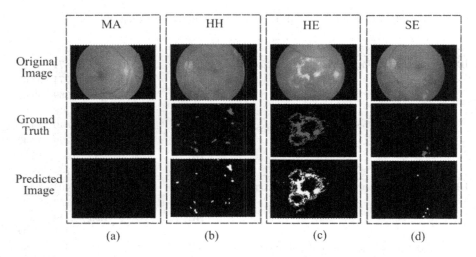

Fig. 3. Segmentation results obtained with the proposed model on IDRiD dataset for different types of DR lesions (a) MA, (b) HE, (c) HH, and (d) SE.

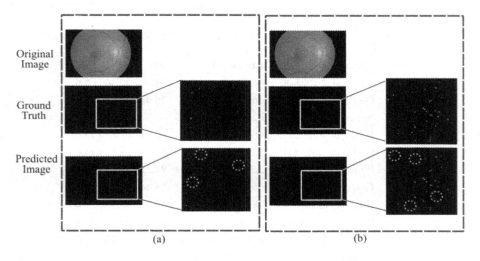

Fig. 4. Segmentation results obtained for MA lesions with the proposed model on (a) IDRiD, and (b) DDR dataset.

The performance of the proposed model for DR lesion segmentation is also analyzed using qualitative results obtained with images of IDRiD dataset as shown in Fig. 3. It can be seen that the proposed model is able to generate lesion segmentation output very near to ground truth, which signifies its high adaptability for practical use. However, Fig. 4 reveals that the proposed model fails to detect some challenging cases of MA lesions comprising a few pixels in the fundus image. These tiny MA lesions have pixel color values very similar to the fundus image background, resulting in misclassification for this lesion class.

6   Conclusion

Diabetic retinopathy is a prevalent condition caused by prolonged diabetes and significantly contributes to irreversible visual impairment worldwide. The manual screening of DR by experts is time-consuming and demands high precision in annotating lesion boundaries. A need for an automated segmentation system arises to determine the severity stages of DR patients effectively.

This work proposes a novel approach based on a lightweight UNet architecture augmented with inverted residual blocks. A shallow U-Net architecture integrated with inverted residual blocks between the encoder and decoder parts of the network is proposed. By combining location information from the downsampling path and contextual information from the upsampling path, the model efficiently predicts a comprehensive segmentation map for the target fundus images. The proposed architecture demonstrates superior performance while maintaining a low memory footprint, outperforming existing state-of-the-art methods for MA, HH, HE, and SE lesions. The proposed model performs better than state-of-the-art methods in most cases. Due to class imbalance and small-sized lesion structures, the segmentation efficiency needs improvement in the case of MA. In the future, the proposed work can be extended to include generative adversarial network (GAN) based synthetic sample generation for handling class imbalance issues. Also, to handle the small-sized structured lesions, attention-based methods can be proposed in the network to give more weight to their precise segmentation.

Acknowledgments. This work is supported by research projects from Khalifa University Ref: CIRA-2021-052 and the Advanced Technology Research Center Program (ASPIRE) Ref: AARE20-279.

References

1. Adem, K.: Exudate detection for diabetic retinopathy with circular hough transformation and convolutional neural networks. Expert Syst. Appl. **114**, 289–295 (2018)
2. Devaraj, D., Suma, R., Kumar, S.P.: A survey on segmentation of exudates and microaneurysms for early detection of diabetic retinopathy. Mater. Today: Proc. **5**(4), 10845–10850 (2018)
3. Guo, S., Wang, K., Kang, H., Liu, T., Gao, Y., Li, T.: Bin loss for hard exudates segmentation in fundus images. Neurocomputing **392**, 314–324 (2020)
4. Guo, T., Yang, J., Yu, Q.: Diabetic retinopathy lesion segmentation using deep multi-scale framework. Biomed. Signal Process. Control 105050 (2023)
5. Huang, S., Li, J., Xiao, Y., Shen, N., Xu, T.: RTNet: relation transformer network for diabetic retinopathy multi-lesion segmentation. IEEE Trans. Med. Imaging **41**(6), 1596–1607 (2022)
6. Huang, Y., et al.: Automated hemorrhage detection from coarsely annotated fundus images in diabetic retinopathy. In: 2020 IEEE 17th International Symposium on Biomedical Imaging (ISBI), pp. 1369–1372. IEEE (2020)
7. Imani, E., Pourreza, H.R.: A novel method for retinal exudate segmentation using signal separation algorithm. Comput. Methods Programs Biomed. **133**, 195–205 (2016)
8. Joshi, S., Karule, P.: A review on exudates detection methods for diabetic retinopathy. Biomed. Pharmacother. **97**, 1454–1460 (2018)

9. Karkuzhali, S., Manimegalai, D.: Retinal haemorrhages segmentation using improved tobog-gan segmentation algorithm in diabetic retinopathy images. Biomed. Res. (0970-938X) (2018)
10. Kaur, J., Mittal, D.: A generalized method for the segmentation of exudates from pathological retinal fundus images. Biocybern. Biomed. Eng. **38**(1), 27–53 (2018)
11. Li, L., et al.: A large-scale database and a CNN model for attention-based glaucoma detection. IEEE Trans. Med. Imaging **39**(2), 413–424 (2019)
12. Li, T., Gao, Y., Wang, K., Guo, S., Liu, H., Kang, H.: Diagnostic assessment of deep learning algorithms for diabetic retinopathy screening. Inf. Sci. **501**, 511–522 (2019)
13. Porwal, P., et al.: IDRiD: diabetic retinopathy-segmentation and grading challenge. Med. Image Anal. **59**, 101561 (2020)
14. Sandler, M., Howard, A., Zhu, M., Zhmoginov, A., Chen, L.C.: MobileNetv2: inverted resid-uals and linear bottlenecks. In: Proceedings of the IEEE Conference on Computer Vision and Pattern Recognition, pp. 4510–4520 (2018)
15. Sarhan, M.H., Albarqouni, S., Yigitsoy, M., Navab, N., Eslami, A.: Multi-scale microa-neurysms segmentation using embedding triplet loss. In: Shen, D., et al. (eds.) MICCAI 2019. LNCS, vol. 11764, pp. 174–182. Springer, Cham (2019). https://doi.org/10.1007/978-3-030-32239-7_20
16. Van Grinsven, M.J., van Ginneken, B., Hoyng, C.B., Theelen, T., Sánchez, C.I.: Fast con-volutional neural network training using selective data sampling: application to hemorrhage detection in color fundus images. IEEE Trans. Med. Imaging **35**(5), 1273–1284 (2016)
17. Xie, Y., Zhang, J., Lu, H., Shen, C., Xia, Y.: SESV: accurate medical image segmentation by predicting and correcting errors. IEEE Trans. Med. Imaging **40**(1), 286–296 (2020)
18. Yan, Z., Han, X., Wang, C., Qiu, Y., Xiong, Z., Cui, S.: Learning mutually local-global U-nets for high-resolution retinal lesion segmentation in fundus images. In: 2019 IEEE 16th International Symposium on Biomedical Imaging (ISBI 2019), pp. 597–600. IEEE (2019)

A Belief Theory Based Instance Selection Scheme for Label Noise and Outlier Detection from Breast Cancer Data

Shameer Faziludeen[(✉)] and Praveen Sankaran

National Institute of Technology Calicut, Kozhikode, Kerala, India
shameer503@gmail.com

Abstract. In case of real datasets, the likelihood of the training data being corrupted with training label noise and outliers arises. Certain classification algorithms including support vector machine (SVM) is sensitive to noise and outlier samples which can degrade their performance. Belief theory which involves an extension of the general probabilistic model and utilises combination rules for information fusion has found good use in the realm of classifiers. In this paper, we propose a belief theory based instance selection (BIS) scheme using the k nearest neighbours (KNN) algorithm for removing outlier and noise samples prior to SVM training to increase classification performance for breast cancer FNAC (Fine needle aspiration cytology) image data features. Our algorithm is tested on the WBCD database from the UCI machine learning repository which contains FNAC image data features. Performance evaluation is done by considering accuracy and confusion matrix measures. Effect of noise is assessed by testing on the datasets after contaminating the training data by random mislabelling. Results are compared with the conventional SVM algorithm for both the noisy and noiseless datasets. The proposed BIS scheme is shown to improve the performance of the SVM classifier considerably under noisy conditions.

Keywords: Support vector machine · belief theory · Dempster Shafer theory · evidential k nearest neighbours · k nearest neighbours · breast cancer · histopathology · FNAC image

1 Introduction

Support vector machine (SVM) is a binary classifier based on statistical learning theory [17]. SVM has been widely used in different classification and regression applications and gives very good generalization performance. It has found utility in a multitude of tasks like face recognition, handwriting recognition, image classification and speech processing [7,9,16].

SVM being a supervised type classifier involves two phases in its operation-training and testing phase. During the training phase, a hyperplane maximizing the distance between the support vectors (boundary vectors) of the two data

H. Kaur et al. (Eds.): CVIP 2023, CCIS 2010, pp. 67–77, 2024.
https://doi.org/10.1007/978-3-031-58174-8_7

classes under consideration is found. This process of maximum margin separation helps the SVM classifier achieve a high generalization performance [11]. In case of real datasets, it is possible that the training data might be contaminated with mislabelled (noise) samples. SVM is sensitive to noise and outlier samples which can affect its performance considerably [13,19]. To deal with outlier and noise data, Lin and Wang developed a fuzzy SVM model [2]. In this model, sample fuzzy membership values are calculated based on which they contribute to the SVM training. Gao and Wang developed a twin SVM formulation [6]. Liu et al. [10] developed a belief theory based formulation to deal with the same. In this approach, basic belief assignments (bba) of the samples are generated using the methodology in evidential c means clustering algorithm and sample weights for SVM training are assigned based on this bba.

Belief theory was introduced by Arthur Dempster and formalized by Glen Shafer [3,14]. It involves the use of Shafer's model and fusion rules for combining information arising from multiple sources. Shafer's model extends the general probability model by incorporating the ignorance condition [14]. Combination rules can be used to effectively combine information from multiple sources, there being different combination rules which can be selected according to the need of the situation [15]. These tools make belief theory extremely useful in classification problems - one of its applications being in the k nearest neighbours (KNN) algorithm by Denoeux [4].

In this paper, we propose a belief theory based instance selection (BIS) scheme for improving the performance of the conventional SVM classifier. The proposed BIS scheme removes outlier and noise samples prior to SVM training. Major contributions are listed below.

1. A method is developed to extract training sample neighbourhood information using combination rules.
2. An outlier detection technique employing Murphy's combination rule is devised.
3. A two-step combination process utilizing Murphy's and Dubois & Prade rule is devised to detect and eliminate noisy samples from the training data.

This paper is organized as follows. Sections 2 and 3 review the theoretical aspects of belief theory and SVM algorithm respectively. Section 4 presents the proposed algorithm. Section 5 describes the experimental setup. Section 6 analyses the results. Section 7 concludes the paper.

2   Belief Theory

Belief theory/ Dempster Shafer theory has two major parts- use of Shafer's model and combination rules for information fusion [14]. Let the classification problem be n class with the classes in the discernment frame C denoted as $C_1, C_2, C_3, ...C_n$. The discernment frame power set, 2^C consists of all the subsets of C and has a cardinality of 2^n [14,15].

2.1   Shafer's Model

In Shafer's model, basic belief assignment, m(.) is such that it satisfies the conditions given in (1).

$$m(\phi) = 0, \quad \sum_{D \in 2^C} m(D) = 1 \tag{1}$$

Here, ϕ indicates the null-set. The assignments are such that collective exhaustivity criteria is imposed on the discernment frame power set unlike in the probability model [14,15]. The difference can be illustrated with the following example. Consider a two class problem with the discernment frame, $C = \{C_1, C_2\}$. Its powerset is given by $2^C = \{C_1, C_2, C_1 \cup C_2, \phi\}$. In the probability model, the assignments are only to the specific classes- C_1 and C_2. Shafer's model provides the flexibility for assignment to an additional ignorance class, $C_1 \cup C_2$. The ignorance class belief measures the uncertainty of the classifier regarding the test data sample label and hence its inclusion helps to represent class relationships better.

2.2   Combination Rules

Combination rules are used to combine information from multiple sources. Different such rules are available. Those relevant to this paper are discussed below.

Dubois and Prade Combination Rule. This rule is commutative but not associative [15]. Conflict between the sources is dealt with by adding the partial conflicting masses to the masses of the corresponding metaclasses [15].

$$\begin{aligned} m(\phi) &= 0 \\ m_{dp}(D) &= \sum_{A \cap B = D} m_1(A)m_2(B) \\ &+ \sum_{A \cap B = \phi, A \cup B = D} m_1(A)m_2(B) \end{aligned} \tag{2}$$

where $A, B, D \in 2^C$ and $A, B, D \neq \phi$. $m_{dp}(.)$ refers to the combined result utilising Dubois and Prade rule with "dp" indicating the rule used here (Dubois and Prade).

Murphy's Combination Rule. Murphy's rule is commutative but not associative. It involves taking the simple arithmetic average of the two belief functions to be combined [12,15].

$$\begin{aligned} m(\phi) &= 0 \\ m_{mp}(D) &= \frac{m_1(D) + m_2(D)}{2} \end{aligned} \tag{3}$$

where $D \in 2^C$ and $D \neq \phi$. $m_{mp}(.)$ refers to the combined result utilising Murphy's rule with "mp" indicating the rule used here (Murphy's rule).

3   Support Vector Machines

Support vector machines work by finding a hyperplane achieving maximal margin separation between the two data classes under consideration in a linearly separable space. This is done during the training phase of the SVM classifier. During the testing phase, data is classified into the respective classes based on the side of the hyperplane in which it falls under [1].

3.1   Training Phase

A general hyperplane equation is given by,

$$y = g.x + b \tag{4}$$

where b is the bias, g is an m dimensional weight vector (data dimensionality is m).

Distance between the nearest point to the plane (support vector) and the plane (margin) is given by $1/\|g\|$ [1,11]. Hence, we maximize,

$$\frac{1}{\|g\|} \quad s.t \atop min|g.x_t + b| = 1 \tag{5}$$

This is equivalent to

$$Minimize \atop \frac{1}{2}\|g\| \quad s.t \atop y_t(g.x_t + b) - 1 >= 0 \ \forall t = 1,..l \tag{6}$$

where l is the number of learning data and x_t is the training data point with t referring to the index of the particular training data point (t varies from 1 to l). The optimization problem can be solved by using a Lagrange formulation as shown in (7). Solution can then be obtained using quadratic programming. Positive values for the Lagrange multipliers indicate that the corresponding points are support vectors [1,11].

$$L(g,b,\lambda) = 1/2\|g\|^2 - \sum_{t=1}^{l} \Lambda_t(y_t(g.x_t - b) - 1) \tag{7}$$

In the case of non-linearly separable data, kernel transformations are used to map the data into a space where linear separability is achievable. RBF (radial basis function) kernel is widely used [1].

3.2   Testing Phase

During the SVM training phase, support vectors are identified and the Lagrange multipliers corresponding to each support vector is calculated. Bias value is also found during training. This information is used in the testing phase of the SVM to compute a score corresponding to each test data sample based on which class assignment is done [1].

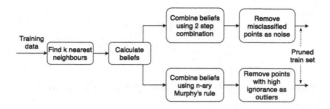

Fig. 1. Proposed BIS scheme

4 Proposed Algorithm

The proposed belief theory based instance selection (BIS) algorithm involves removal of outlier and noise samples prior to training the SVM. Overview of the proposed scheme is shown in Fig. 1. The proposed scheme utilizes the KNN algorithm. The beliefs corresponding to the k nearest neighbours of each training point is calculated. These beliefs are then combined using Murphy's rule for the outlier detection step and a two step combination process utilizing Murphy's and Dubois & Prade rule for noise label detection. Outlier detection is based on the premise that a large mass to the ignorance class indicates that the sample is distant from the typical samples belonging to that class. Noise detection utilizes Dubois & Prade rule also since this rule preserves conflict information. It is based on the premise that if a sample's label is different from that of its k nearest neighbours, it is likely to have been mislabelled. The steps involved in the proposed BIS scheme are described in detail below.

1. Calculation of beliefs corresponding to training data points:

Beliefs corresponding to the training data points are calculated by using the belief function estimation step in the evidential KNN method developed by Denoeux [4]. The k nearest neighbours corresponding to each training data point is found. The euclidean distance metric is used here. Each neighbour has an associated belief function with mass assignments to two classes- either the specific class belonging to the neighbour or the total ignorance class. Let x_h be the training data point and x_i represent the neighbours. Belief function corresponding to the ith neighbour is given in (8).

$$
\begin{aligned}
m^{h,i}(C_p) &= \alpha \\
m^{h,i}(C) &= 1 - \alpha \\
m^{h,i}(D) &= 0 \, \forall D \in 2^C \backslash \{C, C_p\}
\end{aligned}
\tag{8}
$$

where,
$m^{h,i}(C_p)$ is the belief assigned to class C_p.
$m^{h,i}(C)$ is the belief assigned to total ignorance.
α is modelled as an exponentially decreasing function of distance and a limit is set on its maximum value using α_0 [4].

$$\begin{aligned}
\alpha &= \alpha_0 . \phi_p(d^{h,i}) \\
\phi_p(d) &= e^{(-\gamma_p . d^\delta)}, 0 < \alpha_0 < 1 \\
\gamma_p &= \frac{1}{d_p{}^\delta}
\end{aligned} \qquad (9)$$

where d_p is the mean distance between any two training samples belonging to a particular class.

For our use, α_0 is set to 0.95 and δ set to 1. Since SVM is a binary classifier, power set of the hypothesis under consideration always has only three elements.

$$2^C = (C_1, C_2, C_1 U C_2) \qquad (10)$$

2. Combination of belief functions corresponding to each training point:

Combination of belief functions corresponding to each training point is done in two manners so as to remove outliers and noise samples. N-ary Murphy's rule is employed to combine all the belief functions corresponding to each training point and the subsequently obtained belief assignments are used to remove the class outlier samples. For noise sample detection, Murphy's rule is used in conjunction with Dubois & Prade rule as a part of a two step combination strategy. Dubois & Prade rule is used since it preserves partial conflict information improving the classification accuracy. Since it is not associative, it has to be used in the second step after Murphy's rule. The combination steps are described in detail below.

(i) Using Murphy's rule:

General expression for belief combination using Murphy's rule is given in (3). Here, we take the assumption of n-ary associativity (since information from all sources is available together). Using Murphy's rule with n-ary associativity equates to taking the mean of all belief functions considered at once. In our algorithm, we use Murphy's rule in two manners.

1. Murphy's rule is applied to combine the belief functions corresponding to all the k nearest neighbours of a training point under consideration. This step is done to remove outliers. The ignorance class of the final obtained belief function will have high mass assigned to it in case the training point is an outlier. This is since outlier samples are distant from both the classes, hence increasing the ignorance class mass on calculation as per Eq. (8). Murphy's rule involves averaging and hence preserves this ignorance class mass. For our experiments, we remove points with ignorance class mass higher than 0.75 as outliers.
2. We also use Murphy's rule to combine classwise the belief functions of the k nearest neighbours corresponding to each data point in the training set. This step is used as a part of the two step combination process prior to using Dubois & Prade rule and is utilized to detect and remove noise samples.

(ii) Using Dubois & Prade rule:

For noise detection, the classwise belief functions obtained using Murphy's rule are combined using Dubois & Prade rule in a two step process. Since Dubois & Prade rule is not associative, it cannot be used without bringing down the number of belief functions to be combined to two as we did by using Murphy's rule initially. Expression for belief combination using Dubois & Prade rule is given in (2). The training points are classified according to the mass assignments in the obtained belief function. If the assigned label is different from the actual label of the training point, then it is labelled as a noise sample and removed from the training set.

5 Experimental Setup

Testing is done on the WBCD database available from the UCI machine learning repository [5,18]. The proposed BIS algorithm is used for outlier and noise removal from the training data prior to using SVM for classification. RBF kernel is used for the SVM classifier in both cases. Min-max normalization is carried out on both the datasets prior to processing. The number of nearest neighbours k in the proposed algorithm is decided using grid search in the range [1,9] such that minimal LOO (Leave one out) testing error is obtained on the training data.

5.1 Database Description

The WBCD database contains features extracted from FNAC (fine needle aspiration cytology) images. It contains 699 entries, each having nine features associated with it [5,18]. List of the available attributes is given in Table 1. Sixteen of these entries have missing feature values and hence are excluded from current testing. Algorithm is tested on the 683 remaining entries. Data samples belong to either of two classes- normal and abnormal. Of the 683 samples under consideration, 444 belong to the normal category and 239 samples belong to the abnormal class.

We carry out 200 iterations with half the dataset being selected for training and the remaining for testing randomly. 200 iterations are taken so that the number is suitably large so as to capture the expected performance of the proposed model. Effect of noise on algorithm performance is then analysed by repeating the experiments after introducing noise in the training data. This is done by randomly assigning 20% of the training data belonging to each class to the opposite category.

5.2 Performance Metrics

Accuracy. Accuracy of a classifier is defined as the rate of correctly detected samples. It is given by (11).

$$\text{Accuracy} = \frac{T_c}{T_s} \tag{11}$$

Table 1. Wisconsin breast cancer data - Attribute information

Attributes
1. Clump thickness
2. Uniformity of cell size
3. Uniformity of cell shape
4. Marginal adhesion
5. Single epithelial cell size
6. Bare nuclei
7. Bland chromatin
8. Normal nucleoli
9. Mitoses

where T_c is the number of correctly classified samples and T_s is the total number of samples tested by the classifier.

Confusion Matrix. Confusion matrices are widely used for performance analysis of classification algorithms [8]. A typical confusion matrix for a two class problem is given in Fig. 2. Here, the abnormal class is designated as positive and normal class as negative. TN, TP, FN, FP denote the percentage of true negatives, true positives, false negatives and false positives respectively.

Table 2. Confusion matrix for a two class problem

	Normal	Abnormal
Normal	TN	FP
Abnormal	FN	TP

6   Results and Discussion

Table 3 shows comparison of classification error rates obtained using the proposed BIS+SVM method and conventional SVM for the WBCD database under the noiseless and noisy conditions. The proposed belief theory based sample selection scheme improves the performance marginally for the noiseless WBCD dataset and significantly by more than 0.5% for the noisy WBCD dataset as seen in Table 3. The confusion matrix using conventional SVM and the proposed schemes for the noiseless WBCD dataset is shown in Table 4. The confusion matrix for the noisy WBCD dataset is shown in Table 5. For the noisy WBCD database, the BIS scheme improves malignant class accuracy on using SVM by more than 2% while lowering benign class accuracy marginally. SVM performance is known to be affected by training label noise and outliers, with training label noise having more of an impact. The improvement in performance for the proposed algorithm in case of the noise introduced dataset is due to the effectiveness of the designed belief theory based scheme for removing training label noise and also outliers prior to SVM classification. The proposed algorithm is also shown to perform better compared to a belief theory based approach by Liu et al. [10] as seen in Table 6.

Table 3. Classification error rates (in %) using conventional SVM and the proposed method for the WBCD database (noiseless and noisy cases)

	SVM	Proposed (BIS+SVM)
WBCD (noiseless)	2.84	2.72
WBCD (noisy)	3.62	3.06

Table 4. Confusion matrix (values in %) for noiseless WBCD data using a) Conventional SVM b) Proposed BIS+SVM

(a) Conventional SVM

	Benign	Malignant
Benign	96.96	3.04
Malignant	2.46	97.54

(b) Proposed BIS+SVM

	Benign	Malignant
Benign	96.72	3.28
Malignant	1.69	98.31

Table 5. Confusion matrix (values in %) for noisy WBCD data using a) Conventional SVM b) Proposed BIS+SVM

(a) Conventional SVM

	Benign	Malignant
Benign	96.95	3.05
Malignant	4.66	95.34

(b) Proposed BIS+SVM

	Benign	Malignant
Benign	96.51	3.49
Malignant	2.27	97.73

Table 6. Comparison with other approaches on noisy WBCD data

Method	Error rate(%)
Liu [10]	3.46
Proposed	3.06

7   Conclusion

A belief theory based instance selection (BIS) scheme using the k nearest neighbours algorithm has been proposed to effectively deal with noisy data in the SVM classifier. The proposed scheme utilises different combination rules- Murphy's and Dubois & Prade rule for identifying outlier and noise samples prior to training the SVM classifier. Testing is done on the WBCD database which contains FNAC image data features and is available from the UCI machine learning repository. Proposed algorithm is shown to achieve better performance compared to the conventional SVM classifier with the difference being considerable for the case of the noisy datasets.

Future work involves analysing the effect of distance metric selection for improving the performance of the KNN algorithm used in our BIS scheme. Use of kernel based KNN approaches can also be considered. Effect of using different combination rules on outlier and noise detection is to be analysed. An FNAC breast cancer dataset is to be developed in collaboration with a health center/hospital so as to test the applicability of the approach on additional real-time data.

Currently, the algorithm deals with binary classification which focusses on detecting breast cancer. As a future work, deep learning based approaches are to be used for feature extraction with the noise and outlier detection to be done on the deep learned features. Categorization is to be extended to include the different subcategories of malignant and benign tumors rather than the binary class output alone as in the present work. The performance comparison is to be done exhaustively so as to demonstrate conclusively the utility of the proposed approach over other outlier and noise detection approaches.

References

1. Burges, C.J.: A tutorial on support vector machines for pattern recognition. Data Min. Knowl. Disc. **2**(2), 121–167 (1998)
2. Lin, C.-F., Wang, S.-D.: Fuzzy support vector machines. IEEE Trans. Neural Netw. **13**(2), 464–471 (2002)
3. Dempster, A.P.: Upper and lower probabilities induced by a multivalued mapping. Ann. Math. Stat. **38**(2), 325–339 (1967)
4. Denoeux, T.: A k-nearest neighbor classification rule based on dempster-shafer theory. IEEE Trans. Syst. Man Cybern. **25**(5), 804–813 (1995)
5. Dheeru, D., Karra Taniskidou, E.: UCI machine learning repository (2017). http:// archive.ics.uci.edu/ml

6. Gao, B.B., Wang, J.J.: A fast and robust TSVM for pattern classification. arXiv preprint arXiv:1711.05406 (2017)
7. Jia, H., Martinez, A.M.: Support vector machines in face recognition with occlusions. In: 2009 IEEE Conference on Computer Vision and Pattern Recognition, pp. 136–141, June 2009
8. Labatut, V., Cherifi, H.: Accuracy measures for the comparison of classifiers. arXiv preprint arXiv:1207.3790 (2012)
9. Lauer, F., Suen, C.Y., Bloch, G.: A trainable feature extractor for handwritten digit recognition. Pattern Recognit. 40(6), 1816–1824 (2007)
10. Liu, W., Han, D., Yang, Y.: A novel weighted SVM based on theory of belief functions. In: 2017 20th International Conference on Information Fusion (Fusion), pp. 1–6. IEEE (2017)
11. Mostafa, Y.A.: Lectures (2012). https://work.caltech.edu/lectures.html. Accessed 05 Aug 2018
12. Murphy, C.K.: Combining belief functions when evidence conflicts. Decis. Support Syst. 29(1), 1–9 (2000)
13. Pelletier, C., Valero, S., Inglada, J., Champion, N., Marais Sicre, C., Dedieu, G.: Effect of training class label noise on classification performances for land cover mapping with satellite image time series. Remote Sens. 9(2), 173 (2017)
14. Shafer, G.: A Mathematical Theory of Evidence, vol. 42. Princeton University Press, Princeton (1976)
15. Smarandache, F., Dezert, J.: Advances and Applications of DSmT for Information Fusion (Collected Works). American Research Press, Rehoboth, NM, USA (2004)
16. Temko, A., Nadeu, C.: Classification of acoustic events using SVM-based clustering schemes. Pattern Recognit. 39(4), 682–694 (2006)
17. Vapnik, V.: The Nature of Statistical Learning Theory. Springer, New York (2013). https://doi.org/10.1007/978-1-4757-3264-1
18. Wolberg, W.H., Mangasarian, O.L.: Multisurface method of pattern separation for medical diagnosis applied to breast cytology. Proc. Nat. Acad. Sci. 87(23), 9193–9196 (1990)
19. Yang, X., Song, Q., Cao, A.: Weighted support vector machine for data classification. In: Proceedings. 2005 IEEE International Joint Conference on Neural Networks, 2005, vol. 2, pp. 859–864, July 2005

GAN-Based Super-Resolution for Disease Detection in Aerial Images: A Case Study of Potato Crop

Anil Pankaj[✉]⑩, Kalidas Yeturu⑩, and Venkataramana Badarla⑩

Department of Computer Science and Engineering, Indian Institute of Technology
Tirupati, Tirupati, India
{cs21m002,ykalidas,ramana}@iittp.ac.in

Abstract. Precision agriculture requires high-resolution images to monitor crop growth and health effects. However, capturing such images from aerial platforms faces challenges due to altitude, motion blur, and limited resolution. Early detection and identification of these diseases can help prevent their spread and minimize the impact on crop yields. To address the challenge of capturing high-quality images, this paper relies on the new degradation model BSRGAN to enhance low-resolution aerial images of potato crops, initially sized at 750×750, to a higher resolution of 3000×3000. The experimental results indicate that the proposed BSRGAN method surpasses existing super-resolution techniques in terms of visual quality.

The study utilizes the Potato Multispectral Images Dataset, which has dimensions of 750×750. Interpolation methods are then applied to enhance the resolution, resulting in a high super-resolution dataset with dimensions of 3000×3000. Subsequently, the dataset is labeled using the publicly available tool makesense.ai (makesense.ai: https://www.makesense.ai/index.html), based on three categories of crop health: (a) Healthy, (b) Potato Leafroll Virus (PLRV), and (c) Verticillium wilt, as specified by the Potato Disease Identification, Agriculture, and Horticulture Development Board 2023 (AHDB). After labeling the data, we use You Only Look Once version 8 (YOLOv8) for potato crop health detection on the high-resolution dataset with dimensions of 3000×3000. The YOLOv8 algorithm has been trained on a high super-resolution dataset for object detection and classification. It achieves an impressive mAP better than without super-resolution of over 73%, specifically for healthy potato leaves, with an overall mAP of 56% across all three categories. These findings demonstrate the potential of deep learning-based approaches to accurately and efficiently identify potato leaf diseases, empowering farmers to protect their crops.

Keywords: Generative adversarial networks · ESRGAN · BSRGAN · Precision agriculture · Unmanned aerial vehicle · Computer Vision

© The Author(s), under exclusive license to Springer Nature Switzerland AG 2024
H. Kaur et al. (Eds.): CVIP 2023, CCIS 2010, pp. 78–90, 2024.
https://doi.org/10.1007/978-3-031-58174-8_8

1 Introduction

Precision agriculture [1] is an approach to agricultural management that involves collecting, processing, and analyzing temporal, spatial, and individual data. Potato crop disease identification is of utmost importance in ensuring the well-being and productivity of potato crops, which serve as a vital staple food globally. Conventional approaches to detecting diseases in potato crops heavily rely on manual inspection, which is time-consuming, labor-intensive, and prone to human errors. However, the advancements in computer vision and aerial imaging technologies present an opportunity to automate the disease identification process using aerial images. By harnessing the power of computer vision algorithms and machine learning techniques, analyzing aerial images of potato crops and precisely identifying and classifying various diseases becomes feasible. The research on potato crop stress identification in aerial images using deep learning-based object detection [2] focuses on identifying healthy and stressed potato crops. This technological advancement can significantly enhance the efficiency and accuracy of disease identification, empowering farmers to promptly implement preventive or corrective measures to safeguard their potato crops and optimize their yield potential.

The proposed method in this study makes several contributions to potato crop disease identification. We created an aerial dataset of potato crops and obtained high super-resolution images using the Blind Image Super-Resolution (BSRGAN) [3] instead of Bicubic Interpolation [4] and Enhance Super-Resolution Generative Adversarial Network (ESRGAN) [5]. This process enhanced the resolution of the aerial images, resulting in high super-resolution images for the potato crop. Additionally, we labeled the high super-resolution dataset, which includes images of healthy potato leaves and those infected with various diseases such as Potato Leafroll Virus (PLRV) and Verticillium wilt, using the publicly available tool makesense.ai. We trained the YOLOv8 [6] object detection model, released by Ultralytics, to identify diseases in potato crops. It achieves an impressive mAP of over 73% specifically for healthy potato leaves, with an overall mAP of 56% across all three categories.

The dataset[1] comprises aerial images of potato crops, which can be utilized to train computer vision models for precise crop health evaluation in precision agriculture applications. These images were obtained from a field at the Aberdeen Research and Extension Center, affiliated with the University of Idaho. A Parrot Sequoia multispectral camera was mounted on a 3DR Solo drone to capture the images.

The created dataset comprises 360 RGB image patches, each measuring 750×750 pixels, and saved in jpg format. These image patches were obtained by performing cropping, rotating, and resizing operations on the original high-resolution aerial images. The patches specifically correspond to regions containing healthy plants, Potato Leafroll Virus(PLRV) plants, and Verticillium wilt

---

[1] Potato Dataset: https://www.webpages.uidaho.edu/vakanski/Multispectral_Imag es_Dataset.html.

plants. To accurately label the crop regions within the images, we utilized the graphical annotation software makesense.ai. This manual annotation allowed us to classify the crop regions into three categories: healthy, Potato Leafroll Virus(PLRV), and Verticillium wilt[2]. It is important to note that the testing subset of images is entirely separate from the training subset. In other words, the image patches used for model testing were extracted from different aerial images, ensuring an independent evaluation of the trained model's performance. Here, we have referenced several literature sources related to methods for enhancing vision datasets [7–11].

2 Methods

This section includes the subsequent sections focusing on image super-resolution techniques, including bicubic interpolation, ESRGAN, and BSRGAN. Furthermore, the section delves into using the YOLOv8 algorithm for potato plant disease identification on a created customized potato crop dataset.

2.1 Labeled Dataset Creation

After obtaining a high-resolution dataset through the application of the BSR-GAN model instead of bicubic interpolation and the ESRGAN model to a low-resolution potato plant aerial dataset, we proceeded to label the potato crop aerial super-resolution images using the makesense.io tool. The labeling was done based on the following three categories: (a) Healthy, (b) Potato Leafroll Virus (PLRV), and (c) Verticillium wilt.

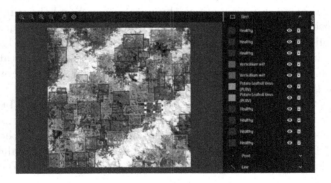

Fig. 1. Label images using makesense.io tool

Figure 1 illustrates the labeled images achieved using the makesense.io tool. To represent the input data in a tensor format, we can consider each line of the

---

[2] Potato Disease Identification, Agriculture and Horticulture Development Board 2023 (AHDB): https://potatoes.ahdb.org.uk/knowledgelibrary/potato-disease-identificat ion.

labeled TXT file as a separate object. Each line contains the following information: [class_label, x_min, y_min, x_max, y_max]

– class_label: Represents the class or label of the object.
– (x_min, y_min): Denotes the coordinates of the top-left corner of the bounding box.
– (x_max, y_max): Denotes the coordinates of the bottom-right corner of the bounding box.

We can extract these values from each line and create an input tensor representing the image's labeled objects. The specific implementation details, such as the tensor shape and data format, will depend on the model's requirements. The novelty of this paper lies in the new degradation model and the potential to utilize existing network structures, as shown in Fig. 2, such as ESRGAN [5], to train a deep blind model. We could select or design "basic blocks" (e.g., residual block [12], dense block [13], RRDB) for better performance.

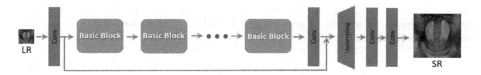

Fig. 2. ESRGAN architecture

2.2 Bicubic Interpolation

Bicubic interpolation [4] is a widely used technique in image processing and computer graphics, primarily for image resampling and altering size or resolution. It estimates new pixel color values by considering neighboring pixels in the original image. However, it should be noted that bicubic interpolation cannot add new details that were not in the original image, meaning the quality of the upscaled image depends on the quality of the original image.

Result of Bicubic Interpolation on Potato Aerial Dataset. We use a bicubic interpolation model to enhance low-resolution aerial images; however, the desired results are not achieved. We take low-resolution input images Fig. 3a, apply the bicubic interpolation method, and obtain a higher-resolution output image Fig. 3b. It is crucial to note that bicubic interpolation does not improve image quality; instead, it simply doubles the dimensions of the input image, resulting in blurred output images. In this context, we present the zoomed region of the input images, showcasing the effects of without interpolation, bicubic interpolation, ESRGAN, and BSRGAN, as depicted in Fig. 3c, Fig. 3d, Fig. 3e, and Fig. 3f.

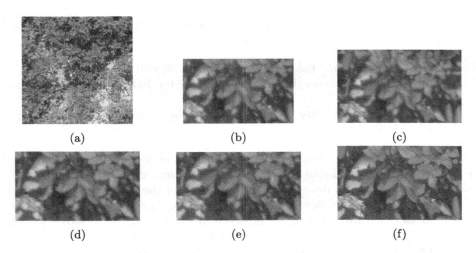

(a)   (b)   (c)

(d)   (e)   (f)

Fig. 3. (a) Low-resolution input image of potato crops; (b) Input image of a zoomed area without super-resolution; (c) image of a zoomed area using without interpolation; (d) Super-resolution image of a zoomed area using bicubic interpolation; (e) Super-resolution image of a zoomed area using ESRGAN; (f) Super-resolution image of a zoomed area using BSRGAN

2.3   Enhanced Super-Resolution Generative Adversarial Network

After deploying the unsatisfactory bicubic interpolation model, we explored ESRGAN as an alternative approach [5]. ESRGAN is an advanced deep-learning model designed for image super-resolution tasks. It enhances low-resolution images, generating high-resolution versions with finer details and improved visual fidelity. ESRGAN utilizes a GAN [14] architecture with a generator and discriminator networks. The generator network transforms low-resolution images into high-resolution ones resembling the ground truth. Meanwhile, the discriminator network differentiates between generated and real high-resolution images.

Result of ESRGAN on Potato Aerial Dataset. Following the failure of the bicubic interpolation method, we have deployed an ESRGAN model to address the low-resolution images with dimensions of 750×750 (see Fig. 4a). However, the expected results have not been achieved, as illustrated in Fig. 4b. The output images have dimensions of 3000×3000, yet they still exhibit low resolution. Considering these challenges, the application of ESRGAN does not produce satisfactory results, as evidenced by the output images.

2.4   Blind Image Super-Resolution

After unsuccessful attempts with bicubic interpolation and ESRGAN, we turned to a different model, BSRGAN [3]. BSRGAN is a specialized Blind Image Super-

(a)   (b)

Fig. 4. (a) Low-resolution input image of potato plants; (b) Super-resolution output image using ESRGAN

Resolution designed for image super-resolution tasks. It incorporates two generators and two discriminators, enabling upscaling and downscaling capabilities. The notable feature of this model is its ability to generate high-resolution images from low-resolution inputs. Moreover, BSRGAN utilizes a perceptual loss function to enhance the visual appeal and realism of the generated images. The BSRGAN model has produced remarkable results in our specific case and dataset.

Result of BSRGAN on Potato Aerial Dataset. In this scenario, we are utilizing a BSRGAN model to address low-resolution aerial images with dimensions of 750×750 Fig. 6a. After obtaining the high super-resolution images, their size increased to 3000×3000, significantly improving the image quality and providing the expected results, as depicted in Fig. 6c. Here, we can observe the leaves in the images, and when zoomed in, we can see the clear details of the leaves compared to the low-resolution images. In low-resolution images, everything appears blurred, and nothing is visible when zoomed in. Thus, BSRGAN proves capable of enhancing the quality of aerial images. With these high super-resolution images, we can now effectively identify diseases in potato plants (Fig. 5).

2.5 YOLOv8

YOLOv8 [6], developed by Ultralytics, the same company that created YOLOv5, was introduced in January 2023. YOLOv8 offers five different scaled versions: YOLOv8n (nano), YOLOv8s (small), YOLOv8m (medium), YOLOv8l (large), and YOLOv8x (extra large). It is a versatile framework capable of handling various vision tasks, including object detection, segmentation, pose estimation, tracking, and classification. YOLOv8 incorporates the CIoU [15] and DFL [16] loss functions to handle bounding box loss, while it utilizes binary cross-entropy for classification loss. These loss functions have demonstrated enhanced object detection capabilities, particularly when confronted with smaller objects.

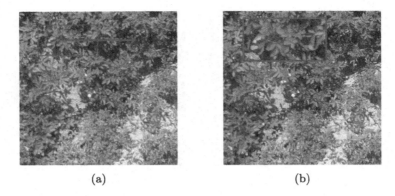

(a)   (b)

Fig. 5. (a) Aerial input image of potato plants with low resolution; (b) High super-resolution output image using BSRGAN

3   Results and Discussion

3.1   Exploring the Efficacy of YOLOv8 Algorithm for Disease Detection in Potato Plants Using High Super-Resolution Images

Various experiments were conducted on the image super-resolution methods and the identification of diseases on the potato plant's customized dataset, as discussed in the method section. This chapter contains the details about the experiments and the results obtained. We analyze our custom high super-resolution created dataset by leveraging the YOLOv8 algorithm. The training process yields batch detections, as depicted in Fig. 6.

Table 1. Performance of the YOLOv8 model on potato crops with high super-resolution using BSRGAN for various diseases.

YOLOv8 Model Performance Metrics Values			
Types of Disease ⟶	Healthy	Verticillium wilt	PLRV
Precision	0.75	0.70	0.51
Recall	0.66	0.49	0.36
mAP	0.73	0.62	0.32

We further evaluate the algorithm's efficacy by conducting predictions on the test images. This comprehensive methodology enables precise identification and localization of objects of interest, thereby demonstrating proficiency in object detection tasks compared to YOLO [17], YOLOv3 [18], and beyond [19] algorithms. Through this analysis, we ascertain the algorithm's accuracy and efficiency in detecting and classifying objects within the dataset, showcasing its potential for various applications in computer vision and image analysis.

In our initial experiment, as shown in the following Table 1, we utilized the YOLOv8 pre-trained model to test the detection capabilities on a 10% sample of aerial images. The objective was to determine if the model could successfully identify diseases. To achieve this, we conducted a training phase using our custom dataset, which consisted of a subset of 10% of the available aerial images. By training the model on our dataset, we aimed to enhance its performance specifically for disease detection in our context. This process involved fine-tuning the model's parameters and optimizing its algorithms to improve its accuracy and sensitivity to disease patterns. The training phase played a crucial role in refining the model's performance and enabling it to effectively identify diseases in our created dataset of aerial images.

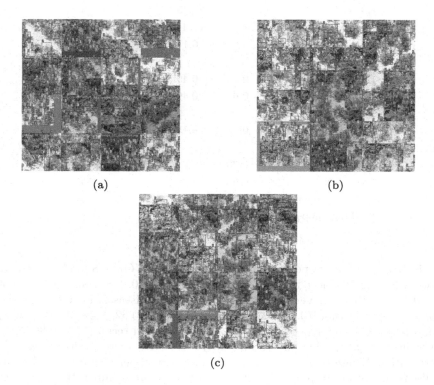

Fig. 6. Consolidated detection output by YOLOv8 on training (a) batch zero; (b) batch one; and (c) batch two

3.2 Comparing Pre-super-resolution to Post-super-resolution Analysis of Aerial Images of Potato Crops

We are experiencing unsatisfactory results regarding image upscaling compared to the high-resolution image. The experiment is yielding very poor performance due to the low quality of the images. The dataset comprises images of varying quality obtained after applying Bicubic Interpolation, ESRGAN, and BSRGAN models on a very low-resolution dataset. The outcome is highly dependent on the image quality.

Table 2. Performance metrics values for YOLOv8 model with and without super-resolution on potato plants. BSRGAN and without interpolation cases are depicted in black, the ESRGAN case in blue, and the Bicubic interpolation case in pink.

	Healthy	Verticillium wilt	PLRV
Precision			
BSRGAN	0.75	0.70	0.51
ESRGAN	0.67	0.45	0.53
Bicubic Interpolation	0.63	0.45	0.48
Without Interpolation	0.3	0.17	0.11
Recall			
BSRGAN	0.66	0.49	0.36
ESRGAN	0.62	0.49	0.49
Bicubic Interpolation	0.57	0.36	0.57
Without Interpolation	0.31	0.15	0.13
mAP			
BSRGAN	0.73	0.62	0.32
ESRGAN	0.66	0.42	0.54
Bicubic Interpolation	0.60	0.36	0.52
Without Interpolation	0.19	0.05	0.08

The Table 2 presents performance metrics for the YOLOv8 model on potato plants. BSRGAN achieved higher precision (0.75, 0.70, 0.51) and recall (0.66, 0.49, 0.36) for Healthy, Verticillium wilt, and PLRV diseases. ESRGAN showed slightly lower precision (0.67, 0.45, 0.53) and recall (0.62, 0.49, 0.49). Bicubic Interpolation had lower precision (0.63, 0.45, 0.48) and recall (0.57, 0.36, 0.57). Precision (0.3, 0.17, 0.11) and recall (0.31, 0.15, 0.13) were the lowest without interpolation. These results highlight the impact of super-resolution techniques on disease detection in potato plants. Consequently, it is imperative to employ super-resolution techniques for accurate disease identification in the customized aerial dataset of potato plants. Table 2 provides a comparative analysis between GAN-based and non-GAN-based methods for crop images depicting PLRV or Verticillium wilt diseases and healthy leaves.

The bar graph 7 illustrates the values representing detection accuracy for three diseases: Healthy, Verticillium wilt, and PLRV (Potato Leafroll Virus). Four different interpolation methods were used for the detection: BSRGAN, ESRGAN, Bicubic, and No Interpolation. The y-axis represents the accuracy values ranging from 0 to 1. The graph shows that BSRGAN achieved the highest accuracy for all three diseases, followed by ESRGAN and Bicubic. The No Interpolation method performed the worst in terms of disease detection accuracy.

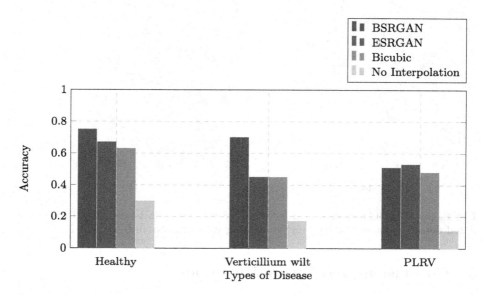

Fig. 7. Comparison of disease detection accuracy using different interpolation methods

3.3 Discussion on Failed Cases

Upon executing the YOLOv8 algorithm, the test images were processed to generate predictions. The predicted output can be observed in Fig. 8b, which displays the consolidated validation batch zero. Figure 8a visualizes the detected labels. The testing image without labels is shown in the first block of Fig. 8a. The algorithm successfully predicted the expected results, as depicted in the first block of Fig. 8b. Moving on to the second block, we have a label image that contains six healthy bounding boxes, 16 verticillium wilt bounding boxes, and three potato leaf roll virus bounding boxes. In Fig. 8b, the algorithm predicts four healthy bounding boxes: three truly positive, one false positive, and two false negatives. Our dataset includes 36 healthy bounding boxes, 59 verticillium wilt bounding boxes, and 23 potato leaf roll virus bounding boxes. Analyzing Fig. 8b, we observe that the algorithm correctly predicts 30 out of 36 healthy bounding boxes, with 25 being true positives, five false positives, and six false negatives. Additionally, it accurately predicts 43 out of 59 verticillium wilt bounding boxes, with 27 being true positives, 12 false positives, and four false negatives. Lastly, it predicts 19 out of 23 potato leaf roll virus bounding boxes correctly, with 13 being true positives, three false positives, and three false negatives.

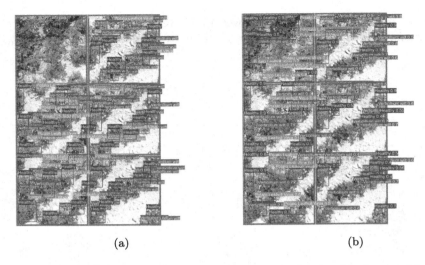

(a)   (b)

Fig. 8. (a) Consolidated detection by YOLOv8 on validation batch zero; (b) Consolidated detection output by YOLOv8 on testing validation batch zero

4   Conclusions and Future Directions

The research presented in this study is focused on enhancing the existing publicly accessible low-resolution aerial dataset of Russet Burbank potato crops, which holds significant importance in precision agriculture for effective crop health assessment. However, the limitations of the low-resolution images pose challenges in accurately evaluating and detecting crop health conditions. To overcome this obstacle, computer vision pre-trained models are employed to generate high-resolution aerial images from the original low-resolution ones. This research uses three distinct models for image super-resolution: ESRGAN[3], BSRGAN[4], and the bicubic interpolation technique. These models leverage the capabilities of deep neural networks to transform low-resolution aerial images into high-resolution versions. By incorporating these models, the researchers aim to enhance the dataset's quality, enabling more precise analysis and assessment of the potato crop's health. Remarkably, the BSRGA model exhibits exceptional outcomes in improving the aerial images' resolution and quality. The model's unique ability to upscale and downscale images prove advantageous for various agricultural applications.

The evaluation of the YOLOv8 algorithm on the custom dataset reveals promising disease detection and classification results. Specifically, for the healthy class, the algorithm achieves a 73% Mean Average Precision, a 75% Precision, and a 66% Recall. In the case of Verticillium wilt, the algorithm attains a 62% mAP score, a 70% Precision score, and a 49% Recall score. Lastly, for the potato

---

[3] GitHub repository for ESRGAN: https://github.com/xinntao/ESRGAN.
[4] GitHub repository for BSRGAN: https://github.com/cszn/BSRGAN.

leafroll virus class, the algorithm obtains a 32% mAP score, a 51% Precision score, and a 36% Recall score. These results successfully demonstrate the algorithm's capability to effectively identify and classify diseases in potato plants based on high super-resolution aerial images. It is worth mentioning that these evaluation results are derived from a subset of the dataset, specifically 10% of the test images. Consequently, further evaluation on a larger scale is imperative to validate the algorithm's performance and robustness in real-world scenarios. The work can be extended to incorporate metrics that support the efficacy of super-resolution techniques such as PSNR, and SSIM.

Acknowledgement. The authors acknowledge computational and funding support from the project numbered *CSE2122001FACEKALI* and titled *Design and Development of Disaster Response Dashboard for India* for carrying out the work.

References

1. Pierce, F.J., Nowak, P.: Aspects of precision agriculture. Adv. Agron. **67**, 1–85 (1999)
2. Butte, S., Vakanski, A., Duellman, K., Wang, H., Mirkouei, A.: Potato crop stress identification in aerial images using deep learning-based object detection. Agron. J. **113**(5), 3991–4002 (2021)
3. Zhang, K., Liang, J., Van Gool, L., Timofte, R.: Designing a practical degradation model for deep blind image super-resolution. In: Proceedings of the IEEE/CVF International Conference on Computer Vision, pp. 4791–4800 (2021)
4. Gavade, A., Sane, P.: Super resolution image reconstruction by using bicubic interpolation. In: National Conference on Advanced Technologies in Electrical and Electronic Systems, vol. 10, p. 1 (2014)
5. Wang, X., et al.: ESRGAN: enhanced super-resolution generative adversarial networks. In: Proceedings of the European Conference on Computer Vision (ECCV) Workshops (2018)
6. Jocher, G., Chaurasia, A., Qiu, J.: Yolo by ultralytics (2023). https://github.com/ultralytics/ultralytics
7. Jiang, Y., Wang, Y., Li, S., Zhang, Y., Zhao, M., Gao, Y.: Event-based low-illumination image enhancement. IEEE Trans. Multimed. 1–12 (2023)
8. Yi, M., Li, W., Elibol, A., Chong, N.Y.: Attention-model guided image enhancement for robotic vision applications. In: 2020 17th International Conference on Ubiquitous Robots (UR), pp. 514–519 (2020)
9. Kim, W.: Low-light image enhancement: a comparative review and prospects. IEEE Access **10**, 84535–84557 (2022)
10. Roy, S.D., Pal, T., Bhowmik, M.K.: Benchmarking of natural scene image dataset in degraded conditions for visibility enhancement. In: 2021 IEEE International Conference on Image Processing (ICIP), pp. 1999–2003 (2021)
11. Yang, K.-F., Zhang, X.-S., Li, Y.-J.: A biological vision inspired framework for image enhancement in poor visibility conditions. IEEE Trans. Image Process. **29**, 1493–1506 (2020)
12. He, K., Zhang, X., Ren, S., Sun, J.: Deep residual learning for image recognition. In: Proceedings of the IEEE Conference on Computer Vision and Pattern Recognition, pp. 770–778 (2016)

13. Huang, G., Liu, Z., Van Der Maaten, L., Weinberger, K.Q.: Densely connected convolutional networks. In: Proceedings of the IEEE Conference on Computer Vision and Pattern Recognition, pp. 4700–4708 (2017)
14. Goodfellow, I., et al.: Generative adversarial networks. Commun. ACM **63**(11), 139–144 (2020)
15. Zheng, Z., Wang, P., Liu, W., Li, J., Ye, R., Ren, D.: Distance-IoU loss: faster and better learning for bounding box regression. In: Proceedings of the AAAI Conference on Artificial Intelligence, vol. 34, pp. 12993–13000 (2020)
16. Li, X., et al.: Generalized focal loss: learning qualified and distributed bounding boxes for dense object detection. Adv. Neural Inf. Process. Syst. **33**, 21002–21012 (2020)
17. Redmon, J., Divvala, S., Girshick, R., Farhadi, A.: You only look once: unified, real-time object detection. In: Proceedings of the IEEE Conference on Computer Vision and Pattern Recognition, pp. 779–788 (2016)
18. Redmon, J., Farhadi, A.: Yolov3: an incremental improvement. arXiv preprint arXiv:1804.02767 (2018)
19. Terven, J., Cordova-Esparza, D.: A comprehensive review of YOLO: from YOLOv1 to YOLOv8 and beyond. arXiv preprint arXiv:2304.00501, 2023

Biogeography Based Band Selection for Hyperspectral Image Classification

Aloke Datta[✉] and Gaurav Niranjan

LNMIIT, Jaipur, India
{aloke.datta,19UCS054}@lnmiit.ac.in

Abstract. Hyperspectral image classification is a widely researched topic in the field of remote sensing. In this context, dimensionality reduction plays an important role as it can affect the efficiency of the learning algorithm and also reduce the redundancy. In this article, a different look on the problem has been explored where application of biogeography based optimization is used for efficient dimensionality reduction in hyperspectral images. After that SVM classification technique is used to categorize the image pixels. Establishing the betterment of the methods, qualitative and quantitative analysis of the methods have been made, which shows a promising result than other existing methods.

Keywords: Hyperspectral image · dimensionality reduction · biogeography based optimization · SVM · RBF kernel

1 Introduction

A hyperspectral image (HSI) is a three dimensional image that contains hundreds or thousands of contiguous narrow wavelength bands, which makes it possible to identify the materials present in an image with a high degree of accuracy. HSI analysis has various applications, from crop analysis to military surveillance [8]. In this perspective, classification is an important task. Hyperspectral image classification (HSIC) is a process that involves assigning categories or classes to pixels in a hyperspectral image.

HSIC faces some difficulties which are primarily related to its high dimensionality, making most learning algorithms inefficient. Since a hypespectral image contains hundreds of bands, not all of them might be useful for classification task. Hence, it is important to filter out the redundant bands through dimensionality reduction techniques. Two important ways of feature reduction is either selection or extraction of features [4,5].

Pal et al. [9] explain why feature selection is an important step in HSIC. They show that SVM classifier's accuracy depends on the no. of features, and that the accuracy might reduce when using more features on a small dataset. Zhang et al. [16] propose a dimensionality reduction algorithm which learns a shared latent

© The Author(s), under exclusive license to Springer Nature Switzerland AG 2024
H. Kaur et al. (Eds.): CVIP 2023, CCIS 2010, pp. 91–101, 2024.
https://doi.org/10.1007/978-3-031-58174-8_9

low dimensional subspace by projecting the spectral and spatial features into a common space through graph Laplacian techniques. Archibald et al. [1] introduce an embedded feature selection algorithm that works by embedding a weighting into the SVM kernel that updates iteratively.

Recent methods on HSIC focus on deep learning approaches to learn high level features in the data through non-linear mappings. These techniques mostly use PCA [3] to reduce the dimensionality of the data through mathematical transformations. Chen et al. [2] propose stacked auto encoders to learn high level features, and then performing classification by logistic regression. Further they design a joint spectral-spatial classification framework, using PCA and neighborhood pixels for better results. Zhong et al. [18] design a residual network of 3D convolution layers which learn spectral and spatial features simultaneously without performing any dimensionality reduction on the dataset. Yang et al. [14] introduce the use of recurrent 2D and 3D CNN architectures, which perform feature learning at multiple levels of input size to leverage the spatial context of every pixel.

Various evolutionary algorithm based band selection methods [7] are experimented in the state-of-the-art techniques exploiting the merits of different evolutionary algorithms like genetic algorithm (GA) [15], particle swarm optimization [11], differential evolution [6], etc. These methods basically use evolutionary methods for selecting the (sub)optimal subset of bands and fitness value of each subset is calculated by either filter method or wrapper method [8]. State-of-the-art evolutionary algorithm methods include artificial bee colony (ABC) algorithm [13], immune clone selection (ICS) algorithm [17] and Ant lion optimizer (ALO) algorithm [12].

In this paper, a new feature selection method is proposed based on biogeography based optimization (BBO) technique. BBO comes from the wide range of evolutionary algorithms and is inspired from the geographical distribution of biological organisms. For classification, SVM is used with RBF kernel function due to its generalization ability and robustness to outliers.

The rest of the paper is structured as follows. First the basic model of the BBO is sketched in Sect. 2, Sect. 3 describes the proposed approach. Section 4 entails experimental details and result analysis. We conclude with Sect. 5.

2   Basics of Biogeography Based Optimization (BBO)

BBO is based on the natural phenomena of distribution of species among neighbouring islands. Introduced by Dan Simon [10], BBO models the extinction and migration of species in different islands mathematically. In the context of an optimization problem, an island refers to a solution and suitability index variable (SIV) refer to features of optimization problem. Based on good set of SIV (features) migration rate will increase. BBO tries to find the optimal set of characteristics/features using two parameters: immigration rate (λ) and emigration rate (μ). Immigration rate signifies how likely are features to be replaced and emigration rate signifies how likely the features will be shared. Hence a more optimal solution will have a higher emigration rate and a lower immigration rate and vice-versa for the least optimal solution.

BBO initializes many solutions by randomly selecting features from the pool of valid features. All solutions are evaluated by some fitness function, which measures the quality of the solutions. The solutions would have different fitness values showing that some solutions are better than others. The fitness of each solution is calculated by some fitness function $F(.)$. If a given solution is considered to modify, then its immigration rate λ is applied to decide whether or not to modify a feature in that solution. If a given feature in a given solution S_i is considered to be modify, then the emigration rates μ of the other solutions is used to decide which of the solutions should migrate a randomly selected feature to S_i.

Initially in the BBO process, each solution contains some randomly selected features from the set of all features. The migration process, governed by emigration and immigration rates, only exchanges the features from one solution to another. This way, the features that weren't selected initially from the set of all features never get a chance to be a part of any solution. To counter this effect, mutation is performed. Mutation changes a random feature from a randomly selected solution. The feature that is introduced can be any feature from the set of all features. In this way, the other features also get a chance to improve the solutions if possible.

In order to preserve the best solution from being changed by mutation, the BBO algorithm incorporates some sort of elitism. Algorithm 1 is the pseudocode of the BBO algorithm used in our implementation. It is important to note that Algorithm 1 is just one cycle of the BBO process without mutation. For the subsequent cycles, the initialization of the variables won't be done again. After each cycle of the BBO migration process, mutation is performed (using P_{mutate}) shown in Algorithm 2.

Algorithm 1 BBO migration process

1: $N :=$ total number of features
2: $n :=$ number of features in each solution
3: $K :=$ total number of solutions (population size)
4: Initialize K solutions by randomly choosing n features from the set of N features
5: $P_{mutate} :=$ mutation probability
6: Calculate fitness $F(K_i)$ of each solution and sort the solutions from most fit to least fit
7: Calculate μ_i and λ_i of each solution S_i
8: $\mu_{sum} := \sum \mu_i$
9: Define $R(.) :=$ random number generator in $(0, 1)$
10: **for** $i = 0$ to K **do**
11:     **for** $j = 0$ to n **do**
12:         **if** $R(.) < \lambda_i$ **then**
13:             RandomNum $:= R(.) * \mu_{sum}$
14:             Select $:= 0$
15:             SelectIndex $:= -1$
16:             **for** $t = 0$ to K **do**
17:                 Select $=$ Select $+ \mu_t$
18:                 SelectIndex $=$ SelectIndex $+ 1$
19:                 **if** RandomNum $\leq$ Select **AND** SelectIndex $< K$ **then**
20:                     j^{th} feature of $K_i := j^{th}$ feature of K_t
21:                     **break**
22:                 **else**
23:                     **continue**
24:         **else**
25:             **continue**

Algorithm 2 BBO mutation

1: Define $R(.) :=$ random number generator in $(0, 1)$
2: After one cycle of BBO algorithm:
3: **for** $i = 0$ to K **do**
4:     **for** $j = 0$ to n **do**
5:         **if** $R(.) < P_{mutate}$ **then**
6:             Set j^{th} feature of K_i as any random feature from the set of all features
7:         **else**
8:             **continue**

---

3   The Proposed Method

The proposed method is basically a two step process. In step 1, BBO based dimensionality reduction has been explained and in step 2 classification using SVM is described.

3.1   Step 1: BBO Based Dimensionality Reduction

In this step, BBO algorithm is employed for band selection that in turn reduces the dimensionality of the data. Since the hyperspectral image contains hundreds of bands, and not all of them are needed, we filter out a subset of these bands which contribute the most to our task of classifying the pixel. So, band selection is the major step in HSIC. We propose band selection through the BBO algorithm and show that it achieves high classification accuracy.

For the BBO algorithm, we need to define a fitness function which tells us how good the solutions are. For our task, we took classification accuracy from an kernel SVM classifier as the fitness measure. As for the initialization parameters: number of bands in each solution (n), population size (K), and mutation probability (P_{mutate}), where all chosen by trail and error from various values. The total number of features N would be the number of bands in the HSI.

We defined the emigration and immigration rates as follows:

$$\mu_i = (N - i) / (N + 1)$$

$$\lambda_i = 1 - \mu_i$$

$$\forall i = 0....N - 1$$

Here i is the index of the solution after sorting the population from most fit to least fit. Hence, for the best solution $i = 0$ and for the worst solution $i = N - 1$. Therefore for the best solution, μ will be very high (close to 1) and λ will be low (close to 0), signifying that the best solution shares its features with other solutions much more and resists a change in its own features. The opposite is true for the worst solution.

3.2   Step 2: SVM Based Classification

After band selection, we classify the pixel using support vector machine (SVM). It is a supervised learning algorithm used for classification and regression problems and is effective in solving complex problems with high-dimensional feature spaces. SVM finds a hyperplane that separates the different classes of the data with the largest possible margin, i.e., it aims to maximize the distance between the decision hyperplane and the closest data points of each class (support vectors). This enables SVMs to have better generalization ability and reduce overfitting.

SVMs can utilize kernel functions that map the data points in higher dimension implicitly. This allows the classifier to fit data that might not be linearly separable in the original lower dimension. For our task, we use the RBF (Radial Basis Function) as kernel function, which measures the similarity between two data points based on their Euclidean distance in the input space. It transforms the data points into a higher-dimensional feature space, where a linear decision boundary can be found. The mathematical formula for the RBF kernel is as follows:

$$K(x, x') = exp(-\gamma * \|x - x'\|^2)$$

Here, x and x' represent two data points and γ is a hyperparameter that controls the influence of each training example on the decision boundary.

4   Experimental Details and Results Analysis

4.1   Description of Dataset

Indian Pine dataset was used to perform all experiments. It is captured by the AVIRIS sensor over the Indian Pine test site in North-western Indiana. It consists of 145 × 145 pixels with each pixel having 200 bands. This dataset contains a total of 16 classes, mostly related to agriculture, forests and vegetation. It is the most widely used benchmark dataset for land cover mapping. Figure 1 shows the map of Indian Pine with different classes colored accordingly. Table 1 contains the different classes in the Indian Pine dataset along with the number of samples in each class.

Table 1. Classes in Indian Pine dataset with their respective samples

#	Class	Samples
1	Alfalfa	46
2	Corn-notill	1428
3	Corn-mintill	830
4	Corn	237
5	Grass-pasture	483
6	Grass-trees	730
7	Grass-pasture-mowed	28
8	Hay-windrowed	478
9	Oats	20
10	Soybean-notill	972
11	Soybean-mintill	2455
12	Soybean-clean	593
13	Wheat	205
14	Woods	1265
15	Buildings-Grass-Trees-Drives	386
16	Stone-Steel-Towers	93

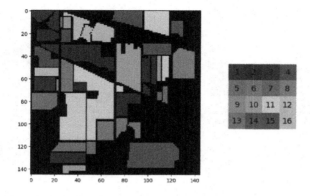

Fig. 1. Indian Pine ground truth with class labels

4.2 Parameter Details

In the proposed method several parameters need to be tuned for the BBO based band learning process. These are n (number of bands), K (population size), P_{mutate} (mutation probability), test split and regularization parameter C for the SVM classifier. The optimal hyperparameters were found by trail and error, keeping parameters constant and changing only one. We obtained: $n = 40$, $K = 40$, $P = 0.10$, $C = 150$ and test-split = 20%.

4.3 The Analysis of Result

In the experiments, classification accuracy and kappa coefficients are evaluated for quantitatively measuring the goodness of the proposed method over the other existing evolutionary (GA and DE) based algorithms on HSIC. Table 2 presents a comparative analysis between the Genetic Algorithm (GA), Differential Evolution (DE) and the biogeography based (BBO) algorithm on the Indian pine data set. The table clearly shows the superiority of the BBO-based approach over the other two methods in terms of accuracy and kappa value.

Table 2. Comparison of classification accuracy and kappa values using GA, DE and BBO based method on Indian Pine dataset

No. of bands	GA		DE		BBO	
	Classification Accuracy	Kappa	Classification Accuracy	Kappa	Classification Accuracy	Kappa
5	82.19%	0.8051	84.13%	0.8270	86.54%	0.8346
10	89.41%	0.8870	91.27%	0.9055	93.37%	0.9114
15	91.02%	0.9004	92.80%	0.9130	93.95%	0.9186
20	91.21%	0.9208	93.07%	0.9296	94.34%	0.9308
25	92.04%	0.9225	93.92%	0.9410	95.71%	0.9439
30	92.48%	0.9300	94.31%	0.9321	96.29%	0.9370
35	93.02%	0.9401	94.86%	0.9488	96.49%	0.9470
40	93.07%	0.9349	95.02%	0.9522	96.68%	0.9543

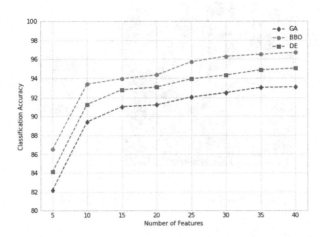

Fig. 2. Comparison of classification accuracy using GA, DE and BBO based method

Table 3. Precision, Recall, F1 score and Intersection over Union(IoU) in each class of Indian Pine dataset for GA and BBO based band selection method.

Class	GA				BBO			
	Precision	Recall	F1 score	IoU	Precision	Recall	F1 score	IoU
1	0.88	0.85	0.87	0.76	0.91	0.90	0.91	0.83
2	0.86	0.88	0.87	0.76	0.92	0.89	0.91	0.82
3	0.72	0.85	0.78	0.64	0.85	0.85	0.85	0.74
4	0.93	0.95	0.94	0.89	0.93	0.96	0.95	0.89
5	0.99	0.99	0.99	0.98	1.00	0.98	0.99	0.98
6	1.00	1.00	1.00	1.00	1.00	1.00	1.00	1.00
7	0.99	1.00	0.99	1.00	0.99	1.00	0.99	1.00
8	1.00	1.00	1.00	1.00	1.00	1.00	1.00	1.00
9	0.86	0.90	0.88	0.78	0.89	0.88	0.88	0.79
10	0.91	0.88	0.89	0.80	0.92	0.92	0.92	0.85
11	0.88	0.92	0.90	0.81	0.91	0.97	0.94	0.88
12	1.00	1.00	1.00	1.00	1.00	0.98	0.99	0.97
13	0.99	0.95	0.97	0.93	0.99	0.97	0.98	0.95
14	0.78	0.90	0.83	0.71	0.95	0.95	0.90	0.81
15	0.95	0.95	0.95	0.90	1.00	0.95	0.98	0.95
16	0.99	0.99	0.99	0.97	1.00	0.99	0.99	0.98
Avg	0.89	0.92	0.90	0.83	**0.94**	**0.95**	**0.94**	**0.88**

Figure 2 gives a graphical representation of classification accuracy with different number of selected bands (from 5 to 40 with interval 5) for all three GA, DE and BBO based methods on the Indian Pine data set. The graph also corroborates our earlier findings. It is also observed that accuracy becomes stable (i.e., rate of increase is slow) whenever number of selected bands is 20 or more for all three methods.

Table 3 provides a comprehensive study of various performance metrics for GA and BBO based band selection methods, over individual classes as well as average over the classes of the Inian Pine dataset. The performance matrics used in this table are precision, recall, F1 Score, and Intersection over Union (IoU). For both GA and BBO, the metrics vary across different classes, indicating varying degrees of success in classifying the pixels. Notably, both algorithms achieve high scores, particularly in classes 6, 7, 8, and 12, where they consistently attain perfect or near-perfect metrics, such as precision and recall. Overall, the table underscores the effectiveness of BBO over GA in HSIC, with BBO outperforming GA across the different classes, as well as, average evaluation metrics.

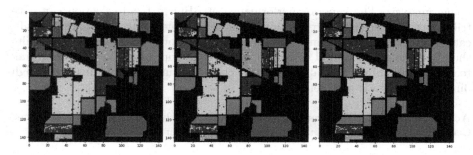

Fig. 3. Classified images using 40 bands by GA, DE, BBO based method, respectively on Indian Pine dataset

For qualitatively analyzing the result, it is better to show the pictorial representation of the methods. Figure 3 gives a pictorial representation of classified images of Indian Pine data for all three GA, DE and BBO based methods with 40 selected bands

GA, DE and BBO filter out the bands that maximize the fitness function, i.e., the classification accuracy of the SVM classifier. From Fig. 2 we can infer than the classification accuracy does not change much after 30 bands. But as we can see, BBO performs slightly better than GA and DE. BBO's migration process, which involves exchanging information between solutions, can facilitate exploration and exploitation effectively.

By comparing the results obtained through BBO with those of GA and DE, we observed that BBO consistently yielded superior classification accuracy. The utilization of BBO for band selection enhanced the discriminative power of the selected bands. These improvements can be attributed to the inherent exploration and exploitation capabilities of BBO, which enable the algorithm to efficiently navigate the solution space and identify (sub)optimal band subsets.

5 Conclusion

This article, initially, explored the effectiveness of biogeography based optimization (BBO) for band selection in hyperspectral images and compared its performance with band selection using genetic algorithms (GA) and differential evolution(DE) based methods. Through experimentation and analysis, it is noticed that BBO outperformed GA and DE based methods in terms of classification accuracy and kappa coefficient when using the same number of bands.

The application of BBO in hyperspectral band selection exhibited notable advantages over other methods. BBO leverages the principles of biogeography, which mimic the dynamics of species migration, to optimize the band selection process. This unique approach proved to be effective in identifying relevant bands that contribute significantly to classification accuracy.

The findings of this research hold significant implications for hyperspectral image analysis. The superior performance of BBO in band selection can contribute to enhanced remote sensing applications, including land cover classification, object detection, and environmental monitoring. Moreover, the results shed light on the potential of biogeography based optimization as a promising technique for addressing feature selection challenges in other domains where high dimensional data is prevalent.

Acknowledgment. This work is partially supported by ISRO Regional Academic Center for Space, MNIT Jaipur through Project Number RAC-S/SP/22-23/04.

References

1. Archibald, R., Fann, G.: Feature selection and classification of hyperspectral images with support vector machines. IEEE Geosci. Remote Sens. Lett. 4(4), 674–677 (2007)
2. Chen, Y., et al.: Deep learning-based classification of hyperspectral data. IEEE J. Sel. Top. Appl. Earth Obs. Remote Sens. 7(6), 2094–2107 (2014)
3. Datta, A., Chakravorty, A.: Hyperspectral image segmentation using multidimensional histogram over principal component images. In: International Conference on Advances in Computing, Communication Control and Networking (ICAC-CCN), pp. 857–862 (2018)
4. Datta, A., Ghosh, S., Ghosh, A.: Combination of clustering and ranking techniques for unsupervised band selection of hyperspectral images. IEEE J. Sel. Top. Appl. Earth Obs. Remote Sens. 8(6), 2814–2823 (2015)
5. Datta, A., Ghosh, S., Ghosh, A.: Supervised band extraction of hyperspectral images using partitioned maximum margin criterion. IEEE Geosci. Remote Sens. Lett. 14(1), 82–86 (2017)
6. Datta, A., Ghosh, S., Ghosh, A.: Wrapper based feature selection in hyperspectral image data using self-adaptive differential evolution. In: Proceedings of the International Conference on Image Information Processing (ICIIP), pp. 1–6 (2011)

7. Ghosh, A., Datta, A., Ghosh, S.: Self-adaptive differential evolution for feature selection in hyperspectral image data. Appl. Soft Comput. **13**(4), 1969–1977 (2013)
8. Jia, X., Kuo, B.-C., Crawford, M.M.: Feature mining for hyperspectral image classification. Proc. IEEE **101**(3), 676–697 (2013)
9. Pal, M., Foody, G.M.: Feature selection for classification of hyperspectral data by SVM. IEEE Trans. Geosci. Remote Sens. **48**(5), 2297–2307 (2010)
10. Simon, D.: Biogeography-based optimization. IEEE Trans. Evolut. Comput. **12**(6), 702–713 (2008)
11. Su, H., et al.: Optimized hyperspectral band selection using particle swarm optimization. IEEE J. Sel. Top. Appl. Earth Obs. Remote Sens. **7**(6), 2659–2670 (2014)
12. Wang, M., et al.: A feature selection approach for hyperspectral image based on modified ant lion optimizer. Knowl.-Based Syst. **168**, 39–48 (2019)
13. Xie, F., et al.: Unsupervised band selection based on artificial bee colony algorithm for hyperspectral image classification. Appl. Soft Comput. **75**, 428–440 (2019)
14. Yang, X., et al. "Hyperspectral image classification with deep learning models. IEEE Trans. Geosci. Remote Sens. **56**(9), 5408–5423 (2018). 12 A. Datta et al
15. Yu, S., Backer, S.D., Scheunders, P.: Genetic feature selection combined with composite fuzzy nearest neighbour classifiers for hyperspectral satellite imagery. Pattern Recognit. Lett. **23**, 183–190 (2002)
16. Zhang, L., et al.: Simultaneous spectral-spatial feature selection and extraction for hyperspectral images. IEEE Trans. Cybern. **48**(1), 16–28 (2016)
17. Zhang, W., Li, X., Zhao, L.: Discovering the representative subset with low redundancy for hyperspectral feature selection. Remote Sens. **11**(11), 1341 (2019)
18. Zhong, Z., et al.: Spectral-spatial residual network for hyperspectral image classification: a 3-D deep learning framework. IEEE Trans. Geosci. Remote Sens. **56**(2), 847–858 (2017)

Uncovering the Extent of Flood Damage using Sentinel-1 SAR Imagery: A Case Study of the July 2020 Flood in Assam

Puviyarasi Thirugnanasammandamoorthi⬤, Debabrata Ghosh$^{(\boxtimes)}$⬤, and Ram Kishan Dewangan⬤

Department of Electronics and Communication Engineering, Thapar Institute of Engineering and Technology, Punjab 147004, India
{pt_phd22,debabrata.ghosh,ram.kishan}@thapar.edu

Abstract. In India, Assam is known for being highly susceptible to floods, with the state being hit by multiple flooding events each year. The floods in Assam in July 2020 were mainly due to the heavy monsoon rainfall in the region. The Brahmaputra River and its tributaries, which pass through the state, received substantial rainfall, leading to a sudden increase in water levels and flooding in multiple districts. The state's topography, hills, and valleys also exacerbated the situation as the mountain water flowed into the plains and inundated low-lying areas. Identifying areas that floods have impacted is of utmost importance in facilitating an efficient response to the flood. The current work focuses on the case study of the 2020 Assam flood and aims to develop an operational methodology for potential flood-damaged area mapping. Sentinel-1 Synthetic Aperture Radar (SAR) images from April 2020 (before the flood) and July 2020 (after the flood) were used to create water masks based on global thresholding. This was followed by an RGB composite image highlighting the inundation extent. The resulting flood map was compared to a ground truth RGB composite generated by stacking the pre- and post-disaster images. The study's methodology can be replicated to map floods in other areas around the world.

Keywords: Flood mapping · Sentinel-1 · SAR image · Backscatter · RGB composite · Water mask · Flood Mask

1 Introduction

One of the most frequent natural disasters in the world is floods, and their devastation affects infrastructure, crop production, and human life worldwide. Climate change has led to an increase in the frequency and unpredictability of flood events in recent years. In the years to come, the price and the number of people impacted by this catastrophe will considerably rise. According to climate change estimates, the number of people affected by floods worldwide will double by 2030, going from 72 million to 147 million per year [1]. The Organization for Economic Cooperation and Development estimates that floods globally inflict more than $40 billion in damage yearly [2].

India, which ranks second in the world regarding the severity of flood damage behind Bangladesh, is responsible for one-fifth of all flood-related fatalities worldwide. During a brief monsoon season that lasts only four months (June-September), nearly 75% of all rainfall in India occurs. This causes the rivers to flow high, resulting in extensive flooding incidents. The National Flood Commission reports that approximately 40 million hectares of land in India are susceptible to flooding, and about 18.6 million hectares of land are affected annually on average. There are around 3.7 million hectares of crops damaged annually on average. In the north and northeast of India, the Ganga, Meghana, and Brahmaputra River basins are the nation's most vulnerable regions to flooding [3]. According to the Water Resources Department of the Government of Assam, the flood-prone area in Assam is four times the national average of flood-prone areas.

Flood mapping is a critical task for disaster management and risk assessment. Traditional methods of flood mapping, such as ground-based surveys and remote sensing, are often time-consuming and expensive. Synthetic aperture radar (SAR) imagery, on the other hand, can be used to rapidly and cost-effectively map floods. SAR is a type of radar that uses microwaves to create images of the Earth's surface. SAR imagery is not affected by clouds or darkness, making it ideal for monitoring floods. Thus, many researchers [4–13] have looked at using SAR data for flood mapping.

Sentinel-1 is a constellation of two SAR satellites operated by the European Space Agency (ESA). Sentinel-1 imagery is freely available and has a high temporal resolution (12 days). This makes it ideal for monitoring floods. Sentinel-1 SAR data can be used for flood mapping by detecting changes in the backscattered signal between pre-flood and post-flood images. This enables differentiating the overflow flood water from the permanent water bodies.

The primary purpose of this study is to map the extent of the July 2020 Assam flood event in some of the severely affected districts using Sentinel-1 SAR data. For this purpose, two different Sentinel-1 datasets have been acquired from the ESA's Copernicus Open Access Hub and pre-processed using the open-source SNAP Tool. While the majority of the SAR imaging-based flood mapping techniques [2, 9, 14–19] involve utilizing AI-ML algorithms to extract features from SAR images and train models to classify water and non-water areas, they have limitations, including the requirement of the extensive training dataset, the necessity for ground truth for model validation. To address these limitations, a novel flood mapping technique has been proposed, which creates water masks from the pre-and post-disaster SAR images, followed by generating an RGB composite image highlighting the inundation extent. To validate the flood mapping results, an RGB composite image generated by stacking the pre- and after-flood images has been used as ground truth.

2 Methodology

2.1 Study Area

The 2020 Assam flood refers to the devastating flood that occurred along the Brahmaputra River during the COVID-19 pandemic. The flood was triggered by heavy monsoon rainfall in the catchment areas of the Brahmaputra River [24]. According to the flood report released on July 20th by the Assam State Disaster Management Authority, more than 2.4 million individuals were impacted by the flood, and over 1.09 lakh hectares of cropland were affected [20]. In addition, the flood had a significant impact on over 900,000 large animals, resulting in the deaths of 113 animals in Kaziranga. Among the 24 districts that were affected, Nagaon, Kamrup, Darrang, Nalbari, Barpeta, and Morigaon experienced severe impact. Moreover, certain state regions were still under a severe flood alert. A study area was chosen, covering a few of the worst affected districts along the Brahmaputra River basin. It includes Nagaon, Darrang, and Morigaon districts in central Assam. Figure 1 shows the study area.

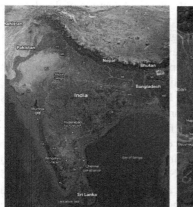

Fig. 1. Study area for the proposed flood mapping

2.2 Materials

The availability of Sentinel-1 SAR images has proven valuable for near real-time emergency response, as the data can be accessed for free within 3 h of acquisition. For systematically archived data, the images are accessible within 24 h. The Copernicus Open Access Hub of ESA provided the Sentinel-1 (Mission S1A) datasets used in this investigation. The specification of the acquired data includes Ground Range Detected (GRD), Interferometric Wide swath (IW), and dual-polarization (Vertical transmit/Vertical receive VV and Vertical transmit/Horizontal receive VH). The dataset has a wide swath width (250 km) and high resolution (10 m), allowing extensive geographical analysis at a large scale [21]. Two datasets (archived) were obtained in the predefined study area to delineate the flood water: one taken on 3rd April 2020 is known as the archive image (before the incidence of the flood), and the other acquired on 20th July 2020 is known as the crisis image (during the flood), both captured when the satellite was ascending. ESA's Sentinel Application Platform (SNAP), an open-source software, along with the S1Tbx toolbox, was used for processing all the datasets. Only the like-polarized (VV) channel of each dataset, retrieved as a Level-1 GRD product, was analyzed in this study. The generated flood map was exported on Google Earth to display as an overlay on the Google Earth optical imagery. It enables seeing the spatial relationship between the flood map and other geographic features.

2.3 Methods

To differentiate the flood overflow regions from permanent water bodies and other land covers, Sentinel-1 SAR raw pictures were pre-processed with the open-source SNAP toolbox. Pre-processing is required for several corrections and adjustments, which make the raw data more usable and accurate for flood mapping. A methodological framework of the proposed work is shown in Figure 2.

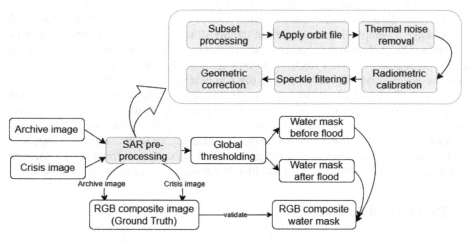

Fig. 2. Framework of the proposed methodology

To generate calibrated level-1 temporal GRD SAR products, a step-wise procedure including subset processing, applying orbit file, thermal noise removal, radiometric calibration, speckle filtering, multi-look processing, and geometric calibration was applied to the raw datasets. Subset processing was performed to extract only a portion of the SAR image. It helped to reduce the processing time and the storage requirement considerably. The apply orbit file operator was used to apply a precise orbit determination (POD) file to the SAR data to produce more accurate georeferenced images. POD contains information about the precise location and velocity of the satellite as it passes over the Earth, which is used to correct the SAR data for any errors introduced by the satellite's motion. Thermal noise removal was employed to remove the noise caused due to the random variations in the electronic components of the SAR instrument.

Radiometric calibration was used to convert the raw pixel digital number (DN) values to radar backscatter values (sigma naught σ^0). A 7 x 7 Boxcar speckle filter was used to lessen speckle noise inherent to SAR data. Multi-look processing was used to reduce the speckle noise further and improve image interpretability. The number of looks for the range and azimuth directions was set to 5 and 1, respectively. A geometric correction was applied to the SAR data to correct geometric distortions caused by the imaging geometry [22]. For this, Range-Doppler Terrain Correction was used based on SRTM-3 digital elevation model (DEM) along with bilinear interpolation and WGS84 map projection. Finally, a radiometric conversion of the backscatter coefficient values to a dB scale was conducted to improve the compatibility and interpretability of the SAR data. Batch processing was performed using Graph Builder to automatically apply the operations as mentioned above to both the archive image and the crisis image.

Water masks were created using both the processed archive image and the processed crisis image by employing band math in the SNAP tool. A global threshold value was determined by analyzing the characteristics of water pixels over several polygons placed across the region of interest (ROI). A threshold value close to the mean pixel intensity over the water polygons was chosen to discriminate the water bodies from non-water bodies in the SAR images. An RGB composite image was generated using the two water masks: the crisis water mask for the red band and the archive water mask for the green and blue bands. This composite image acts as the proposed flood map as it highlights the inundation extent. To validate the flood mapping accuracy, an RGB composite image was further generated using the archive image and the crisis image: the red band is assigned to the archive image, and the green and blue bands are assigned to the crisis image.

3   Results and Discussion

The proposed methodology uses simple steps to extract the flood-affected locations in the study area. Pre-processing the GRD product using SNAP software generates the archive and crisis images (shown in VV polarization), as shown in Figure 3. The permanent water bodies appear uniformly dark in the SAR images.

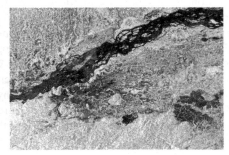

a) Archive image   b) Crisis image

Fig. 3. SAR Pre-processed (subset processing, application of orbit files, thermal noise removal, radiometric calibration, speckle filtering, and geometric correction) images

Specular reflection over these smooth water surfaces causes the reflected radar signal to go away from the sensor, resulting in a very low backscatter. Flood water, on the other hand, appears brighter in SAR images. However, flood water may appear differently depending on the timing and extent of the flood. During the early stages of the flood (Fig. 3b), when the water is shallow, and the surface is relatively smooth, flood water appears dark. As the flood water becomes more profound and more turbulent, it scatters radar signals in multiple directions, resulting in a brighter appearance. Other land covers, with very high backscatter values, appear in tones of grey in the SAR images. Histograms of before- and after-flood SAR images (both in VV polarization) are shown in Fig. 4. They can provide valuable information about the extent and severity of the flooding. The water mode (i.e., the shorter tail at the low end of the histogram) of the after-flood image's histogram is more prominent than before flood image's histogram. Furthermore, the water mode of the after-flood image's histogram is shifted to the left compared to the before-flood images' histogram due to the decrease in the overall backscatter coefficient of water with the emergence of flood water. The pixel counts in the non-water mode (i.e., the long tail at the high end of the histogram) is reduced in the after-flood image compared to the before-flood image due to the inundation of land covers.

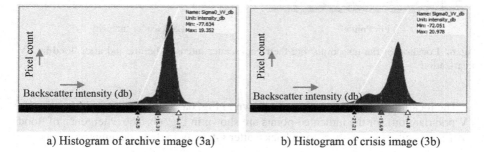

a) Histogram of archive image (3a)   b) Histogram of crisis image (3b)

Fig. 4. Histograms of Pre-processed images

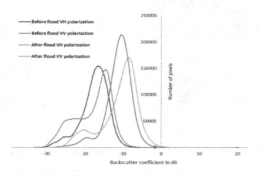

Fig. 5. Histograms of VV and VH polarized archive and crisis images

The histograms of the backscatter coefficients in the archive and the crisis images (both in VV and VH polarization) are shown in Fig. 5. Cross-polarization (VH) appears weaker than like-polarization (VV) in both images. This could be attributed to the fact that only a tiny part of the radar signal returns polarized (vertical turning horizontal) to the sensor over flat surfaces (for example, water bodies). Consequently, VV polarization images were only used for all the analyses in this study. Ten points were considered on the flood-affected areas within the ROI to compare their backscatter intensity before and after the flood [23].

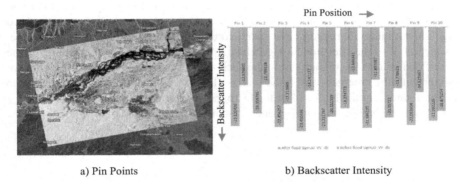

a) Pin Points   b) Backscatter Intensity

Fig. 6. Location of the ten points and their backscatter intensity before and after flood in VV polarization

The location map of these points is shown in Fig. 6a. The backscatter intensities (in VV polarization) for the indicated points are shown in Fig. 6b. The emergence of flood water has resulted in a reduction in backscatter intensity in these designated points.

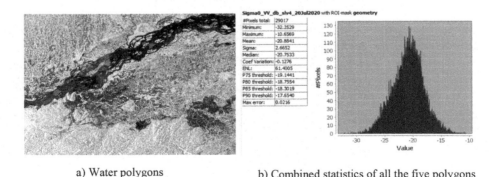

a) Water polygons   b) Combined statistics of all the five polygons

Fig. 7. Location of water polygons over the crisis image and combined statistics of all the five polygons shown in Fig. 7a

By examining the statistics of the water pixels in the archive image, a global threshold value was experimentally determined to construct water masks. Histograms of the before and after flood images, as seen in Fig. 4, exhibit a bimodal distribution where one mode represents the water bodies and the other represents the non-water bodies. Based on this inherent bimodal nature of the data, a carefully chosen global thresholding approach was opted to differentiate between water and non-water contents in the mask creation process. For empirical selection of the threshold value, 5 polygons (Fig. 7a) were placed over the water bodies across the archive image. The overall statistics of these water polygons are shown in Fig. 7b. A threshold value (−20 dB) close to the average backscatter intensity of the water pixels over these polygons was selected to delineate water bodies from the SAR images.

The raster-band math tool of the SNAP software was used to create two binary masks using the archive image and the crisis image. In our band math expression, backscatter values below −20 dB indicate the water bodies (i.e., permanent and flooded water), whereas values above −20 dB indicate other land covers. The archive and crisis water masks are shown in Figs. 8a and b. The difference between the water masks created from the after and before flood images are computed and shown in Fig. 9. The resulting difference map provides valuable information about the flood-damaged areas.

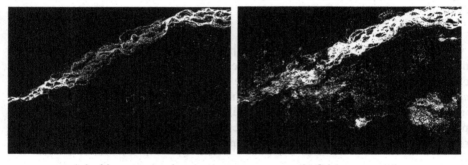

a) Archive water mask   b) Crisis water mask

Fig. 8. Water masks created using global thresholding

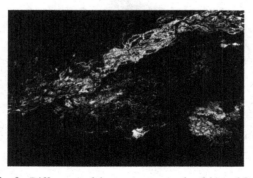

Fig. 9. Difference of the two water masks: 8 b) and 8 a)

An RGB composite image (Fig. 10) was created using the archive water mask and the crisis water mask to differentiate between the flood water and the permanent water bodies. We treat this image as our produced flood map. The composite image was obtained by selecting the crisis water mask for the red channel and the archive water mask for the green and blue channels. The difference between the crisis water mask and the archive water mask (i.e., the flood water only) appears red.

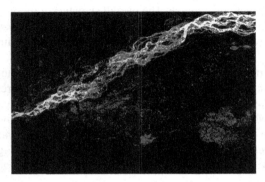

Fig. 10. RGB composite of archive and crisis water masks (i.e., generated flood map). (Color figure online)

The permanent water bodies, which are present in both the archive water mask and the crisis water mask, appear white because these pixels are high (i.e., 1) in all three channels. Some areas in the RGB composite image appear in tones of cyan (green-blue combined), indicating high values (i.e., 1) in the archive mask but low values (i.e., 0) in the crisis mask. One possible reason could be that some water bodies which were present in the archive image had receded or evaporated after the flood. Another possible reason could be that the ground or vegetation had absorbed the water bodies.

Fig. 11. RGB composite of archive and crisis images (i.e., ground truth). (Color figure online)

The resulting flood map was evaluated using a ground truth RGB composite image (Fig. 11) generated by selecting an archive image for the red band and a crisis image for the green and blue bands. In the archive image, there is high backscatter from the no-flooded areas (areas surrounding the river). However, in the crisis image, low backscatter occurs over these areas since they are flooded. As a result, these areas appear in red, with high responses in the red channel and low responses in the green and blue channels. The surrounding areas, where there are no floods, will appear in tones of grey. Because the backscatter response of these regions is similar in both the archive and the crisis image, making similar responses in red, green, and blue bands. The permanent water appears very dark because of the low backscatter in the archive and the crisis image. So, all three channels indicate a dark tone. Some surrounding areas appear in tones of cyan, indicating high backscatter response in the crisis image than in the archive image. These may be attributed to the ground cover changes as the flood water recedes. Or roughening of the water surface created by heavy wind, causing higher backscattering.

A quantitative comparison of the generated flood map RGB composite and the ground truth RGB composite is presented in Table 1. Ten regions of interest (ROIs, Fig. 12) were identified from both these images, and the percentage of floodwater pixels in each ROI was calculated. Fig. 13 shows the statistics of the two datasets. The mean ± standard deviation values of the two datasets were calculated as 21.7 ± 10.26 and 21.6 ± 10.07. Data from the produced flood map were compared with those obtained from the ground truth. Percentage error was calculated for each ROI. The average percentage error across all the ROIs was 1.08%.

Table 1. Quantitative comparison of ROIs in the generated flood map and the ground truth

ROI	Flood water pixel % in produced flood map	Flood water pixel % in ground truth	% error
ROI1	16.83	16.53	1.81
ROI2	37.91	37.54	0.98
ROI3	39.4	38.95	1.15
ROI4	15.41	15.77	2.28
ROI5	24.38	24.36	0.08
ROI6	13.34	13.24	0.75
ROI7	25.71	25.25	1.82
ROI8	20.4	20.61	1.02
ROI9	8.81	8.84	0.34
ROI10	14.87	14.95	0.53

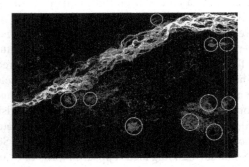

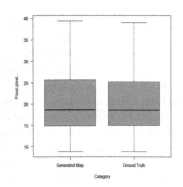

Fig. 12. ROIs identified on the generated flood map used in Table 1

Fig. 13. Box plots of the two datasets: flood water pixel % in generated flood map and in ground truth

4 Conclusions

The focus of this study is to explore the potential of using Sentinel-1 SAR data acquired over Assam in between April 2020 and July 2020 to identify flooded areas. To achieve this, the pre- and post-disaster SAR data were pre-processed with the aid of the SNAP Tool. This was followed by water mask creation and RGB composite image generation for inundation mapping. The resulting flood map was then compared to a ground truth RGB composite image generated by stacking the pre- and post-disaster images. Upon quantitative assessment, the global thresholding-based water mask creation followed by RGB composite generation was found to have performed quite accurately (with an average error of 1.08%) mapping the Assam flood. The methodology can be replicated to map floods in other areas around the world.

References

1. Islam, M.T., Meng, Q.: An exploratory study of Sentinel-1 SAR for rapid urban flood mapping on Google Earth Engine. Int. J. Appl. Earth Observ. Geoinf. **113**, 103002 (2022). https://doi.org/10.1016/j.jag.2022.103002, ISSN 1569-8432
2. Palomba, G., Farasin, A., Rossi, C.: Sentinel-1 flood delineation with supervised machine learning. In: ISCRAM 2020 Conference Proceedings-17th International Conference on Information Systems for Crisis Response and Management, pp. 1072-1083 (2020)
3. Flood Hazard Atlas of Odisha, National Disaster Management Authority (NDMA). https://ndma.gov.in/flood-hazard-atlases
4. Vargas-Cuentas, N.I., Roman-Gonzalez, A.: Sentinel 1 SAR-based flood detection and mapping: Myanmar two consecutive years case. Int. J. Eng. Trends Technol. **70**(12), 59–66 (2022). https://doi.org/10.14445/22315381/IJETT-V70I12P207.
5. Polat, A.B., Akçay, Ö.: Rapid flood mapping with Sentinel-1 SAR images: a case study of Maritsa River . In: 2nd Intercontinental Geoinformation Days (IGD), pp. 123-126, Mersin, Turkey (2021)
6. Zhang, M., Chen, F., Liang, D., Tian, B., Yang, A.: Use of Sentinel-1 GRD SAR images to delineate flood extent in Pakistan. Sustainability. **12**, 5784 (2020). https://doi.org/10.3390/su12145784

7. Uddin, M.: Meyer: operational flood mapping using multi-temporal Sentinel-1 SAR images: a case study from Bangladesh. Remote Sens. **11**, 1581 (2019). https://doi.org/10.3390/rs11113 1581

8. Nasirzadehdizaji, R., Akyuz, D.E., Cakir, Z.: Flood mapping and permanent water bodies change detection using sentinel SAR data, Int. Arch. Photogramm. Remote Sens. Spatial Inf. Sci. **XLII-4/W18**, 797–801 (2019). https://doi.org/10.5194/isprs-archives-XLII-4-W18-797-2019

9. Amitrano, D., Di Martino, G., Iodice, A., Riccio, D., Ruello, G.: Unsupervised rapid flood mapping using Sentinel-1 GRD SAR images. IEEE Trans. Geosci. Remote Sens. **56**(6), 3290–3299 (2018). https://doi.org/10.1109/TGRS.2018.2797536

10. Liang, J., Liu, D.: A local thresholding approach to flood water delineation using Sentinel-1 SAR imagery. ISPRS J. Photogramm. Remote Sens **159**, pp. 53-62 (2020). https://doi.org/10. 1016/j.isprsjprs.2019.10.017, ISSN 0924-2716

11. Bioresita, F., Puissant, A., Stumpf, A.J., Malet, J.: A method for automatic and rapid mapping of water surfaces from Sentinel-1 imagery. Remote Sens. **10**, 217 (2018)

12. Grimaldi, S., Xu, J., Li, Y., Pauwels, V.R.N., Walker, J.P.: Flood mapping under vegetation using single SAR acquisitions. Remote Sens. Environ. **237**, 111582 (2020). https://doi.org/ 10.1016/j.rse.2019.111582, ISSN 0034-4257

13. Tavus, B., Kocaman, S., Nefeslioglu, H.A., Gökçeoğlu, C.: Flood mapping using Sentinel-1 SAR data: a case study of Ordu 8 August 2018 Flood. Int. J. Environ. **6**, 333–337 (2019)

14. Liao, L., Du, L., Guo, Y.: Semi-supervised SAR target detection based on an improved faster R-CNN. Remote Sens. **14**, 143 (2021). https://doi.org/10.3390/rs14010143

15. Benoudjit, A., Guida, R.: A novel fully automated mapping of the flood extent on SAR images using a supervised classifier. Remote Sens. **11**(7), 779 (2019). https://doi.org/10.3390/rs1107 0779

16. Kang, W., Xiang, Y., Wang, F., Wan, L., You, H.: Flood detection in Gaofen-3 SAR images via fully convolutional networks. Sens. (Basel Switz.) **18**(9), E2915 (2018). https://doi.org/ 10.3390/s18092915.PMID:30200546;PMCID:PMC6165191

17. Ghosh, B., Garg, S., and Motagh, M.: Automatic flood detection from SENTINEL-1 data using deep learning architectures. ISPRS Ann. Photogramm. Remote Sens. Spatial Inf. Sci. **3**, 201–208 (2022). https://doi.org/10.5194/isprs-annals-V-3-2022-201-2022

18. Jiang, X., et al.: Rapid and large-scale mapping of flood inundation via integrating spaceborne synthetic aperture radar imagery with unsupervised deep learning. ISPRS J. Photogramm. Remote Sens. **178**, pp. 36-50 (2021). https://doi.org/10.1016/j.isprsjprs.2021.05.019, ISSN 0924-2716

19. Huang, M., Jin, S.: Rapid flood mapping and evaluation with a supervised classifier and change detection in Shouguang using Sentinel-1 SAR and Sentinel-2 optical data. Remote Sens. **12**, 2073 (2020). https://doi.org/10.3390/rs12132073

20. Daily report on flood from Assam state Disaster Management Authority. https://asdma.assam. gov.in/resource/assam-flood-report

21. Tran, K.H., Menenti, M., Jia, L.: Surface water mapping and flood monitoring in the Mekong delta using Sentinel-1 SAR time series and Otsu threshold. Remote Sens. **14**, 5721 (2022). https://doi.org/10.3390/rs14225721

22. Vanama, V.S.K., Rao, Y.S., Bhatt, C.M.: Change detection based flood mapping using multi-temporal earth observation satellite images: 2018 flood event of Kerala. Ind. Eur. J. Remote Sens. **54**(1), 42–58 (2021)

23. Carreño Conde, F., De Mata Muñoz, M.: Flood monitoring based on the study of Sentinel-1 SAR images: the Ebro River case study. Water **11**, 2454 (2019). https://doi.org/10.3390/w11 122454

24. Roy, S., Kumar Ojah, S., Nishant, N., Pratap Singh, P., Chutia, D.: Spatio-temporal Analysis of Flood Hazard Zonation in Assam. In: Gupta, D., Goswami, R.S., Banerjee, S., Tanveer, M., Pachori, R.B. (eds.) Pattern Recognition and Data Analysis with Applications. Lecture Notes in Electrical Engineering, vol. 888, pp. 521–531. Springer, Singapore (2022). https://doi.org/10.1007/978-981-19-1520-8_42.

Robust Unsupervised Geo-Spatial Change Detection Algorithm for SAR Images

Mrinmoy Sarkar[1]([✉])[iD], Subhojeet Roy[2][iD], and Rudrajit Choudhuri[2][iD]

[1] Techno International New Town, Kolkata, India
mrin2ksarkar@gmail.com
[2] St. Thomas' College of Engineering & Technology, Kolkata, India

Abstract. Geo-spatial change detection plays a crucial role in identifying alterations on the earth's surface over time intervals. This paper introduces a novel unsupervised grid graph generation algorithm specifically designed for change detection using Synthetic Aperture Radar (SAR) images. The proposed technique encompasses a multi-step process: starting with an improved log-ratio based difference image generation, followed by shortest path vector computation and thresholding from the generated grid graph utilizing Dijkstra's algorithm. Furthermore, a voting-major based tuning approach is employed to effectively eliminate any residual noisy corruptions. The algorithm is rigorously evaluated on qualitative and quantitative scales using standard image data and is benchmarked against state-of-the-art methods. Results demonstrate the resilience and superior performance of the proposed method in comparison to existing approaches in terms of robustness and speed.

Keywords: Remote Sensing · Unsupervised Change Detection · Graph Theoretic Algorithm

1 Introduction

Geo-spatial change detection (CD) helps identify changes on the earth's surface by analyzing the difference between satellite images acquired over different temporal periods [22]. The domain has wide practical applications ranging from urban research and monitoring [20,27], to the assessment of natural disasters [13]. Robust change detection algorithms have profound potential in improving rescue operations and damage assessment. There are three broad categories of CD algorithms: supervised [29], semi-supervised [28], and unsupervised [16]. Supervised and semi-supervised approaches are resilient as they model temporal relationships between images by treating CD as a classification problem. However, training these models requires large sets of labeled training data which is often not available in the context of remote sensing images. On the other hand, unsupervised algorithms treat CD as a change/non-change pixel map generation problem, eliminating the need for any prior information or labeled ground truth. Thus, these approaches are popular when it comes to remote sensing change

H. Kaur et al. (Eds.): CVIP 2023, CCIS 2010, pp. 115–127, 2024.
https://doi.org/10.1007/978-3-031-58174-8_11

detection. Traditionally, unsupervised methods follow a three-step approach for CD: (1) It starts with a pre-processing step where image denoising and geometric corrections are made to ensure that the pixels across different temporal snapshots correspond to the exact geographic location. (2) Next, a difference image is generated by comparing bi-temporal images. (3) Finally, the difference images are thresholded to obtain the final change map. Nevertheless, unsupervised CD methods have their own set of limitations. Multiplicative speckle noise [14], which is a grainy salt-and-pepper pattern present in radar imagery, is quite abundantly present in Synthetic Aperture Radar (SAR) [17] images. This reduces the quality of the produced difference image, introducing inaccuracies in the final change map [12]. Unsupervised methods also often pose hyper-parameter tuning problems, thus limiting the generalizability across multiple use cases.

The domain of CD has been tackled from several angles over the years. Initial approaches included traditonal clustering methods including Fuzzy C Means (FCM) [6] and PCA-K Means [4]. These methods are highly sensitive to initialization of hyperparameters and thus require granular tuning based on the nature of the images.

In 2019, Gao et al. proposed a Convolutional-wavelet neural network (CWNN) framework [9], a supervised method that uses a virtual sample generation technique to generate training samples for model training. Previous research has highlighted that the potential of network learning for this method is not fully released [19]. Other unsupervised methods like the Nonlocal self-similarity-based method (NPSG) [25], Improved Non-local Patch-based Graph (INLPG) [26], Iterative Robust Graph and Markovian Co-Segmentation (IRG-McS) [23] have also been proposed over the years. These methods however, have been show to have the following shortcomings: First of all, these methods compare the edges or vertices and ignore the structural information that the graph holds. Second, most of these strategies employ one of the local or nonlocal structural links. Excluding the relationships results in limitations in detection outcomes [5] [24].

In this paper, we tackle these limitations in literature and propose a novel unsupervised geo-spatial change detection algorithm for Synthetic Aperture Radar (SAR) [17] images. Unlike other optical devices, SAR sensors use their own energy to illuminate the ground and record what is reflected back to them from the surface. Since no sunlight is required, this offers the special benefit of enabling image acquisition both during the day and at night. Nevertheless, SAR images also have their disadvantages. They inherently have high levels of intrinsic multiplicative speckle noise [14], which is a grainy salt-and-pepper pattern present in the radar imagery. To reduce the influence of this noise we use an improved log-ratio method [17] to compute the difference image (DI). After generating the difference image, we construct a weighted non-directional grid graph. Each pixel in the DI corresponds to a vertex in the graph and the absolute difference of the intensities of the neighboring pixels are assigned as weights of the connected edges. Next, we employ Dijkstra's algorithm to obtain the shortest-path vector in the graph which is then utilized to compute a threshold value. This value is used to segment the DI by classifying each pixel as either changed/unchanged, to generate an intermediate binary change map. Finally, a voting-major based tuning method is used to smooth out the intermediate binary change map and remove noise corruptions to obtain the final change map. We compare this algorithm against the current state-of-the-art methods on three standard SAR datasets. The performance of the proposed technique is highlighted as indicated by the qualitative and the quantitative scales. The presented technique stands out in terms of resiliency and speed.

The rest of the paper is structured as follows: Sect. 2 summarizes the related works relevant to CD in SAR images. The proposed methodology is presented in Sect. 3. The experiment results and analysis are discussed in Sect. 4. Finally, the conclusion inferred is in Sect. 5.

2   Related Work

The field of change detection in remote sensing images has been fairly investigated. Various approaches been proven to detect changes in remote sensing images having varying degrees of robustness. In this section, we briefly describe the evolution over the years along with their limitations.

Initial approaches including the Fuzzy C-Means (FCM) [6] clustering and PCA K-means [4] are two of the most primitive techniques that have been used. PCA K-means segments the DI to separate the image into distinct regions based on similarities in their pixel intensities. It first uses Principal Component Analysis (PCA) to transform the original high-dimensional pixel space into a lower-dimensional feature space. Next, the K-means algorithm is used to cluster the feature vectors obtained from the PCA transformation. FCM on the other hand is a soft clustering algorithm that allows flexibility for each pixel in an image to belong in multiple clusters with varying probability, instead of hard assigning each pixel to a single cluster. Both FCM and PCA suffer from high sensitivity in terms of the initialization of the respective hyperparameters. The initial cluster centroids can significantly affect the final segmentation results, and it is often challenging to determine the optimal initialization parameters.

In 2019 Gao et al. [9] proposed a method for detecting changes in sea ice from SAR images using convolutional-wavelet neural networks (CWNNs). The method introduces dual-tree complex wavelet transform into convolutional neural networks to distinguish between the changed and unchanged pixels. This decreases the effect of speckle noise to some extent. To generate samples for training the CWNN, a virtual sample generation method is used. Although the method generates decent results it requires many samples for model training. Additionally, the potential of network learning is not fully released [19].

Next in 2021, a nonlocal self-similarity-based method (NPSG) for heterogeneous CD was proposed by Sun, Y. et. al [25]. The method exploits the structural information of bi-temporal images to construct nonlocal patch similarity graphs (NPSG) using image patches, that are then used to compute a forward and a backward difference image. The two difference images are combined to form a final difference image. Next, the final difference image is treated as an image binary segmentation problem and thresholded to obtain the final change map. The same year, the authors improved on their previous method and proposed an Improved Non-local Patch-based Graph (INLPG) [26]. The authors used a structural consistency-based method for change detection, which detects changes by comparing the structures of the two images rather than the pixel values of the images.

More recently in 2021, Sun, Y. et al. [23], suggested an unsupervised, iterative CD method: Iterative Robust Graph and Markovian Co-Segmentation (IRG-McS). The method first segments the input bi-temporal images into several super-pixels. Then they take advantage of the inherent structural consistency of the input SAR images to create a robust, adaptive K-nearest neighbor (KNN) graph that describes the image's structure, using the previously generated super-pixels, in an iterative framework. They then compare the graphs to determine the differences between the two images. Finally, a superpixel-based Markov random field (MRF) co-segmentation model is used to merge the difference images.

Although, these newer methods have been shown to be effective, they have two common shortcomings: Firstly, these approaches compare the edges or vertices of the KNN graph and do not take into account all of the structural data that the graph contains. Second, only one of the local or nonlocal structural relationships is used by the majority of these techniques. Neglecting the informational richness of both relationships limits the detection outcomes [5] [24].

3   Proposed Methodology

In this section, we detail our proposed algorithm. We start with the difference image generation. Next, we explain the grid graph generation process and shortest path vector computation based on Dijkstra's algorithm. Finally, we present the threshold value computation and the voting-major based tuning process. We summarize the proposed framework in Fig. 1 and the corresponding algorithm is presented in Algorithm 1.

3.1   Difference Image Genearation

There are several techniques for generating difference images (DI), including the subtraction method, ratio method, and the log ratio method [3]. Ratio methods have proven to be better suited for getting the DI from SAR images because they can lessen the impact of calibration and radiometric problems [15] [18] [21]. However, the inherent speckle noise in SAR images restrict the precision of change detection. Given the multiplicative nature of speckle noise, the log ratio approach is preferred. This is because the logarithmic transformation both condenses the value range of the ratio method and converts the multiplicative noise into additive noise [3] [2] [7] [10].

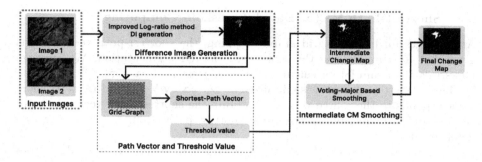

Fig. 1. Illustration of the proposed framework.

We utilize the improved log ratio (ILR) [17] method to generate the difference image, owing to its robust performance [30] against multiplicative speckle noise [1], and calibration errors [18]. The difference image (DI) is generated using Eq. (1).

$$DI = ln\left\{1 - \frac{min(I_1(x), I_2(x))}{max(I_1(x), I_2(x))}\right\} \tag{1}$$

where $I_1(x)$ and $I_2(x)$ be the pixel intensities for the respective bi-temporal images I_1 and I_2 at position x.

3.2   Grid-Graph Generation

In the next step, a grid-graph is constructed from the generated difference image. We describe the image-to-graph conversion process henceforth. We convert all the pixels of the difference image I into a set of vertices V of a graph G such that:

$$G = \{V_k, E_k, W_k; \forall k \in [0, M \times N]\} \tag{2}$$

where,

$$V_k = \{I_{(i,j)}; \forall i \in [0, N] \ and \ \forall j \in [0, M]\} \tag{3}$$

$$E_k = \{(V_{(i,j)}, V_{(i+1,j-1)}), (V_{(i,j)}, V_{(i+1,j)}), (V_{(i,j)}, V_{(i+1,j+1)}), (V_{(i,j)}, V_{(i,j+1)})\} \tag{4}$$

$$W_k = \{|I_{(i,j)} - I_{(i+1,j-1)}|, |I_{(i,j)} - I_{(i+1,j)}|, |I_{(i,j)} - I_{(i+1,j+1)}|, |I_{(i,j)} - I_{(i,j+1)}|\} \tag{5}$$

V_k represents each individual vertex in the graph. These vertices represent the spacial position of the corresponding pixels in the difference image. E_k represents the set of edges between a vertex corresponding to the pixel $I_{(i,j)}$ and its surrounding neighboring pixels, and W_k are the weights associated with each of those edges. Mapping every neighbor for all the internal vertices generates multiple redundant edges. Therefore, to reduce these redundancies only the top-right, right, bottom-right, and bottom neighbors are considered. Finally, an un-directed weighted grid-graph having $M \times N$ vertices is obtained, where M and N are the dimensions of the difference image.

3.3   Shortest-Path Vector Based Threshold Computing

After successful image-to-grid graph mapping, the shortest-path vector (D) is generated to compute the threshold value for DI segmentation. We leverage Dijkstra's algorithm [8] for calculating the shortest-path vector.

The shortest-path vector is initialized as $D_V = \infty$, $\forall$ V$\in$ G and $D_s = 0$, where s corresponds to the source vertex. To obtain the shortest-path vector, a set of vertices (S) is maintained, whose final shortest paths from source s are to be determined.

In the first iteration, the source s is added to S and all the edges from the source are relaxed and the shortest-path vector component of the adjacent vertices are updated according to Eq.(6). In every iteration, a vertex $u \in (G - S)$ with the minimum shortest path estimate is added to S, and all edges from u are relaxed and the shortest-path vector component of the neighboring vertex is again updated. This process is repeated for $|G| - 1$ times until all the vertices in G are added to S.

$$D_v = min\{D_v, W_{u,v} + D_v\} \tag{6}$$

After obtaining the final shortest-path vector D, the threshold value is obtained using Eq. (7). An intermediate segmented image I_{thresh} is generated by thresholding the difference image DI using the computed threshold value as shown in Eq. (8).

$$thresh = \frac{min(D) + max(D)}{N \times M} \tag{7}$$

$$I_{thresh(i,j)} = \begin{cases} 255, & \text{if } intensity(DI_{(i,j)}) > thresh. \\ 0, & \text{otherwise.} \end{cases} \tag{8}$$

3.4   Calibartion Using Voting-Major Based Technique

After the generation of the segmented image, we propose a voting-major-based technique focused at fine-tuning the intermediate image. For each of the pixels in the segmented image I_{thresh}, a window of 3×3 pixels is considered, and a voting measure(VM), that represents the pixel intensity of the pixel set with the maximum cardinality in the selected window, is calculated as shown in Eq. (9). This is then applied to each of the pixels in I_{thresh} to get the final change map as described in Eq. (10):

$$VM_{(i,j)} = \begin{cases} 225, & \text{if } |I_{thresh(255)}| \geq |I_{thresh(0)}|. \\ 0, & \text{otherwise.} \end{cases} \tag{9}$$

$|I_{thresh(255)}|, |I_{thresh(0)}|$ represent the cardinality of the sets of pixels whose intensities are 255 and 0 respectively.

$$I_{CM(i,j)} = \begin{cases} VM_{(i,j)}, & \text{if } I_{thresh(i,j)} \neq VM. \\ I_{thresh(i,j)}, & \text{otherwise.} \end{cases} \tag{10}$$

Algorithm 1: Graph Theoretic Image Segmentation

---

1 **Input:** Input images, I_1 and I_2 are two bi-temporal images acquired in the same geographical area at two different times
2 **Output:** Binary Change map I_{CM}
3 Calculate improved log-ratio difference image (DI) using Eqn.(1)
4 Map difference image DI to an undirected graph G based on Eqn.(2)
5 Set s to be the source vertex and Let $S = \emptyset$ be a set of vertices, whose shortest path from s have been determined
6 **while** $(/G/ - 1) \neq 0$ **do**
7   Fetch the vertex v with minimum distance D_v
8     $S \cup \{v\}$
9   **for** *each vertex u adjacent to v* **do**
10       $D_u \leftarrow min(D_u, W_{(u,v)+D_u})$
11   **end**
12 **end**
13 Find the threshold value using Eqn.(7) and threshold the difference image DI to obtain the intermediate image I_{thresh} [Eqn.(8)]
14 Compute voting-major (VM) for each pixel in I_{thresh} using Eqn.(9)
15 Generate the final image I_{CM} from I_{thresh} using the function described in Eqn.(10)

---

4 Experimental Results and Discussion

In this section, we present our experimental results. We first summarize our data acquisition process, followed by listing the quantitative and qualitative metrics used for comparing the performance of the methods. Next, we analyze the performance of the presented method in comparison to the existing benchmarks. The proposed approach surpasses its peers in terms of algorithmic robustness. The algorithms were implemented in Python and all the experiments were run on a machine with an Intel i5 1.6 GHz processor, 8 GB of RAM, and running Windows 10 operating system.

4.1 Data Acquisition

We test the algorithms on a set of three benchmark bi-temporal image data. A brief description of the three datasets, including their location, date of occurrence, and the sensors used to capture them are outlined in Table 1. The datasets depict three natural phenomena: forest fires (Dataset 1 from Elba Island), lake expansion (Dataset 2 from Italy), and flooding (Dataset 3 from Ottawa, Canada). The images vary in size, with heights and widths ranging from 290 to 450 pixels. The performance of the methods on these sets provide sufficient implications about the robustness of the methods.

Table 1. Description of the dataset

Image	Sensor	Location	Dates	Event
Dataset 1	Landsat-TM4	Elba Island	Aug 1992 - Aug 1994	Forest fire
Dataset 2	Landsat-5	Italy	Sept 1995 - July 1996	Lake expansion
Dataset 3	Radarsat-1	Ottowa	July 1997 - Aug 1997	Flooding

4.2   Metrics Used

Selection of the correct set of evaluation metrics (both quantitative and qualitative) is critical to correctly assess the performance of any CD algorithm. First, we use the receiver operating characteristics (ROC) curves to evaluate the quality of the generated DIs against the ground truth. The ROC takes the probability of change detection as a function of the probability of false alarm. Furthermore, the area under the curve (AUC) is used to quantify the results of the ROC curves. To assess the algorithm's performance, we used accuracy as an overall indicator. Additionally, root mean squared error (RMSE), is used to measure the deviation between the output images and the ground truth that further serves to triangulate the results. It is quite well known that CD data, by its nature, is quite imbalanced [11]. The number of changed pixels is far lower than the number of unchanged pixels. Hence, to account for this issue, we considered precision, recall, F1 score, intersection over union (IoU), and Cohen's Kappa score metrics.

4.3   Performance Evaluation

This section entails the performance of the presented technique on the dataset and compares it to the existing approaches. To gain a qualitative understanding of the robustness of the improved log-ratio method, we present the difference images alongside the ground truth in Fig. 2.

For quantitative evaluation, we present the ROC curves of these DIs in Fig.(5). The high quality of these plots indicates high sensitivity i.e. the DI is successfully able to identify pixels that have a high probability of change; decreasing the false alarm rate. Hence, it can be concluded that the improved log-ratio method is able to successfully capture the differences in the input images and then highlight them in the DIs. These observations are further backed up by the high corresponding AUC values (Dataset 1: 0.97, Dataset 2: 0.94, Dataset 3: 0.97).

Next, we compare the binary change maps generated by the different methods. Figure 3 presents the change maps generated by the following techniques: FCM, PCA-K Means, INLPG, IRG-McS, CWNN, and NPSG along with the proposed method. By comparing all of the changed and unchanged areas in Fig. 3 and Fig. 4 with the ground truth, we can observe that the proposed method has successfully detected the changed and unchanged pixels with a relatively low false negative and false positive rate, compared to the other methods.

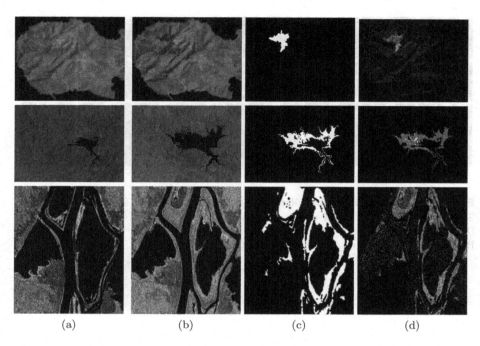

Fig. 2. Difference images: (a) Pre-event Image, (b) Post-event Image, (c) Binary Ground Truth Image, (d) Difference Image

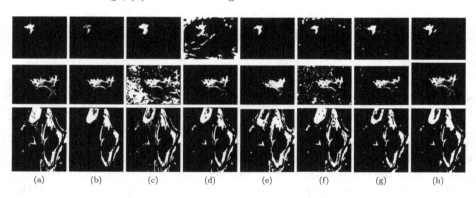

Fig. 3. Final Change maps for different methods: (a) Ground Truth (b) FCM, (c) PCA K-means, (d) CWNN, (e)NPSG, (f)INLPG , (g) IRG-McS, (h) Proposed method

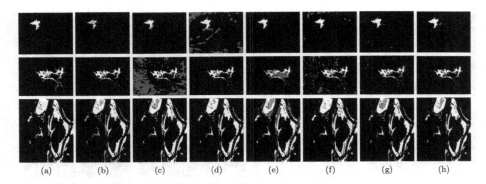

Fig. 4. Final Change maps for different methods with similarity criterion: (a) Ground Truth (b) FCM, (c) PCA K-means, (d) CWNN, (e)NPSG, (f)INLPG, (g) IRG-McS, (h) Proposed method; In the binary CMs, Black: true negative, White: true positive, Red: false positive, Green: false negatives (Color figure online)

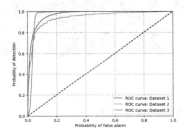

Fig. 5. ROC curves of DIs generated using the Proposed method.

On quantitative evaluation, we find that the presented method surpasses all its peers in terms of robustness. Table 2 - 4 presents the quantitative metrics corresponding to the three images. We present the accuracy, RMSE, Precision, Recall, F1-Score, IoU, and Kappa scores. It can be observed that the outputs generated by the proposed technique has the least deviation from the ground truth images (in terms of RMSE). To triangulate this finding, we observe that all other the quality metrics including accuracy (average: 97.78%), F1-score (average: 0.91), Precision, Recall, IoU, and Kappa score are maximum for the output images generated by the presented technique. These findings indicate that the changed and unchanged pixels in the generated final change maps and the ground truth have a high degree of overlap. Therefore, the resiliency of the proposed method is duly highlighted both on qualitative and quantitative scales. Furthermore, we present the computation time required by each algorithm (in seconds). As it can be noticed from Table 5, the proposed method consistently takes less computation time and yields results faster. Overall, the robustness and the speed of the algorithm is highlighted.

Table 2. Metrics for Dataset 1

	Accuracy	RMSE	Precision	Recall	F1-Score	IoU	Kappa
NPSG	98.025	23.803	0.888	0.793	0.838	0.721	0.825
INLPG	97.857	26.383	0.456	0.737	0.563	0.392	0.553
IRG-McS	79.804	92.137	0.729	0.851	0.785	0.647	0.781
CWNN	86.945	37.327	0.115	0.892	0.176	0.113	0.176
FCM	98.482	21.345	0.991	0.427	0.597	0.332	0.475
PCA-Kmeans	98.853	20.335	0.752	0.983	0.852	0.732	0.753
Proposed	99.416	19.484	0.983	0.951	0.859	0.994	0.866

Table 3. Metrics for Dataset 2

	Accuracy	RMSE	Precision	Recall	F1-Score	IoU	Kappa
NPSG	92.389	60.911	0.503	0.562	0.531	0.361	0.427
INLPG	90.221	71.299	0.398	0.874	0.547	0.376	0.452
IRG-McS	94.594	47.676	0.739	0.722	0.731	0.576	0.566
CWNN	95.737	31.659	0.953	0.963	0.958	0.724	0.735
FCM	96.447	27.209	0.934	0.921	0.927	0.684	0.719
PCA-Kmeans	67.282	141.211	0.132	0.948	0.233	0.154	0.152
Proposed	97.843	25.052	0.970	0.967	0.969	0.941	0.755

Table 4. Metrics for Dataset 3

	Accuracy	RMSE	Precision	Recall	F1-Score	IoU	Kappa
NPSG	75.946	79.561	0.457	0.758	0.571	0.521	0.344
INLPG	79.803	57.915	0.852	0.857	0.824	0.608	0.414
IRG-McS	80.035	57.844	0.976	0.778	0.826	0.728	0.363
CWNN	80.499	52.781	0.912	0.763	0.851	0.565	0.413
FCM	80.297	52.821	0.993	0.822	0.901	0.456	0.367
PCA-Kmeans	79.731	53.275	0.854	0.834	0.844	0.557	0.395
Proposed	96.082	50.469	0.944	0.915	0.929	0.764	0.809

Table 5. Computation Times(seconds)

	Dataset 1	Dataset 2	Dataset 3
NPSG	1.912	5.959	3.779
INLPG	2.975	43.221	9.063
IRG-McS	7.943	7.943	24.221
CWNN	655.250	3562.355	1996.222
FCM	1.874	10.191	5.711
PCA-Kmeans	2.616	14.223	7.971
Proposed	1.038	5.644	3.162

5   Conclusion

A novel unsupervised geo-spatial image segmentation technique with a voting-major based fine-tuning mechanism is presented for change detection in bi-temporal remote sensing images. The robustness of the proposed technique is demonstrated after rigorous experiments carried out on standardized images. Future work can leverage this technique owing to the simplicity and scalability of the approach, and it can be integrated with hardware systems in the future for real-time change detection in the domain of satellite imaging.

References

1. Argenti, F., Alparone, L.: Speckle removal from SAR images in the undecimated wavelet domain. IEEE Trans. Geosci. Remote Sens. **40**(11), 2363–2374 (2002)
2. Bovolo, F., Marin, C., Bruzzone, L.: A hierarchical approach to change detection in very high resolution SAR images for (2013)
3. Bovolo, F., Bruzzone, L.: A detail-preserving scale-driven approach to change detection in multitemporal SAR images. IEEE Trans. Geosci. Remote Sens. **43**(12), 2963–2972 (2005)
4. Celik, T.: Unsupervised change detection in satellite images using principal component analysis and k-means clustering. IEEE Geosci. Remote Sens. Lett. **6**(4), 772–776 (2009)
5. Chen, H., Yokoya, N., Chini, M.: Fourier domain structural relationship analysis for unsupervised multimodal change detection. ISPRS J. Photogramm. Remote. Sens. **198**, 99–114 (2023)
6. Chuang, K.S., Tzeng, H.L., Chen, S., Wu, J., Chen, T.J.: Fuzzy c-means clustering with spatial information for image segmentation. Comput. Med. Imaging Graph. **30**(1), 9–15 (2006)
7. Dekker, R.: Speckle filtering in satellite SAR change detection imagery. Int. J. Remote Sens. **19**(6), 1133–1146 (1998)
8. Dijkstra, E.W.: A note on two problems in connexion with graphs. In: Edsger Wybe Dijkstra: His Life, Work, and Legacy, pp. 287–290 (2022)
9. Gao, F., Wang, X., Gao, Y., Dong, J., Wang, S.: Sea ice change detection in SAR images based on convolutional-wavelet neural networks. IEEE Geosci. Remote Sens. Lett. **16**(8), 1240–1244 (2019)
10. Gong, M., Cao, Y., Wu, Q.: A neighborhood-based ratio approach for change detection in SAR images. IEEE Geosci. Remote Sens. Lett. **9**(2), 307–311 (2011)
11. Huang, Z., Dumitru, C.O., Pan, Z., Lei, B., Datcu, M.: Classification of large-scale high-resolution SAR images with deep transfer learning. IEEE Geosci. Remote Sens. Lett. **18**(1), 107–111 (2020)
12. Jiang, H., et al.: A survey on deep learning-based change detection from high-resolution remote sensing images. Remote Sens. **14**(7), 1552 (2022)
13. Joyce, K.E., Belliss, S.E., Samsonov, S.V., McNeill, S.J., Glassey, P.J.: A review of the status of satellite remote sensing and image processing techniques for mapping natural hazards and disasters. Prog. Phys. Geogr. **33**(2), 183–207 (2009)
14. Lee, J.S.: Speckle analysis and smoothing of synthetic aperture radar images. Comput. Graph. Image Process. **17**(1), 24–32 (1981)
15. Lu, D., Mausel, P., Brondizio, E., Moran, E.: Change detection techniques. Int. J. Remote Sens. **25**(12), 2365–2407 (2004)

16. Moser, G., Serpico, S.B.: Unsupervised change detection from multichannel SAR data by Markovian data fusion. IEEE Trans. Geosci. Remote Sens. **47**(7), 2114–2128 (2009)
17. Oliver, C., Quegan, S.: Understanding synthetic aperture radar images. SciTech Publishing (2004)
18. Rignot, E.J., Van Zyl, J.J.: Change detection techniques for ERS-1 SAR data. IEEE Trans. Geosci. Remote Sens. **31**(4), 896–906 (1993)
19. Shafique, A., Cao, G., Khan, Z., Asad, M., Aslam, M.: Deep learning-based change detection in remote sensing images: a review. Remote Sens. **14**(4), 871 (2022)
20. Si Salah, H., Ait-Aoudia, S., Rezgui, A., Goldin, S.E.: Change detection in urban areas from remote sensing data: a multidimensional classification scheme. Int. J. Remote Sens. **40**(17), 6635–6679 (2019)
21. Singh, A.: Digital change detection techniques using remotely-sensed data 1989. Int. J. Remote Sens. **10**(6), 100–989 (1990)
22. Singh, A.: Review article digital change detection techniques using remotely-sensed data. Int. J. Remote Sens. **10**(6), 989–1003 (1989)
23. Sun, Y., Lei, L., Guan, D., Kuang, G.: Iterative robust graph for unsupervised change detection of heterogeneous remote sensing images. IEEE Trans. Image Process. **30**, 6277–6291 (2021)
24. Sun, Y., Lei, L., Guan, D., Kuang, G., Liu, L.: Graph signal processing for heterogeneous change detection part i: vertex domain filtering. arXiv preprint arXiv:2208.01881 (2022)
25. Sun, Y., Lei, L., Li, X., Sun, H., Kuang, G.: Nonlocal patch similarity based heterogeneous remote sensing change detection. Pattern Recogn. **109**, 107598
26. Sun, Y., Lei, L., Li, X., Tan, X., Kuang, G.: Structure consistency-based graph for unsupervised change detection with homogeneous and heterogeneous remote sensing images. IEEE Trans. Geosci. Remote Sens. **60**, 1–21 (2021)
27. Willis, K.S.: Remote sensing change detection for ecological monitoring in united states protected areas. Biol. Conserv. **182**, 233–242 (2015)
28. Yuan, Y., Lv, H., Lu, X.: Semi-supervised change detection method for multi-temporal hyperspectral images. Neurocomputing **148**, 363–375 (2015)
29. Zerrouki, N., Harrou, F., Sun, Y., Hocini, L.: A machine learning-based approach for land cover change detection using remote sensing and radiometric measurements. IEEE Sens. J. **19**(14), 5843–5850 (2019)
30. Zhuang, H., Tan, Z., Deng, K., Fan, H.: It is a misunderstanding that log ratio outperforms ratio in change detection of SAR images. Eur. J. Remote Sens. **52**(1), 484–492 (2019)

Automatic Diagnosis of Age-Related Macular Degeneration via Federated Learning

Movya Sonti⬤ and Priyanka Kokil$^{(\boxtimes)}$⬤

Advanced Signal and Image Processing (ASIP) Lab, Department of Electronics and Communication Engineering, Indian Institute of Information Technology, Design and Manufacturing, Kancheepuram, Chennai 600127, India
{edm19b017,priyanka}@iiitdm.ac.in

Abstract. Artificial intelligence has taken healthcare a step forward by providing quick diagnosis and treatment recommendations. The traditional machine-learning approach requires massive data to train the model for better diagnosis. But, due to policy regulations, medical data is always guarded by the barricades of the law, making data accessibility difficult for researchers. To address this issue, a data-decentralized collaborative framework known as federated learning is adopted that reaps the benefits of huge private data without aggregating it into a single common store. A pre-trained model is employed to diagnose age-related macular degeneration and performance of the proposed framework is compared with other two model architectures, namely, MobileNet and InceptionV3. To investigate the effectiveness of the proposed framework, a comparison is made with a data-centralized learning approach. Using the MobileNet model, the federated and centralized frameworks have achieved an accuracy of 95% and 92%, respectively. These findings encourage clinicians around the globe to utilize wealthy private data without violating privacy laws using federated learning to build a powerful model for classifying any disorders while maintaining data privacy.

Keywords: Federated learning · Privacy · Data-security · Data-decentralization · Pre-trained models · Age-related macular degeneration

1 Introduction

At least 2.2 billion people worldwide suffer from near- or distance-vision impairment, and among them, at least 1 billion have avoidable vision loss [1]. The main factors that lead to vision loss and blindness are refractive errors, cataract , diabetic retinopathy, glaucoma, age-related macular degeneration (ARMD or AMD) [1–3]. The prevalence, price, and accessibility of eye care services, as well as the general level of education in the population, all have an impact on the causes of visual impairment, which vary significantly within and within nations. For

H. Kaur et al. (Eds.): CVIP 2023, CCIS 2010, pp. 128–136, 2024.
https://doi.org/10.1007/978-3-031-58174-8_12

instance, in low- and middle-income countries, untreated cataracts account for a greater proportion of vision impairment. The prevalence of diseases like glaucoma and age-related macular degeneration is generally higher in high-income countries. According to a comprehensive review and analysis of studies, it has been found that around 8.7% of the global population experiences AMD. Additionally, there are predictions that the number of individuals affected by AMD will increase from an estimated 196 million in 2020 to approximately 288 million by the year 2040 [5]. AMD is regarded as the main source of irreversible blindness globally [1], with age being the major risk factor [4,6,7]. The severity of the condition increases as the stage passes. Though there is no cure for this condition, early detection of the disease is important to hinder its adverse effects. The traditional method of machine learning requires a large volume of data to train the model effectively. But, regulations such as the Health Insurance Portability and Accountability Act (HIPAA) in the USA and the General Data Protection Regulation (GDPR) in the European Union have imposed strict rules on data access. These policies protect medical data, making it challenging for scientists to access the extensive clinical data necessary for training machine learning models. This lack of access has contributed to the inconsistent findings in artificial intelligence research [8]. To overcome this limitation and benefit from private data, a privacy-preserving approach is needed. Federated learning (FL) [9] is a technique in deep learning that enables the collaborative training of models using decentralized data. In FL, each clinical institute acts as a node and trains the shared model using its own data. Once training is complete, solely the model parameters are sent to the central server, ensuring that no data is leaked. Since each node has data generated with different patterns, there may be heterogeneity in the data distribution. For instance, node1 may generate more data compared to node2 and also node1 may have images considered with different features to that of node2. Since the whole data is aggregated at one common store in the traditional machine learning approach, there will be no variation in data distribution, whereas in FL the distribution could be *a*) non-independent and identically distributed (non-IID) or *b*) unbalanced distribution. Due to this data heterogeneity, the model doesn't converge, and the overall performance is affected. To deal with naturally raised cases like non-IID and unbalanced data distributions, the FDIC algorithm is used for better convergence of the model. In their groundbreaking work in 2017, McMahan et al. [9] introduced the pioneering concept of the federated averaging (FedAvg) algorithm.

2 Methodology

In this work, a federated learning framework for diagnosing AMD using a pretrained model is proposed and the results are compared with the data-centralized learning model. To replicate the real-world scenario, we considered a non-IID label skew distribution in which each node has equal data samples but different proportions of classes. Convolutional neural networks (CNN) are widely used in image classification tasks [13]. However, a disadvantage of CNN addresses the requirement of huge labeled training samples for weight parameters learning and the need for power GPU to accelerate the learning process [14]. People with fewer data samples, low computational power, and time cannot have the iconic advantage of CNN. The common solution for using CNNs on a small dataset is through transfer learning in which the weights are transferred from previously trained CNN on a large dataset namely, ImageNet [15]. Compared to traditional ML, transfer learning can be faster, more accurate, and even need fewer data datasets [15] We chose two pre-trained architectures, MobileNet and InceptionV3 as our model backbone. As far as our knowledge extends, this study represents the first attempt to tackle the challenge of federated learning specifically for the AMD detection using retinal fundus images. The main contributions of this paper are:

1. A collaborative framework is implemented using a pre-trained model to diagnose an eye disorder that utilizes the goodness of rich private data in a decentralized fashion.
2. To validate the effectiveness of our proposed framework, we compare the results with a data-centralized learning model.
3. To analyze the performance dependency of our framework on the client count, we experiment with 5 client settings and tabulate the observed results.

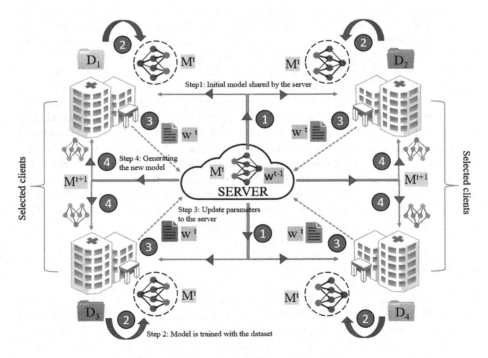

Fig. 1. Federated learning architecture

In our work, we proposed a client-server architecture as shown in Fig. 1. The main objective of this architecture is to promise privacy by using private data in a decentralized fashion in which each client has their own data and it is never been shared with the central server. For model optimization, stochastic gradient descent (SGD) is used on the client side and the FedAvg algorithm on the server side. There are four main steps involved in this implementation and is represented in Fig. 1.

1. A global model M^r, is initially trained at the server-side with weights w^{r-1}, which is then shared with the subset K randomly selected clients.
2. Each selected client c trains the received model M^r with a mini-batch of data size b, from their private data of size S^c, using the SGD optimization algorithm as shown in Algorithm 2.
3. After completion of local training for E epochs with a learning rate l, each client updates the model weights w^r to the main central server.
4. Then, this central server aggregates all the weights received from selected clients to update the shared model M^r using the FedAvg algorithm as shown in Algorithm 1.

The updated model M^{r+1} is now shared with the selected clients for the next training round. This process of aggregating all the received weights and sharing the updated global model with the clients is repeated as per the number of communication rounds mentioned.

Two main architectures namely, MobileNet and InceptionV3 are trained and evaluated with various numbers of participating clients. This works accounts for a total of 10 experiments ($=$ 2 architectures $*$ 5 client settings). A different number of participating clients is considered to replicate the real-life scenario. While 5 clients could represent 5 hospitals in a small town associating to learn a global model, 100 clients could represent a state-level collaboration. The main focus of our current work has been to develop and validate a system that utilizes federated learning for the purpose of detecting AMD. This particular aspect serves as the

---

Algorithm 1. Federated Averaging: There are K clients, F is the fraction of clients participating in each round, B is the local mini-batch size, l_r is the learning rate, D_n is the local training dataset, t is the number of rounds

Server Executes:
  initialize w^0
  for round $t = 1, 2, 3, ...r$ **do**
    $m \leftarrow max(F \cdot K, 1)$
    $S_m \leftarrow$ (random set of m clients)
    for each client $n \in S_m$ in parallel **do**
      Send w^{t-1} to client n
      $w_n^t \leftarrow$ Client Update (n, w^{t-1})
    end for
    $w^t \leftarrow \sum_{n=1}^{K} \left(\frac{D_n}{D} \right) w_n^t$
  end for

Algorithm 2. Client-side execution

ClientUpdate: (n, w)
  $M \leftarrow$ (Split D_n into batches of size B)
  for batch b in M **do**
    $w \leftarrow w - l_r \nabla l(w, b)$
  end for
  return w to the server

---

foundation for all the innovative elements presented in this article. For federated learning, we have chosen two different architectures, MobileNet and InceptionV3 with weights pre-trained on ImageNet [15]. Instead of utilizing the existing fully connected layer in these models, we incorporated two additional fully connected (FC) layers with Rectified Linear Unit (ReLU) and Softmax activation functions, respectively. The weights of the CNN backbone for both architectures are frozen because the main aim here is to train only the newly added FC layers. A significant accuracy rate is mandatory for diagnosing any disease to detect and take necessary actions to hinder its spread to the next stage of the condition. To minimize the loss function and update the network parameters we used the standard optimizer known as SGD. We also took 0.01 as the local learning rate, and the batch size to 3 to make the computation feasible (Fig. 2).

The dataset that we utilized contains 327 AMD and 873 normal images respectively collected from ODIR [10], ARIA [11], and RFMiD [12] datasets. All the images are converted to a jpg version and pre-processed to 224×224 pixels. The whole data is randomly partitioned into training and testing data. Maintaining the ratio of 9:1 the entire data of 1200 samples are divided into 90% training set and 10% testing set accounting for 1080 training images and 120 testing images. Since we focused on label-skew distribution, the data is splitted among the clients equally with different proportions of class data. For instance, the number of AMD images differs from client1 to client2 but both have equal samples of total data.

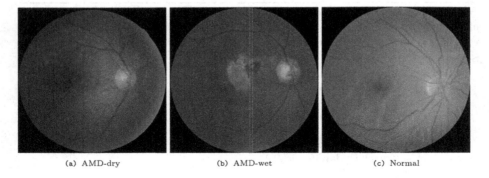

(a) AMD-dry   (b) AMD-wet   (c) Normal

Fig. 2. Sample images taken from the ODIR dataset [10]

3   Discussion

In our work, we conducted two sections of experiments. In the first section, we compared the results of federated learning and centralized learning. We took client $C = 10$ for comparison. The quality of the model is assessed by accuracy plots on the vertical axis and communication rounds on the horizontal axis as shown in Fig. 3.

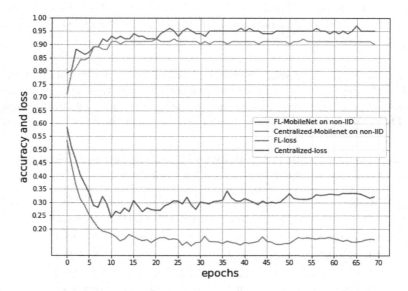

Fig. 3. Accuracy and loss curve of federated learning and data-centralized learning with MobileNet architecture when $C = 10$ in a non-IID data distribution

For comparison, we took client participation $C = 10$ for both federated and data-centralized training for 70 epochs. Figure 3 shows that our proposed model outnumbered centralized learning because of collaborative training simultaneously. The blue curve represents FL, which has higher accuracy compared to the orange curve, which is centralized training.

In the second section, we analyzed the dependency of model performance on client count in both learnings. Table 1 highlights the changes in framework accuracy with an increase in client count when trained using MobileNet and InceptionV3 architectures.

Table 1. Accuracy (in %) of federated learning vs. data-centralized learning in non-IID data distribution after 70 communication rounds using MobileNet and InceptionV3 architectures

Architecture	Training	Client Count				
		5	10	20	40	80
MobileNet	Federated	93.1	95.5	93.2	90.6	91.4
	Data-centralized	90.2	92.0	91.3	88.7	90.0
InceptionV3	Federated	87.5	88.6	89.8	88.2	86.3
	Data-centralized	86.0	85.5	86.2	86.6	87.2

The table depicts that with an increase in client count, there is an incremental change in the performance of the model to a certain extent, and thereby a decline in performance is observed. This is due to the fixed number of total samples of data. The quality measures of the model are shown in the table 2.

Table 2. Class-wise Accuracy, Sensitivity, and Specificity values of federated learning and data-centralized learning recorded after the last round.

Method	Accuracy		Sensitivity		Specificity	
	AMD	Normal	AMD	Normal	AMD	Normal
FL-MobileNet	92.3	96.2	98.1	86.2	86.0	98.1
CL-MobileNet	92.3	93.2	98.4	75	75.8	98.5
FL-InceptionV3	85.4	90.3	92.0	83.1	83.2	92.4
CL-InceptionV3	89.7	86.5	95.3	72.4	72.6	95.4

4   Conclusions

In this paper, we presented a collaborative framework to classify AMD and healthy retinal fundus images using pre-trained CNN architectures, MobileNet and InceptionV3. Despite non-IID distribution, the proposed model showed a competitive performance compared to the centralized training model. Then we also analyzed the significance of the client's ratio with the performance. The decrease in accuracy is observed with an increase in clients which is due to a fixed number of data samples. However, this may not be the case in real-world, due to the availability of huge data. Despite the client dependency and heterogeneity, the proposed method provides a reliable means to train the model with huge private data while maintaining privacy.

The proposed method holds the promise of linking various independent medical establishments, hospitals, or devices to enable them to exchange their insights and work together while ensuring data privacy for various other diseases such as cataract [3], kidney abnormalities [16], fetal abnormal growth [17], etc.

Acknowledgement. The research reported in this paper was supported by the Department of Science and Technology (DST) under the Fund for Improvement of S&T Infrastructure (FIST), Govt. of India, under the grant SR/FST/ET-I/2020/578 and Science and Engineering Research Board (SERB), grant no. EEQ/2021/000804.

Data Availibility Statement. The dataset analyzed during the current study is available in the repositories ODIR [7], ARIA [8], and RFMiD [9].

Declarations. The authors have no conflicts of interest to declare.

References

1. Vision Impairment and Blindness. https://www.who.int/news-room/fact-sheets/detail/blindness-and-visual-impairment. Accessed 20 Jan 2023
2. Pratap, T., Kokil, P.: Computer-aided diagnosis of cataract using deep transfer learning. Biomed. Sign. Process. Control **53**, 101533 (2019)
3. Pratap, T., Kokil, P.: Automatic cataract detection in fundus retinal images using singular value decomposition. In: 2019 International Conference on Wireless Communications Signal Processing and Networking (WiSPNET), pp. 373–377. IEEE (2019)
4. Stahl, A.: The diagnosis and treatment of age-related macular degeneration. Dtsch. Arztebl. Int. **117**(29–30), 513 (2020)
5. Wong, W.L., et al.: Global prevalence of age-related macular degeneration and disease burden projection for 2020 and 2040: a systematic review and meta-analysis. Lancet Glob. Health **2**(2), e106–e116 (2014)
6. Bressler, N.M., Bressler, S.B., Fine, S.L.: Age-related macular degeneration. Surv. Ophthalmol. **32**(6), 375–413 (1988)
7. Mitchell, P., Liew, G., Gopinath, B., Wong, T.Y.: Age-related macular degeneration. Lancet **392**(10153), 1147–1159 (2018)
8. Feki, I., Ammar, S., Kessentini, Y., Muhammad, K.: Federated learning for COVID-19 screening from Chest X-ray images. Appl. Soft Comput. **106**, 107330 (2021)
9. McMahan, B., Moore, E., Ramage, D., Hampson, S., Arcas, B.A.: Communication-efficient learning of deep networks from decentralized data. In: Artificial Intelligence and Statistics, pp. 1273-1282. PMLR (2017)
10. International Competition on Ocular Disease Intelligent Recognition. https://odir2019.grand-challenge.org/dataset/. Accessed 18 Nov 2021
11. Automated Retinal Image Analysis (ARIA) Data Set - Damian JJ Farnell. https://www.damianjjfarnell.com/?pageid=276. Accessed 14 May 2023
12. Pachade, S., et al.: Retinal Fundus Multi-disease Image Dataset (RFMiD). IEEE Dataport (2020). https://doi.org/10.21227/s3g7-st65
13. Krishna, S.T., Kalluri, H.K.: Deep learning and transfer learning approaches for image classification. Int. J. Recent Technol. Eng. (IJRTE), **7**(5S4), 427–432 (2019)
14. Han, D., Liu, Q., Fan, W.: A new image classification method using CNN transfer learning and web data augmentation. Expert Syst. Appl. **95**, 43–56 (2018)
15. Deng, J., Dong, W., Socher, R., Li, L.J., Li, K., Fei-Fei, L.: ImageNet: a large-scale hierarchical image database. In: 2009 IEEE Conference on Computer Vision and Pattern Recognition, pp. 248–255. IEEE (2009)

16. Kokil, P., Sudharson, S.: Automatic detection of renal abnormalities by Off-the-shelf CNN features. IETE J. Educ. **60**(1), 14–23 (2019)

17. Krishna, T.B., Kokil, P.: Automated classification of common maternal fetal ultrasound planes using multi-layer perceptron with deep feature integration. Biomed. Signal Process. Control **86**, 105283 (2023)

FResFormer: Leukemia Detection Using Fusion-Enabled CNN and Attention

Murukessan Perumal[1(✉)], E. Goutham[2], U. Shivani Sri Varshini[1],
M. Srinivas[1], and R.B.V. Subramanyam[1]

[1] National Institute of Technology, Warangal, Telangana, India
muruap87@student.nitw.ac.in
[2] Institute of Aeronautical Engineering, Dundigal, Hyderabad, Telangana, India

Abstract. In this paper, the binary classification of normal and abnormal (malignant) cells from the microscopic images is done. It is quite challenging due to the appearance of both cells morphologically similar. In particular, manual identification of malignant and benign cells from the microscopic images in early stages is difficult because of the similar resemblance of both cells in their appearance. This early diagnosis process requires advanced techniques like flow cytometry that are currently used and more expensive and, therefore, are not accessible in all places. Additionally, a medical expert is also required. Therefore, by using automated diagnostic tools, we can perform better diagnoses with low-cost microscopic image data. In this paper, we propose a classification of normal and malignant cells in the lymphocytes using a fusion-enabled CNN and Attention-based neural network, which we named Fusion-based Residual Transformer (FRESFORMER) architecture. Our proposed model tops the performance on the benchmark ISBI 2019 challenge dataset. The proposed model achieves an F1-Score of 84.89.

Keywords: Acute Lymphoblastic Leukemia · Chronic Leukemia · Deep Learning · Transformers · Computer Vision

1 Introduction

The challenges in computer-assisted diagnostic tools have been studied with great interest in the medical image processing community. The healthcare's dependence on modern medical imaging techniques for disease diagnosis [20] is increasing daily. On this point, cell classification using image processing techniques to develop an efficient computer-assisted diagnosis for identifying blood disorders like leukemia is necessary for better disease diagnosis and progression. Developing a computer-assisted diagnostic tool to automatically identify malignant cells with better accuracy is one of the challenging problems. Binary classification of normal and cancerous cells from the microscopic images is difficult since their appearances are morphologically similar [7,8]. Blood malignancies

Supported by Ministry of Education, India.

that begin in the bone marrow tissue are called leukemia. An issue in generating immature blood cells that enter the circulation may cause it to manifest. And it usually affects the white blood cells. Leukemia may be divided into two groups, Acute leukemia, and Chronic leukemia, depending on how immature they are. The fast expansion of immature cells generated in the bone marrow leads to acute leukemia. Thus, this crowding situation of immature cells affects the functioning of the bone marrow to produce cells with less hemoglobin. It is mostly diagnosed among children. Chronic leukemia, in contrast to acute leukemia, progresses gradually due to the creation of aberrant white blood cells. Most cases of chronic leukemia are diagnosed in adults. Other classifications of these two types of leukemia include lymphoblastic or lymphocytic leukaemia and myeloid or myelogenous leukemia. When B or T cells transform malignantly, lymphocytic leukemia is discovered (WBC). In this paper, we are working on Acute Lymphoblastic Leukemia (ALL).

According to the American Cancer Society [18], 6,540 people of all ages (3,660 men and boys and 2,880 women and girls) will be diagnosed with ALL in the United States this year. And the estimated death rate for ALL is high. The major challenges or difficulties to identifying abnormal cells are: Manual identification of malignant and benign cells from the microscopic images in early stages is hard because of how similar they appear [5]. Another problem in leukemia is detected in advanced cancer stages by understanding the process by which cancer cells begin to grow unrestrictedly. Hence, they are present in much larger numbers as compared to their numbers in a healthy person. Figure 1 shows some examples of normal and malignant cells.

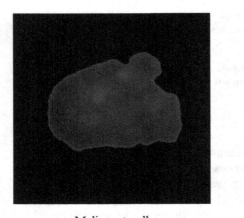
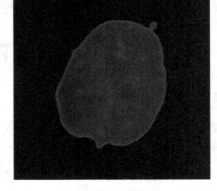

Malignant cell   Normal Cell

Fig. 1. Sample images of normal and malignant cells

However, Early stage detection of such ALL is crucial for better treatment. This early diagnosis process requires advanced techniques like flow cytometry to be present that are more expensive and not accessible at all the places and requires a medical expert [3,4]. Therefore, by using automated diagnostic tools, we can perform better diagnoses with low-cost microscopic image data.

The Fusion-based Residual Transformer (FRESFORMER) model, which we use to classify normal and cancerous cells, is a CNN with fusion functionality combined with an attention-based neural network. Our approach, FRES-FORMER, projects the benefits of residual learning and transformer-based self-attention on a combined novel feature space, which also has early layers fused features from both residual blocks and transformer hidden layers. Spatially local features from residuals and long-range features from transformer blocks, along with their early layers' features, form a novel feature space that outperforms other models in the challenging cancer image classification task of the ISBI 2019 challenge.

2   Related Work

The current literature survey has shown that classification tasks can be successfully applied by using convolutional neural networks (CNNs), especially in ISBI 2019 challenge [11,12,15,16,21]. By using discriminative feature representations from pre-trained CNN models from huge datasets, modifications in layers and fine-tuning approaches have given a lot of significant improvements in medical image classification tasks. Moreover, advanced deep learning methods have shown outstanding improvement in medical image applications [1,19]. It has better classification accuracy than traditional machine learning methods that adopt handcrafted features. Previously, there have been many approaches made in this field of detecting and classifying cancer disease. Particularly for detecting a malignant tumor in lymphocytes.

In the nucleus of ALL cells, V. Singhal et al. [17] have noticed a change in the texture of chromatin distribution, and they employed Local Binary pattern and Gray Level Co-occurrence Matrix for Support Vector Machine(SVM) identification of ALL cells. The method proposed by W. Yu et al. [22] has used different Convolutional Neural networks such as ResNet50, Inception V3, VGG 16, VGG 19, and Xception to extract features and a voting mechanism is used to select the best among them. Images were pre-processed from RGB color space to YCbCr color space to extract Cb and Cr color coefficients for the segmentation process, which was helpful in getting various features of the nucleus and cytoplasm. These features were fed into the Random Forest classifier. The ensemble model [13] was employed in the model presented by Mohapatra et al. to identify leukemia in stained blood smears and bone marrow microscopic images. Implementation of Squeeze and excitation modules with Resnext architecture on the dataset by SBI lab has given some satisfactory results proposed by Jonas Prellberg et al. [14]. Kassani et al. [10] proposed a model that collects the features from MobileNet architecture's five different convolution layers to form a feature vector with the concatenated features of VGG-16 and MobileNet architectures for better prediction. A stain deconvolution layer(SD-layer) [6] was applied to the images and found to have improved the classification results through CNNs.

However, a major question arises of how transformers come into the picture here in the recent scenario. Also, CNNs are prone to the locality of spatially connected features, unlike long-range attention in transformers. We address these issues in our work.

3   Proposed Method

In this study, we show a method for classifying healthy and cancerous lymphocyte cells utilizing an attention and CNN-based neural network that can fuse early layer features, which we call the Fusion-based Residual Transformer (FRES-FORMER) architecture. To get better and optimized detection, we have pre-processed our dataset using pre-processing techniques like normalization and SD-Layer. For training our model without over-fitting on a smaller dataset, we have used augmentation methods like random-axis-flipping, random-affine(rotate, shear, translate), and Gaussian-blur. These will help instruct our model by generalizing the feature qualities. We have fed the designed FRESFORMER model with the pre-processed and augmented data.

Our proposed model, FRESFORMER, deploys layers of residual blocks that consist of CNNs to extract spatially local features and layers of transformer encoders to extract long-range features. Additionally, early layer features from residual blocks and transformers [CLS] tokens are globally averaged to form more features. This novel feature space results in overall better metrics. All the features are concatenated and fed into further dense layers and, thereby, final binary classification (Fig. 2).

FRESFORMER is a CNN and Attention-based model that makes use of early layers' features as well features from residual layers and transformer encoder layers to form an efficient feature space to predict the microscopic images as cancerous or normal. The image input is scaled to [0–1] float value and then normalized for transformer encoders, whereas they are further processed through an SD layer before passing to residual layers. There is a novel feature space vector formed by concatenating transformer encoder features and their early layer averaged features, residual layer features, and their early layer globally averaged features. This feature space is then projected through two successive linear projections with ReLU and softmax activations, respectively. The final layer has two dense neurons for predicting cancer or normal.

Residual learning [9] has significantly contributed to computer vision and has become the benchmark for all standard image-related tasks. Introducing skip connections in residual networks made deep CNNs a reality, mitigating the vanishing gradient problem in deeper networks. However, CNNs are short-sighted, with spatial locality as a major inductive bias. This is overcome in the self-attention-based transformer encoders. The transformer encoder [2] is known for relating long-range features in the image and, therefore, superior or complementary to CNNs. Still, transformers suffer from the need for huge training data due to no inductive bias. Also, in the microscopic images, features from early layers are helpful in the final prediction. So, forming a novel feature space from

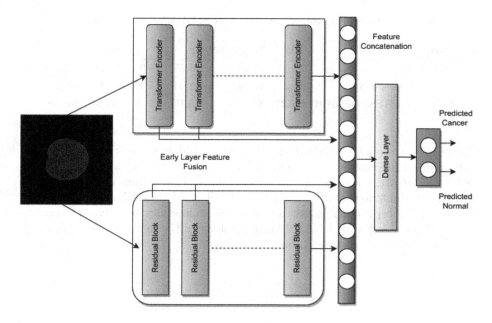

Fig. 2. Overview of the proposed method (FRESFORMER)

the residual learning, transformer encoders, and their fused early layer feature results in a finer prediction of the proposed model FRESFORMER.

4   Experimental Results and Evaluation

4.1   Dataset

For the B-ALL white blood cancer microscopic Imaging (CNMC) challenge in ISBI 2019, we classified Normal versus Malignant cells using the dataset made available by SBI Lab. Pictures were 2560 by 1920 pixels and were in raw BMP format. After segmenting the whole dataset from the given photos, stain normalization was performed. Images that have been segmented are 450 by 450 pixels in size, but they have been center-cropped to 224 by 224 pixels to extract key information before being sent to the model. The training dataset includes 3389 normal cells from 26 participants and 7272 malignant cells from 47 patients. Augmentation techniques such as random-axis-flipping, random-affine(rotate, shear, translate), and Gaussian-blur are applied to the train set. Augmentation will help in making our model more accurate and robust to over-fitting. Center-wise cropping is to remove the uninformative background. We have also added the translating, shearing, and zooming parameters in random-affine for enhancing the features and have them captured in the feature maps. The training set is divided into seven equal stratified folds for cross-validation. Efforts are made to ensure no same patient images are found across train and validation folds.

Table 1. Comparison of proposed model FRESFORMER in test metrics(%)

Model	TA	Macro TA	Sp	P	R	F1
SDNet [6]	74.93	65.33	80.71	74.93	77.27	71.29
VGGMobileNet [10]	81.37	77.01	80.04	81.37	81.15	80.62
Proposed FRESFORMER	**85.27**	**81.7**	**85.05**	**85.27**	**85.23**	**84.89**

The proposed model FRESFORMER is cross-validated and evaluated on the preliminary test dataset. An ensemble and weighted voting approach is used on FRESFORMER for the final test evaluation. The preliminary test data is used due to the unavailability of final test labels, and the evaluation server also has stopped accepting submissions. Also, the preliminary test dataset consists of 1867 images, out of which 1219 images belong to the malignant category and 648 images are normal ones (Table 1).

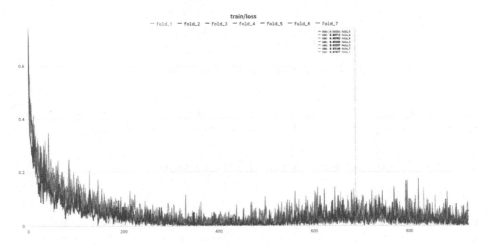

Fig. 3. Training loss across 7-folds of FRESFORMER

4.2 Performance Evaluation and Results

The performance of FRESFORMER was assessed using several measures, including accuracy (AC), precision (P), sensitivity (SE), specificity (SP), and $F1 - score$. Also, we computed the True Positive (TP), True Negative (TN), False Positive (FP), and False Negative (FN) values to do this. Since the dataset is imbalanced, weighted, micro, and macro metrics are tabulated. Different metrics are calculated using the equations as follows:

$$AC = \frac{TP + TN}{TP + TN + FP + FN} \tag{1}$$

$$SP = \frac{TN}{TN + FP} \tag{2}$$

$$SE = \frac{TP}{TP + FN} \tag{3}$$

The F1-score is calculated as follows:

$$precision = \frac{TP}{TP + FP} \tag{4}$$

$$recall = \frac{TP}{TP + FN} \tag{5}$$

$$F1 = 2 \times \frac{precision \times recall}{precision + recall} \tag{6}$$

In each cross-validation fold, 6-folds are in the training set, and the remaining 7th fold is in the validation set. After training all the folds and cross-validation, each fold's model weights are saved for inference in test data. Two alternative, cutting-edge models, SD-Net [6] and VGG-Mobilenet [10], are compared with the proposed model. For a fair comparison, the SD-Net and VGG-Mobilenet are rerun in our setting, and the results are reported. In the ensemble type of models SD-Net and the proposed FRESFORMER, weighted voting is used for test set evaluation. In contrast, in the simple model hybrid VGG16-Mobilenet, the average of all cross-validated models' performance is compared.

Since the training data is imbalanced, weighted cross-entropy loss is used. Adam is the optimizer, and its initial learning rate is 0.0001. For the proposed model, a batch size 48 was used, and each fold was run for 25 epochs. The learning curve of the training loss for all folds is shown in Fig. 3. Since there was insufficient improvement over 25 epochs, we early stopped the training. This is evident in the validation accuracy over epochs for all folds shown in Fig. 4. We used a Tesla P100 GPU for training.

A fair comparison of the proposed model FRESFORMER is made with two of the state-of-the-art models, SD-Net and VGGMobileNet. The FRESFORMER beats the other models in all metrics, such as Test Accuracy(TA), Macro Test Accuracy, Weighted Specificity(Sp), Weighted Precision(P), Weighted Recall(R), and Weighted F1. The FRESFORMER achieves an F1-Score of 84.89

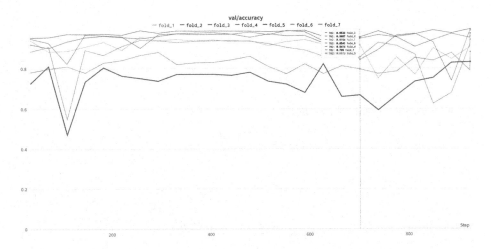

Fig. 4. Validation accuracy across 7-folds of FRESFORMER

5 Conclusion

Diagnosing illness is becoming increasingly dependent on modern medical diagnostic imaging techniques. On this point, cell classification using image processing techniques to build efficient computer-assisted diagnosis for identifying blood disorders like leukemia is necessary for better disease diagnosis and progression. To this end, we propose the novel FRESFORMER architecture. The model is one more step forward in clinical research getting into clinical practice.

References

1. Donahue, J., et al.: Decaf: a deep convolutional activation feature for generic visual recognition. In: International Conference on Machine Learning, pp. 647–655. PMLR (2014)
2. Dosovitskiy, A., et al.: An image is worth 16×16 words: Transformers for image recognition at scale. arXiv preprint arXiv:2010.11929 (2020)
3. Duggal, R., Gupta, A., Gupta, R.: Segmentation of overlapping/touching white blood cell nuclei using artificial neural networks. CME Series on Hemato-Oncopathology, All India Institute of Medical Sciences (AIIMS), New Delhi, India (2016)
4. Duggal, R., Gupta, A., Gupta, R., Mallick, P.: SD-layer: stain deconvolutional layer for CNNs in medical microscopic imaging. In: Descoteaux, M., Maier-Hein, L., Franz, A., Jannin, P., Collins, D.L., Duchesne, S. (eds.) MICCAI 2017. LNCS, vol. 10435, pp. 435–443. Springer, Cham (2017). https://doi.org/10.1007/978-3-319-66179-7_50
5. Duggal, R., Gupta, A., Gupta, R., Wadhwa, M., Ahuja, C.: Overlapping cell nuclei segmentation in microscopic images using deep belief networks. In: Proceedings of the Tenth Indian Conference on Computer Vision, Graphics and Image Processing, pp. 1–8 (2016)

6. Gehlot, S., Gupta, A., Gupta, R.: SDCT-AuxNet*θ*: DCT augmented stain deconvolutional CNN with auxiliary classifier for cancer diagnosis. Med. Image Anal. **61**, 101661 (2020)

7. Gupta, A., et al.: GCTI-SN: geometry-inspired chemical and tissue invariant stain normalization of microscopic medical images. Med. Image Anal. **65**, 101788 (2020). https://doi.org/10.1016/j.media.2020.101788

8. Gupta, R., Mallick, P., Duggal, R., Gupta, A., Sharma, O.: Stain color normalization and segmentation of plasma cells in microscopic images as a prelude to development of computer assisted automated disease diagnostic tool in multiple myeloma. Clin. Lymphoma Myeloma Leuk. **17**(1), e99 (2017)

9. He, K., Zhang, X., Ren, S., Sun, J.: Deep residual learning for image recognition. In: Proceedings of the IEEE Conference on Computer Vision and Pattern Recognition (CVPR) (2016)

10. Kassani, S.H., kassani, P.H., Wesolowski, M.J., Schneider, K.A., Deters, R.: A hybrid deep learning architecture for leukemic b-lymphoblast classification (2019). https://doi.org/10.48550/ARXIV.1909.11866, https://arxiv.org/abs/1909.11866

11. Khan, M.A., Choo, J.: Classification of cancer microscopic images via convolutional neural networks. In: Gupta, A., Gupta, R. (eds.) ISBI 2019 C-NMC Challenge: Classification in Cancer Cell Imaging. LNB, pp. 141–147. Springer, Singapore (2019). https://doi.org/10.1007/978-981-15-0798-4_15

12. Mohajerani, P., Ntziachristos, V.: Classification of normal versus malignant cells in B-ALL microscopic images based on a tiled convolution neural network approach. In: Gupta, A., Gupta, R. (eds.) ISBI 2019 C-NMC Challenge: Classification in Cancer Cell Imaging. LNB, pp. 103–111. Springer, Singapore (2019). https://doi.org/10.1007/978-981-15-0798-4_11

13. Mohapatra, S., Patra, D., Satpathy, S.: An ensemble classifier system for early diagnosis of acute lymphoblastic leukemia in blood microscopic images. Neural Comput. Appl. **24**, 1887–1904 (2014)

14. Prellberg, J., Kramer, O.: Acute lymphoblastic leukemia classification from microscopic images using convolutional neural networks (2019). https://doi.org/10.48550/ARXIV.1906.09020, https://arxiv.org/abs/1906.09020

15. Shah, S., Nawaz, W., Jalil, B., Khan, H.A.: Classification of normal and leukemic blast cells in B-ALL cancer using a combination of convolutional and recurrent neural networks. In: Gupta, A., Gupta, R. (eds.) ISBI 2019 C-NMC Challenge: Classification in Cancer Cell Imaging. LNB, pp. 23–31. Springer, Singapore (2019). https://doi.org/10.1007/978-981-15-0798-4_3

16. Shi, T., Wu, L., Zhong, C., Wang, R., Zheng, W.: Ensemble convolutional neural networks for cell classification in microscopic images. In: Gupta, A., Gupta, R. (eds.) ISBI 2019 C-NMC Challenge: Classification in Cancer Cell Imaging. LNB, pp. 43–51. Springer, Singapore (2019). https://doi.org/10.1007/978-981-15-0798-4_5

17. Singhal, V., Singh, P.: Texture features for the detection of acute lymphoblastic leukemia. In: Satapathy, S.C., Joshi, A., Modi, N., Pathak, N. (eds.) Proceedings of International Conference on ICT for Sustainable Development. AISC, vol. 409, pp. 535–543. Springer, Singapore (2016). https://doi.org/10.1007/978-981-10-0135-2_52

18. Society, A.C.: Key statistics for acute lymphocytic leukemia (ALL). https://www.cancer.org/cancer/acute-lymphocytic-leukemia/about/key-statistics.html (2023). Accessed 17 Feb 2023

19. Srinivas, M., Lin, Y.Y., Liao, H.Y.M.: Deep dictionary learning for fine-grained image classification. In: 2017 IEEE International Conference on Image Processing (ICIP), pp. 835–839 (2017). https://doi.org/10.1109/ICIP.2017.8296398
20. Srinivas, M., Naidu, R.R., Sastry, C., Mohan, C.K.: Content based medical image retrieval using dictionary learning. Neurocomputing **168**, 880–895 (2015). https://doi.org/10.1016/j.neucom.2015.05.036
21. Verma, E., Singh, V.: ISBI challenge 2019: convolution neural networks for B-ALL cell classification. In: Gupta, A., Gupta, R. (eds.) ISBI 2019 C-NMC Challenge: Classification in Cancer Cell Imaging. LNB, pp. 131–139. Springer, Singapore (2019). https://doi.org/10.1007/978-981-15-0798-4_14
22. Yu, W., et al.: Automatic classification of leukocytes using deep neural network. In: 2017 IEEE 12th International Conference on ASIC (ASICON), pp. 1041–1044. IEEE (2017)

S-Net: A Lightweight Real-Time Semantic Segmentation Network for Autonomous Driving

Saquib Mazhar$^{(\boxtimes)}$, Nadeem Atif , M.K. Bhuyan ,
and Shaik Rafi Ahamed

Indian Institute of Technology, Guwahati, Assam, India
{saquibmazhar,atif176102103,mkb,rafiahamed}@iitg.ac.in

Abstract. Semantic segmentation of road-scene images for autonomous driving is a dense pixel-level prediction task performed in real-time. Deep learning models make extensive efforts to improve segmentation accuracy, among which network architecture design is essential. In edge devices, this becomes more challenging due to limited computing power. While very deep encoder-decoder-based networks perform fairly accurately, their slow inference speed and many parameters make them unsuitable for small devices. Decoder-less models are fast but suffer from accuracy loss. To this end, we propose a novel architecture with a shallow decoder. We propose a building block for our network, which leverages a multi-scale feature pyramid model. The block efficiently learns semantic and contextual features based on which we design our network. It benefits from uniquely placed encoder skip connections, which are responsible for retaining low-level features to preserve boundary information, often lost in deep networks. Experiments on highly competitive *Cityscapes* and *CamVid* datasets show the efficiency of our proposed architecture. Our model gets a mean intersection-over-union score of 72.5% and 67.5% on the Cityscapes and CamVid test set, with only 0.6 Million parameters running in real-time.

Keywords: Computer vision · Autonomous driving · Semantic segmentation · Deep learning

1 Introduction

Semantic segmentation is a computer vision task of pixel classification. It amounts to assigning each pixel an object class label. It forms the fundamental step in several image-understanding applications like oncology through biomedical images, satellite imagery, virtual reality, and autonomous driving, to name a few. Modern algorithms for semantic image segmentation include deep neural networks for their above-human-level accuracy. These neural networks are often marked by their huge computation requirements and large size [2,17]. However, applications like autonomous driving work in a resource-constrained

© The Author(s), under exclusive license to Springer Nature Switzerland AG 2024
H. Kaur et al. (Eds.): CVIP 2023, CCIS 2010, pp. 147–159, 2024.
https://doi.org/10.1007/978-3-031-58174-8_14

environment on devices with limited power. In addition, being time-critical, the low latency requirement further constricts the deployment of large-scale networks. Hence, network design plays a crucial role in meeting these requirements.

While [7,16,19,20,29] have achieved a decent performance in small real-time networks, a significant gap exists between lightweight and regular deep networks for semantic segmentation. In the following paragraphs, we discuss the existing methods and introduce our work.

We classify the existing methods in four network topologies shown in Fig. 1. Initial algorithms were based on ImageNet [4] classification backbone and mostly followed a deep encoder-decoder model. However, to gain faster inference speed, the asymmetric design (Fig. 1(a)) gave way to a shallow decoder [11,16,19,20]. ENet [19] highly optimised FCN [24] for mobile devices. ERFNet [20] exploited local-semantic and contextual features for effective semantic segmentation through their two-branched basic block design. FRNet [15] and LAANet [35] used similar basic modules with added convolution layers in a shallow structure. In addition, LAANet used a lightweight asymmetric pyramid pooling module after the decoder to regain the context information. DFANet [11] used three ImageNet pre-trained MobileNet [8] backbones with fully connected layers retained to achieve better class-wise segmentation accuracy.

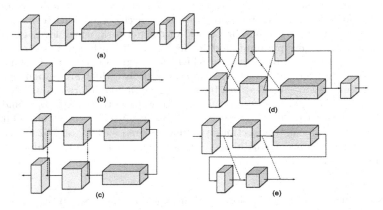

Fig. 1. Illustration of some semantic segmentation network architectures. (a) Asymmetric encoder-decoder based (b) Only encoder based (c) UNet based (d) Multipath based (e) Proposed. The dimension of the cube represents the feature map size. The dotted line represents a skip connection. The same colour represents the same 'HxW' of the feature map.

DABNet [10], CGNet [30], MFNet [14], followed the second topology (Fig. 1(b)). They discarded the decoder in favour of faster inference speed. CGNet used an efficient bottleneck design in the basic block. The context information was learned with dilated convolution kernels. DABNet was built over CGNet with a redesigned basic block with two asymmetric convolutions in each branch. LRNNet [9] added a channel-wise pyramid pooling (PP) module after the encoder for context aggregation. EDANet [12] used harmonic connections to improve RAM (random access memory) utilization, thus leading to decreased latency.

The third structure, shown in Fig. 1(c), is based on UNet [21] architecture. It proposes an encoder-decoder-based model with a dense symmetric decoder having lateral skip connections. Networks like FASSDNet [22], ESPNet [16], and SS-UNet [37] are based on this topology. FASSDNet used HarDNet blocks with a pyramidal fusion module between the encoder and decoder that used 1D dilated convolutions to reduce the size. ESPNet used pyramid-based basic blocks to split the input channels among the branches. The processed feature maps from all branches were concatenated hierarchically to reduce the gridding effect.

Several methods like HRNet [25], DDRNet [7], and BiSeNet [33] are based on multi-path network topology (Fig. 1(d)). This method processes the input image at different resolutions in a parallel setup. While BiSeNet and DDRNet used two branches in the encoder, HRNet used four. The high-resolution input is applied to a shallow context branch, whereas the low-resolution input is for a deeper semantic branch. The features from both branches are fused in the final stage before bilinear upsampling.

Methods discussed above vary significantly in their network structures. Nevertheless, they have specific limitations for real-time deployment on resource-constrained edge devices. The current methods based on Transformers [2,31,34] require large memory and computing resources and, hence, are not fully optimized for edge device deployment. While deep encoder-decoder-based methods use an ImageNet backbone or a custom-designed structure, the deep decoder reduces the inference speed and adds to the computation load. Decoder-less design opts for a direct upsampling of the encoded feature map; this causes accuracy loss due to the absence of any learnable parameters. UNet-based models are deep and require feature maps from different stages to be stored hierarchically, leading to high memory requirements. Multi-branch structures calculate the same image features multiple times, thus learning some redundant features. To solve these problems, we propose a lightweight encoder-decoder-based deep network for real-time applications and call it S-Net due to its structure. The significant contributions of our work are summarized below:

1. We design a novel pyramid-based basic block to effectively learn local semantics and global context features at the block level. Specifically, our Multi-scale Context Aggregation Pyramid (MCAP) module uses dilated kernels to learn features at multiple scales.
2. Based on this module, we propose a novel encoder-decoder backbone structure for real-time applications.
3. Our shallow decoder design and uniquely placed skip connections (see Fig. 1 (e)) further improve the accuracy of the proposed network.

In the following sections, we discuss the proposed method and experimental results.

2   Proposed Method

We first illustrate the proposed network in this section. Following this, we elaborate on the structure of our Multi-scale Context Aggregation Pyramid (MCAP) module. Finally, we explain the complete architecture of our network in detail. The overview of our network is given in Fig. 2.

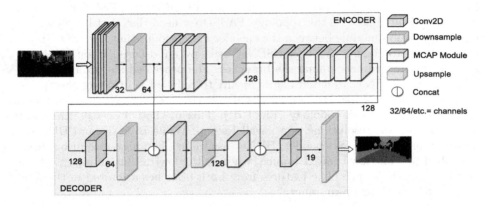

Fig. 2. Overview of the proposed S-Net.

2.1   MCAP Module

Accurate labelling of pixels in semantic segmentation calls for effective learning of local semantics and global context. Methods [9,16,20,30], combined both these feature learning in the basic block. At the same time, it is a common practice to append a pyramid pooling module after a deep encoder [7,22,25]. However, low-level information such as image boundaries and textures cannot be fully recovered at such depths. We solve this problem by incorporating a feature pyramid in the basic block design shown in Fig. 3. It is a three-branched structure with different dilations. We use inverted residual bottlenecks from [23]. This increases the number of input channels inside the block for preserving the information in the input manifold of interest [23]. While we use stacked dilated convolution kernels in two branches, we do not apply any dilation in the top kernel. The top convolution kernel learns the local semantics around the centre pixel. Stacking kernels with different dilation rates increases the effective field of view. Consequently, it can extract multi-scale features. We add the output from all three branches and convolve with a 3×3 kernel to restore the channel count, followed by batch normalization to normalize different levels of feature representations [33]. A larger kernel is used instead of pointwise convolution for effective context learning. Finally, we add a residual connection for gradient flow.

2.2   Proposed Network Architecture

We design the S-Net based on the MCAP module as a basic functional block. It follows the encoder-decoder model with a shallow decoder for faster inference.

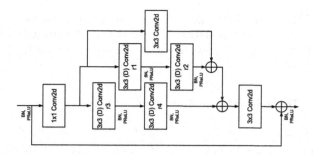

Fig. 3. Multi-scale Context Aggregation Pyramid (MCAP) module. (D) Conv2d: Dilated convolution; r1/r2/r3/r4: dilation rate; BN: Batch Norm.; PReLU: Parametric ReLU. '+': element wise addition.

The detailed structure of our network is given in Table 1. The encoder has three stages with 32, 64, and 128 channels, respectively. While the first consists of three 2D convolution kernels of 3 × 3, the second and third stages comprise MCAP modules. The downsampler is made of a similar 3 × 3 kernel, albeit with a stride of 2 [19]. As the first kernel in stage-1 downsamples the feature map by 2, the resolution of the final encoded output is 1/8× of the input size following three downsampling operations throughout. The decoder processes the encoder output to obtain the final feature maps. The number of channels in the output conforms with the number of object classes (19 in this case). A softmax layer predicts the final class label from these feature maps. In the next paragraph, we describe our decoder structure.

Decoder: In addition to the final encoder output, we use two additional low-level feature maps from different stages. This has a twofold advantage; first, it adds context features to high-level semantic features and then improves the gradient flow during backpropagation. As the first operation in the decoder, we reduce the number of channels through a pointwise convolution to match channels with the encoder skip connection. The feature maps are concatenated and applied to an MCAP module for effective feature blending. This process is repeated in the second decoder stage. After the final projection layer, the feature maps are bilinearly upsampled to restore the resolution. The uniqueness of our decoder lies in the position from which skip connections are taken. In [7,16,21,25], the skip connections come from the end of each stage, whereas in our design, they are taken from the beginning of the stage. The high-frequency image details, such as boundary and texture, are distinctive to low-level features. Our approach preserves these features better because, with increasing depth, some of them are lost due to the low-pass filtering effect of the convolution kernel.

3   Experimental Results

We evaluate the proposed network on the competitive Cityscapes [3] and CamVid [1] dataset. We first give a brief introduction to these datasets. The implementation details follow this. In the next subsection, we conduct an extensive ablation study on the Cityscapes dataset to show the effectiveness of our design choices. Finally, we compare our work with the state-of-the-art methods on these datasets.

Table 1. Detailed structure of the proposed S-Net.

	Layer	Operation	Mode	Channel	Output size
Encoder	1	3×3 Conv	stride=2	32	384×768
	2	3×3 (G) Conv	stride=1	32	384×768
	3	3×3 (G) Conv	stride=1	32	384×768
	4	Downsampling	stride=2	64	192×384
	5–7	3xMCAP Module	d=(2,4,8,16)	64	192×384
	8	Downsampling	stride=2	128	96×192
	9–14	6xMCAP Module	d=(2,4,8,16)	128	96×192
Decoder	16	1×1 Conv	stride=1	64	96×192
	18	Upsampling	scale=2	64	192×384
	19	MCAP Module	d=(1,2,1,2)	64	192×384
	20	Downsampling	scale=2	128	96×192
	21	MCAP Module	d=(1,2,1,2)	128	96×192
	22	1×1 Conv	stride=1	19	96×192
	23	Upsampling	factor=8	19	768×1536

(G) Conv- Group convolution; d=(r1,r2,r3,r4) is the dilation rate, refer Fig. 3.

3.1 Datasets

Cityscapes. It is a high-resolution urban scene dataset for autonomous driving. It contains 5000 finely annotated images of resolution 1024×2048. Out of 35 labelled classes in the dataset, 19 are used for training and evaluation. The images are divided into 2975 training, 1525 testing and 500 validation. We randomly crop the images to 768×1536 for training.

CamVid. The CamVid dataset contains 701 images selected from a two-hour-long driving video sequence. The images are divided into 367 for training, 233 for testing and 101 for validation. The 720×960 resolution images are annotated with 11 object classes for training.

3.2 Implementation Details

We implement the network in PyTorch v1.11 on a system equipped with Nvidia-V100 GPU running with an Intel-Xeon-Silver 4110 processor. We use Adam optimizer with an initial learning rate of 5×10^{-4}, a polynomial schedule with weight decay of 10^{-4}, and a warmup strategy to train for 400 epochs, with a batch size of 8. Random crops, flips and translations, with a maximum shift of 2 pixels, are among the data augmentation strategies.

3.3 Evaluation Metrics

We use three metrics for the performance evaluation of our model. They are segmentation accuracy, inference speed and model size. The accuracy is measured using the mean intersection-over-union (mIoU) score. The inference speed is measured in segmented frames per second (fps). The model size is reported in terms of the number of parameters (Params) in Million (M).

3.4 Ablation Study

We perform a series of ablation experiments to verify the effectiveness of our design choices. All the experiments are performed using the Cityscapes training set, with results reported on its validation set.

MCAP Module. To show the overall effectiveness of our basic module, we replace it with two similar modules from FRNet [15] and LAANet [35] in our backbone design (Fig. 4). Table 2 shows that using the FRNet module reduces the parameters and improves the inference speed. However, it also drops the accuracy by 2.8%. The LAANet module has better accuracy but with reduced inference speed and increased parameters. This shows that our MCAP module gives the best balance between accuracy, size and speed.

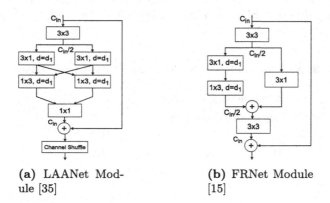

(a) LAANet Module [35]   (b) FRNet Module [15]

Fig. 4. Overview of some modules for ablation studies. 'C_{in}': Number of input channels. '3×1' is the convolution kernel size. 'd': Dilation rate. '+' denotes element-wise addition.

Dilation Rates: We use different sets of dilation rates in the MCAP module of the encoder. To begin with, we use (r1,r2,r3,r4)=(1,1,1,1); refer Fig. 3 for kernel locations. This essentially means no dilation and gives the least accuracy, as seen in Table 2. This reinforces the claim for the need for dilated kernels in semantic

Table 2. Ablation study for MCAP module on Cityscapes validation set.

Ablation Study	Type	mIOU (%)	fps	Params (M)
Basic Module	MCAP	71.8	65	0.6
	FRNet	69.2	76.1	0.52
	LAANet	72.5	58.7	0.78
Dilation rates	(1,1,1,1)	68	67.3	0.6
	(2,2,2,2)	69.5	66.5	0.6
	(1,2,1,2)	69.1	67.1	0.6
	(2,4,8,16)	71.8	65	0.6

segmentation. For the next set, (2,2,2,2) is used. Though this setting improves over the first, as all kernels have the same dilation rate, multi-scale features are not learned. Similar performance is obtained for (1,2,1,2). The best accuracy is obtained by (2,4,8,16) with a slight drop in speed due to large dilation rates.

Decoder. We use two skip connections in our decoder to gather context information from the encoder. Initially, we take the features from the end of stage 1 and stage 2 of the encoder. Table 3 shows that this configuration has reduced accuracy. While for the second experiment, we move the connections to the beginning of the stages. This increases the accuracy by 1.6%. As stated earlier, the reason may be attributed to better retaining low-level image features such as object boundary and texture. The qualitative improvement in the segmented image can be seen in Fig. 5. We also experimented with the position of the MCAP module in the decoder. Shifting it from the last to the second stage improves the accuracy by 0.8%.

Table 3. Ablation study for the decoder on Cityscapes validation set.

Ablation Study	Type	mIOU (%)
skip connections	after	70.2
	before	71.8
MCAP module	last stage	71.0
	second stage	71.8

3.5   Comparison on the Cityscapes Benchmark

In this sub-section, we report the performance of our method on the Cityscapes benchmark and compare it with other state-of-the-art lightweight real-time methods. Table 4 reports the result. The techniques with the highest accuracy

(ViT-Adapter-L [2], Trans4trans [34], SegFormer [31]) are in the top section and are mainly transformer [26] based. They are marked by large size and high floating point operations (FLOPs), making them unsuitable for small devices. We use a resolution of 768×1536 and achieve a mIoU of 72.5% running at 65 fps. LRNNet [9] has similar accuracy and model size but uses a smaller resolution, so it runs faster. HyperSeg [17], LBN [5] and DDRNet [7] achieve better accuracy but are significantly large. FASSDNet [22], and BiSeNet [33] run faster by 68 and 40 fps, respectively, but are 4x and 9.5x larger. Their inference speed is due to conventional 3×3 convolution, which is hardware-optimized but has many parameters. DABNet [10] and CFPNet [13] have higher accuracy by abysmal speed due to 1.5× input image size than ours. Thus, our method can effectively balance the speed, size, and accuracy, which is critical to resource-constrained devices.

Table 4. Comparison with state-of-the-art on the Cityscapes test benchmark.

Method	FLOPs(G)	InputSize	mIoU (%)	FPS	Params (M)
ViT-Adapter-L [2]	-	896×896	**84.9**	< 1	347.9
Trans4trans [34]	94.25	768×1536	81.5	27.3	49.5
SegFormer-B5 [31]	1447.60	1024×1024	84.0	2.5	84.7
Hyperseg-M [17]	7.5	512×1024	75.8	36.9	10.1
LBN-AA [5]	49.5	448×896	73.6	51	6.2
DDRNet-Slim [7]	35.78	1024×2048	**77.4**	108.8	5.7
BiSeNet [33]	14.8	768×1536	68.4	105.8	5.8
FASSD-Net-L2 [22]	45.1	1024×2048	72.1	**133.1**	2.3
ERFNet [20]	21.0	512×1024	68.0	41	2.1
ESNet [29]	27.49	512×1024	69.1	63	1.66
MLFNet-MobileV2 [6]	4.67	512×1024	71.5	90.8	3.99
AGLNet [36]	13.88	512×1024	70.1	52	1.12
LEDNet [28]	11.44	512×1024	70.6	71.0	0.94
DABNet [10]	10.60	1024×2048	70.1	27.7	0.76
LRNNet [9]	8.48	512×1024	72.2	71.0	0.68
CFPNet [13]	14.7	1024×2048	70.1	30	0.55
CGNet [30]	7.14	512×1024	64.8	50	0.5
ENet [19]	**3.8**	640×360	58.3	52	0.39
ESPNet [16]	4.5	512×1024	60.3	112	**0.39**
S-Net (Ours)	6.24	768×1536	72.5	65	0.6

"-" indicates that the method does not report the result.

3.6   Comparison on the CamVid Benchmark

We also evaluate the performance of our method on the CamVid dataset. The results are reported in Table 5. Our method achieves a mIoU of 67.5% for an input size of 960 × 720 at 92 fps. RTFormer [27] achieves the highest accuracy but is 8× larger than our model. While LAANet [35] achieves similar accuracy, it has a half-size input image. CGNet [30] is smaller but has 2% less accuracy. These results further demonstrate the efficacy of our method.

Table 5. Comparison with state-of-the-art on the CamVid test benchmark.

Method	InputSize	mIoU (%)	FPS	Params (M)
RTFormer-Slim [27]	960 × 720	81.4	190.7	4.8
EDANet [12]	480 × 360	66.4	40.75	0.7
DFANet [11]	960 × 720	59.3	116	7.8
SwiftNet-MN [18]	960 × 720	65.0	27.7	11.8
BiSeNet [33]	960 × 720	65.6	175	5.8
BiSeNetV2-L [32]	960 × 720	**73.2**	32.7	-
MLFNet-Res34 [6]	960 × 720	69.0	57.2	4.0
LAANet [35]	480 × 360	67.9	**112.5**	0.7
CGNet [30]	960 × 720	65.6	59.0	**0.5**
FASSDNet [22]	960 × 720	69.3	80.0	2.85
DABNet [10]	480 × 360	66.4	101.3[*]	0.76
S-Net (Ours)	960 × 720	67.5	92	0.6

[*]Denotes that the specific metric is calculated by us using the open-source code. "-" indicates that the method does not report the result.

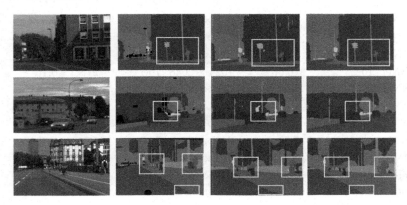

Fig. 5. Qualitative results of our method for different positions of encoder skip connection on the Cityscapes validation set. Column 1: Input Image; Column 2: Ground truth; Column 3: Before; Column 4: After. (Ref. Sec. 4.4 Decoder for more detail.). Critical regions are shown in the box.

4 Conclusion

In this paper, we design a novel multi-branch basic block based on a dilation pyramid which learns semantic and context features for effective segmentation. Based on it, we propose a lightweight encoder-decoder network, S-Net. Our novel decoder uses unique skip connections to add low-level features while achieving state-of-the-art performance on Cityscapes and CamVid benchmarks. In future, we will extend our work by (i) validating our network on a more diverse segmentation dataset, (ii) adding an attention mechanism to restore features during decoding, and (iii) applying methods like knowledge distillation and pruning to reduce the model size.

Acknowledgment. We acknowledge the Science and Engineering Research Board, Department of Science and Technology, Government of India, for the financial support for Project CRG/2022/003473.

References

1. Brostow, G.J., Fauqueur, J., Cipolla, R.: Semantic object classes in video: a high-definition ground truth database. Pattern Recogn. Lett. **30**(2), 88–97 (2009)
2. Chen, Z., et al.: Vision transformer adapter for dense predictions (2022). https://arxiv.org/abs/2205.08534
3. Cordts, M., et al.: The cityscapes dataset. In: CVPR Workshop on The Future of Datasets in Vision (2015)
4. Deng, J., Dong, W., Socher, R., Li, L., Kai, L., Fei-Fei, L.: ImageNet: a large-scale hierarchical image database. In: IEEE Conference on Computer Vision and Pattern Recognition, pp. 248–255 (2009)
5. Dong, G., Yan, Y., Shen, C., Wang, H.: Real-time high-performance semantic image segmentation of urban street scenes. IEEE Trans. Intell. Transp. Syst. **22**(6), 3258–3274 (2021)
6. Fan, J., Wang, F., Chu, H., Hu, X., Cheng, Y., Gao, B.: MLFNet: multi-level fusion network for real-time semantic segmentation of autonomous driving. IEEE Trans. Intell. Veh. **8**(1), 756–767 (2023)
7. Hong, Y., Pan, H., Sun, W., Jia, Y.: Deep dual-resolution networks for real-time and accurate semantic segmentation of road scenes. arXiv preprint arXiv:2101.06085 (2021)
8. Howard, A.G., et al.: MobileNets: Efficient Convolutional Neural Networks for Mobile Vision Applications. CoRR **abs/1704.04861** (2017)
9. Jiang, W., Xie, Z., Li, Y., Liu, C., Lu, H.: LRNNET: a light-weighted network with efficient reduced non-local operation for real-time semantic segmentation. In: 2020 IEEE International Conference on Multimedia and Expo Workshop (ICMEW), pp. 1–6. IEEE Computer Society, Los Alamitos, CA, USA (2020)
10. Li, G., Yun, I.Y., Kim, J., Kim, J.: DABNet: depth-wise asymmetric bottleneck for real-time semantic segmentation. In: BMVC (2019)
11. Li, H., Xiong, P., Fan, H., Sun, J.: DFANet: deep feature aggregation for real-time semantic segmentation. In: 2019 IEEE/CVF Conference on Computer Vision and Pattern Recognition (CVPR), pp. 9514–9523 (2019)

12. Lo, S.Y., Hang, H.M., Chan, S.W., Lin, J.J.: Efficient dense modules of asymmetric convolution for real-time semantic segmentation. In: Proceedings of the ACM Multimedia Asia, pp. 1–6 (2019)
13. Lou, A., Loew, M.: CFPNET: channel-wise feature pyramid for real-time semantic segmentation. In: 2021 IEEE International Conference on Image Processing (ICIP), pp. 1894–1898 (2021)
14. Lu, M., Chen, Z., Liu, C., Ma, S., Cai, L., Qin, H.: MFNet: multi-feature fusion network for real-time semantic segmentation in road scenes. IEEE Trans. Intell. Transp. Syst. **23**(11), 20991–21003 (2022)
15. Lu, M., Chen, Z., Wu, Q.M.J., Wang, N., Rong, X., Yan, X.: FRNet: factorized and regular blocks network for semantic segmentation in road scene. IEEE Trans. Intell. Transp. Syst. **23**(4), 3522–3530 (2022)
16. Mehta, S., Rastegari, M., Caspi, A., Shapiro, L., Hajishirzi, H.: ESPNet: efficient spatial pyramid of dilated convolutions for semantic segmentation. In: Proceedings of the European Conference on Computer Vision (ECCV) (2018)
17. Nirkin, Y., Wolf, L., Hassner, T.: HyperSeg: patch-wise hypernetwork for real-time semantic segmentation. In: 2021 IEEE/CVF Conference on Computer Vision and Pattern Recognition (CVPR), pp. 4060–4069 (2021)
18. Oršić, M., Šegvić, S.: Efficient semantic segmentation with pyramidal fusion. Pattern Recogn. **110**, 107611 (2021)
19. Paszke, A., Chaurasia, A., Kim, S., Culurciello, E.: ENet: a deep neural network architecture for real-time semantic segmentation. In: 4th International Conference on Learning Representations, ICLR (2018)
20. Romera, E., Álvarez, J.M., Bergasa, L.M., Arroyo, R.: ERFNet: efficient residual factorized ConvNet for real-time semantic segmentation. IEEE Trans. Intell. Transp. Syst. **19**(1), 263–272 (2018)
21. Ronneberger, O., Fischer, P., Brox, T.: U-Net: convolutional networks for biomedical image segmentation. In: Navab, N., Hornegger, J., Wells, W.M., Frangi, A.F. (eds.) MICCAI 2015. LNCS, vol. 9351, pp. 234–241. Springer, Cham (2015). https://doi.org/10.1007/978-3-319-24574-4_28
22. Rosas-Arias, L., Benitez-Garcia, G., Portillo-Portillo, J., Olivares-Mercado, J., Sanchez-Perez, G., Yanai, K.: FASSD-Net: fast and accurate real-time semantic segmentation for embedded systems. IEEE Trans. Intell. Transp. Syst., 1–12 (2021)
23. Sandler, M., Howard, A., Zhu, M., Zhmoginov, A., Chen, L.C.: MobileNetV2: inverted residuals and linear bottlenecks (2018)
24. Shelhamer, E., Long, J., Darrell, T.: Fully convolutional networks for semantic segmentation. In: IEEE Transaction on Pattern Analysis and Machine Intelligence(PAMI), vol. 39, pp. 640–651. USA (2017)
25. Sun, K., Xiao, B., Liu, D., Wang, J.: Deep high-resolution representation learning for visual recognition. IEEE Trans. Pattern Anal. Mach. Intell. **43**(10), 3349–3364 (2021)
26. Vaswani, A., et al.: Attention is all you need. In: Advances in Neural Information Processing Systems (NIPS), vol. 30. Curran Associates, Inc. (2017)
27. Wang, J., et al.: RTFormer: efficient design for real-time semantic segmentation with transformer. In: Oh, A.H., Agarwal, A., Belgrave, D., Cho, K. (eds.) Advances in Neural Information Processing Systems (2022)
28. Wang, Y., et al.: LEDNet: a lightweight encoder-decoder network for real-time semantic segmentation. In: 2019 IEEE International Conference on Image Processing (ICIP), pp. 1860–1864 (2019)

29. Wang, Yu., Zhou, Q., Xiong, J., Wu, X., Jin, X.: ESNet: an efficient symmetric network for real-time semantic segmentation. In: Lin, Z., et al. (eds.) PRCV 2019. LNCS, vol. 11858, pp. 41–52. Springer, Cham (2019). https://doi.org/10.1007/978-3-030-31723-2_4

30. Wu, T., Tang, S., Zhang, R., Cao, J., Zhang, Y.: CGNet: a light-weight context guided network for semantic segmentation. IEEE Trans. Image Process. **30**, 1169–1179 (2021)

31. Xie, E., Wang, W., Yu, Z., Anandkumar, A., Alvarez, J.M., Luo, P.: SegFormer: simple and efficient design for semantic segmentation with transformers. In: Advances in Neural Information Processing Systems (2021)

32. Yu, C., Gao, C., Wang, J., Yu, G., Shen, C., Sang, N.: BiSeNet V2: bilateral network with guided aggregation for real-time semantic segmentation. Int. J. Comput. Vision **129**(11), 3051–3068 (2021)

33. Yu, C., Wang, J., Peng, C., Gao, C., Yu, G., Sang, N.: BiSeNet: bilateral segmentation network for real-time semantic segmentation. In: Ferrari, V., Hebert, M., Sminchisescu, C., Weiss, Y. (eds.) Computer Vision – ECCV 2018. Springer, Cham (2018)

34. Zhang, J., Yang, K., Constantinescu, A., Peng, K., Müller, K., Stiefelhagen, R.: Trans4trans: efficient transformer for transparent object and semantic scene segmentation in real-world navigation assistance. IEEE Trans. Intell. Transp. Syst. **23**(10), 19173–19186 (2022)

35. Zhang, X., Du, B., Wu, Z., Wan, T.: LAANet: lightweight attention-guided asymmetric network for real-time semantic segmentation. Neural Comput. Appl. **34**(5), 3573–3587 (2022)

36. Zhou, Q., et al.: AGLNet: towards real-time semantic segmentation of self-driving images via attention-guided lightweight network. Appl. Soft Comput. **96**, 106682 (2020)

37. Zhu, F., Cui, J., Zhu, B., Li, H., Liu, Y.: Semantic segmentation of urban street scene images based on improved U-Net network. Optoelectron. Lett. **19**(3), 179–185 (2023)

Segmentation and Labeling of Vertebra Using SegFormer Architecture

Archan Ghosh[1], Debgandhar Ghosh[2](✉), Somoballi Ghoshal[1],
Amlan Chakrabarti[1], and Susmita Sur-Kolay[3]

[1] University of Calcutta, Kolkata, India
`acakcs@caluniv.ac.in`
[2] Maulana Abul Kalam Azad University of Technology, Kolkata, India
`debgandhar4000@gmail.com`
[3] Indian Statistical Institute, Kolkata, Kolkata, India
`ssk@isical.ac.in`

Abstract. Vertebra segmentation and labeling in MR images of the spine play a vital role in the identification of diseases or anomalies. MRI captures the tissue structure of a spine accurately, hence it is essential to demarcate and identify the vertebra in the MRI image. There are both supervised and unsupervised methods for vertebra segmentation and labeling. However, the acquisition of requisite data is a challenge to designing methods with very high accuracy. In this work, we have modified a transformer-based architecture called Segformer for semantic segmentation of 3D sliced data. Our method leverages transfer learning on low-population data. With a new advanced masking logic, we achieve 99% accuracy for segmentation and labeling of lumbar spine MR images.

Keywords: Semantic segmentation of image · Vertebra labeling · Transfer learning · Segformer architecture

1 Introduction

MR imaging has become the preferred modality for diagnosing various spinal disorders such as degenerative disc diseases or spinal stenosis, due to its excellent soft tissue contrast and no ionizing radiation [1]. One of the most important tasks for spine disease detection and analysis is to segment and label the vertebral column.

Recently, with the rapid development of convolution neural networks (CNN), deep learning-based methods have achieved remarkable performance in semantic segmentation. For medical images, a CNN model trained with complete annotation can obtain accuracy which is at par with that of clinical specialists [20]. In [8], the authors convert the images into spectral/spatio-spectral domains by using discrete cosine transform and discrete wavelet transform. Then, these features are projected into a lower dimension through the Convolutional Neural Network (CNN), and those three types of projected features are then fed to

H. Kaur et al. (Eds.): CVIP 2023, CCIS 2010, pp. 160–171, 2024.
https://doi.org/10.1007/978-3-031-58174-8_15

Multilayer Perceptron (MLP) for final prediction. The combination of the three types of features yielded superior performance than any of the features when used individually. However, manual annotation is laborious and time-consuming which makes it costly, and thus limited annotated data is available within the scope of current literature. Furthermore, due to data sensitive nature of CNN, it can easily fail if it does not have access to different variations during its training procedure. In cases of variations or data obtained from different settings, the model may fail and require retraining on newly obtained data, which thereby increases the overall complexity.

Vertebra segmentation and labeling have been a challenge in deep learning due to the limitation of properly labeled open datasets in the medical domain. The authors in [17] introduced the SpineNetV2 which has achieved impressive results with the help of a restructured U-Net and multi-modal architecture. In comparison, the study in [21] employed three different architectures, namely BN-U-NET, FCN and U-Net to find the best possible labels. In [15], the authors pioneered using U-Net but added an attention mechanism for better feature realization. The authors of [11] combined the rule-based method with a CNN architecture to differentiate multiple parts of the spine including the vertebrae, and intervertebral discs. Alternatively, in [16] a cascading FCN that can easily detect the desired segmentation masks for the vertebrae has been proposed.

Our proposed method here uses transfer learning instead, to help in a faster training process, yield results with less noise, and to be able to tackle situations with limited data access, employing the weights and features learned by the pre-trained model. We use semantic segmentation in place of bounding box-based object detection as in existing works based on RCNN, UNET, FCN, and Mask RCNN [12,14] We have used a semantic segmentation architecture along the lines of Segformer [19] to detect the location of a vertebra with the help of its corresponding novel type of mask.

Our Contributions: We have proposed a framework for automatic semantic segmentation of vertebrae from 3D MRI images reconstructed from a sequence of 2D slices with different slice gaps, using a transformer-based sub-supervised learning approach. The novelties of our method in particular are as follows:

- a centroid-based masking technique to generate masks for each 2D slice of MR images.
- incorporating multilabel masking for classifying the vertebra after 3D volume reconstruction with interpolation from a sequence of 2D slices along the sagittal plane;

2   Preliminaries

We first describe the semantic segmentation of images briefly and then about Segformer [19], a transformer-based architecture for semantic segmentation. It partly uses ViT [4] at its core, since it excels in vision tasks.

2.1   Semantic Segmentation

Semantic segmentation studies several elements in an image and labels them. Unlike using a bounding box, here we directly follow the natural shape of the target label present in an image. The vertebra segments were assigned to a particular pixel intensity based on their class, hence semantic segmentation was employed to achieve pixel-wise classification.

2.2   Segformer

Segformer [19] as shown in Fig. 1 consists of two main parts, a hierarchical encoder based on the transformer architecture [18], and a lightweight multi-layer perceptron (MLP) decoder.

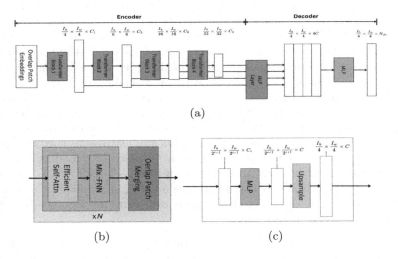

Fig. 1. (a) Segformer architecture, (b) a transformer block, and (c) details of the MLP decoder.

The encoder part of Segformer acts as a feature extractor, that can capture both high-level fine features and low-level coarse features, thereby boosting the granularity of the model. It uses a series of patch-based modules based on the resolution of the image for the extraction of features. The Mix Transformer(MiT) based encoder helps generate multi-label feature maps similar to a CNN, unlike that of ViT [7] which can only generate a single feature map. More elaborately, for a given image of size $I_h \times I_w \times 3$ (there are three channels in RGB), patch merging is performed to generate a hierarchical feature map F_i, having a resolution $\frac{I_h}{2^{i+1}} \times \frac{I_w}{2^{i+1}} \times C_i$, where $i \in \{1, 2, 3, 4\}$, C is the number of channels per i^{th} transformer, and C_{i+1} is greater than C_i.

Efficient Self-Attention. Finally being an entirely transformer-based network, another major bottleneck inherently present within Segformer is the presence of

Self-Attention. For multi-head self-attention, each of the heads, Q, K, V have the same dimensions $N \times C$, where $N = H \times W$ is the length of the sequence, and self-attention is estimated by the following formula:

$$Attention\,(Q, K, V) = Softmax \left(\frac{QK^T}{\sqrt{d_{head}}} \right) V \qquad (1)$$

Following this, after sequence reduction, we are able to obtain:

$$K = Linear(C \cdot R, C)(\hat{K}), \qquad (2)$$

because of this the new K dimensions of $\frac{N}{R} \times C$ and as a result the order of complexity of this attention is reduced by a factor of R, to $O(\frac{N^2}{R})$ from $O(N^2)$. The faster inference is supported by the usage of an MLP decoder which generates the prediction masks. The lightweight decoder ensures that the inference is faster but also sampled like a CNN prediction mask which is usually returned from a UNet or FCN-based architecture.

$$x_{out} = MLP(GELU(Conv_{3\times3}(MLP\,(x_{in})))) + x_{in} \qquad (3)$$

As presented in the original work Segformer is available in 5 formats depending on the size of parameters, for our work, we have used the B0 version, which has 3.8 million parameters. The encoder part of SegFormer [19] is pre-trained on ImageNet-1K [6] and the decoder part is randomly initialized. The Segformer b0 Model is then trained on ADE20K [23] dataset. The advantage of Segformer is its scalability and efficiency, which are exponentially better compared to previous approaches. [19] Apart from outperforming standard transformer-based architectures, Segformer has also been able to outscore FCN-based architectures, on two standard datasets ADE20K [23] and Cityscapes [5], which induced us to leverage this for our use case.

3   Our Proposed Methodology for Segmentation

Figure 2 gives the block diagram of the proposed methodology. The green dotted lined boxes denote the blocks of our contribution. The input is a set of consecutive 2D slices along a single axis (sagittal) of the MRI spine with a gap of 3 or 5 mm between two consecutive slices. We first reconstruct a complete 3D image by judicious and methodical interpolation in the significant gap between slices, applying the algorithm as in [10] to generate the missing data between two consecutive slices or all the slices. Now, treating this as a 3D matrix and extracting the slices along the sagittal plane with an increment of the index by 1, we get all possible slices with a gap as small as desired and described in [9]. Then, we work with the 2D slices, segment and label the vertebrae in each slice, and again stack the labeled data into a 3D matrix, thus we get a 3D labeled vertebra along the sagittal plane.

For each 2D slice, a proposed centroid-based method for masking is applied to generate the mask. Next, these labeled vertebrae are mapped to the original

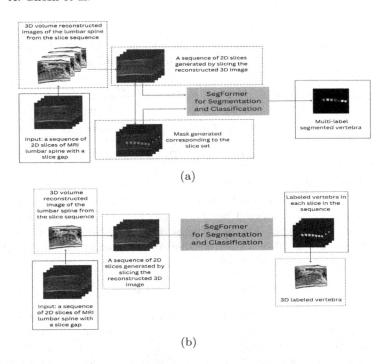

(a)

(b)

Fig. 2. Block diagram of our proposed method – (a) Training process, and (b) Prediction process

2D slice, to get the labeling in the original 2D image. All the 2D slices along the sagittal plane are thus generated and stacked to get the 3D labeled vertebra and then each image with its mask is fed to the Segformer architecture [19].

3.1 Multilabel Semantic Mask Using Centroid-Based Masking

Our proposed method is based on a multilabel semantic mask using a centroid-based masking procedure. Our dataset consists of T2-weighted MRI. So we prepared a semantic mask, more specifically, a multilabel semantic mask that could be used by the model for a feature-rich segmentation. For the required segmentation masks, we first identified and isolated the slices that were properly annotated and had more than one label. The dataset had in total seven labels, five from the lumbar region numbered L1 to L5, and two from the thoracic region numbered T11 and T12. Following this, each of the labels is given a pixel intensity value that ranges from 1 to 7 representing the seven labels respectively. Next, the task is to capture the exact position of a vertebra that is present within the slice. We have information about the centroid and coordinates of two corner points from the centroid for each vertebra per slice. For the intermediate slices that we have reconstructed, we have defined the centroids and the corresponding coordinates based on the projection of its pre-defined slice. Initially, based on the centroid and two corner coordinates we sketch a bounding box around the vertebrae and then trace the boundary of each vertebra by excluding the "0" valued or black pixels from the bounding box. The pixels in this bounded region are then changed to the corresponding class intensity value as per the defined label. Figure 3 shows the stepwise masking process.

$$[x_c, y_c] = \sum_{i=W_1^c}^{W_2^c} x_i \times \sum_{j=H_1^c}^{H_2^c} y_j \tag{4}$$

$$\begin{aligned} if\ (x, y) > 0, then\ [x_c, y_c] = L \\ elseif\ (x, y) = 0, then\ [x_c, y_c] = 0 \end{aligned} \tag{5}$$

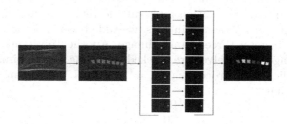

Fig. 3. Proposed masking process

Next, all the slices corresponding to one MRI image are stacked into its 3D structure, providing us with 3D planar information, and the same is done for the mask to provide 3D planar target masks. As the images are inherently grayscale, the individual slices are normalized and cropped. Secondly, while creating the boundary before masking, it is ascertained that for each such step, the boundaries are tightly defined on each side and not a single pixel is more or less than the original size of the vertebra in the MRI scan.

MultiLabel Approach for Segmentation: The T2 weighted images that are used for training, have 30 to 45 slices per scan level. However, not all of them are usable for segmentation. Any slice that is at the beginning or at the end is discarded, for better quality-of-life slices being used in training. Further, we need to create a multilabel image containing more than two labels per image. For this, we club the different labels that are present per slice allowing us to achieve this. If we have an image I containing slices S_n, for each slice S_i, we can have K labels out of all the labels. *Let us take the following sample as an example:*

There is an image I_1 where slice S_{20} has labels $= [K_{L1}, K_{L2}, K_{L3}]$. Each of the labels $[K_{L1}, K_{L2}, K_{L3}]$ are first masked using Eqs. 4 and 5 producing three individual sub-slices, that can be represented as $S_{20}^{K_{L1}}$, $S_{20}^{K_{L2}}$, $S_{20}^{K_{L3}}$. These three separate sub-slices are then merged to form the original slice containing all the masked labels, $S_{20}^{[K_{L1}+K_{L2}+K_{L3}]}$. This gives us multi-label slices that contain K masked labels. Finally, the intensity per label is adjusted, which is predefined for each label.

3.2 Implementation and Training

In this subsection, we present the details of the implementation of our proposed method and the training process. Segformer is available in five formats depending on the size of the parameters. For our work, we have implemented the B0 version having 3.8 million parameters as it suffices our requirement of vertebra segmentation. Feature-wise the mask and the image have to be identical in size and dimension. In our case, as we are dealing with MRI images, we only have access to ground truth images which are $I_h \times I_w \times 1$. Segformer extracts features like a CNN, by moving over the patches of images. Thus, having more channels always results in more information retrieval and retention, and to overcome the challenge of having just grayscale images, we added two padding layers that imitated the image being a three-channel image. Another key point to note is the fact that the images themselves are stacked, resulting in a 3D image.

Initial S = slice after processing: $S_k = I_h \times I_w \times 1$. Creating false channels for padding, we have:

$$
C_f = \begin{bmatrix} 00 \cdots 0 \\ 00 \cdots 0 \\ \cdots \cdots \\ \cdots \cdots \\ 00 \cdots 0 \end{bmatrix}_{\{I_h \times I_w\}} \tag{6}
$$

After merging the false channels to the slice $S_k = I_h \times I_w \times 3$ we have also implemented the B0 model of Segformer [19], primarily for the following reasons. The B0 model already has 3.8 million parameters, and considering the data volume we have, it is not necessary to use a larger model compared to this, as the training time would not have any effect on accuracy. Instead, we may end up with the problem of vanishing gradients. The B0 model due to its size uses restricted information from the last encoder, thereby reducing the noise being generated by super low grain patches. By using transfer learning, we are using partially frozen weights of the B0 variant which reduces the chances of exploding gradients, on coarse features. Moreover, Transfer Learning helps in the faster training process and yields better results as the pre-trained model leverages the features, previously learned by the pre-trained model.

We have also used a feature extractor based on the original implementation which helps us in using the stacked slices. The feature extractor pairs each ground truth image to its corresponding mask and then stacks them based on each consecutive slice that belongs to the ground truth image. This is then propagated through the input encoder to create the discerned embedding. The labels of each mask are also serialized and changed to a multi-label approach as discussed previously. Each label has its distinct pixel value which has a 1-to-1 mapping to the stated label and is used in the prediction head during classification.

The model was trained on a Tesla V100 GPU having 32GB of Vram with a batch size of 2, and an epoch range of 40. For the training, the data is feature extracted and batched before training itself. This helps us gain a slight advantage in time by reducing the patch-wise traversal of the attention heads. The model configuration is another key step, that helps ensure that the training is smooth for the given data.

The model is first loaded from a binary graph to ensure that the weights are properly inserted at each node, following which it is restructured based on the given data dimensions of $H \times W \times C$, and class labels of n. For model optimization, we have used AdamW [13] optimizer with a learning rate of $6e^{-5}$, as it gave us the best results. AdamW [13] tackles the problem of weight decay when using pre-trained weights. We also used a bilinear interpolation kernel for the up-sampling of the prediction logits. During training we did an in-loop evaluation, to ensure the model performance was optimum and to minimize the chances of exploding gradients.

3.3   Evaluation Metrics

We have chosen three separate metrics during the training process. For the prediction of correct masking topology, Intersection-over-Union (IoU) has been chosen. As we are also dealing with a 3D multi-class classification problem, we have taken class-based accuracy. Finally, there was logit loss which is used to measure the overall performance of the model for per-pixel classification.

In our case, if the image has a vertebra that is correctly identified, then it comes under TP. If a vertebrae is in the image but could not be identified at all then it comes under FN. If some other vertebrae or some other tissue is falsely identified in place of a vertebrae then it comes under FP, and if there is no vertebra in the image and it is not identified, it comes under TN. IoU is expressed as a function of true positive(TP), true negative(TN), false positive (FP), and false negative (FN): $IoU = \frac{TP}{TP+FP+FN}$. It is taken as the mean over all the training samples in a batch. For training, step mean IoU is calculated over a range, thereby giving the model feedback during a single step and correcting them over the next batch.

3D multi-class accuracy is given by: $ClassAccuracy = \frac{TN+TP}{TN+TP+FP+FN}$.

We also take into account the loss of the model over its training process and represent it as an average loss in Fig. 7. The model is trained with native pixel-to-pixel cross-entropy loss [22]. Cross entropy can be defined as: $L_{CE} = -\sum_{i=1}^{n} t_i \log(p_i)$. Here t_i represents the true class value of each pixel that has been labeled, and p_i is the Softmax probability of the ith class predicted by the model.

4   Our Results and Analysis

We have applied our algorithm on PACS 24 T2 MRI lumbar spine labeled data set [2], eight T2 MRI lumbar spine [3], and on twenty real-life T2 MRI data of lumbar spine collected from Bangur Institute of Neurosciences, Kolkata. Our proposed model has been trained with 80% of the dataset, and the rest 20% is used for testing. For training and testing, the images were randomly chosen and fed to our model. For testing, we obtained the 3D volumetric image set by combining the 2D slices along the sagittal plane. The model is then used to predict the mask on a per-slice basis along the sagittal axis, thereby allowing us to obtain the full volumetric mask. Figure 4 is an example of output obtained by applying our proposed approach on a 2D slice.

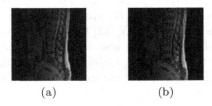

(a)   (b)

Fig. 4. Example 1 for Vertebra labeling in 2D lumbar sagittal slice – (a) Input image, (b) Output labeled vertebra

After the experimentation, we have taken the multi-level segmentation results from the evaluation set. During training, we evaluated the model in 3 steps, one of which was after training on a few samples, representing sub-sampling 1. The second evaluation was done when we had trained the model on at least 50% of the data for that epoch, represented by sub-sampling 2, and finally, the third evaluation was done after the full batch was trained for that epoch, represented by sub-sampling 3. We have captured and illustrated in Figs. 5, 6, and 7 the overall performance of our model for the three different metrics that were taken into consideration. The multi-level segmentation also shows us how our model performs over 3D non-annotated images, being trained over a minimal subset of 3D annotated images.

As we were dealing with a multi-label classification problem, we used IoU as it helped us to understand both performances on 2D as well as 3D planes. While the model is training, IoU is measured over each 2D slice extracted and divulged, while evaluating the IoU is measured over each 3D stack. This gives a whole new aspect of un-supervision to our approach and also increases the model's overall semantic separation capabilities. In Fig. 7, we observe that there are specific spikes during the fine-tuning process, indicating the divergence present within the different shapes of the vertebral sections, yet the final score clearly portrays that the model is adapting over the 3D segment masks.

Figure 8 shows an example of a 3D-labeled vertebra. The comparison of accuracy by our method with two earlier approaches appears in Fig. 9. We have applied and compared UNET, Attention UNET Methods, and SegFormer Architecture to our dataset and achieved an accuracy of 96%, 97%, and 99% respectively. The various algorithms used in the related works could not be compared with our proposed approach as the algorithms used in the works are not open source.

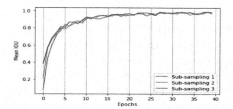
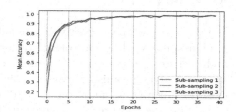

Fig. 5. IoU Score   **Fig. 6.** Class Accuracy

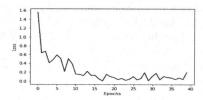

Fig. 7. Average loss over the epochs for our dataset

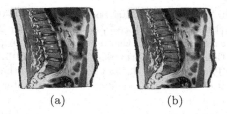

(a)   (b)

Fig. 8. An example of vertebra labeling in 3D MRI spine – (a) 3D reconstructed image from slices, and (b) vertebra labeled 3D image

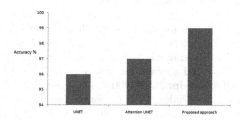

Fig. 9. Comparison of our method with earlier approaches

5   Conclusion

In this work, we have effectively carried out segmentation of vertebrae from 3D lumbar spine MRI and also labeled them accurately with the help of Segformer architecture. The comparative results as shown in Fig. 9 show that our proposed approach gives promising results with respect to accuracy. Since we have used transfer learning, we get to our desired results with relatively fewer data with less noise. Since we have reconstructed full 3D volumetric data from the available 2D slices along the sagittal plane there is no missing information in between slices and all the slices are labeled without loss of information. This can be further improved by incorporating more features like morphological features etc.

Acknowledgement. We would like to acknowledge and express our gratitude towards Dr. Alok Pandit, Bangur Institute of Neurosciences, Mr. Sameer Kundu, Technician, MRI Unit, IPGMER, and Dr. Ambhuranjan Santra, NRS Medical College and Hospital for validating our results and guiding us with the real-life implementation of our approach. We would also like to thank Mr. Ritwik Deb, a student of M.B.B.S at Calcutta Medical College, who helped us with our initial understanding of vertebral tissue and structure.

References

1. Mri physics: Diffusion-weighted imaging. http://xrayphysics.com/dwi.html. Accessed 07 Jan 2023
2. http://dx.doi.org/10.5281/zenodo.22304 , accessed: 2023-03-07
3. http://spineweb.digitalimaginggroup.ca/ . Accessed 01 Mar 2017
4. Carion, N., Massa, F., Synnaeve, G., Usunier, N., Kirillov, A., Zagoruyko, S.: End-to-end object detection with transformers. CoRR **abs/2005.12872** (2020)
5. Cordts, M., et al.: The cityscapes dataset for semantic urban scene understanding. In: Proceedings of the IEEE Conference on Computer Vision and Pattern Recognition (CVPR), June 2016
6. Deng, J., Dong, W., Socher, R., Li, L.J., Li, K., Fei-Fei, L.: Imagenet: a large-scale hierarchical image database. In: 2009 IEEE Conference on Computer Vision and Pattern Recognition, pp. 248–255 (2009). https://doi.org/10.1109/CVPR.2009.5206848
7. Dosovitskiy, A., et al.: An image is worth 16 × 16 words: transformers for image recognition at scale. CoRR **abs/2010.11929** (2020)
8. Ghosh, S., Das, S., Mallipeddi, R.: A deep learning framework integrating the spectral and spatial features for image-assisted medical diagnostics. IEEE Access **9**, 163686–163696 (2021). https://doi.org/10.1109/ACCESS.2021.3133338
9. Ghoshal, S., Banu, S., Chakrabarti, A., Sur Kolay, S., Pandit, A.: 3D reconstruction of spine image from 2DMRI slices along one axis. IET Image Process. **14** (2020). https://doi.org/10.1049/iet-ipr.2019.0800
10. Ghoshal, S., Goswami, S., Chakrabarti, A., Sur-Kolay, S.: Fast 3d volumetric image reconstruction from 2D MRI slices by parallel processing (2023)
11. Kuang, X., et al.: Spine-GFlow: a hybrid learning framework for robust multi-tissue segmentation in lumbar MRI without manual annotation. Comput. Med. Imaging Graph. **99**, 102091 (2022). https://doi.org/10.1016/j.compmedimag.2022.102091

12. Li, H., et al.: Automatic lumbar spinal MRI image segmentation with a multi-scale attention network. Neural Comput. Appl. **33**, 1–14 (2021). https://doi.org/10.1007/s00521-021-05856-4
13. Loshchilov, I., Hutter, F.: Fixing weight decay regularization in Adam. CoRR **abs/1711.05101** (2017). http://arxiv.org/abs/1711.05101
14. Minaee, S., Boykov, Y., Porikli, F., Plaza, A., Kehtarnavaz, N., Terzopoulos, D.: Image segmentation using deep learning: a survey. IEEE Trans. Pattern Anal. Mach. Intell. **44**(7), 3523–3542 (2022). https://doi.org/10.1109/TPAMI.2021.3059968
15. Wang, S., Jiang, Z., Yang, H., Li, X., Yang, Z.: Automatic segmentation of lumbar spine MRI images based on improved attention U-Net. Comput. Intell. Neurosci. **2022**, 4259471 (2022)
16. Whitehead, W., Moran, S., Gaonkar, B., Macyszyn, L., Iyer, S.: A deep learning approach to spine segmentation using a feed-forward chain of pixel-wise convolutional networks. In: 2018 IEEE 15th International Symposium on Biomedical Imaging (ISBI 2018), pp. 868–871 (2018). https://doi.org/10.1109/ISBI.2018.8363709
17. Windsor, R., Jamaludin, A., Kadir, T., Zisserman, A.: Spinenetv2: automated detection, labelling and radiological grading of clinical MR scans (2022). https://doi.org/10.48550/ARXIV.2205.01683
18. Wolf, T., et al.: Transformers: State-of-the-art natural language processing. In: Proceedings of the 2020 Conference on Empirical Methods in Natural Language Processing: System Demonstrations, pp. 38–45. Association for Computational Linguistics, Online, October 2020
19. Xie, E., Wang, W., Yu, Z., Anandkumar, A., Alvarez, J.M., Luo, P.: Segformer: simple and efficient design for semantic segmentation with transformers. CoRR **abs/2105.15203** (2021)
20. Yadav, S., Jadhav, S.: Deep convolutional neural network based medical image classification for disease diagnosis. J. Big Data **6** (2019). https://doi.org/10.1186/s40537-019-0276-2
21. Zhang, Q., Du, Y., Wei, Z., Liu, H., Yang, X., Zhao, D.: Spine medical image segmentation based on deep learning. J. Healthc. Eng. **2021**, 1–6 (2021). https://doi.org/10.1155/2021/1917946
22. Zhang, Z., Sabuncu, M.: Generalized cross entropy loss for training deep neural networks with noisy labels. In: Bengio, S., Wallach, H., Larochelle, H., Grauman, K., Cesa-Bianchi, N., Garnett, R. (eds.) Advances in Neural Information Processing Systems, vol. 31. Curran Associates, Inc. (2018)
23. Zhou, B., Zhao, H., Puig, X., Fidler, S., Barriuso, A., Torralba, A.: Scene parsing through ADE20K dataset. In: 2017 IEEE Conference on Computer Vision and Pattern Recognition (CVPR), pp. 5122–5130 (2017). https://doi.org/10.1109/CVPR.2017.544

CNN Based Tropical Cyclone Intensity Estimation Using Satellite Images Around Indian Subcontinent

Parag Jha[✉], S. Sumam David, and Deepu Vijayasenan

Department of Electronics and Communication Engineering, National Institute
of Technology Karnataka, Surathkal 575025, India
paragjha111@gmail.com

Abstract. In this work, we have used deep learning models for estimating tropical cyclone (TC) intensity using satellite images. This is
an image to regression problem, where an image is given as input and
intensity value is estimated as output. In the literature, various deep
learning methods have been proposed for TC intensity estimation but
their focus on cyclones around the Indian subcontinent is limited. We
have implemented three models: regression model, classification model,
and a multitask model having regression and classification output as
two tasks. We have worked with two sets of input data. One set of data
contains single channel input containing infrared (IR) brightness temperature satellite image. Another set of data contains two channel inputs
having infrared (IR) brightness temperature satellite image as one of the
channels, and rain rate derived from passive microwave (PMW) satellite
image as another channel. We have used satellite images for cyclones
occurring in the Atlantic, Northeast Pacific, and North Central Pacific
regions from 2006 through 2016. For cyclones around the Indian subcontinent, we have used satellite images from 2005- 2016.

Keywords: Multi-task learning · CNN · Weather prediction · Cyclone
prediction · Cyclone intensity estimation

1 Introduction

Tropical cyclones (TC) cause huge loss of lives and livelihood for people living
around coastal areas. Thus, cyclones need to be predicted in advance to issue
cyclone alerts and perform precautionary actions like evacuations. India has a
coastline of around 7000 km. Thus, a large population is at risk of being affected
by harsh weather events like cyclones.

Usually, TC intensity is defined in terms of maximum sustained wind speed
(MSW) or minimum sea level pressure at the center of a cyclone, but the definition varies depending on the region and there is no standard definition. In intensity estimation, the goal is to estimate cyclone intensity using given features or
parameters. In the literature, satellite image-based techniques have proven to be

© The Author(s), under exclusive license to Springer Nature Switzerland AG 2024
H. Kaur et al. (Eds.): CVIP 2023, CCIS 2010, pp. 172–185, 2024.
https://doi.org/10.1007/978-3-031-58174-8_16

highly effective methods for real-time intensity estimation. With recent progress in deep learning models, there have been attempts to apply these techniques to TC intensity estimation.

Indian Meteorological Department uses Advanced Dvorak Technique for estimating intensity using satellite images [5]. There is large scope for improvement in intensity estimation as highlighted in the literature [2]. Hence, we attempt to use deep learning models for cyclone intensity estimation. Further, existing deep learning-based estimation literature does not focus on the estimation of cyclones around the Indian subcontinent.

Contributions. We have implemented three models: a regression model (TCReg-Net), a classification model (TCClassNet), and a multitask model (TCMultiNet) having regression and classification output as two tasks. We trained the models on satellite images from HURSAT dataset [6] and labels from HURDAT2 dataset [7]. Further, we created two channel inputs by combining satellite images from HURSAT dataset and CMORPH Climate Data Record dataset [14], and used them to train the model. We used the model for the estimation of cyclones occurring around the Indian subcontinent.

This paper contains 6 sections. In Sect. 2, we discuss the background of the problem and explored existing methodologies present in the literature. In Sect. 3, we discuss model architectures in detail. In Sect. 4, we discuss the dataset used. In Sect. 5, we discuss experiments performed and the results obtained. In Sect. 6, we present the conclusion.

2   Literature Survey

With faster computing power availability, weather prediction problems are attempted by data-driven methods [12]. To solve weather prediction problems, the meteorology research community is trying to adopt deep learning technologies which has potential to solve such problems. In the literature, it is noted that machine learning methods may not be adequate for solving weather prediction problems having a complex statistical nature [11]. It encourages the use of deep learning methods that shows the potential to solve such problems.

The most popular technique for intensity estimation is Dvorak Technique [4]. The underlying principle of this technique is that pattern formed by the clouds is related to the cyclone's intensity - not the amount of cloud in the pattern as shown in Fig. 1. This techniques assigns a Tropical number(T-number) to the storm depending on the intensity. Features of the pattern used to estimate are the storm center and the overcast around the center. This is a subjective method and requires an expert forecaster to predict the intensity.

The availability of computers in the 1980s gave rise to objective methods that can be run on computers [8]. The current state-of-the-art technique is Advanced Dvorak Technique (ADT) and is used by almost every meteorological department. ADT is a regression-based technique, where features are selected based on the region of the cyclone.

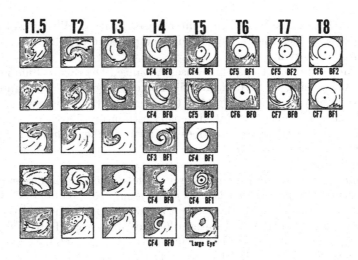

Fig. 1. Cloud pattern of cyclone at various stages during formation and development, and corresponding tropical number (T-number) [3]

Cyclone intensity estimation has been attempted using deep learning, both as a classification problem [9,13] and as a regression problem [1].

Pradhan el al. developed a eight-class classification model and these class predictions were converted to regression output by taking the weighted average of the two highest categories during inference [9]. They used satellite images from the tropical cyclone repository of the Marine Meteorology Division of U.S. Naval Research Laboratory, and labels from HURDAT2 dataset. Their model contained five convolution layers with max pooling followed by three fully connected layers. They reported root mean squared error (RMSE) value of 10.18 knot for the Atlantic region and Pacific region.

DeepMicroNet model based on AlexNet, developed by Wimmers et al., formulated the intensity estimation as classification problem [13]. Maximum sustained winds (MSW) value from 10 to 170 knot was divided in 33 classes by stepping up 5 knot in each class. For actual prediction task, only 29 out of 33 classes were used. They used passive microwave images in 37-GHz and 89-GHz band as their dataset. RMSE of 10.6 knot was reported on test dataset.

Chen et al. developed a regression deep learning model named CNN-TC based on AlexNet. They used GridSat dataset along with passive microwave image and RMSE of 10.59 knot was reported.

Zhang et al. proposed TCICENet model based on Inception-ResNet and AlexNet [15]. It divided the problem into two stages. First, it classified intensity into three broad categories using a classifier. Then, it estimated the intensity as a regression task. It used Infrared satellite images as dataset. RMSE of 8.60 knot and MAE of 6.67 knot was reported.

3   Methodology

We have implemented both classification and regression based models. We have implemented a multi-task model having two outputs, which are averaged to get a single output regression model. In this section, we discuss the implemented models.

3.1   Regression Model (TCRegNet)

We have implemented regression CNN model containing 11 individual layers, which can be grouped together in 7 blocks, as shown in Table 1. Figure 2 shows feature maps obtained at the output of each block. Input to model is $128 \times 128 \times 2$ image and maximum sustained wind speed is used as label. Block 1 contains convolution layer with ReLU activation function, followed by max pooling layer and batch normalization layer. Block 2, 3 and 4 contains convolution layer with ReLU activation function, followed by max pooling layer. Block 5, 6 and 7 contain fully connected layer. Block 5 and 6 is activated with ReLU function. No activation function is used on the last block. During training, we used Adam optimizer with a a learning rate of 0.0001. Mean squared error (MSE) is used as loss function. Root mean squared error (RMSE) is used to evaluate the model performance.

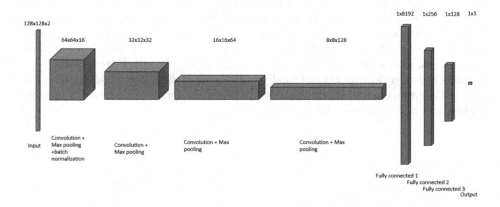

Fig. 2. TCRegNet feature maps

3.2   Classification Model (TCClassNet)

We have implemented a classification CNN model containing 11 individual layers, which can be grouped in 7 blocks, as shown in Table 2. We have divided output into steps of 5 knot from 15 to 185 giving 35 classes. We one-hot encoded the labels for the classification model. Figure 3 shows feature maps obtained at the output of each block. Input to model is $128 \times 128 \times 2$ image. Block 1 contains

Table 1. TCRegNet architecture

Layer	Type	Filter Size	Stride	Activation
In	Input			
C1	Convolution	4 × 4	1	ReLU
P1	Max pooling	-	2	-
BN1	Batch normalization	-	-	-
C2	Convolution	3 × 3	1	ReLU
P2	Max pooling	-	2	-
C3	Convolution	3 × 3	1	ReLU
P3	Max pooling	-	2	-
C4	Convolution	3 × 3	1	ReLU
P4	Max pooling	-	2	-
FC1	Fully connected	-	-	ReLU
FC2	Fully connected	-	-	ReLU
FC3	Fully conected	-	-	None

a convolution layer with ReLU activation function, followed by a max pooling layer and batch normalization layer. Block 2, 3 and 4 contains a convolution layer with ReLU activation function, followed by a max pooling layer. Blocks 5, 6, and 7 contain a fully connected layer. Layers 5 and 6 are activated with the ReLU activation function. Softmax activation is used on the last block. During training, we used Adam optimizer with a learning rate of 0.001. Categorical cross-entropy is used as loss function. Usually, classification models are evaluated based on prediction accuracy. As our problem is a regression one, we have computed RMSE to evaluate the model performance.

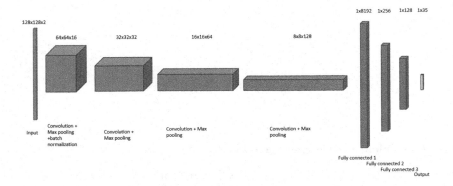

Fig. 3. TCClassNet feature maps

Table 2. TCClassNet architecture

Layer	Type	Filter Size	Stride	Activation
In	Input			
C1	Convolution	4×4	1	ReLU
P1	Max pooling	-	2	-
BN1	Batch normalization	-	-	-
C2	Convolution	3×3	1	ReLU
P2	Max pooling	-	2	-
C3	Convolution	3×3	1	ReLU
P3	Max pooling	-	2	-
C4	Convolution	3×3	1	ReLU
P4	Max pooling	-	2	-
FC1	Fully connected	-	-	ReLU
FC2	Fully connected	-	-	ReLU
FC3	Fully connected	-	-	Softmax

3.3   Multitask Model (TCMultiNet)

The idea behind multitask model is to train the model to perform multiple tasks simultaneously. In these models, some layers and parameters are shared between tasks. We have implemented two task model having a classification output and a regression output. Figure 4 shows implemented multitask model (TCMultiNet) with first four stages as shared convolution stage, followed by two separate fully connected branches (each branch has three fully connected layer), where upper branch is a regression branch, and lower branch is classification branch. During inference, outputs from both tasks are averaged together to give a single output model. Categorical cross-entropy is used as loss function in classification branch. Mean squared error (MSE) is used as loss function in the regression branch.

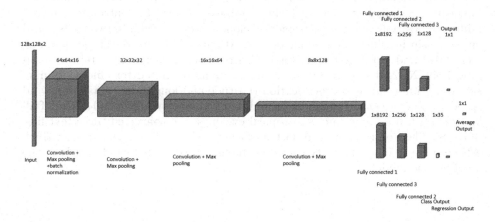

Fig. 4. TCMultiNet feature maps

4   Datasets

In this work, we have used dataset from four different sources, as listed below.

1. HURSAT dataset [6]
2. HURDAT2 dataset [7]
3. CMORPH Climate Data Record (CDR) [14]
4. Best track estimate data from Regional Specialized Meteorological Centre (RSMC), Delhi [10]

In this section, we will look at these datasets in detail.

4.1   HURSAT Dataset

Hurricane satellite (HURSAT) dataset [6] provides satellite images of tropical cyclones for the period of record from 1978 to 2016. The data is provided in netCDF format, and all the files for one cyclone are archived in zip format. These cyclones are organized as per their year of occurrence. The data is collected by geostationary satellites of Japan, Europe, and US, and is re-calibrated to minimize the differences due to the data acquisition instruments in the different satellites. Each file contains a 301 × 301 brightness temperature value (in kelvin) captured in infrared (IR) window channel and has a resolution of 0.07° × 0.07° (latitude×longitude). Figure 5 shows some of the sample images from the dataset. We used images of tropical cyclones that occurred during 2006–2016 from HURSAT dataset for this work, cyclone images from 2006 was used as the validation dataset, 2011 images as the test dataset, and the remaining as the training dataset.

4.2   HURDAT2 Dataset

Hurricane database (HURDAT2) dataset [7] provides best track estimates, analyzed by National Hurricane Center (NHC). These estimates are calculated by hurricane specialists at NHC. It includes intensity (in knot), central pressure (in millibar), position, and size of tropical cyclones. It is divided into two parts based on the basin in which the cyclone occurs: Atlantic hurricane database spanning 1851–2022 and Northeast and North Central Pacific hurricane database spanning 1949–2022. It is provided as a single comma-delimited text file containing six-hourly information on the location (latitude and longitude), maximum wind speed (in knot), central pressure (in millibar), and (starting in 2004) size of all known tropical cyclones and subtropical cyclones. We converted these text files into CSV files and then merged both files (for two basins) into a single best track estimate file. We use intensity (given as maximum sustained wind speed) as the label for the models.

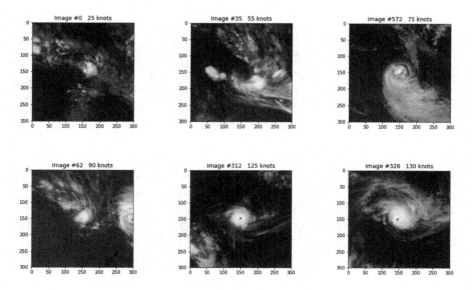

Fig. 5. IR satellite image samples from HURSAT dataset

4.3   CMORPH Climate Data Record (CDR)

CMORPH Climate Data Record (CDR) dateset [14] contains rain rate estimates, also known as precipitation estimates (rain rate in mm per unit time) provided by NOAA. Low-orbit satellites are used to capture microwave observations. These microwave observations are used to estimate the rain rate. Due to lower orbit, these data are available less frequently. Geostationary IR satellites can capture data more frequently compared to low-orbit satellites. Therefore, the CMORPH technique combines data from these two satellite sources [14]. Data is provided in 3 spatial-temporal resolutions. Full-resolution CMORPH data covers spatial resolution of $8km \times 8km$ with a temporal resolution of 30 min, giving rain rate in mm/hour. Hourly CMORPH covers spatial resolution of 0.25° lat/lon with a temporal resolution of 1 h, giving rain rate in mm/hour. Daily CMORPH covers spatial resolution of 0.25° lat/lon with a temporal resolution of 1 day, giving rain rate in mm/day. We have used hourly CMORPH data, cropped it to 128×128 image size, and upscaled it using linear interpolation to resolution of 0.07° lat/lon. Figure 6 shows some of the sample images from the dataset.

4.4   Best Track Estimate Data from RSMC, Delhi

Regional Specialized Meteorological Centre (RSMC), Delhi [10] publishes best track estimates for cyclones originating in the North Indian Ocean region. It contains intensity estimates, central pressure estimate (in hectopascal), pressure drop (in hectopascal), CI number (or T number), pressure drop, cyclone grade,

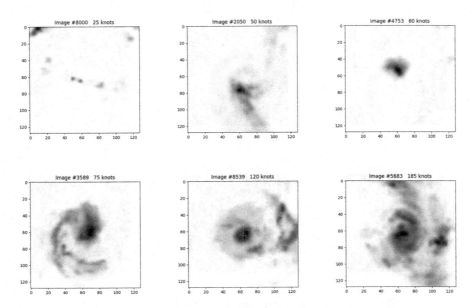

Fig. 6. Passive microwave derived rain rate samples from CMORPH Climate Data Record dataset

latitude, longitude, time and date of occurrence of cyclones over a period in 1982–2022, in Excel file format. We created a CSV file from the best track estimate file for our use.

5   Experiments and Results

We have performed two sets of experiments with three models. In one set of experiments, infrared brightness temperature satellite images were used as single channel input. In another set of experiments, the infrared brightness temperature satellite image and rain rate satellite image were stacked together as two-channel input. We have used satellite images from year 2006–2016 (11000 images), with the year 2011 images as the validation set (1000 images), and the year 2006 images as the test set (1000 images). As the number of images is less, we use data augmentation techniques to increase the number of images during training. Augmentation techniques used are image zooming (maximum scaling of 120%), horizontal and vertical shifting, image rotation (maximum rotation of 360°), vertical and horizontal flipping, and feature-wise normalization. We have used Keras deep learning library for implementation.

5.1 Single Channel Input Models

We have trained all models with a learning rate of 0.01 using Adam optimizer. We trained TCRegNet and TCClassNet models for 200 epoch, and TCMultiNet model for 300 epoch. Figure 7 shows RMSE curve of TCRegNet model. Figure 8 shows RMSE curve of TCClassNet model. Figure 9 and fig. 10 shows RMSE curve for regression and classification branches, respectively of TCMultiNet model. Table 3 shows results obtained for different models on test dataset. Comparing the result of three models, TCClassNet model performs worse than other two models.

Table 3. Result of models on single channel input

Model	RMSE (in knot)
TCRegNet model	11.0150
TCClassNet model	12.4552
TCMultiNet model	11.0322

5.2 Two Channel Input Models

As seen in the case of single channel experiments, TCClassNet model perform worse than other two models. Hence, we did not consider this model for further experiments and proceeded with TCRegNet and TCMultiNet models. We have trained both models with a learning rate of 0.0001 using Adam optimizer for 300 epoch. Then, we trained both the models for further 600 epoch with a learning rate of 0.00001. Figure 11 shows RMSE curve of TCRegNet model. Figure 12 and fig. 13 show RMSE curve of regression and classification branch, respectively of TCMultiNet model. Comparing results of single channel input and two channel input, we observe that two channel input performs better, showing that model is able to learn comparatively more features in two channel case. Figure 14 shows residual plot of TCMultiNet model. We observe that images that are underestimated have smaller error compared to images that are overestimated. In other words, model predicts with larger value of error when it overestimates.

Table 4. Result of models on two channel input

Model	RMSE (in knot)
TCRegNet model	10.8431
TCMultiNet model	10.8664

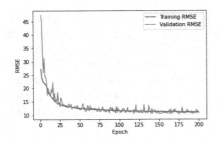

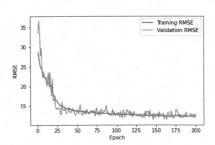

Fig. 7. RMSE of single channel TCReg-Net model

Fig. 8. RMSE of single channel TCClass-Net model

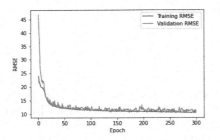

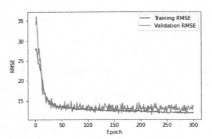

Fig. 9. RMSE of regression branch of single channel TCMultiNet model

Fig. 10. RMSE of classification branch of single channel TCMultiNet model

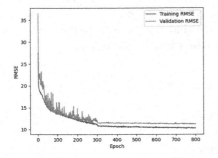

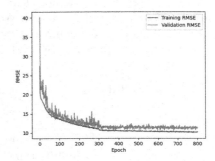

Fig. 11. RMSE of two-channel TCReg-Net model

Fig. 12. RMSE of regression branch of two-channel TCMultiNet model

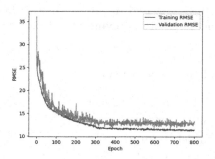

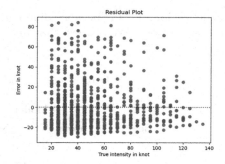

Fig. 13. RMSE of classification branch of two-channel TCMultiNet model

Fig. 14. Residual plot of two-channel TCMultiNet model

5.3   Improvement in TCMultiNet Model

As observerd earlier, TCClassNet performs worse than the other two models. Prediction strategy for TCClassNet is to predict the class with highest possibility. This prediction approach is used in classification branch of TCMultiNet. It was expected that changing the prediction strategy for classification branch may help in improving the model performance. We modified the prediction strategy of classification branch of TCMultiNet to include the weighted average of top six classes with weights being 0.3, 0.2, 0.2, 0.1, 0.1 and 0.1. RMSE of 10.3847 was reported on test dataset. As seen in Table 5, our model (TCMultiNet) performance is very close to state-of-art single stage deep learning based estimation methods.

Table 5. Performance comparison with state-of-art intensity estimation models

Model	RMSE (in knot)
TCMultiNet	**10.3**
DeepMicroNet [13]	10.6
CNN-TC [1]	10.6
Pradhan et al. [9]	10.2

5.4   Result for Cyclones Around Indian Subcontinent

We have divided cyclone images into two time periods, 2005–2010 (600 images) and 2011–2016 (800 images). We used images for 2011–2016 to test our model, and results without fine-tuning are shown in table 6. We fine-tuned the model by using images from the year 2005–2010 at a learning rate of 0.000001 for 150 epochs, and tested our model on images from 2011–2016. The final results after fine-tuning are shown in table 6. Without fine-tuning, the result of cyclones around the Indian subcontinent is relatively poor compared to the Atlantic and

Pacific region. This is because different satellites are used to capture images in different regions. We observe that fine-tuning helps in improving model performance.

Table 6. Result of model on Indian cyclone data

	Model	RMSE (in knot)
Before fine tuning	TCRegNet model	19.7080
	TCMultiNet model	18.8020
After fine tuning	TCRegNet model	14.4513
	TCMultiNet model	14.0190

6   Conclusion

In this work, we have used three CNN models to estimate cyclone intensity using satellite images: TCRegNet model, TCClassNet model, and TCMultiNet model. We used 9000 IR brightness temperature images of cyclones occurring in the Atlantic and Pacific region to train the model. We observed that the TCClass-Net model performs worse than the other two models. We modified the input to a two-channel image containing an IR image and a rain rate image. We observe that two-channel input performs better showing that the model can learn comparatively more features in two-channel cases. We improved TCMultiNet model performance by changing the prediction strategy. On comparison, we noted that TCMultiNet performs as good as any state-of-art single stage estimation model. Further, We conclude that images that are underestimated have smaller errors compared to images that are overestimated. For cyclones around the Indian subcontinent, results have improved after fine-tuning the model.

References

1. Chen, B., Chen, B.F., Lin, H.T.: Rotation-blended CNNs on a new open dataset for tropical cyclone image-to-intensity regression. In: Proceedings of the 24th ACM SIGKDD International Conference on Knowledge Discovery and Data Mining, pp. 90-99 (2018). https://doi.org/10.1145/3219819.3219926
2. Chen, R., Zhang, W., Wang, X.: Machine learning in tropical cyclone forecast modeling: a review. Atmosphere **11**(7) (2020)
3. Dvorak, V.F.: Tropical cyclone intensity analysis and forecasting from satellite imagery. Mon. Weather Rev. **103**(5), 420–430 (1975)
4. Dvorak, V.F.: Tropical cyclone intensity analysis using satellite data. NOAA Technical Report (1984)
5. Goyal, S., Mohapatra, M., Kumari, P., Dube, S.K., Rajendra, K.: Validation of advanced Dvorak technique (ADT) over north Indian ocean. MAUSAM **68**(4), 689-698 (2017). https://doi.org/10.54302/mausam.v68i4.768, https://mausamjournal.imd.gov.in/index.php/MAUSAM/article/view/768 https://doi.org/10.54302/mausam.v68i4.768https://mausamjournal.imd.gov.in/index.php/MAUSAM/article/view/768

6. Knapp, K.R., Kossin, J.P.: New global tropical cyclone data set from ISCCP B1 geostationary satellite observations. J. Appl. Remote Sens. **1**(1), 013505 (2007). https://doi.org/10.1117/1.2712816
7. Landsea, C.W., Franklin, J.L.: Atlantic hurricane database uncertainty and presentation of a new database format. Mon. Weather Rev. **141**(10), 3576–3592 (2013). https://doi.org/10.1175/MWR-D-12-00254.1
8. Olander, T.L., Velden, C.S.: The advanced Dvorak technique: continued development of an objective scheme to estimate tropical cyclone intensity using geostationary infrared satellite imagery. Weather Forecast. **22**(2), 287–298 (2007). https://doi.org/10.1175/WAF975.1
9. Pradhan, R., Aygun, R.S., Maskey, M., Ramachandran, R., Cecil, D.J.: Tropical cyclone intensity estimation using a deep convolutional neural network. IEEE Trans. Image Process. **27**(2), 692–702 (2018). https://doi.org/10.1109/TIP.2017.2766358
10. Regional Specialised Meteorological Centre (RSMC) Tropical Cyclones, N.D.: Best track data of tropical cyclonic disturbances over the north Indian ocean. https://rsmcnewdelhi.imd.gov.in
11. Reichstein, M., et al.: Deep learning and process understanding for data-driven earth system science. Nature **566**(7743), 195–204 (2019)
12. Schultz, M.G., et al.: Can deep learning beat numerical weather prediction? Philos. Trans. Royal Soc. A Math. Phys. Eng. Sci. **379**(2194), 20200097 (2021). https://doi.org/10.1098/rsta.2020.0097
13. Wimmers, A., Velden, C., Cossuth, J.H.: Using deep learning to estimate tropical cyclone intensity from satellite passive microwave imagery. Mon. Weather Rev. **147**(6), 2261–2282 (2019). https://doi.org/10.1175/MWR-D-18-0391.1
14. Xie, P., et al.: NOAA climate data record (CDR) of CPC morphing technique (CMORPH) high resolution global precipitation estimates (2019). https://www.ncei.noaa.gov/data/cmorph-high-resolution-global-precipitation-estimates/access/
15. Zhang, C.J., Wang, X.J., Ma, L.M., Lu, X.Q.: Tropical cyclone intensity classification and estimation using infrared satellite images with deep learning. IEEE J. Select. Top. Appl. Earth Observ. Remote Sens. **14**, 2070–2086 (2021). https://doi.org/10.1109/JSTARS.2021.3050767

MuSTAT: Face Ageing Using Multi-scale Target Age Style Transfer

Praveen Kumar Chandaliya[1]([✉]), Kiran Raja[1], Gharat Snehal Rajendra[2], Neeta Nain[2], Raghavendra Ramachandra[1], and Christoph Busch[1]

[1] Norwegian University of Science and Technology (NTNU), Gjøvik, Norway
{praveen.k.chandaliya,kiran.raja,raghavendra.ramachandra,
christoph.busch}@ntnu.no
[2] Malaviya National Institute of Technology Jaipur, Jaipur, Rajasthan, India
{2019pcp5150,nnain.cse}@mnit.ac.in

Abstract. Most existing bottleneck-based Generative Adversarial Networks suffer from ghosting artifacts or blur for generating ageing results with an increased age gap. Although this can be solved using data collected over long age spans, it is challenging and tedious. This work proposes a multi-scale target age-based style face ageing model using an encoder-decoder architecture to generate high-fidelity face images under ageing. Further, we propose using skip connections with selective transfer units (STU) in the encoder-decoder architecture to adaptively select and modify the encoder feature to enhance face ageing results. Unlike conditional GAN (cGAN) approaches that rely on age as a condition to train the generator, we used style information gathered from a random image of the target age group to train the generator. The qualitative and quantitative results on public datasets show that our model can generate photo-realistic synthetic face images of the target age group. The proposed model can also generate diverse age groups for age progression and regression tasks. Furthermore, the analysis using six different Face Recognition Systems (FRS) also indicates the ability of the proposed approach to preserve the identity resulting in 89.82% False Non Match Rate (FNMR) at False Match Rate (FMR) of 0.0001%.

Keywords: Face ageing · Face recognition · Style transfer · Age estimation

1 Introduction

Face age progression finds its application in wide domains, such as finding missing children, digital entertainment, post-cosmetic surgery, and cross-age face recognition, to name a few. Conventional approaches for face ageing are technically classified into two categories such as prototype model and physical model. The former approach aims to simulate ageing on a given image using images for different ages and the mean face across ages [15,25] to derive a prototype and extract a texture difference between the prototypes. The latter synthesizes

H. Kaur et al. (Eds.): CVIP 2023, CCIS 2010, pp. 186–199, 2024.
https://doi.org/10.1007/978-3-031-58174-8_17

realistic age-progressed images by considering the anatomy, facial muscles, and wrinkles of skin [31].

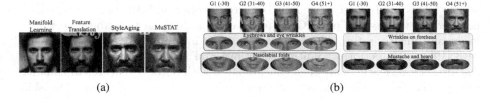

(a)   (b)

Fig. 1. Fig (a) Illustration of ageing uniformity by GAN-driven ageing approaches as compared to MuSTAT and Fig (b) Illustration of ageing pattern effect by MuSTAT.

However, these approaches generally require longitudinal face sequences of the same subject with a broad range of ages and this type of data collection is arduous and expensive to collect in practice. To handle this issue, several deep learning-based GAN-driven face ageing approaches have been developed [32, 33, 36]. These approaches usually employ (i) manifold learning, and (ii) feature translation with source image and target attribute vector as input.

Despite their extensive deployment, manifold networks [3, 36] remain insufficient for preserving identity. To optimize face ageing while preserving identity, researchers have used feature-translation-based methods [32, 33]. However, the feature translation networks fail in generating face-age progression with high fidelity due to altered on ageing related pattern. Therefore, many researchers have suggested adding skip connections between the encoder and decoder layers of the base generator in GAN as a remedy [19]. Despite improving the quality of facial age progression, skip connections harm the attribute manipulation abilities of the feature translation models. Another possible solution is to employ an attention block to allow for attribute-specific region modification. However, such an approach is effective only for local face regions and is not designed for global attribute manipulation [23, 35] (e.g., beard, wrinkle on adult and old-age groups). In particular, the encoders in earlier works [3, 36] utilized only the source image as input to produce a latent vector and concatenate the age attribute with this vector. The decoder utilizes both latent and age vectors to generate age-progressive faces. In contrast, feature translation requires input from the source image and target age vector. Selecting the target age group to be modified while editing an individual's face age is important. Taking the entire target attribute into account may have a detrimental effect on the results.

More recent GAN-enabled frameworks fail to synthesize faces of extreme age ranges [32, 33]. Additionally, facial synthesis based on a single label (one hot vector) ignores the intra-class diversity of each age class and collapses it into a single ageing pattern. Consequently, conditioning face ageing synthesis on a single label ignores the intra-class diversity of each age class and results in images with a non-diverse ageing pattern. Therefore, GAN-based methods produce a single ageing per face biased by training data. Due to these deficiencies, such methods are ineffective for enhancing diversity in data since they tend to result in algorithmic bias when trained on biased synthetic datasets [8].

To address these issues, this study proposes the use of Selective Transfer Units (STUs) and skip connections between encoder and decoder layers, which inspired by the success of STGAN and taking a difference attribute vector as input and incorporating selective transfer units into an encoder-decoder structure [19]. STUs perform adaptive selections and modifications of the encoder features. These features are then concatenated with decoder features to enhance the quality and capture local and global ageing-related attributes. The skip connections between the encoder and decoder layers typically result in training stability. In recent studies, multi-level facial features extracted from images were found to contain more texture and style features if multiple scales of discriminators were employed and can force the generator to synthesize by adversarial loss to produce vivid ageing effects [14,33]. As shown in Fig. 1(a) a manifold learning-based model, feature translation, and StyleAging do not preserve identity in the presence of hair, mustache, or beard effects in the 50+ age group. Our MuSTAT model captures a more ageing pattern while preserving identity.

The contributions of this work are as follows:

 (i) A proposed Multi-Scale Target Age Style Transfer (MuSTAT) approach that is novel to transfer face age model and can generate more realistic results than prior models.
(ii) A selective transfer unit is incorporated at the initial layers of the encoder-decoder to capture local and global face ageing patterns simultaneously. Furthermore, the proposed approach uses skip connection to provide training stability as an inherent advantage. MuSTAT can generate faces with large intra-class diversity while preserving the identity by focusing on the target image instead of a target class.
(iii) Our model can retain identity information while preserving gender, hairstyle and background. The experiments on FRS indicate 89.82% False Non Match Rate (FNMR) at False Match Rate (FMR) of 0.0001% using Elastic-Cos+ [2] while we obtain a $FNMR = 100\%$ at $FMR = 0.01\%$ using Probabilistic Face Embedding (PFE) [30].
(iv) The experiment results indicate that the proposed approach can capture face ageing. While existing models can create ageing images up to 50 years, our model is able to capture ageing beyond 60 years.

2   Related Works

2.1   Encoder-Decoder Architecture

Hinton et al. [11] proposed an autoencoder network consisting of an encoder and decoder to map the input into a latent vector and a decoder to recover from the latent vector. Subsequently, denoising autoencoders were proposed to learn representations robust to partial corruption. Kingma et al. [16] suggested a Variational autoencoder (VAE) which validates the feasibility of encoder architecture to generate unseen images. Recent studies [26] between encoder and decoder layers usually provide training stability and visual quality. StarGAN [6] adopted an encoder-decoder structure, where spatial pooling or downsampling are essential to obtain a high-level abstract representation for attribute manipulation. Unfortunately, downsampling irreversibly diminishes spatial resolution and fine details of feature maps due to transposed convolution which results in blurry or missing information. STGAN [19] developed selective transfer units (STU) to adaptively transform encoder features guided by attributes to be changed and enhance the image quality of editing.

2.2 Generative Adversarial Networks

Goodfellow et al. [9] proposed Generative Adversarial Networks (GANs) for various applications, including image generation, image super-resolution, text-to-image synthesis, and image-to-image translation, following the min-max rule to train the network. Several works were presented to improve GAN image quality and stability. First, Radford et al. [24] introduced the deep convolutional generative adversarial network architecture (DCGAN). To overcome the vanishing gradient, mode collapse and improve network stability, methods like LSGAN [28] and WGAN [1] are proposed. The conditional generative adversarial network (cGAN) [21] is a variant of GAN, which uses a class label as a condition to synthesize a target image. Face ageing can be considered a sub-problem of image-to-image translation, which involves converting an input image from one domain to another while preserving its original identity. Isola et al. [13] introduced pix2pix, which requires paired datasets to learn picture-to-picture translations. On the one hand, it is impractical to collect paired images with and without desirable attributes (e.g., female and male face images of the same person in different age). CycleGANs [37] have recently been successfully used for image-to-image translation tasks, overcoming the need for a paired dataset and achieving reliable results. In the most recent trend of style transfer work, style content is modulated explicitly at different layers with Adaptive Instance Normalization [7].

2.3 Style Transfer

Style transfer is a computer vision approach that allows us to impose the style of one image on the other image content. It takes two images as input content and style images and merges them so that the resulting output image keeps the essential components of the content image. However, the results tend to appear as "painted" in the style of the reference image. Gatys et al. [7] introduced the first neural style transfer algorithm by integrating feature statistics in convolutional layers of a DNN which resulted in impressive style transfer. However, given a slow optimization process, subsequent works were proposed to improve style transfer speed and quality. Li et al. [18] demonstrated that several other statistics are similarly beneficial for style transfers, including the channel-wise mean and variance. Huang et al. [12] proposed a method to resolve the slow optimization process and presented an adaptive instance normalization concept that aligns the mean and variance of content and style attributes.

2.4   Face Ageing

Traditional methods such as physical model-based and prototype-based models are computationally expensive and require large paired datasets at varying ages [10]. Recently, deep learning-based approaches using GANs and its variant Conditional GANs (cGANs) [21] have made a breakthrough in generating high-quality images and image translation. Several studies for facial ageing based on GANs [33] and cGANs [4,32,36] have been proposed, using unpaired datasets and generating good results. These methods learn the ageing patterns between two groups and map functions to translate faces, given target age as a condition. However, the generated results often show ghosting artifacts due to the increasing age gap (See Fig. 1(a). Due to the intrinsic complexities (like gender, race, and expressions) of face ageing, these approaches do not guarantee smooth ageing results. Further, they do not preserve age-invariant attributes and suffer from identity loss. To preserve identity, recent works have introduced identity consistency [32,33,36].

3   Proposed Network Architecture

To tackle the limitations listed in related works, we used a style-based face ageing model, where instead of passing just age as a condition, a style image of the target age is used along with the source image. We further introduce a selective transfer unit block to transfer selective attributes from encoder to decoder. Instead of passing just age as a condition, we pass a style image of the target age along with the source image. In addition to protecting identity information, we focus on improving the diversity of intra-class ageing patterns based on distinct intrinsic and extrinsic factors using a multi-scale age discriminator.

Our proposed MuSTAT model comprises two components, i.e., a style generator (G) and multi-scale age discriminator (D). Figure 2 illustrates the network architecture of G consisting of encoder G_{enc} for latent abstract representation and a decoder G_{enc} for target image generation with ageing effect. (D) is incorporated to synthesize an image of desired target age, given a source image of a particular age and a style image of desired target age. The source face image $x_s \in \mathbb{R}^{h \times w \times 3}$, of age s along with a style image $\hat{x}_t \in \mathbb{R}^{h \times w \times 3}$ of desired target age t; is passed through the generator and discriminator (where h and w are the height and width of image), to obtain a target image $\tilde{x}_t$ with ageing effects of target class.

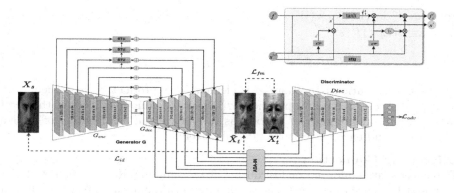

Fig. 2. The architecture of proposed MuSTAT model. The block on the top right corner shows the STU used in the proposed architecture.

3.1   Style Generator

The generator, as shown in Fig. 2 follows an auto-encoder architecture, with an encoder G_{enc} and decoder G_{dec}. The encoder G_{enc} takes input a source image x_s and generates a feature map z; $z = G_{enc}(x_s)$. The encoder having E^l as intermediate layer, can be formulated as $G_{enc} = E^N \circ E^{N-1} \circ \cdots \circ E^1$, where the symbol $\circ$ denotes function composition. The output for layers $l \in \{1, N\}$ is $f^l = E^l(f^{l-1})$; *where* $f^0 = x_s$ and so, $z = f^N$. Similarly, the decoder having D^l as intermediate layer, can be formulated as $G_{dec} = D^N \circ D^{N-1} \circ \cdots \circ D^1$ and, the multi-scale age discriminator (D_{msa}) having C^l as intermediate layer, can be formulated as $D_{msa} = C^{N+1} \circ C^N \circ C^{N-1} \circ \cdots \circ C^1$. The discriminator output for layers $l \in \{1, N\}$ is $g^l = C^l(g^{l-1})$; *where* $g^0 = \hat{x}_t$ The target age style is extracted from $\hat{x}_t$ by all layers of multi-scale age discriminator (D_{msa}). The age style is then injected into the decoder of the style generator (G) using adaptive instance normalization (AdaIN) [12].

Selective Transfer Unit (STU). We introduced the Selective Transfer Unit (STU) block in the skip connections to capture local and global face ageing patterns simultaneously. At the first three layers of this skip connection, we added the STU blocks [19], which selectively transform the encoder feature and pass it to the decoder. Thus, for layer $l \in \{1, 3\}$ -

$$h^l = AdaIN(D^l(h^{l-1} + STU(f^{N-l+1}, s^{N-l+2})), g^{N-l+1});$$
$$where \ h^0 = z \ and \ s^4 = f^4 \tag{1}$$

And for any layer $l \in \{1, N\}$,

$$h^l = AdaIN(D^l(h^{l-1} + f^{N-l+1}), g^{N-l+1}) \tag{2}$$

Figure 2 shows the architecture of the GRU-based STU unit. For l^{th} layer, where f^l is the feature output from l^{th} layer of encoder and s^{l+1} is the hidden state from $l + 1^{th}$ layer. $r^l = \sigma(W_r * [f^l, s^{l+1}])$, $z^l = \sigma(W_z * [f^l, s^{l+1}])$, $s^l = r^l \otimes s^{l+1}$, $\hat{f}_t^l = \tanh(W_h * [f^l, s^l])$

$$STU(f^l, s^{l+1}) = (1 - z^l) \otimes s^{l+1} \oplus z^l \otimes \hat{f}_t^l \qquad (3)$$

here, $*$ is convolution operation; $\otimes$ is element wise product; $\oplus$ is element wise sum; $[.,.]$ is concatenation operation; $\sigma(.)$ sigmoid function. Adding the reset gate (r^l) and update gate (z^l) allows us to manage the contribution of hidden state (s^{l+1}) and encoder features (f^l) selectively.

U-Net Skip Connection
To recover spatial information lost during down-sampling, Ronneberger et al. [26] proposed U-Net skip connections in the encoder-decoder architecture. Output from each layer of encoder is element-wise added to each corresponding layer of decoder. The decoder takes the feature map z as input along the skip connections and adds up style information passed from discriminator using the Adaptive Instance Normalization (AdaIN) [12] layer to give a synthesized image $\tilde{x}_t$ as output. So the output of decoder for any layer $l \in \{1, N\}$: $h^l = AdaIN(D^l(h^{l-1} + f^{N-l+1}), g^{N-l+1})$

3.2   Multi-scale Age Discriminator

A discriminator detects whether an image belongs to a real or fake image. As the images are classified into four age groups, we used a few-shot unsupervised multi-task discriminator [20]. To detect whether an image is a real one belonging to class s_i or a generated one. The discriminator output is $y = C^{N+1}(g^N)$, where y yields the score for the s_i class to which it corresponds or is the target class. The resulting network captures features representing both the "realness" of the faces and their age. (D_{msa}) is mirrored G_{dec} of G to maintain correspondence between features at different scales.

4   Loss Function

The aim is to optimize the MuSTAT to achieve four main goals of ageing: (i) Better quality of the synthesized image, (ii) Diversity in the ageing pattern, (iii) Enforcing cycle consistency, and (iv) Preserving the identity of the original image. Therefore, we used four respective types of loss functions for training:

Adversarial Loss: To achieve a better quality of synthesized image, we train the network with the min-max loss. The generator tries to minimize the loss given in Eq. (4) while the discriminator tries to maximize it. Given an input face image x_s of source age s and a style image $\hat{x}_t$ of target age t, to generate $\tilde{x}_t$ the synthesized image from $\tilde{x}_t = G(x_s, \hat{x}_t)$, the adversarial loss is calculated as:

$$\mathcal{L}_{adv} = \mathbb{E}_{x_s}[\log(D_{msa}(x_s))] + \mathbb{E}_{x_s, \hat{x}_t}[\log(1 - D_{msa}(\tilde{x}_t))] \qquad (4)$$

Feature Matching Loss: The model would not converge and cause a mode collapse problem due to the greedy nature of optimization in the min-max game between generator and discriminator. During the training of the multiscale age model, it is important to identify the features that discriminate between real data and synthesized data in MuSTAT model. We therefore use feature loss [28] that modifies the generator's cost function to minimize the statistical difference between real and synthesized image features. As a result, feature matching broadens the aim beyond defeating the opponent to matching features in real-world images. We train the generator to match the expected value of the features on an intermediate layer of the discriminator. The loss is calculated between input style image $\hat{x}_t$ and the synthesized image $\tilde{x}_t$. The feature loss is -

$$\mathcal{L}_{fm} = \mathbb{E}_{\tilde{x}_t} \|g(\hat{x}_t) - g(\tilde{x}_t)\|_2^2 \tag{5}$$

$g(x)$ is the feature vector extracted from an intermediate layer of the multi-scale age discriminator D_{msa}.

Cycle Consistency Loss: Cycle GAN [37] uses the forward cycle consistency loss to learn mapping and $M : x_s \rightarrow \tilde{x}_t$ and $N : \tilde{x}_t \rightarrow x_s$. We want to enforce the intuition that these mappings should be preserved between x_s and x_t. This loss ensures that $N(M(x_s)) \approx x_s$ and $M(N(\tilde{x}_t)) \approx \tilde{x}_t$.

$$\mathcal{L}_{cc} = \mathbb{E}_{x_s, \tilde{x}_t} \|x_s - G(x_s, \tilde{x}_t)\|_1 \tag{6}$$

Identity Loss: The adversarial loss makes the generator generate faces from the target distribution. The resulting face can resemble any person in the target age group. The identity of the synthesized image therefore must be preserved for face recognition applications. Along with the adversarial loss we added the identity loss, calculated between the original face image and the synthesized image.

$$\mathcal{L}_{id} = \mathbb{E}_{x_s, \tilde{x}_t}[\|x_s - \tilde{x}_t\|_1] \tag{7}$$

Regularization: The R1 regularization technique is used to stabilize the discriminator. The discriminator is penalized for diverging from the Nash Equilibrium solely based on real data. The gradient penalty assures that the discriminator cannot construct a non-zero gradient orthogonal to the data manifold without losing the GAN min-max game when the generator distribution yields the genuine data distribution and the discriminator is equal to 0 on the data manifold. They apply the following regularization term on the synthesized image $\tilde{x}_t$ and add to the discriminator loss.

$$\mathcal{L}_{gp} = \lambda_{gp} \mathbb{E}_x \|\nabla D_{msa}(\tilde{x}_t)\|_1 \tag{8}$$

Objective Function: To train the generator G they use the feature matching loss (5), cycle consistency loss (6) and the identity loss (7). The generator loss $\mathcal{L}_G$ is:

$$\mathcal{L}_G = \mathcal{L}_{fm} + \lambda_{cc}\mathcal{L}_{cc} + \lambda_{id}\mathcal{L}_{id} \tag{9}$$

And, train the discriminator with adversarial loss (4), and add a regularization term (8) to stabilize the discriminator using $\mathcal{L}_{D_{msa}}$ loss. Where, $\lambda_{cc} = 0.01$, $\lambda_{id} = 10^{-4}$, $\lambda_{gp} = 10.0$.

$$\mathcal{L}_{D_{msa}} = \mathcal{L}_{adv} + \mathcal{L}_{gp} \tag{10}$$

Fig. 3. Ageing results generated by IPCGAN, CPAVAE, Georgopoulos et al. [8] and our MuSTAT on two images from CACD dataset (Zoom for better view).

5   Experiments and Results

5.1   Dataset

Cross-Age Celebrity Dataset: CACD [5] dataset is the largest publicly available cross-age face dataset, consisting of over $160,000$ images of $2,000$ celebrities aged 16 to 62 [5]. We used 90% of the dataset for training and 10% for testing purposes. The dataset has significant variations in pose, illumination, and even style. For data pre-processing, we used MTCNN [34] to detect the five landmarks points (two eyes, nose, and two mouth corners) used for proper alignment and to crop the images to a resolution of 128×128 pixels before passing images into MuSTAT model. For our experiments, the dataset was divided into four age groups such as $G1(0-30)$, $G2(31-40)$, $G3(41-50)$, and $G4(50+)$, respectively. **FGNET:** To inspect the robustness of our proposed MuSTAT approach, we also adopt FGNET [17] for the testing phase only. FG-NET contains $1,002$ face images from 82 subjects, with age ranging from 0 to 69 and an age gap up to 45 years.

5.2   Implementation Details

To evaluate the proposed model, we compare MuSTAT with IPCGAN [32], CPAVAE [22], CAAE [36] and Georgopoulos et al. [8] on two datasets explained before. Our proposed model is trained using Adam optimizer ($\beta_1 = 0.5, \beta_2 = 0.0.999$) with a learning rate 0.0001 and hyperparameters with $\lambda_{cc} = 0.01$, $\lambda_{id} = 10^{-4}$, $\lambda_{gp} = 10.0$.

6 Qualitative Evaluation

6.1 Experiment I: CACD Dataset

Figure 3 presents sample results on face ageing using three state-of-the-art models for a male and a female subject. It can be noted from the figures that the manifold learning-based CPAVAE model beautifies images and does not preserve skin color. It removes wrinkles when synthesizing old faces from young face source input due to pre-trained VGG19 perceptual loss. CPAVAE generates relatively smooth images with less age progression effects. IPCGAN based on feature translation approach alters the face region alone to preserve the identity but cannot generate better-ageing effects such as wrinkles, hair and variation in skin texture. While Georgopoulos et al. [8] can generate both young and old-aged faces with ageing effects, artifacts appear near the eyes and produce unrealistic the moustache and beard concerning age group (Ref Fig. 3). However, the proposed MuSTAT model can produce results of higher visual fidelity, especially if the last age group ($G4$) is considered. A similar trend can also be noticed for a female subject as shown in Fig. 3. Compared to the Georgopoulos et al. [8] model, our proposed approach results in high-fidelity images by preserving the identity occluded forehead. While IPCGAN and CPAVAE produce unrealistic colors hair colors, our approach can preserve realistic hair color. Further, looking at the results for $G1$ category, one can note that our proposed approach can preserve gender identity compared to Georgopoulos et al. [8]. We take a detailed look at the results as shown in Fig. 1(a), where one can note the superiority of the proposed approach. Specifically, the proposed approach can handle nasolabial folds, facial skin changes, adjusted moustache and beard, and detailed wrinkles.

7 Quantitative Evaluation

Our experiments are benchmarked against three state-of-the-art face-ageing models [8, 22, 32] using the publicly available DEX [27] age estimator model. We further employ 6 different FRS models for establishing the results of Identity Preservation.

7.1 Ageing Variation

To measure the ageing variation of proposed approach, we first generate images corresponding to different age categories for each image. We measure the Mean-Absolute difference across different age groups to measure the variation from generated images computed from DEX age estimator model. Figure 4a and Fig. 4b show the estimated ages calculated using the age estimator on the generated images for each age group. It shows that IPCGAN and CPAVAE's estimated ages on the generated images have overlapping distribution for all age groups and can mainly generate images between 20–40 age intervals. The proposed method can diversify its range and generate images in different age groups. Figure 4a shows that CPAVAE fails to produce aged and beyond 40 year age group when used for age-progression while the proposed MuSTAT is able to generate image in larger age groups (G3 and G4). Further, considering a age-regression scenario, one can also note that the proposed approach is able to generate younger age images from an older age group as shown in Fig. 4b. The results indicate the ability of MuSTAT model to capture the central distribution density in terms of age categories.

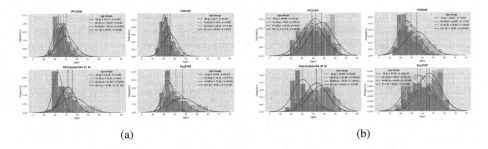

(a)   (b)

Fig. 4. Distribution of estimated ages on generated images for (a) age progression (b) age regression with i) IPCGAN ii) CPAVAE iii) Georgopoulos et al. [8] and iv) MuSTAT.

7.2   Identity Preservation Using Face Recognition

To evaluate the identity preservation of the proposed approach and compare it against state-of-the-art models, we employ six different FRS namely, FaceNet [29], PFE [30], and four variant of ElasticFace [2]. We specifically evaluate the FRS performance on CACD test datasets by creating impostor and genuine image pairs. Genuine pairs are formed using generated images of the largest age category (G4) against lowest age category (G1) for age progression and vice versa for regression. We present the results of FRS evaluation using FNMR at various FNMR as provided in Table 1. Our proposed MuSTAT model competes with IPCGAN and Georgopoulos et el. [8] when evaluated using different FRS on CACD. MuSTAT and Georgopoulos et el. achieve 100% verification rates at 0.1% FNMR using PFE and ElasticFace, respectively. The legacy models like CAAE and CPAVAE across all FRS have very low accuracy as they modify local and global face attributes. It is also evident that MuSTAT achieves far better accuracy than IPCGAN, CAAE and CPAVAE while competing equally with Georgopoulos et al. It can be seen from the results that the face verification accuracy is better when recent models like Elastic-Arc, Elastic-Cos, Elastic-Arc+, and Elastic-Cos+ are used as compared to relatively older FaceNet and PFE.

Table 1. Face verification (%) of different face aging models using FRS on CACD.

Ageing	FaceNet			PFE			Elastic-Arc			Elastic-Cos			Elastic-Arc+			Elastic-Cos+		
	FNMR@FMR			FNMR@FMR			FNMR@FMR			FNMR@FMR			FNMR@FMR			FNMR@FMR		
	1e−2	1e−3	1e−4	1e−2	1e−3	1e−4	1e−2	1e−3	1e−4	1e−2	1e−3	1e−4	1e−2	1e−3	1e−4	1e−2	1e−3	1e−4
IPCGAN	99.89	99.26	78.87	99.93	99.26	99.67	77.96	98.80	99.93	99.91	99.67	90.65	99.93	98.80	75.85	9.95	99.65	90.04
CPAVE	34.27	13.03	2.84	30.12	12.23	2.88	29.33	10.30	3.51	33.64	13.18	3.66	30.60	11.47	3.62	34.81	13.70	4.68
CAAE	52.66	29.28	10.95	53.08	30.91	17.28	49.28	25.92	13.16	55.57	32.77	16.48	51.06	26.96	12.29	56.05	32.47	14.81
Georgopoulos	99.84	98.35	81.93	99.97	98.85	99.97	**100.0**	98.59	89.80	**100.0**	99.21	94.33	**100.0**	98.52	88.24	**100.0**	99.32	94.14
MuSTAT	99.80	97.20	88.55	**100.0**	96.68	85.40	99.97	94.96	86.50	99.97	94.96	86.50	99.97	96.65	89.26	99.97	97.09	89.82

8   Conclusion and Future Work

In this paper, we have proposed a multi-scale age-style transfer for face ageing. Our MuSTAT approach leverages selective transfer in a GAN framework. The proposed model can achieve progressive and regressive ageing effects with a high-fidelity visual appearance. Further, the model can transfer selective effects related to ageing to the real image using the style images. Experimental results on public datasets demonstrate that MuSTAT can produce ageing details in a superior manner compared to existing state-of-the-art works. We verify the diversity of face age generated using the proposed approach by employing DEX age estimator. In addition, we also evaluate the general application for face recognition using six different FRS to establish the identity preservation ability of the proposed approach. Future works in this direction should consider extending this idea to 3D facial age modeling and simulation for cross-age face recognition.

Acknowledgement. This work was supported by the European Union's Horizon 2020 Research and Innovation Program under Grant 883356.

References

1. Arjovsky, M., Chintala, S., Bottou, L.: Wasserstein GAN (2017)
2. Boutros, F., Damer, N., Kirchbuchner, F., Kuijper, A.: ElasticFace: elastic margin loss for deep face recognition. In: Proceedings of the IEEE/CVF Conference on Computer Vision and Pattern Recognition (CVPR) Workshops, pp. 1578–1587 (2022)
3. Chandaliya, P.K., Nain, N.: ChildGAN: face aging and rejuvenation to find missing children. Pattern Recogn. **129**, 108761 (2022)
4. Chandaliya, P.K., Sinha, A., Nain, N.: ChildFace: gender aware child face aging. In: BIOSIG 2020, pp. 255–263 (2020)
5. Chen, B.-C., Chen, C.-S., Hsu, W.H.: Cross-age reference coding for age-invariant face recognition and retrieval. In: Fleet, D., Pajdla, T., Schiele, B., Tuytelaars, T. (eds.) ECCV 2014. LNCS, vol. 8694, pp. 768–783. Springer, Cham (2014). https://doi.org/10.1007/978-3-319-10599-4_49
6. Choi, Y., Choi, M., Kim, M., Ha, J.W., Kim, S., Choo, J.: StarGAN: unified generative adversarial networks for multi-domain image-to-image translation. In: Proceedings of the IEEE Conference on Computer Vision and Pattern Recognition (2018)
7. Gatys, L.A., Ecker, A.S., Bethge, M.: A neural algorithm of artistic style (2015)

8. Georgopoulos, M., Oldfield, J., Nicolaou, M.A., Panagakis, Y., Pantic, M.: Enhancing facial data diversity with style-based face aging (2020)
9. Goodfellow, I., Pouget-Abadie, J., Mirza, M., Xu, B., Warde-Farley, et al.: Generative adversarial nets. In: NIPS, pp. 2672–2680 (2014)
10. Grimmer, M., Ramachandra, R., Busch, C.: Deep face age progression: a survey. IEEE Access **9**, 83376–83393 (2021). https://doi.org/10.1109/ACCESS.2021.3085835
11. Hinton, G.E., Zemel, R.S.: Autoencoders, minimum description length and Helmholtz free energy. In: Proceedings of the 6th International Conference on Neural Information Processing Systems, NIPS 1993, pp. 3–10. Morgan Kaufmann Publishers Inc. (1993)
12. Huang, X., Belongie, S.: Arbitrary style transfer in real-time with adaptive instance normalization (2017)
13. Isola, P., Zhu, J.Y., Zhou, T., Efros, A.A.: Image-to-image translation with conditional adversarial networks (2018)
14. Karras, T., Laine, S., Aila, T.: A style-based generator architecture for generative adversarial networks. In: CVPR, pp. 4396–4405 (2019)
15. Kemelmacher-Shlizerman, I., Suwajanakorn, S., Seitz, S.M.: Illumination-aware age progression. In: CVPR, pp. 3334–3341 (2014)
16. Kingma, D.P., Welling, M.: Auto-encoding variational bayes. In: ICLR (2016)
17. Lanitis, A., Taylor, C., Cootes, T.: Toward automatic simulation of aging effects on face images. IEEE Trans. Pattern Anal. Mach. Intell. **24**(4), 442–455 (2002). https://doi.org/10.1109/34.993553
18. Li, Y., Wang, N., Liu, J., Hou, X.: Demystifying neural style transfer. In: AAAI, pp. 2230–2236 (2017)
19. Liu, M., et al.: STGAN: a unified selective transfer network for arbitrary image attribute editing. In: CVPR (2019)
20. Liu, M.Y., et al.: Few-shot unsupervised image-to-image translation. In: CVPR, pp. 1–8 (2019)
21. Mirza, M., Osindero, S.: Conditional generative adversarial nets (2014). http://arxiv.org/abs/1411.1784
22. Praveen, K.C., Neeta, N.: Conditional perceptual adversarial variational autoencoder for age progression and regression on child face. In: ICB, pp. 1–8 (2019)
23. Chandaliya, P.K., Kumar, V., Harjani, M., Nain, N.: SCDAE: ethnicity and gender alteration on CLF and UTKFace dataset. In: CVIP, pp. 294–306 (2019)
24. Radford, A., Metz, L., Chintala, S.: Unsupervised representation learning with deep convolutional generative adversarial networks (2016)
25. Ramanathan, N., Chellappa, R.: Modeling age progression in young faces. In: CVPR, pp. 387–394 (2006)
26. Ronneberger, O., Fischer, P., Brox, T.: U-Net: convolutional networks for biomedical image segmentation. In: Navab, N., Hornegger, J., Wells, W.M., Frangi, A.F. (eds.) MICCAI 2015. LNCS, vol. 9351, pp. 234–241. Springer, Cham (2015). https://doi.org/10.1007/978-3-319-24574-4_28
27. Rothe, R., Timofte, R., Van Gool, L.: Deep expectation of real and apparent age from a single image without facial landmarks. Int. J. Comput. Vis. **126**(2), 144–157 (2018)
28. Salimans, T., Goodfellow, I., Zaremba, W., Cheung, V., Radford, A., Chen, X.: Improved techniques for training GANs (2016)
29. Schroff, F., Kalenichenko, D., Philbin, J.: FaceNet: a unified embedding for face recognition and clustering. In: CVPR (2015)

30. Shi, Y., Jain, A.: Probabilistic face embeddings. In: ICCV, pp. 6901–6910 (2019)
31. Tazoe, Y., Gohara, H., Maejima, A., Morishima, S.: Facial aging simulator considering geometry and patch-tiled texture. In: ACM SIGGRAPH 2012 Posters, pp. 90:1–90:1 (2012)
32. Wang, Z., Tang, X., Luo, W., Gao, S.: Face aging with identity-preserved conditional generative adversarial networks. In: CVPR (2018)
33. Yang, H., Huang, D., Wang, Y., Jain, A.K.: Learning face age progression: a pyramid architecture of GANs. In: CVPR, pp. 31–39. IEEE Computer Society (2018)
34. Zhang, K., Zhang, Z., Li, Z., Qiao, Y.: Joint face detection and alignment using multitask cascaded convolutional networks. IEEE Signal Process. Lett. **23**(10), 1499–1503 (2016)
35. Zhang, K., Su, Y., Guo, X., Qi, L., Zhao, Z.: Mu-GAN: facial attribute editing based on multi-attention mechanism, vol. 8, p. 1614 (2021). https://doi.org/10. 1109/JAS.2020.1003390
36. Zhang, Z., Song, Y., Qi, H.: Age progression/regression by conditional adversarial autoencoder. In: CVPR, pp. 4352–4360. IEEE Computer Society (2017)
37. Zhu, J.Y., Park, T., Isola, P., Efros, A.A.: Unpaired image-to-image translation using cycle-consistent adversarial networks. In: ICCV, pp. 2242–2251 (2017)

Efficient Contextual Feature Network for Single Image Super Resolution

Inderjeet$^{(\boxtimes)}$ (iD) and J. S. Sahambi

Indian Institute of Technology Ropar, Rupnagar 140001, Punjab, India
inderjeet.20eez0028@iitrpr.ac.in

Abstract. The field of efficient super-resolution techniques has witnessed significant progress, with advancements in reducing parameters
and FLOPs and enhancing feature utilization through complex layer
connections. However, these methods may not be suitable for resource-
constrained devices due to their computational demands. We propose a
novel approach called Efficient Contextual Feature Network (ECFN) to
address this issue. ECFN utilizes two convolutional layers to learn residual contextual local features, striking a balance between model effectiveness, inference speed, and efficiency. These updates improve performance compared to previously reported efficient super-resolution models
for Single Image Super-Resolution (SISR), offering faster runtime without compromising high PSNR or SSIM.

Keywords: Efficient Single Image Super Resolution · Convolutional
Neural Network · Efficient Contextual Feature Extraction

1 Introduction

In computer vision, the goal of the Single Image Super-Resolution (SISR) task
is to recreate a high-resolution image from a low-resolution one. It can be used
in many contexts, including but not limited to visual computing, data visualization, and video compression. Although deep learning-based approaches have
demonstrated impressive performance in SISR, many of these models are computationally expensive, making it difficult to deploy on resource-constrained devices
for practical use. Therefore, developing SISR models that strike a good balance
between image quality and inference time while remaining lightweight and efficient is important.

Effective SISR models have been proposed by several previous studies
[1, 2, 7, 11, 20], typically by decreasing the number of model parameters or FLOPs
(Floating Point Operations). Though recursive networks using weight-sharing
strategies have seen widespread use in the quest to shrink model parameters,
their complex graph topology means they may not always result in fewer operations and shorter inference times. Although depth-wise convolutions, feature
splitting, and shuffling have all been used to decrease FLOPs, their ability to
boost computational efficiency is not always assured. In addition, recent studies

H. Kaur et al. (Eds.): CVIP 2023, CCIS 2010, pp. 200–212, 2024.
https://doi.org/10.1007/978-3-031-58174-8_18

have shown that the runtime efficiency of models is not necessarily improved by reducing the number of parameters and FLOPs. For this reason, it is important to work on efficient SISR models that emphasize faster inference speed rather than simply reducing parameters or FLOPs to satisfy the real world better.

Our goal in this research was to find a better balance between reconstructed image quality and inference time by reevaluating the state-of-the-art efficient SISR model RFDN [10] (Residual Feature Distillation Network) & RLFN [21] (Residual Local Feature Network). We revisit the effectiveness of various RLFB-proposed residual local feature block parts.

We propose a new Efficient Contextual Feature Network (ECFN) that can consolidate different parts of the network without diminishing the overall power of the model. We further improve its performance using a loss function based on mean absolute errors. Additionally, we look into the feature extractor's intermediate feature selection process and discover that feature extraction from shallow layers preserves more precise details, contextual details, and textures. Given this finding, we developed a feature extractor to pull out edges and details despite blur.

Our contributions to this study can be summarized as follows:

1. To accomplish fast and accurate single-image super-resolution (SISR), we introduce a highly efficient and compact Contextual Feature Network (ECFN). Our method outperforms state-of-the-art SR techniques despite using many fewer parameters.
2. To more effectively extract the intermediate features with contextual details, we proposed a novel architecture based on residual contextual feature extraction.
3. We examine intermediate features extracted by the feature extractor of the combined loss and discover that features from shallow layers are indispensable. This motivates us to create an innovative feature extractor to pull more data, including edges, textures, and the overall scene.

2   Related Work

Recently, models based on deep learning have made significant progress in image SR. Dong *et al.* [1] established the foundation by using a three-layer convolutional neural network SRCNN to optimize the complete process from beginning to end, including feature extraction, non-linear mapping, and image reconstruction. Following this, Kim *et al.* [3] proposed the very deep super-resolution (VDSR) network, which uses 20 convolutional layers to enhance the SR performance. Kim *et al.* [14] presented DRCN, a method for reducing model complexity by repeatedly recursively applying the feature extraction layer (16 times). To boost performance while reducing the number of parameters, DRRN [5] combines the recursive and residual network schemes. The original LR images are used as input for the Laplacian pyramid super-resolution network (LapSRN), which progressively reconstructs the sub-band residuals of HR images to solve the speed and accuracy problem proposed by Lai *et al.* [4]. With the persistent memory network (MemNet), Tai *et al.* [6] addressed the long-term dependency issue present in earlier CNN architectures when applied to image restoration tasks. Because most of the computation can be done in the low-dimensional feature space, Shi *et al.* [18] developed an efficient sub-pixel convolution to upsample the resolutions of feature maps at the end of SR models. This allows for faster testing and lower computational costs. Fast SRCNN (FSRCNN) was proposed by Dong *et al.* [2] to achieve the same goal; it uses transposed convolution as upsampling layers to perform SR after the data has been upsampled. After that, Lim *et al.* [15] proposed EDSR and MDSR, which made major advancements by omitting modules from standard residual networks. After implementing EDSR, Zhang *et al.* [17] proposed the residual dense network (RDN) by adding dense links to the residual nodes. Additional models, such as the Residual Non-Local Attention Network (RNAN) [19] and the Very Deep Residual Attention Network (RCAN) [20], were also proposed. Dai *et al.* could rescale them adaptively by considering higher-order statistics for features. To improve the functionality of SR models, Guo *et al.* devised a dual regression scheme by introducing an extra constraint that allows the mappings to form closed-loop and LR images to be reconstructed. While CNN-based methods have seen a lot of success, they typically aren't optimized for use on mobile devices. Ahn *et al.* [8] proposed the CARN-M model for mobile scenarios using a cascading network architecture to address this issue. To further dissect the previously extracted features, Hui *et al.* [7] proposed the information distillation network (IDN). After the success of the IDN-based fast and lightweight information multi-distillation network (IMDN) [9], which won the AIM 2019 constrained image super-resolution challenge, researchers [7] and [10] improved the information distillation mechanism and proposed a residual feature distillation block, respectively, which went on to win the AIM 2020 Efficient SR Challenge.

3   Proposed Network

3.1   Network Architecture

Figure 1 illustrates the overall architecture of our proposed Efficient Contextual Feature Network (ECFN). ECFN comprises three main components: the initial Low-Level Feature Extraction (LLFE) convolution, multiple stacked efficient contextual feature blocks (ECFBs), and the reconstruction module. The input to ECFN is denoted by I_{LR}, and the output super-resolved image is denoted by I_{SR}.

In the first stage, we utilize a single 3×3 convolution layer to extract coarse features, given by

$$F_0 = H_{LLFE}(I_{LR}), \tag{1}$$

where $H_{LLFE}(.)$ denotes the convolution operation for Low-Level Feature Extraction (LLFE), F_0 is the extracted feature maps. Next, we employ multiple ECFBs in a cascade manner for intermediate feature extraction, which can be expressed as;

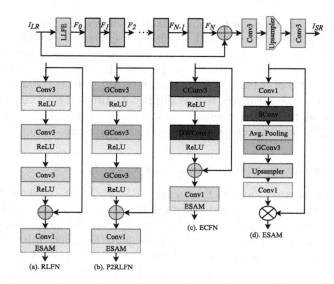

Fig. 1. In our proposed model, we utilize various convolutional layers. These layers are represented by different names: Conv1 for the 1×1 convolution operator, Conv3 for the 3×3 convolution operator, GConv3 for the 3×3 group convolution operator, CConv3 for the 3×3 contextual convolutions operator, and SConv3 for the 3×3 stride convolution operator. Our model consists of two main components: (a) RLFB, which refers to the residual local feature block, and (b) P2RLFN, which stands for parallel processing residual local feature block. Additionally, we have the ECFB (Efficient Contextual Feature block) where DWConv represents the Depthwise convolution operator, and (d) ESAM, which stands for Enhanced Spatial Attention Module.

$$F_N = H_{ECFN}^N(H_{ECFN}^{N-1}(\ldots H_{ECFN}^0(F_0)\ldots)), \tag{2}$$

where $H_{ECFN}^N(.)$ represents the N-th ECFN function, and F_N is the N-th output feature maps.

Additionally, we apply a 3×3 convolution layer to smooth the gradually refined deep feature maps. Finally, the reconstruction module is generate the final output I_{SR}, which is obtained by combining the smoothed deep feature maps with the initial feature maps, as

$$I_{SR} = H_{rec}((Conv(F_N) + F_0)). \tag{3}$$

Here, $H_{rec}(.)$ represents the reconstruction module consisting of two 3×3 convolution layers and one sub-pixel operation.

3.2 Parallel Processing Residual Local Feature Block

Parallel processing residual local feature block (PPRLFB) is a technique that effectively reduces the time required for inference while maintaining the model's capacity, in comparison to RLFN [21] and RFDN [10]. RLFB comprises stacked

GConv+ReLU layers for local feature extraction, eliminating the need for multiple feature distillation connections. Each feature refinement module in PPRLFB consists of a 3×3 group convolution layer followed by a ReLU activation function layer. The input features (F_{in}) undergo multiple steps of local feature refinement to obtain refined features. The final refined output features are obtained by adding the last refined features to the skipped features. These refined features are passed through a 1×1 convolution layer and an ESAM block. PPRLFB significantly enhances the efficiency of the model while preserving its capacity.

3.3   Efficient Contextual Feature Extraction Block

An efficient Contextual Feature Extraction (ECFE) block consists of a Group Convolution layer with Contextual Details Enhancement. This block takes an input feature map and applies convolutional operations and activations, ultimately returning an enhanced output feature map. The motivation behind this function is to leverage the power of convolutional neural networks (CNNs) to extract and enhance features from the input tensor. CNNs are particularly effective at processing grid-like data (such as images), as they can identify patterns and features at different scales and complexities.

The ECFE block receives input from the LLFE layer blok. Contextual convolution-based dilation rate performs this operation in groups of 4. Group convolution reduces computational complexity and increases network capacity by creating input channel subgroups and applying convolutions to each subgroup separately. A ReLU (Rectified Linear Unit) activation function is applied following the convolution operation. This introduces non-linearity into the model, allowing it to learn more complex patterns. Next, a depthwise convolutional layer is applied. A depthwise convolution is a type that processes each input channel independently of the others. This can aid in further simplifying computational complexity without sacrificing the ability to learn intricate patterns. The residual connection is made by summing the depthwise convolution's output with the input tensor. The vanishing gradient problem in deep networks can be mitigated with the help of residual connections, allowing the model to learn more efficiently. A final 1×1 convolution and ESAM (Enhanced Spatial Attention) block are then applied. The feature maps' dimensionality is altered with the help of 1×1 convolution, and their spatial details are improved with the help of an ESAM block.

3.4   Enhanced Spatial Attention Module

This module focuses the model on the most informative parts of the input feature map X_{in}, improving its performance. A 1×1 convolution operation often changes the tensor's filter count without changing its spatial dimensions. After this, a stride convolution (SConv) and avg. pooling operation downsamples the feature map, reducing its spatial dimensions and computational complexity as:

$$F_1 = F_{AP}(F_{SConv}(F_{Conv1}(X_{in}))), \tag{4}$$

Table 1. Quantitative comparison with state-of-the-art methods on benchmark datasets. The best and second-best performances are in *Red* and *Blue* colors, respectively. 'Multi-Add' is calculated with 1280 × 720 GT (Ground Truth) image.

Method	Scale	Params [K]	Multi-Adds [G]	Set5 [13] PSNR/SSIM	Set14 [16] PSNR/SSIM	BSD100 [22] PSNR/SSIM	Urban100 [23] PSNR/SSIM
Bicubic	×2	–	–	33.66/0.9299	30.24/0.8688	29.56/0.8431	26.88/0.8403
SRCNN [1]		8	52.7	36.66/0.9542	32.45/0.9067	31.36/0.8879	29.50/0.8946
FSRCNN [2]		13	6.0	37.00/0.9542	32.63/0.9088	31.53/0.8920	29.88/0.9020
VDSR [3]		666	612.6	37.53/0.9587	33.03/0.9124	31.90/0.8960	30.76/0.9140
LapSR [4]		251	29.9	37.52/0.9591	32.99/0.9124	31.80/0.8952	30.41/0.9103
DRRN [5]		298	6796.9	37.74/0.9591	33.23/0.9136	32.05/0.8973	31.23/0.9188
MemNet [6]		678	2662.4	37.78/0.9597	33.28/0.9142	32.08/0.8978	31.31/0.9195
IDN [7]		553	124.6	37.83/0.9600	33.30/0.9148	32.08/0.8985	31.27/0.9196
CARN [8]		1592	222.8	37.76/0.9690	33.52/0.9166	32.09/0.8978	31.92/0.9256
IMDN [9]		694	158.8	38.00/0.9605	33.63/0.9177	32.19/0.8996	32.17/0.9283
RFDN [10]		534	95.0	38.05/0.9606	33.68/0.9184	32.16/0.8994	32.12/0.9278
BSRN [11]		332	73.0	38.10/0.9610	33.74/0.9193	32.24/0.9006	32.34/0.9303
FeNet [24]		351	77.9	37.90/0.9602	33.45/0.9161	32.09/0.8995	31.75/0.9257
ACDN [25]		408	82	37.87/0.9593	33.57/0.9172	32.15/0.8990	32.13/0.9280
P2RLFN (Ours)	2	211.78	29.235	**38.05/0.9802**	**33.70/0.9190**	**32.20/0.8901**	**32.31/0.9289**
ECFN(Ours)	2	195.22	12.293	38.11/0.9812	33.76/0.9197	32.26/0.9011	32.35/0.9304
Bicubic	×4	–	–	28.42/0.8104	26.00/0.7027	25.96/0.6675	23.14/0.6577
SRCNN [1]		8	52.7	30.48/0.8626	27.50/0.7513	26.90/0.7101	24.52/0.7221
FSRCNN [2]		13	4.6	30.72/0.8660	27.61/0.7550	26.98/0.7150	24.62/0.7280
VDSR [3]		666	612.6	31.35/0.8838	28.01/0.7674	27.29/0.7251	25.18/0.7524
LapSRN [4]		813	149.4	31.54/0.8852	28.09/0.7700	27.32/0.7275	25.21/0.7562
DRRN [5]		298	6796.9	31.68/0.8888	28.21/0.7720	27.38/0.7284	25.44/0.7638
MemNet [6]		678	2662.4	31.74/0.8893	28.26/0.7723	27.40/0.7281	25.50/0.7630
IDN [7]		553	32.4	31.82/0.8903	28.25/0.7730	27.41/0.7297	25.41/0.7632
CARN [8]		1592	90.9	32.13/0.8937	28.60/0.7806	27.58/0.7349	26.07/0.7837
IMDN [9]		715	40.9	32.21/0.8948	28.58/0.7811	27.56/0.7353	26.04/0.7838
RFDN [10]		550	23.9	32.24/0.8952	28.61/0.7819	27.57/0.7360	26.11/0.7858
BSRN [11]		352	19.4	32.35/0.8966	28.73/0.7847	27.65/0.7387	26.27/0.7908
FeNet [24]		366	20.4G	32.02/0.8919	28.28/0.7764	27.47/0.7319	25.75/0.7747
ACDN [25]		421	22.5	32.17/0.8937	28.60/0.7809	27.55/0.735	26.07/0.7852
P2RLFN(Ours)	4	211.78	29.235	**32.74/0.8970**	**28.74/0.7850**	**27.60/0.7371**	**26.23/0.7824**
ECFN(Ours)	4	195.22	12.293	32.80/0.9098	28.78/0.7901	27.84/0.7388	26.28/0.7910

where, $F_{SConv}(.)$ denotes the Stride Convolution operator, $F_{Conv1}(.)$ denotes the pointwise convolution operator, $F_{AP}(.)$ is Average pooling layer and F_1 is the output feature map. The downsampled tensor is then convolution-upsampled to match the original spatial dimensions. This process can extract and restore coarse-grained spatial information for tasks that require spatial structure understanding. The original and upsampled feature maps must be added to merge the fine-grained and coarse-grained spatial information. A final 1 × 1 convolution and sigmoid activation function scale output values as:

$$F_2 = \sigma(F_{Conv1}(F_{upsampler}(F_{GConv}(F_1)))), \qquad (5)$$

where, ($F_{GConv}(.)$ is the group convolution layer, $F_{upsampler}(.)$ is the Upsampler operator, $\sigma(.)$ denotes the sigmoid function. The original feature map X_{in} multiplies the sigmoid function output. This step is crucial because it applies the learned attention weights to the original feature map, allowing the model to focus on the most informative input.

The ESAM block is a spatial attention mechanism that can enhance CNN performance by directing it to the most relevant parts of the input. The original input feature map is modified by adding learned attention weights and combining fine- and coarse-grained spatial information.

4   Results and Discussion

In this section, a brief overview of the training and testing datasets, as well as the experimental implementation, will be provided before proceeding to the ablation study. After that, the proposed network will be compared with state-of-the-art models on four benchmark datasets, and visual results will be presented at varying scales.

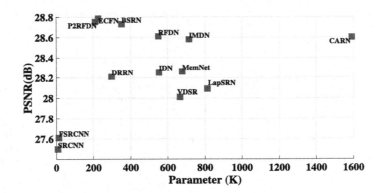

Fig. 2. PSNR vs Parameter [K].

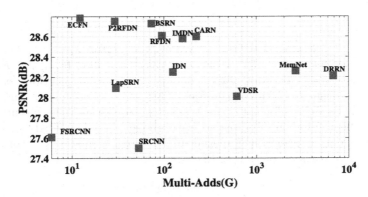

Fig. 3. Performance (in terms PSNR) vs Multi-Adds (G).

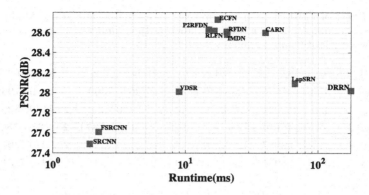

Fig. 4. PSNR vs Runtime [ms], where 'ms' is in milli-seconds.

4.1 Training Details

The input and output data are in RGB image format for this study. The training process utilized a batch size of 1. The proposed model was trained using the ADAM [12] optimizer with $\beta_1 = 0.9$, $\beta_2 = 0.9999$, an epsilon value of 10^{-8}, a learning rate of 10^{-3}, and 100–200 epochs. Training the proposed model for each scaling factor took approximately 3–4 h. All models were implemented on a single NVIDIA P100 GPU. To showcase the effectiveness of our proposal, we utilize the commonly used L_2 loss as our objective function. During the training process, we work with a training set $\{\mathcal{I}_{LR}, \mathcal{I}_{HR}\}_{s=1}^{S}$, which consists of $\mathcal{S}$ degraded LR inputs and their corresponding HR labels. The cost function for training the RFCA network is defined as follows: $\mathcal{L}(\theta) = \frac{1}{\mathcal{S}} \sum_{s=1}^{\mathcal{S}} \| \mathcal{I}_{HR}^{s} - \mathcal{M}_{ECFN})(\mathcal{I}_{LR}^{s}) \|$ Here, θ represents the learnable parameters, and $\mathcal{M}_{ECFN})(.)$ refers to the overall function of our proposed network.

4.2 Datasets

The BSDS500 dataset, on which the proposed model was trained, contains 200 high-quality images used for training and an additional 150 images used for validation and testing. During testing, we relied on four widely-used benchmark datasets, each of which has its quirks: Set5 [13], Set14 [16], BSD100 [22] and Urban100 [23]. Images of people and the natural world predominate in Set5, Set14, and BSD100, while Urban100 features 100 photographs of actual cities. Results for structural similarity (SSIM) and peak signal-to-noise ratio (PSNR) are computed on the Y channel of the transformed YCrCb color space for the final SR images. The HR image is blurred with bicubic downsampling to create the LR image.

4.3 Ablation Study

This section discusses the effects of various P2RLFN stages, ECFE stages, and model complexity.

Table 2. Effect of P2RLFN (parallel processing residual local feature) Module stages on proposed architecture where Stage N indicates the number of blocks cascaded proposed network. "**Bold**" values denote the best result.

P2RLFN	Set5 [13]	Set14 [16]	BSD100 [22]	Urban100 [23]
Stage 1	32.19/0.8998	28.08/0.7720	27.36/0.7309	24.21/0.7796
Stage 2	32.69/0.9021	27.57/0.7760	27.51/0.7336	25.11/0.7826
Stage 3	**32.80/0.9098**	**28.78/0.7901**	**27.60/0.7371**	**26.23/0.7824**
Stage 4	31.94/0.8987	28.27/0.7833	27.51/0.7353	25.32/0.7801
Stage 5	31.69/0.8951	28.43/0.7860	27.30/0.7291	25.22/0.7731

Table 3. Impact of ECFE (Efficient Contextual Feature Extraction) block stages on proposed architecture where **ECFE$_N$** indicates the number of blocks cascaded proposed network. "**Bold**" values denote the best result.

ECFE	Set5 [13]	Set14 [16]	BSD100 [22]	Urban100 [23]
ECFE$_1$	31.76/0.8861	27.85/0.7803	26.07/0.7349	25.10/0.7731
ECFE$_2$	31.28/0.8839	28.63/0.7887	26.35/0.7324	25.62/0.7812
ECFE$_3$	31.73/0.8859	27.49/0.7701	27.18/0.7300	25.90/0.7891
ECFE$_4$	32.40/0.8959	28.61/0.7835	27.81/0.7361	26.21/0.7900
ECFE$_5$	**32.74/0.8970**	**28.74/0.7850**	**27.84/0.7388**	**26.28/0.7910**

Table 4. Effect of different combinations Convolution, Depth-wise convolution, and contextual convolution layers ECFE (Efficient Contextual Feature Extraction) on proposed architecture, "**Bold**" values denote the best result.

Layers Effect on ECFN	Set5 [13]	Set14 [16]
Consecutive Conv3	31.93/0.8916	27.31/0.7790
1 Conv3 & 1 DWconv3	32.22/0.8993	27.89/0.7823
1 Conv3 & 1 CConv3	32.31/0.9003	28.01/0.7845
1 DWconv3 & 1 CConv3	**32.80/0.9098**	**28.78/0.7901**

Impact of P2RLFN Stages: Table 2 shows the effect of the P2RLFN (parallel processing residual local feature) module stages on a proposed architecture for single image super-resolution. The proposed architecture was tested on four datasets: Set5, Set14, BSD100, and Urban100. The results are presented as PSNR and SSIM metrics. The table shows that increasing the number of stages in the P2RLFN module generally leads to better results, as seen by the increase in PSNR and SSIM metrics in most cases. However, in some cases, performance may decrease, such as in Stage 4 for the Set5 dataset, where the PSNR metric decreases slightly compared to Stage 3. Overall, the table provides a comparison of the performance of the proposed architecture with different stages of the P2RLFN module on different datasets, which can help to choose the best configuration for their specific application (Table 4).

Impact of ECFE Blocks: Table 3 shows the impact of different stages of the Efficient Contextual Feature Extraction (ECFE) block on the proposed architecture. The stages are evaluated using four datasets: Set5, Set14, BSD100, and Urban100. The performance of each stage is measured using metrics such as PSNR and SSIM. The table demonstrates how each ECFE block stage affects the architecture, with the fifth stage performing the best across all datasets. This analysis helps us understand the effectiveness of each stage and can guide future improvements. Table 2 illustrates the impact of different combinations of Convolution, Depth-wise convolution, and contextual convolution layers on the architecture, with the best results highlighted in bold.

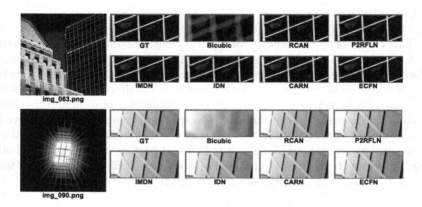

Fig. 5. Visual comparison of P2RFLN and ECFN with the state-of-the-art methods on ×4 SR.

4.4   Model Complexity Analysis

Figure 2 compares PSNR vs Parameters on Set14 [16] dataset. The models depicted in Fig. 2 SRCNN [1], FSRCNN [2], VDSR [3], LapSRN [4], DRRN [5], MemNet [6], IDN [7], CARN [8], IMDN [9], RFDN [10], BSRN [11], ACDN [25] and FeNet [24]. When evaluating a lightweight model, the number of parameters is a key factor. From Table 1, we can observe that our ECFN achieves comparable or better performance when compared with state-of-the-art lightweight models with fewer parameters. As shown in Fig. 2, though RFDN [10] achieves prominent improvement compared with previous methods, such as IDN [7], and CARN [8], it has more parameters than most of the lightweight models. In contracts, our ECFN achieves better performance than VDSR [3], LapSRN [4], DRRN [5], MemNet [6], IDN [7], CARN [8], IMDN [9], RFDN [10], and BSRN [11]. To get a more comprehensive understanding of the model complexity, we also show the comparison of PSNR vs Multi-Adds and PSNR vs. Run time on Set14 ×4 in Figs. 3 and 4. Our method has fewer calculations than the RFDN [10] and saves more energy.

4.5   Comparison with State-of-the-art Methods

We compare the proposed P2RFDN & ECFN with various lightweight SR methods on ×2 and ×4 scales, SRCNN [1], FSRCNN [2], VDSR [3], LapSRN [4], DRRN [5], MemNet [6], IDN [7], CARN [8], IMDN [9], RFDN [10], and BSRN [11]. Table 1 shows the quantitative comparisons on the four benchmark datasets. We can find that the proposed P2RFDN & ECFN can make a better trade-off. Figure 5, shows the visual comparison. The improvement in dB for different datasets compared to BSRN [11] is as follows: Set5 - 0.5 dB, Set14 - 0.1 dB, BSD100 - 0.3 dB, and Urban100 - 0.2 dB.

5   Conclusion

This paper examines the efficacy of the Efficient Contextual Feature Extraction Network (ECFN) and the residual local feature in parallel processing for lightweight image super-resolution. Then, we propose a lightweight and versatile Efficient Contextual Feature Extraction block as an alternative to the residual feature distillation network (RFDN). The contextual convolution and the depthwise convolution based on the skip connections are also proposed to improve the super-resolution performance further. Extensive experiments have demonstrated that the proposed approach yields state-of-the-art performance metrics and qualitative outcomes. In addition, our model's parameters, multi-adds, and run times are kept to a minimum to facilitate portability to mobile devices.

References

1. Dong, C., Loy, C.C., He, K., Tang, X.: Image super-resolution using deep convolutional networks. IEEE Trans. Pattern Anal. Mach. Intell. **38**(2), 295–307 (2016). https://doi.org/10.1109/TPAMI.2015.2439281
2. Dong, C., Loy, C.C., Tang, X.: Accelerating the super-resolution convolutional neural network. In: Leibe, B., Matas, J., Sebe, N., Welling, M. (eds.) ECCV 2016, Part II. LNCS, vol. 9906, pp. 391–407. Springer, Cham (2016). https://doi.org/10.1007/978-3-319-46475-6_25
3. Kim, J., Lee, J.K., Lee, K.M.: Accurate image super-resolution using very deep convolutional networks. In: Proceedings of the IEEE Conference on Computer Vision and Pattern Recognition (2016)
4. Lai, W.-S., et al.: Deep Laplacian pyramid networks for fast and accurate super-resolution. In: Proceedings of the IEEE Conference on Computer Vision and Pattern Recognition (2017)
5. Tai, Y., Yang, J., Liu, X.: Image super-resolution via deep recursive residual network. In: Proceedings of the IEEE Conference on Computer Vision and Pattern Recognition (2017)
6. Tai, Y., et al.: MemNet: a persistent memory network for image restoration. In: Proceedings of the IEEE International Conference on Computer Vision (2017)

7. Hui, Z., Wang, X., Gao, X.: Fast and accurate single image super-resolution via information distillation network. In: Proceedings of the IEEE conference on Computer Vision and Pattern Recognition (2018)
8. Ahn, N., Kang, B., Sohn, K.-A.: Fast, accurate, and lightweight super-resolution with cascading residual network. In: Proceedings of the European Conference on Computer Vision (ECCV) (2018)
9. Hui, Z., et al.: Lightweight image super-resolution with information multi-distillation network. In: Proceedings of the 27th ACM International Conference on Multimedia (2019)
10. Liu, J., Tang, J., Wu, G.: Residual feature distillation network for lightweight image super-resolution. In: Bartoli, A., Fusiello, A. (eds.) ECCV 2020, Part III. LNCS, vol. 12537, pp. 41–55. Springer, Cham (2020). https://doi.org/10.1007/978-3-030-67070-2_2
11. Li, Z., et al.: Blueprint separable residual network for efficient image super-resolution. In: Proceedings of the IEEE/CVF Conference on Computer Vision and Pattern Recognition (2022)
12. Kingma, D.P., Ba, J.: Adam: a method for stochastic optimization. arXiv preprint arXiv:1412.6980 (2014)
13. Bevilacqua, M., Roumy, A., Guillemot, C., Alberi-Morel, M.L.: Low-complexity single-image super-resolution based on nonnegative neighbor embedding, p. 135-1 (2012)
14. Kim, J., Lee, J.K., Lee, K.M.: Deeply-recursive convolutional network for image super-resolution. In: Proceedings of the IEEE Conference on Computer Vision and Pattern Recognition (2016)
15. Lim, B., et al.: Enhanced deep residual networks for single image super-resolution. In: Proceedings of the IEEE Conference on Computer Vision and Pattern Recognition Workshops (2017)
16. Zeyde, R., Elad, M., Protter, M.: On single image scale-up using sparse-representations. In: Boissonnat, J.-D., et al. (eds.) Curves and Surfaces 2010. LNCS, vol. 6920, pp. 711–730. Springer, Heidelberg (2012). https://doi.org/10.1007/978-3-642-27413-8_47
17. Zhang, Y., et al.: Residual dense network for image super-resolution. In: Proceedings of the IEEE Conference on Computer Vision and Pattern Recognition (2018)
18. Shi, W., et al.: Real-time single image and video super-resolution using an efficient sub-pixel convolutional neural network. In: Proceedings of the IEEE Conference on Computer Vision and Pattern Recognition (2016)
19. Zhang, Y., et al.: Residual non-local attention networks for image restoration. arXiv preprint arXiv:1903.10082 (2019)
20. Zhang, Y., et al.: Image super-resolution using very deep residual channel attention networks. In: Proceedings of the European Conference on Computer Vision (ECCV) (2018)
21. Kong, F., et al.: Residual local feature network for efficient super-resolution. In: Proceedings of the IEEE/CVF Conference on Computer Vision and Pattern Recognition, pp. 766–776 (2022)
22. Martin, D., Fowlkes, C., Tal, D., Malik, J.: A database of human segmented natural images and its application to evaluating segmentation algorithms and measuring ecological statistics. In: Proceedings Eighth IEEE International Conference on Computer Vision, ICCV 2001, vol. 2, pp. 416–423. IEEE (2001)
23. Huang, J.-B., Singh, A., Ahuja, N.: Single image super-resolution from transformed self-exemplars. In: Proceedings of the IEEE Conference on Computer Vision and Pattern Recognition, pp. 5197–5206 (2015)

24. Wang, Z., et al.: FeNet: feature enhancement network for lightweight remote-sensing image super-resolution. IEEE Trans. Geosci. Remote Sens. **60**, 1–12 (2022). https://doi.org/10.1109/TGRS.2022.3168787. Art no. 5622112
25. Wu, J., Wang, Y., Zhang, X.: Lightweight asymmetric convolutional distillation network for single image super-resolution. IEEE Signal Process. Lett. **30**, 733–737 (2023). https://doi.org/10.1109/LSP.2023.3286811

T-Fusion Net: A Novel Deep Neural Network Augmented with Multiple Localizations Based Spatial Attention Mechanisms for Covid-19 Detection

Susmita Ghosh[✉] and Abhiroop Chatterjee

Jadavpur University, Kolkata, India
susmita.ghoshde@jadavpuruniversity.in

Abstract. Recent years have witnessed significant advancements in image classification tasks, primarily driven by the increasing capabilities of deep neural networks. Nonetheless, the growing complexity of datasets and the ongoing pursuit of enhanced performance necessitate innovative approaches. In this study, we introduce a novel deep neural network, referred to as the "T-Fusion Net," which incorporates multiple spatial attention mechanisms based on localizations. This attention mechanism enables the model to concentrate on pertinent regions within the images, thus bolstering its discriminative abilities. To further elevate image classification accuracy, we employ a homogeneous ensemble of these T-Fusion Nets. This ensemble technique involves multiple instances of individual T-Fusion Nets, and the fusion of their outputs is achieved through a fuzzy max fusion process. We meticulously optimize this fusion process by selecting appropriate parameters to ensure a balanced contribution from each individual model. Experimental assessments conducted on a well-documented dataset of COVID-19 (SARS-CoV-2 CT scans) were utilized to assess the efficacy of both the T-Fusion Net model and its ensemble counterpart. The results indicate that our T-Fusion Net and its ensemble model consistently surpass existing approaches, demonstrating remarkable accuracy rates of 97.59% and 98.4%, respectively.

Keywords: Convolutional neural network · spatial attention · ensemble model · fuzzy max fusion · Covid-19 detection

1 Introduction

Earlier techniques in image analysis often drew inspiration from the widespread applicability of artificial neural networks [1, 2] (Fig. 1) and nature-inspired algorithms [3], mimicking how humans perceive and interpret visual information and how nature works in an optimum manner. While effective for various tasks, the advent of deep learning [4, 5] has largely surpassed these traditional approaches, offering more flexibility and superior performance in complex image classification tasks. In the realm of medical image analysis [6, 7], where the stakes are high, the integration of attention mechanisms [8] becomes even more necessary. Medical images often contain intricate details and

© The Author(s), under exclusive license to Springer Nature Switzerland AG 2024
H. Kaur et al. (Eds.): CVIP 2023, CCIS 2010, pp. 213–224, 2024.
https://doi.org/10.1007/978-3-031-58174-8_19

subtle patterns that are crucial for accurate diagnosis and treatment planning. Therefore, researchers are actively investigating ways to leverage attention mechanisms within deep learning models for better feature extraction and enhanced feature representation.

In the context of this research, the introduction of (*T-Fusion Net*), a deep neural network (DNN) combined with MLSAM (multiple localizations based spatial attention mechanisms), addresses the need for improved feature extraction and representation in complex image analysis tasks, particularly in medical domain. The utilization of a homogeneous ensemble model with varying kernel sizes for introducing spatial attention aims to harness the collective power of multiple model instances, enhancing the network's ability to capture diverse scales of image details which is crucial for accurate medical image analysis. The motivation behind introducing T-Fusion Net equipped with MLSAM and an ensemble of varying spatial attention mechanisms is to achieve better feature representation. Enhanced feature representation is essential for unlocking deeper insights from complex image data, particularly in medical applications, where fine-grained details and diverse scales of information play a pivotal role in accurate analysis and diagnosis.

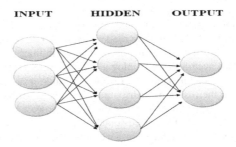

Fig. 1. An artificial neural network

Our proposed approach's effectiveness is assessed through experiments conducted on the widely recognized SARS-CoV-2 CT scan dataset, a benchmark in Covid-19 detection [9]. We perform performance analysis with various other DNN models, revealing the superior accuracy of our proposed T-Fusion Net, enhanced with spatial attention, and its ensemble using fuzzy max fusion. The remainder of this paper is organized as follows: In Sect. 2, we delve into a review of the related literature in the domain of image classification using deep learning. Section 3 details our methodology, encompassing a comprehensive explanation of the multiple localizations-based spatial attention block, its integration into the T-Fusion Net architecture, and the ensemble mechanism achieved through fuzzy max fusion. In Sect. 4, we elaborate on the experimental setup, including the dataset utilized, the evaluation metrics employed, the image preprocessing techniques applied, and the parameter specifics. Section 5 is dedicated to the analysis of our results. Finally, in Sect. 6, we draw conclusions based on our findings.

2 Related Research

Attention mechanisms in deep learning models allow the network to focus on specific regions or channels of input data that are most relevant for making predictions. Spatial attention helps the model concentrate on important spatial regions, while channel attention emphasizes important channels in the feature maps. Zhang et al. [10] proposed a hybrid attention method that combined both spatial and channel attention mechanisms. The approach demonstrated significant performance gains compared to conventional methods, making it a state-of-the-art technique at the time of its publication. Huang et al. [11] introduced a fuzzy fusion technique as an effective way to combine outputs from individual models. Ensemble methods, such as model fusion, are commonly used to boost the performance of machine learning models. In the context of image classification, multiple models may produce different predictions for the same image, and combining their outputs can lead to improved accuracy and robustness. Zheng et al. [12] proposed a hierarchical fusion approach that combined multiple levels of features for image classification. It is to be noted that in deep nets, features are hierarchically learned at different layers of the network. In line with these advancements, our research presents a novel DNN model (termed as, *T-Fusion Net*) which integrates a new spatial attention method. By incorporating attention mechanisms into each of such individual models, we aim to capture diverse and discriminative features from images. Thereafter, using fuzzy max fusion, our model optimally combines the strengths of individual T-Fusion Net, leading to improved classification accuracy.

3 Proposed Methodology

In the present work, the architecture of the proposed model is designed using Convolutional Neural Networks (CNNs) to extract meaningful features from images. Spatial attention is incorporated by adding convolutional layers with different kernel sizes. We call it multiple localizations. The outputs of these attention-enhanced convolutional layers are concatenated to capture discriminative features from images. Since the proposed network model looks like the English alphabet "T", we termed it as, *T-Fusion Net*. Additionally, we develop an ensemble model with a fuzzy max function to further improve the performance of the T-Fusion Net. Each of the modules of the T-Fusion Net is described below in detail.

3.1 Multiple Localizations Based Spatial Attention Mechanism

The objective of the proposed Multiple Localizations-Based Attention Mechanism (MLSAM) is to bolster the model's receptive capabilities by directing its attention selectively toward significant regions within the input feature map.

The MLSAM module in Fig. 2 takes an input feature map and applies convolutional operations to capture local and global patterns at different scales by varying kernel sizes. It consists of three parallel branches, each performing convolution with different kernel sizes: 3×3, 5×5, and 7×7. These branches generate feature maps with 4 channels each, resulting in a concatenated feature map with a total of 12 channels.

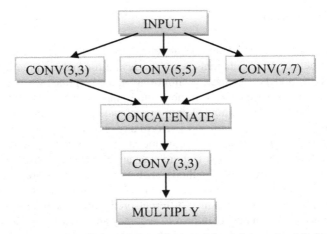

Fig. 2. MLSAM: Multiple Localizations based Spatial Attention Mechanism.

The concatenation of the feature maps is performed along the channel axis, allowing the model to capture diverse information from different kernel sizes. This step is crucial for acquiring multi-scale feature extraction. Subsequently, a convolutional layer with a 3 × 3 kernel size is applied to the concatenated feature map. This layer decreases the total number of channels to one using sigmoid activation function. The resultant output is a spatial attention map that represents the importance of different spatial locations within the input feature map. Finally, the spatial attention map is combined with the input feature map through element-wise multiplication. This operation selectively amplifies informative regions while suppressing less relevant ones.

3.2 Architecture of the T-Fusion Net

The neural network architecture in Fig. 3 outlined is designed for image classification tasks with input images of dimensions (224, 224, 3), representing width, height, and RGB color channels. The initial layers consist of three parallel convolutional layers, each employing 16 filters and the Rectified Linear Unit (ReLU) activation function. These convolutional layers use different kernel sizes (3 × 3, 5 × 5, 7 × 7) to capture information at various spatial scales. The outputs from these convolutional layers are concatenated along the channel axis, enabling the model to capture diverse features at multiple scales. Batch normalization is applied to the concatenated feature maps to improve model convergence by normalizing the activations. A crucial component of this architecture is the Multiple Localizations based Spatial Attention Mechanism (MLSAM), which selectively highlights important spatial regions while suppressing irrelevant or noisy information. MLSAM is introduced in the Feature extractor and Sub-sampling Block 1, which is positioned between Batch Normalization and Max Pooling layers. Max Pooling is then performed on the spatially attended feature maps with a 2 × 2 kernel size. This operation reduces the spatial dimensions and computational complexity while retaining important features. Following Max Pooling, there are four additional convolutional layers applied sequentially, forming the "Feature extractor and Sub-sampling

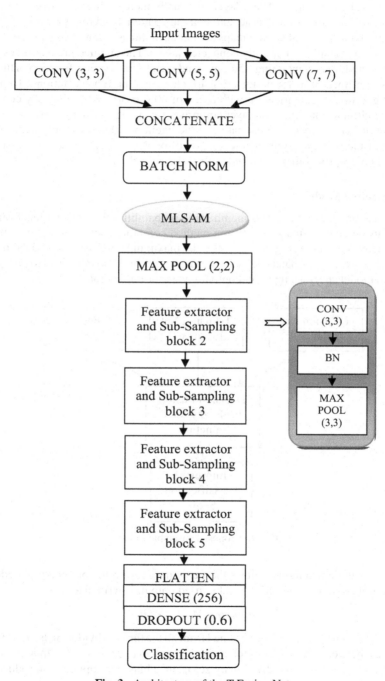

Fig. 3. Architecture of the T-Fusion Net.

block." These layers have 64, 128, 256, and 256 filters, respectively, each using a 3x3 kernel and ReLU activation. These layers gradually increase the receptive field, allowing the model to learn more abstract and complex patterns and relationships within the input image data. The final feature maps are flattened into a 1-dimensional vector, which serves as input for subsequent fully connected layers. The architecture continues with a fully connected layer containing 256 units and a ReLU activation function. This layer performs non-linear transformations to learn class-specific representations. To prevent overfitting, dropout regularization with a rate of 60% is applied to the fully connected layer. The ultimate classification layer comprises two nodes utilizing a Softmax activation function. These nodes are indicative of the likelihood that the input image pertains to either of the two categories, namely, 'Covid' or 'Non-Covid.' The class associated with the highest probability is chosen as the predicted class.

3.3 Ensemble Model

The Softmax layer provides class membership probabilities. To fuse outputs from multiple T-Fusion Nets, a fuzzy max fusion method combines individual net outputs. The homogeneous ensemble (Fig. 4) computes the maximum value across models' outputs, and the fused output is balanced with α, augmented by ϵ, and a bias B (Eq. 1). The ensemble model specifies input and output layers for integration.

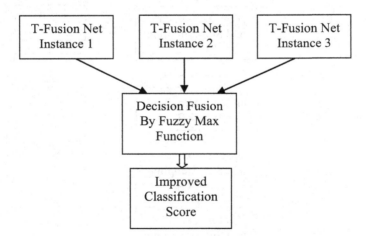

Fig. 4. Proposed ensemble model.

This ensemble technique utilizes the fuzzy max fusion to combine the predictions from multiple individual models. F_o, the fused output, is written as:

$$F_o = \alpha * M_o + \varepsilon + B, \tag{1}$$

where, M_o is the maximum value obtained from all the three individual nets, α determines the balance between the output of the individual model and the fused output. ε is a small constant introduced to avoid division by zero, and a bias B is applied to introduce some offset and ensure numerical stability.

4   Experimental Setup

To evaluate the efficacy of the proposed network and subsequently its homogeneous ensemble, we conducted experiments employing the SARS-CoV-2 CT scan dataset. The comprehensive details of the experimental configuration are elaborated below.

4.1   Dataset Used

In our study, we utilized the SARS-CoV-2 CT scan dataset, which is detailed in Fig. 5 and originally sourced from reference [9]. This dataset comprises a total of 1252 images depicting COVID-19 cases and an additional 1230 images showcasing non-COVID-19 cases, as summarized in Table 1. Sample images from both categories are provided in Fig. 5.

Table 1. The images used in this study were sourced from the SARS-CoV-2 CT scan dataset [9].

Different Classes	Total Images for each class
Non Covid-19	1230
Covid-19	1252
Total Images	**2482**

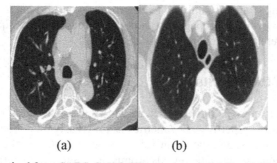

(a)   (b)

Fig. 5. Images acquired from SARS-CoV-2 CT scan dataset. (a) Covid-19, (b) Non Covid-19.

4.2   Image Preprocessing

We resized each input image to a fixed dimension of 224x224 pixels and performed pixel value normalization to the range [0,1] by dividing the original pixel values by a factor of 255.

4.3   Performance Metrics Used

We assessed the models' performance using a range of metrics, including Accuracy and loss values. In addition, we incorporated other performance evaluation criteria such as Precision, Recall, F1-score, and Top-1% error. We also presented the Confusion matrix and the IoU (Intersection over Union) curve.

4.4 Parameters Used

In Table 2, we provide a detailed listing of the parameters used in our experiments along with their respective values. Additionally, we fixed the values of α, ε, and B at 0.8, 0.0001, and 20, respectively, although we conducted experiments with different values for these parameters.

Table 2. Experimental configuration.

Parameters	Values
Batch Size	16
Learning Rate	0.0001
Maximum Epochs	50
Optimizer Used	Adam
Loss Function	Categorical Cross-entropy

4.5 Training the Model

We partitioned the dataset into training and testing subsets, utilizing a 20% test size while implementing stratified sampling to ensure class equilibrium. During the training process, we employed back-propagation and gradient descent techniques to update the model weights, thereby minimizing the loss function.

5 Analysis of the Results

To assess the effectiveness of the proposed network and its ensemble with fuzzy fusion, we employed a range of performance metrics as previously mentioned. We conducted a total of 20 simulations, and the mean values for each metric in the ensemble model are presented in Table 3. The table reveals promising results across various performance indices, with an impressive accuracy of 98.4% achieved for the ensemble of T-Fusion Nets. These experiments were conducted utilizing the NVIDIA A100 tensor core GPU.

As described earlier, in the present paper, we propose a new soft segmentation approach called, MLSAM, for image classification tasks. MLSAM aims to enhance the interpretability and accuracy (Table 3) of soft segmentation models. This is achieved by incorporating multiple localizations based spatial attention mechanisms, which allow the model to selectively focus on different regions of the image at various levels of granularity. Figure 6 shows how our MLSAM module segments the original image.

Figures 7 and 8 depict training and validation accuracies, as well as training and validation losses for the T-Fusion Net. Both training and validation accuracies show upward trends across epochs, indicating effective data generalization and accurate predictions, with stabilization as training progresses. Loss values also exhibit a stabilizing pattern over epochs, as seen in Fig. 8. In Fig. 9, IoU (Intersection over Union) bar plots for two

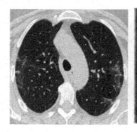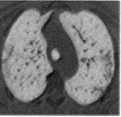

Fig. 6. Original input image is represented in left while the visualization of the intermediate feature representation after the proposed MLSAM module in T-Fusion Net is shown in right.

Table 3. Results from SARS-CoV-2 CT scan dataset [9].

Metrics	Ensemble Model (rounded)
Recall	0.98
Precision	0.98
F1-score	0.98
Accuracy (%)	98.0
Top-1 error (%)	2.0

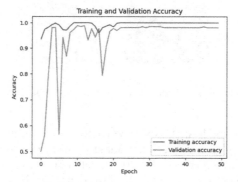

Fig. 7. Variation in training and validation accuracies with epochs for T-Fusion Net.

classes are presented. IoU measures overlap between predicted and true positives, commonly used in object detection and image segmentation. For Covid-19, IoU is 0.9538, and for Non Covid-19, it's 0.9522, reflecting a high overlap between predicted and true positive classes in both cases.

The confusion matrix obtained using the proposed T-Fusion Net (augmented with MLSAM) is shown in Fig. 10. The entries in the matrix depict the best result obtained out of 20 simulations. The resultant matrix indicates that the proposed model is performing very well for Covid-19 detection.

To establish the efficacy of our proposed network, performances of the T-Fusion Net and also its ensemble have been compared with four pre-trained (on ImageNet

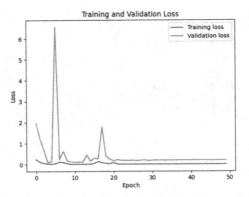

Fig. 8. Variation in training and validation loss values with epochs for T-Fusion Net+MLSAM.

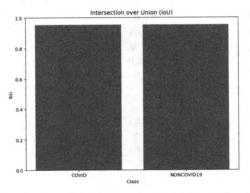

Fig. 9. IoU (Intersection over Union) curves for Covid-19 and Non Covid-19 classes.

dataset) deep learning models: AlexNet, VGG-16, VGG-19, and DenseNet201. The corresponding accuracy scores are given in Table 4. The last 3 rows of the table (marked as bold) depict the results (averaged over 20 simulations) obtained through our proposed network under different configurations. In this connection it is to be noted that, the proposed network is trained from scratch, and not pre-trained. This table demonstrates that T-Fusion Net exhibits superior performance in Covid-19 detection, even when not used in an ensemble.

The T-Fusion Net architecture, with and without MLSAM, achieves a remarkable 97.59% accuracy, surpassing existing methods (Table 4). It also maintains a low parameter count (4,221,947) compared to state-of-the-art networks. The Ensemble T-Fusion Net with MLSAM excels with the highest accuracy of 98.40%, outperforming all other models and approaches.

Table 4. Comparison of the classification performance of our proposed model with other state-of-the-art models on the SARS-CoV-2 CT scan dataset [9].

Methods Used	Accuracy (%)
VGG-16 (Pre-trained on ImageNet) [13]	94.62
AlexNet (Pre-trained on ImageNet) [13]	93.71
VGG-19 (Pre-trained on ImageNet) [13]	93.56
DenseNet201based deep TL [14]	96.25
T-Fusion Net (baseline, no MLSAM)	**96.59**
T-Fusion Net (with MLSAM)	**97.59**
Ensemble of T-Fusion Net (with MLSAM)	**98.40**

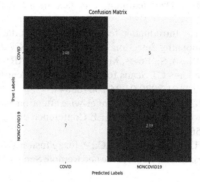

Fig. 10. Confusion matrix representation for Covid-19 detection for the proposed T-Fusion Net (with MLSAM).

6 Conclusion and Future Works

This work introduces the novel T-Fusion Net and the innovative MLSAM spatial attention mechanism. An ensemble of these nets, employing fuzzy max fusion, is utilized for Covid-19 and Non Covid-19 image classification. Evaluation using various metrics demonstrates their effectiveness, with individual T-Fusion Net achieving 97.50% accuracy and the ensemble achieving 98.4%. These results hold promise for Covid-19 diagnosis using multiple localizations based spatial attention. However, further research and model refinement are needed for broader applications. Future studies should expand datasets to encompass diverse Covid-19 cases, imaging modalities, and disease stages. Fine-tuning and optimization can enhance model performance and generalization capabilities.

Acknowledgement. A portion of this research has received support from the IDEAS - Institute of Data Engineering, Analytics, and Science Foundation, as well as The Technology Innovation Hub at the Indian Statistical Institute, Kolkata, under Project No /ISI/TIH/2022/55/ dated September 13, 2022.

References

1. Haykin, S.: Neural Networks and Learning Machines. Pearson (2009)
2. Mondal, A., Ghosh, S., Ghosh, A.: Partially camouflaged object tracking using modified probabilistic neural network and fuzzy energy-based active contour. Int. J. Comput. Vision **122**, 116–148 (2017)
3. Dehuri, S., Ghosh, S., Cho, S.B. (eds.): Integration of Swarm Intelligence and Artificial Neural Network, vol. 78. World Scientific (2011)
4. Goodfellow, I., Bengio, Y., Courville, A.: Deep Learning. MIT Press (2016)
5. LeCun, Y., Bengio, Y., Hinton, G.: Deep learning. Nature **521**(7553), 436–444 (2015)
6. Panigrahi, S., Nanda, B. S., Bhuyan, R., Kumar, K., Ghosh, S., & Swarnkar, T.: Classifying histopathological images of oral squamous cell carcinoma using deep transfer learning. Heliyon **9**(3) (2023)
7. Shen, D., Wu, G., Suk, H.I.: Deep learning in medical image analysis. Annu. Rev. Biomed. Eng. **19**, 221–248 (2017)
8. Ghosh, S., Chatterjee, A.: Introducing feature attention module on convolutional neural network for diabetic retinopathy detection. arXiv preprint arXiv:2308.02985 (2023)
9. Soares, E., Angelov, P., Biaso, S., Froes, M.H., Abe, D.K.: SARS-CoV-2 CT-scan dataset: A Large Dataset of Real Patients CT Scans for SARS-CoV-2 Identification. MedRxiv 2020-04 (2020). https://doi.org/10.1101/2020.04.24.20078584
10. Chen, L., et al.: SCA-CNN: Spatial and channel-wise attention in convolutional networks for image captioning. In: Proceedings of the IEEE Conference on Computer Vision and Pattern Recognition, pp. 5659–5667 (2017)
11. Kuo, B.C., Huang, C.S., Liu, H.C., Hung, C.C.: A fuzzy fusion algorithm to combine multiple classifiers. In: IEEE International Geoscience and Remote Sensing Symposium. 3, pp. III–685. IEEE (2009)
12. Ma, N., Zhang, X., Zheng, H.T., Sun, J.: ShuffleNet v2: Practical guidelines for efficient CNN architecture design. In: Proceedings of the European Conference on Computer Vision (ECCV), pp. 116–131 (2018)
13. Bhattacharyya, A., Bhaik, D., Kumar, S., Thakur, P., Sharma, R., Pachori, R.B.: A deep learning based approach for automatic detection of COVID-19 cases using chest X-ray images. Biomed. Signal Proc. Control, **71**, 103182 (2022)
14. Jaiswal, A., Gianchandani, N., Singh, D., Kumar, V., Kaur, M.: Classification of the COVID-19 infected patients using DenseNet201 based deep transfer learning. J. Biomol. Struct. Dyn. **39**(15), 5682–5689 (2021)

DCT-SwinGAN: Leveraging DCT and Swin Transformer for Face Synthesis from Sketch and Thermal Domains

Haresh Kumar Kotadiya, Satish Kumar Singh, Shiv Ram Dubey$^{(\boxtimes)}$, and Nand Kumar Yadav

Computer Vision and Biometrics Lab (CVBL), Indian Institute of Information Technology, Allahabad, Prayagraj, India
info.hareshkotadiya@gmail.com, {sk.singh,srdubey,pis2016004}@iiita.ac.in

Abstract. Face generation remains a crucial task owing to its applications in crime investigation, entertainment, etc. Sketch to face synthesis is an important task accomplished using Generative Adversarial Network (GAN) models. The generator of the GAN is usually designed using Convolutional Neural Networks (CNNs). GANs are able to deliver promising outcomes in some cases but fail in others. Owing to the local nature of CNN, it is unable to keep track of long range dependencies, limiting the model to local information and delivering underwhelming results. However, recently developed Transformers encode the global context having long range dependencies. Swin Transformer is designed to be suitable for images with promising performance on several vision tasks. We utilize the Swin Transformer along with Discrete Cosine Transform (DCT) in the GAN framework and propose DCT-SwinGAN for face synthesis from sketch and thermal domains. DCT-SwinGAN comprises a multi scale discriminator paired with a generator comprising an attention module, DCT ResNet Convolution, Deconv decoder, and Swin Transformer. The proposed model captures not only local but also global information to generate realistic face images. The generated model outperforms the existing state-of-the-art models on CUHK sketch-to-face and the WHU-IIP thermal-to-face datasets.

Keywords: Face Synthesis · Sketch · Thermal · GAN · DCT · Swin Transformer · Multi Scale Discriminator · Image Translation

1 Introduction

In the area of image processing and computer vision, generating new images brings in a lot of new challenges. It is a cross-domain task that has multiple use cases including image-to-image translation, facial recognition, image synthesis, etc. The image to image translation is one such use case of image generation tasks. The problem at hand is the sketch and thermal to visible image translation. The solution to this problem is inspired by language translation and presents deep learning models. In unsupervised learning, a Generative Adversarial Network (GAN) [1] is used to generate new images using a Convolutional Neural Network (CNN) [29]. GAN comprises two neural networks as shown in Fig. 1.

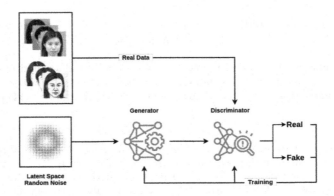

Fig. 1. Generative Adversarial Network. Facial sketches and facial images are taken from CUHK Dataset [17].

CNN fails to generate good-quality images owing to the fact that it is not able to catch long-term dependencies in the images. Self-attention [7] modules can be used to overcome the problem of CNN. The main purpose of the attention module in the generator of the image synthesis task is to concentrate on important features and details of the input images. A sketch image has fewer details as compared to colored images owing to the change in focus on the edge of the sketch for generating a high-quality result. Self-attention module is capable of capturing long-range dependencies, but for higher quality images and to capture the global dependency, Transformer models can be used.

The Transformer model [3] is inspired by natural language processing and suitable for capturing sequential details hence ideal for capturing global dependencies in images. In recent years, Transformers have been very actively utilized for vision tasks [30]. Transformer [7] consists of an encoder and a decoder. Transformer leverages a self-attention module to capture long range dependencies as well as global dependencies in images. With all the advantages that the Transformer brings in, the computational complexity is also quite significant in comparison to the GAN model. To decrease the computational complexity Shifted Window (Swin) Transformer [16] is used. It works by hierarchical merging patches neighboring to each other as one goes deeper into a Transformer model. Thus, the complexity becomes linear corresponding to the size of feature maps.

The motivation of the proposed work is to generate images corresponding to given sketches with reduced artifacts and minimize the time complexity. This would aid in rapid prototyping, artistic visualization, crime investigation, and many other such domains. Our model successfully generates images with reduced artifacts in comparison to SOTA models.

The contributions of the proposed work are:

- In this paper, a novel combination of DCT Convolution and Swin Transformer is exploited in the generator architecture of the proposed DCT-SwinGAN. A multi-scale discriminator is utilized to train the generator model.
- The proposed model better encodes the global relationship between images as compared to the existing GAN models and leads to improved visual quality, accurately representing the input image with enhanced details and texture.
- The proposed model is validated using two datasets, namely the CUHK sketch-to-face and WHU-IIP thermal-to-face dataset with improved results. The analysis of loss functions is also performed to justify the used losses.

2 Related Work

The GAN is also utilized for image-to-image translation in Pix2Pix [20]. The ConditionalGAN [8] explicitly provides a condition with the standard input to generate output with a given input condition. The CycleGAN [9] utilizes a cyclic consistency adversarial network model with the help of the cycle consistency loss to train the model. The Identity-aware CycleGAN [11] utilizes the CycleGAN model face photo-sketch synthesis and recognition. A DualGAN model [13] is different from the CycleGAN in terms of the construction loss.

Kancharagunta et al. [5] developed a cyclic-synthesized generative adversarial network (CSGAN) using the CycleGAN framework [9]. CSGAN uses the cyclic synthesized loss to generate more realistic images. Kancharagunta et al. have also exploited the perceptual loss in PCSGAN [22]. A composition-aided GAN architecture is proposed in [12] for face photo-sketch synthesis by exploiting the compositional reconstruction loss. Coupled generative adversarial networks [15] have the ability to understand the pattern that humans cannot understand or learn directly.

The self-attention [3] mechanism has been extensively exploited for several tasks, including vision applications. Several attention-guided GANs are proposed for image synthesis [2,4,14,24,25]. The GAN with cycle-synthesized attention is exploited in CSA-GAN model [24]. In TVA-GAN [25], attention-guided synthesis is utilized to convert thermal pictures into visible images. TVA-GAN exploits the recurrent inception block with an attention mechanism to learn the local and focused sparse structure. The attention module utilizes the spatial attention maps and important regions' information from the image in [14]. A self-attention GAN is proposed in [4] by preserving the global dependencies through the dissimilarity among different pixels in an image, i.e., spatial locations. Though the attention mechanism is exploited with GANs for image synthesis, the performance is still limited due to the CNN based networks.

Recent methods try to explore the Transformer based GANs for image synthesis. CNN fails to capture the structural and global details of the input. The Vision Transformer (ViT) model [10] works on images by dividing the image into patches which are considered as the tokens. ViT captures the long-range dependencies with outstanding performance but fails to handle the low-level vision tasks. Global and local self-attention is exploited in [7] for face photo-sketch synthesis. The ViT model is improved to Swin Transformer in [16]. The authors [31] have employed Cycle Swin transformer to convert infrared images to high resolution images. The authors [32] make use of a double attention based Swin Gan transformer model to generate images which is scalable and can be leveraged to bigger systems as well. The Swin Transformer is utilized with Fast Fourier Transform (FFT) in GAN framework [23] to capture the local and global dependencies in the images for face photo-sketch synthesis. Recently, Discrete Cosine Transform is also exploited with transformer for image applications [28,33,34]. In this paper, we utilize the Swin Transformer with Discrete Cosine Transform in GAN framework for sketch/thermal face to visible face synthesis.

In computer vision, CNN models are heavily used. However, due to the failure of CNN models to capture the long range dependencies, the self-attention models have gained recent popularity. Self-attention models capture long-range dependencies and produce relatively better quality output. The transformer can be used to capture global dependencies in images, but due to the higher complexity of the transformer, a better solution is required. Swin Transformer facilitates an output of similar quality with a reduction in time complexity. Moreover, in our case of conversion from a sketch to an image, the features of the input sketch tend to be highly correlated making feature extraction an important attribute of the model. Hence, we have used DCT, as DCT is used to extract features having strong frequency domain correlations.

3   Proposed DCT-SwinGAN Model

In this paper, we propose a Swin Transformer and DCT based GAN model that performs sketch/thermal face to visible face synthesis as depicted in Fig. 2. From the given input sketch image let's say x, and we have to generate $G(x)$ using the generator. Here, we use the paired dataset which contains the ground truth images and the corresponding input sketch/thermal images. Discriminator network helps in generating more realistic images by differentiating between ground truth and generated images. The generator is a combination of an improved attention block, Discrete Cosine Transform (DCT) ResNet convolution network, Swin Transformer block in the deconvolution layer, and a deconvolutional decoder block.

If the input sketch/thermal image has insufficient information, then the resultant image will be blurry or noisy and we will get artifacts. So, we add the attention block to the generator, which resolves this issue and generates the spatial attention map containing the information of input features. In image synthesis, capturing the global contexts of the input plays a very important role. However, CNN fails to capture long-range dependencies in images and hence generates poor-quality images. The input image, i.e., the sketch/thermal data, holds the global structure and information that are essential for generating the resulting

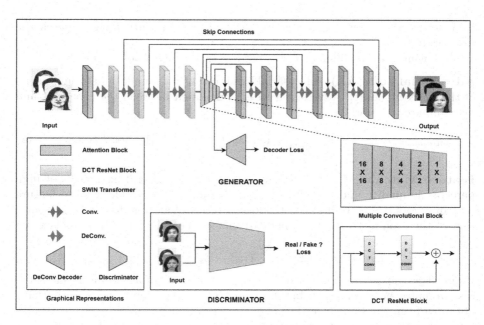

Fig. 2. Proposed Network for Image Synthesis. The dimension of the image and sketch image is 256 × 256. The main blocks of architecture are the attention module, the DCT ResNet module for the encoder, and the Swin Transformer in the decoder. To obtain an optimal SSIM Score dimension of the output image has been converted to the power of two.

image. DCT convolution is crucial for capturing long-range context. DCT block can capture the global and local context of the image by converting the input into the frequency domain from the spatial domain. The spatial domain is converted into the frequency domain, as the frequency domain is able to work with more global domains in comparison to the spatial domain to get optimal results. Also, the frequency domain removes the noisy frequency elements from the data.

Due to the failure of CNN to capture long-term dependencies, one solution for that is to exploit the Transformer network. However, the computational complexity of traditional Transformers is too high. Instead, we use the Swin Transformer [16], which splits the image into nonoverlapping windows, restricting the self attention computation to that part only, unlike a traditional Transformer. In the network, sometimes there is a chance of a vanishing gradient. Introducing the deconv decoder, it is fed with the input by the preceding convolution part and generates the synthesized image. It further calculates the loss for intermediate feature maps. In the network, we use skip connections to preserve the feature information and stabilize the training network. We use a multi-scale discriminator to distinguish between ground truth and generated images. Also, discriminator output influences the SSIM score. When we make the discriminator's output power of two then it aligns with the image resolution and leads to a better SSIM score as the generated and ground truth images match the resolution.

Following are the different losses used to train the proposed model:

Adversarial Loss (AL): Adversarial loss is one of the foundational components of the GAN model [1]. Adversarial loss is calculated between the generator and discriminator network as

$$\mathcal{L}_{minmax} \min_{G} \max_{D} = \mathbb{E}_{x \sim p_{\text{data}}(x)}[\log D(x)] + \mathbb{E}_{z \sim p_z(z)}[1 - \log D(G(z))]. \quad (1)$$

Feature Matching Loss (FML): This results in generating images of high perceptible quality and leads to the stabilization of GAN. The goal of feature matching loss [18] is to diminish the loss in terms of average feature representation of the ground truth and generated images. Feature matching loss is given as,

$$\mathcal{L}_{feature} = \left\| \mathbb{E}_{x \sim p_{\text{data}}} \mathbf{f}(x) - \mathbb{E}_{z \sim p_z(z)} \mathbf{f}(G(z)) \right\|_2^2 \quad (2)$$

where, $\mathbf{f}(x)$ represents the feature vector obtained from a specific layer of the discriminator network for an input x and $\mathbf{f}(G(z))$ represents the feature vector obtained from the same layer for a generated sample $G(z)$.

Perceptual Loss (VPL): Perceptual loss [19] is calculated by comparing the feature map of input and output images. The perceptual loss is given as,

$$\mathcal{L}_{Perceptual} = \sum_i w_i^* d(F(r), F(g)) \quad (3)$$

where $F(r)$ and $F(g)$ are the feature maps of the VGG model for reference and generated images, and w_i is the weight for i^{th} layer.

Decoder Loss (DL): Decoder loss is calculated between the real image and intermediate generated image from the deconv decoder. Decoder loss is represented as a reconstruction loss [21] which is often represented using a distance or dissimilarity metric as,

$$\mathcal{L}_{decoder} = \frac{1}{n} \sum_{i=1}^{n} (x_i - G(z)_i)^2. \quad (4)$$

The training procedure becomes more stable by including the relevant losses, such as adversarial loss, perceptual loss, feature matching loss, and decoder loss providing supplementary information to create high quality images.

4   Experimental Results

4.1   Experimental Settings

For the validation of the generated model, the CUHK Sketch-to-Face synthesis dataset is exploited [17]. It consists of 188 image pairs. This dataset is widely

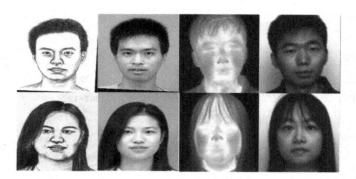

Fig. 3. Sample paired images of 256 × 256 dimension. From left to right: CUHK Sketch Face, CUHK Visible Face, WHU-IIP Thermal Face, and WHU-IIP Visible Face images.

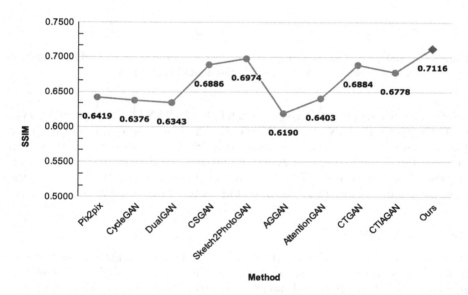

Fig. 4. Comparisons of SSIM score of various SOTA methods on CUHK face dataset. A higher value of the SSIM score is nearer to the ground truth images

used amongst researchers for image translation and synthesis. The size of each of the images is 200 × 250 pixels which have been resized to 256 × 256 dimensions images. The proposed model is also validated using a Thermal-to-Visible dataset, i.e., WHU-IIP [26]. The sample images of the dataset are shown in Fig. 3.

The proposed model is trained by the Adam optimizer with $\beta_1 = 0.5$ and $\beta_2 = 0.999$, respectively, in the PyTorch framework. The batch size is used as 2. The training is performed using an Nvidia GTX 1080TI GPU [27]. The proposed DCT-SwinGAN model is compared with various state-of-the-art (SOTA) image-to-image translation models, including Pix2pix [20], CycleGAN [9], Dual-

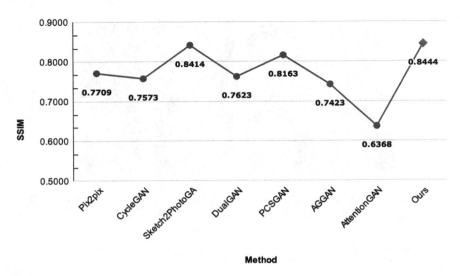

Fig. 5. Comparisons of SSIM score of various SOTA methods on WHU-IIP dataset. A higher value of the SSIM score is nearer to the ground truth images

GAN [13], CSGAN [5], AGGAN [14], Sketch2PhotoGAN [23], AttentionGAN [4], CTGAN [6], CTIAGAN [6], and PCSGAN [22]. The structural similarity index (SSIM) score is used to evaluate the model. SSIM calculates the similarity gap between the ground truth and generated images. SSIM score takes into consideration a few parameters while comparing the images, i.e., contrast variance, the luminance parts of the data, and most importantly, the structure of the image.

4.2   Result Analysis

In Fig. 4, a comparison chart corresponding to the CUHK Face dataset is presented. It contains the SSIM scores of the various aforementioned SOTA methods in comparison to the proposed model. In comparison to our model, the percentage change in SSIM scores is 10.85%, 11.60%, 12.18%, 3.34%, 2.03%, 14.95%, 11.13%, 3.37%, and 4.98% less for Pix2pix, CycleGAN, DualGAN, CSGAN, Sketch2PhotoGAN, AGGAN, AttentionGAN, CTGAN and CTIAGAN, respectively. It is clear that DCT-SwinGAN model notably outperforms other GAN approaches for sketch-to-face synthesis.

In order to test the dataset generalization ability of the DCT-SwinGAN, we also validate the results for thermal-to-face synthesis. Figure 5 presents the comparison chart of SSIM scores in correspondence to the WHU-IIP dataset. In comparison to our model, the percentage change in SSIM scores is 9.53%, 11.50%, 0.35%, 10.77%, 3.44%, 13.75%, 32.60% less for Pix2pix, CycleGAN, Sketch2PhotoGAN, DualGAN, PCSGAN, AGGAN, AttentionGAN, respectively. It noticed that the proposed model is also able to outperform the existing GAN models for thermal-to-face image synthesis.

Figure 6 depicts the qualitative results in terms of the generated face images using the proposed DCT-SwinGAN model. The left half of the figure contains the sketch image, synthesized image, and ground truth image corresponding to the samples taken from the CUHK dataset. It can be stated that the generated image is quite similar to the ground truth image with a very minute difference in color. The right half of the figure contains the thermal input image, the synthesized image, and the ground truth image for the sample images taken from WHU-IIP dataset. The ground truth image and the synthesized image look structurally similar, leading to a good SSIM score. The generated image is softer and missing details like the shape of eyebrows and facial wrinkles, which don't create much difference optically in thermal images.

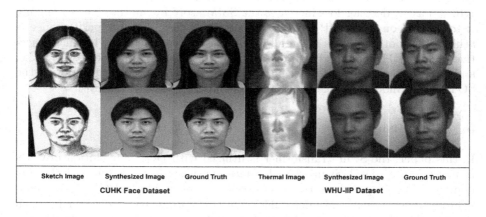

Fig. 6. From left to right: CUHK Face dataset result and WHU-IIP dataset result.

4.3 Loss Ablation Study

We have used adversarial loss (AL), feature matching loss (FML), VGG perceptual loss (VPL), and decoder loss (DL) to create the best quality images for the corresponding input sketch or thermal face images. Table 1 shows the effect of different combinations of losses used to train the proposed DCT-SwinGAN model in terms of the SSIM scores generated for the CUHK and WHU-IIP datasets. Initially, we use only adversarial loss, which gives an SSIM score of 61.98% on the CUHK dataset, which is much lower than the SSIM score of the proposed model. Then feature matching loss is added to the objective function, increasing the SSIM score by 10.40%. To further improve the training, VGG perceptual loss is added leading to an increase in the SSIM score by 1.72%. Lastly, when decoder loss is added to the objective function, the SSIM score is increased by 2.22%, making it 71.16% on the CUHK dataset. Similarly, on WHU-IIP dataset, we use only adversarial loss, which gives an SSIM score of 71.79%, which is much

Table 1. Comparison of various losses on CUHK and WHU-IIP datasets.

Losses	SSIM on CUHK	SSIM on WHU-IIP
AL	0.6198	0.7179
AL + FML	0.6843	0.8299
AL + FML + VPL	0.6961	0.8391
AL + FML + VPL + DL	0.7116	0.8444

lower than the SSIM score of the proposed model. Then feature matching loss is added to the objective function, increasing the SSIM score by 15.6%. Next, VGG perceptual loss is added which leads to an increase in the SSIM score by another 1.10%. Lastly, decoder loss increases the SSIM score by another 0.63%, making it to 84.44% on WHU-IIP dataset. It is noticed that the best performance is achieved on both datasets when all four losses are combined in the final objective function. Thus, it can be stated that due to the use of multiple losses, DCT, and Transformer model, the proposed DCT-SwinGAN model outperforms the SOTA GAN models for sketch/thermal face to visible face synthesis.

5   Conclusion

In this paper, the Swin Transformer is utilized with DCT convolution in GAN framework (i.e., DCT-SwinGAN) for face synthesis from sketch and thermal domains. The proposed model integrates an attention block, DCT ResNet convolution block, deconv decoder, and Swin Transformer based decoder block in a generator for capturing local as well as global information and a multi-scale discriminator. The DCT-SwinGAN is validated on two benchmark face synthesis datasets, namely the CUHK sketch-to-face dataset and the WHU-IIP thermal-to-face dataset. The proposed model outperforms the existing models in terms of the SSIM score on both datasets. The analysis of different losses is also presented which justifies the use of adversarial, feature matching, VGG perceptual, and decoder losses in the objective function. Overall, the proposed model is able to generate high-quality and realistic faces from sketch and thermal faces.

Acknowledgement. The authors acknowledge the funding and facilities provided by IIIT Allahabad to facilitate this research work.

References

1. Goodfellow, I., et al.: Generative adversarial networks. Commun. ACM **63**(11), 139–144 (2020)
2. Lei, Y., Du, W., Hu, Q.: Face sketch-to-photo transformation with multi-scale self-attention GAN. Neurocomputing **396**, 13–23 (2020)
3. Vaswani, A., et al.: Attention is all you need. In: Advances in Neural Information Processing Systems, vol. 30 (2017)

4. Tang, H., Xu, D., Sebe, N., Yan, Y.: Attention-guided generative adversarial networks for unsupervised image-to-image translation. In: IEEE International Joint Conference on Neural Networks, pp. 1–8 (2019)

5. Kancharagunta, K.B., Dubey, S.R.: CSGAN: cyclic-synthesized generative adversarial networks for image-to-image transformation. arXiv preprint arXiv:1901.03554 (2019)

6. Cao, B., Wang, N., Li, J., Hu, Q., Gao, X.: Face photo-sketch synthesis via full-scale identity supervision. Pattern Recogn. **124**, 108446 (2022)

7. Yu, W., Zhu, M., Wang, N., Wang, X., Gao, X.: An efficient transformer based on global and local self-attention for face photo-sketch synthesis. IEEE Trans. Image Process. **32**, 483–495 (2022)

8. Mirza, M., Osindero, S.: Conditional generative adversarial nets. arXiv preprint arXiv:1411.1784 (2014)

9. Zhu, J.Y., Park, T., Isola, P., Efros, A.A.: Unpaired image-to-image translation using cycle-consistent adversarial networks. In: IEEE International Conference on Computer Vision, pp. 2223–2232 (2017)

10. Dosovitskiy, A., et al.: An image is worth 16×16 words: transformers for image recognition at scale. In: International Conference on Learning Representations (2020)

11. Fang, Y., Deng, W., Du, J., Hu, J.: Identity-aware CycleGAN for face photo-sketch synthesis and recognition. Pattern Recogn. **102**, 107249 (2020)

12. Yu, J., et al.: Toward realistic face photo-sketch synthesis via composition-aided GANs. IEEE Trans. Cybern. **51**(9), 4350–4362 (2020)

13. Yi, Z., Zhang, H., Tan, P., Gong, M.: DualGAN: unsupervised dual learning for image-to-image translation. In: IEEE International Conference on Computer Vision (2017)

14. Alami Mejjati, Y., Richardt, C., Tompkin, J., Cosker, D., Kim, K.I.: Unsupervised attention-guided image-to-image translation. In: Advances in Neural Information Processing Systems, vol. 31 (2018)

15. Liu, M.Y., Tuzel, O.: Coupled generative adversarial networks. In: Advances in Neural Information Processing Systems, vol. 29 (2016)

16. Liu, Z., et al.: Swin transformer: hierarchical vision transformer using shifted windows. In: IEEE International Conference on Computer Vision, pp. 10012–10022 (2021)

17. Wang, X., Tang, X.: Face photo-sketch synthesis and recognition. IEEE Trans. Pattern Anal. Mach. Intell. **31**(11), 1955–1967 (2008)

18. Salimans, T., Goodfellow, I., Zaremba, W., Cheung, V., Radford, A., Chen, X.: Improved techniques for training GANs. In: Advances in Neural Information Processing Systems, vol. 29 (2016)

19. Johnson, J., Alahi, A., Fei-Fei, L.: Perceptual losses for real-time style transfer and super-resolution. In: Leibe, B., Matas, J., Sebe, N., Welling, M. (eds.) ECCV 2016. LNCS, vol. 9906, pp. 694–711. Springer, Cham (2016). https://doi.org/10.1007/978-3-319-46475-6_43

20. Isola, P., Zhu, J.Y., Zhou, T., Efros, A.A.: Image-to-image translation with conditional adversarial networks. In: IEEE Conference on Computer Vision and Pattern Recognition, pp. 1125–1134 (2017)

21. Ganguli, S., Garzon, P., Glaser, N.: GeoGAN: a conditional GAN with reconstruction and style loss to generate standard layer of maps from satellite images. arXiv preprint arXiv:1902.05611 (2019)

22. Babu, K.K., Dubey, S.R.: PCSGAN: perceptual cyclic-synthesized generative adversarial networks for thermal and NIR to visible image transformation. Neuro-computing **413**, 41–50 (2020)

23. Liu, H., Xu, Y., Chen, F.: Sketch2Photo: synthesizing photo-realistic images from sketches via global contexts. Eng. Appl. Artif. Intell. **117**, 105608 (2023)

24. Yadav, N.K., Singh, S.K., Dubey, S.R.: CSA-GAN: cyclic synthesized attention guided generative adversarial network for face synthesis. Appl. Intell. **52**(11), 12704–12723 (2022)

25. Yadav, N.K., Singh, S.K., Dubey, S.R.: TVA-GAN: attention guided generative adversarial network for thermal to visible image transformations. Neural Comput. Appl. 1–21 (2023)

26. Wang, Z., Chen, Z., Wu, F.: Thermal to visible facial image translation using generative adversarial networks. IEEE Signal Process. Lett. **25**(8), 1161–1165 (2018)

27. Owens, J.D., Houston, M., Luebke, D., Green, S., Stone, J.E., Phillips, J.C.: GPU computing. Proc. IEEE **96**(5), 879–899 (2008)

28. Zhang, J., Liao, Y., Zhu, X., Wang, H., Ding, J.: A deep learning approach in the discrete cosine transform domain to median filtering forensics. IEEE Signal Process. Lett. **27**, 276–280 (2020)

29. Gatys, L.A., Ecker, A.S., Bethge, M.: Image style transfer using convolutional neural networks. In: IEEE Conference on Computer Vision and Pattern Recognition, pp. 2414–2423 (2016)

30. Dubey, S.R., Singh, S.K.: Transformer-based generative adversarial networks in computer vision: a comprehensive survey. arXiv preprint arXiv:2302.08641 (2023)

31. Zhao, M., Feng, G., Tan, J., Zhang, N., Lu, X.: CSTGAN: cycle swin transformer GAN for unpaired infrared image colorization. In: 3rd International Conference on Control, Robotics and Intelligent System, pp. 241–247 (2022)

32. Zhang, B., et al.: StyleSwin: transformer-based GAN for high-resolution image generation. In: IEEE Conference on Computer Vision and Pattern Recognition, pp. 11304–11314 (2022)

33. Li, X., Zhang, Y., Yuan, J., Lu, H., Zhu, Y.: Discrete cosin transformer: image modeling from frequency domain. In: IEEE Winter Conference on Applications of Computer Vision, pp. 5468–5478 (2023)

34. Scribano, C., Franchini, G., Prato, M., Bertogna, M.: DCT-former: efficient self-attention with discrete cosine transform. J. Sci. Comput. **94**(3), 67 (2023)

Optimum Selection of Image Object Attributes for Object-Based Image Analysis and High Classification Accuracy

Ganesh Khadanga$^{(\boxtimes)}$ (ID) and Kamal Jain (ID)

IIT Roorkee, Roorkee 247667, India
ganesh@nic.in

Abstract. Object-based image analysis (OBIA) is extensively used for the classification of High-Resolution Satellite Imagery (HRSI). The various attributes of the image segments like spectral, spatial and textural, can be generated for analysis and classification purposes. However, the use of all these attributes may not lead to attaining high classification accuracy. Experiments have shown that, a suitable set of these features need to be identified for faster and accurate classification of imageries. The filter based methods like Chi-Square, Information-gain and ReliefF are extensively used for identification and ranking the best set of parameters. The random tree based Boruta machine learning feature ranking method is also used in identifying the feature ranking along with the above algorithms. Subsequently, a learner is fused with a filter and the resultant receiver operating characteristic (ROC) plot of the model has been used to identify the best accuracy and the minimal set of attributes for identifying an individual feature like roads, trees, grass, buildings and shadow. The best set of parameters for a class is identified by the best ROC plot. The best parameters are identified from Boruta feature analysis. The results indicate that the identified smaller feature set helps in enhancing classification accuracy.

Keywords: HRSI · OBIA · Boruta · Feature Selection · SVM

1 Introduction

The OBIA techniques were increasingly used for the classification of images because of their contribution in increasing the accuracy of classification. In object-based techniques the image is divided into homogeneous segments [1, 2, 11]. The attributes of these segments were processed for spatial, spectral and textural analysis. Thus in OBIA technique, the classification of the image objects are done rather than the pixels. The images objects are the essential element in OBIA based analysis. The objects have a large of number feature sets and lead to higher dimensional feature space. It needs to identify a suitable minimal set of attributes for classification and for attaining higher classification accuracy [9, 24]. Hence the efforts are made to identify the minimal set of features using the filter based and wrapper based techniques [22]. The most widely used filter based techniques are Chi square, Information gain and ReliefF. The Filter based

H. Kaur et al. (Eds.): CVIP 2023, CCIS 2010, pp. 237–251, 2024.
https://doi.org/10.1007/978-3-031-58174-8_21

approach uses the heuristic scoring technique and it does not depend on any classifier. The filter based methods are also very fast and computationally efficient.

The wrapper method [3, 13] uses a search strategy to identify the candidate feature subset, and then a classifier is used to evaluate the candidate feature set. Thus the method is computationally intensive. The Random Tree based Boruta [20] machine learning feature raking method is also used in this study for identifying the feature ranking.

The authors in paper [3] applied filter-based Chi-square, information gain and ReliefF methods in OBIA based image classification using Pan-sharpened 0.5 m spatial resolution multispectral WorldView-2 imagery. The performances of feature selection algorithms on the identified features were generated using, nearest neighborhood (NN), Support Vector Machine (SVM) and Random Forest (RF) classifiers. The highest classification accuracy is achieved by the smallest feature data set identified by information gain filter using the SVM classification.

The author in paper [21] used correlation-based feature selection (CFS) method to choose the best features from the LiDAR Data. Higher accuracy was achieved with the identified smaller set of features and the same was used for identifying the shallow and deep-seated landslides.

The paper [14] used five filter methods (Gain ratio, Chi-square, SVM-RFE, CFS, and ReliefF), two wrapper methods (RF wrapper and SVM wrapper), and one embedded method (RF) for feature selection with ranked list of features. The analysis indicates that SVM classifier benefits more from a feature selection analysis with a smaller set of training data.

The authors in [5] analyzed a World View 2 image using the RFE and SVM tools for identifying the bamboo patches. The authors have identified the principal component 1 and 2 along with GLCM Mean of the six bands as important 10 features for achieving higher classification accuracy in the OBIA technique.

The comparative analysis of different attribute selection methods are indicated in [12]. It has shown Jeffreys-Matusita distance generates the highest classification accuracy. It was also indicated that feature space optimization (FSO) tool as available in eCognition is treated as a black-box in nature and has achieved the lowest accuracies. The studies as done by authors in reference [18] indicate, that most of the large number of features in OBIA are strongly correlated.

As per Hughe's effect the accuracy of the classification gets decreased when the number of parameters gets increased [6, 8]. The number of training samples also needs to be increased as per the increase in the dimensionality of features, to improve the accuracy of the classification.

The objective of this paper is to identify a suitable set of features using the openly available algorithm to identify a minimal set of features for attaining the best classification accuracy. Further, the object identification relating to single feature has recently gained importance and much literature is also not available on this subject. After the identification of individual objects the edge preserving approach [27] may be used for finding the edges of the objects. The wrapper-based and filter-based feature selection methods like Maximum relevance minimum redundancy (MRMR), ReliefF, Neighborhood component analysis (NCA) are used in [28] to find the initial ten percent of the primary features and then the artificial neural network (ANN), SVM, and RF classifiers are used for identifying the efficiency of these parameters. Through this paper, an attempt is made to find the optimal set of parameters for an individual class using the ROC [17] approach with foreground and background images.

2 Study Area

Delhi is the capital city of India extended approximately from the northern latitudes 28^0 25' to 28^0 53' and eastern longitudes 28^0 25' to 76^0 30'. The (Fig. 1) shows the geographic location of the study area. It is well connected with major airlines. It is also a major destination of international and national tourist. The study area is having a number of urban features (tree, road, building, grass) and is a representative area of the most of the urban features.

The Multispectral data (0.8 meter resolution) of SkySat Satellite with red, green, blue and near-infrared (NIR) band (dated 28 Jan 2018) as available is taken up for the analysis purpose.

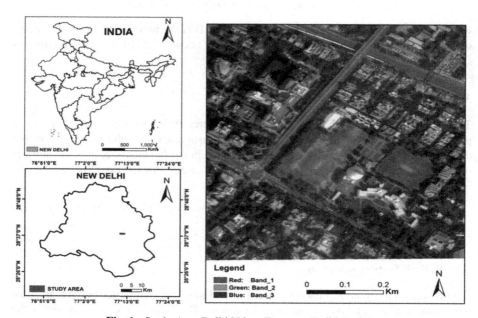

Fig. 1. Study Area Delhi Urban Features (Delhi, India)

3 Methodology

The HRSI of the study area was segmented using the multi-resolution segmentation technique as available in eCognition. Each segment was processed through the software and the values of the 50 attributes as indicated in Table 1 are assigned.

The spectral features like mean of the layers (4 layers) and the standard deviation of the layers, the maximum difference and the brightness is taken up. The geometrical features (like area and length/width) and shape parameters like compactness, elliptic fit, rectangular fit, shape index are taken as attributes of the objects. The texture features of this study are based on the grey-level co-occurrence matrix (GLCM) and grey-level difference vector (GLDV) and are in directions from 0^0, 45^0, 90^0, 135^0 and all direction. Texture features are derived from texture after Haralick based on the Grey-Level Co-occurrence Matrix or Grey-Level Difference Vector.

3.1 Chi-square feature evaluation

The Chi Square statistics measure the lack of independence between two variables [3]. The statistic value is calculated using the two-way contingency table of feature t and the class (c) by Eq. (1):

$$\chi^2(t,c) = \frac{N(AD - BC)^2}{(A + B)(B + D(A + B)(C + D)} \tag{1}$$

where A is the number of times t and c co-occurs, B is the number of time the t occurs without c, D is the number of times neither c nor t occurs and N is the total number of samples.

3.2 Information Gain feature selection

The Info Gain feature selection algorithm measures the reduction in entropy of the predication of class (c) by the changes of the observed values the feature (t) in the dataset [3.26]. Let $\{ci\}_{i=1}^m$ denote the set of classes in the target space, m is the number of classes, the information gain of a feature (t) is measured by the Eq. (2)

$$IG(t) = -\sum_{i=1}^m P_r(c_i)logP_r(c_i) + P_r(t)\sum_{i=1}^m P_r(c_i|t)logP_r(c_i|t) + P_r(\bar{t})\sum_{i=1}^m P_r(c_i|\bar{t})logP_r(c_i|\bar{t}) \tag{2}$$

3.3 ReliefF feature selection

ReliefF is another feature ranking algorithm and has provided better performance for many applications of feature ranking evaluation. The ReliefF method calculates the quality of all the features using the training instances randomly sampled from data. The ReliefF searches for a set of its neighbours from the same class and named as nearest hits. Then searchers are for the k nearest neighbours from each of the different classes named as nearest misses. If a neat hit has a different value for a certain feature, that feature appears is considered irrelevant and the weight of that feature is decreased. If a near miss has a different value, the feature is considered relevant and the weight of that feature is increased. More details of ReliefF can be found from literature [17, 25].

3.4 Boruta feature selection

In Boruta [10] method of feature selection first, a duplicate copies of all the independent variable are made and shuffled. The new set of duplicate variables is known as shadow variable. A random forest classifier is used to find the variable importance. This score is also known as Z score (mean accuracy loss/ standard deviation of accuracy loss). Then a threshold is decided for the Z score (Maximum of the shadow variable to decide the shadow variable) to identify important and not important. The list of the attributes as per the Z score is shown in Table 2. The Boruta is feature selection wrapper algorithm, capable of working with any classification method and indicates the importance measure of the attributes. Boruta is based on Random Forest (Fig. 2).

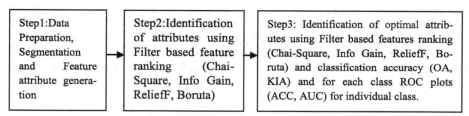

Fig. 2. Workflow for Feature Attribute Identification using OBIA for classification, Object extraction and Accuracy

For classification of the HRSI, all these parameters are not necessary to be taken for analysis. A set of suitable parameters needs to be identified for classification for better performance without hampering the accuracy of classification. For that purpose, the Boruta library as available in R is taken up for identification of a best set of parameters.

No of classes (Tree, Road, Building, Built-up, Grass, Shadow) is taken up as per the observed ground truth. The details of the attributes of the 712 segment (scale: 250, shape: 0.7, compactness: 0.6) features generated using the best set of segment parameters for scale, shape, compactness using the eCognition (Ver 8.3) software. The weights for the scale, color/shape and smoothness/compactness are the same in all the trial cases and bands. There are 50 attributes and these attributes can be grouped into 9 categories. The details of the attributes are shown in Table 1.

SVM has been extensively used in remote sensing as one of non-parametric classification algorithm. In SVM the optimal decision boundary is found for classification between two classes that minimizes the error [23]. The radial basis kernel function was taken up in this study. The SVM is a classifier increasingly popular in remote sensing applications [19]. The radial basis function (RBF) kernel as available in eCognition is taken up for analysis.

The MLR package of R helps in performing machine learning tasks. One can create a task for loading the data. An algorithm can be chosen to learn the tasks from the data and train them. The linear discriminant analysis (LDA) is used for training and prediction. The ACC (assess the quality of the prediction) and AOC (area under the curve) is used to access the quality of the perdition of individual objects or feature class.

R package named MLR, which is absolutely incredible at performing machine learning tasks. This package includes the entire machine learning (ML) algorithms which we use frequently.

4 Results and Analysis

The raking of the features (50 attributes) based on the different algorithms (Information Gain, ReliefF, Chi-Square, Boruta) was done using the R implementations. The raking of the features using different algorithms is shown in Table 2. The feature ranks as generated using Boruta feature analysis is shown in (Fig 3). The classification of the HRSI data (Fig. 4) is done with SVM classifier. The classification with all the attributes is (50 attributes) is shown in (Fig. 5).

Table 1. Object Attribute Category and list of attributes of the dataset.

Feature Category	Number of attributes	Features
Mean Layer	6	MeanLayer1,MeanLayer2,MeanLayer3,Meanlayer4, BrightBrightness, Maxdiff.
Standard deviation	4	StandarddeviationLayer1,StandarddeviationLayer2, StandarddeviationLayer3, StandarddeviationLayer4
Geometry (extent, shape)	6	Aea(Pxl),Length/Width,EllipticFit,Compactness,Roundness,Shapeindex.
Customized	4	NDVI, RVI, NDWI, TotalReflentance.
GLCM Contrast	5	GLCMContrastalldir, GLCM Contrast0, GLCM Contrast45, GLCM Contrast90, GLCM Contrast135.
GLCM Entropy	5	GLCM Entropyalldir, GLCM Entropy0, GLCM Entropy45, GLCM Entropy90, GLCM Entropy135.
GLCM Homogeneity	5	GLCMHomogenietyalldir, GLCMHomogeniety0, GLCMHomogeniety45, GLCMHomogeniety90, GLCMHomogeniety135.
GLCM Mean	5	GLCM Meanalldir, GLCM Mean0, GLCM Mean45, GLCM Mean90, GLCM Mean135.
GLDV Contrast	5	GLDV Contrastalldir, GLDV Contrast0, GLDV Contrast45, GLDV Contrast90, GLDV Contrast135.

Table 2. Feature ranking by different Algorithms (v51 is the class category).

Sl	Object Attributes Rankwise	Bo-ruta	Object Attributes Rankwise	Info Gain	Object Attributes Chi-Sqaure Rankwise	Chi-Square	Object Attributes Rankwise	ReliefF
v1	MeanLayer1	13	MeanLayer1	13	MeanLayer1	13	StandarddevLayer1	17
v2	Totalreflectance	48	Totalreflectance	48	Totalreflectance	48	MeanLayer3	15
v3	Ndvi	45	MeanLayer2	14	Meanlayer2	14	Totalreflectance	48
v4	Rvi	47	MeanLayer3	15	Meanlayer3	15	StandarddevLayer2	18
v5	MeanLayer2	14	Brightness	5	Brightness	5	MeanLayer1	13
v6	StandarddevLayer4	20	MeanLayer4	16	GLCMContrast0	29	MeanLayer2	14
v7	MeanLayer3	15	Ndvi	45	GLDVContrast0	30	Brightness	5
v8	MeanLayer4	16	Rvi	47	GLDVContrast45	22	StandarddevLayer3	19
v9	Brightness	5	Ndwi	46	GLCM Contrast45	32	Ndwi	46
v10	Ndwi	46	StandarddevLayer1	17	GLDVEntropy45	44	Ndvi	45
v11	Maxdiff	34	StandarddevLayer2	18	StandarddeviationLayer2	18	GLDVEntropy45	44
v12	StandarddevLayer1	17	Maxdiff	34	Ndvi	45	Rvi	47
v13	StandarddevLayer2	18	GLCMMeanalldir	11	Rvi	47	MeanLayer4	16
v14	StandarddevLayer3	19	GLCMMean45	6	GLDVContrast90	24	GLCMHomogeneity90	21
v15	GLCMContrast0	29	StandarddevLayer3	19	GLCMContrast90	38	GLCMHomogeneityalldir	43
v16	GLCMMeanalldir	11	GLCMMean90	37	GLCMHomogeneity45	42	GLDVEntropy135	9
v17	GLDVContrast0	30	GLCM Mean0	3	GLDVEntropy90	41	GLDVEntropyalldir	10
v18	GLDVEntropyalldir	10	GLCMMean135	39	GLCMMean135	39	GLCMMean135	39
v19	GLCMMean45	6	GLDVEntropyalldir	10	GLDVContrastalldir	25	Roundness	4
v20	GLCM Mean0	3	GLDVContrastalldir	25	GLCMContrastalldir	35	GLCM Mean0	3
v21	GLCMMean135	39	GLCMContrastalldir	35	MeanLayer4	16	GLDVEntropy0	33
v22	GLDVContrastalldir	25	GLDVEntropy0	33	GLDVEntropyalldir	10	GLCMHomogeneity0	26
v23	GLDVEntropy0	33	GLCMContrast0	29	StandarddevLayer1	17	StandarddevLayer4	20
v24	GLCMContrastalldir	35	GLDVContrast0	30	GLCMHomogeneityalldir	43	GLDVContrast135	1
v25	GLDVContrast90	24	GLDVContrast45	22	GLDVEntropy0	33	GLCMContrast135	49
v26	GLDVContrast45	22	GLCM Contrast45	32	GLCMMeanalldir	11	GLCMMeanalldir	11
v27	GLCMMean90	37	StandarddevLayer4	20	StandarddeviationLayer3	19	GLDVEntropy90	41
v28	GLCM Contrast45	32	GLDVEntropy45	44	Ndwi	46	GLCMMean45	6
v29	GLCMContrast90	38	GLDVContrast90	24	GLCMMean45	6	EllipticFit	40
v30	GLDVEntropy45	44	GLCMContrast90	38	GLCM Mean0	3	Shapeindex	12
v31	GLCMHomogeneityalldir	43	GLCMHomogeneity0	26	GLCMMean90	37	GLCMHomogeneity45	42
v32	GLCMHomogeneity45	42	GLDVContrast135	1	StandarddevLayer4	20	GLCMMean90	37
v33	GLDVEntropy90	43	GLCMContrast135	49	GLCMHomogeneity0	26	GLDVContrast45	22
v34	GLCMHomogeneity0	26	GLCMHomogeneity45	42	Maxdiff	34	GLCM Contrast45	32
v35	GLDVEntropy135	9	GLCMHomogeneity90	21	GLDVEntropy135	9	Maxdiff	34
v36	GLCMHomogeneity90	21	GLDVEntropy90	41	GLDVContrast135	1	GLCMContrast0	29
v37	GLDVContrast135	1	GLCMHomogeneityalldir	43	GLCMContrast135	49	GLDVContrast0	30
v38	GLCMContrast135	49	GLCMEntropyall dir	8	GLCMHomogeneity90	21	GLDVContrastalldir	25
v39	GLCMEntropyall dir	8	GLCMEntropy45	23	AreaPxl	2	GLCMContrastalldir	35
v40	GLDVContrast45	23	GLDVEntropy135	9	GLCMEntropy135	27	LengthWidth	28
v41	AreaPxl	2	AreaPxl	2	GLCMEntropy45	23	GLCMHomogeneity135	31
v42	GLCMEntropy90	36	GLCMEntropy135	27	GLCMEntropy90	36	Compactness	7
v43	GLCMEntropy0	50	GLCMEntropy90	36	GLCMHomogeneity135	31	GLDVContrast90	24
v44	GLCMEntropy135	27	GLCMEntropy0	50	GLCMEntropy0	50	GLCMContrast90	38
v45	GLCMHomogeneity135	31	GLCMHomogeneity135	31	GLCMEntropyall dir	8	AreaPxl	2
v46	LengthWidth	28	Shapeindex	12	Shapeindex	12	GLCMEntropy0	50
v47	Shapeindex	12	LengthWidth	28	LengthWidth	28	GLCMEntropy45	23
v48	EllipticFit	40	Roundness	4	Roundness	4	GLCMEntropy90	36
v49	Compactness	7	EllipticFit	40	EllipticFit	40	GLCMEntropy135	27
v50	Roundness	4	Compactness	7	Compactness	7	GLCMEntropyall dir	8

Table 3. SVM Classification with different features and with different algorithms.

SL	Algorithm	No of Features	SVM(OA%)	SVM(KIA)
1	Boruta	15	0.843	0.805
2	ReliefF	15	0.843	0.805
3	Info-gain	20	0.823	0.779
4	Chi Square	41	0.802	0.753
		All Features (50)	0.802	0.753

Table 4. Algorithms and the best identified features

SL	Borura (15 Parameters)	ReliefF (15 Parameters)	Info-gain (20 Parameters)
1	MeanLayer1 MeanLayer2 MeanLayer3 MeanLayer4 Brightness Maxdiff	MeanLayer1 MeanLayer2 MeanLayer3 MeanLayer4 Brightness	MeanLayer1 MeanLayer2 MeanLayer3 MeanLayer4 Brightness Maxdiff
2	StandarddeviationLayer1 StandarddeviationLayer2 StandarddeviationLayer3 StandarddeviationLayer4	StandarddeviationLayer1 StandarddeviationLayer2 StandarddeviationLayer3	StandarddeviationLayer1 StandarddeviationLayer2 StandarddeviationLayer3
3	NDVI RVI (NIR/R) NDWI TotalReflectance (R+G+B)	NDVI RVI (NIR/R) NDWI Total Reflectance (R+G+B)	NDVI RVI (NIR/R) NDWI
4	GLCM Contrast0	GLDVentropy45 GLCM homogeneity 90 GLCM homogenityalldir	GLCM Mean0 GLCM Mean45 GLCM Mean90 GLCM Mean135 GLCMMeanalldir GLDVEntropyalldir GLDVContrastalldir
5			Roundness

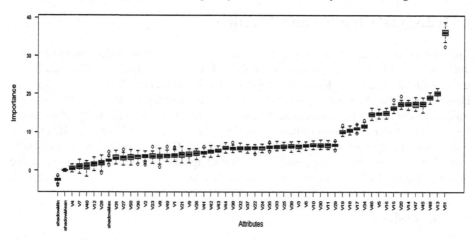

Fig. 3. Boruta Analysis for identification of important attributes.

5   SVM classification with reduced set of attributes

Classification using SVM and different set of object attributes as generated using Information Gain, Chi-Square, ReliefF and Boruta algorithm is carried out in a SVM Classifier. The accuracy results (Overall Accuracy (OA) and Kappa Index of Agreement (KIA)) of the classification as found with 50 attributes and limited set of parameters with different attributes as per rank and algorithm is shown below in Table 3. The classification with all the attributes is shown in (Fig. 5). The result of SVM classification with top 15 attributes as identified in Boruta Feature Ranking is shown in (Fig. 6). The result of SVM classification with top 15 attributes as identified in ReliefF Feature Ranking is shown in (Fig. 7). The result of SVM classification with top 20 attributes as identified in information Gain Feature Ranking is shown in (Fig. 8). The Chi-Square method (Fig. 9) needs a larger set of attributes (41 attributes) to achieve accuracy similar to that of all the 50 attributes. For other algorithms, the accuracy parameters are higher with a limited smaller set of attributes. The best classification is achieved through the Boruta feature selection algorithm with 15 attributes. The overall classification accuracy is achieved is 84.5% with 15 attributes. This accuracy achieved is higher than the accuracy achieved with all the attributes (80.2%). The KIA is also higher in case of the smaller set (80.5%). The ReliefF has also generated a similar accuracy. The reduced set of features are limited to mean reflectance, standard-deviation of layers and one texture values in case of Boruta feature analysis. In case of ReliefF three texture attributes are ranked higher (GLDVetropy45, GLCMHomogenity90 and GLCMHomegenityalldir). Features are better classified in case of Boruta feature analysis.

6 Individual Class Feature detection

The data set was reassigned with identified class as the foreground class and rest of the attributes are taken as background. Then the ML analysis is done for identification of the classification and the ROC Curve for the foreground class. With R programming language and the MLR package the task was built to describe the data and the model is trained on the complete dataset. The data set was reassigned with identified class as the foreground class and rest of the attributes are taken as background. Then the ML analysis is done for identification of the classification and the ROC Curve for the foreground class. With R programming language and the MLR package the task was built to describe the data and the model is trained on the complete dataset.

7 Discussions

It has been demonstrated that OBIA based classification leads to a higher classification accuracy in case of high-resolution satellite images. But each object has numerous attributes related to spatial, spectral, textural, contextual properties. An effective set of these attributes also needs to be identified for achieving better classification accuracy and fast computations.

Out of the 50 attributes as identified for the image, the SVM classification achieves a better classification accuracy using the Boruta and reliefF feature selection techniques using only 15 features. The Boruta algorithm has identified six mean layers, four standard deviation of layers, four customized and one texture property GLCM Contrast0 properties as shown in Tables 2 and 4. The reliefF has identified five mean layers, three standard deviation of layers, four customized and three texture property (GLDVentropy45, GLCM homogeneity 90, GLCM homogenityalldir). ReliefF has not identified, Maxdiff, Standard deviation layer4 and GLCM Contrast 0) as identified by Boruta. Information gain feature selection needs 20 attributes to achieve a greater accuracy than all features. The additional seven texture features that are identified in case of information gain algorithm are GLCM Mean0, GLCM Mean45, GLCM Mean90, GLCM Mean135, GLCM Meanalldir, GLDVEntropyalldir, GLDVContrastalldir along with six mean layer, three standard deviation, four customized properties. Thus it leads to a conclusion that the parameters like standard deviation of layer 4, GLCM Contrast0, GLDVentropy45, GLCM homogeneity 90, GLCM homogenityalldir which are part of minimum set (15 paprmeters) leads to higher classification accuracy along with the common parameters as shown in SL no 1 and 2 of Table 4. In fact as the imagery belongs to urban area and full of manmade features and the textural features, are good in identifying the distinction between the classes like building, roads and trees. The standard deviation of layer4 also got a good priority in case of Boruta feature analysis. This analysis also in line with the fact that for the SVM classifier, 10-20 input features generally produce the best result [15].

The Chi-Square algorithm needs higher number of features to achieve the accuracy higher than all the features. Thus it is not identified as a suitable feature selector.

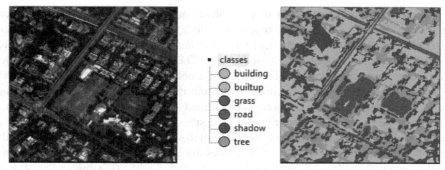

Fig. 4. Original Image of the Study Area

Fig. 5. Classification with all 50 attributes

Fig. 6. Classification with 15 Attributes (Boruta)

Fig. 7. Classification with 15 Attributes (ReliefF)

Fig. 8. Classification with 20 Attributes (InfoGain)

Fig. 9. Classification with 41 Attributes (Chi-quare)

It was observed that a smaller set of attributes are sufficient for an image classification. But to identify an individual object or a single class type, much literatures are not available. An approach for using the ROC curve analysis for the object feature as foreground and other classes as background is tried. The ranked features are again analysed with foreground and background classes with the help of the linear discriminate analysis of the ranked features by the algorithms (feature ranking) as indicated above. During the feature identification process only an identified set of features are taken an absolute number of items. The ROC for the fitted classifier, ACC and AUC for the feature is recorded in Fig. 10. The accuracy achieved with the minimal set of attributes and all the attributes are also shown in Fig. 10. The trees are identified better using the info gain analysis with 10 attributes. The roads are best identified with 10 features as per Boruta algorithm. Grass is identified by top 8 Chi Square ranked features. The shadow is identified by top 20 Boruta features. The built-up areas are identified by top 15 features. It is observed that the Boruta identifies the individual features with minimal set of feature attributes and with greater accuracy for shadow, grass, road and built-up cases. In case of tree features the ACC and AOC of limited set of attributes are almost matching with all the attributes in case of info gain. It is not higher as in other cases. It might be because of the low distinction between tree and shadow. One ROC plot for tree feature with 50 attributes and 25 attributes is shown in Fig. 11.

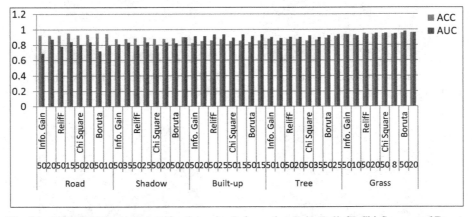

Fig. 10. Individual Feature Identification using Information Gain, ReliefF, Chi-Square and Boruta Method with ACC and AUC from ROC Curve

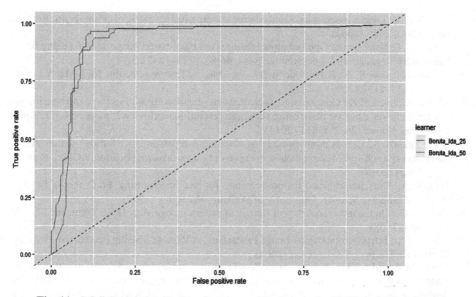

Fig. 11. ROC Curve plot for Tree features and background with 50 and 25 attributes

8 Conclusion

In this study, filter-based feature selection algorithms like Information Gain, Chi Square, ReliefF and the random forest based Boruta feature selection algorithm were tested for the data set. The additional use of Boruta feature selection algorithm is the special feature of this paper. The analysis of accuracy was better in Boruta and Information gain based algorithms. The highest classification accuracy is achieved with a smaller set of attributes. Further, individual feature identification was also done using the same data set with one as the identified feature (foreground) and rest as background using the identified feature selection algorithm. Then, the linear discriminate analysis (LDA) is used as a classification algorithm. The analysis indicates that, the Boruta produces a better classification of individual features (objects) with better accuracy for a smaller set of attributes. This can also be treated as object extraction. For OBIA analysis, the feature selection using the above machine learning techniques should be done as a pre-processing step for identification of most relevant features for getting fast and better classification accuracy. The current methodology is based on, one classifier like SVM in case of classification and one classifier for identifying the individual features. Multiple classifier algorithms and ensemble machine learning algorithms can also be experimented.

References

1. Baatz, M., Schape, A.: Multi resolution segmentation: an optimization approach for high quality multi scale image segmentation. Angew. Geogr. Informations Verarb. **12**, 12–23 (2000)

2. Blaschke, T.: Object based image analysis for remote sensing. ISPRS J. Photogram. Remote Sens. **65**(1), 2–16 (2001)
3. Colkesen, I.: Selection of Optimal object features in object-based image analysis using filter-based algorithms. Jo. Ind. Soc. Remote Sens. **46**(8), 1233–1242 (2018)
4. Guyon, I., Elisseeff, A.: An introduction to variable and feature selection. In: J. Mach. Learn. Res. **3**, 1157–1182 (2003)
5. Ghosh, A., Joshi, P. K.: Comparison of selected classification algorithms for mapping bamboo patches in lower gangetic plain using very high resolution worldview2 imagery. Int. J. Appl. Earth Obs. Geoinf, **26**, 298-311 (2014)
6. S. Georganos, S.: Less is more: optimizing classification performance through feature selection in a very-high-resolution remote sensing object-based urban application. J.GISci. Remote Sens. **55**(2) (2018)
7. Hall, M.A.: Correlation-based feature selection for machine learning. Ph.D. thesis. Department of Computer Science, University of Waikato, Hamilton. (1999)
8. Hughes, G.: On the mean accuracy of statistical pattern recognizers. IEEE Trans. Inf. Theory **14**, 55-63 (1968)
9. Jensen, J.R.: Introductory Digital Image Processing: A Remote Sensing Perspective, 3rd edn. PrenticeHall, Upper Saddle River (2004)
10. Kursa, M.B.: R Package 'Boruta'. https://cran.r-project.org/web/packages/Boruta/Boruta.pdf
11. Lang., S.: Object-based image analysis for remote sensing applications: modeling reality—dealing with complexity. In: Blaschke, T., Lang, S., Hay, G.J. (eds.) Object-Based Image Analysis. Lecture Notes in Geoinformation and Cartography, pp. 3–27. Springer, Heidelberg (2008). https://doi.org/10.1007/978-3-540-77058-9_1
12. Laliberttea, A.S.: A compearision of three feature selection methods for object-based classification of sub-decimenter resolution UltraCam-L imagery. Int. J. Appl. Earth Observ. Geoinf. **15**, 70-78 (2012)
13. Liu, C.: A new feature selection method based on a validity index of feature subset. Patt. Recogn. Lett. **92**, 1-8 (2017)
14. Li, M.C.: A systematic comparison of different object-based classification techniques using high spatial resolution imagery in agricultural environments. Int. J. Appl. Earth Observ. Geoinf. **49**, 87–98 (2016)
15. Ma., L.: Evaluation of feature selection methods for object-based land cover mapping of unmanned aerial vehicle imagery using random forest and support vector machine classifiers. ISPRS Int. J. Geo-Inf. **6**, 51 (2017)
16. Ma, L.: A review of supervised object-based land-cover image classification. ISPRS J. Photogram. Remote Sens. **130**, 277–293 (2017)
17. Maxion, R.A., Roberts, R.R.: Proper use of ROC curves in intrusion/Anomaly detection proper use of ROC Curves in intrusion. Technical report series, School of Computing Science, University of Newcastle, UK (2004).
18. Ma. L.: Training set size scale, and features in Geographic Object-Based Image Analysis of very high resolution unmanned aerial vehicle imagery. ISPRS J. Photogram. Remote Sens. **102**, 14–27 (2015)
19. Otukei, J.R., Blaschke, T.: Land cover change assessment using decision trees, support vector machines and maximum likelihood classification algorithms. Int. J. Appl. Earth Obs. Geoinf. **12**(1), S27–S31 (2010)
20. Rajbhandari, S.: Leveraging machine learning to extend Ontology-Driven Geographic Object-Based Image Analysis (O-GEOBIA): a case study in forest-type mapping, Remote Sens. **11**, 503 (2019)
21. Rmezall, M., Pradhan, B.: Correlation-based feature optimization and object-based approach for distinguishing shallow and deep-seated landslides using high resolution airborne laser scanning data. IOP Conf. Ser.: Earth Environ. Sci. **169**, 012048 (2018)

22. Talavera, L.: An evaluation of filter and wrapper methods for feature selection in categorical clustering. In: Famili, A.F., Kok, J.N., Peña, J.M., Siebes, A., Feelders, A. (eds.) Advances in Intelligent Data Analysis VI. IDA 2005. Lecture Notes in Computer Science, vol. 3646, pp. 440–451. Springer, Berlin (2005). https://doi.org/10.1007/11552253_40
23. Vapnik, V.N.: The Nature of Statistical Learning Theory. Springer, New York (1995). https://doi.org/10.1007/978-1-4757-2440-0
24. Witten, I.H.: Data Mining: Practical Machine Learning Tools and Techniques, 3rd edn. Morgan Kaufmann, Burlington (2011)
25. Wu, B.: A comparative evaluation of filter-based feature selection methods for hyper spectral band selection. Int. J. Remote Sens. **34**(22), 7974-7990 (2013)
26. Yang, Y., Pedersen, I.O.: A comparative study on feature selection in text categorization, In: Proceedings of the Fourteenth International Conference on Machine Learning, Nashville, Tennessee, USA, 8-12 July (1997)
27. Suresh, M., Kamal Jain, K.: Calorimetry-based edge preservation approach for color image enhancement, In. J. Appl. Remote Sens **10**(3), 035011 (2016). https://doi.org/10.1117/1.JRS.10.035011
28. Saboori, M., Homayouni, S., Shah-Hosseini, R., Zhang, Y.: Optimum feature and classifier selection for accurate urban land use/cover mapping from very high resolution satellite imagery. Remote Sens. **14**, 2097 (2022). https://doi.org/10.3390/rs14092097

xDFPAD: Explainable Tabular Deep Learning for Fingerprint Presentation Attack Detection

Shaik Dastagiri[1], Kongara Sireesh[2], and Ram Prakash Sharma[3]([✉])

[1] Leegality, Gurgaon, India
[2] Cleveland State University, Cleveland, USA
[3] National Institute of Technology Hamirpur, Hamirpur, India
ram.psharma28@gmail.com

Abstract. Security of fingerprint authentication system is compromised when they are exposed to the Presentation Attacks (PAs). To detect these PAs under any attack conditions, an efficient Fingerprint Presentation Attack Detection (FPAD) technique is required. This work presents an explainable deep learning based FPAD (xDFPAD) method to prevent any possible PAs using any novel Presentation Attack Instrument (PAI). Our proposed method will use a tabular deep learning model called Tab-Net for the detection of PAs using the fingerprint quality feature based tabular data. This method combines the benefits of quality feature based FPAD solutions with the deep learning to make it white-box instead of its intrinsic block-box nature. Our proposed deep learning based TabNet model provides instance wise explainable reasoning of the output results. Performance of the method is tested on the LivDet 2017 competition database. Results indicates that our method is able to perform significantly better than the existing techniques for realistic unknown sensor or material attacks conditions. Also, our method provide the benefit of instance wise explanation of the predicted class which is not provided by the existing block-box deep learning solutions.

Keywords: Fingerprint · Presentation Attacks · Explainability · TabNet

1 Introduction

Authentication using the fingerprints is a widely used biometric authentication technology due to their unique characteristics which make them stand out as a reliable, high performing, and efficient biometric solution. The cost of fingerprint recognition technology has also reduced significantly over the years, which made its accessibility to a wide range of applications i.e., attendance systems, banking, border control, criminal investigation, personal identity etc. This increasing use of fingerprint recognition system also increases the possibility of various security concerns. One of the possible security threat is the vulnerability

H. Kaur et al. (Eds.): CVIP 2023, CCIS 2010, pp. 252–262, 2024.
https://doi.org/10.1007/978-3-031-58174-8_22

of fingerprint recognition systems to Presentation Attacks (PAs), also known as spoofing attacks. In PAs, an attacker presents a fake fingerprint made of different Presentation Attack Instruments (PAIs) to obtain unauthorized access. These PAIs include a variety of materials, including rubber, silicone, playdoh, latex, and even 3D-printer to fabricate the artificial replica of an genuine fingerprint. To protect fingerprint-based recognition systems from PAs, an efficient Presentation Attack Detection (PAD) module is required. These PAD methods are categorized in hardware and software based techniques. The hardware based methods involve analysing the physical properties of the spoof fingerprint, such as its reflectance, surface roughness, or temperature, to identify anomalies that may indicate the presence of a spoof/fake fingerprint impression. Software based methods utilizes various techniques to detect the authenticity of a fingerprint, such as analyzing the texture, curvature, and minutiae of the fingerprint etc. Software based methods also involve using machine learning and deep learning based algorithms to analyse the live and fake fingerprint's visual appearance and to identify spoof fingerprints. In this work, we will be proposing a software based solution for the PAD in fingerprint recognition systems.

The existing software based solutions for the PAD are based on handcrafted feature [1,11–13] or deep learning techniques [4,5,19]. Despite the high performance of majority of the existing deep learning models, it doesn't provide an explainable solution to justify the predicted results. In this work, we have proposed an explainable model for the detection of PAs in the fingerprint recognition systems. We are using an attentive interpretable deep learning model called TabNet for the PAD in fingerprint systems. TabNet model takes the traditional tabular features as input to the model instead of images as required by the deep learning models. We have extracted 9 fingerprint quality features which plays an important role in examining the intrinsic properties of fingerprint images. These features are fed to the TabNet model in which the extracted features are passed through the different layers. The trained model outputs the predicted class (live or fake) and feature importance for each instance encountered to the trained model. Our model uses the sequential attention mechanism which enable it to select most important features at each decision step, thus, providing explanation of each decision provided by the model.

2   Related Work

This section provides a brief study of some of the well known software based PAD solutions. Use of deep learning model in the fingerprint PAD models is initially done by Nogueira et al. [6]. They have extracted features with two different techniques in which one of them was using deep convolution network with random weights and another one with LBP technique. In results, they have observed improvement of over 35% as compared with previously published traditional techniques. Following the new trend of deep learning, Wang et al. [16], have used a voting strategy based Deep Convolution Neural Network (DCNN). Their method was also able to perform better than handcraft feature based techniques. Park et al. [10] have proposed a patch based CNN approach in which majority voting approach is followed to classify the fingerprint images as live or fake. Another similar patch based voting approach using the score level fusion of patches is proposed by Toosi et al. [14]. Jung et al. [8] proposed a new CNN model which doesn't uses the fully connected layers but employs squared regression error for each receptive field. This modified CNN architecture improves the performance for the task of fingerprint PAD. Zhang et al. [19] has presented a lightweight CNN model called Slim-ResCNN consisting of stack of series of improved residual block. These blocks provides an advantage of avoiding the overfitting problem and takes less processing time as compared with traditional CNN based FPAD systems. Their method achieves the best performance on fingerprint liveness detection competition 2017 databases and also improves the performance of PAD on older LivDet databases. In 2020, Uliyan et al. [15] have proposed the use of Discriminative Restricted Boltzmann Machines to recognize bonafied fingerprints against the fingerprint fabricated with various spoof materials such as playdoh, latex, woodglue etc. Zhang et al. [18] have proposed FLDNet which is a lightweight and efficient network architecture to enhance the generalization ability and reduce the complexity of the PAD model. Their designed model is compact and also improves the performance of the detection of PAs. Zhang et al. [17] have proposed a study where fingerprint matching score is fused with the fingerprint liveness score. Matching score is computed using Octantal Nearest-Neighborhood Structure (ONNS) and liveness score using the modified Residual Network (Slim-ResCNN). The approach for fingerprint spoof detection proposed by Anusha et al. [2] provides evaluations on cross sensor and cross material databases. In their study they have used global and local feature descriptors computed using DenseNet which improves the performance for cross sensor, material, and data-set scenarios using the proposed algorithm. They have also proposed a novel attention network to locate most discriminative patches in identification of bonafied presentation or imposter presentation.

3   Proposed Work

The explainable deep learning solution proposed in this work utilizes tabular features to detect the PAs. This enable our proposed method to combine the benefits of the traditional feature based approaches and deep learning methods. In this work, we are exploring the benefits of using fingerprint quality features as input to TabNet [3] which is a feature based deep learning model. The overall flow diagram of the approach is shown in Fig. 1. Our approach works in two different modules, (i) extraction of quality features from both the training and testing sets, and (ii) training the tabular data driven deep learning model TabNet. The trained TabNet model is used for classification of testing data-set features in live and fake classes. In the first module, both the training and testing data-set are fed to the block-wise feature extraction unit. In this unit, after segmenting the foreground of the fingerprint image, block-wise features are extracted which are later aggregated to obtain a single feature value for a fingerprint image. This block-wise feature extraction is done for all the features considered in this work.

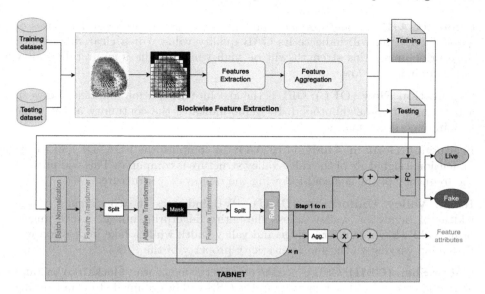

Fig. 1. Schematic diagram of proposed explainable FPAD.

After successfully executing the module one of the proposed framework, we will get both the training and testing data-sets feature files containing all features of each and every individual fingerprint image. The training file is then fed to the TabNet encoder network. The TabNet process the input file through Batch Normalization (BN), feature transformer, and then through the multi-step unit containing the attentive transformer, feature transformer, attention mask, and ReLU. The output of the multi-step unit is ensembled and passed to the Fully Connected (FC) layer which acts as a classifier for the testing data-set features file. Attention mask of the network provides instance wise feature attribute mask. The ensembling property of the TabNet model provides a robust and efficient decision. Description of various internal modules of xDFPAD are provided below.

3.1   Quality Feature Extraction

Training of the TabNet model requires tabular feature data. In this study, we have considered the most efficient fingerprint quality based features for the detection of PAs using TabNet. The quality features considered in this work are extracted from the fingerprint images using Olsen et al. [9]. All the features are computed in a block wise manner. A brief information of the extracted features are provided below to understand and decode the output results of the proposed method using the significance of each feature.

Orientation Certainty Level (OCL): OCL indicates the magnitude of the energy concentration along the primary ridge flow orientation in different blocks of the fingerprint image.

Gabor (GAB): Strength of the standard deviation of pixel-wise responses of gabor filter bank will indicate its GAB quality value. For a clear ridge valley fingerprint image this strength will be high while for the unclear ridge-valley structure it will be low.

Orientation Flow (OFL): OFL is the absolute orientation difference between a block and its 8-neighborhood. Its value indicates the continuity of the ridge flow in fingerprint images.

Frequency Domain Analysis (FDA): To compute the FDA, DFT of the 1-dimensional signature of the ridge-valley structure is computed. This will provide the frequency of the sinusoid following the ridge-valley structure.

Ridge Valley Uniformity (RVU): RVU indicates the consistency of the widths of ridges and valley across the entire fingerprint image. A live fingerprint will be having uniform ridge and valley width while a fake impression will be having varying width due to elasticity property of the PAIs.

Gabor Shen (GSH): GSH is used to classify the fingerprint blocks into bad and good quality classes. The final value of the GSH will be obtained after subtracting ratio of number of foreground blocks and the number of poor quality foreground blocks marked as poor from 1.

Standard Deviation (SD): This feature provides the standard deviation of the grayscale pixel values in the input image.

Mean (M): The mean indicates the arithmetic mean of the grayscale pixel values of the input image.

Local Clarity Score(LCS): The LCS feature will represent the clarity of ridges and valleys. It will be computed by applying linear regression to get a grey-level threshold for identifying pixels as ridge or valley.

3.2   TabNet: An Explainable Deep Learning Model

TabNet [3] is a deep learning model developed by Google research for tabular data. It is an extension of the attention mechanism, which was originally introduced in natural language processing tasks and has since been applied to a wide range of machine learning tasks. TabNet is designed to handle tabular data, which consists of rows and columns of data, similar to a spreadsheet. It is particularly well-suited for tasks such as regression and classification, where the goal is to predict a target variable based on a set of input features. One key feature of TabNet is its attention mechanism, which allows the model to automatically learn which features are most important for the task at hand. This is done by assigning different weights to each feature, based on how much the model thinks they contribute to the final prediction. The attention mechanism is implemented using a self-attention layer, which takes in the input features and calculates the importance of each feature using a set of learnable parameters. Another key feature of TabNet is its ability to handle categorical variables, which are variables that can have a limited number of values. These variables are often found in tabular data and can be difficult to model using traditional machine learning methods. TabNet is able to handle categorical variables by representing them as embeddings, which are low-dimensional vectors that capture the relationships between different categories.

TabNet also includes a feature selection mechanism, which allows the model to automatically select the most important features for the problem to be solved. This helps to reduce the number of input features and makes the model more efficient, as well as improves the interpret-ability of the model. TabNet is a powerful tool for working with tabular data and has shown strong performance on a range of tasks. It is particularly useful for tasks where interpretability and feature selection are important, as well as for handling categorical variables.

TabNet Encoder Architecture: The architecture of TabNet for encoding tabular features data is provide in Fig. 1. The TabNet encoder architecture works in a supervised learning approach for the classification of data. The architecture of TabNet encoder consists of sequential multi-steps where output of one step is passed to the another step as an input. In the first step of encoder, the raw data-set containing the features is passed to the model without any feature engineering. This raw data is provided to the Batch Normalization (BN) layer, which normalizes the various feature values in the data-set. The output of the BN layer is passed to the feature transformer unit as input. Encoding of the tabnet is based on the sequential multi-step processing with N_{steps} decision steps. Task of the feature transformer and all subsequent units of TabNet encoder is provided below.

Feature transformer: Feature transformer is a 4 layers network in which 2 are shared across all the decision steps and 2 are decision independent. Each layer have a Fully Connected (FC) layer, Batch Normalization layer, and Gated Linear Unit (GLU) which is then connected to a normalized residual connection with normalization. Normalization value of $\sqrt{0.5}$ is used as it helps to stabilize the learning by avoiding any sudden change is variance throughout the network.

Attentive Transformer: Attentive transformer is a single layer block which contains a FC layer, BN layer with prior scale information. Prior scale information is used to know how much each feature has been used till the current decision step. Finally sparse max layer is used for normalization of the coefficient which results in the sparse selection of most important features.

Attention Mask: In each sequential multi-step, output from the Attentive transformer is fed as input to the Attention mask. This mask provides explainable information about the most important features based on the model's functionality. All the sequential multi-step masks can be aggregated to obtain global feature importance attribute.

4   Experimental Results

Table 1. Database description of LivDet 2017

| Database | LivDet 2017 | | | | | |
| | Train | | | Test | | |
	Live	Spoof	Materials	Live	Spoof	Materials
Digital Persona	999	1199	Wood Glue, Body Double, Ecoflex	1700	2028	Gelatin, Liquid Ecoflex, Latex
GreenBit	1000	1200	Wood Glue, Body Double, Ecoflex	1700	2040	Gelatin, Liquid Ecoflex, Latex
Orcanthus	1000	1200	Wood Glue, Body Double, Ecoflex	1700	2018	Gelatin, Liquid Ecoflex, Latex

Experimental evaluations of the proposed xDFPAD are performed on publically available liveness detection competition database of 2017 (LivDet 2017). This database is composed of three different data-sets captured with Digital persona, GreenBit, and Orcanthus sensor. All the three data-sets are divided in separate fixed training and testing sets. The fake samples of the training and testing sets are captured with different PAIs to observe the effectiveness of the PAD models on unknown PAIs attacks. The overall composition of the LivDet 2017 database is provided in the Table 1. Some sample fingerprint images of live and fake class (Gelatin, Latex, and Liquid Ecoflex) are shown in Fig. 2.

Fig. 2. Sample live and fake (Gelatin, Latex, and Liquid Ecoflex-left to right) fingerprint images from Digital Person sensor of LivDet 2017.

4.1   Evaluation Protocol:

The performance of the xDFPAD is tested using the ISO/IEC 30107-3:2023 [7] standards. In particular, two parameters, Attack Presentation Classification Error Rate (APCER) and Bonafied Presentation Classification Error Rate (BPCER) are used to evaluate the proposed PAD method performance. Here, APCER is the rate of attack presentation which are wrongly classified as bonafied presentation while BPCER is the bonafied presentations which are wrongly classified as attack presentation. The average performance of the model is represented using the Average Classification Error (ACE) rate which is the average of APCER and BPCER.

4.2   Baseline Results on LivDet 2017

The baseline results are obtained using the predefined training and testing set provided in all the three data-sets of the LivDet 2017. The results of all three data-sets are reported in Table 2. Our model achieved APCER of 8.72 and BPCER of 15.17 for the Digital Persona sensor of LivDet 2017. The (APCER, BPCER) value for GreenBit and Orcanthus sensor is (5.93, 11.05) and (14.71, 12.05). The ACE for all three sensor Digital Persona, Green Bit, and Orcanthus sensor is 11.66, 8.26, and 13.50, respectively.

Table 2. Results of TabNet model on LivDet 2017 database.

Sensor	APCER	BPCER	ACE
Digital Persona	8.72	15.17	11.66
GreenBit	5.93	11.05	8.26
Orcanthus	14.71	12.05	13.50

4.3   Cross-Sensor Evaluations

We have also investigated performance of our proposed method under the cross-sensor attacks. In these evaluation, we have trained the model using the training set of one specific sensor and tested the sensor specific trained model with the testing data-set of other (except the training sensor) sensors. Table 3 provides the cross-sensor attack evaluation results. The results indicated in table shows that our proposed xDFPAD model is able to achieve good performance even for the unknown sensor attack scenarios. This performance achievement of our model indicates that our method is capable of detecting any sensor attacks irrespective of whether it has been already seen during the training or not.

Table 3. Cross sensor evaluation results on LivDet 2017 database

Training Sensors	Testing Sensor	APCER	BPCER	ACE
Digital Persona	GreenBit	24.11	20.11	22.29
Digital Persona	Orcanthus	30.42	18.88	25.14
GreenBit	Digital Persona	5.12	39.82	20.94
GreenBit	Orcanthus	13.23	62.52	35.77
Orcanthus	Digital Persona	2.76	66.76	31.94
Orcanthus	GreenBit	29.65	29.23	29.46

Table 4. Comparative study of baseline results on LivDet 2017.

Various methods	Orcanthus	DigitalPersona	GreenBit	Average
Slim-ResCNN [5, 17]	6.07	7.11	4.80	5.99
FSB [4,5]	5.49	4.88	3.32	5.56
ResNet-50+SVM [1]	9.84	9.13	12.89	10.62
VGG-19+SVM [1]	12.71	19.41	12.70	14.94
Proposed method	13.50	11.66	8.26	11.14

Table 5. Comparative study of cross-sensor results on LivDet 2017 database.

Training (Testing)	Slim-ResCNN [5,17]	FSB [4,5]	ResNet-50+SVM [1]	VGG-19+SVM [1]	Proposed approach
Digital Persona (GreenBit)	12.10	10.46	–	–	22.29
Digital Persona (Orcanthus)	55.70	50.68	–	–	25.14
GreenBit (Digital Persona)	19.61	10.63	30.33	37.85	20.94
GreenBit (Orcanthus)	56.02	50.57	–	–	35.77
Orcanthus (Digital Persona)	31.70	42.01	52.77	34.71	31.94
Orcanthus (GreenBit)	31.18	30.07	44.16	40.49	29.46
Average	34.38	32.40	42.12	37.68	27.59

4.4   Comparative Analysis

The results obtained by our proposed approach are compared with some state-of-art methods. We have compared our method in both the baseline attack and cross-sensor attack conditions. The baseline comparative analysis of the performance of proposed method is provided in Table 4 while the cross sensor performance comparison is provided in Table 5. The performance of our proposed method is comparable or better for the baseline attack conditions where a sensor specific attacks are required to be detected. In case of realistic conditions of cross-sensor attacks, our method preforms significantly much better as compared with any other existing methods in literature. This property of our method clearly indicates that it will be best to use our proposed method in the real world cases of attacks where the intruder can use any sensor or material to subvert the authentication module of the recognition system.

4.5   Instance-Wise Attentive Feature Importance

The attentive transformer unit at each step in the TabNet model provides the feature importance for each instance presented to the trained TabNet model. Feature importance masks generated from the three steps of the model are provided in Fig. 3. This figure shows the instance wise importance of each feature in the overall decision at each step. Brighter blocks in the figure represents more importance of a particular feature while the darker blocks represents less importance. For example, in Mask 0, for image number 1, feature number 5 (GSH) and 6 (STD) have highest importance in detecting the live or fake class of the image. This feature importance masks is further refined in the future steps based on the feedback provided from the previous steps.

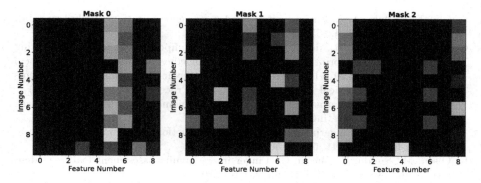

Fig. 3. Feature importance masks of 10 random images of Digital Persona sensor in different decision steps. Brighter blocks represents more importance while the darker blocks represents less importance of feature in the decision process. X-axis refers to the feature number (order is as mentioned in Sect. 3.1, OCL-0 to LCS-8) while the Y-axis refers to the sample image number from 0 to 9.

5   Conclusion

We have presented an explainable deep learning based technique for the detection of PAs in the fingerprint recognition systems. Our proposed tabular deep learning solution takes handcrafted features as input which converts our proposed method in an explainable solution rater than a non-explainable block-box solution. The model is based on TabNet which provides an attentive instance wise feature based learning. The results obtained on LivDet 2017 exhibits that our model is able to operate well in the realistic conditions of PAs where any sensor or material can be utilized to deceive the security provided by the authentication system. This work is a preliminary study in combining the inherently explainable nature of feature based technique and performance of deep learning techniques. In future, we would like to improve and extend this study for other possible realistic attack scenarios to further enhance the security of the existing fingerprint based authentication systems.

References

1. Agarwal, S., Rattani, A., Chowdary, C.R.: A comparative study on handcrafted features v/s deep features for open-set fingerprint liveness detection. Pattern Recogn. Lett. **147**, 34–40 (2021)
2. Anusha, B., Banerjee, S., Chaudhuri, S.: DeFraudNet:End2End fingerprint spoof detection using patch level attention. In: 2020 IEEE Winter Conference on Applications of Computer Vision (WACV), pp. 2684–2693 (2020)
3. Arik, S., Pfister, T.: TabNet: attentive interpretable tabular learning. In: AAAI Conference on Artificial Intelligence, vol. 35, pp. 6679–6687 (2019)
4. Chugh, T., Cao, K., Jain, A.K.: Fingerprint spoof buster: use of minutiae-centered patches. IEEE Trans. Inf. Forensics Secur. **13**(9), 2190–2202 (2018)

5. Chugh, T., Jain, A.K.: Fingerprint spoof detector generalization. IEEE Trans. Inf. Forensics Secur. **16**, 42–55 (2021)
6. Frassetto Nogueira, R., de Alencar Lotufo, R., Campos Machado, R.: Evaluating software-based fingerprint liveness detection using convolutional networks and local binary patterns. In: 2014 IEEE Workshop on Biometric Measurements and Systems for Security and Medical Applications (BIOMS) Proceedings, pp. 22–29 (2014)
7. ISO/IEC3010-3: Information technology – biometric presentation attack detection—part 3: Testing and reporting (2023)
8. Jung, H., Heo, Y.: Fingerprint liveness map construction using convolutional neural network. Electron. Lett. **54**(9), 564–566 (2018)
9. Olsen, M., Šmida, V., Busch, C.: Finger image quality assessment features - definitions and evaluation. IET Biometrics **5** (2016)
10. Park, E., Kim, W., Li, Q., Kim, J., Kim, H.: Fingerprint liveness detection using CNN features of random sample patches. In: 2016 International Conference of the Biometrics Special Interest Group (BIOSIG), pp. 1–4 (2016)
11. Sharma, R.P., Anshul, A., Jha, A., Dey, S.: Investigating fingerprint quality features for liveness detection. In: Purushothama, B.R., Thenkanidiyoor, V., Prasath, R., Vanga, O. (eds.) MIKE 2019. LNCS, vol. 11987, pp. 296–307. Springer, Cham (2020). https://doi.org/10.1007/978-3-030-66187-8
12. Sharma, R., Dey, S.: Fingerprint liveness detection using local quality features. Vis. Comput. **35**, 1393–1410 (2019)
13. Sharma, R., Dey, S.: A comparative study of handcrafted local texture descriptors for fingerprint liveness detection under real world scenarios. Multimed. Tools Appl. **80**, 9993–10012 (2021)
14. Toosi, A., Cumani, S., Bottino, A.: CNN patch-based voting for fingerprint liveness detection. In: International Joint Conference on Computational Intelligence (2017)
15. Uliyan, D.M., Sadeghi, S., Jalab, H.A.: Anti-spoofing method for fingerprint recognition using patch based deep learning machine. Int. J. Eng. Sci. Technol. **23**(2), 264–273 (2020)
16. Wang, C., Li, K., Wu, Z., Zhao, Q.: A DCNN based fingerprint liveness detection algorithm with voting strategy. In: Yang, J., Yang, J., Sun, Z., Shan, S., Zheng, W., Feng, J. (eds.) Biometric Recognition, pp. 241–249 (2015)
17. Zhang, Y., Gao, C., Pan, S., Li, Z., Xu, Y., Qiu, H.: A score-level fusion of fingerprint matching with fingerprint liveness detection. IEEE Access **8**, 183391–183400 (2020)
18. Zhang, Y., Pan, S., Zhan, X., Li, Z., Gao, M., Gao, C.: FLDNet: light dense CNN for fingerprint liveness detection. IEEE Access **8**, 84141–84152 (2020)
19. Zhang, Y., Shi, D., Zhan, X., Cao, D., Zhu, K., Li, Z.: Slim-ResCNN: a deep residual convolutional neural network for fingerprint liveness detection. IEEE Access **7**, 91476–91487 (2019)

Gaze Classification on Redacted Videos

Shubham Chitnis[1], Bhismadev Chakrabarti[2], and Sharat Chandran[1(✉)]

[1] Indian Institute of Technology Bombay, Mumbai, India
{190020033,sharat}@iitb.ac.in
[2] University of Reading, Reading, UK
b.chakrabarti@reading.ac.uk

Abstract. Videos have become prevalent, and a dominant mode of communication and consumption, providing *rich content*. On the other hand, stemming from privacy considerations, the process of redaction masks prominent individuals, or conversely the background, and *conceals* information. These two concepts takes us in opposing directions. In this work we highlight the importance of feature preserving face redaction in videos in the context of behavioral analysis.

Specifically, we consider a well known non-verbal assessment method commonly used in studying the development of young children. Several pairs of social and nonsocial videos are presented on a mobile device, and using the front camera, the proportion of gaze directed to the social videos are analyzed. Can a redacted video taken by the care-giving parent sent to a server be automatically analyzed without identifying the child? We answer this question in the affirmative – gaze classification can be done with about equal, significantly high accuracy for both the redacted and the original, non-redacted video.

1 Introduction

Redaction refers to the process of hiding sensitive information present in a photograph in order to preserve privacy. Sensitive information can be present in the foreground or the background of the image. An example of the redaction of the foreground is the face redaction problem which aims to hide the identities of the subjects present in the videos. There are several ways in which the faces can be redacted, e.g., by blurring, pixelating, or blackening out multiple faces, swapping the face with the face of another person, or overlaying a mesh of facial landmarks. Example modalities are demonstrated in Fig. 1.

What useful information can be conveyed by redacted images? For this we turn to the difficult problem of quantifying child behavior when confronted with social stimuli. In a typical task paradigm two competing social and non-social stimuli—one of each type—are simultaneously presented while participants' gaze is tracked [13]. Studies have demonstrated that typically developing children and adults gaze longer [3] at social than non-social stimuli and show that social

---

Please see our acknowledgements of support.

H. Kaur et al. (Eds.): CVIP 2023, CCIS 2010, pp. 263–277, 2024.
https://doi.org/10.1007/978-3-031-58174-8_23

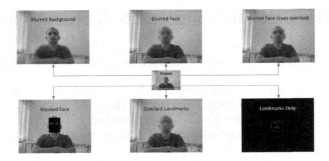

Fig. 1. Example redaction modalities. At one extreme only landmarks are provided, whereas in others, simple Gaussian blurring has been used. See Table 2 for results from this paper.

stimuli are the more likely to be fixated first. Neurotypical individuals thus seem to assign greater reward value to social stimuli.

The tedious part in the experiments is of course gaze classification, and is often done in the laboratory. Gaze refers to the direction in which an individual is looking and focusing at, in an application running on a computer. The subject looking at the screen is captured in the form of a video. The gaze is then classified as Left or Right (termed Two-Way classification in this paper, Fig. 2). Note that the Left and Right gaze labels are the subject's left and right orientation.

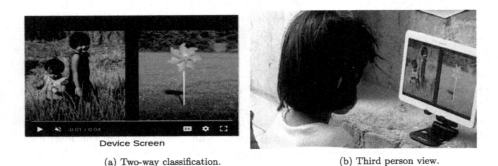

(a) Two-way classification.   (b) Third person view.

Fig. 2. In the Two-Way Classification task, the subject looks at various social and non-social shown on the device screen. The images are from a live, in-the-wild experiment conducted at Nottingham.

Gaze classification becomes more difficult when the video capture is done on casual devices such as a mobile phone or a tablet. Nevertheless, gaze classification has been reported to be automatically performed with potentially reasonable accuracy using methods such as the eye-tracking work in [8]. In this work we are not seized with the idea of improving the accuracy, rather, the scientific problem addressed is "How can we do gaze classification on redacted videos?" In this paper, we resolve the above problem. To establish this claim, we need relevant data that is described in the next section.

1.1 Ground Truth in the Lab

For the purpose of ground truth, an Android app [12] was created. The app randomly displays objects in the left, middle and right regions of the screen, one at a time, as shown in Fig. 3. The subject's gaze is expected to be directed to the different regions while the front camera records the face of the subject. More details of this dataset appear in Sect. 2.3.

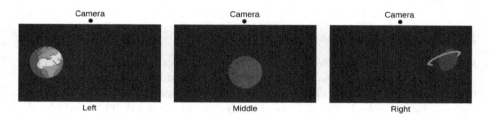

Fig. 3. Our custom app [12] that provides stimuli and is used to capture ground truth. See Sect. 2.3 for details.

1.2 In-the-wild Data

Data was collected in Nottingham as the first preliminary part [5] of the START Project. See Fig. 2 for an example. More details of this dataset appear in Sect. 2.3.

1.3 Contributions

We outline our major contributions here. Up until now, it was not clear if gaze classification can be done with redacted data. At first glance, this seems to be quite difficult. We settle this matter in this paper. In particular:

1. We demonstrate the utility of a face redacted dataset by performing several experiments and ablation studies for gaze classification using 200 videos (around 0.4 million images) present in the ground truth dataset collected in the lab. Specifically, we achieve a classification accuracy of 96% with both redacted and unredacted data. This shows that redaction doesn't hamper the model performance provided eyes are given as input.

2. With respect to the in-the-wild data, after manual annotation to establish ground truth, we show that our approach to gaze classification works equally well on face redacted data as it does on the unredacted data. We test our approach on the uncurated Nottingham data collected and achieve a classification accuracy of 93% with redacted faces.

The rest of this paper is as follows. First in Sect. 2 we survey various methods that are likely to be useful in the creation of the redacted data in the first place. We settle on Retina face [4] after detailed investigations. We also describe our dataset in more detail in this section. Next, in Sect. 3 we discuss our method and follow up with results in Sect. 4 where we present our findings, including various ablation studies that shows the utility of our method. We conclude in the final section.

1.4   Related Work

Most of the work related to redaction is oblivious to the gaze, and is primarily intended for applications such as surveillance. The survey paper [16] gives the broad overview of the problem. In particular, a video database is envisaged which is being probed. The objects of interest is then defined. This could be the principal actor in a frame, or all the persons in the frame, or even objects such as noticeboards. Object identification is carried out using typical deep learning methods such as You Only Look Once (YOLO) [15]. Next, the type of obfuscation is defined (examples are shown in Fig. 1). The database is then made available publicly. However as mentioned in [1] "even a modest goal of 95% recall with 95% precision remain beyond the reach of any current algorithm". Therefore [1] focuses on using a team of human workers to identify areas to be identified as blurred, i.e., the object detection is done manually. The approach in our paper is *different* in that we prefer to work with off-the-shelf detectors since our use case is in the two-way classification task. In [6], the opposite scenario is considered, namely, reconstruction of the identities from blurred faces using deep learning methods. Because we can work with blackened faces (albeit with eyes) (see Sect. 4) the premise of the counter attack on redaction does not apply.

Considerable work has been done in using gaze for gaming and for virtual reality applications. For example [2] uses prototype privacy preserving gaze estimation. However, the work is in a limited context since the paper uses synthetic images, and that too, of eyes only to demonstrate their work. EyeKeys [11] is a system that was developed to control computers using eyes. For example, a wink could signify an action such as a mouse click. The focus of the work is not redaction. Similarly [17] uses the GazeCapture [8] database to build an appearance based method for gaze regression. Our work is similar, except that our focus is on showing the results on redacted images. *Thus we see that largely the problem of gaze classification using redacted images has not got the attention it deserves.*

2   Background

In this section, we provide the background to lay the basis for our methods. First, in order to redact an image, one has to decide the foreground portion, which, in our case of gaze classification, are the eyes. There are a plethora of face detection algorithms starting from the erstwhile Viola-Jones [18] face detector, and recent deep-learning based detectors. We embark on the journey of finding a suitable face detector for the task at hand.

Next, in a subsequent subsection, we need a method of quantifying gaze classification results, and here we briefly describe as a baseline, the gaze regressor from [8].

Finally in the last subsection we provide more details of the dataset used since data forms the corner pin of deep learning algorithms.

2.1   Face Detector Comparisons

Figure 4 compares the precision-recall curves of various detectors. Note that the ground truth face bounding boxes were manually annotated in 20 two-way classification videos. The results and the precision-recall curves are obtained on this subset containing 53,217 frames. From these results, it can be seen that Dual Shot Face Detector (DSFD) [9] works the best on our dataset, with the highest Average Precision (AP) score at various Interseciton over Union (IoU) thresholds. Other detectors like Retina Face [4], Single Shot Scale-invariant Face Detector (S3FD) [10], and Light and Fast Face Detector (LFFD) [7] are competitive with DSFD, and at a reasonable Intersection over Union (IoU) threshold of 0.5 or 0.6, the difference in Average Precision (AP) scores is not very significant. But the YOLOv5 Face detector [14] performs the worst among all. A reasonable explanation could be that all others are dedicated face detectors with dedicated pipelines for face detection, whereas YOLOv5 Face is just an extension of the YOLOv5 object detector.

Out of all detectors used, DSFD is the slowest (Fig. 5), as expected from the study of its architecture. It has a 2-stage pipeline, namely Original Feature Shot and Enhance Feature Shot which increases the runtime of DSFD. On the other hand, YOLOv5 Face and LFFD are the fastest detectors and can be used for real-time face detection applications. For an effective accuracy-speed trade-off, Retina Face is an excellent detector. So for all extractions in our experiments, we used the Retina Face detector.

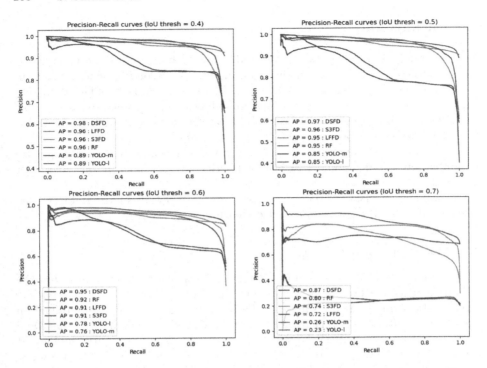

Fig. 4. Comparison of the accuracy of various, recent face detectors to determine choice of detector.

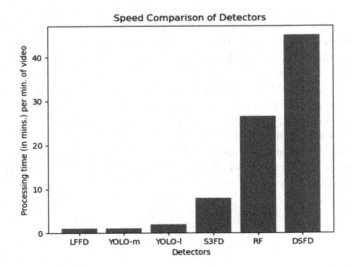

Fig. 5. Computational speed of the various detectors mentioned in Sect. 2.1.

2.2   Baseline Gaze Detection

The ITracker Neural Network proposed in [8] is a deep convolutional neural network (CNN) that takes the face, crops of the eye and a face grid as inputs and predicts the XY gaze coordinates on the screen w.r.t. the camera as output. The X-coordinate and Y-coordinate axes are oriented rightwards and upwards, respectively, with the camera located at the origin of this reference frame. The camera location is an important factor in the device specifications because the gaze of the subject (either XY coordinates or gaze classes) are defined w.r.t. the camera. In the case of XY coordinate regression, the origin is defined at the camera location, and in the case of gaze classification, the divisions of the screen region are assigned taking into consideration the location of the camera. We leverage this model for our purposes of classification of gaze by replacing the final XY gaze regression layer with a gaze classification layer to output the gaze class labels.

2.3   Details of Datasets

In each of the datasets described below, careful attention is made to ensure that subjects in the 'train' subset do not appear in the 'test' subset.

Reading Dataset. This dataset (termed Reading Dataset) was collected at the University of Reading from an Android app [12] created at IIT Bombay. The app displays objects in the left, middle and right regions of the screen, one at a time, as shown in Fig. 3. The subject is asked to keep track of the object as it appears on the screen in different regions while the front camera records the face of the subject. The objects appear in the left, right and middle regions for a fixed duration of 3, 3 and 2 s, respectively, which helps in obtaining the ground truth gaze labels. This pattern repeats for 16 cycles resulting in a video recording of around 128 s. The cue to look at left, or right is at random, from the point of view of the subject.

Fig. 6. Examples of subjects using our app to collect ground truth data for the Reading dataset.

The device used for the collection of data is Huawei MediaPad M3 Lite 10 tablet. The camera in this device is located at the center of the long edge of the screen.

The dataset contains 23 different subjects (samples shown in Fig. 6), each performing the task several times at different locations and in different lighting conditions, poses, etc. By discarding the frames with "middle" as the ground truth, we obtain a curated dataset with well separated left and right regions. In this sense, we do not consider this data to be "in-the-wild". The resulting dataset has about 200 videos with a total of 0.4 million image frames which are split into the train, validation and test in a ratio of approximately 7:1:2.

Nottingham Dataset. The Nottingham dataset is created with the Two-Way classification task being performed by children in Nottingham as a part of the START Project [5]. The app displays a social and a non-social video clip simultaneously on the screen; one displayed on the left and the other on the right side of the screen, randomly, as shown in Fig. 2. By recording the face and gazes, this task gauges the social preference of the children.

This data was manually annotated. It contains one of the two class labels (Left or Right) for each image frame. The device used for the collection of data is Samsung Note 10 SM P600 tablet (also referred to as *START device* here onwards). It has different dimensions compared to the one used to collect the Reading dataset, and the camera in this device is located at an offset of 2 cm towards the left from the center of the long edge of the screen.

The dataset contains 11 videos, in which the children perform the Two-way Classification task. It contains a total of around 8,000 frames which are split into the train, validation and test in a ratio of approximately 7:1:2.

3   Methodology

In this section, we outline the method used to justify our contributions.

As part of the study, we work with data collected in two contrasting settings. The Reading dataset comprises of 23 students looking at objects randomly displayed on the device for pre-decided intervals. Although, the data is measured in a lab setting, we allow for variations in the lighting and subject's posture to diversify the training data. The lab setting and the choice of students enables ground truth. In the second Nottingham data, we ask children to carry out the Two-way classification task and annotate the generated videos manually for ground truth. There is less control over the subjects and the capturing conditions making this our "in-the-wild" dataset.

Our investigation of the data captured above started with a survey of numerous face detection systems available for the purpose of redacting the faces. We justified our choice of detector with two criteria: model performance (using precision-recall curves) and detection speed. Using the preferred detector, we are able to extract and process face landmarks and bounding boxes for our video data. This and our ground truth labels form the dataset that we further use for gaze analysis. We pose gaze as a two-way classification problem with the subject either looking to the left or the right of the screen. We base our convolutional neural architecture on the ITracker regression network used to track gaze coordinates. The relevant questions we ask are:

1. Can we use the baseline neural net regression model [8] for classification using the dimensions of the device? In other words, is this model truly "gaze tracking for everyone" as stated in the title of the paper? The answers (Table 1 and

Table 3) turns out to be less than satisfying since the classification results are about chance.

2. Can we use the data collected from [8]) and adopt a transfer learning approach for classification? Will this work on redacted data? The results (Table 2 and Table 4) in this paper is that yes, it does work!

Note that our results work on uncurated data collected in Nottingham. In the following section, we explain our training setup, obtained results, and ablation studies in more detail.

4   Results

Results are reported in multiple subsections below.

4.1   Extraction and Training Details

We used Retina Face [4] for the detection and extraction of face and eye crops for each frame in the Reading and the Nottingham dataset. For the extraction of around 0.4 million frames present in the Reading dataset, Retina Face takes around 37 h and for 8,000 frames present in the START Nottingham data, Retina Face takes around 30 min at an extraction rate of around 4 frames/s.

The classification model takes a training time of around 5.3 h per epoch on the "train" split of the Reading dataset. In order to reduce the training time, we trained on 2.5% subset resulting in around 1.2 h for 10 epochs.

For training the classification model, we use the cross-entropy loss function with the Stochastic Gradient Descent (SGD) algorithm. We used a batch size of 100 for training purposes, which consumes approximately 3.5 GB memory on NVIDIA GeForce GTX 980 Ti GPU. We trained the models with a learning rate of 0.001, a momentum of 0.9 and a weight decay of 0.0001.

4.2   Baseline Classification

Since the baseline regression model outputs XY gaze coordinates, it is easy to perform a classification of the regressed coordinates into gaze classes according to the device screen dimensions and camera location. This method is the most straightforward way for classification, given a regression model.

Table 1. The regression model provided in [8] does no better than chance. We need something more.

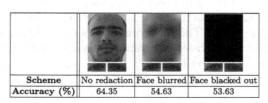

Scheme	No redaction	Face blurred	Face blacked out
Accuracy (%)	64.35	54.63	53.63

Table 1 shows that the method of classification post-regression does not work accurately for classification, and the regression model under-performs on the classification task. A possible explanation for this is the non-generalizability of the regression model due to domain shift in data distribution (note that the regression model is trained on data collected by MIT on iPhones/iPads, whereas testing is done on the Reading data collected on the Huawei MediaPad).

4.3   Transfer Learning

We need to tune the regression model on the Reading data to adapt to the data distribution shift between the data on which the regression model is trained and data on which Two-Way classification is targeted. We train (i.e., tune) the model on a subset of the Two-Way Reading data (2.5% of the "train" set containing 7,195 frames). This helps to make the training faster as well as check if the model is able to fit properly with a small amount of data.

Table 2. Transfer learning results in the model successfully able to work with both unreadacted and redacted videos.

Scheme	No redaction	Face blurred	Black Face	Black Eyes	Dummy eyes
Accuracy (%)	96.77	96.78	96.75	74.93	75.63

The results in Table 2 show that our proposed tuning model is as accurate on redacted faces as a model on unredacted faces. We also perform ablation studies by redacting the eyes with different variations instead of the face in order to decide if we really need to provide eye crops in our face redacted dataset (i.e., to check the accuracy of possible approaches a client would use with our dataset if we don't provide eye crops). The above results clearly demonstrate that eye crops are important for gaze classification, and the model is able to learn to focus on eye crops.

4.4   Gaze Classification on Uncurated Data

The Reading dataset is a curated dataset that is collected by the data collection app [12]. it is important to test our approach on the in-the-wild dataset. In this direction, we test our methods on the "test" set of the Nottingham dataset (containing 1,585 frames). The following subsections demonstrate the experiments performed on this dataset (containing 11 videos with approximately 8,000 frames) for gaze preserving redaction.

Baseline. Similar to the classification-post-regression method adopted earlier, we perform the procedure on the output of the base regression model. Note that, unlike the device used in Reading, the device used (see Fig. 7) in Nottingham has its camera at an offset of 2 cm towards the left of the center of the long edge of the device. So the demarcation for left and right gaze labels for this device does not go through the optical center of the camera.

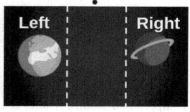

(a) Two-Way Stimuli for in-the-wild data collection.   (b) Device used in University of Reading for ground truth.

Fig. 7. Contrast between Nottingham stimuli and ground truth stimuli in the Reading data. Note the approximate location of the camera shown with a black dot.

The results shown in Table 3 for classification without transfer learning show results consistent with Table 1. This further strengthens our argument that the method of post-classification does not work accurately for classification, and the regression model under performs on the classification task due to the non-generalizability of the regression model arising because of the domain shift in data distribution.

Table 3. The regression model provided in [8] is unsuitable in that results are similar to chance (although if the data is not redacted, we get better results).

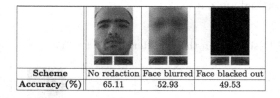

Scheme	No redaction	Face blurred	Face blacked out
Accuracy (%)	65.11	52.93	49.53

Second Transfer Learning. As before we tune the regression model on the Nottingham data. Note that we train (i.e., tune) the model on a subset of Nottingham data (i.e., 10% of the "train" set containing 554 frames) to check the effectiveness of tuning the model with a small amount of data. This helps to make the training faster, check if the model is able to fit properly with a small amount of data, and make a fair comparison with the tuning results on the Two-Way app-based data presented in Sect. 4.3.

Table 4. Our method works on in-the-wild data as well.

Scheme	No redaction	Face blurred	Face blacked out
Accuracy (%)	93.94	94.07	93.94

As compared to tuning results on the Reading data (Table 2), the tuning results on the Nottingham data (Table 4) are approximately 2–3% lower since the Nottingham videos are in-the-wild videos as compared to the well-curated filtered Two-Way Reading data. But the overall accuracy results show that our gaze preserving face redaction approach works well on the Nottingham data as well.

4.5   Ablation: Alternate Testing Paradigm

Figure 7 shows the differences between the device used in Nottingham and the Reading device. The camera is located at an offset of 2 cm towards left from the center, as opposed to the camera located at the center of the device in Reading. Since the Reading data is conceptually different from the Nottingham data, it is imperative that we train the model on the Reading data, and test it on the Nottingham data. This also helps in inferring the generalizing potential with respect to variability in the subject's age. In this part, we tune the baseline regression model on the Reading data and directly, that is without further tuning, test it on the Nottingham data.

Table 5. Classifier on in-the-wild data when trained on app driven data.

Scheme	No redaction	Face blurred	Face blacked out
Accuracy (%)	93.12	93.00	93.00

Device Independence. The result in the Table 5 establishes an important result that the classifier trained by tuning the model on a particular device is device-independent (given the devices are not wildly different in terms of the screen size and camera location) and generalizes well enough to yield accuracy above 93%. This is contrary to the behavior of the baseline regression model, which does not seem to generalize well to other devices (as seen in Table 1 and Table 3).

Achieving Higher Accuracy. As showcased above, we are able to generalize well across datasets that aren't poles apart in terms of their device setup. We can take another step further and fine-tune the previously trained model on 10% of the Nottingham train data. It is observed that we get an accuracy bump of another 2–3% doing this (Table 6). Our performance is also better than when we just perform fine-tuning on START data, meaning that the additional training data from Reading helps.

Table 6. Results when we fine tune on 2.5% of the train set of the Reading data, followed by a subsequent fine tuning on 10% of the in-the-wild data, and test on 100% of the test subset of the in-the-wild Nottingham data.

Scheme	No redaction	Face blurred
Accuracy (%)	95.77	95.84

5   Conclusion and Future Work

Videos have become the lingua franca of modern communication, but in the nature of the media, sometimes reveal more information than is needed. Redaction is the process of concealing private information. In this paper we demonstrate gaze classification can be done with redacted videos.

Specifically we have collected for the purposes of gaze classification ground truth data using a specialized self-created Android app. Using this app, we can tell when a subject looked at a social stimuli, or a non-social stimuli with confidence. We redacted the videos of 23 subjects using this app, and we were able to predict the gaze with an accuracy comparable to that of unredacted videos.

We also performed a similar experiment on a novel in-the-wild data collected on children in Nottingham for the two-way classification task. This task is often administered in understanding social preferences of young children. Our results on this in-the-wild data are comparable to that of the curated data set.

In all cases, our accuracy was over 93%. We conclude that it is possible to both conceal information, and reveal significant relevant information.

In this work, we discuss a particular aspect of face redaction in videos for gaze classification. It will be interesting to consider alternate modalities and other computer vision tasks on redacted videos.

Acknowledgements. The START consortium project was supported by Medical Research Council, UK (MR/PO23894/1). START Consortium members are listed here in alphabetical order: Bhismadev Chakrabarti, Debarati Mukherjee, Gauri Divan, Georgia Lockwood-Estrin, Indu Dubey, Jayashree Dasgupta, Mark Johnson, Matthew Belmonte, Rahul Bishain, Sharat Chandran, Sheffali Gulati, Supriya Bhavnani, Teodora Gliga, Vikram Patel.

Special thanks to Aditya Modi who developed the app on which the Reading dataset was collected, Rachel Sanders for collecting the data in Reading, Rahul Bishain who wrote the first version of the gaze classifier code based on the iTracker codebase, and Abhinav Kumar who wrote the second version, and the section on the face detector comparisons (and declined to be a co-author).

References

1. Alshaibani, A., Carrell, S., Tseng, L.H., Shin, J., Quinn, A.: Privacy-preserving face redaction using crowdsourcing. In: Proceedings of the AAAI Conference on Human Computation and Crowdsourcing, vol. 8, pp. 13–22 (2020)
2. Bozkir, E., Ünal, A.B., Akgün, M., Kasneci, E., Pfeifer, N.: Privacy preserving gaze estimation using synthetic images via a randomized encoding based framework. In: ACM Symposium on Eye Tracking Research and Applications, pp. 1–5 (2020)
3. Chakrabarti, B., Haffey, A., Canzano, L., Taylor, C.P., McSorley, E.: Individual differences in responsivity to social rewards: insights from two eye-tracking tasks. PLOS ONE (2017)
4. Deng, J., Guo, J., Ververas, E., Kotsia, I., Zafeiriou, S.: Retinaface: single-shot multi-level face localisation in the wild. In: Proceedings of the IEEE/CVF Conference on Computer Vision and Pattern Recognition (CVPR), pp. 5203–5212 (2020)
5. Dubey, I., et al.: Quantifying preference for social stimuli in young children using two tasks on a mobile platform. PLOS ONE **17**(6) (2022)
6. Hao, H., Güera, D., Horváth, J., Reibman, A.R., Delp, E.J.: Robustness analysis of face obscuration. In: 2020 15th IEEE International Conference on Automatic Face and Gesture Recognition (FG 2020), pp. 176–183. IEEE (2020)
7. He, Y., Xu, D., Wu, L., Jian, M., Xiang, S., Pan, C.: LFFD: a light and fast face detector for edge devices (2019). https://doi.org/10.48550/ARXIV.1904.10633
8. Krafka, K., et al.: Eye tracking for everyone. In: Proceedings of the IEEE Conference on Computer Vision and Pattern Recognition (CVPR), pp. 2176–2184 (2016)
9. Li, J., et al.: DSFD: dual shot face detector. In: Proceedings of the IEEE/CVF Conference on Computer Vision and Pattern Recognition (CVPR), pp. 5060–5069 (2019)
10. Liu, W., et al.: S3FD: single shot scale-invariant face detector. In: Proceedings of IEEE International Conference on Computer Vision (ICCV) (2017)
11. Magee, J.J., Scott, M.R., Waber, B.N., Betke, M.: EyeKeys: a real-time vision interface based on gaze detection from a low-grade video camera. In: 2004 Conference on Computer Vision and Pattern Recognition Workshop, pp. 159–159. IEEE (2004)

12. Modi, A., Bishain, R., Chandran, S.: Experimenting gaze detection on mobile (android) devices. CS-691 Course Project (2019). https://github.com/AdiModi96/Gaze-Catcher

13. Pierce, K., Conant, D., Hazin, R., Stoner, R., Desmond, J.: Preference for geometric patterns early in life as a risk factor for autism. Arch. Gen. Psychiatry **69**(1), 101–109 (2011)

14. Qi, D., Tan, W., Yao, Q., Liu, J.: Yolov5 face: why reinventing a face detector. arXiv:2105.12931v2 (2021)

15. Redmon, J., Divvala, S., Girshick, R., Farhadi, A.: You only look once: unified, real-time object detection. In: Proceedings of the IEEE Conference on Computer Vision and Pattern Recognition, pp. 779–788 (2016)

16. Sah, S., Shringi, A., Ptucha, R., Burry, A., Loce, R.: Video redaction: a survey and comparison of enabling technologies. J. Electron. Imaging **26**(5), 051406–051406 (2017)

17. Sharma, J., Campbell, J., Ansell, P., Beavers, J., O'Dowd, C.: Towards hardware-agnostic gaze-trackers. arXiv preprint arXiv:2010.05123 (2020)

18. Viola, P., Jones, M.J.: Robust real-time face detection. Int. J. Comput. Vis. **57**, 137–154 (2004)

Drug Recommendation System for Cancer Patients Using XAI: A Traceability Perspective

Plavani Sahoo[1], Dasari Prashanth Naidu[1], Mullapudi Venkata Sai Samartha[1],
Shantilata Palei[1], Biswajit Jena[2], and Sanjay Saxena[1(✉)]

[1] International Institute of Information Technology, Bhubaneswar 751003, Odisha, India
sanjay@iiit-bh.ac.in
[2] Institute of Technical Education and Research, SOA University, Bhubaneswar 751030,
Odisha, India

Abstract. Implementing Artificial Intelligence (AI) in cancer drug recommendations holds promise for advancing personalized cancer therapy. However, a key challenge faced by current AI-based drug recommendations is their lack of transparency, which hinders understanding and trust among doctors and patients. Explainable Artificial Intelligence (XAI) is a research field dedicated to designing AI systems that provide transparent explanations for their decisions. XAI addresses the black-box nature of many AI models, aiding in humans' interpretation of internal workings and decision-making processes. This paper presents a modular approach that combines XAI techniques with a drug recommendation system based on cancer omics data. The primary objective of this approach is to offer transparent and interpretable drug recommendations specifically tailored to precision oncology. By leveraging the traceability perspective, our proposed methodology enhances the explainability of drug recommendations, thereby improving their accuracy, reliability, and trustworthiness. By incorporating XAI techniques, this research aims to bridge the gap between AI-based drug recommendations and the understanding of clinicians and patients. The traceability rate, a metric indicating the proportion of recommendations accompanied by explainable justifications, achieved a rate of 59.24%. A total of 70,211 drug recommendation predictions were made, with associated probabilities available for 41,593 predictions. The results of this study demonstrate the successful integration of cancer omics data and XAI techniques, effectively enhancing the transparency and interpretability of AI-driven drug recommendations in cancer research. This advancement contributes significantly to precision oncology by enabling informed decision-making and fostering trust in AI-based drug recommendations.

Keywords: Drug Recommendation · Explainable AI · Knowledge Graph · Multistep Prediction Model · Explainability · Reinforcement Learning

1 Introduction

Cancer has been the world's top cause of death in the past few years. Personalized cancer therapy has the potential to improve patient outcomes [1]. AI can recommend drugs, but current systems are black boxes [2, 3]. In our study, we propose an explainable AI

H. Kaur et al. (Eds.): CVIP 2023, CCIS 2010, pp. 278–287, 2024.
https://doi.org/10.1007/978-3-031-58174-8_24

drug recommendation inference approach that leverages cancer omics data for precision oncology [4]. Our system is based on a traceability perspective that enables transparent and auditable tracking of the decision-making process, thereby enhancing the interpretability and trustworthiness of the AI model. This model can improve the translation of cancer omics data [5, 6] into clinical decision-making and patient outcomes.

The primary purpose of the above work is to emphasize the importance of creating AI systems for recommending explainable cancer drugs. The motivation for this study stems from the urgent requirement for explainability in AI-driven drug recommendations for cancer treatment. Although existing AI models can effectively predict drug recommendations, their decision-making processes resemble black boxes, creating a challenge in gaining the trust of clinicians and patients [7, 8]. Recognizing that AI algorithms often face challenges related to their black-box nature, especially in critical domains like healthcare, we aim to bridge this gap [21, 22]. The primary objective is to propose utilizing Explainable Artificial Intelligence (XAI) techniques [23, 24]. By leveraging XAI, we seek to provide transparent and interpretable explanations for the drug recommendations generated by AI algorithms [25]. We focus on enhancing our understanding of how these algorithms analyze and interpret cancer omics data. Ultimately, we strive to empower healthcare professionals and researchers with actionable insights, enabling them to make informed decisions and enhance patient care within cancer treatment.

Our contribution to this study:

- Assess the suggested framework using a real-life dataset comprising individuals diagnosed with cancer.
- Demonstrate that implementing Explainable AI in drug recommendation models can provide accurate and explainable results.
- Discuss the implications of the XAI framework for developing personalized cancer therapy.

Our paper is organized into various sections. The literature survey is explained in Sect. 2, and Datasets and methodology give an insight into the materials and methods in Sect. 3. Section 4 shows the results, the discussion is explained in Sect. 5, and the Conclusion is described in Sect. 6.

2   Literature Survey

The most relevant paper used for our study reference is Cancer omic data based explainable AI drug recommendation inference: A traceability perspective for explainability, Xi et al. [4] established a traceability-based XAI framework for cancer drug recommendation. The paper established a traceability-based XAI framework for cancer drug recommendation. While going through the literature, we can conclude that there has been substantial comparison with various existing models [2, 3]. And conclude that the proposed framework can potentially improve people's trust and reliability on AI-based cancer drug recommendation systems [20]. Gogleva et al. [9] introduced the knowledge graph early for medical purposes and found that KG-Rec could identify genes involved in EGFRi resistance with high accuracy. Link prediction in complex networks, applied in drug discovery, was proposed by Abbas et al. [10] argue that network link prediction can identify potential drug targets and drug-cell interactions, which can help accelerate the drug discovery process. Genomics of drug sensitivity in cancer (GDSC): a resource for therapeutic biomarker discovery in cancer cells, was proposed by Yang et al. [6]. The data preparation was performed meticulously in the paper and is a pivotal part of the work. Bayesian network meta- analysis of the efficacy of targeted therapies and chemotherapy for treating triple- negative breast cancer, Chen et al. [11] presented a Bayesian network meta-analysis that evaluates the effectiveness of targeted therapies for treating breast cancer. Importance of interpretability and visualization in machine learning for applications in medicine and health care. Vellido et al. [3] highlighted the significance of interpretability and visualization in machine learning models. How much can deep learning improve the prediction of the responses to drugs in cancer cell lines Chen et al. [12] investigated the potential of deep learning to enhance drug response prediction in cancer cell lines, providing insights into the predictive capabilities of these models. In a genome-wide association study of Alzheimer's disease using random forests and enrichment analysis, Zou et al. [13] utilized random forests and enrichment analysis in a genome-wide association study to investigate the genetic factors associated with Alzheimer's disease. Improving drug response prediction by integrating multiple data sources: matrix factorization, kernel, and network-based approaches, Paltun et al. [14] focused on enhancing drug response prediction by integrating multiple data sources and employing matrix factorization, kernel methods, and network-based approaches to improve the accuracy and reliability of predictions. Explainable Artificial Intelligence (XAI) approaches and deep meta-learning models, Daglarli et al. [15] highlighted the importance of interpretability in deep learning models. They discussed how XAI approaches can enhance the transparency and explainability of these complex models. After studying the papers, we get some limitations. We try to overcome those issues through our work.

3 Methodology

3.1 The Datasets

The data sets used for our study were obtained from The Cancer Cell Line Encyclopaedia (CCLE) [5] and Genomics of Drug Sensitivity in Cancer (GDSC) [6]. They provide researchers with comprehensive genomic and pharmacological data for diverse cancer cell lines. This resource aids in identifying potential biomarkers of drug sensitivity, understanding drug mechanisms, and guiding personalized cancer treatment development. Our study used four types of data: Copy Number Alteration Data (1039 cell lines × 1026 genes), Mutation Data (716 cell lines × 217 genes), DNA Hypermethylation Data (332 cell lines × 109 genes), DrugInteraction Data (991 samples × 531 genes), and Drug Sensitivity Data (1002 cell lines × 268 samples) [4].

The Cancer Cell Line Encyclopedia (CCLE) is an extensive compilation of genetic and pharmacological data related to diverse cancer cell lines. It is a valuable resource aiding cancer research and the exploration of new drugs. The CCLE project characterized and analysed over 1,000 cancer cell lines derived from various tissue origins. The CCLE dataset provides essential information such as gene expression, copy number variations, mutations, and drug sensitivity for each cancer cell line, contributing to the comprehension of diverse biomarkers. GDSC, which stands for Genomics of Drug Sensitivity in Cancer, signifies a collaborative initiative seeking to comprehend the genetic elements influencing the response of cancer cells to different anti-cancer medications. By integrating genomic and pharmacological data, the GDSC project aims to identify genetic markers and molecular characteristics associated with drug sensitivity or resistance in specific cancer types. This understanding aids researchers in gaining deeper insights into the mechanisms of action of anti-cancer drugs and facilitates the development of more specific and effective treatment strategies.

3.2 Methods

The data sets were available in CSV (Comma separated value) format in n-by-m matrix format [14]. We used Pandas data frames to extract the data from them. We achieve our source data to extend our work by integrating these five data sets (Copy Number Alteration Data, Mutation Data, DNA Hypermethylation Data, Drug Interaction Data, and Drug Sensitivity Data). The methodology implemented in the code combines copy number alteration (CNA) data, interaction data, methylation data, drug response data and mutation data to predict drug sensitivity in cell lines. The process entails combining and preparing the copy number alteration (CNA) data, creating bipartite graphs for CNA data, methylation data, drug response data, mutation data and interaction data, merging them into a knowledge graph, and dividing the data into separate training and testing sets of 80% and 20%. To measure the connections between genes, drugs, and drug responses, the Adamic-Adar index, a graph-based model, is utilized. The index calculates the inference path based on the common neighbours between nodes in the knowledge graph. This path represents the strength of the association between a gene, a drug, and the corresponding drug response. The traceability perspective is applied to the entire methodology. It involves documenting the lineage and processing of the data, algorithms, and decisions made throughout the drug recommendation process. This perspective ensures transparency and allows for tracking and explaining the connections, decisions, and processes involved in drug recommendation inference. The methodology followed by our study is broadly divided into three components:

 (i) Formation of knowledge graphs [9]
 (ii) Multi-step prediction model [16]
(iii) Traceability analysis [4]

The knowledge graph utilized in this study is an interconnected system consisting of nodes and edges. These nodes symbolize the entities pertinent to the paper, specifically cancer genes, drugs, and targets. The edges represent relationships between entities, such as 'targets', 'sensitive', and 'resistive' [13]. The knowledge graph is also used to improve the accuracy of AI predictions. By providing insights into the relationships between cancer genes, drugs, and drug targets, the knowledge graph can help to identify the most relevant features for AI prediction models [7]. This can lead to more accurate and reliable AI predictions and provide doctors and patients with much-needed insight into drug recommendations. The paper describes a multi-step prediction model, a machine-learning model designed to forecast the effectiveness of drugs for cancer patients by utilizing their genomic data. The model is trained in a multi-step fashion. During the initial stages of preparing the multi-step model, the model undergoes training to predict the cancer genes found within a specific patient's tumor [17]. Subsequently, in the next stage, the model forecasts the drug targets associated with the cancer genes identified in the tumor. Finally, based on the drug targets connected to the cancer genes present in the tumor, the trained model predicts the effectiveness of the drug for the given patient. Figure 1 shows the workflow of our study.

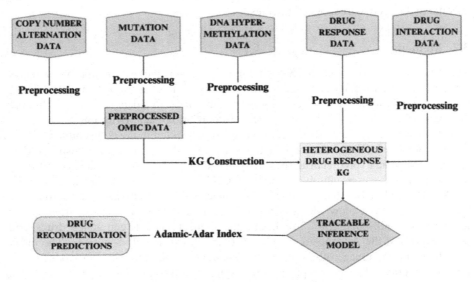

Fig. 1. Workflow of the study

For the traceability analysis, the predictions above a particular threshold are considered for the analysis from the predictions obtained by the multi-step model. The inference paths of the prediction are extracted with the help of earlier-used models. The relevant features are identified and later analyzed using the traceable inference model [18, 19].

4   Results

4.1   Environmental Setup

The environment used for our work was set up on a MacBook Air M2. The technical specs are an 8-core CPU with four performance and four efficiency cores. It has an 8-core GPU with a 16-core Neural Engine and 100 GB/s bandwidth. The operating system on our device is MacOS. The work environment was set up using a Python 3.8 virtual environment. We installed the necessary functional libraries, such as Pandas, Networks, and Scikit.

$$\text{Traceability Rate} = \frac{\sum_{pi} I\{(e_1^i \in p_i, e_L^i \in p_i) | (e_1^i, e_L^i) \in S_{GT}\}}{\#(S_{GT})} \tag{1}$$

where p is the inference paths across the existing links in the KG. L is the predefined length of paths. pi is the i th inference path in the KG. I{.} is the Indicator function. e i 1 the first entity of the i th path. e i L is the last entity of the i th path. SGT is the ground-truth response set. #{.} is the cardinality of a set [4].

4.2 Results of Our Study

We have obtained probability scores and identifiable paths for our study's predictions. By setting a probability threshold of 0.5, we selected traceable paths with accurate predictions to determine the proportion of these paths in the ground-truth outcomes. The choice of 0.5 as the threshold was due to its everyday use for probabilities since the scores obtained were probabilities. We tested the model on the omics data set five times to check robustness, and the average traceability rate during testing was 59.24%. The representation of the traceability rate for each trial can be observed by using a bar graph in Fig. 2. As an illustration, we present some examples of the predicted traceable inferences. A typical inference involves starting from a tested sample cell line, tracing through aberration genes, further linking to other samples, and finally resulting in drug recommendations. To find specific examples, we recommend referring to Table 1, which provides a comprehensive collection of instances. Among the examples listed, one instance worth mentioning are as follows: [(CellLine: NCI-H82), (Gene: ADCK3), ('Resistive', 'Drug Name: Vorinostat')].

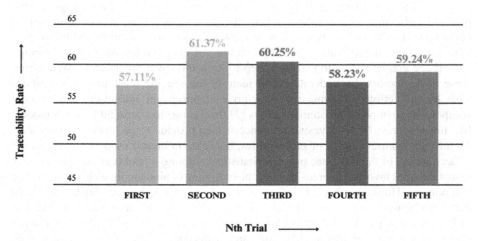

Fig. 2. Traceability Rates of different trails

Table 1. Traceable Inference Drug Recommendation with prediction results

Probability	Gene Name	Cell Line Name	Drug Name	Sensitivity
0.615008	SPSB1	SUIT-2	FMK	Sensitive
0.550684	DRAXIN	SK-MM-2	OSI-930	Sensitive
0.922299	CLCNKA	WSU-DLCL2	GSK429286A	Sensitive
0.963847	AURKAIP1	SNU-489	CX-5461	–
0.835302	ACOT11	Daudi	BMS-708163	–
0.588884	CELA3A	HCC2157	HG-5-88-01	–
0.519423	TMEM59	LU99	SB 216763	–
0.711860	MTHFR	Raji	WZ3105	–
0.645980	EFHD2	A-673	Ruxolitinib	–
0.503093	C1orf87	COR-L23	KIN001-236	Resistive

5 Discussion

5.1 Comparison with Traditional Methods

The traceable inference model offers a distinctive advantage over existing drug recommendation models in recent times. These advantages make it a superior choice for achieving explainability in drug recommendation tasks. Compared to similarity- based models, which calculate similarity scores based on distances between drug- sample pairs, traceable inference models stand out due to their detailed coherence with existing knowledge. Unlike similarity-based models, which lack explainability and fail to provide insight into the reasoning behind predictions, traceable inference models leverage knowledge graphs (KGs) to establish step-by-step inference procedures. By utilizing these KGs, doctors can understand and identify the specific reasoning steps responsible for predictions, allowing space for error identification and adjustment of local components to improve recommendations [2]. In contrast to statistical learning models like linear regression or Bayesian inference, which provide some level of explainability through feature weights or probabilities, traceable inference models offer a deeper understanding of the inference process. Statistical learning models can only sometimes reveal the steps involved in predictions or the reasoning behind giving weights to specific components. However, traceable inference models employ KGs to establish transparent pathways between drugs and samples. By comprehending the intermediate knowledge and inference steps, doctors can identify errors, adjust the model, and enhance the accuracy of drug recommendations [11]. Compared to deep learning models, which are often considered black boxes due to their lack of transparency, traceable inference models provide interpretable pathways and steps within KGs. Deep learning models need to offer a clearer understanding of the reasoning process. In contrast, traceable inference models provide prediction results and the corresponding paths within KGs. This traceability allows doctors to trace the reasoning process, identify critical steps for generalizability, and precisely locate errors. Additionally, traceable inference models do not rely on vast amounts of data for parameter adjustments, making them more suitable for explainable drug recommendations [8, 12]. There is a need to enhance the accuracy of prediction in explainable AI drug recommendation models by leveraging advanced machine learning techniques and an increased spectrum of datasets. Striking a delicate balance between model performance and explainability is also pivotal, ensuring the recommendations are highly accurate while maintaining transparent and traceable inference paths.

Our traceable inference model differs from other drug recommendation methods in several significant ways. Its improved explainability compared to other models is one of its main merits. Unlike similarity-based and deep learning models, our approach uses knowledge graphs to create step-by-step inference processes, frequently requiring more transparency. This gives medical professionals vital insight into the recommendation process by enabling them to comprehend and pinpoint the precise reasoning steps responsible for forecasts. Our model also exhibits excellent congruence with existing knowledge. It creates visible routes between medications and samples by utilizing knowledge graphs, guaranteeing that reliable data support recommendations (Table 2).

Table 2. Comparison of various state of methods

Model → Aspect ↓	Statistical Based Model [2]	Similarity Based Model [11]	Deep Learning Based Model [8, 12]	Traceable Inference Model
Transparency	It varies depending on the statistical approach used	Transparency may vary based on similarity measures and weighting schemes	Transparency may vary due to deep neural network complexity	High transparency due to traceable inference
Trustworthiness	Trust varies based on statistical model assumptions and data quality	Trust may vary based on the quality of similarity measures and data coverage	Trust may depend on the depth and complexity of the neural network	Enhanced trust due to traceable explanations
Explainability	Limited explanations often rely on statistical correlations	Limited explanations based on similarity scores	Limited explanations due to black-box nature of deep learning	Detailed explanations through traceability
Traceability	Limited traceability as it lacks explicit paths of inference	Limited traceability as it relies on similarity scores	Limited traceability in deep neural networks	High traceability through explicit inference paths
Generalizability	Generalizability may depend on statistical model robustness, performs reasonably on new datasets	Generalizability may depend on the diversity of similarity measures, may struggle with rare cases	Generalizability may depend on data size and network design, tends to excel with large datasets	Achieves good generalizability, performs well on diverse patient populations

One drawback of our traceable inference model is that there can still be difficulties with generalizability. Doctors and patients may need time and effort to comprehend the intermediate knowledge and inference processes the model offers. Those less familiar with knowledge graphs or with fewer resources for training and education may find this a hurdle. Furthermore, while our approach provides insight into explainability and logic, it's crucial to remember that it provides only a 59.24% traceability rate. The effectiveness of our model is still dependent on the reliability of the knowledge graphs and the accuracy of the underlying datasets. As a result, even though our model has many advantages in terms of explainability, consistency with the body of knowledge, and the balance between model performance and explainability, it is important to acknowledge its drawbacks in terms of generalizability, user expertise requirements, and the potential impact of outside factors on accuracy. We may work to deliver solid and trustworthy drug recommendations for medical professionals and patients alike by addressing these constraints and continuously enhancing the model.

6 Conclusion

The existing AI drug recommendation models have shown remarkable precision in their predictions. However, gaining the trust of medical professionals and patients is difficult due to their need for more transparency. In contrast, our model includes traceable inference paths in addition to recommendations. By aligning inference with known facts, traceable routes can increase accuracy and prevent irrational predictions. Moreover, unlike black-box models, these traceable paths enable doctors to quickly identify and rectify errors in incorrect predictions. To evaluate our model's efficacy, we propose using a traceability rate as an evaluation measure to assess the effectiveness of explainable AI-based drug recommendation systems. In the experiments conducted on a drug knowledge graph, we achieved a traceability rate of 59.24%. Even if this rate is insufficient for clinical applications, due to the impracticality and expense of annotating each step, our suggested solution cannot fully align every step of the connected paths with doctors' labels, even though it significantly increases explainability. Future research will improve prediction accuracy while preserving the traceability of justifiable inference processes.

References

1. Costello, J.C., et al.: A community effort to assess and improve drug sensitivity prediction algorithms. Nat. Biotechnol. **32**(12), 1202–1212 (2014)
2. Tjoa, E., et al.: A survey on explainable artificial intelligence (xai): toward medical xai. IEEE Trans. Neural Netw. Learn. Syst. **32**(11), 4793–4813 (2020)
3. Vellido, A.: The importance of interpretability and visualization in machine learning for applications in medicine and health care. Neural Comput. Appl. **32**(24), 18069–18083 (2020)
4. Xi, J., et al.: Cancer omic data based explainable AI drug recommendation inference: a traceability perspective for explainability. Biomed. Signal Process. Control **79**, 104144 (2023)
5. Barretina, J., et al.: Addendum: the cancer cell line encyclopedia enables predictive modeling of anticancer drug sensitivity. Nature **565**(7738), E5–E6 (2019)
6. Yang, W., et al.: Genomics of Drug Sensitivity in Cancer (GDSC): a resource for therapeutic biomarker discovery in cancer cells. Nucleic Acids Res. **41**(D1), D955–D961 (2012)
7. Pu, Q., et al.: Local feature for visible-thermal PReID based on transformer. In: Huang, DS., Jo, KH., Jing, J., Premaratne, P., Bevilacqua, V., Hussain, A. (eds.) Intelligent Computing Theories and Application. ICIC 2022. LNCS, vol. 13393, pp. 352–362. Springer, Cham (2022). https://doi.org/10.1007/978-3-031-13870-6_29
8. Wang, F., et al.: Deep learning in medicine—promise, progress, and challenges. JAMA Intern. Med. **179**(3), 293–294 (2019)
9. Gogleva, A., et al.: Knowledge graph-based recommendation framework identifies drivers of resistance in EGFR mutant non-small cell lung cancer. Nat. Commun. **13**(1), 1667 (2019)

10. Abbas, K., et al.: Application of network link prediction in drug discovery. BMC Bioinform. **22**, 1–21 (2021)
11. Chen, H., et al.: A Bayesian network meta-analysis of the efficacy of targeted therapies and chemotherapy for treatment of triple-negative breast cancer. Cancer Med. **8**(1), 383–399 (2019)
12. Chen, Y., et al.: How much can deep learning improve prediction of the responses to drugs in cancer cell lines? Brief. Bioinform. **23**(1), bbab378 (2022)
13. Zou, L., et al.: A genome-wide association study of Alzheimer's disease using random forests and enrichment analysis. Sci. China Life Sci. **55**, 618–625 (2012)
14. Paltun, G., et al.: Improving drug response prediction by integrating multiple data sources: matrix factorization, kernel and network-based approaches. Brief. Bioinform. **22**(1), 346–359 (2021)
15. Dağlarli, E.: Explainable artificial intelligence (xAI) approaches and deep meta learning models. Adv. Appl. Deep Learn. **79** (2020)
16. Xian, Y., et al.: Reinforcement knowledge graph reasoning for explainable recommendation. In: Proceedings of the 42nd International ACM SIGIR Conference on Research and Development in Information Retrieval (2019)
17. Yang, J., et al.: A novel approach for drug response prediction in cancer cell lines via network representation learning. Bioinformatics **35**(9), 1527–1535 (2019)
18. Yu, Z., et al.: SimuSCoP: reliably simulate Illumina sequencing data based on position and context dependent profiles. BMC Bioinformatics **21**, 1–18 (2020)
19. Yuan, Y., et al.: Objective reduction in many-objective optimization: evolutionary multiobjective approaches and comprehensive analysis. IEEE Trans. Evolut. Comput. **22**(2), 189–210 (2017)
20. Huang, X., et al.: A survey of safety and trustworthiness of deep neural networks: verification, testing, adversarial attack and defense, and interpretability. Comput. Sci. Rev. **37**, 100270 (2020)
21. Saxena, S., et al.: Role of artificial intelligence in radiogenomics for cancers in the era of precision medicine. Cancers **14**(12), 2860 (2022)
22. Suri, J.S., et al.: Cardiovascular/stroke risk stratification in Parkinson's disease patients using atherosclerosis pathway and artificial intelligence paradigm: a systematic review. Metabolites **12**(4), 312 (2022)
23. Das, S., et al.: Brain tumor segmentation and overall survival period prediction in glioblastoma multiforme using radiomic features. Concurr. Comput. Pract. Exp. **34**(20), e6501 (2022)
24. Sinha, P., et al.: Medical image segmentation: hard and soft computing approaches. SN Applied Sciences 2 (2020): 1-8
25. Suri, J.S., et al.: Five strategies for bias estimation in artificial intelligence-based hybrid deep learning for acute respiratory distress syndrome COVID-19 lung infected patients using AP (AI) Bias 2.0: a systematic review. IEEE Transactions on Instrumentation and Measurement (2022)

LiteFace: A Light-Weight Multi-person Face Detection Model

Kanupriya Anand[1][✉], Nirmala Murali[2], and Deepak Mishra[2]

[1] RV College of Engineering, Bangalore, India
kanupriya_anand@outlook.com
[2] IIST, Thiruvananthapuram, India

Abstract. Deep neural network based face detection models have made remarkable progress in recent years. One-stage detectors have been widely used due to their balance between speed and accuracy. In this study, a light-weight face detection model, LiteFace, that uses YOLOv5 model as a baseline is proposed. This model detects and counts the faces in a given image with the addition of the focal loss function to mitigate the problem of imbalanced training data. Wasserstein loss is used to focus on small-scale faces, while Intersection over Union (IoU) loss is used for large-scale and medium-scale face detection. In order to achieve receptive field enhancement of the upper pyramid layers of the network, an Inception module is introduced at the top of the bottom-up pathway. A Convolutional Block Attention Model is added before the detection heads to help the network focus on regions of interest. This network is trained on a subset of the training images from the WIDER FACE dataset and achieves an improved training time with an accuracy of 94.1% on the easy subset of WIDER FACE.

Keywords: Face Detection · YOLO · Loss functions · Attention

1 Introduction

Face detection is known to be a fundamental computer vision task since it may be applied to face recognition, verification, expression and attribute analysis. As a result, this field has been studied widely from several perspectives. This study of face detection finds applications in crowd management and surveillance with the aim of obtaining the person count in an image. Some earlier works use annotated landmarks as an additional supervision signal and other face detectors focus more on the network design or on different data augmentation techniques and loss functions [30,32]. The task of face detection is widely studied, and detector accuracy has improved significantly with the increased use of deep neural networks, in which the methods of general object detection are applied to the task of detecting faces [4]. Though the field is widely studied, the challenge of detecting faces with varied poses, scales, occlusion, illumination, blur etc., still remains.

H. Kaur et al. (Eds.): CVIP 2023, CCIS 2010, pp. 288–300, 2024.
https://doi.org/10.1007/978-3-031-58174-8_25

A variety of one-stage detectors have been presented to improve detection speed and to mitigate the problems faced by cascading deep learning networks. A problem arises when the search space is to be divided with a finer granularity for small objects. This causes the problem of an imbalance of samples in the dataset which is usually dominated by easy examples. These are not iteratively filtered out in one-stage detectors, and as a result, during training, the model tends to overfit the easily detectable faces. To deal with this, Gradient Harmonizing Mechanism (GHM) [34] was proposed to suppress the gradients from simple samples so that more informative samples were focused on. Similar to GHM, Focal Loss [4] dynamically assigns higher weights to difficult training points. In YOLOv5, FPN [35] fuses the features of the upper three pyramid layers. For smaller objects, pixel information is lost after multiple convolution layers, and the remaining semantic information is insubstantial [2]. Increasing the feature map resolution can improve the model's response to small-scale faces [2–4]. Additionally, the sensitivity of certain popular loss functions like IoU and L1/L2 loss varies depending on the scale of objects. In order to increase sensitivity to smaller faces, Wasserstein Distance Loss [14] is used in this work. However, it is important to ensure large-scale object information is not lost at a finer granularity. In an image, the receptive field is the region that influences activation of a particular neuron in a convolutional layer. Through receptive field expansion, models can capture more global contextual information and better understand the relationships between different parts of an image. Receptive field enhancement modules [1, 2] solve this issue using dilated convolutions.

Faces in the wild also face the problem of occlusion. This is the main cause of decline in accuracy of face detectors. In RetinaFace [6], a model that uses the ResNet [28] backbone, context modules are applied on feature maps from each pyramid level in the network to increase the receptive field. Works like FAN [9] attempt to solve this problem using anchor-level attention. However, FAN ignores information between channels. In contrast, CBAM [5] captures inter-channel relationships and highlights important spatial regions. The use of context information in all these works improves the accuracy of face detectors. To better explore these ideas and challenges, generic object detection-based method is employed in this study to detect faces using the WIDER FACE dataset [27].

The contributions of this work can be summarized as follows:

- Providing a strong but simple baseline method for person count and bounding box detection of faces using a modified YOLOv5 network. Modules and functions used in this architecture are based on modules for general object detection.
- To detect faces at different scales, the idea employed is to increase the receptive field using an Inception Module. Imbalance in the dataset is ameliorated using Focal Loss, and Wasserstein Distance Loss is used to detect small faces. The CBAM module incorporated improves the context awareness of the network.
- With this model called "LiteFace", 94.1% precision on the easy subset of WIDER FACE is achieved. In comparison to current state-of-the-art detec-

tors, the model is light-weight and has significantly fewer parameters. It should be noted that while there are lighter-weight models for face detection, our architecture achieves higher accuracy at the cost of a small increase in number of parameters.

2 Related Work

Face Detection. Earlier methods for face detection relied on statistical learning of various facial features such as LBP [19] and HOG [37]. The pioneering work of the Viola-Jones [17] in 2001 uses the concept of Haar-like features to learn rectangular regions at specific parts of the face, introducing a new way to represent faces as an integral image. However, the Viola-Jones detector is slow to train and does not detect faces with variation in pose. CascadeCNN [35] uses a three-tier cascaded structure of CNNs that predict facial landmarks and locations of faces in an image. MTCNN [16] or Multi-Task Cascaded Convolutional Neural Networks aligns the face landmarks and detects the location of faces in an image by employing a similar architecture. However, these early algorithms for face detection have the disadvantage of slow training and low accuracy. More recently, rather than using certain features to describe facial patterns of the eyes, nose, mouth, etc., the facial features can be learnt automatically by the neural network using deep learning techniques. Newer face detection algorithms such as SSD [7], Faster R-CNN [8], Mask-RCNN [39] and RetinaNet [4] make use of general object detection algorithms for face detection. SRN [24], which is based on the RefineDet [25] and RetinaNet [4] for the purpose of detecting faces, achieves increased accuracy by implementing a dual stage classification and regression which is slower. This network also improves the effect of receptive fields which reduce in the bottom-up pathway of a feature pyramid network by using a multi-branch model. To handle problem of multiple scales, YOLO-based architectures [1,11,33,42] introduce anchor matching strategies.

YOLO. You Only Look Once is a powerful generic object detector that has revolutionized computer vision applications. All versions of the existing YOLO [1,11,18,33,42] architectures use a single-shot approach to object detection-bounding box predictions and confidence or class probability predictions are made directly using CNNs. The algorithm is as follows: the input image is divided into an S × S grid, the model makes a certain number of bounding box predictions of a given class along with class probabilities for each grid cell. The confidence score, coordinates of the center of the box and its height and width relative to the image dimensions are the components of a bounding box prediction. The output of the model is the above tensor followed by non-maximum suppression in case of duplicate detections. YOLOv1 [11] has 24 layers of convolutions followed by two fully-connected layers, but the model makes localization accuracy errors and is not sensitive to tiny object detection. YOLOv2 [33] made improvements by introducing anchor boxes for prediction and using batch-normalization and multi-scale training. The third version [11] uses a different backbone (Darknet-53) and spatial pyramid pooling. Several YOLO versions have been released at present, each with slightly varying architecture and advantages.

In recent years, YOLOv5 has gained widespread popularity as a general object detector due to its high accuracy and efficiency. Hence, we have used YOLOv5 for face detection along with additional modules with the goal of addressing some of the common challenges in this field, such as detecting small faces and handling face occlusion. The YOLOv5 architecture comprises three key components: the backbone, neck, and detection heads. For the backbone, we adopt the CSPDarknet53 architecture, which enables the fusion of multi-scale features by fusing P3, P4 and P5 layers. The neck component has the structure of the Spatial Pyramid Network [20] and Path Aggregation Network [10] modules. Finally, the heads are responsible for classifying the target category and regressing its location, and we make the addition of a branch before the detection heads to improve the network's ability to detect occluded faces.

Figure 1 shows a schematic representation of our detector. The part 1(a) represents the network backbone, consisting of CSP blocks that are feature extractors along with the Inception Module at the top of the bottom-up network for receptive field enhancement. Figure 1(b) is the neck layers, comprising SPP and PAN modules. In addition, we introduce the CBAM to improve the detection of occluded faces after the neck layer output.

Receptive Field Enhancement and Attention. Large face scale variations and occlusions have a marked impact on performance of the model and is one of the major problems with images of faces in the wild. In YOLO-FaceV2 [2], the YOLOv5 architecture is used for face detection and a scale-aware RFE module to increase the receptive field, and a multi-head SEAM attention network to identify occluded faces is added to the model. Similarly, TinaFace [3] achieves state-of-the-art accuracy on the WIDER FACE dataset using a ResNet-50 backbone. Ideas in TinaFace are based on existing object detection modules. The network makes an Inception module similar to RFE.

Loss Functions. L1/L2 loss, smooth L1 loss and IoU loss are used most commonly for face detection. Other loss functions have been introduced to solve the problem of imbalanced datasets and multi-scale objects. In YOLO-FaceV2, a sample-weighting (Slide) function is used to balance the hard and easy samples and NWD loss [22] is used to improve the detector performance on small faces. Focal Loss [4] also addresses this imbalance problem. It assigns more weights to hard samples, thereby modifying Cross-Entropy Loss to handles the imbalance problem. TinaFace uses an IoU-aware branch and DIoU [41] loss which addresses the problem of small faces by minimizing distance between prediction box and ground truth box centers.

Inspired by these works, the current light-weight architecture and loss functions are proposed for face detection using YOLOv5.

3   Methodology

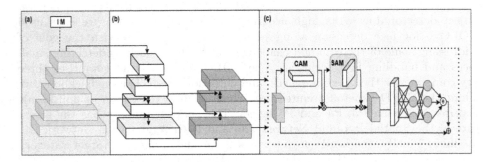

Fig. 1. Architecture of LiteFace model with (a) Backbone: a feed-forward CSPDark-net53 network that extracts feature maps at multiple scales, the top of the bottom-up pathway contains the Inception Module (IM) (b) Neck: Spatial Pyramid Pooling (SPP) layers that separate out the most significant context features (c) Head: CBAM attention network (consisting of CAM- Channel Attention Module and SAM-Spatial Attention Module) connected to fully connected layers.

3.1   Inception Module

A challenge in the detection of faces in the wild is the multi-scale variance. One common way to approach this is multi-scale training in the Feature Pyramid Network. The Inception module (IM) shown in Fig. 2 is inspired by that of GoogLeNet [1], which addresses the large computational cost of earlier Inception modules using 1×1 convolutions before using larger filters. The Inception module serves as a receptive field enhancement block in our network. Before its introduction, the question of selecting which convolution filter size to leverage posed a challenge. Inception mitigates the need to make such decisions as it uses 1×1, 3×3 and 5×5 filter sizes. This forms features of different receptive fields, which together help capture faces as well as multi-scale context. This ensures that semantic information is not lost in the bottom-up pathway of the FPN. The 1×1 filters help learn patterns across the depth of the input. The 3×3 and 5×5 filter sizes help to learn spatial patterns across all dimensions of the input. The concatenation of the feature maps thus obtained increases the representational power of the proposed model.

3.2   Attention Module

The Convolutional Block Attention Module abbreviated as CBAM [5] has emerged as a powerful mechanism in deep learning architectures, enhancing the discriminative power and attentional capabilities of CNNs. CBAM incorporates

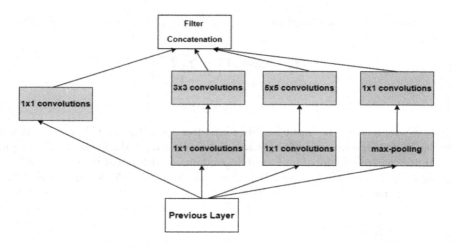

Fig. 2. Inception Block architecture

two key components, namely the Channel Attention Module (CAM) and the Spatial Attention Module (SAM), to selectively focus on informative features and spatial locations, respectively. The CAM enables the network to adaptively recalibrate the channel-wise feature responses by capturing interdependencies across different channels. This is achieved through a combination of global average pooling, a shared fully connected layer and subsequent activations, which generate attention weights. Element-wise multiplication is performed between attention weights and the original feature maps, emphasizing important channels while suppressing less relevant ones. On the other hand, the SAM exploits interdependencies in spatial dimensions, attending to informative spatial regions in a given feature map. It utilizes a learnable convolutional kernel to generate spatial attention maps, which are combined with the original feature maps. This mechanism encourages the model to focus on relevant spatial locations while suppressing less important ones. By combining CAM and SAM, CBAM enables CNNs to dynamically adapt their feature representations, facilitating improved discriminability and context awareness. F'_{cam} (the output feature map of CAM) can be computed as shown below. F' represents the input feature map of size $C \times H \times W$. C represents channels, H and W are height and width of the feature map respectively. $\otimes$ is element-wise multiplication.

$$M_c = \text{sigmoid} \left(\frac{1}{H \cdot W} \sum_{i=1}^{H} \sum_{j=1}^{W} F'_{ijc} \right) \tag{1}$$

$$F'_{\text{cam}} = M_c \otimes F' \tag{2}$$

The feature map obtained from SAM (F''_{sam}) can be computed as follows:

$$M_s = \text{sigmoid} \left(\frac{1}{C} \sum_{c=1}^{C} F''_c \right) \tag{3}$$

$$F''_{sam} = M_s \otimes F'' \tag{4}$$

where F'' represents the input feature map after applying the CAM. CBAM has demonstrated significant performance gains for certain tasks in computer vision. Its ability to capture global and local dependencies within feature maps has been exploited by incorporating the CBAM module before the detection heads of the YOLOv5 network.

3.3 Focal Loss

$$\text{Cross Entropy}(p_t) = -log(p_t) \tag{5}$$

$$\text{Focal Loss}(p_t) = -(1 - p_t)^\gamma log(p_t) \tag{6}$$

Focal Loss [4] has emerged as a powerful and effective loss function for addressing the issue of class imbalance in deep learning models, particularly in object detection and classification tasks. Developed by Lin et al. in 2017, Focal Loss is designed to mitigate the dominant influence of easy examples that overwhelm the training process in imbalanced datasets. Focal Loss assigns dynamically weighted importance to each training sample during the optimization process. This is achieved by introducing a modulating factor called the "focusing parameter". By using the focusing parameter, Focal Loss down weighs the contribution of easy examples and gives higher weight to challenging samples that are often misclassified. The formulation of Focal Loss is a modification of Binary Cross Entropy loss, which includes an additional term that adjusts the loss contribution of each example based on its predicted probability. The modulating factor is a function of predicted probability, with a higher value assigned to low-confidence but more informative predictions. Easy and hard samples are distinguished on the basis of the IoU of the predicted bounding box and ground-truth box. This weighting strategy enables Focal Loss to effectively prioritize the learning of challenging face examples from WIDER FACE, leading to improved performance for face detection.

3.4 Wasserstein Loss

Wasserstein distance is the distance metric derived from the Optimal Transport Theory [29]. Optimal Transport Theory deals with transporting the source data to the destination in an efficient way. A transport map is computed to know which parts of the source are mapped to corresponding parts of the destination, and then the work done for the transport is calculated by finding the product of the mass transferred and the distance between the source and destination points.

In machine learning, Wasserstein distance has seen numerous applications in comparing distributions of data. Wasserstein distance [38] can be computed as follows,

$$WD(F^s, F^t) = min \sum_{i}^{p} \sum_{j}^{p} S_{ij}.C(f_i^s, f_j^t) \quad (7)$$

The model transports some amount of mass, S_{ij} from i to j. The ground cost values are given in the cost matrix, C. The map is computed between the source feature vector F^s and the target feature vector F^t. Several methods exist to transport the source distribution to the target distribution. But the objective function tries to find the transport map that results in minimum cost. Wasserstein distance gives a good perceptual view to the model as it finds the work done instead of just finding the distance between the two distributions.

4 Experiments and Results

4.1 Dataset

A subset of the WIDER FACE dataset was used to train the model, consisting of 16000 images, including approximately 150,000 faces. The WIDER dataset consists of three parts: the training, verification, and test set divided in the ratio 4:1:5. The dataset is classified into easy, medium and hard subsets on the basis of how challenging the samples are. Amongst these, the hard set has the most difficult samples, and its predictions on this subset are a stronger indicator of the effectiveness of a detector. We evaluate our model using the WIDER FACE validation and test set.

4.2 Implementation Details

We conduct comprehensive experiments on the proposed method, including the effectiveness of the Inception module and loss functions. We also compare the accuracy of our LiteFace detector with current state-of-the-art detectors in Table 1. The YOLOv5 is used as a baseline, and all modules and methods are implemented in TensorFlow. For training, we use the Adam optimizer. An initial learning rate of 0.008 is set and Cosine Annealing is used to decay the learning rate. The model is trained on an NVIDIA Tesla V100 GPU using a batch size of 32. The threshold of IoU for NMS is set to 0.3.

Anchor Settings. All images are resized to dimensions of 640 × 640 before training. The following anchor box dimensions are used : [[8., 9.], [16., 24.], [28., 58.], [41., 25.], [58., 125.], [71., 52.], [129., 97.], [163., 218.], [384., 347.]]

4.3 Discussion

Our LiteFace detector obtains an accuracy of 94.1%, 91.2%, and 84.8% on the Easy, Medium, and Hard subsets of the dataset, respectively. Figure 3, 4 and

Table 1. AP (Average Precision) performance of different detectors on the validation set of WIDER FACE

Detector	Backbone	Easy	Medium	Hard	Params(M)
HAMBox [36]	ResNet50 [28]	0.952	0.937	0.767	30.24
DSFD [21]	ResNet152 [28]	0.969	0.957	0.904	120.06
YOLOv5n0.5 [31]	ShuffleNetv2-0.5 [40]	0.907	0.881	0.738	0.447
yolov5n [31]	ShuffleNetv2 [40]	0.936	0.915	0.805	1.726
YOLOv5s [31]	YOLOv5-CSPNet [18]	0.943	0.926	0.831	7.075
YOLOv5m [31]	YOLOv5-CSPNet [18]	0.953	0.937	0.852	21.063
YOLOv5l [31]	YOLOv5-CSPNet [18]	0.959	0.944	0.845	46.627
RetinaFace [6]	ResNet50 [28]	0.969	0.961	0.918	29.50
TinaFace [3]	ResNet-50 [28]	0.963	0.957	0.930	37.980
LiteFace (our model)	YOLOv5-CSPNet [18]	0.941	0.912	0.848	**7.399**

(a) Single large-scale face detected   (b) partially-occluded face detected

Fig. 3. Results on images with large-scale faces from WIDER FACE

(a) All medium scale faces detected ac- (b) All medium scale faces detected but
curately   with false positive detections

Fig. 4. Results on medium-scale faces from WIDER FACE

5 show some of the images tested along with the number of persons detected. Figure 3(a) shows bounding box detection of a single large-scale along with the person count. Figure 3(b) shows the detection of a partially occluded face with a noisy background. In Fig. 4(a), the model accurately detects and counts all 25

(a) multiple faces detected with scale-variation

(b) small-scale faces in a noisy image detected

Fig. 5. Results on small to medium-scale faces from WIDER FACE Test set

medium-scale faces. The detection of smaller faces in Fig. 5 is attributed to the use of Wasserstein loss as well as the use of the Attention module. Some faces with harsh illumination in this image are not detected. In noisy images like Fig. 5(b), the model predicts small-scale, partially-occluded faces well.

Table 2. Variation of AP depending on the presence of Inception Module

Inception Module	Easy	Medium	Hard
With Inception Module	0.941	0.912	0.848
Without Inception Module	0.939	0.909	0.829

Table 3. Variation of AP depending on γ value.

γ	Easy	Medium	Hard
0	0.924	0.896	0.821
0.5	0.928	0.908	0.827
1.5	0.936	0.910	0.832
2	0.941	0.912	0.848

Comparison with Current State-of-the-Art. As shown in Table 1, in comparison to current state-of-the-art such as TinaFace [3] and RetinaFace [6], there is a trade-off between parameters and precision with the detection on the Easy and Medium subsets being comparable. As can be observed from the table, the TinaFace detector has over 5 times the number of parameters compared to our detector. In comparison to the YOLO-FaceV2 [2] model- which achieves 98.7%, 97.2%, and 87.7% on the respective subsets- our model is more light-weight at the cost of slightly reduced accuracy. While lighter models exist, LiteFace achieves higher accuracy with only a slight increase in parameters when compared to YOLOv5n0.5 and yolov5n [31]. The bar charts in Fig. 6 compare the accuracy of the subsets against the number of parameters of the detector.

Effect of Inception Block. The Inception block is the receptive field enhancement module. By using this block, we make up for the semantic information lost in the bottom-up network of the FPN. Table 2 shows the results of using this module.

Effect of Focal Loss. The variation in accuracy with the value of γ in focal loss [4] is shown in Table 3. The γ value reduces the loss for easy examples. When the value is 0.2, accuracy is the highest.

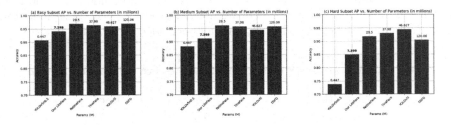

Fig. 6. (a-c) Comparison of AP on Easy, Medium and Hard subsets based on number of parameters (in millions)

5   Conclusion

In this paper, we design "LiteFace"- a light-weight face detector using YOLOv5 as the baseline. The proposed model can be easily deployed in surveillance applications due to its light-weight nature. The detector also outputs the number of faces in an image which can be adapted for the purpose of crowd management. An extensive analysis is conducted on the WIDER FACE dataset. The network is simple and has fewer parameters than state-of-the-art while achieving significant performance on WIDER FACE. In order to further enhance face detection performance, future improvements will focus on addressing the challenge of scale variation of faces in the same image with special attention to larger faces among several smaller faces. Additionally, to adapt the model for real-time crowd-surveillance footage, further research can be conducted on optimizing the network architecture for efficient detection as well as recognition of faces.

References

1. Szegedy, C., et al.: Going deeper with convolutions. In: 2015 IEEE Conference on Computer Vision and Pattern Recognition (CVPR), Boston, MA, USA (2015)
2. Yu, Z., Huang, H., Chen, W., Su, Y., Liu, Y., Wang, X.: Yolo-facev2: a scale and occlusion aware face detector. arXiv preprint arXiv:2208.02019 (2022)
3. Zhu, Y., Cai, H., Zhang, S., Wang, C., Xiong, Y.: Tinaface: strong but simple baseline for face detection. arXiv preprint arXiv:2011.13183 (2020)
4. Lin, T.Y., Goyal, P., Girshick, R., He, K., Dollár, P.: Focal loss for dense object detection. In: Proceedings of the IEEE International Conference on Computer Vision, pp. 2980–2988 (2017)
5. Woo, S., Park, J., Lee, J.Y., Kweon, I.S.: Cbam: convolutional block attention module. In Proceedings of the European Conference on Computer Vision (ECCV), pp. 3–19 (2018)
6. Deng, J., et al.: Retinaface: single-stage dense face localisation in the wild. arXiv preprint arXiv:1905.00641 (2019)
7. Liu, W., et al.: SSD: Single shot MultiBox detector. In: Leibe, B., Matas, J., Sebe, N., Welling, M. (eds.) ECCV 2016 Part I. LNCS, vol. 9905, pp. 21–37. Springer, Cham (2016). https://doi.org/10.1007/978-3-319-46448-0_2
8. Ren, S., He, K., Girshick, R., Sun, J.: Faster r-cnn: towards real-time object detection with region proposal networks. In: Advances in Neural Information Processing Systems, vol. 28 (2015)
9. Wang, J., Yuan, Y., Yu, G.: Face attention network: an effective face detector for the occluded faces. arXiv preprint arXiv:1711.07246 (2017)
10. Liu, S., Qi, L., Qin, H., Shi, J., Jia, J.: Path aggregation network for instance segmentation. In: IEEE Conference on Computer Vision and Pattern Recognition (2018)
11. Redmon, J., Farhadi, A.: Yolov3: an incremental improvement. In: arXiv preprint arXiv:1804.02767 (2018)
12. Wu, S., Li, X., Wang, X.: IoU-aware single-stage object detector for accurate localization. In: Image and Vision Computing, p. 103911 (2020)
13. Zhang, S., et al.: S3fd: single shot scale-invariant face detector. In: Proceedings of the IEEE International Conference on Computer Vision, pp. 192–201 (2017)
14. He, R., Wu, X., Sun, Z., Tan, T.: Wasserstein CNN: learning invariant features for NIR-VIS face recognition. IEEE Trans. Pattern Anal. Mach. Intell. (2018)
15. Wang, J., Xu, C., Yang, W., Yu, L.: A normalized gaussian wasserstein distance for tiny object detection (2021)
16. Zhang, K., Zhang, Z., Li, Z., Qiao, Y.: Joint face detection and alignment using multitask cascaded convolutional networks. IEEE Signal Process. Lett. **23**(10), 1499–1503 (2016)
17. Viola, P., Jones, M..: Rapid object detection using a boosted cascade of simple features. In: Proceedings of the 2001 IEEE Computer Society Conference on Computer Vision and Pattern Recognition, pp. I–I. CVPR 2001, Kauai, HI, USA (2001). https://doi.org/10.1109/CVPR.2001.990517
18. YOLOv5, "Yolov5" https://github.com/ultralytics/yolov5
19. Pietikãinen, M.: Local binary patterns. Scholarpedia **5**(3), 9775 (2010)
20. He, K., Zhang, X., Ren, S., Sun, J.: Spatial pyramid pooling in deep convolutional networks for visual recognition. IEEE Trans. Pattern Anal. Mach. Intell. (2014)
21. Li, J., et al.: DSFD: dual shot face detector. In: 2019 IEEE/CVF Conference on Computer Vision and Pattern Recognition (CVPR), pp. 5055–5064. Long Beach, CA, USA (2019). https://doi.org/10.1109/CVPR.2019.00520

22. Wang, J., Xu, C., Yang, W., Yu, L.: A normalized Gaussian Wasserstein distance for tiny object detection. arXiv:2110.13389 (2021)
23. Zhang, S., Zhu, X., Lei, Z., Shi, H., Wang, X., Li, S.Z.: Faceboxes: a CPU real-time face detector with high accuracy. In: (IJCB), IEEE (2017)
24. Ke, W., Chen, J., Jiao, J., Zhao, G., Ye, Q.: SRN: side-output residual network for object symmetry detection in the wild. IEEE Trans. Neural Netw. Learn. Syst. (2021)
25. Zhang, S., Wen, L., Bian, X., Lei, Z., Li, S.Z..: Single-shot refinement neural network for object detection. In 2018 IEEE/CVF Conference on Computer Vision and Pattern Recognition (2018)
26. Felzenszwalb, P., McAllester, D., Ramanan, D.: A discriminatively trained, multiscale, deformable part model. In: IEEE Conference on Computer Vision and Pattern Recognition, vol. 2008, pp. 1–8. IEEE (2008)
27. Yang, S., Luo, P., Loy, C.C., Tang, X.: Wider face: a face detection benchmark. In: IEEE, pp. 5525–5533 (2016)
28. He, K., Zhang, X., Ren, S., Sun, J.: Deep residual learning for image recognition. In: CVPR (2016)
29. Peyré, G., Cuturi, M.: Computational Optimal Transport (2020)
30. Rezatofighi, H., Tsoi, N., Gwak, J.Y., Sadeghian, A., Savarese, S.: Generalized intersection over union: a metric and a loss for bounding box regression. In: (CVPR) (2019)
31. Qi, D., Tan, W., Yao, Q., Liu, J.: YOLO5Face: why reinventing a face detector. In: Karlinsky, L., Michaeli, T., Nishino, K. (eds.) ECCV 2022. LNCS, vol. 13805, pp. 228–244. Springer, Cham (2022). https://doi.org/10.1007/978-3-031-25072-9_15
32. Zhang, Y.F., Ren, W., Zhang, Z., Jia, Z., Wang, L., Tan, T.: Focal and efficient IOU loss for accurate bounding box regression. Neurocomputing **506**, 146–157 (2022)
33. Redmon, J., Farhadi, A.: Yolo9000: Better, faster, stronger. In: IEEE Conference on Computer Vision and Pattern Recognition (2017)
34. Chen, M., Ren, X., Yan, Z.: Real-time indoor object detection based on deep learning and gradient harmonizing mechanism. In: (DDCLS) (2020)
35. Lin, T.Y., Dollár, P., Girshick, R., He, K., Hariharan, B., Belongie, S.: Feature pyramid networks for object detection (2017)
36. Liu, Y., et al.: HAMBox: delving into mining high-quality anchors on face detection. In: (CVPR) (2020)
37. Albiol, A., Monzo, D., Martin, A., Sastre, J., Albiol, A.: Face recognition using HOG-EBGM. Pattern Recognit. Lett. **29**(10), 1537–1543 (2008)
38. Solomon, J.: Computational optimal transport (2017)
39. Cakiroglu, O., Ozer, C., Gunsel, B.: Design of a deep face detector by mask R-CNN. In: Signal Processing and Communications Applications Conference (2019)
40. Ma, M., Zhang, X., Zheng, H., Sun, J.: Shufflenet v2: practical guidelines for efficient cnn architecture design. ArXiv preprint **11164**, 2018 (1807)
41. Zheng, Z., et al.: Distance-IoU Loss: faster and better learning for bounding box regression. In: AAAI, pp. 12993–13000 (2020)
42. Redmon, J., Divvala, S., Girshick, R., Farhadi, A.: You only look once: unified, real-time object detection. In: Proceedings of the IEEE Conference on Computer Vision and Pattern Recognition, pp. 779–788 (2016)

Synthesis of Glioblastoma Segmentation Data Using Generative Adversarial Network

Mullapudi Venkata Sai Samartha[1], Gorantla Maheswar[1], Shantilata Palei[1], Biswajit Jena[2], and Sanjay Saxena[1(✉)]

[1] Department of Computer Science and Engineering, International Institute of Information Technology, Bhubaneswar 751003, Odisha, India
sanjay@iiit-bh.ac.in

[2] Institute of Technical Education and Research, SOA University, Bhubaneswar 751030, Odisha, India

Abstract. Background: The application of machine learning and deep learning techniques in medical imaging encounters a significant limitation due to the limited availability of high-quality medical imaging data. The reluctance to share patient information for research purposes poses a substantial challenge in this regard. While traditional approaches like data augmentation and geographical alterations have been employed to address this issue, Generative Adversarial Networks (GANs) offer a promising solution for generating realistic synthetic medical images. GANs can create believable images from original, unlabeled photographs by learning the underlying data distribution from training examples, mitigating the risk of overfitting on small datasets. These generated images exhibit high realism, even though they may differ from the originals while still conforming to the same data distribution.

Method: In this study, we utilize a Generative Adversarial Network (GAN) framework that has undergone training using the BraTS 2020 dataset, specifically focused on the segmentation of brain tumors. The primary objective is to create synthetic MRI scans of brain tumors and their corresponding masks. Subsequently, we evaluate the influence of dataset augmentation by integrating these synthetic images into a segmentation network based on the U-Net architecture.

Result: The results of our investigation demonstrate a noteworthy improvement in segmentation performance when utilizing the augmented dataset. Specifically, the testing accuracy increased from 0.90 for the original dataset to 0.94 for the augmented one.

Conclusion: Our study underscores the potential of GANs in creating visually authentic medical images, as well as their capacity to enhance the performance of segmentation networks. This research addresses the critical need for more extensive and diverse medical imaging data in healthcare analysis, ultimately advancing the medical image analysis and diagnosis field.

Keywords: GAN · MRI · Pix2Pix GAN · Segmentation

1 Introduction

The brain, a vital constituent of the Central Nervous System (CNS), can develop an aberrant neoplasm known as brain tumor, identified explicitly as Glioblastoma Multiforme (GBM), classified as a Grade-IV brain tumor by the World Health Organization (WHO) [1, 2]. GBM manifests as an aggressive tumor that rapidly disseminates within the cerebrum, the principal region of the brain. According to data obtained from the Surveillance, Epidemiology, and End Results (SEER) program, approximately 24,810 cases of neuro-oncological pathology are anticipated in 2023, constituting 1.30% of all cancer cases, with approximately 18,990 fatalities (3.1% of cancer-related deaths) attributed to these malignant neoplasms [3]. GBM patients exhibit a median survival time of only nine months, which may be extended to 15–16 months through standard-of-care surgical intervention and adjuvant chemoradiation [4].

The diagnostic process for brain tumors is complicated by variations in size, shape, location, and appearance, particularly during the initial stages when the precise nature of the tumor is arduous to ascertain. Nonetheless, early detection facilitates timely treatment initiation and augments prognosis. Treatment modalities, including chemotherapy, radiation therapy, and surgery, are tailored to the specific characteristics of the tumor [5].

Deep learning and computer vision have emerged as promising avenues for automating meticulous and time-consuming medical imaging tasks, particularly in medical image segmentation, which aids in patient diagnosis and complex decision-making [29–31]. However, limited access to medical data presents a challenge due to legal and security constraints. Neuroimaging datasets that encompass both images and segmentations, enriched with data sourced from a cohort exceeding 100 patients, are notably scarce [6, 7]. Deep learning algorithms offer a solution by generating synthetic data through the utilization of Generative Adversarial Networks (GANs), thereby mitigating the scarcity of patient data within medical databases. GANs, introduced in 2014, represent a category of deep learning frameworks that exhibit the ability to generate highly realistic data when trained on appropriate distributions [28]. These networks have shown notable potential across various applications [32]. The present study aims to address the following objectives:

1. To explore the potential of GANs in synthesizing visually authentic magnetic resonance (MR) brain images.
2. To assess whether including these synthesized images can enhance the performance of a segmentation network when amalgamated with a dataset comprising real-world images.

In this paper, Sect. 2 overviews the literature of GANs in field of interest. Section 3 describes the methods used in this study to achieve the aforementioned objectives. Section 4 shows the results obtained in the analyses performed on the data, and Sect. 5 implies a critical discussion section that includes the challenges faced during the implementation. Finally, in Sect. 6, we conclude the study.

2   Literature Survey

Ali et al. [8] provide an encompassing overview of GAN benefits in brain MRI and their application in addressing focal brain disorders. Creswell et al. [9] delve into the training intricacies of GANs, including the challenge of mode collapse. Ronneberger et al. [10] introduce the U-Net architecture, a convolutional neural network pivotal in brain tumor segmentation. Dong et al. [11] propose a dedicated convolutional network for brain tumor segmentation inspired by U-Net. Xue et al. [12] present an end-to-end adversarial network for brain tumor segmentation, utilizing a Fully Connected Neural Network (FCNN) generator. Isola et al. [13] introduce conditional GANs (cGANs) with a U-Net-based generator for image-to-image translation. Rezaei et al. [14] extend cGANs for MRI-based brain tumor segmentation. Simonyan et al. [15] leverage convolutional classification networks for generating realistic images. Elazab et al. [33] introduce 3D GANs (GP-GAN) for glioma progression forecasting. Neelma et al. [34] demonstrate tumor detection with GANs. Güven et al. [35] enhance Brain-MRI segmentation with GANs. Liu et al. [36] propose a multi-modal MRI fusion GAN (BTMF-GAN) for optimizing fusion quality in brain tumors. Aslan et al. [37] employ probabilistic deep belief networks in a GAN framework for classifying disorders in brain MR data. These studies collectively shape the landscape of GAN applications in medical imaging, with ongoing efforts focused on addressing emerging challenges in this dynamic field.

3   Materials and Methodology

3.1   Dataset

The Multimodal Brain Tumor Image Segmentation Benchmark dataset includes volumetric MR images and tumor segmentations from patients with low- and high-grade gliomas in the Neuroimaging Informatics Technology Initiative (NIfTI) format. We utilized the 2020 dataset version [16–19] which comprised 369 sets of MRI scans in the training section. Each set contained four modalities: T1-weighted (T1), contrast-enhanced T1-weighted (T1c), T2-weighted (T2), and T2-weighted FLAIR image (FLAIR). We chose only the FLAIR modality as it provided a good contrast between healthy tissue and tumor region. Figure 1 shows Multi-parametric MR scans (T1, T2, FLAIR, T1-GD) with whole tumor (GBM) with subregions (different color coding) BG, red: TC, blue: ET, and green: ED. Each set of scans also has a segmentation mask with four regions. They are:

0. Background (BG)
1. Necrotic and non-enhancing tumor core (NCR/NET)
2. Peritumoral edema (ED)
3. GD-enhancing tumor (ET).

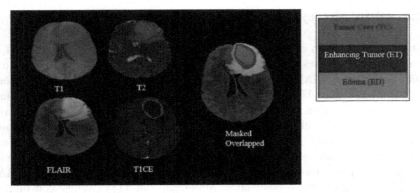

Fig. 1. Multi-parametric MR scans (T1, T2, FLAIR, T1-GD) with whole tumor (GBM) with subregions (different color coding) BG, red: TC, blue: ET, and green: ED [27].

3.2 Workflow

The data were first preprocessed, detailed in (Sect. 3.3). Pix2pix GAN (Sect. 3.5) was used to generate FLAIR images from corresponding mask images generated by vanilla GAN (Sect. 3.4). Then the fake FLAIR and corresponding fake mask images were augmented into the real dataset in an equal ratio with respect to the real ones. The purely 'real' and augmented data were then sent into a segmentation network, and the results were compared (Sect. 3.6). The workflow of the study is depicted in Fig. 2.

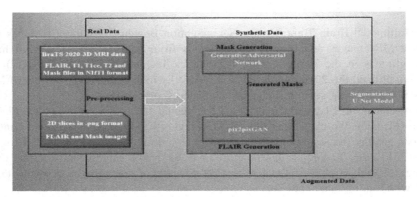

Fig. 2. A step-by-step method for accomplishing the project: The real data is pre-processed and then using GAN, synthetic data is created. Both the real and augmented data (combination of real and synthetic data) are segmented using U-Net model and their results are compared.

3.3 Preprocessing

The dataset used in this study (BraTS) consisted of 369 3D-MRI images and associated masks in the '.nii' file format in the training part. After removing 19 corrupted image sets, a total of 350 image sets were available for analysis. The FLAIR modality was utilized for the experiments. Preprocessing involved normalization using a min- max scalar, cropping each image to $128 \times 128 \times 128$ voxels, slicing them axially into 128 2D slices, and selecting the center 50 slices (they contained most information), resulting in 17,500 'real' FLAIR 2D slices. Corresponding masks were also preprocessed in a similar fashion, resulting in 17,500 corresponding mask 2D slices. The mask values were converted to categorical variables, representing different parts of the brain tumor, with non-zero pixels set to 1 for binary segmentation purposes.

3.4 Implementation of GAN

In 2014, Goodfellow et al. [20] introduced the Generative Adversarial Network (GAN), a deep learning architecture that learns and mimics the probability distribution of given data by generating artificial examples that closely resemble the natural distribution. GANs have various forms, including vanilla GAN, Style GAN, and pix2pix GAN. In the vanilla GAN architecture, two neural networks, namely the generator (G) and the discriminator (D), engage in a competitive game. In our study, discriminator took an image (mask) as input, while the generator received a latent vector space of random integers (size: 128). The discriminator outputted a $1 \times 1 \times 1$ tensor, utilizing multiple iterations of a kernel (size: 4) and a stride (size: 2) with padding (size: 1). To handle negative values, we employed LeakyReLU as the activation function with a coefficient of 0.2 for the independent variable. The generator, in turn, generated the fake mask using a process called transposed convolution achieved through substantial input padding. For activation, we used ReLU. The loss function was a binary-cross entropy function. The GAN model underwent training for 50 epochs. Fig. 3 visually represents the GAN utilized in our study. This methodology enabled the creation of 17,500 fake masks from 17,500 preprocessed real masks.

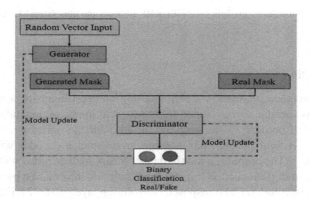

Fig. 3. An illustration of the GAN.

3.5 Implementation of pix2pix GAN

Traditional deep learning frameworks, such as convolutional neural networks (CNNs) or autoencoders, have limitations when it comes to image translation tasks. Frameworks such as pix2pix GAN have proven to be highly effective. In our study, we employed the pix2pix GAN for image translation purposes. The generator component utilized a U-Net architecture, while the discriminator employed a 'patch GAN' approach. The generator took the mask generated from the vanilla GAN as input to produce synthetic FLAIR images. These synthetic FLAIR images were then combined with the mask input to form the fake input for the discriminator. Additionally, the mask image and the FLAIR image were provided as real input to the discriminator. The discriminator utilized a patch GAN with a receptive field size of 70. The loss function was a binary-cross entropy function. Training the model involved 50 epochs with a learning rate of 0.0002. Fig. 4 provides a visual representation of the pix2pix GAN utilized in our study. Through this approach, we generated 17,500 fake FLAIR images corresponding to the 17,500 fake masks created by the vanilla GAN.

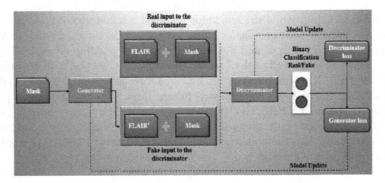

Fig. 4. Illustration of pix2pix GAN. FLAIR' denotes the generated FLAIR image

3.6 Segmentation

Conventional image segmentation algorithms rely on pixel intensity, while the U-Net architecture was specifically developed for biomedical image segmentation tasks, such as identifying cell borders. U-Net employs an auto-encoder structure, comprising an encoder with convolutional and max pooling layers, and a decoder with transposed convolution layers. The output is a multi-channel binary map encoded with one-hot representation, where skip connections retain high-resolution information by connecting the corresponding convolution and transposed convolution layers [21, 22]. Fig. 5 represents the U-Net employed in the study.

The dataset comprised 17,500 FLAIR 2D images and their respective masks. To augment the dataset, real and generated data were combined, resulting in a total of 31,000 FLAIR images and masks. The Keras implementation of the U-Net architecture employed a four-level encoder, with incrementally increasing convolutional filters (16,

32, 64, and 128) and accompanying max pooling layers. The fifth level served as the connection point between the encoder and the decoder. In the decoder, there were four classes with decreasing filter numbers (128, 64, 32, and 16), and transposed convolution layers were utilized. For classification purposes, a final convolution layer was included, with filters corresponding to the classes in the dataset. The spatial dimensions were preserved using the same padding technique, and the weights were initialized using the 'He normal' method. A testing set consisting of 2000 'real' images and 4000 augmented images was reserved. The loss function was a binary-cross entropy function. The training employed the Adam optimization method with a batch size of 16 and a validation split of 0.1. The model underwent 50 epochs of training, with separate training instances using either only real data or a combination of real and synthetic data.

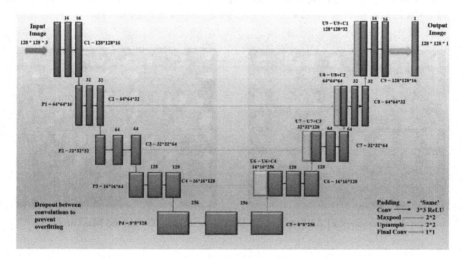

Fig. 5. Illustration of U-Net architecture.

4   Results

In this Section, we present the results obtained after following the processes mentioned in Sect. 3. Losses are one of the most intuitive ways to judge the performance of GAN-based networks. A general thumb of rule for understanding the performance of a GAN model is that the discriminator loss must be non-increasing corresponding to epochs, whereas the generator loss should be decreasing. Fig. 6 and Fig. 7 are the "Losses vs epoch" graphs obtained while generating the FLAIR and mask images. Fig. 8 and Fig. 9 show a sample of generated FLAIR and mask image results. Fig. 10 and Fig. 11 show the losses with respect to each dataset. Fig. 12 and Fig. 13 show the accuracies with respect to each dataset.

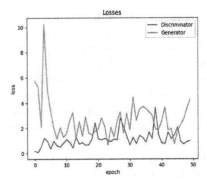

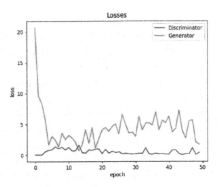

Fig. 6. Discriminator and Generator Losses for FLAIR images through epochs

Fig. 7. Discriminator and Generator Losses for mask images through epochs.

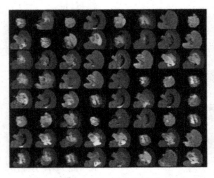

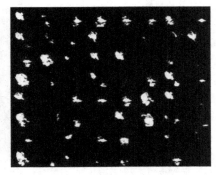

Fig. 8. Generated FLAIR images

Fig. 9. Generated Mask images

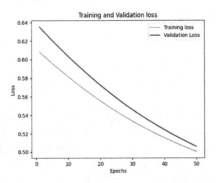

Fig. 10. Losses for the real dataset.

Fig. 11. Losses for the augmented dataset

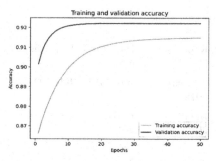

Fig. 12. Accuracies for the real dataset.

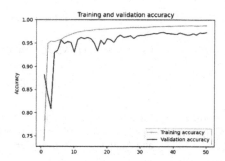

Fig. 13. Accuracies for the augmented data

After the training and validation phase, we ran the segmentation model on real and augmented datasets. The test accuracies were recorded as 0.90 and 0.94 respectively for each dataset. From the above results after segmentation, we inferred that the inclusion of synthetic data improved the performance of the segmentation model.

5 Discussion

Deep learning experiments were carried out on a computer equipped with an Intel 11th generation Core i5 processor, and the duration of training varied from 2 to 10 hours. The synthetic segmentation masks generated by the GAN exhibited a visually convincing appearance, but they suffered from notable distortions and noise. This issue likely stemmed from the inherent differences in slice sizes present in the real dataset, which posed a significant challenge for the generator. To tackle this limitation in future investigations, an interesting avenue would involve training separate instances of the GAN on distinct subsets of the real dataset, thereby enabling specialization in learning specific slice ranges [23, 24]. The augmented dataset exhibited higher loss values, indicating a noticeable discrepancy between the real and synthetic datasets, potentially attributed to the presence of noisy masks. To overcome this challenge, advanced image preprocessing techniques could be explored. For instance, leveraging the knowledge gained from the trained discriminator or involving medical experts for manual review could significantly improve the quality of the synthetic masks. Unfortunately, due to the substantial training times required, cross-validation of the test results was not performed. Nevertheless, efforts were made to calculate the error across the entire test set for each iteration, providing insights into the performance of the models. The following table (Table 1) is a benchmarking table comparing our study to others.

Table 1. Benchmarking Table

Attributes	Dong et al. [11]	Wang et al. [25]	Rezaei et al. [14]	Hussain et al. [26]	Samartha et al. (proposed)
Date	June 2017	August 2019	February 2018	July 2017	July 2023
Journal/ Conference	Medical Image Understanding and Analysis	Frontiers in Computational Neuroscience	BrainLes 2017	EMBC 2017	CVIP-2023
References	29	55	26	25	37
Model used Dataset	U-Net Brats 2015	CNN Brats 2017 and	cGAN Brats 2017	DCNN Brats 2013	pix2pix GAN, U-Net Brats 2020

6 Conclusion

The results of the segmentation analysis demonstrate a modest improvement in test scores when using synthetic data, underscoring the potential of GANs for data augmentation in datasets with limited samples. While these preliminary findings are encouraging, additional testing is required to optimize the quality of the generated images. Furthermore, it would be valuable to investigate the advantages of conducting similar experiments on artificial datasets that possess higher visual fidelity, as this could offer additional insights and potentially yield more accurate and reliable results. Exploring such avenues could greatly contribute to advancing the field of medical imaging analysis and its applications in clinical settings.

References

1. Jena, B., et al.: Brain tumor characterization using radiogenomics in artificial intelligence framework. Cancers **14**(16), 4052 (2022)
2. Tamimi, A.F., et al.: Epidemiology and Outcome of Glioblastoma, pp. 143–153. Exon Publications, Brisbane City (2017)
3. Jena, B., et al.: An empirical study of different machine learning techniques for brain tumor classification and subsequent segmentation using hybrid texture feature. Mach. Vis. Appl. **33**(1), 6 (2022)
4. Foroozandeh, M., et al.: GAN-Based Synthesis of Brain Tumor Segmentation Data: Augmenting a dataset by generating artificial images, ed, 2020
5. Saxena, S., et al.: Advanced approaches for medical image segmentation. Appl. Biomed. Eng. Neurosci. 153–172 (2019)
6. Jena, B., et al.: Maximum payload for digital image steganography obtained by mixed edge detection mechanism. In: 2019 International Conference on Information Technology (ICIT), pp. 206–210. IEEE (2019)
7. Bardosi, Z., et al.: Metacarpal bones localization in x-ray imagery using particle filter segmentation, arXiv preprint arXiv:. 2014
8. Ali, H., et al.: The role of generative adversarial networks in brain MRI: a scoping review. Insights Imaging **13**(1), 98 (2022)

9. Creswell, A., et al.: Generative adversarial networks: an overview. IEEE Signal Process. Mag. **35**(1), 53–65 (2018)

10. Ronneberger, O., et al.: U-net: convolutional networks for biomedical image segmentation. In: Navab, N., Hornegger, J., Wells, W., Frangi, A. (eds.) Medical Image Computing and Computer-Assisted Intervention – MICCAI 2015. MICCAI 2015. LNCS, vol. 9351, pp. 234–241. Springer, Cham (2015). https://doi.org/10.1007/978-3-319-24574-4_28

11. Dong, H., et al.: Automatic brain tumor detection and segmentation using U-Net based fully convolutional networks. In: Valdés Hernández, M., González-Castro, V. (eds.) Medical Image Understanding and Analysis. MIUA 2017. CCIS, vol. 723, pp. 506–517. Springer, Cham (2017). https://doi.org/10.1007/978-3-319-60964-5_44

12. Xue, Y., et al.: Adversarial learning with multi-scale loss for skin lesion segmentation. In: 2018 IEEE 15th International Symposium on Biomedical Imaging (ISBI 2018), pp. 859–863. IEEE (2018)

13. Isola, P., et al.: Image-to-image translation with conditional adversarial networks. In: Proceedings of the IEEE Conference on Computer Vision and Pattern Recognition, pp. 1125–1134 (2017)

14. Rezaei, M. et al.: A conditional adversarial network for semantic segmentation of brain tumor. In: Crimi, A., Bakas, S., Kuijf, H., Menze, B., Reyes, M. (eds.) Brainlesion: Glioma, Multiple Sclerosis, Stroke and Traumatic Brain Injuries. BrainLes 2017. LNCS, vol. 10670, pp. 241–252. Springer, Cham (2018). https://doi.org/10.1007/978-3-319-75238-9_21

15. Simonyan, K., et al.: Very deep convolutional networks for large-scale image recognition, arXiv preprint arXiv:. 2014

16. Bakas, S., et al.: Advancing the cancer genome atlas glioma MRI collections with expert segmentation labels and radiomic features. Sci. Data **4**(1), 1–13 (2017)

17. Menze, B.H., et al.: The multimodal brain tumor image segmentation benchmark (BRATS). IEEE Trans. Med. Imaging **34**(10), 1993–2024 (2014)

18. Bakas, S., et al.: Identifying the best machine learning algorithms for brain tumor segmentation, progression assessment, and overall survival prediction in the BRATS challenge, arXiv preprint arXiv:.02629 (2018)

19. Bakas, S.: Segmentation labels and radiomic features for the pre-operative scans of the TCGA-GBM collection, July 2017. org/10. K, vol. 9

20. Goodfellow, I., et al.: Generative adversarial networks. Commun. ACM **63**(11), 139–144 (2020)

21. Jena, B., et al.: Effect of learning parameters on the performance of the U-Net architecture for cell nuclei segmentation from microscopic cell images. Microscopy (2022)

22. Jena, B., et al.: Analysis of depth variation of U-NET architecture for brain tumor segmentation. Multimed. Tools Appl. **82**(7), 10723–10743 (2023)

23. Jena, B., et al.: High-Performance computing and its requirements in deep learning. In: High-Performance Medical Image Processing: Apple, pp. 255–288. Academic Press (2022)

24. Saxena, S., et al.: Study of parallel image processing with the implementation of VHGW algorithm using CUDA on NVIDIA'S GPU framework. In: Proceedings of the World Congress on Engineering, vol. 1 (2017)

25. Wang, G., et al.: Automatic Brain Tumor Segmentation using Cascaded Anisotropic Convolutional Neural Networks, arXiv.org, 2018. https://arxiv.org/abs/1709.00382. Accessed 28 Jun 2023

26. Hussain, S., et al.: Brain tumor segmentation using cascaded deep convolutional neural network. In: 2017 39th Annual International Conference of the IEEE Engineering in Medicine and Biology Society (EMBC), Jeju, Korea (South), pp. 1998–2001 (2017). https://doi.org/10.1109/EMBC.2017.8037243

27. Saxena, S., et al.: Prediction of O-6-methylguanine-DNA methyltransferase and overall survival of the patients suffering from glioblastoma using MRI-based hybrid radiomics signatures in machine and deep learning framework. Neural Comput. Appl. **35**(18), 13647–13663 (2023)

28. Suri, J.S., et al.: Five strategies for bias estimation in artificial intelligence-based hybrid deep learning for acute respiratory distress syndrome COVID-19 lung infected patients using AP (AI) Bias 2.0: a systematic review. IEEE Trans. Instrum. Meas. (2022)

29. Saxena, S., et al.: An intelligent system for segmenting an abdominal image in multi core architecture. In: 2013 10th International Conference and Expo on Emerging Technologies for a Smarter World (CEWIT). IEEE (2013)

30. Sinha, P., et al.: Medical image segmentation: hard and soft computing approaches. SN Appl. Sci. **2**, 1–8 (2020)

31. Das, S., et al.: Brain tumor segmentation and overall survival period prediction in glioblastoma multiforme using radiomic features. Concurr. Comput. Pract. Exp. **34**(20), e6501 (2022)

32. Suri, J.S., et al.: Cardiovascular/stroke risk stratification in Parkinson's disease patients using atherosclerosis pathway and artificial intelligence paradigm: a systematic review. Metabolites **12**(4), 312 (2022)

33. Elazab, A., et al.: GP-GAN: brain tumor growth prediction using stacked 3D generative adversarial networks from longitudinal MR Images. Neural Netw. **132**, 321–332 (2020). https://doi.org/10.1016/j.neunet.2020.09.004

34. Neelima, G., Chigurukota, D.R., Maram, B., Girirajan, B.: Optimal DeepMRSeg based tumor segmentation with GAN for brain tumor classification. Biomed. Signal Process. Control **74**, 103537 (2022). https://doi.org/10.1016/j.bspc.2022.103537

35. Altun Güven, S., Talu, M.F.: Brain MRI high resolution image creation and segmentation with the new GAN method. Biomed. Signal Process. Control 80, 104246 (2023). https://doi.org/10.1016/j.bspc.2022.104246

36. Liu, X., et al.: BTMF-GAN: a multi-modal MRI fusion generative adversarial network for brain tumors. Comput. Biol. Med. **157**, 106769 (2023). https://doi.org/10.1016/j.compbiomed.2023.106769

37. Aslan, N., Dogan, S., Koca, G.O.: Automated classification of brain diseases using the restricted Boltzmann machine and the generative adversarial network. Eng. Appl. Artif. Intell. **126**, 106794 (2023). https://doi.org/10.1016/j.engappai.2023.106794

A Machine Learning Approach for Risk Prediction of Cardiovascular Disease

Shovna Panda[1], Shantilata Palei[1], Mullapudi Venkata Sai Samartha[1], Biswajit Jena[2], and Sanjay Saxena[1(✉)]

[1] International Institute of Information Technology, Bhubaneswar 751003, Odisha, India
sanjay@iiit-bh.ac.in
[2] Institute of Technical Education and Research, SOA University, Bhubaneswar 751030, Odisha, India

Abstract. Worldwide, Cardiovascular Diseases (CVD) continue to be the most prevalent cause of fatality and morbidity, claiming the lives of approximately 20.5 million individuals annually. Timely and accurate risk prediction is crucial in identifying high-risk individuals and implementing preventive measures. Leveraging Machine Learning (ML) techniques and unbiased data analysis can enhance the efficacy of risk forecasting by uncovering new risk determinants and understanding complex relationships among them. In this study, publicly available data from the University of California Irvine (UCI) repository was utilized to detect CVD. Four ML methodologies, namely K-Nearest Neighbor (KNN), Multi-Layer Perceptron (MLP), Support Vector Machine (SVM), and Extreme Gradient Boosting (XGBoost), were employed, along with hyperparameter tuning techniques to improve predictive accuracy. The models were trained and evaluated using Grid Search Cross-Validation. The results demonstrated promising predictive capabilities for each classifier. The KNN model achieved an AUC value of 0.9821, the MLP model achieved 0.9935, the SVM had an AUC score of 0.9464, and the XGBoost performed exceptionally well with an AUC score of 0.9978. Consequently, the XGBoost model was recommended for automated CVD detection. This study highlights the potential of ML techniques in the healthcare sector, offering an alternative to conventional visual inspection methods. The widespread adoption of ML technology empowers medical professionals to diagnose CVD more accurately by evaluating complex traits and features, thereby improving patient prognosis and treatment.

Keywords: Cardiovascular Disease · Cross Validation · Feature Selection · Machine Learning

1 Introduction

Cardiovascular Disease (CVD) pertains to several ailments that impact the functioning of the heart and blood vessels, such as blood clots, structural deviations, and vascular damage. The potential effects of CVD can be severe, resulting in vascular and heart failure, physical impairment, or even death. It is crucial to identify CVD early on to save

H. Kaur et al. (Eds.): CVIP 2023, CCIS 2010, pp. 313–323, 2024.
https://doi.org/10.1007/978-3-031-58174-8_27

lives. A medical diagnosis identifies illnesses or abnormalities contributing to symptoms and ambiguous indicators, typically determined through health records and physical examinations and confirmed by trained physicians [1]. Many patients fail to receive an appropriate diagnosis because of the lack of necessary health experts [2]. Conventional diagnostic processes frequently involve human interaction, which might be constrained by a person's capacity, but ML-based solutions are not [29]. The expanding utilization of ML approaches in healthcare domains for detecting medical conditions accentuates the technology's efficacy in this field [3, 27, 28]. However, there is still room for improvement in reliability and precision in the existing studies, with challenges like unbalanced data, ML comprehension, and ML conduct principles [4]. A promising area for development is the ethical combination of routine clinical data with ML methods to predict CVD. Unfortunately, a thorough study that incorporates these components has not yet been carried out, despite its potential advantages [5, 6].

Cardiologists struggle with early patient diagnosis and treatment due to limitations in the current medical system. Conventional risk-assessment techniques, like coronary angiography, are intrusive and risky and oversimplify complex correlations between risk factors. This study aims to provide the predictive performance of four reliable ML models, such as KNN, MLP, SVM, and XGBoost, filling the gap between traditional and cutting-edge technology to detect CVD, by analyzing and establishing connections between intricate relationships and outcomes associated with CVD. The prediction model offers a revolutionary method for early and enhanced diagnosis of CVD, reducing fatality rates and saving money and time in cardiovascular healthcare procedures, thereby improving the quality and accuracy of clinical decision-making and preventative healthcare [7].

Our contribution to this study:

- ML approaches for the timely detection of cardiovascular diseases.
- Determine and analyze the ML algorithm that yields the best results and whether machine learning could increase the precision of cardiovascular risk prediction in health care for the general public.
- Understand how data range affects CVD predictions by providing a rigorous statistical analysis of input datasets.

The rest of this study is organized in the following order: Sect. 2 overviews the literature survey. The methods proposed in this study are described in Sect. 3, whereas Sect. 4 displays the results. A critical discussion of the study is in Sect. 5, and in Sect. 6 we conclude the paper.

2 Literature Survey

Many researchers worked on this CVD detection from this we reviewed important papers. Pal et al. [5] investigated the effectiveness of MLP and KNN for detecting CVD using the CVD Dataset from the UCI repository and suggested using MLP by obtaining an accuracy of 82.47%. Kaur et al. [8] created a system that generates suggestions based on historical and empirical data using ML techniques and publicly available healthcare datasets and detected CVD using MLP with an accuracy of 47.54%. Beunza et al. [9]

used R-Studio and Rapid Miner and got an AUC value of 0.75 using an SVM technique on the Framingham heart database for predicting CVD. Kamencay *et al.* [10] studied a novel approach using PCA-KNN, a scale-invariant component frequently applied in scaling medical images. When trained using 200 images, they attained 83.6% accuracy. In a study by Pouriyeh *et al.* [11], where they used a Boosting SVM, an AUC value of 0.8846 was obtained. MLP was used by Bhatt *et al.* [12] to predict CVD, and the results showed an accuracy of 87.28%. MLP and SVM techniques were utilized by Gudadhe *et al.* [13] to classify heart diseases, where they obtained an accuracy of 80.41%. Johnson *et al.* [14] explored predictive modeling ideas in cardiology, including feature selection and incorrect dichotomization, and the potential of deep learning in precision cardiology to enhance the care of patients. El-Bialy *et al.* [15] applied a fast decision tree and a pruned C4.5 tree to achieve 78.06% classification accuracy. An Artificial Neural Network and a Fuzzy Neural Network were combined to create a hybrid neural network in a study by Kahramanli *et al.* [16] on the Cleveland heart disease dataset, and K-fold cross-validation yielded an accuracy of 86.8%. Yang *et al.* [17] presented SVM-based approaches, with PCA-SVM attaining an accuracy of 88.24%. Budholiya *et al.* [18] achieved an AUC score of 0.9134 by using an improved XGBoost classifier to predict CVD. Zhang *et al.* [19] suggested a method for predicting CVD by combining embedded feature selection based on Linear SVC and deep neural networks and achieved an AUC score of 0.983. Supervised ML techniques for forecasting heart diseases were investigated by Upadhyay *et al.* [20] using the UCI ML repository. They found that logistic regression had the highest AUC score of 0.87 of all the tested algorithms.

Our study improves CVD categorization and risk prediction by developing ML models with optimized hyperparameters via Grid Search cross-validation, resulting in substantially higher accuracy and AUC scores compared to the previous research.

3   Proposed Method

This study uses KNN, MLP, SVM, and XGBoost to analyze cardiovascular risk prediction. The following is the flow of the proposed work.

- The Heart Disease dataset [21] from the UCI Repository is collected to train and test the aforementioned ML models.
- Exploratory Data Analysis was performed on the dataset to comprehend the data better.
- Data pre-processing was performed on the data to reduce the skewed measurements and increase the accuracy and then, it was scaled and transformed.
- 13 attributes out of the 76 in the dataset were considered for the training and testing of the ML models.
- The ML models were trained and the accuracy was aimed to be increased by hyperparameter tuning using Grid Search cross-validation (cv).
- The models are then tested by predicting the classes as CVD or No CVD.
- A collection of performance measures is used to evaluate and compare the performance and potential of the ML algorithms.

The flow of the proposed study is shown in Fig. 1.

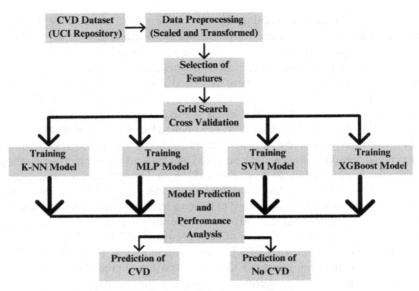

Fig. 1. Flow of the Proposed Work

3.1 The Dataset

The dataset used in this study for the creation of the detection models, obtained from the University of California Irvine (UCI) repository, is the CVD Cleveland dataset [21]. It has been changed to a comma-separated file (.csv) format. The dataset has 303 samples and 76 attributes. Out of those 76 attributes, 13 are considered for training and testing the models after the data preprocessing and selection of features. They are chest pain, sex, age, resting blood pressure, fasting blood sugar, cholesterol, resting electrocardiographic result, exercise-induced angina, maximum heart rate, ST depression, number of major vessels, the slope of peak ST segment, thallium stress result, and one target output [5, 21].

3.2 Exploratory Data Analysis

The main goal in the exploratory data analysis stage is to comprehend the data better, spot anomalies, and produce insights that can guide future analysis and modeling decisions. Here in this study, missing values, outliers, and inconsistencies were identified and removed from the data. The mean, median, mode, and standard deviation were analyzed, offering insights into the dataset's central patterns, variability, and distribution. All features correlated with the target output were found, to know about the linear association between quantitative features. Selecting qualities that correlate favorably with the desired variable is typically better. A few severely negatively connected features were to be removed from the data collection. For this, a Heatmap was plotted, as shown in Fig. 2.

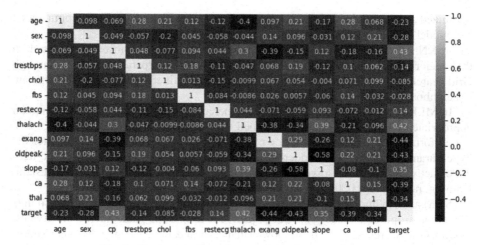

Fig. 2. Heatmap to show the correlation between features.

A Pairplot was also plotted to understand the pairwise relationship between the attributes. Scatter plots were also plotted to see the relationship between each feature and another. It was also found that the dataset has 165 patients who had CVD and 138 patients who did not have CVD.

3.3 Data Preprocessing and Feature Selection

Pre-processing of the dataset [21], including smoothing, standardization, and aggregation, reduced skewed measurements. The correlation matrix and Heatmap indicated if the features are favorably or negatively associated. According to all these factors, only the 13 most important attributes were used in building the model out of the given 76 biomarkers. The categorical variables i.e., chest pain, sex, resting electrocardiographic result, fasting blood sugar, exercise-induced angina, number of major vessels, the slope of peak ST segment, and thallium stress result, are transformed into dummy values. The variables age, resting blood pressure, ST depression, maximum heart rate, and cholesterol are scaled and transformed using the Standard Scaler.

3.4 Training the Models

KNN, MLP, SVM, and XGBoost were trained on the CVD dataset from the UCI library [21]. The dataset was split into 80% for the training and 20% for the testing.

The dataset [21] was divided into training and validation subgroups during training. GridSearch cv was used to optimize and find the best hyperparameters for each model to maximize the AUC score from the ROC curve. The models were trained on the training data set with a 10-fold cv, ensuring thorough training and performance assessment using multiple data subsets. Each model underwent iterative data fitting and performance evaluation using the prescribed hyperparameter grid, which was carefully defined and optimized as it significantly impacts predictive model performance. The recommended ML model was the one with the highest AUC ROC score.

In KNN, the k nearest neighbors to the new data point are chosen [22]. Based on their majority class, the label of the class is allocated. By hyperparameter tuning, through Grid Search with a cv of 10, the optimal parameters identified were metric – Manhattan, n_neighbors (= k) – 9, and weights – uniform.

In MLP, a structured arrangement of the perceptrons forms distinct layers, and an appropriate collection of outputs is mapped from a set of input datasets [12, 23, 24]. On performing Grid Search with a cv of 10, the best parameters ascertained after the hyperparameter tuning were: hidden_layer_sizes – (400, 400, 400, 400, 400), max_iter– 2000, activation – tanh, solver – adam, alpha – 0.0001, learning_rate – constant, learning_rate_init – 0.0001 and early_stopping - true.

SVM aims to find an N-dimensional space hyperplane that partitions the data points into the appropriate classes [17]. Our objective is to find the plane having the greatest margin. Grid Search with a cv of 10 showed that the best parameters after the hyperparameter tuning were: Penalty Parameter C, which governs the balance between minimizing training errors and maximizing margin width, – 1, gamma – scale, kernel – poly, and probability - true.

Through the technique of gradient boosting, XGBoost sequentially constructs classifiers by training decision trees on the gradient of the loss obtained from the preceding tree [25, 26]. On performing hyperparameter tuning using Grid Search cross-validation with a cv of 10, the optimal parameters determined were: gamma – 1.5, max_depth – 4, min_child_weight – 5, n_estimators – 100, and subsample – 0.6.

3.5   Prediction of Class

The models are then tested by predicting the classes, 1 for CVD and 0 for No CVD. To assess the prospective value of ML algorithms, a set of performance metrics is used.

3.6   Performance Analysis

The potential of all the ML algorithms is assessed using a set of performance metrics. They are primarily evaluated using the AUC Score calculated from the ROC Curve. The accuracy, recall, precision, and F1-Score are also calculated. The Confusion Matrix is also generated for the result of each ML model.

4   Results

4.1   Environmental Setup

For our study, the Python 3.11 virtual environment was used. Pandas, NumPy, sklearn, and matplotlib were the few python libraries that were installed, using the virtual environment on Jupyter Notebook, to visualize and analyze the data. It was set up on HP Pavilion Intel Core i7 7th Gen. The operating system on our device is Windows 10 OS.

4.2 Results of the ML Models Used in Our Study

The Results section provides a comprehensive overview of the performance metrics for each ML model we evaluated in our study. Table 1 presents the testing accuracy, validation accuracy, and the AUC scores achieved by the models, providing a clear comparison of their predictive capabilities.

Table 1. Accuracy, Validation Accuracy, and AUC Scores of the Models used in our study

Algorithm	Testing Accuracy (%)	Validation Accuracy (%)	AUC Score (considered metric in our study)
KNN	98.36	90.23	0.9821
MLP	96.72	91.42	0.9935
SVM	95.08	89.67	0.9464
XGBoost (the recommended approach in our study)	98.36	91.96	0.9978

According to the above results, it is observed that the XGBoost Model with the parameters obtained after cross-validation and hyperparameter tuning performs the best, with an AUC score of 0.9978. The ROC Plot of the XGBoost Model in Fig. 3 shows an AUC Score of 0.9978.

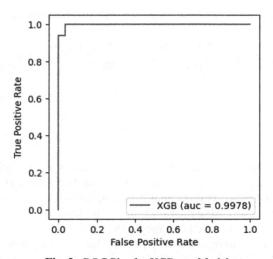

Fig. 3. ROC Plot for XGBoost Model

The developed XGBoost Model also gives increased TPs and TNs and fewer FPs and FNs, with 27 TPs and 1 FP, 0 FNs, and 33 TNs, out of the 61 instances the models were tested on. The confusion matrix of the XGBoost model is shown in Fig. 4.

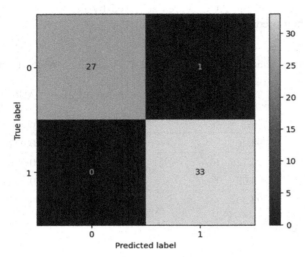

Fig. 4. Confusion Matrix of XGBoost Model

The accuracy, recall, precision, and F1-Score are also calculated for the XGBoost model and are shown in Table 2.

Table 2. Precision, Recall, F1-Score, Accuracy, and AUC Score for the XGBoost Model

Precision	Recall	F1-Score	Accuracy (%)	AUC Score
0.96	1.00	0.98	98.36	0.9978

5 Discussion

AUC metric considers probabilities of category prediction. As a result, the models can be more accurately assessed and contrasted. Using probabilities and AUC, probability thresholds can be tuned and our models can be strengthened even further. Thus, our study uses the AUC ROC as a scoring metric for model performance evaluation. In Fig. 5, a comparison of the AUC scores and accuracy values between our recommended approach and the other models we have studied is enlisted. The outcomes show how the four ML models performed differently on the CVD dataset. The results presented indicate that with an AUC Score of 0.9978 and an accuracy of 98.36%, the XGBoost model, which is our recommended approach in this study, had the best result, followed by MLP (AUC = 0.9935), KNN (AUC = 0.9821), and SVM (AUC = 0.9464).

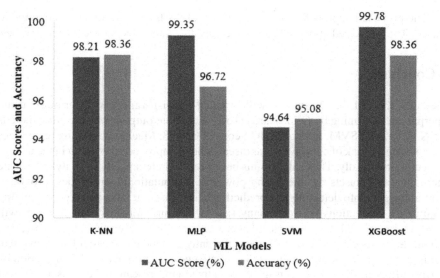

Fig. 5. Comparison of the AUC Scores and Accuracy of the ML Models we have studied in this research

In Table 3 a comparison of AUC scores between our suggested approach and previously published studies is provided. Our approach surpasses previous studies by achieving a higher AUC Score and better risk prediction for CVD.

Table 3. AUC-ROC Score Comparison of our proposed approach with existing studies

Research Studies	Approaches Studied	AUC-Score	Reference
Pal *et al.*, 2022	MLP	0.8641	[5]
Pouriyeh *et al.*, 2017	Boosting SVM	0.8846	[11]
Budholiya *et al.*, 2022	XGBoost	0.9134	[18]
Zhang *et al.*, 2021	Linear SVC and DNN	0.983	[19]
Upadhyay *et al.*, 2023	Logistic Regression	0.87	[20]
Our Proposed Approach	XGBoost with Hyperparameter Tuning and Cross- Validation of 10	0.9978	–

Data preprocessing and GridSearch cross-validation, used to tune the hyperparameters, greatly enhanced the performance of all the models we used in our study. Searching for the ideal hyperparameter values improved each model's AUC Score, accuracy, and resilience.

Our study's limitation is that the dataset [21] employed in our research is comparatively smaller. However, the established models may be used with vast amounts of data. The proposed approach is anticipated to help the healthcare industry continue to advance. The suggested approach can also be used to categorize various other diseases.

6 Conclusion

This study showed that XGBoost, with optimal hyper-parameters, determined using Hyperparameter Tuning by Grid-Search cross-validation, outperforms the other models - KNN, MLP, and SVM, with an AUC Score 0f 0.9978. Machine Learning techniques for predicting the risk of cardiovascular diseases have improved innovation in the healthcare sector profoundly. These algorithms have proven their capacity to analyze intricate patterns within datasets by integrating powerful computational techniques, providing essential insights into detecting and predicting cardiovascular risks and comprehending the complex interactions between many risk factors and ailments. Our methods will allow for more specialized and targeted approaches to illnesses, early identification, prevention, therapy, and course of treatment. Recently conducted research has shown that there is still room for improvement in the effectiveness of automated CVD detection by utilizing different ML models. It is to be noted that in this research, the dataset used was comparatively smaller. By collaborating with medical experts, gaining access to hospital databases in the future, and performing extensive studies on routine patient data, we hope to improve the research work further and enable a more thorough and practical assessment of the suggested methods for predicting cardiovascular and other diseases.

References

1. Kim, E.E., et al.: Current medical diagnosis and treatment. J. Nucl. Med. **50**(1), 165 (2009)
2. Suri, J.S., et al.: Five strategies for bias estimation in artificial intelligence-based hybrid deep learning for acute respiratory distress syndrome COVID-19 lung infected patients using AP (AI) Bias 2.0: a systematic review. IEEE Trans. Instrum. Meas. (2022)
3. Jena, B., et al.: An empirical study of different machine learning techniques for brain tumor classification and subsequent segmentation using hybrid texture feature. Mach. Vis. Appl. **33**(1), 6 (2022)
4. Jena, B., et al.: Artificial intelligence-based hybrid deep learning models for image classification: the first narrative review. Comput. Biol. Med. **137**, 104803 (2021)
5. Pal, M., et al.: Risk prediction of cardiovascular disease using machine learning classifiers. Open Med. **17**(1), 1100–1113 (2022)
6. Nagavelli, U., et al.: Machine learning technology-based heart disease detection models. J. Healthc. Eng. **2022** (2022)
7. Alaa, A.M., et al.: Cardiovascular disease risk prediction using automated machine learning: a prospective study of 423,604 UK Biobank participants. PLoS ONE **14**(5), e0213653 (2019)
8. Kaur, P., et al.: A healthcare monitoring system using random forest and internet of things (IoT). Multimed. Tools Appl. **78**, 19905–19916 (2019)
9. Beunza, J.-J., et al.: Comparison of machine learning algorithms for clinical event prediction (risk of coronary heart disease). J. Biomed. Inform. **97**, 103257 (2019)
10. Kamencay, P., et al.: Feature extraction for object recognition using PCA-KNN with application to medical image analysis. In: 2013 36th International Conference on Telecommunications and Signal Processing (TSP), pp. 830–834. IEEE (2013)

11. Pouriyeh, S., et al.: A comprehensive investigation and comparison of machine learning techniques in the domain of heart disease. In: 2017 IEEE Symposium on Computers and Communications (ISCC), pp. 204–207. IEEE (2017)
12. Bhatt, C.M., et al.: Effective heart disease prediction using machine learning techniques. Algorithms 16(2), 88 (2023)
13. Gudadhe, M., et al.: Decision support system for heart disease based on support vector machine and artificial neural network. In: 2010 International Conference on Computer and Communication Technology (ICCCT), pp. 741–745. IEEE (2010)
14. Johnson, K.W., et al.: Artificial intelligence in cardiology. J. Am. Coll. Cardiol. 71(23), 2668–2679 (2018)
15. El-Bialy, R., et al.: Feature analysis of coronary artery heart disease data sets. Procedia Comput. Sci. 65, 459–468 (2015)
16. Kahramanli, H., et al.: Design of a hybrid system for the diabetes and heart diseases. Expert Syst. Appl. 35(1–2), 82–89 (2008)
17. Yang, C., et al.: Heart-disease diagnosis via support vector machine-based approaches. In: 2018 IEEE International Conference on Systems, Man, and Cybernetics (SMC), pp. 3153–3158. IEEE (2018)
18. Budholiya, K., et al.: An optimized XGBoost based diagnostic system for effective prediction of heart disease. J. King Saud Univ.-Comput. Inf. Sci. 34(7), 4514–4523 (2022)
19. Zhang, D., et al.: Heart disease prediction based on the embedded feature selection method and deep neural network. J. Healthc. Eng. 2021, 1–9 (2021)
20. Upadhyay, S., et al.: Heart disease prediction model using various supervised learning algorithm. In: 2023 IEEE 12th International Conference on Communication Systems and Network Technologies (CSNT), pp. 197–201. IEEE (2023)
21. Asuncion, A., et al.: UCI machine learning repository. ed: Irvine, CA, USA, 2007
22. Wang, L., et al.: Research and implementation of machine learning classifier based on KNN. In: IOP Conference Series: Materials Science and Engineering, vol. 677, no. 5, p. 052038. IOP publishing (2019)
23. Mohanty, M.D., et al.: Verbal sentiment analysis and detection using recurrent neural network. In: Advanced Data Mining Tools and Methods for Social Computing, pp. 85–106. Elsevier (2022)
24. Wu, C.C., et al.: Prediction of fatty liver disease using machine learning algorithms. Comput. Methods Programs Biomed. 170, 23–29 (2019)
25. Opitz, D., et al.: Popular ensemble methods: an empirical study. J. Artif. Intell. Res. 11, 169–198 (1999)
26. Chen, T., et al.: Xgboost: a scalable tree boosting system. In: Proceedings of the 22nd ACM SIGKDD International Conference on Knowledge Discovery and Data Mining, pp. 785–794 (2016)
27. Saxena, S., et al.: Role of artificial intelligence in radiogenomics for cancers in the era of precision medicine. Cancers 14(12), 2860 (2022)
28. Suri, J.S., et al.: Cardiovascular/stroke risk stratification in Parkinson's disease patients using atherosclerosis pathway and artificial intelligence paradigm: a systematic review. Metabolites 12(4), 312 (2022)
29. Sinha, P., et al.: Medical image segmentation: hard and soft computing approaches. SN Appl. Sci. 2, 1–8 (2020)

Automatic Segmentation of Hard Exudates Using LAB Color Space Contours Edge Detection and Morphological Operation

Shree Prakash and Jagadeesh Kakarla[✉]

Department of Computer Science and Engineering, Indian Institute of Information Technology, Design and Manufacturing, Chennai, Tamil Nadu, India
{coe19d002,jagadeeshk}@iiitdm.ac.in

Abstract. Diabetic retinopathy is a serious medical condition that affects people across the world and diminishes the quality of life. Hard exudates are one of the most common and early signs of diabetic retinopathy. Segmentation of hard exudates is a challenging task due to the wide diversity in features such as irregular shape, size, and location. This paper proposes an efficient and accurate approach for the segmentation of hard exudates from RGB (Red, Green, Blue) fundus images. An unsupervised approach partitions the fundus image into disjoint and mutually exclusive regions. With this approach, the system is flexible enough to use different methods in diverse regions. Luminance and A-axis component generates a new image and adaptive threshold extracts the exudates in one region. In other regions, the unsupervised multi-stage algorithm detects the region of exudates. Morphological operation followed by contour features enhances the exudates region and removes the outliers. The proposed approach obtains 0.913, 0.981, 0.975 of recall, specificity, and accuracy on the ISBI IDRiD dataset.

Keywords: Hard exudates · Luminance · Unsupervised · Adaptive threshold · Morphology · Contours

1 Introduction

Diabetic Retinopathy (DR) is a progressive, chronic, and leading cause of blindness. Hard exudates (HE) is one of the biomarkers in diabetic retinopathy [1–3]. Additionally, it contributes to the development of macular edema, which impairs the clearest vision of the eye [4]. The color appearance of HE are yellow deposits, which can range in size from tiny specks to massive patches illustrated in Fig. 1(a). The characteristics of HE are not fixed and its structure is irregular. It can be greater than the optic disc and smaller than blood vessels. The position of HE is unknown. It can be anywhere in the fundus image as shown in Fig. 1(b). It takes a lot of effort and expertise for humans to detect HE [5]. Blindness can develop from exudates that are detected too late, particularly in places with poor medical infrastructure. It is necessary to develop a tool for automatic segmentation and detection of the exudates.

Several approaches have been put forth throughout the years for the segmentation of HE from RGB fundus images [6–8,10–16]. Basha *et al.* [6] proposed a methodology to identify the region having HE using morphological operation, fuzzy logic and several color space. It performs the segmentation of exudates in presence of optic disc and gives few false positives due to the color similarity with optic disc. Imani *et al.* [7] separate the vessels from lesions using the green channel of fundus image. Morphological Component Analysis (MCA) [8] and dynamic thresholding are utilized to segregate lesions from retinal anatomy. Exudates border is extracted using morphological operation. However, some portions of the lesion are not completely separated. In [10], the initial seed is chosen as HE using a supervised multilayer perceptron. The initial seeds are clustered using K-means clustering mechanism to prevent fault detection. Exudates are segmented using the graph cut technique. Further, the authors have achieved less sensitivity because it is unable to distinguish between pixels, particularly those that are on the edge of patches of HE. In [11], the fully convolutional network model (FCN-8) with shortcuts is used to segment exudates. Further, it eliminates the optic disc from the retinal image before processing the hard exudates by locating the area with a Faster R-CNN based on the AlexNet [9]. However, the achieved sensitivity is 81.6%. Garifullin *et al.* [12] presents a Bayesian framework for the detection of hard exudates. The architecture utilized is dense-FCN [13]. However, the sensitivity achieved is 76.7%. In [14], the network architecture and results of a grand competition on "Diabetic Retinopathy Segmentation and Grading", on Biomedical Imaging (ISBI 2018) is reported. The Indian Diabetic Retinopathy Image Dataset(IDRiD) [14] is used for the challenge. It consists of three sub-challenges. Sub-challenge 1(Task -2) deals with the segmentation of hard exudates. Several participants have presented their methodologies which are developed using deep neural networks. The maximum sensitivity achieved is 88.5%. Guo *et al.* [15] presents a two stage training lightweight encoder decoder

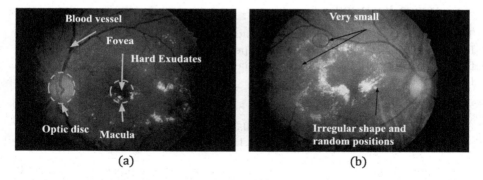

(a)   (b)

Fig. 1. Pathological sample of hard exudates: (a) Anatomical structure in eye fundus image, (b) Challenges in hard exudates segmentation

model with Multi-scale feature to increase filter size and decrease parameters. However, the achieved sensitivity is 78.03%. Zhang *et al.* [16] presents a super-resolution multi-scale feature module to improve the detection of tiny lesions and boundaries. Multi-scale Attention Fusion (MAF) module reduces the noise due to super-resolution and enhances the localization of small lesions and boundaries. Still, the achieved accuracy and sensitivity are 85.96% and 69.39% respectively. Our key contribution are as follows:

- We proposed an automatic effective method for the segmentation of hard exudates.
- An unsupervised approach partition the image into disjoint and mutually exclusive regions. It makes the system flexible to adapt multiple approach in different regions.
- Luminance and A-axis component highlight the exudates from its environs and adaptive threshold is utilized to segment the exudates from one region, while multistage edge detection method followed by morphological operation and contour feature detects the exudates in other regions.

The rest of this paper is structured as follows. An overview of the proposed approach and descriptions of the algorithms are provided in Sect. 2. Section 3 covers Results and Discussion. Section 4 concludes the proposed work.

2   Methodology

The proposed block diagram shown in Fig. 2 depicts the work flow of the segmentation of hard exudates and the steps are provided in Algorithm 1. The proposed approach is broadly divided into two parts. (a) Unsupervised approach is utilized for the partition of RGB fundus image. (b)This makes the system flexible to implement different approaches on the partitioned fundus RGB image. The detailed description of approach is as follows.

2.1   Image Partition

The eye fundus image input in RGB space is transformed into LAB color space. It is perceptually uniform, device independent, separate the color information from gray information, and resembles the logarithmic behaviour of the eye [19]. It is computed as

$$\begin{bmatrix} L \\ A \\ B \end{bmatrix} = \begin{bmatrix} 1 \\ 1.4749 \\ 0.6249 \end{bmatrix}^T \odot \left(\begin{bmatrix} 0.2126 & 0.2213 & 0.1949 \\ 0.7152 & -0.3390 & -0.6057 \\ 0.0722 & 0.1177 & -0.8066 \end{bmatrix} \begin{bmatrix} R \\ G \\ B \end{bmatrix} \right) + \begin{bmatrix} 0 \\ 128 \\ 128 \end{bmatrix} \quad (1)$$

After computing $2 * L + A$, colour quantization [20, 21] is applied to the image. It is performed by adaptive quantization followed by inverse color mapping. It is a method of scaling down the excessive number of colors. The first step is to choose fewer colors to portray the colors of the input image, known as the color palette.

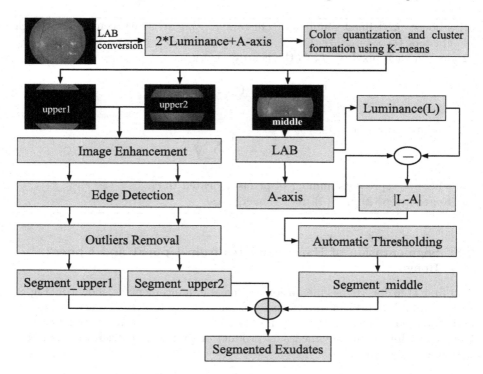

Fig. 2. Proposed block diagram for the segmentation of hard exudates

In the second step, every input pixel is allocated to one of the colors known as pixel mapping. The two primary categories of quantization algorithms are (i) post-clustering method, which generates a set of K members that are improved by the iterative process, and (ii) pre-clustering approach, that partition set of colors and assign one representative to each cluster. K-mean clustering is one of the most efficient and widely used unsupervised clustering techniques [22]. It is an iterative, adaptive quantization and post clustering technique implemented in our work. The process is repeated until local solution is found. Let I is an input image, set I_p represents the pixel of I, and N denotes the total number of pixels. The number of desired colors in a quantize image is K and the number of color channels is G. The pseudo-code for K-means is given below.

2.2 Extraction of Hard Exudates from Cluster Image

The output of the Algorithm 1 (step1) is upper1, upper2, and middle image respectively as shown in Fig. 2. Algorithm 1 (step2) lists the step of extraction of exudates from upper1 and upper2 clusters and Algorithm 1 (step3) provide the segmentation step from middle cluster.

1: Choose predefined number of clusters K and arbitrary centroid for each clusters $\{c_1, c_2, c_3, ..., c_k\}$.

2: Assign each pixel q ϵ I_p to the nearest center c_i,

$$q \leftarrow argmin_{z\epsilon\{c_1,c_2,...,c_k\}} \|z - q\|$$

3: Update cluster centers,

$$c_i \leftarrow \frac{1}{n_i} \sum_{q\epsilon p_i} q$$

where n_i represents number of pixels allocated to c_i.

4: Repeat step (2) and (3) until convergence.

2.3 Segmentation of Hard Exudates from Upper1 and Upper2 Image

The first step for HE segmentation is image enhancement as shown in Fig. 2. Gabor filter has been acknowledged as an efficient tool for image processing and computer vision, particularly for texture analysis, and image enhancement [23]. It is a linear filter defined as a product of sinusoidal carrier and Gaussian envelope given in Eq. 2.

$$exp[\frac{-(x^2 + \gamma^2 y^2))}{2\sigma^2}].exp[i(\frac{2\pi x}{\lambda} + \phi)] \tag{2}$$

Here (x, y) is the spatial co-ordinate, σ is the variance. λ, γ, and ϕ represents the wavelength, aspect ratio, and phase of the sinusoidal carrier. θ defines the orientation of Gabor kernel. It defines the direction in which edges will be highlighted. In our proposed work, a filter bank is created for different orientations ranging from 0 to π with the step size of $\frac{\pi}{number\ of\ filters}$. Edges represent the boundaries with sudden changes in brightness between different regions. Over the years, several edge detection methods have been developed [24,25]. One of the popular edge detection technique is Canny edge detection [26]. It is a multistage, linear, and first-order derivative filter. The stages are: smoothing the image using the Gaussian function, calculating the image gradient magnitude and direction for image de-noising, non-maxima suppression in accordance with gradient direction to eliminate any extraneous pixels that might not be the edge, and utilizing the double threshold approach to detect and link edges. The double threshold (upper threshold, lower threshold) step identifies the strong, weak, and irrelevant pixels. The pixel with very high intensity and it is certain that it contributes to the edge is known as a strong pixel. Weak pixels are those that are neither sufficiently strong to be regarded as such nor insignificantly small to be regarded as irrelevant for edge detection. Other pixels are viewed as being irrelevant to the edge. The intensity values greater than the upper threshold determine the strong pixel. The intensity values smaller than the lower threshold represent the

---

Algorithm 1. Segmentation of hard exudates

Input: *RGB image* $(m \times n \times 3)$
Output: *Segment Exudate Region Image (SERI)* $(m \times n)$

1: Partition the image using K-means clustering mechanism
   (i) Compute A-axis and Luminance component from RGB image.
   (ii) $imageLA \leftarrow 2 * Luminance + A - axis$
  (iii) Perform color quantization on image $imageLA$. Compute the clusters using K-means algorithm. The value of K is 3.
  (iv) Label the clusters. Let the label is upper1,upper2, and middle.
   (v) Compute connected components in each cluster using 4-connectivity method. Middle cluster containing the optic disc have $K - 1$ connected components. For each cluster, extract the matching RGB image (upper1, upper2, and middle).

2: Perform the following operations for image $i \; \epsilon$ (upper1 and upper2) clusters.
   (i) **for** *each image* $i \; \epsilon \; (upper1, upper2)$ **do**
   (ii)   Enhance the image i using Gabor filter
  (iii)   Perform automatic canny edge detection,
     (a) $BE_1 \leftarrow cannyedge(lowerthresh1, upperthreshq11, i)$ ▷ Extract border
     (b) $BE_2 \leftarrow cannyedge(lowerthresh2, upperthresh2, i)$ ▷ Extract HE
     (c) $EDGE_i \leftarrow |BE_1 - BE_2|$
  (iv)   Fill the $EDGE_i$ using Flood Fill Algorithm [28],

$$F_i \leftarrow Fillimage(EDGE_i)$$

   (v)   Remove the outliers using contour approximation,

$$Segment\_upper_i \leftarrow approxcontour(F_i)$$

  (vi) **end for**

3:    Perform the following operation for middle clusters.
   (i)   Compute A-axis and Luminance component.
   (ii)   Determine the absolute difference of A-axis and Luminance component,

$$absLA \leftarrow |L - A|$$

  (iii)   Perform automatic thresholding using Yen method,

$$Segment\_middle \leftarrow Yen(absLA)$$

  (iv)   Set the pixel value to zero for optic disc region in $BinLA$ image.

4:    Combine the image obtained from step (2) and step(3),

$$SERI \leftarrow Segment\_middle + Segment\_upper_i$$

---

non-relevant pixels. The intensity value between these two thresholds is considered as weak pixels. Hysteresis mechanism is applied to convert weak pixels into strong or irrelevant pixels. It converts the weak pixel into a strong one if at least one of the pixels around is a strong pixel using the 8-neighborhood method. The value of the *lowerthresh1, upperthresh1* is (0,255).The value of *upperthresh2* is obtained by applying Otsu's threshold [27] on the gray scale image of clusters. The value of *lowerthresh2* is computed using 0.3* *upperthresh2*. The next step is to fill the extracted region using flood fill algorithm [28]. The outliers are removed using the contour approximation method [29]. The assumption is that a curve can be roughly represented by a collection of line segments. This approach aims to use fewer points to simplify a complex polygon or curve. The extent of simplification is determined by the tolerance parameter [30]. The two parameters for this method are the tolerance level (a), which is the greatest distance between the contour and the approximate contours, and the contour length or contour perimeter. The value of the tolerance is $a \times perimeter\ of\ contour$, where a is constant. Finally, the bitwise AND operation is performed to remove the outliers.

2.4   Segmentation of Hard Exudates from Middle Cluster

Segmentation of HE is a challenging task due to irregular illuminations, color variation, and similar brightness and color properties with the optic disc. Segmentation of HE frequently includes the optic disc area that needs to be excluded. In this paper, optic disc is excluded using three-level automatic segmentation by Prakash et al. [31]. Absolute difference of Luminance and A-axis is computed to highlight the HE region and Adaptive Yen thresholding [32] is utilized to extract the HE region. Finally, HE regions obtained from all the three clusters are combined.

3   Results and Discussion

The proposed methodology is carried out using Python on an Intel processor with 3.30 GHz clock speed and 16 GB of RAM.

3.1   Dataset Description

The effectiveness of the proposed work is illustrated by running experiments on the ISBI IDRiD dataset. The dataset is made available to the public by an eye facility in Nanded, (M.S.), India. The resolution of RGB fundus image is 4288 × 2848 pixels. Each image is in JPG format. The hard exudates have ground truth annotations for a total of 81 images. The effectiveness of the proposed approach is evaluated using Sensitivity/Recall, Specificity, Predicted Positive Value(PPV), F-1 score, Intersection over Union(IoU), Dice Coefficient, and Accuracy metrics [33].

3.2   Experimental Results

We have applied our Algorithm 1 and the visual results are shown in Fig. 3, Fig. 4, and Fig. 5 respectively. Figure 3 (a) shows the extracted cluster(upper2). The

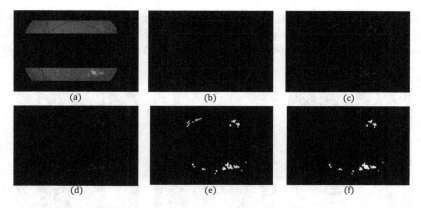

Fig. 3. Segmentation of HE from upper2 cluster: (a) Upper2 cluster in RGB format, (b) Boundary edge detection, (c) Exudates region detection, (d) Removal of boundary region, (e) Filling of exudates region with pixel value 255, and (f) Removal of outliers.

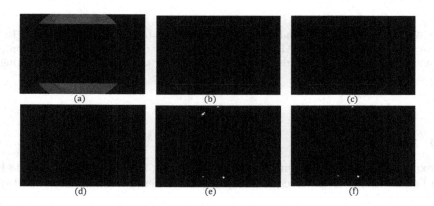

Fig. 4. Segmentation of exudates from upper1 cluster: (a) Upper1 cluster in RGB format, (b) Boundary edge detection, (c) Exudates region detection, (d) Removal of boundary region, (e) Filling of exudates region with pixel value 255, and (f) Removal of outliers.

boundary edge and the region are extracted using edge detection method illustrated in Fig. 3 (b) and Fig. 3 (c) respectively. The outliers like boundary edge are removed which is demonstrated in Fig. 3 (d). Figure 3 (e) shows the region filled with pixel value 255. However the outliers are still present and it is removed by approximation using arc of contour shown in Fig. 3 (f). Similarly the regions are extracted from upper 1 cluster and the step wise visualization is shown in Fig. 4 (a–f). The extraction of exudates from middle cluster is shown in Fig. 5. The middle cluster is in RGB color space and converted into LAB color space (shown in Fig. 5(a–b)). The extracted Luminance and A-axis component are demonstrated in Fig. 5 (c) and Fig. 5(d) respectively. It is visible that the intensity of exudates pixel and its environs are much similar. Figure 5 (e) shows the |L-A| to highlight exudates pixels from the rest of fundus image. Figure 5 (f) shows the segmented exudates utilizing automatic Yen thresholding method.

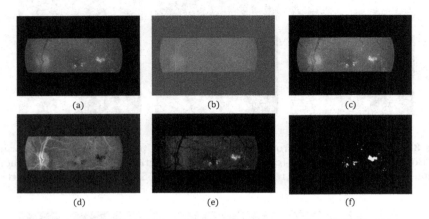

Fig. 5. Segmentation of exudates from middle cluster: (a)Middle cluster (RGB space), (b) Middle cluster (LAB space), (c) Luminance component (L) Extraction,(d) A-axis component, (e) Highlight of exudates region by taking |L-A|, and (f) Segmentation of exudates.

3.3 Discussion

In experiments conducted with the IDRiD datasets, the segmentation results for hard exudates of varying irregular shapes under different illumination conditions is shown in Fig. 6.

The size of the input data is $4288 \times 2848 \times 3$. Table 1 presents a comparison of performance metrics for the segmentation of hard exudates with existing techniques. Our proposed algorithm is superior in terms of higher recall, F1-score, dice coefficient, and IoU values. It surpasses them by 10% of the recall, 6.65% of F1-score, 6.85% of dice coefficient, and 19 % percent of IoU metrics. One of the reasons is that the experiments are conducted on the original resolution of RGB fundus image. It is demonstrated that the suggested method functions effectively in a variety of lighting conditions, irregular shapes, and exudates positions. The limitation of the study is the segmentation of very tiny hard exudates. The value of tolerance level (a) is empirically set at 0.1.

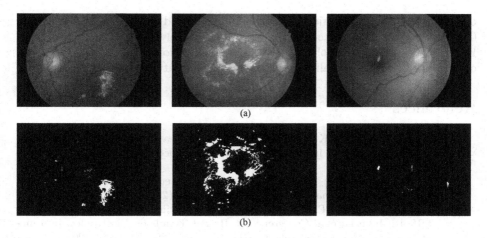

Fig. 6. Predicted hard exudates at different illumination, position, and irregular shape: (a) RGB fundus image, (b) Segmented exudates by the proposed approach considering IDRiD dataset.

Table 1. Obtained accuracy values for segmentation of hard exudates (HE) using proposed and existing approaches. The symbol (-) indicates that the metrics is not reported in the paper.

Methodology	Performance metrics						
	Recall	Precision	F1-score	Specificity	Dice Coefficient	IoU	Accuracy
Azat *et al.* [12]	0.767	0.753	-	0.997	-	-	-
Zhang *et al.* [16]	0.6939	-	-	-	0.7255	0.5693	0.8596
Guo *et al.* [15]	0.7803	-	-	-	0.7815	-	-
Ali *et al.* [18]	0.7553	0.8354	0.7933	-	-	-	-
Hamad *et al.* [17]	0.81	-	-	0.992	-	-	0.9920
Proposed	**0.913**	0.8108	**0.8589**	0.981	**0.850**	**0.750**	0.9750

4   Conclusions

An critical stage in the early diagnosis of retinal disorders is the segmentation of hard exudates from the RGB fundus image. It is challenging task due to artifacts and a range of image irregularities. We propose an effective and a reliable approach for automatic segmentation of hard exudates. First, RGB fundus image is partitioned into three disjoint and mutually exclusive regions. The motivation behind this unsupervised approach is to implement different methodologies on regions. Edge detection algorithm is applied on the regions which does not contain the optic disc (upper1 and upper2). The region contains optic disc(middle region) is transformed into LAB space and the difference of component A-axis and luminance is computed to highlight the exudates region. The proposed approach effectively avoids the influence of complex structures and segment the desired hard exudates region. The proposed method achieves 0.913 of recall, 0.981 of specificity, and accuracy of 0.975, respectively on the IDRiD database. However, there are still problems with missclassification in our study, and developing solutions to this challenge will be one of our future research focuses.

References

1. Verma, S.B., Yadav, A.K.: Hard exudates detection: a review. emerging technologies in data mining and information security. In: Proceedings of IEMIS 2020, vol. 1, pp.117–124 (2021)
2. Joshi, S., Karule, P.T.: A review on exudates detection methods for diabetic retinopathy. Biomed. Pharmacother. **97**, 1454–1460 (2018)
3. Dixit, A.K., Prabhakar, P.: Hard exudate detection using linear brightness method. In: 2019 4th International Conference on Recent Trends on Electronics, Information, Communication & Technology (RTEICT), pp. 980–984. IEEE (2019)
4. Kumar, A., Tewari, A.S., Singh, J.P.: Classification of diabetic macular edema severity using deep learning technique. Res. Biomed. Eng. **38**(3), 977–987 (2022)
5. Guo, S., Wang, K., Kang, H., Liu, T., Gao, Y., Li, T.: Bin loss for hard exudates segmentation in fundus images. Neurocomputing **392**, 314–324 (2020)
6. Basha, S.S., Prasad, K.S.: Automatic detection of hard exudates in diabetic retinopathy using morphological segmentation and fuzzy logic. Int. J. Comput. Sci. Netw. Secur. **8**(12), 211–218 (2008)
7. Imani, E., Pourreza, H.R.: A novel method for retinal exudate segmentation using signal separation algorithm. Comput. Methods Programs Biomed. **133**, 195–205 (2016)
8. Starck, J.L., Elad, M., Donoho, D.L.: Image decomposition via the combination of sparse representations and a variational approach. IEEE Trans. Image Process. **14**(10), 1570–1582 (2005)
9. Alom, M.Z., et al.: The history began from alexnet: a comprehensive survey on deep learning approaches. arXiv preprint arXiv:1803.01164 (2018)
10. Kusakunniran, W., Wu, Q., Ritthipravat, P., Zhang, J.: Hard exudates segmentation based on learned initial seeds and iterative graph cut. Comput. Methods Programs Biomed. **158**, 173–183 (2018)
11. Qomariah, D.U.N., Tjandrasa, H., Fatichah, C.: Exudate segmentation for diabetic retinopathy using modified FCN-8 and dice loss. Int. J. Intell. Eng. Syst. **15**(2) (2022)
12. Garifullin, A., Lensu, L., Uusitalo, H.: Deep Bayesian baseline for segmenting diabetic retinopathy lesions: advances and challenges. Comput. Biol. Med. **136**, 104725 (2021)
13. Jégou, S., Drozdzal, M., Vazquez, D., Romero, A., Bengio, Y.: The one hundred layers tiramisu: Fully convolutional densenets for semantic segmentation. In: Proceedings of the IEEE Conference on Computer Vision and Pattern Recognition Workshops, pp. 11–19 (2017)
14. Porwal, P., et al.: Idrid: diabetic retinopathy-segmentation and grading challenge. Med. Image Anal. **59**, 101561 (2020). https://doi.org/10.21227/H25W98
15. Guo, S., Li, T., Wang, K., Zhang, C., Kang, H.: A lightweight neural network for hard exudate segmentation of fundus image. In: Artificial Neural Networks and Machine Learning-ICANN, pp. 189–199 (2019)

16. Zhang, J., Chen, X., Qiu, Z., Yang, M., Hu, Y., Liu, J.: Hard exudate segmentation supplemented by super-resolution with multi-scale attention fusion module. In 2022 IEEE International Conference on Bioinformatics and Biomedicine (BIBM), pp. 1375–1380 (2022)
17. Hamad, H., Dwickat, T., Tegolo, D., Valenti, C.: Exudates as landmarks Identified through FCM Clustering in Retinal Images. Appl. Sci. **11**(1), 142 (2020)
18. Ali, M.Y.S., Abdel-Nasser, M., Jabreel, M., Valls, A., Baget, M.: Exu-Eye: retinal exudates segmentation based on multi-scale modules and gated skip connection. In: 2022 5th International Conference on Multimedia, Signal Processing and Communication Technologies (IMPACT), pp. 1–5 (2022)
19. Schwarz, M.W., Cowan, W.B., Beatty, J.C.: An experimental comparison of RGB, YIQ, LAB, HSV, and opponent color models. ACM Trans. Graph. (TOG) **6**(2), 123–158 (1987)
20. Abernathy, A., Celebi, M.E.: The incremental online k-means clustering algorithm and its application to color quantization. Expert Syst. Appl. **207**, 117927 (2022)
21. Palus, H., Frackiewicz, M.: New approach for initialization of k-means technique applied to color quantization. In: 2010 2nd International Conference on Information Technology,(2010 ICIT), pp. 205–209. IEEE (2010)
22. Gan, G., Ma, C., Wu, J.: Data clustering: theory, algorithms, and applications. Soc. Ind. Appl. Math. (2020)
23. Kamarainen, J.K., Kyrki, V., Kalviainen, H.: Invariance properties of Gabor filter-based features-overview and applications. IEEE Trans. Image Process. **15**(5), 1088–1099 (2006)
24. Jing, J., Liu, S., Wang, G., Zhang, W., Sun, C.: Recent advances on image edge detection: a comprehensive review. Neurocomputing (2022)
25. Owotogbe, J.S., Ibiyemi, T.S., Adu, B.A.: Edge detection techniques on digital images-a review. Int. J. Innov. Sci. Res. Technol **4**(11), 329–332 (2019)
26. Rong, W., Li, Z., Zhang, W., Sun, L.: An improved CANNY edge detection algorithm. In: 2014 IEEE International Conference on Mechatronics and Automation, pp. 577–582 (2014)
27. Hamdaoui, F., Sakly, A., Mtibaa, A.: An efficient multi level thresholding method for image segmentation based on the hybridization of modified PSO and Otsu's method. Comput. Intell. Appl. Model. Control, 343–367 (2015)
28. Kumar, B., Tiwari, U.K., Kumar, S., Tomer, V., Kalra, J.: Comparison and performance evaluation of boundary fill and flood fill algorithm. Int. J. Innov. Technol. Explor. Eng **8**, 9–13 (2020)
29. Pinheiro, A.M., Ghanbari, M.: Piecewise approximation of contours through scale-space selection of dominant points. IEEE Trans. Image Process. **19**(6), 1442–1450 (2010)
30. Ramer, U.: An iterative procedure for the polygonal approximation of plane curves. Comput. Graphics Image Process. **1**(3), 244–256 (1972)
31. Prakash, S., Kakarla, J.: Three level automatic segmentation of optic disc using LAB color space contours and morphological operation. Int. J. Imaging Syst. Technol (2023)
32. Yen, J.C., Chang, F.J., Chang, S.: A new criterion for automatic multilevel thresholding. IEEE Trans. Image Process. **4**(3), 370–378 (1995)
33. Muller, D., Soto-Rey, I., Kramer, F.: Towards a guideline for evaluation metrics in medical image segmentation. BMC. Res. Notes **15**(1), 1–8 (2022)

A Novel Facial Expression Recognition (FER) Model Using Multi-scale Attention Network

Chakrapani Ghadai[✉], Dipti Patra, and Manish Okade

National Institute of Technology, Rourkela, Rourkela, India
{520ee7014,dpatra,okadem}@nitrkl.ac.in

Abstract. Facial Expression Recognition (FER) faces significant challenges, primarily due to significant variations within classes and subtle visual differences between classes, and limited dataset sizes. Real-world factors such as pose, illumination, and partial occlusion further hinder FER performance. To tackle these challenges, multi-scale and attention-based networks have been widely employed. However, previous approaches have primarily focused on increasing depth while neglecting width, resulting in an inadequate representation of granular facial expression features. This study introduces a novel FER model. A multi-scale attention network (MSA-Net) is designed as a more extensive and deeper network that captures features from various receptive fields through a parallel network structure. Each parallel branch in the proposed network utilizes channel complementary multi-scale blocks, e.g., left multi-scale (MS-L) and right multi-scale (MS-R), to broaden the effective receptive field and capture features having diversity. Additionally, attention networks are employed to emphasize important regions and boost the discriminative capability of the multi-scale features. The performance evaluation of the proposed method was carried out on two popular real-world FER databases: AffectNet and RAF-DB. Our MSA-Net has reduced the impact of the pose, partial occlusions and the network's susceptibility to subtle expression-related variations, thereby outperforming other methods in FER.

Keywords: Facial expression recognition (FER) · Deep learning · Muti-scale · Attention · receptive field

1 Introduction

The ability to interpret facial expressions is essential for humans to communicate their emotions and intentions. Identifying facial expressions from images is a well-known challenge in computer vision. It holds significant research potential in advanced medical treatments, lie detection, online education, and more. FER has experienced notable advancements in machine learning and computer vision, with a plethora of methods emerging. These methods commonly categorize expressions into six fundamental emotions: anger, disgust, fear, surprise,

© The Author(s), under exclusive license to Springer Nature Switzerland AG 2024
H. Kaur et al. (Eds.): CVIP 2023, CCIS 2010, pp. 336–346, 2024.
https://doi.org/10.1007/978-3-031-58174-8_29

sadness, and happiness. Most FER studies largely concentrate on feature extraction and classifier development. The FER studies are classified as static FER and dynamic FER approaches. Static FER models [23,27] are designed to analyse individual static images for FER and employ classifiers like random forests, support vector machines, and Softmax classifiers. On the other hand, dynamic FER approaches are tailored for facial video sequences. These methods extract relevant temporal features from the sequence, improving recognition performance. In practical applications, multimodal systems integrating additional modalities, such as physiological and audio channels, have also enhanced FER accuracy and effectiveness. Historically, facial expression recognition (FER) methods commonly depended on manually crafted features or shallow learning approaches. These approaches include the use of SIFT [21], sparse learning [20], and non-negative matrix factorization [1]. These techniques aimed to capture distinctive characteristics of facial expressions through manual feature engineering or simple learning algorithms. The performance of traditional methods using sparse feature representations can be further enhanced. Emotion recognition competitions Emotion Recognition in the Wild [2,3], and FER2013 [8] have facilitated the collection of abundant training data in challenging scenarios from the real-world. This shift has implicitly encouraged the transition of FER from controlled laboratory environments to more realistic and uncontrolled settings. Moreover, the rapid advancement of chip processing and the advancement of CNNs have prompted the adoption of deep learning methods in various research domains.

Recently, a surge is seen in the adoption of deep learning methodologies, with CNNs [15,18] emerging as particularly prominent tools, for FER. Deep learning has demonstrated significant performance improvements compared to traditional shallow learning methods. Deeper CNN architectures with enhanced generalization capabilities have been employed; however, they are susceptible to overfitting when confronted with external factors, including pose variations, illumination changes, occlusions, and more. To address this, attention networks have been integrated into the CNN backbone [14] to focus on important regions, enabling more robust FER in real-world scenarios. Furthermore, some approaches have utilized DenseNet, a type of the inception architecture [9], and pyramid structures [22] to extract multi-scale features. These methods leverage multi-scale features to provide context and facilitate learning more discriminative features. These methods suffer from limitations in diversity and the effective receptive field for feature learning.

2   Key Contributions

To address the challenges outlined earlier, a novel parallel structured two-branch approach called the Facial expression using multi-scale attention networks (MSA-Net) is proposed. The Key contributions include:

1. The MSA-Net is engineered to capture features from diverse receptive fields. Subsequently, the features from each branch are fused together. This fusion process can effectively mitigate the influence of external factors such as pose and occlusions.

2. The multi-scale module hierarchically integrates features extracted from various receptive fields within a unified block. This approach helps reduce the FER's susceptibility to large between class and with in class variations caused by external factors.

3. Within each pathway, an attention module is integrated into the deeper layers to highlight critical regions, thereby augmenting the discriminative nature of expression-related features.

The rest sections are outlined as follows: Sect. 3 discusses a comprehensive overview of the MSA-Net. Section 4 delves into the experimental details. Section 5, concludes with closing remarks.

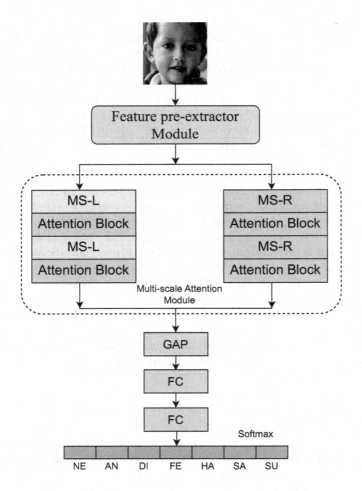

Fig. 1. The proposed MSA-Net framework

3   Proposed Method

3.1   Framework Overview

The MSA-Net, as proposed, is depicted in Fig. 1. It is made up of a feature pre-extractor, a multi-scale attention module, and a fusion and classification. The feature pre-extractor comprises conv1 to conv3 of ResNet-18 [10] to extract mid-level features of size $128 \times 28 \times 28$. These feature maps are fed into two parallel branch networks, each consisting of a MSA module. Within the MSA module, a multi-scale block is connected in cascade with an attention block, and the arrangement is repeated twice in the multi-scale attention module. Two types of multi-scale blocks, left multi-scale (MS-L) and right multi-scale (MS-R), complementary along the channel, are used in the left and right branches, respectively. Ultimately, the features from two pathways are integrated and subjected to softmax classification to produce the results.

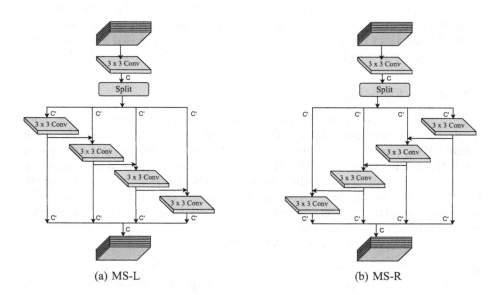

(a) MS-L   (b) MS-R

Fig. 2. Multi-scale blocks. Where C and C' are the number of channels of the feature maps

3.2   Multi-scale Module

The multi-scale blocks are illustrated in Fig. 2a and Fig. 2b. Specifically designed for FER, our multi-scale blocks, MS-L and MS-R, draw inspiration from Res2Net [7]. The multi-scale block utilizes a hierarchy of basic convolution blocks to extract features at various receptive fields. The first convolution layer within each multi-scale block regulates the spatial dimensions. Let us denote the feature map after first 3×3 convolution as 'X'. Following this, 'X' is partitioned into 'n' equal subsets of features along the channel axis, denoted as X_i, where $i \in \{1, 2, ..., n\}$. Consequently, all subsets X_i have identical spatial sizes, with the number of channels (C') being $\frac{1}{n}$ of the total channels(C) in 'X'. Furthermore, the subsets X_i undergo parallel processing through four separate convolution layers. Let the 3×3 convolution on each of X_i can be represented by $P_i^p(.)$, where $p \in \{L, R\}$, p represents the location of the multi-scale block. Y_i^p represents the output of $P_i^p(.)$ i.e.

$$Y_i^L = \begin{cases} P_i^L(X_i), & i = 1 \\ P_i^L(X_i) + Y_{i-1}^L, & 1 < i \le n \end{cases} \tag{1}$$

$$Y_i^R = \begin{cases} P_i^R(X_i), & i = n \\ P_i^R(X_i) + Y_{i+1}^R, & 1 \le i < n \end{cases} \tag{2}$$

The output of multi-scale blocks is obtained by concatenating the elements Y_i^p. It can be verified that the left multi-scale block exhibits a higher effective receptive field in higher channels and a lower receptive field in lower channels. Similarly, the right multi-scale block demonstrates an increased effective receptive field in lower channels and a lower receptive field in higher channels.

3.3   Attention Module

The features acquired from each parallel pathway following the multi-scale module undergo further processing through an attention network. Specifically, a convolutional block attention module (CBAM) [25] is employed in this instance as the attention network. The CBAM is used to enhance the feature extraction capability of CNNs by integrating attention mechanisms directly into the architecture. CBAM focuses on both spatial and channel-wise attention, allowing the network to selectively emphasize informative spatial locations and channel-wise features within each convolutional block.

Here's a breakdown of how CBAM works:

1. Channel Attention: In this component, CBAM computes the channel-wise attention map by performing global average pooling followed by two fully connected (FC) layers. The channel-wise attention weights are generated from the output of the FC layers, which are applied to each feature map across channels.
2. Spatial Attention: Spatial attention is computed by first applying max pooling and average pooling operations to each feature map separately. The resulting max-pooled and average-pooled feature maps are then concatenated and processed through another set of FC layers. Again, these weights are added to the original feature maps to accentuate significant spatial locations while suppressing less relevant ones.
3. Integration: Finally, the channel-wise and spatial attention maps are combined using element-wise multiplication, producing the final attention-enhanced feature maps. These maps capture both channel-wise and spatial

contextual information, effectively guiding the network to suppress redundant features.

By incorporating CBAM modules within convolutional blocks, CNNs can learn to adaptively attend to informative spatial locations and channel-wise features, which has been used in many machine vision tasks like image enhancement [17], classification, segmentation, etc. CBAM has demonstrated its effectiveness in enhancing the discriminative power across different datasets and applications.

3.4 Fusion Strategy and Loss Function

A simple concatenation operation is used along the channel to fuse the features from the parallel pathways. This concatenation combines the feature maps into a single feature map. Following this, the fused attention feature maps undergo the global average pooling. This operation computes the average value of each channel across the spatial dimensions, resulting in a vector. The model is trained with the cross-entropy loss function. The loss function is given below.

$$L_{CA} = -\frac{\alpha}{M} \sum_{0}^{M-1} \log \frac{e^{w_k^T u_k + b_k}}{\sum_{0}^{C-1} e^{w_l^T u_l + b_l}}, \tag{3}$$

where M is the batch size; C is the number of classes; b and W, are the bias and weight terms of the fully connected layer; u_k is the input to the fully connected layer at k^{th} sample. α is the hyperparameter of the loss function.

4 Results and Discussion

4.1 Datasets and Implementation Details

The experiments were conducted using two widely used FER datasets: RAF-DB [12] and Affectnet [16]. The RAF-DB dataset consists of 29,672 images annotated with basic or compound expressions. It includes 12,264 training samples and 3,061 testing samples. The samples are taken from basic expressions. There are 283,901 images available for training and 2,992 images for testing in the Affectnet dataset. For the experiments, we focused on seven basic expression categories. The images in both datasets are resized to 224×224 pixels. To augment the data, we employed simple techniques such as extracting random crops (central, corner) and applying horizontal flips. Stochastic gradient descent (SGD) is used as the optimizer during the training, utilizing a batch size of 32. The training process spanned 100 epochs, with an initial learning rate at 0.001. The experiments were carried out utilizing the PyTorch framework and executed on an NVIDIA GeForce RTX 3060 GPU.

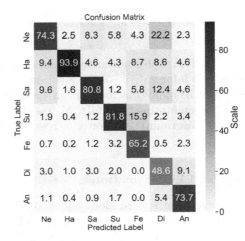

Fig. 3. Confusion matrix on RAF-DB

4.2 Study on RAF-DB Dataset

Table 1 compares results in the RAF-DB dataset across seven emotion categories. The suggested approach attains an accuracy of 86.47%. Analyzing the confusion matrix depicted in Fig. 3, it is evident that fear and disgust pose significant recognition challenges, with 15.9% of fear instances incorrectly classified as a surprise and 22% of disgust misclassified as neutral. This observation can be attributed to the overlapping facial muscle movements and recognition patterns exhibited by both fear and surprise.

Table 1. Comparison of results on RAF-DB dataset.

Method	Accuracy (%)
RLPS [11]	72.89
IE-DBN [26]	84.75
ALT [6]	84.50
gACNN [14]	85.07
RAN [24]	85.53
Proposed	86.47

4.3 Study on AffectNet Dataset

AffectNet is presently recognized as the most extensive dataset for facial expressions. However, accurate recognition poses a significant challenge due to the intricate and varied nature of facial images within AffectNet. Hence the experiments were conducted on AffectNet dataset to thoroughly validate the efficacy of the proposed method on the seven emotion categories. The outcomes achieved using different methods are presented in Table 2. Our method exhibits superior performance for the seven primary emotion categories, surpassing the previously leading DDA-Loss method [5]. Figure 4 shows the confusion matrix. Neutral, sad, surprise, and angry are difficult expressions to recognize.

Table 2. Comparison of on Affectnet dataset

Method	Accuracy (%)
gACNN [14]	58.78
IDFL [13]	59.2
ESR-9 [19]	59.3
OADN [4]	61.89
DDA-Loss [5]	62.34
Proposed	63.61

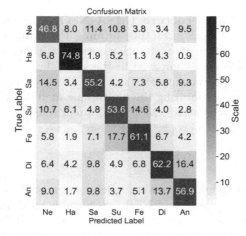

Fig. 4. Confusion matrix on Affectnet

4.4 Ablation Study

Ablation study is carried out to assess the efficacy of different modules utilized. The findings presented evaluate the efficacy of the proposed method in Table 3. The one pathway structure is taken as baseline. Observations reveal that MSA-net, featuring two parallel branch structures, yielded the most superior results.

Baseline (One Branch). The one-branch structure considered from the proposed method is called the baseline. The baseline attains the accuracy of 85.21% and 62.33% on RAF-DB and AffectNet databases, respectively.

Multi-scale Structure (MS). The impact of the multi-scale structure in the proposed method, without the attention module, was investigated. As shown in Table 3, it can be observed that the multi-scale (MS) structure reduces the performance from the baseline by 1.3% on RAF-DB, and 1.51% on AffectNet, respectively. This is due to the attention module being embedded in the baseline structure.

Table 3. Ablation study on RAFDB and Affectnet

Component	Accuracy (%) on RAF-DB	Accuracy (%) on Affectnet
Baseline	85.21	62.33
MS	84.10	61.39
Proposed (MSA-net)	86.47	63.11

Multi-scale Attention Structure (MSA-Net). The attention blocks are considered with a multi-scale structure forming the proposed framework, i.e. MSA-net. The incorporation of an attention network within a multi-scale module evidently enhances accuracy compared to the standalone multi-scale structure, achieving a notable improvement of 2.74%, and 2.72% on RAF-DB and Affect-Net, respectively. By incorporating the multi-scale module, it becomes easier to extract features at various scales. Moreover, integrating the attention network enhances the discriminative properties of these features even more.

5 Conclusion

We proposed a novel facial expression model using a multi-scale attention network to address the challenges of FER, specifically tackling within-class and between-class variations present in the FER datasets. Utilizing a multi-scale module, the proposed approach attains proficiency in learning features across various receptive fields, thereby mitigating the effects of pose variations and partial occlusions during inference. Moreover, the attention module facilitates selective attention to salient regions while filtering out irrelevant areas, thereby extracting features at a more nuanced level. Consequently, this diminishes the network's vulnerability to subtle expression-related deviations. Our proposed method has better accuracy on the RAF-DB and AffectNet datasets, with results of 86.47% and 63.11%, respectively. In future work, we aim to delve into subtle intra-class visual differences by exploring the correlation between two paths and adaptive learning techniques.

References

1. Ali, H.B., Powers, D.M., Jia, X., Zhang, Y.: Extended non-negative matrix factorization for face and facial expression recognition. Int. J. Mach. Learn. Comput. **5**(2), 142 (2015)
2. Dhall, A., Goecke, R., Joshi, J., Hoey, J., Gedeon, T.: Emotiw 2016: video and group-level emotion recognition challenges. In: Proceedings of the 18th ACM International Conference on Multimodal Interaction, pp. 427–432 (2016)
3. Dhall, A., Ramana Murthy, O., Goecke, R., Joshi, J., Gedeon, T.: Video and image based emotion recognition challenges in the wild: Emotiw 2015. In: Proceedings of the 2015 ACM on International Conference on Multimodal Interaction, pp. 423–426 (2015)
4. Ding, H., Zhou, P., Chellappa, R.: Occlusion-adaptive deep network for robust facial expression recognition. In: 2020 IEEE International Joint Conference on Biometrics (IJCB), pp. 1–9. IEEE (2020)
5. Farzaneh, A.H., Qi, X.: Discriminant distribution-agnostic loss for facial expression recognition in the wild. In: Proceedings of the IEEE/CVF Conference on Computer Vision and Pattern Recognition Workshops, pp. 406–407 (2020)
6. Florea, C., Florea, L., Badea, M.S., Vertan, C., Racoviteanu, A.: Annealed label transfer for face expression recognition. In: BMVC, p. 104 (2019)
7. Gao, S.H., Cheng, M.M., Zhao, K., Zhang, X.Y., Yang, M.H., Torr, P.: Res2net: a new multi-scale backbone architecture. IEEE Trans. Pattern Anal. Mach. Intell. **43**(2), 652–662 (2019)
8. Goodfellow, I.J., et al.: Challenges in representation learning: a report on three machine learning contests. In: Lee, M., Hirose, A., Hou, Z.-G., Kil, R.M. (eds.) ICONIP 2013. LNCS, vol. 8228, pp. 117–124. Springer, Heidelberg (2013). https://doi.org/10.1007/978-3-642-42051-1_16
9. Hardjadinata, H., Oetama, R.S., Prasetiawan, I.: Facial expression recognition using xception and densenet architecture. In: 2021 6th International Conference on New Media Studies (CONMEDIA), pp. 60–65. IEEE (2021)
10. He, K., Zhang, X., Ren, S., Sun, J.: Deep residual learning for image recognition. In: Proceedings of the IEEE Conference on Computer Vision and Pattern Recognition, pp. 770–778 (2016)
11. Li, H., Xu, H.: Deep reinforcement learning for robust emotional classification in facial expression recognition. Knowl.-Based Syst. **204**, 106172 (2020)
12. Li, S., Deng, W., Du, J.: Reliable crowdsourcing and deep locality-preserving learning for expression recognition in the wild. In: Proceedings of the IEEE Conference on Computer Vision and Pattern Recognition, pp. 2852–2861 (2017)
13. Li, Y., et al.: Learning informative and discriminative features for facial expression recognition in the wild. IEEE Trans. Circuits Syst. Video Technol. **32**(5), 3178–3189 (2021)
14. Li, Y., Zeng, J., Shan, S., Chen, X.: Occlusion aware facial expression recognition using CNN with attention mechanism. IEEE Trans. Image Process. **28**(5), 2439–2450 (2018)
15. Liu, K., Zhang, M., Pan, Z.: Facial expression recognition with CNN ensemble. In: 2016 International Conference on Cyberworlds (CW), pp. 163–166. IEEE (2016)
16. Mollahosseini, A., Hasani, B., Mahoor, M.H.: Affectnet: a database for facial expression, valence, and arousal computing in the wild. IEEE Trans. Affect. Comput. **10**(1), 18–31 (2017)

17. Panda, S.K., Sa, P.K.: Integrating graph convolution into a deep multi-layer framework for low-light image enhancement. IEEE Sens. Lett. (2024)
18. Shin, M., Kim, M., Kwon, D.S.: Baseline CNN structure analysis for facial expression recognition. In: 2016 25th IEEE International Symposium on Robot and Human Interactive Communication (RO-MAN), pp. 724–729. IEEE (2016)
19. Siqueira, H., Magg, S., Wermter, S.: Efficient facial feature learning with wide ensemble-based convolutional neural networks. In: Proceedings of the AAAI Conference on Artificial Intelligence, vol. 34, pp. 5800–5809 (2020)
20. Song, M., Tao, D., Sun, S., Chen, C., Bu, J.: Joint sparse learning for 3-d facial expression generation. IEEE Trans. Image Process. **22**(8), 3283–3295 (2013)
21. Soyel, H., Demirel, H.: Improved sift matching for pose robust facial expression recognition. In: 2011 IEEE International Conference on Automatic Face & Gesture Recognition (FG), pp. 585–590. IEEE (2011)
22. Vo, T.H., Lee, G.S., Yang, H.J., Kim, S.H.: Pyramid with super resolution for in-the-wild facial expression recognition. IEEE Access **8**, 131988–132001 (2020)
23. Wadhawan, R., Gandhi, T.K.: Landmark-aware and part-based ensemble transfer learning network for static facial expression recognition from images. IEEE Trans. Artif. Intell. **4**(2), 349–361 (2022)
24. Wang, K., Peng, X., Yang, J., Meng, D., Qiao, Y.: Region attention networks for pose and occlusion robust facial expression recognition. IEEE Trans. Image Process. **29**, 4057–4069 (2020)
25. Woo, S., Park, J., Lee, J.Y., Kweon, I.S.: Cbam: convolutional block attention module. In: Proceedings of the European Conference on Computer Vision (ECCV), pp. 3–19 (2018)
26. Zhang, H., Su, W., Yu, J., Wang, Z.: Identity-expression dual branch network for facial expression recognition. IEEE Trans. Cogn. Dev. Syst. **13**(4), 898–911 (2020)
27. Zhong, L., Bai, C., Li, J., Chen, T., Li, S., Liu, Y.: A graph-structured representation with brnn for static-based facial expression recognition. In: 2019 14th IEEE International Conference on Automatic Face & Gesture Recognition (FG 2019), pp. 1–5. IEEE (2019)

Imitation Learning of Long-Horizon Manipulation Tasks Through Temporal Sub-action Sequencing

Niharika Singh[1], Samrat Dutta[2], Aditya Jain[2], Ravi Prakash[1],
Anima Majumder[2], Rajesh Sinha[2], Laxmidhar Behera[1],
and Tushar Sandhan[1(✉)]

[1] Indian Institute of Technology Kanpur, Kanpur, Uttar Pradesh, India
{niharika20,lbehera,sandhan}@iitk.ac.in
[2] TCS Research, Bengaluru, Karnataka, India
aditya14129@iiitd.ac.in

Abstract. This research proposes an approach to long-horizon manipulation which uses video and kinesthetic demonstrations to imitate human actions. The task learning process involves two stages. To learn the sequence of the sub-actions in the video demonstration, the *Task Sequencing Network (TSNet)* - a hybrid neural network made up of Convolutional Neural Network (CNN), Recurrent Neural Network (RNN), and Connectionist Temporal Classification (CTC) loss, is used in the first stage. Through dynamic movement primitive (DMP) models, task-agnostic task primitives are learned in the second stage via kinesthetic demonstrations. To encode the semantic relationship between the sub-actions and the objects, a Multi-relational Embedding Network (MRE) using YOLOv4 for object detection is used to estimate the affordances associated with the objects in the scene. For tasks like liquid pouring, table cleaning and object placement, the proposed imitation learning approach learns task planning and execution in a decoupled manner, resulting in effective sub-action sequencing and quicker and more precise learning of sub-action execution.

Keywords: Sequence labeling · Connectionist temporal classification · Convolutional Neural Network · Multi-relational embedding

1 Introduction

Humans possess exceptional capability to learn difficult *long horizon*[1] tasks from observations [21,24] and replicate them with ease by connecting the task primitives (learned since childhood) in the appropriate sequence while leveraging the knowledge about the objects to be manipulated. Imitation Learning (IL) enables

---

[1] tasks like table cleaning, water pouring, table arrangement that involve multiple and precise object manipulations over a long time span.

H. Kaur et al. (Eds.): CVIP 2023, CCIS 2010, pp. 347–361, 2024.
https://doi.org/10.1007/978-3-031-58174-8_30

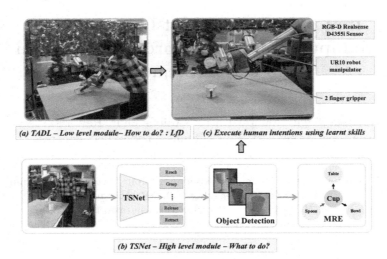

Fig. 1. Decoupled imitation learning architecture: (a) TADL based low level module: skill generation for generic robotic manipulation using learning from demonstrations, (b) TSNet based high level module: primitive actions segmentation present in the video of a human activity e.g. liquid pouring and (c) Realtime execution of the segmented actions using learnt skills in its own context.

robots to obtain similar capabilities while avoiding rigorous robot programming. However, imitating long-horizon and *complex*[2] tasks from observation is still a challenge and current trends in IL is to solve such problems [2,3,9]. In this work, we develop a decoupled architecture where task planning and task execution are separated as opposed to end-to-end architectures. We argue that this kind of architecture is appropriate for long-horizon task learning as a long-horizon task can be decomposed into multiple sub-actions. The proposed approach learns the implementation of the sub-actions using kinesthetic teaching and the order of execution of these sub-actions is learned from video demonstrations. As the semantic relationship between the objects and the sub-actions is very important for execution of the overall task, the proposed algorithms jointly comprehends human intentions and actions by creating a *knowledge graph* representation that models the semantic information.

The proposed architecture is depicted in Fig. 1. The contributions of this work are summarized as follows:

– A decoupled imitation learning approach to teach a robot how to replicate set of human actions is presented. A high-level controller (TSNet) separates out the basic actions in the video of a human demonstration, and a low-level controller (TADL) executes those motions sequentially on the robot for liquid pouring, table cleaning and object placement tasks.

---

[2] tasks are the combinations of multiple task primitives.

- The proposed TSNet employing RNN and CNN is trained using videos of demonstrations of human tasks while minimising CTC loss [7] function to predict the right task primitive sequence in human demonstrations.
- The high-level module is integrated with YOLOv4 (*You Only Look Once version 4*) [4] that detects the objects in the videos and *Multi-relational Embedding Network* (MRE Network) [6] which models semantic knowledge of the task primitives and the objects as knowledge triples *(head, relation, tail)* serving as common sense for guiding the network to select the object to act upon.
- Low-level controller, termed as Task Agnostic DMP library (TADL) is designed which stores the DMPs associated to sub-tasks, that are trained by collecting kinesthetic robot demonstrations (RD) for each primitive action.
- A commercially available manipulator for simulating liquid pouring, table cleaning, and object placement tasks is used to validate the suggested design.

2   Related Work

Studies on decoupled architectures for imitation learning that use quite different approaches yet seem to be comparable exist. Our work is closely connected to that of Chella et al. [5], who tracks the position and orientation of the human hand during demonstrations and group it with the manipulable item into action primitives. Sharma et al [17]'s proposal for decoupling uses a modified version of GAN [19] to translate the immediate target state in robot view from video of human demonstrations. The low-level controller is then used to carry out the translation after being trained with kinesthetic robot demonstrations. [18]'s modular approach for IL uses behaviour cloning to learn low-level control from examples and CTC for sub-task alignment. Although action sequence identification from videos using CTC has been explored separately [8,12].

In Chen Jiang et al. [10], they use a Vision-Language model to automatically interpret task evolution and robotic actions semantically into a linguistic dynamic knowledge graph filled with commonsense knowledge. A novel technique is presented by Karinne et al. [15] for inferring human coordinated actions using semantic representations to derive the meaning of the observed job by taking relevant information from the observations. Then using the acquired semantics it deduces the observed human behaviours to activate a robot's motion primitives carrying out the demonstrated task. To our knowledge, this is the first time that robotic imitation learning has used CTC for basic action sequence segmentation from videos combined with a general set of DMPs with implementation on a real robot for three complex tasks.

3   System Architecture

We outline the proposed decoupled strategy and address two task execution-related queries: a) *What to do?* (high-level controller) and *How to do?* (low-level controller). By predicting the most likely sequence of sub-actions in the input video, the objects to be acted upon, and potential affordances for imitating the *long-horizon* and *complex* task from the context of the robot, the higher level controller (TSNet) assists in decision-making. TADL the lower level controller of the proposed algorithm, preserves the tasks primitives learned by DMPs. The task primitives are executed as per the sequence predicted by the TSNet and on Yolov4's [4] detected objects. Figure 2 shows the overall architecture of the system.

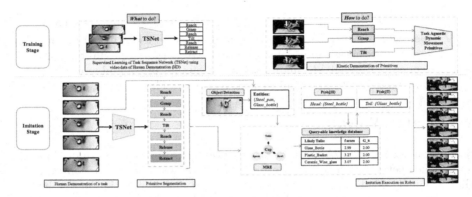

Fig. 2. Decoupled system architecture shows training stage of TADL and TSNet and imitation stage of robot imitating human activity from a video input. In the Training stage, we address two task execution-related queries: a) *What to do?* and *How to do?* TSNet is trained using videos of demonstrations of human tasks to predict the right task primitive sequence in real human demonstrations. TADL preserves the tasks primitives learned by DMPs. In the Imitation stage, by predicting the most likely sequence of sub-actions in the input demonstration video of a complex task (pouring), the objects to be acted upon (glass bottle, steel pan), and potential affordances for imitating the *long-horizon* and *complex* task from the context of the robot, TSNet assists in decision-making. YOLOv4 detects the objects and MRE Network models semantic knowledge of the sub-tasks and the objects as knowledge triples (glass bottle, tilt, steel pan) serving as query-able knowledge database. The task primitives are executed as per the sequence predicted by the TSNet on Yolov4's detected objects.

3.1   Primitive Segmentation Using TSNet: What to Do?

We build a hybrid neural network with three parts: 1) CNN - to extract features from video frames; 2) RNN - to learn the temporal relationship between frames; and 3) Connectionist Temporal Classification (CTC) - to deal with the issues of output label variability and non-alignment between input video and label sequence. We have the final sequence of primitives used in each human demonstration.

TSNet: Let us consider $\mathcal{D}$ as the set of human demonstrations from a distribution of task $\mathcal{H}_{\mathcal{F} \times \mathcal{S}}$. Here $\mathcal{F} \in \Re^n$ is the n-dimensional feature space of all the sequences and $\mathcal{S} = \mathbf{L}$ is the set of all associated subtask/task primitives which has the labels from $\mathbf{L}$. Each element in $\mathcal{D}$ is a tuple of $\{\mathbf{F}, \mathbf{s}\}$ with $\mathbf{F} = \{\mathbf{x}_1, \mathbf{x}_2, ..., \mathbf{x}_V\}$ being a particular demonstration of length V and the associated subtask sequence is provided in $\mathbf{s} = \{s_1, s_2, ..., s_T\}$ of length T where $T \leq V$. The idea is to learn a temporal map $g: \mathcal{F} \longmapsto \mathcal{S}$ using the demonstrations $\mathcal{D}$ to predict the sequencing of subtask involved in the novel inputs sampled from the distribution $\mathcal{H}_{\mathcal{F} \times \mathcal{S}}$ while minimizing an appropriate loss function.

To have a probability distribution over label sequences, the network uses a softmax output layer with two extra labels, the 'blank label' and the 'padding' other than the number of primitives. The new set of labels L^{aug} includes extra labels in L. This helps to compute the probability of all possible sequence of stitching the task primitives to form a *complex* and *long-horizon* task. Let $\boldsymbol{\Gamma}: (\Re^n)^T \longmapsto (\Re^v)^T$ is a continuous map that maps an $n-$dimensional input sequence to a $v-$dimensional output sequence of length T. The weights of $\boldsymbol{\Gamma}$ is trained using the demonstrations $\mathcal{D}$ such that the output

$$\mathbf{u} = \boldsymbol{\Gamma}(\mathbf{x}), \quad \forall \mathbf{x} \in \Re^n \tag{1}$$

where, u_i^t is the ith element of $\mathbf{u}$, represents the activation of ith node at tth time instant. It gives the probability of occurrence of the ith label at time t. Then the probability distribution over $(L_{aug})^T$ of T sequences can be found using (1).

$$p(l|\mathbf{x}) = \prod_{t=1}^{T} u_{l_t}^t, \quad \forall l \in L^{aug} \tag{2}$$

The additional labels need to be removed from the predicted labels to get the possible set of sequences L^{final}. The conditional probability $p(\boldsymbol{\ell}|\mathbf{x})$ of all $\boldsymbol{\ell} \in L^{final}$ can be obtained by summing up all the probabilities of all the *subtask-groups* associated to it. The classifier $\mathbf{g}(\mathbf{x})$ predicts the maximum probable sequence of the task primitives for a given input as

$$\mathbf{g}(\mathbf{x}) = arg \max_{\boldsymbol{\ell} \in L^{final}} p(\boldsymbol{\ell}|\mathbf{x}) \tag{3}$$

Decoding Network Output: The output of the TSNet needs processing before it computes the probabilities $p(\boldsymbol{\ell}|\mathbf{x})$ of all $\boldsymbol{\ell} \in L^{final}$ by discarding the extra blank token. First the task primitives with highest probability at every time step is chosen resulting in a sequence of length 50 primitives. In the second stage, a decoding process is followed: Let us consider the task primitives are labeled as: 1-reach, 3-retract, 4-grasp, 5-release.

Here, $\varnothing$ is the blank token used when repetition of labels are required and l is the length of a task in terms of subtasks. The adjacent duplicate task primitives are merged into one. (step: 1 to 2). The blank token $\varnothing$ is removed (step: 2 to 3) and then the padded label '0' is removed (step: 3 to 4). The labels are padded with a '0' to equalise the primitive sequences lengths before training.

Table 1. Dataset Labelling

Task	Label
Liquid Pouring	Reach - Grasp - Reach - Tilt - Reach - Release - Retract
Stack	Reach - Grasp - Reach - Release - Retract
Push	Reach - Reach - Retract
Pick	Reach - Grasp - Reach - Reach - Release - Retract
Liquid Mixing	Reach - Grasp - Reach -Stir- Reach - Release - Retract
Table Cleaning	Reach - Grasp - Wipe - Release - Retract
Place in Basket	Reach - Grasp - Reach - Release - Retract
Object Rotation	Reach - Grasp - Rotate - Release - Retract
Poke	Reach - Press - Retract

Decoding Process	
1: 1 1 1 ∅ 4 4 1 1 ∅ 1 1 ... 5 3 3 0 0 0	▷ $l = 50$
2: 1 ∅ 4 1 ∅ 1 5 3 0	▷ $l = 9$
3: 1 4 1 1 5 3 0	
4: 1 4 1 1 5 3	▷ $l = 6$

Object Identification: YOLOv4 [4] is a convolutional network that predicts multiple bounding boxes and class probabilities. YOLOv4 model examines the video input of the demonstration and detects entities present in the video to give the list, eg., entities = {'Cup','Container'}. YOLOv4 is trained in our research using objects from the MIME [16] dataset and the Amazon Peaking Challenge dataset (lab created data consisting of daily objects) that adds up to 147 classes. We manually annotate the ground truth objects using bounding boxes.

MRE (Query-Able Knowledge Database): In our work, we use RoboCSE [6] as MRE that allows us to represent the semantic knowledge of the task primitives and the objects involved in tasks as *knowledge triples* (h, r, t) i.e., *(head, relation, tail)*, for eg., *(steel pan, reach, container)*. The MRE learns a continuous vector representation of a knowledge graph $\mathcal{G}$ [14,23] to model semantic knowledge while utilising a scoring function $f(h, r, t)$ [13]. The resulting knowledge representation can be used by the robot as a query-able database that gives us the likely tails ranked according to the scoring function f.

We manually create the domain-constrained ground truth knowledge triples. The conditional probability of entities detected by YOLOv4 is calculated to decide the head object, i.e., giving us the object to be manipulated without human intervention. The head object and the sequence primitives (as relations) from TSNet are passed to MRE giving us the likely affordances of tail. The conditional probabilities of a given entity as head or a tail are calculated as follows:

$$P_H(H|obj_i) = \frac{Nh_i}{N_i}, \ P_T(T|obj_i) = \frac{Nt_i}{N_i} \qquad (4)$$

Table 2. TADL vocabulary

DMP	Definition
Reach	end-effector moves from given 6D start to end pose
Grasp	two finger grippers closes
Release	two finger grippers open
Tilt	end-effector roll motion
Displace	end-effector moves an item along a plane (e.g. a table)
Retract	end-effector moves to a home pose from any start pose
Wipe	end-effector wipes along a plane (e.g. a table)
Press	end-effector presses an item
Rotate	end-effector yaw motion
Stir	end-effector moves along a circle in horizontal plane

where, Nh_i is the number of times i^{th} object becomes head and Nt_i is the number of times i^{th} object becomes tail in the ground truth knowledge triples. The total number of times i^{th} object used in the ground truth knowledge triples is given by N_i, i.e., $N_i = Nh_i + Nt_i$.

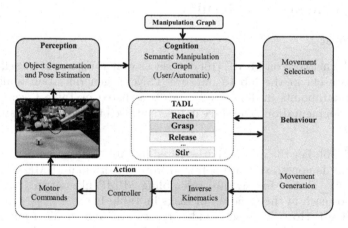

Fig. 3. TADL based low level controller. Given a segmented semantic manipulation graph from high level controller, the execution of the task using the low level controller is sketched which involves several components.

3.2   TADL Generation: How to Do?

TADL, a task-independent DMP library, is a collection of DMP models that have been trained using robot demonstrations for all the 10 primitive actions listed in Table 2. Kinesthetic robot demonstrations are collected by manually actuating the manipulator robotic arm for each primitive action (ex. grasp, tilt, wipe etc.). During RD, the manipulator states are recorded and are used to train the DMP model for every action. The following cartesian DMP formulation, developed by Ude [22], is used in this framework to model a shown movement:

$$\tau \dot{z} = \alpha_z(\beta_z(g - y) - z) + f(x) \tag{5}$$

$$\tau \dot{y} = z \tag{6}$$

where x is the phase variable, z is the scaled velocity of the movement, g is the desired final position on the movement, and f is a nonlinear forcing term. With the choice $\tau > 0$ and $\alpha_z = 4\beta_z$, the linear part of equation system (5) becomes critically damped and y, z monotonically converge to a unique attractor point at $y = g, z = 0$. We gather expert kinesthetic demonstration using a UR10 manipulator arm which are then used to train DMP models for each of the movement primitives and stored in TADL. The execution of the task *(how to do?)* is depicted in Fig. 3.

4   Experiments and Results

4.1   Dataset

We train the network on MIME [16] dataset as well as on two more self-collected realistic datasets in the lab to improve TSNet's generalisation abilities. The number of datapoints in datasets 2) and 3) as listed in Table 3 were increased using data augmentation. The three datasets utilised to train TSNet are depicted in Fig. 4 as:

1. **MIME [16]:** For the nine activities listed in Table 1, third-person view videos of human demonstration are obtained from the original MIME dataset.
2. **Imitaton_Data:** In our lab, resembling MIME-like setting, we collected videos for each of the same set of tasks in Table 1.
3. **Real_Imitation:** This set's video recordings were made from a realistic perspective. For this set, we have recorded videos for five tasks.

4.2   TSNet

We run the following TSNet module experiments using the three datasets in 80/20 split for train and test sets for each experiment: (a) TSNet trained on MIME [16]; (b) Combination of MIME and Imitation_Data, randomly divided and TSNet trained on this mixed pool; and (c) Trained model from (b) is fine tuned using Real_Imitation data.

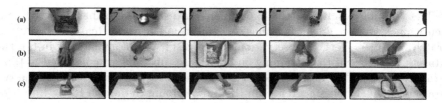

Fig. 4. Dataset: (a) MIME, (b) Imitation_Data and (c) Real_Imitation

Table 3. Dataset for Experimentation

Dataset	Tasks	Total Points
MIME [16]	All 9 in Table 1	4003
Imitation_Data (Ours)	All 9 in Table 1	458
Real_Imitation (Ours)	liquid pouring, pushing, table cleaning, picking, place in basket	224

Table 4. Training Results

Experiment	Test Accuracy
a) MIME [16]	94.38%
b) Mix of MIME and Imitation_Data	91.37%
c) Fine tuning with Real_Imitation	88.89%

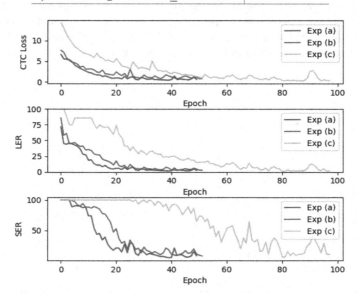

Fig. 5. Test metrics for the three experiments across three parameters: CTC Loss, LER and SER. We use early stopping if the loss does not improve for 10 consecutive epochs, hence the curves end at different times for each of the experiments.

The training results for the experiments are shown in Table 4. Over-fitting occurs quickly when TSNet is trained on Imitation Data and Real Imitation from scratch. We made several observations. As a result of a domain shift in the two datasets, experiment (b)'s training outcomes are substandard compared to those of (a). It is clear that despite the fact that the task's nature is same in the two data sets, the CTC loss is greater in (b). Low amount of data in Real_Imitation is the cause of experiment (c)'s decreased accuracy.

Three metrics-CTC loss, Sequence Error Rate (SER), and Label Error Rate (LER)-are used to assess TSNet. The metrics for the test set for each experiment are shown in Fig. 5. SER is the percentage of incorrectly classified sequence i.e., complement of accuracy. LER is the mean normalised edit distance between the prediction and the target.

4.3   TADL

Demonstration for each primitive action in Table 2 was chosen to train the DMP model and subsequently added to TADL. In Fig. 6, the black trajectories represent the demonstrated movement in the robot workspace used to train DMP and blue lines are generalisation of the learnt model for different goal positions.

As the HD of liquid pouring is passed through TSNet, it predicts the sequence of primitives: *reach - grasp - reach - tilt- reach - release - retract*. First, the DMP parameters of *reach* are searched in TADL and the trajectory is regenerated by the robot for given start and goal position. After the semantic segmentation of the robot's environment, the object bottle is chosen by YOLOv4 and MRE. 6D pose of the bottle is estimated and given as the goal position for *reach* DMP [1, 11] and *reach* is then executed. It follows for all the primitives given by TSNet. Fig. 9 shows the task of cleaning a table using TADL.

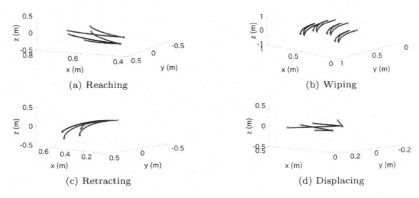

(a) Reaching   (b) Wiping

(c) Retracting   (d) Displacing

Fig. 6. Figure shows components of TADL Vocabulary like reaching, wiping, retracting and displacing. ▬ shows the human demonstrated robot trajectory for the task which is used to train the corresponding DMP model and ▬ represents the generated robot trajectory using learnt DMP models for varying goal parameters. ● and ● represents the beginning and endpoint of the trajectories respectively. (Color figure online)

4.4   Ablation Studies

By varying convolutional and bi-directional LSTM layers in our TSNet architecture, we conduct an ablation study on the MIME [16] dataset to examine the performance.

1. **Varying convolutional layers:** We performed 3 experiments a), b) and c) as shown in Table 5 to train the TSNet model. The accuracy is at its best in a) as seen in Fig. 7. We can extract more features by adding more layers, but this tends to overfit the data, which introduces errors like false positives and lowers the accuracy.
2. **Varying bi-directional LSTM layers:** As depicted in Fig. 8, the TSNet model is trained with different numbers of Bi-LSTM layers. Table 5's experiments a), d), and e) display the test accuracy obtained. The accuracy is at its best in a). The accuracy is still excellent with three layers, but the training does not end as early as it does with only two layers, as illustrated in Fig. 8.

Table 5. Ablation Study Results for MIME [16] dataset

Experiment	Test Accuracy
a) 4 Conv layers + 2 Bi-LSTM layers	94.38%
b) 3 Conv layers + 2 Bi-LSTM layers	91.88%
c) 5 Conv layers + 2 Bi-LSTM layers	91.64%
d) 4 Conv layers + 3 Bi-LSTM layers	93.13%
e) 4 Conv layers + 1 Bi-LSTM layers	91.01%

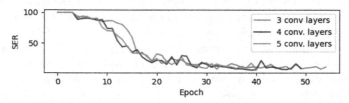

Fig. 7. Effect on SER (sequence error rate) with varying number of convolutional layers while training TSNet

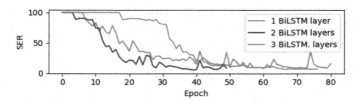

Fig. 8. Effect on SER (sequence error rate) with varying number of bi-directional LSTM layers while training TSNet

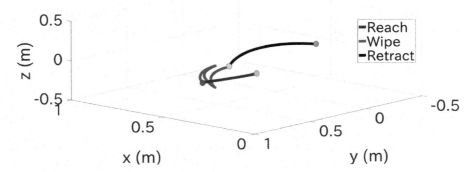

Fig. 9. Task of cleaning a table using TADL (•—• Reach - • Grasp - •—• Wipe - ◦ Release - ◦—◦ Retract) (Color figure online)

4.5   Imitation Test Experiments:

Experimental Setup: We use a 6 DOF UR 10 robot manipulator with a RGBD Realsense-D435i sensor mounted on eye-in-hand configuration (Fig. 1(c)). A 2-finger gripper built using Grabber Reacher with rotating jaw [20] is mounted to the robot end-effector. A table with 10 objects for object manipulation is placed in the robot workspace. We test the proposed imitation learning framework for three robotic manipulation tasks of liquid pouring, table cleaning and object placing. We provide human demonstration videos from Real_Imitation dataset for each of the three tasks to test on a real robot. TSNet predicts the sequence of primitives as mentioned in Table 1 for each of the mentioned tasks.

These primitives in manipulation graph is attached with semantic goals using perception module to generate semantic manipulation graph (i.e., *table, cup,* and *bottle* in case of liquid pouring, see Fig. 10(b, c, d)). The bottle is selected as the object to be manipulated through YOLOv4 [4] and MRE. The probability of objects as head is calculated by the MRE ground truth knowledge database (Fig. 2). After obtaining head (*bottle*) and relations (*reach, grasp, tilt, etc.*), the MRE knowledge base gives most likely tails - *glass, pan, cup,* if the tail object is unknown. Finally the semantic manipulation graph is executed by low level controller using TADL as shown in Fig. 11.

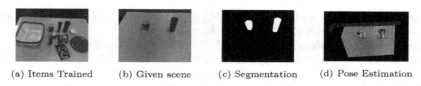

(a) Items Trained   (b) Given scene   (c) Segmentation   (d) Pose Estimation

Fig. 10. Perception module for low level TADL based controller.

Fig. 11. Imitation test on robot (a) table cleaning, (b) object placing and (c) liquid pouring. Each case show human video demonstration and robot execution steps.

5   Conclusions

We present a decoupled architecture for imitation learning. A high-level module does action segmentation using a CTC loss function that avoids the tedious task of frame-wise labelling while the low-level controller does sequential action execution on the robot. It is integrated with MRE Network to model semantic knowledge and YOLOv4 network for detecting the objects. A universal set of DMPs is proposed for the low-level control. The system's efficacy is tested on a real robot for imitation of three complex tasks.

Identification of partially occluded objects in a real-world scene is a challenging problem that we faced using YOLOv4 [4] trained object identification module. At the moment, our system considers TADL's movement primitives to be universal. Additional research ought to make it possible to identify novel primitives in human demonstrations that might then be included in TADL.

References

1. Abdulla, W.: Mask R-CNN for object detection and instance segmentation on Keras and TensorFlow (2017). https://github.com/matterport/Mask_RCNN
2. Argall, B.D., Chernova, S., Veloso, M., Browning, B.: A survey of robot learning from demonstration. Robot. Auton. Syst. **57**(5), 469–483 (2009). https://doi.org/10.1016/j.robot.2008.10.024

3. Behera, L., Kumar, S., Patchaikani, P.K., Nair, R.R., Dutta, S.: Intelligent Control of Robotic Systems. CRC Press, Boca Raton (2020)
4. Bochkovskiy, A., Wang, C.Y., Liao, H.Y.: YOLOv4: optimal speed and accuracy of object detection. arXiv preprint arXiv:2004.10934 [cs.CV] (2020)
5. Chella, A., Dindo, H., Infantino, I.: A cognitive framework for imitation learning. Robot. Auton. Syst. **54**(5), 403–408 (2006). https://doi.org/10.1016/j.robot.2006.01.008
6. Daruna, A., Liu, W., Kira, Z., Chernova, S.: RoboCSE: robot common sense embedding. arXiv preprint arXiv:1903.00412 [cs.RO] (2019). https://doi.org/10.48550/ARXIV.1903.00412
7. Graves, A., Fernández, S., Gomez, F., Schmidhuber, J.: Connectionist temporal classification: labelling unsegmented sequence data with recurrent neural networks. In: Proceedings of the 23rd International Conference on Machine Learning, pp. 369–376 (2006)
8. Huang, D.-A., Fei-Fei, L., Niebles, J.C.: Connectionist temporal modeling for weakly supervised action labeling. In: Leibe, B., Matas, J., Sebe, N., Welling, M. (eds.) ECCV 2016. LNCS, vol. 9908, pp. 137–153. Springer, Cham (2016). https://doi.org/10.1007/978-3-319-46493-0_9
9. Hussein, A., Gaber, M.M., Elyan, E., Jayne, C.: Imitation learning: a survey of learning methods. ACM Comput. Surv. (CSUR) **50**(2), 1–35 (2017)
10. Jiang, C., Dehghan, M., Jagersand, M.: Understanding contexts inside robot and human manipulation tasks through a vision-language model and ontology system in a video stream. arXiv preprint arXiv:2003.01163 [cs.CV] (2020)
11. Kumar, A., Behera, L.: Semi supervised deep quick instance detection and segmentation. In: 2019 International Conference on Robotics and Automation (ICRA), pp. 8325–8331. IEEE (2019)
12. Lin, M., Inoue, N., Shinoda, K.: CTC network with statistical language modeling for action sequence recognition in videos. In: Proceedings of the on Thematic Workshops of ACM Multimedia 2017, pp. 393–401 (2017)
13. Liu, H., Wu, Y., Yang, Y.: Analogical inference for multi-relational embeddings. In: Precup, D., Teh, Y.W. (eds.) Proceedings of the 34th International Conference on Machine Learning. Proceedings of Machine Learning Research, vol. 70, pp. 2168–2178. PMLR (2017)
14. Nickel, M., Murphy, K., Tresp, V., Gabrilovich, E.: A review of relational machine learning for knowledge graphs. Proc. IEEE **104**(1), 11–33 (2016)
15. Ramirez-Amaro, K., Dean-Leon, E., Cheng, G.: Robust semantic representations for inferring human co-manipulation activities even with different demonstration styles. In: 2015 IEEE-RAS 15th International Conference on Humanoid Robots (Humanoids), pp. 1141–1146 (2015). https://doi.org/10.1109/HUMANOIDS.2015.7363496
16. Sharma, P., Mohan, L., Pinto, L., Gupta, A.: Multiple interactions made easy (mime): large scale demonstrations data for imitation. arXiv preprint arXiv:1810.07121 (2018)
17. Sharma, P., Pathak, D., Gupta, A.: Third-person visual imitation learning via decoupled hierarchical controller. arXiv preprint arXiv:1911.09676 (2019). https://doi.org/10.48550/ARXIV.1911.09676
18. Shiarlis, K., Wulfmeier, M., Salter, S., Whiteson, S., Posner, I.: TACO: learning task decomposition via temporal alignment for control. In: International Conference on Machine Learning, pp. 4654–4663. PMLR (2018)

19. Smith, L., Dhawan, N., Zhang, M., Abbeel, P., Levine, S.: AVID: learning multi-stage tasks via pixel-level translation of human videos. arXiv preprint arXiv:1912.04443 (2019). https://doi.org/10.48550/ARXIV.1912.04443
20. Solutions, R.R.M.: RMS - 26" yellow grabber reacher with rotating head (2021). https://www.myrmsstore.com/collections/reachers-grabbers/products/26-yellow-grabber-reacher-with-rotating-head
21. Tomasello, M., Savage-Rumbaugh, S., Kruger, A.C.: Imitative learning of actions on objects by children, chimpanzees, and enculturated chimpanzees. Child Dev. **64**(6), 1688–1705 (1993)
22. Ude, A., Nemec, B., Petri?, T., Morimoto, J.: Orientation in cartesian space dynamic movement primitives. In: 2014 IEEE International Conference on Robotics and Automation (ICRA), pp. 2997–3004 (2014). https://doi.org/10.1109/ICRA.2014.6907291
23. Wang, Q., Mao, Z., Wang, B., Guo, L.: Knowledge graph embedding: a survey of approaches and applications. IEEE Trans. Knowl. Data Eng. **29**(12), 2724–2743 (2017). https://doi.org/10.1109/TKDE.2017.2754499
24. Yang, Y., Li, Y., Fermuller, C., Aloimonos, Y.: Robot learning manipulation action plans by "watching" unconstrained videos from the world wide web. In: Proceedings of the AAAI Conference on Artificial Intelligence, vol. 29, no. 1 (2015)

Adversarial Learning Based Semi-supervised Semantic Segmentation of Low Resolution Gram Stained Microscopic Images

Harshal Singh[1]([✉]), Vidyashree R. Kanabur[1], S. David Sumam[1],
Deepu Vijayasenan[1], and Sreejith Govindan[2]

[1] National Institute of Technology Karnataka, Surathkal, Karnataka, India
harshalsingh78@gmail.com
[2] Department of Basic Medical Sciences, MAHE, Manipal, Karnataka, India

Abstract. Urinary tract infections (UTIs) are infections that affect the urinary system. It is usually caused by bacteria and pus cells. Analyzing urine samples, including examining pus cells, is a standard method for diagnosing and monitoring UTIs. However, manually detecting bacteria or pus cells in microscopic urine images is a time-consuming and labour-intensive task for microbiologists. Therefore, the segmentation of microscopic pus cell images will ease the process of detecting UTI. Especially low resolution microscopic images are hard to annotate; therefore, in this study, we propose an adversarial learning based semi-supervised segmentation method for segmentation of pus cell images at low resolution i.e. 40× using labeled high resolution images i.e. 100×. The proposed methodology aims to ease the process of UTI detection by automating the segmentation of pus cell images. The results of the proposed methodology demonstrate an increase in the Dice coefficient score percentage by 1%, 1.6% and 2.4% on 40× images when compared to fully supervised segmentation model trained on only 100× data using three different architectures- Unet, ResUnet++, and PSPnet, respectively.

Keywords: Pus cell image segmentation · Semi-supervised Learning · Generative Adversarial Network · Fully convolutional networks (FCN) · Deep Learning

1 Introduction

Urinary tract infections (UTIs) are infections that affect the urinary system. UTI [1] can be diagnosed and monitored through the analysis of urine samples, including the examination of pus cells. Segmenting and quantifying pus cells in urine samples can provide valuable information for diagnosing and monitoring UTIs. The manual detection of bacteria or the pus cells in microscopic images of urine test requires lot of time and effort for the microbiologists, especially for

© The Author(s), under exclusive license to Springer Nature Switzerland AG 2024
H. Kaur et al. (Eds.): CVIP 2023, CCIS 2010, pp. 362–373, 2024.
https://doi.org/10.1007/978-3-031-58174-8_31

the low resolution images. The examination of pus cells involves the analysis of images captured at various magnifications, including resolutions ranging from $40\times$ to $100\times$. The main goal of this study is to segment the pus cell at low-resolution, i.e. the ones magnified at $40\times$, which are more challenging to label.

Traditional methods for segmenting gram-stained pus cell images often rely on fully supervised machine learning and deep learning techniques [2], which require segmentation maps for each image. Creating these maps manually is a time-consuming task. The challenges in this task include the variability in staining quality, the presence of artefacts and debris, and the diverse morphology of pus cells. In [3] a machine learning algorithm based on color-based segmentation of Gram-stained sputum smear images using K-Means clustering was developed. The majority of existing bacterial images or pus cells image segmentation techniques are fully supervised [2], meaning that a segmentation map is required for every image.

The field of semi-supervised segmentation of low-resolution gram-stained pus cell images is relatively unexplored in the existing literature. While various segmentation techniques have been developed for other types of medical images, the specific task of semi-supervised segmentation of low-resolution gram-stained pus cell images has not received significant attention.

Semi-supervised segmentation refers to a segmentation approach that utilizes both labeled and unlabeled data for training a model. It combines the advantages of supervised learning (using labeled data) and unsupervised learning (leveraging unlabeled data) to improve the accuracy and robustness of the segmentation process.

There are various semi-supervised methods described in the literature to reduce the dependence on ground truth mask. Semi-supervised learning, typically combines entropy minimization and consistency regularization techniques to train models. Entropy minimization techniques, such as Pseudo label [4] and Noisy student [5], aim to minimize uncertainty in the model's predictions. On the other hand, consistency regularization techniques, including Temporal Ensembling [6], Mean Teacher [7], and Virtual Adversarial Training [8], encourage consistent predictions across different perturbations of the same input. Hybrid approaches, such as FixMatch [9] and MixMatch [10], have also been proposed in the literature, incorporating both entropy minimization and consistency regularization. Hung et al. [11] proposed an Adversarial network for semi-supervised semantic segmentation. Their approach utilizes a generator based on DeepLabV3 to generate a label map. Meanwhile, a discriminator in the form of Fully Convolutional Network (FCN) is employed to distinguish between the generated probability map distribution from the generator and the ground truth probability distribution. This research area holds promise for addressing the challenges posed by expensive and time-consuming labeling tasks, particularly in medical image segmentation. In medical image segmentation, the adversarial learning based network is used to do the semi-supervised semantic segmentation for effusion cytology [12]. We chose to work on an Adversarial based network because it offers several advantages. Adversarial learning based networks can improve the performance of segmentation model by leveraging the discriminator network. The discriminator helps discriminate between the ground truth probability map and the generated probability map, encouraging the generator (segmentation model) to produce more accurate segmentation.

2   Adversarial Learning Based Semi-supervised Image Semantic Segmentation Methodology

The methodology comprises two key networks: a generator network, which can be any segmentation network such as U-Net [13], responsible for performing the image segmentation, i.e. generating masks and a discriminator network which is a Fully Convolutional Network (FCN) that receives probability maps from either the generated distribution or the ground truth distribution. It then generates a probability map of dimension $X \times Y \times 1$.

Figure 1 visually encapsulates the interplay between the generator and discriminator networks in our training approach.

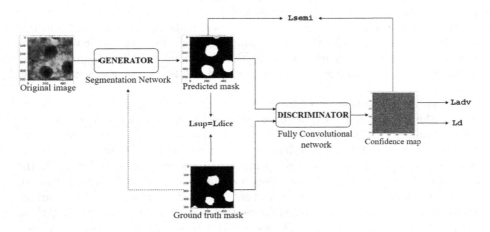

Fig. 1. Proposed methodology overview.

When the generator network is fed with an image having a label, the generator generates its corresponding mask, and the supervised segmentation loss L_{sup} is computed between the generated mask and the ground truth mask. Here loss L_{sup} can be binary-cross entropy loss L_{bce}, or any other segmentation loss such as Dice loss L_{dice}. The discriminator receives both the generated mask and the original mask. For the original masks, loss L_d is calculated by comparing them to a tensor of all 1's, representing real samples. For the generated maps, loss L_d is computed by comparing them to a tensor of all 0's, representing fake samples. Here the loss L_d is binary-cross entropy loss. The training of discriminator is done by doing backpropagation on the loss L_d. The combine loss L_d with the loss L_{bce}, is referred to as L_{adv}. The training of generator is done by doing backpropagation based on this combined loss, $L_{seg} = L_{sup} + k_{adv} \times L_{adv}$, where k_{adv} is hyper-parameter to balance the overall loss.

When dealing with unlabeled images, it is not possible to compute the loss L_{sup} as there are no available ground truth labels. In this scenario, the generated mask is directly given as input to the discriminator. By applying a threshold T_{semi} on the discriminator's output map, a confidence map is generated. Only the labels with high confidence from the confidence map are considered, loss L_{semi} is calculated between this generated confidence map and the predicted probability map generated from generator, here loss L_{semi} is binary-cross entropy loss. This loss L_{semi} term, along with the adversarial loss L_{adv}, is combined and utilized for training the generator.

2.1 Network Architecture

Adversarial networks comprise of two models, i.e. a generator model and a discriminator model. The generator's role is to generate predictions or outputs, while the discriminator aims to differentiate between inputs belonging to the ground truth distribution or the probability distribution that comes from the generator's output. We used a similar adversarial network as proposed by Hung et al. [11], with different segmentation architectures. Below are descriptions of the generator and discriminator networks employed in our training process.

Generator Network. Three segmentation architectures, U-Net [13], ResUNet+− [14], and PSPNet [15], have been used as generators in our different experiments for semi-supervised semantic segmentation. PSPNet has demonstrated significant improvements in performance on the BraTS dataset and CVC-10 dataset. U-Net has been demonstrated to be effective even when trained on a small number of images and in semi-supervised settings [16]. In contrast, ResUNet++ offers faster training times and achieves impressive performance on medical image data with reduced parameter redundancy. Hence these three models are chosen as generator network for generating masks.

Discriminator Network. The discriminator network employed in our model is a Fully Convolutional Network (FCN) as shown in Fig. 2, which is same as FCN architecture used by Hung et al. [11]. It comprises of 5 convolutional layers and the output layers have channel dimensions of 64, 128, 256, 512, and 1, respectively and each convolutional layer is followed by a Leaky-ReLU activation function.

2.2 Loss Function

We denote the input image as x_m, which has dimension $X \times Y \times 3$. The generator network, represented by G(), when fed with image x_m produces an output $G(x_m)$ with dimensions $X \times Y \times 1$. The discriminator network, represented by

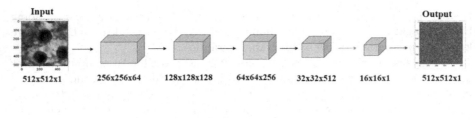

Input

Output

512x512x1   256x256x64   128x128x128   64x64x256   32x32x512   16x16x1   512x512x1

$\longrightarrow$ Conv2d with leaky relu as activation function
$\dashrightarrow$ up-sampling with scale factor of 32
$\longrightarrow$ classifier conv2d

Fig. 2. A Fully Convolutional Network based discriminator [11].

D(), accepts either the ground truth mask y_m or the generator's output probability map $G(x_m)$ of size $X \times Y \times 1$ as input. It generates a probability map $D(G(x_m))$ or $D(y_m)$ with dimensions $X \times Y \times 1$. The training of generator network is based on combined loss term, L_{seg}, as defined in Eq. (1), which consists of three components: L_{sup}, L_{adv}, and L_{semi}. L_{sup} is supervised loss between y_m and $G(x_m)$. We used L_{sup} as Dice loss L_{dice} described in Eq. (2), since models trained using L_{dice} shown better results than L_{bce}. L_{adv} is the adversarial loss, and L_{semi} is the semi-supervised loss. The loss terms are weighted using hyper-parameters k_{adv} and k_{semi} to balance their contributions to the overall loss.

$$L_{seg} = L_{sup} + k_{adv} \times L_{adv} + k_{semi} \times L_{semi} \tag{1}$$

$$L_{dice} = 1 - \frac{2 \times \text{Intersection}}{\text{Union} + \text{Intersection}} \tag{2}$$

To train the segmentation network to deceive the discriminator, the adversarial loss for the FCN D() is utilized. Eq. (3) represents the loss L_{adv} for the predicted mask and Eq. (4) represents the loss L_{adv} for the original mask. These adversarial loss terms play a role in training the generator network to generate segmentation maps that can fool the discriminator.

$$L_{adv} = -\sum \log\left(D(G(x_m))\right) \tag{3}$$

$$L_{adv} = -\sum \log\left(D(y_m)\right) \tag{4}$$

In the case of training with unlabeled data in a semi-supervised manner, the availability of ground truth labels is limited. Therefore, the loss term L_{sup}, which requires the ground truth, cannot be calculated. However, the adversarial loss term L_{adv} can still be calculated as it only requires discriminator's output. In addition to loss L_{adv}, the discriminator is also trained using a self-supervised framework. By applying a threshold T_{semi} to the discriminator's output probability distribution $D(G(x_m))$, a high-confidence map can be generated. This process helps to generate a ground truth approximation based on the confidence of the generated segmentation map. The semi-supervised loss term is defined in Eq. (5). The self-supervised ground truth, denoted by $\hat{y}_m$ is obtained according to Eq. (6), where f() is a function defined in Eq. (7). We took the value of $T_{semi}=0.2$, as in Hung et al. [11] best result is achieved when value T_{semi} is taken as 0.2 from range of 0.1 to 0.3.

$$L_{semi} = -\sum\sum f(D(G(x_m)) > T_{semi}).\hat{y}_m \log(G(x_m)) \qquad (5)$$

$$\hat{y}_m = \begin{cases} 1, & \text{if } \sigma(G(x_m)) > 0.5 \\ 0, & \text{otherwise} \end{cases} \qquad (6)$$

$$f(.) = \begin{cases} \hat{y}_m, & \text{if } D(G(x_m))_{ij} > T_{semi} \\ 1 - \hat{y}_m, & \text{otherwise} \end{cases} \qquad (7)$$

3   Dataset

The dataset consists of low-resolution (40×) and high-resolution (100×) gram-stained urine microscopic images containing pus cells. The data for research purposes is taken from a tertiary hospital. There are total of 40 pus cell images at 100× resolution and 19 images at 40× resolution and all the images have a size of 1200 × 1600 pixels, as shown in Table 1. The masks of pus cell images are prepared and validated by the microbiologists. The mask contains background with black colour and foreground i.e. pus cells shown with white colour, i.e. it is a binary segmentation task. The size of the images is high, therefore, the patches of shape 512 × 512 pixels as given in Table 2 are created for ease of memory management and also helps introduce more effective data augmentation.

First, the dataset is divided into training, validation and testing. Then, overlapping patches are created for training purposes by moving over the original images to increase the dataset for training, and non-overlapping patches are created for validation and testing. Also, for images at 40× resolution, the images are first up-sampled to 2.5 times their original size to match the resolution of images at 100×, and then the patches are created. For the purpose of image up-sampling, the bi-cubic filter available in the OpenCV library was utilized.

Table 1. Dataset Details.

Magnification	No. of Image	Image shape
100×	40	1200 × 1600
40×	19	1200 × 1600

Table 2. Dataset distribution after creating patches.

Magnification	Training	Validation	Testing
100×	214	48	36
40× re-sampled	325	–	–

4   Experiments and Results

As we are doing adversarial learning based semi-supervised segmentation, using both labeled 100× and unlabeled 40× data for training and our main motivation is to do semantic segmentation of pus cell at 40× resolution, we conducted two experiments by taking different amounts of labeled 100× data. To compare the results of adversarial learning based semi-supervised semantic segmentation, we have also done fully supervised segmentation using only 100× labelled data and tested on the 40× images.

For both the experiments we used UNet, ResUNet++, and PSPNet as segmentation architectures to train three different models. In addition to the standard size of encoder and decoder blocks in U-Net and Resunet++, we experimented with smaller-sized blocks with channel depths of 16, 32, 64, 128, and 256 for the encoder and decoder blocks, which showed better results than the standard size. So for all model training using U-net and Resunet++, we have taken smaller-sized encoder-decoder blocks, and we utilized a standard ResNet encoder as the encoder part for the PSPNet architecture. Patches containing at least 5% of pus cells in an image are used for training purposes. While for test purposes, the entire image is considered. Also, before creating patches, all 40× images are stain normalised using a specific image from the 100× set since gram-stained pus cell images have variations in the stain. Also data augmentation techniques such as random crop and pad, random shift, random horizontal and vertical flip and random rotation are used to increase the dataset's diversity. For all segmentation architectures and for FCN i.e. discriminator, we used the Adam optimizer and the leaky ReLU activation function. The hyper-parameters used for the optimizer included a maximum learning rate of 10^{-3} and β_1 and β_2 values of 0.9 and 0.99, respectively. Furthermore, we used k_{semi} and k_{adv} as 0.1 and 0.001, respectively, [11]. We trained all the models for 150 epochs. We used IoU (Intersection-Over-Union) and Dice coefficient as evaluation parameters. The model which is having the lowest loss L_{sup} on validation data is saved.

4.1   Experiment 1

For fully supervised segmentation, the segmentation architectures are trained on 214 patches of 100× labelled data and the model is tested on 100× test data and all images of 40× data. As discussed, three different segmentation architectures (Unet, RessUnet++, PSPnet) are trained with loss $L_{sup}{=}L_{dice}$. In the case of semi-supervised segmentation, a 1:1 ratio of labeled and unlabeled data is used. Since there are a total of 214 patches of 100× data available as labeled data, an equal number of 214 patches from the total of 325 patches of 40× data are used to maintain the 1:1 ratio. For 40× data a 3-fold cross-validation scheme is implemented to train the network, i.e. in each fold 214 patches are taken for training and remaining 111 images for testing. Since we have limited 40× data, therefore 3-fold cross validation scheme enables us to make the most efficient use of available 40× data. The IoU scores and dice coefficient scores are calculated for the 100× test data, and the average IoU and dice coefficient scores across the 3-fold cross-validation are calculated and tabulated in Table 3.

From Table 3 it is observed that for 40× images, there is an increase in IoU scores from 62.5% to 63.9%, 60.6% to 62.1% and 62% to 65.2% for models trained using Unet, ResUnet++, and PSPnet, respectively. Similarly, there is an increase in the Dice coefficient score of 75.5% to 76.5%, 74.2% to 75.8, and 75.6% to 78% for models trained using Unet, ResUnet++, and PSPnet, respectively. Although, for 100× test images, there are no improvements in IoU and Dice scores, our main objective is to improve the segmentation of 40× images which are difficult to label, and the proposed scheme shows improvements for 40× images. Among the three segmentation architectures the PSPnet has shown better IoU and Dice scores compared to Unet and ResUnet++. The predictions of a image taken from 100× and 40× test set is shown in Figs. 3 and 4.

Table 3. Evaluation parameters when models trained on equal amount of 100× data and 40× data

Segmentation Architecture	Model	100× test data		40× test data	
		IoU	Dice coefficient	IoU	Dice coefficient
U-Net	L_{sup}	0.697	0.82	0.625	0.755
	$L_{sup} + L_{adv} + L_{semi}$	0.665	0.798	**0.639**	**0.765**
ResUnet++	L_{sup}	0.68	0.81	0.606	0.742
	$L_{sup} + L_{adv} + L_{semi}$	0.63	0.77	**0.621**	**0.758**
PSPnet	L_{sup}	0.69	0.82	0.62	0.756
	$L_{sup} + L_{adv} + L_{semi}$	0.662	0.73	**0.652**	**0.78**

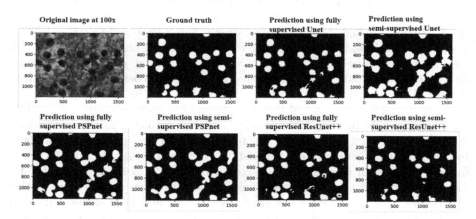

Fig. 3. 100× Predictions for models (fully supervised and semi-supervised) when models trained using equal amount of 100× and 40× data.

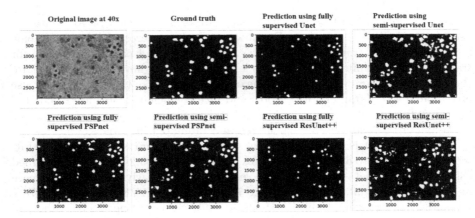

Fig. 4. 40× Predictions for models (fully supervised and semi-supervised) when models trained using equal amount of 100× and 40× data.

4.2 Experiment 2

Experiment 1 shows that the Adversarial learning based technique shown improvement in IoU and Dice scores, therefore in this experiment we have reduced the labeled dataset(100×) to half amount compared to unlabeled dataset(40×) In this experiment we utilized 107 patches of 100× and 214 patches of 40×. i.e. the semi-supervised model is trained with half amount of 100× data compared to 40× data and rest all parameters are kept constant as in experiment 1. For fully supervised segmentation, the segmentation architectures are trained on 107 patches of 100× labelled data and the model is tested on 100× test data and all images of 40× data. The IoU scores and dice coefficient scores are calculated for 100× and 40× test data, and tabulated in Table 4. In the case of semi-supervised segmentation, 107 patches out of 214 of 100× labeled data and 214 patches from the total of 325 patches of 40× data are used to maintain the 1:2 ratio. A 3-fold cross-validation scheme is implemented to train the network, i.e. in each fold 214 patches are taken for training and remaining for test for 40× without label. The IoU scores and dice coefficient scores are calculated for the 100× test data, and the average IoU and dice coefficient scores across the 3-fold cross-validation are calculated, and tabulated in Table 4.

From Table 4, it is observed that for 40× images, there is an increase in IoU scores from 60.2% to 61%, 59% to 62.2% and 62% to 63.6% for models trained using Unet, ResUnet++, and PSPnet, respectively. In this experiment, for 100× test images also, there are improvements in IoU and Dice scores. For 100× test images, there is an increase in IoU score percentage of 3.4%, 0.3%, and 8.3% for models trained using Unet, ResUnet++, and PSPnet, respectively. In this experiment also, the PSPnet has shown better IoU and Dice scores compared to Unet and ResUnet++. The predictions of a image taken from 100× and 40× test set is shown in Figs. 5 and 6.

Table 4. Evaluation parameters when models trained on half amount of 100× data compared to 40× data

Segmentation Architecture	Model	100× test data		40× test data	
		IoU	Dice coefficient	IoU	Dice coefficient
U-Net	L_{sup}	0.597	0.745	0.602	0.737
	$L_{sup} + L_{adv} + L_{semi}$	**0.631**	**0.765**	**0.61**	**0.743**
ResUnet++	L_{sup}	0.638	0.778	0.59	0.73
	$L_{sup} + L_{adv} + L_{semi}$	0.635	0.774	**0.622**	**0.76**
PSPnet	L_{sup}	0.58	0.73	0.62	0.75
	$L_{sup} + L_{adv} + L_{semi}$	**0.663**	**0.794**	**0.636**	**0.769**

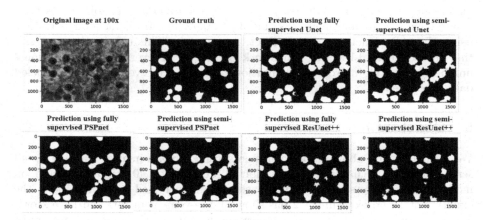

Fig. 5. 100× Predictions for models (fully supervised and semi-supervised) when models trained using half amount of 100× data compared to 40× data.

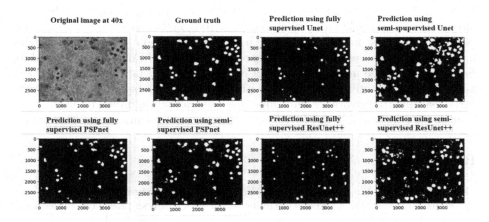

Fig. 6. 40× Predictions for models (fully supervised and semi-supervised) when models trained using half amount of 100× data compared to 40× data.

The results of experiment 2 also shows that the Adversarial learning based technique for semi-supervised semantic segmentation shows improvement in IoU and Dice scores. In experiment 2, when half amount of labeled data is used compared to unlabeled data, for 40× test images, the adversarial learning based semi supervised technique yields IoU scores with a difference of 2.9%, 0.1% and 1.6% only compared to IoU scores obtained in experiment 1 for models trained using Unet, ResUnet++, and PSPnet, respectively. For 100× test data, there is decrease in IoU scores of 1%, 4.2% and 11% from experiment 1 to experiment 2 for models trained using Unet, ResUnet++, and PSPnet, respectively in a supervised way, since for supervised semantic segmentation the performance is decreased as we reduce the training data. And for the same 100× test data tested for models trained using adversarial training, the difference in IoU scores from experiment 1 and experiment 2 is only 3.4%, 0.5% and 0.1% for models trained using Unet, ResUnet++, and PSPnet, respectively. This observation suggests that the adversarial learning framework is effective in leveraging the additional unlabeled data to improve segmentation performance, even when the labeled data is reduced.

5   Conclusion

We evaluated the above two experiments using an adversarial learning-based semi-supervised semantic segmentation approach. For 40× images tested on models using Adversarial learning based semi-supervised approach, both the experiment 1 and experiment 2 has shown improvement in IoU and Dice scores compared to models trained in a supervised way using 100× labeled data only. The proposed methodology demonstrates an increase in the Dice coefficient score by 1%, 1.6% and 2.4% on 40× images when compared to fully supervised segmentation model trained only on 100× data using the three different architectures-Unet, ResUnet++, and PSPnet, respectively. Also in experiment 2 when we have utilized half the amount of labeled data(100×) compared to unlabeled data (40×), for 40× test images, the adversarial learning based semi supervised technique yields IoU scores with a difference of 2.9%, 0.1% and 1.6% only compared to IoU scores obtained in experiment 1 for models trained using Unet, ResUnet++, and PSPnet, respectively. Thus even with a reduction in labeled data, the adversarial learning framework for semi-supervised segmentation proves to be effective in utilizing the available unlabeled data to improve segmentation performance.

References

1. Chinnnusamy, N., Arumugam, V., Vedachalam, D.: A study on analysis of the sputum gram staining and culture in patients with lower respiratory tract infections attending a tertiary care hospital. Indian J. Microbiol. Res. **3**, 24–26 (2016)
2. Reddy, C., Reddy, P., Kanabur, V., Vijayasenan, D., David, S., Govindan, S.: Semi-automatic labeling and semantic segmentation of gram-stained microscopic images from DIBaS dataset. ArXiv Preprint ArXiv:2208.10737 (2022)

3. Sirohi, M., Lall, M., Yenishetti, S., Panat, L., Kumar, A.: Development of a Machine learning image segmentation-based algorithm for the determination of the adequacy of gram-stained sputum smear images. Med. J. Armed Forces India **78**, 339–344 (2021)
4. Seibold, C., Reiß, S., Kleesiek, J., Stiefelhagen, R.: Reference-guided pseudo-label generation for medical semantic segmentation. ArXiv Preprint ArXiv:2112.00735 (2021)
5. Xie, Q., Luong, M., Hovy, E., Le, Q.: Self-training with noisy student improves ImageNet classification. In: Proceedings of the IEEE/CVF Conference on Computer Vision and Pattern Recognition, pp. 10687–10698 (2020)
6. Laine, S., Aila, T.: Temporal ensembling for semi-supervised learning. ArXiv Preprint ArXiv:1610.02242 (2016)
7. Tarvainen, A., Valpola, H. Mean teachers are better role models: Weight-averaged consistency targets improve semi-supervised deep learning results. In: Advances in Neural Information Processing Systems, vol. 30 (2017)
8. Miyato, T., Maeda, S., Koyama, M., Ishii, S.: Virtual adversarial training: a regularization method for supervised and semi-supervised learning. IEEE Trans. Pattern Anal. Mach. Intell. **41**, 1979–1993 (2018)
9. Sohn, K., et al.: FixMatch: simplifying semi-supervised learning with consistency and confidence. In: Advances in Neural Information Processing Systems, vol. 33, pp. 596–608 (2020)
10. Berthelot, D., Carlini, N., Goodfellow, I., Papernot, N., Oliver, A., Raffel, C.: MixMatch: a holistic approach to semi-supervised learning. In: Advances in Neural Information Processing Systems, vol. 32 (2019)
11. Hung, W., Tsai, Y., Liou, Y., Lin, Y., Yang, M.: Adversarial learning for semi-supervised semantic segmentation. CoRR abs/1802.07934 (2018). http://arxiv.org/abs/1802.07934
12. Rajpurohit, M., Aboobacker, S., Vijayasenan, D., Sumam David, S., Suresh, P., Sreeram, S.: Semi-supervised semantic segmentation of effusion cytology images using adversarial training. In: Tistarelli, M., Dubey, S.R., Singh, S.K., Jiang, X. (eds.) Computer Vision and Machine Intelligence. LNNS, vol. 586, pp. 539–551. Springer, Singapore (2023). https://doi.org/10.1007/978-981-19-7867-8_43
13. Ronneberger, O., Fischer, P., Brox, T.: U-net: convolutional networks for biomedical image segmentation. In: Navab, N., Hornegger, J., Wells, W.M., Frangi, A.F. (eds.) MICCAI 2015. LNCS, vol. 9351, pp. 234–241. Springer, Cham (2015). https://doi.org/10.1007/978-3-319-24574-4_28
14. Jha, D., et al.: ResUNet++: an advanced architecture for medical image segmentation. In: 2019 IEEE International Symposium On Multimedia (ISM), pp. 225–2255 (2019)
15. Zhao, H., Shi, J., Qi, X., Wang, X., Jia, J.: Pyramid scene parsing network. In: Proceedings of The IEEE Conference on Computer Vision and Pattern Recognition, pp. 918–926 (2017)
16. Ullah, Z., Usman, M., Latif, S., Khan, A., Gwak, J.: SSMD-UNet: semi-supervised multi-task decoders network for diabetic retinopathy segmentation. Sci. Rep. **13**, 9087 (2023)

Novel Dataset Creation of Varieties of Banana and Ripening Stages for Machine Learning Applications

T. N. Manasa[(✉)] ⓘ and M. P. Pushpalatha

JSS Science and Technology University, Mysore, India
manasa20tn@gmail.com

Abstract. India holds the title of being the top banana producer globally, contributing approximately 25% of the total banana production. However, exporting it can be a challenge because of its shelf-life. To propose the best possible shelf-life extension methodology, it is important to classify based on the banana varieties and ripening stages to ensure sustainable growth and nutritional value. There are still not enough data sets with different varieties of bananas and their respective ripening stages. A review of research publications from the last five years has been conducted using electronic databases like Scopus, Google Scholar, and Research-Gate, as well as the details of publicly accessible dataset repository sites. The dataset captures images of different varieties of banana fruit as well as its respective different stages of ripening. Banana varieties considered include Robusta (MusaAA), Dwarf Cavendish (Musaacuminata), Nanjangud bananas, and Red bananas (Musa acuminata). The dataset contains over 41,900 processed images. In this paper, the authors provide researchers with an opportunity to develop and investigate machine learning and deep learning algorithms that are used to predict and extend the shelf life of banana fruits.

Keywords: Machine learning · Banana type classification · Ripening Stages Classification · Image processing

1 Introduction

Banana (Musa acuminate L) is globally recognized as the most widely cultivated and distributed fruit, playing a significant role in ensuring food security, particularly in developing regions. Bananas are often considered a high-energy food source due to their elevated levels of antioxidants, such as vitamins A, C, and E, β-carotene, and polyphenols, which contribute to their high antioxidant capacity (Ummarat, Matsu-moto, Wall, & Seraypheap, 2011) [1]. However, bananas have a short shelf life at tropical ambient temperatures due to the changes associated with climacteric ripening. These changes include rapid softening, senescence spotting, the development of off-odors, the occurrence of anthracnose and crown rot diseases, and the risk of chilling injury when stored below 13 °C [2]. The perishable nature of bananas makes them susceptible to spoilage, especially during transport and export.

H. Kaur et al. (Eds.): CVIP 2023, CCIS 2010, pp. 374–381, 2024.
https://doi.org/10.1007/978-3-031-58174-8_32

Extending the shelf life of bananas during export is of paramount importance for several reasons. Firstly, it ensures that bananas reach their destination in optimal condition, enhancing their value and marketability. This can result in better prices for the bananas and increased revenue for exporters. Secondly, prolonging the shelf life of bananas during export can contribute to the reduction of waste. When bananas spoil during transport, they may become unfit for consumption or sale, resulting in financial losses for exporters and contributing to food waste.

To address this concern and maintain freshness and shelf life, it is important to understand the stage of bananas and then propose the best possible shelf-life extension methodology, which helps both domestic and international exports.

Bananas can be categorized into various varieties based on their external characteristics, such as shape, size, and color, through the application of computer vision and deep learning techniques [2]. The Banana dataset was developed to encompass Indian bananas, along with their quality parameters, focusing on those varieties that are extensively consumed or exported.

It consists of 4 varieties of Indian banana fruit namely Robusta (MusaAAA), Dwarf cavendish (Musaacuminata), Nanjangud banana, and Red banana (Musa acuminata). They are further categorized based on the ripening stages. The fruit images were captured in diverse settings, featuring various backgrounds and experiencing varying lighting conditions, encompassing both indoor and outdoor environments. The dataset is divided into 4 folders based on the variety of banana. Each folder is further divided into seven subfolders, each representing a different stage of ripening. These subfolders are named as follows:

1. All Green
2. Light Green
3. Half Green Half Yellow
4. More Yellow than Green
5. Yellow with Green Tips
6. Full Yellow
7. Yellow with Brown Flecks

Fig. 1. Shows the sample images of the Robusta banana images from the dataset.

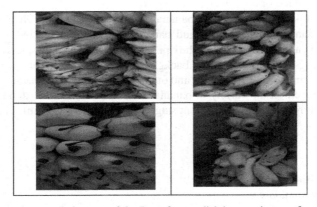

Fig. 2. Shows the sample images of the Dwarf cavendish banana images from the dataset.

Fig. 3. Shows the sample images of the Najangud Rasabale images from the dataset.

2 Purpose of Creating Banana Datasets

It consists of 4 varieties of Indian banana fruit namely Robusta (MusaAAA), Dwarf cavendish(Musaacuminata), Nanjangud banana, and Red banana(Musa acuminata). They are further categorized based on the ripening stages. The fruit images were captured in diverse settings, featuring various backgrounds and experiencing varying lighting conditions, encompassing both indoor and outdoor environments. The dataset is divided into 4 folders based on the variety of banana. Each folder is further divided into seven subfolders, each representing a different stage of ripening. These subfolders are Huge datasets are essential to train machine learning and deep learning models to evaluate the accuracy of the models [4]. There are several dataset repositories that are available publicly and few are patented which requires permission to access the same and some are not downloadable. There was no specific dataset found for different varieties of bananas. Few existing repositories like Kaggle are restricted to generic banana images. As there is a hierarchy of images required, the first hierarchy being varieties of bananas and second layer of hierarchy with different ripening stages in each variety this dataset was created.

Larger the dataset more the precision of algorithm and hence here the main purpose to create banana dataset is that we cannot find specific datasets of banana type like Nanjangud Rasabale or Red banana. Hence the main purpose here is to collect this special variety banana dataset along with its different stages which would help in precise shelf-life prediction.

The dataset provided here is a collection of different varieties of banana fruit images with different ripening stages in each variety. These varieties of banana are majorly found in Karnataka state and southern parts of India. The data will be useful to classify the different varieties of banana images and know which stage of ripening it is so that its shelf life can be calculated, and necessary actions be taken to extend its shelf life. By finding the right shelf life of banana would help the agriculturists in segregating and shipping the right product at right time which would reduce the wastage.

The Banana dataset consists of 41900 + processed images, which are not restricted to any specific background or lighting. The main reason to use different backgrounds and lighting is to train the model under different circumstances and differentiate the background from the image.

3 Properties of Banana Datasets

The standard dataset should have certain properties to achieve the best performance of the algorithm [2]:

- Stability: The Performance of the algorithms should not degrade when it is tested on datasets captured in various scenarios like angle, background, light
- Precise: Datasets should be exact according to the research requirements.
- Relevance: Datasets should be appropriate and suitable for the work.

Apart from the above properties a good dataset should consist of following attributes.

- The dataset should be diverse.
- Represent the real life as much as possible.

- For image annotation projects, it's crucial to possess high-quality data that accurately reflects real-life scenarios. This doesn't necessarily entail high-resolution or crystal-clear images. Instead, high-quality data should align with the specific requirements of the machine learning image processing task. For instance, if the goal is to recognize people in low-light conditions or vehicles driving in foggy weather, high-quality images would be those that closely resemble these challenging real-world situations.
- Very minimal bias
- Searchable and organized. Should be easy to navigate through.

4   Challenges

Capturing images or videos of the banana fruit from various vendors and markets and farms considering parameters is a challenging task. [3]. The following were common challenges.

- Creation of huge various datasets
- Data Cleaning
- Data Labelling
- Availability of all ripening stages

The other challenges that we faced while collecting the dataset is as follows:

- Not all datasets are available in marketplaces especially the banana varieties which is been chosen here and hence we had to target the producers and finding the right cultivators to get these data was a huge task and eventually managed to find the right images of banana for all varieties.
- Once the data/images were collected structuring it was a time-consuming task but an essential part of the objective to sort the right images into different folders for training the model
- Data Labelling was the next task which had to be cautiously done to manage the dataset well and accessible.
- The major challenge that was faced was to differentiate and collect all the 7 stages of ripening of banana of each variety. During this activity not all stages were available at once but had to wait till we get the right ripening stage and then capture the image.
- We even faced challenges with lighting and background was also a challenge as the data was collected directly from the cultivators.

5   Proposed System

In this work, an effort has been employed in the formation of a large & good quantity of banana images datasets with following characteristics [5].

- Completely different background
- Location invariant
- Background invariant (Few on tables, ground farms etc.)
- Distance invariant

The images were captured using the iPhone 13 mobile phone camera, featuring dual 12-megapixel sensors. The images have been captured manually as per the above characteristics.

5.1   Methods of Capturing Data

For banana images datasets raw images were captured from different districts of Karnataka. The 4 different types of banana Robusta (MusaAAA), Dwarf Cavendish (Musaacuminata), Nanjangud banana, and Red banana (Musa acuminata) images were captured from wholesale markets, horticulture land, retail markets. The images were captured using a mobile phone camera under different lighting conditions [4]. All the details of the camera has been captured in Table 1. The image dataset is stored in RGB format and saved in the.jpg file format. The images have been organized into distinct folders, each corresponding to different banana varieties and their respective ripening stages. Initially, the images had dimensions of 3096 × 4128. To facilitate easier processing, they were resized to 256 × 256 dimensions using Python programming.

The images have undergone verification by various agricultural experts and banana plantation farmers. The verification of the images by banana plantation farmers are as below.

- The image collection process involved sorting them into various banana varieties and distinct ripening stages.
- The images were meticulously labeled, and farmers were consulted to verify the banana variety and ripening stage by visually inspecting the images.
- Farmers were presented with around 100 images representing diverse banana varieties and ripening stages. Their accurate recognition of these images provided assurance regarding the dataset's reliability (Tables 2, 3, 4).

Table 1. Camera Specifications used to capture images.

Sl. No	Camera Specifications	Details
1	Camera Producer	Apple
2	Camera Model	iPhone 12
3	Focal Length	4 mm
4	Flash Mode	No Flash

Table 2. Steps for Data acquisition

SL. NO	Process	Time	Work
1	Image Capture	Mar to May (2023)	Images captured during the sunlight and with different backgrounds and also in shaded lights
2	Preparation of Dataset	June (2023)	The original image dimensions, which were initially 3096 × 4128, were resized to the dimensions of 256 × 256. Subsequently, these resized images were categorized into separate folders

Table 3. Details of the existing data for comparative study

Name of the Datasets	Background type	Data Volume
r7issn0oi8sblxc8uga6an.zip(Kaggle)	Complex	1557 images
zk3tkxndjw-2.zip	Complex	1165 images
Fayoum_University_Banana _Classes-20230203T102753Z-001(Kaggle)	Uniform (White Background)	273 images

Table 4. Represents the details of the images captured manually for research work.

Name of the Datasets	Sub Datasets	Data Volume
Robusta	All Green	1500
	Light Green	1350
	Half Green Half Yellow	1420
	More Yellow than green	1620
	Yellow with green tips	1450
	Full Yellow	1420
	Yellow with brown Flecks	1650
Dwarf cavendish	All Green	1415
	Light Green	1550
	Half Green Half Yellow	1420
	More Yellow than green	1370
	Yellow with green tips	1480
	Full Yellow	1550
	Yellow with brown Flecks	1620
Nanjangud banana	All Green	1390
	Light Green	1430
	More Yellow than green	1515
	Yellow with green tips	1560
	Full Yellow	1600
	Yellow with brown Flecks	1520
	More Yellow than green	1600
Red banana	All Green	1410
	Light Green	1385
	Half Green Half Yellow	1620
	More Yellow than green	1512
	Yellow with green tips	1510
	Full Yellow	1600
	Yellow with brown Flecks	1480

6   Conclusion

This paper introduces a self-generated dataset comprising images of four different banana varieties, each encompassing seven distinct ripening stages. The primary objective of this endeavor is to gain insights into the shelf life of bananas. The image capture process was meticulously conducted, considering various parameters, including consistent background, color accuracy, distance, and precise positioning.

In this paper, we delve into an analysis and discussion of the characteristics and challenges associated with standard datasets. Furthermore, we provide a detailed explanation of the setup used for capturing the images to build this dataset.

Looking ahead, as part of the future directions for this research, we anticipate that this dataset can be harnessed for Machine Learning research purposes. Specifically, it can aid in understanding and predicting the precise shelf life of bananas, thereby assisting both agriculturists and exporters in making informed decisions regarding product shipment.

References

1. Dueben, P.D., Schultz, M.G., Chantry, M., Gagne, D.J., Hall, D.M., McGovern, A.: Challenges and benchmark datasets for machine learning in the atmospheric sciences: definition status and outlook. Artif. Intell. Earth Syst. **1**(3), 1–11 (2022). https://doi.org/10.1175/aies-d-21-0002.1
2. Subudhi, P., Mukhopadhyay, S.: A statistical active contour model ineractive clutter image segmentation using graph cut optimization. Sign. Process. **184**, 108056 (2021). https://doi.org/10.1016/j.sigpro.2021.108056
3. Wahome, C.N., Maingi, J.M., Ombori, O., Kimiti, J.M., Njeru, E.M.: Banana production trends, cultivar diversity, and tissue culture technologies uptake in Kenya. Int. J. Agron. **2021**, 6634046 (2021). https://doi.org/10.1155/2021/6634046
4. Cheng, D., Li, S., Zhang, H., Xia, F., Zhang, Y.: Why dataset propoerties bound the scalability of parallel machine learning traning algorithms. IEEE Trans. Parallel Distrib. Syst. **32**(7), 1702–1712 (2021). https://doi.org/10.1109/TPDS.2020.3048836
5. Meshram, V., Patil, K.: FruitNet: Indian fruits image dataset with quality for machine learning applications. https://doi.org/10.1016/j.dib.2021.107686
6. Medhi, E., Deb N.: PSFD-Musa: a dataset of banana plant, stem, fruit, leaf, and disease. https://doi.org/10.1016/j.dib.2022.108427
7. Dwivany, F.M., et al.: Dataset of Cavendish banana transcriptome in response to chitosan coating application. https://doi.org/10.1016/j.dib.2021.107686
8. https://www.kaggle.com/datasets/saranchandar/standard-classification-banana-dataset
9. https://www.abcfruits.net/banana-varieties-production-and-season-in-india/
10. Adebayo, S.A., Hashim, N., Abdan, K., Hanafi, M., Zude-Sasse, M.: Prediction of banana quality attributes and ripeness classification using artificial neural network. In: Acta Horticulturae, Proceedings of the III International Conference on Agricultural and Food Engineering, p. 335
11. Mendoza, F., Aguilera, J.M.: Application of image analysis for classification of ripening bananas. J. Food Sci. **69**(9), 471–477 (2004)
12. Banana Dataset - Datasets - OpenDroneMap Community: https://community.opendronemap.org/t/banana-dataset/2516
13. khoje, S.A., Bodhe, S.K., Adsul, A.: Automated skin defect identification system for fruit grading based on discrete curvelet transform. Int. J. Eng. Technol. **5**(4), 3251–3256 (2013)

DeYOLO: A CNN Based Novel Approach for Classification and Localization of Pneumonia in Chest Radiographs

Murukessan Perumal[1]([✉]), E. Goutham[2], Debraj Das[3], and M. Srinivas[1]

[1] National Institute of Technology, Warangal, Warangal, Telangana, India
`muruap87@student.nitw.ac.in`
[2] Institute of Aeronautical Engineering, Dundigal, Hyderabad, Telangana, India
[3] Indian Institute of Engineering Science and Technology (IIEST), Shibpur, India

Abstract. This paper describes an approach for pneumonia classification and localization of the infected part in the chest radiograph (CXR) images. Localization of pneumonia-infected CXR needs to be in real-time and accurate. Object detection systems like YOLO that are real-time efficient are inaccurate, and there is a trade-off. The proposed DeYOLO model addresses this trade-off by being accurate and real-time with a two-stage detection pipeline. DeYOLO classifies and localizes pneumonia in CXR in real-time with accuracy. DeYOLO is a deep learning model developed using modified neural networks for classification and object detection. Our proposed method, DeYOLO, demonstrates promising experimental results compared with other well-known methods. DeYOLO achieves an ROC score of 0.968 and mAP of 0.209 in the RSNA Pneumonia Detection dataset. DeYOLO can be installed as a web service serving endless users in real-time.

Keywords: Pneumonia · COVID-19 · Localization · Radio-graph · Object detection · Convolutional Neural Networks · Classification

1 Introduction

Recent advancements in the digital world and computer vision demonstrate that convolutional neural network (CNN) architectures have achieved human-level performance. The various tasks, including image processing, classification, segmentation, and object detection, are where AI has proved its strength. As an extension, many ongoing efforts will leverage the capabilities of artificial intelligence techniques in medical imaging. Clinicians utilize deep learning and machine learning algorithms to assist in anomaly detection in various medical imaging modalities [17] and analysis [29]. Recent advanced deep learning works in the medical domain are [1,14,19]. Moreover, CNNs have achieved performance on par with board-certified dermatologists for the classification of skin cancer on

Supported by Ministry of Education, India.

biopsy-proven clinical images [4] and board-certified radiologists for pathology detection in computerized tomography head scans [15].

Being a lung infection, pneumonia causes inflammation and fluid build-up in the alveoli. The build-up causes symptoms such as chest pain, fever, and severe cough. Death may occur in severe cases or if the patient has a weaker immune system and is in advanced stage [13,23]. The main issues and challenges with pneumonia detection are: Diagnosing pneumonia is very difficult and requires trained and specialized technicians. It requires a review of a chest radiograph (CXR) by highly trained specialists and confirmation through clinical history, vital signs, and laboratory exams. Pneumonia usually manifests as an area of increased opacity [6] on CXR. Analysis of CXR image is complicated because of many other lung conditions, such as fluid overload, which we term pulmonary edema, bleeding, atelectasis, lung cancer, post-radiation, and surgical changes. Fluid in the pleural space (pleural effusion) also appears as an increased opacity on CXR. However, our proposed method will be able to identify the infected patches in the lungs.

Severe pneumonia is one of the symptoms in COVID-19-affected persons. Analysis of CXR images will be instrumental in efficiently detecting pneumonia in COVID-19 patients [16]. Automated diagnosis of CXR through deep learning will be a way cheaper method than usual for detecting COVID-19-infected patients [2]. Localization with a bounding box and heat map generation on a pneumonia-positive radio-graph sample image will corroborate the explainable diagnosis of the disease.

To address the challenges of real-time detection and accuracy, we propose a two-stage model for Pneumonia detection and localization called the DeYOLO method. DeYOLO uses convolutional neural networks to process CXR images. It gives the output bounding boxes to localize the regions indicating evidence for pneumonia. DeYOLO uses the Densenet backbone for classification and YOLO for object detection in two stages. DeYOLO uses YOLOv3 for faster inference. Our final model correctly classifies the images of a person with a pneumonia infection. It locates the area in the radio-graphs where the pneumonia is most likely to be specified. For better results, we have used five-fold cross-validation on the training set to detect patchy surfaces. The classification results and information from detecting infected regions have been ensembled to generate better localization outcomes. The proposed method alleviates the requirement of trained, specialized technicians and a review of a chest radiograph (CXR) by highly trained specialists and makes classification much more efficient. We have also tried another deep neural network combination where we used mask-RCNN as a platform for object detection and localization. DeYOLO provides better results for the combination than the mask-RCNN and state-of-the-art results. To improve our classification results and detection performance, we have modified the DenseNet121 and YOLOv3 models.

2   Related Work

Convolutional networks (ConvNets) have significantly enjoyed great success in large-scale image and video recognition applications. The exploration of network architectures has been a part of neural network research since their initial discovery. The recent resurgence in the popularity of neural networks has also revived the use of convoluted layers in deep neural networks to advance other fields like the healthcare research domain.

P. Viola and M. Jones [26] introduced the first efficient object detection algorithm. He explained the facial recognition algorithm using an integral image, which is a novel image representation. Half a decade later, N. Dalal and B. Triggs outperformed existing feature sets by developing a Histogram of Oriented Gradient (HOG) for pedestrian detection. Felzenszwalb et al. [5] had also worked in a similar domain and developed the Deformable Parts Model (DPM). DPM is using a mixture model of deformable parts to recognize the objects.

In 2012, Kriszhevsky et al. [12] used convolutional neural networks (CNN) to outperform every other algorithm on the ImageNet dataset. After the achievement, significant advancements have been made in object detection. Many more advanced techniques have been developed for detecting the objects in real-time applications [3, 8, 9, 11, 25, 28, 30]. Sermanet et al. [24] proposed an integrated framework using deep neural networks for object detection in 2014. Many other networks have been developed since then, for example, Fast-RCNN [7], and Faster-RCNN [22]. Mask R-CNN [21] is an intuitive extension of Faster R-CNN, yet constructing the mask branch properly is critical and crucial for better results. One of the most essential features of Faster RCNN is that it has not been designed for pixel-to-pixel alignment between network inputs and outputs. These complex pipelines are slow and hard to optimize because each component must be trained separately. YOLO [20] has re-framed object detection as a single regression problem, straight from image pixels to bounding box coordinates and class probabilities. Using this system, "You Only Look Once" (YOLO) at an image to predict what objects are present and where they are. This algorithm gave a new dimension to the real-world object detection task, and nowadays, it is heavily used to create the brain of autonomous vehicle standards. However, YOLO is less accurate but faster in inference.

Recent advancements in image classification show that Deep CNN architectures have been successfully used for medical image classification and localization. CheXnet, a 121-layer densenet architecture model, has achieved an F1 score of 0.435 when classifying 14 different pulmonary conditions, including pneumonia, which was marked higher than the 0.387 average of radiologists [18]. However, prior works do not address the problem of real-time inference and classification accuracy. We proposed DeYOLO to address this gap with two-stage detection of high accuracy and real-time inference.

3   Proposed Method

The two-stage classification and localization scheme DeYOLO typically consists of three phases - classification, object detection, and localization. We have represented the building blocks of our proposed work in Fig. 1.

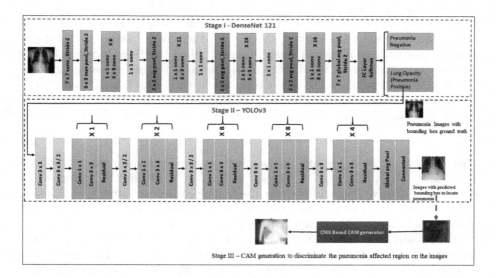

Fig. 1. Block Diagram of our proposed (DeYOLO) model

DeYOLO addresses the research gap in the accurate and real-time detection of pneumonia. The model has been developed on the platform of combined DenseNet121 and YOLO. The YOLO network has been modified by adding extra convoluted and hidden layers for state-of-the-art accuracy. DeYOLO consists of two stages for optimal detection of pneumonia in chest radiograph (CXR) images. We have modified DenseNet121 by adding extra hidden layers for our first stage. It helped us classify the X-ray images of patients with pneumonia infection. In the second stage of our model, the region in the lung got pneumonia infection has been localized. For this, we have been supplying those classified images to another network. It has been developed over the modified YOLOv3, a modified DarkNet53 architecture as its foundation. On feeding the generated images to modified CNN, the network refines the bounding boxes over the region having opacity in the lungs. For better accuracy and efficient localization of patched surfaces, we have augmented the training images before feeding into the architecture. It helps in training our model in the best way. In the final stage, we supply those bounding boxes containing images to architecture to generate a class activation mapping-based heatmap. It uses feature maps to enhance the opacity of the localized part in the radio-graphs. This gives us a better intuition about the exact location of pneumonia in the lungs.

3.1   Detailed DeYOLO Architecture

DeYOLO is an efficient model developed for accurate and real-time pneumonia detection.

Classification Approach. Classification will be done by feeding the data images to the first network of our DeYOLO model based on DenseNet121. The feeding data consists of images of normal people and people infected with pneumonia. We have used 121 layered, dense neural networks having several dense blocks along with pooling and linear layers. It then has been followed by the soft-max activation layer, which detects the image of the patient suffering from pneumonia. In dense block l^{th} layer accepts the feature maps from all the preceding layers marking, a_0, a_1, ..., a_{l-1} as inputs. The mathematical function of taking input in terms of previous layers' inputs has been shown in an equation:

$$a_l = F_l([a_0, a_1, ..., a_{l-1}]) \tag{1}$$

where $[a_0, a_1, ..., a_{l-1}]$ results in the concatenation of feature maps produced in the layers 0, 1, ..., l-1. $F_l([a_0, a_1, ..., a_{l-1}])$ defines the composition of three consecutive operations where the first operation is batch normalization (BN) followed by an activation function called rectified linear unit (ReLU) and then has been followed by a convolution of 3×3 kernels.

This pneumonia detection task is a binary classification where we must define the lung image as the front view of CXR images (A). The output has been described as binary label $z \in \{1, 0\}$, which indicates pneumonia's presence or absence. For any single image in the training dataset, we have defined the weighted binary cross-entropy loss optimizer in the equation as:

$$Loss(A, z) = -C_+ 1_{z=1} logp(Z = 1|A) - C_- 1_{z=0} logp(Z = 0|A) \tag{2}$$

where $p(Z = x|A)$ indicates the probability that our classifier has assigned to the labels known as x, $1_{z=1}$ is 1 for $z = 1$ and 0 otherwise, similarly for $1_{z=0}$, $C_+ = |Q|/(|P| + |Q|)$ and $C_- = |P|/(|P| + |Q|)$, $|P|$ and $|Q|$ represents the number of positive and negative samples evidence of having pneumonia in the training data respectively.

We have normalized the resulting images depending on the mean and standard deviation of images on the ImageNet training data. We have also downscaled the radiographic images before feeding the images to our classifying network. The proposed network has been trained in two different variations. The first technique we have to train our proposed network using the preinitialized weights from the ImageNet dataset. The second one is by training the network without using any pre-trained weights. We have augmented the images to avoid over-fitting problems to ensure better accuracy and premier detection. The images have been augmented using augmentation techniques like random horizontal flipping and cropping. Finally, the resulting pre-processed images have been used for training the model over a continuously decreasing learning rate. As an optimizer, Adam has been implemented just for tackling sparse gradients over the noisy data by giving the better minima.

Object Detection. The resulting classified images have been supplemented to the following network for localizing the infected part in the second stage of our DeYOLO architecture. In this work, we have used object detection-based localization techniques for drawing bounding boxes on images carrying sufficient evidence of pneumonia. We have developed the network at its base over YOLOv3 [18]. It has features concurrent with Darknet53, with more layers stacked onto the backbone.

The main advantage of creating a network having YOLO as a base lies in understanding the loss function. A five-term multi-part loss captures error probability in height, width, coordinates, class, and confidence. The function utilizes the regression approach for drawing the bounding boxes and its refinement. We have also used regression in predicting the confidence of the model. Five-term multi-part loss is defined so that if an object is present in that particular grid cell, only that cell will penalize the classification error. The multi-part loss function has been optimized during the training phase, and a mathematical explanation of this optimization has been described in [20].

Our network is a one-pass detection network, resulting in a simpler and computationally cheaper pipeline generation. Due to the faster inference, a network similar to YOLOv3 has been considered an appropriate choice for localization of the pneumonia-infected regions present in the lungs. The model weights have been initialized with the weights taken from the Darknet53, which has been trained on Imagenet datasets.

Pneumonia Localization

$$M_{\text{pneumonia}}(x, y) = \sum_i w_i^{\text{pneumonia}} \times f_i(x, y) \tag{3}$$

The Class Activation Map(CAM) technique obtains the heatmap on the input image. The above formula gives the mathematical formulation, where the activation map of class pneumonia for pixel position x, y is $M_{\text{pneumonia}}(x, y)$. It equals the weighted aggregation of final classification layer weights of class pneumonia with corresponding global average pooled feature map outputs of the last convolution layer for each pixel at location (x, y). The image is upsampled and overlayed on the input image to obtain a CAM heatmap image.

4 Experimental Results

As our task was dual, i.e., classification and localization using a bounding box, we evaluated our model using AUC and ROC scores for classification and mean average precision(mAP) for localization. We have trained our model over data having a batch size of 32 with a continuously decreasing learning rate in the range 0.001–1e08

4.1   Dataset and Features

The CXR images and the accompanying bounding box labels are sourced from the Radiological Society of North America (RSNA) via the RSNA Pneumonia Detection Kaggle competition [10,27]. This data has been categorized into data labeled about 32% pneumonia-positive and 68% normal. Images labeled as pneumonia-positive have bounding boxes for abnormalities included. Compared to previously used research datasets such as NIH, the RSNA datasets have been claimed to be more precisely labeled. The CXRs are stored in digital imaging and communication in medicines (DICOM) format having 1024×1024 resolution. These images have been converted to PNG format and scaled down to images having (256×256) resolution for further analysis. We have split the training data having 30,227 images into train, validation, and test sets having 80%, 10%, and 10%, respectively. For example, Pneumonia positive sample images and their corresponding ground truth bounding box label have been shown on the left side of Fig. 2 whereas the predicted output label has been shown on the right side.

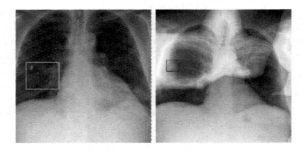

Fig. 2. Sample localization images with bounding box and heatmap generation on a pneumonia-positive radiograph. The left image is the ground truth label, and the right image is the predicted label.

4.2   Stage I: Classification Scores

Stage one classification results are analyzed with the help of ROC score. ROC score defines the area under the receiver operating characteristic curve from the prediction scores. For binary classification, if we assume a threshold T, then the instance is classified as "positive" for the cases where $predicted score > T$, and "negative" for the other cases. Probability distribution $g_0(x)$ denotes the instance x actually belongs to the "negative" class, and in other cases, it is $g_1(x)$. Therefore, we can define the rate of true positive as $M(T) = \int_T^\infty g_1(x)dx$ and the rate of false positive as $N(T) = \int_T^\infty g_0(x)dx$. When we have used normalized units, the area under the curve is often given by the mathematical modeling explained in the below equation

$$Area = \int_{x=0}^{1} M(N^-1(x))dx = P(X_1 > X_0) \qquad (4)$$

where X_1 denotes the score for a positive instance, X_0 denotes the score for a negative instance.

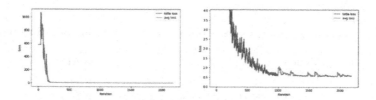

Fig. 3. Performance of Total and average loss on train and validation sets

We have also used various models with and without trained weights and freezing layers for classifying pneumonia and normal chest radiographs. We have found that the proposed DeYOLO method with pre-trained weights from the ImageNet dataset and frozen layers has given promising results for classifying the disease compared to the models with randomly initialized weights. The Performance of total and average loss on train and validation sets with the proposed method are shown in Fig. 3. For each model, the results on the test dataset are as follows:

Table 1. Performance of the Stage one classification results

Models	ROC Score
AlexNet	0.91
Vgg16	0.943
DenseNet121	0.932
NasNet	0.951
ResNet152	0.921
ResNet152 (pre-trained)	0.965
Proposed Method	**0.968**

From Table 1, we can see the highest score is given by our proposed network, which is concurrent to Densenet121, while it has been trained using pre-trained weights taken from the ImageNet dataset. We have carried the results this model gave for inference in stage two. Also, we have compared our results with different models frequently used for object detection.

4.3   Stage 2: Localization Scores

Average Precision (AP) is the area under the Precision-Recall curve over various Intersection Over Union (IoU) thresholds. Mean Average Precision (mAP) is the mean of all per class AP. The mAP is the benchmark metric for all object detection systems and is employed to evaluate and compare models.

The best score is generated by assembling predictions from 5-fold cross-validation. Each model's aggregated mean results on the test dataset are shown in Table 2.

Table 2. Performance results of object localization using bounding box

Models	mAP
YOLOv3	0.141
Mask-RCNN (ResNet50 as backbone)	0.155
Mask-RCNN (DenseNet121 as backbone)	0.172
ResNet152+YOLOv3	0.189
Proposed DeYOLO	**0.209**

This table shows the localization results generated when we trained our second neural network in the DeYOLO model (based on YOLOv3) on the pneumonia-positive radio-graphs.

Our model DeYOLO outperforms all the single models, including Mask-RCNN, a region-based state-of-the-art model for generating localization results. DenseNet121 classifier showed better performance for classification results against the localization algorithms. The ensembled proposed DeYOLO method has shown increased precision compared to a single YOLO model trained on only the positive images. In the case of Mask-RCNN, only pixel-to-pixel information is used for segmenting the bounding boxes over the regions containing the opacity. But YOLOv3 used more boundary and edge information to predict the bounding box regressively, which has turned out to be most effective in our experiments. The primary reason for DeYOLO using YOLOv3 is for inference speed.

DeYOLO, which was trained on only the pneumonia-positive images containing the bounding boxes, showed better classification and localization when tested with both positive and negative images than the models(YOLOv3 and Mask-RCNN with different backbone models) that were trained on the whole dataset.

Class Activation Mapping-based generated heatmaps using the DenseNet121 model's features show that the network usually focuses on the right areas, but in some cases, it looks at extraneous regions. The generated CAMs are shown in Fig. 4. These cases are varied for the quality of the different chest radio-graphs. This can be improved by adding some deformable layers to identify the offset.

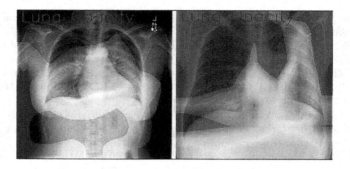

Fig. 4. Generated CAMs of DenseNet121 model to verify classification weighted important regions as evidence of pneumonia.

5   Conclusion

Our model, DeYOLO, successfully fetched information about the evidence of pneumonia from the radiographs and drew the bounding boxes on the opaque pneumonia-related regions. Classifying the pneumonia-positive images with a robust classifier like the DenseNet121 model and training the YOLOv3 on those datasets with 5-fold cross-validation and averaging the results significantly improved the localization metrics. Due to the low computational cost and faster inference, DeYOLO can be deployed in a web server, serving many real-time requests. Owing to its computationally inexpensive nature, YOLO can run in near real-time and on low-resolution data, producing significant results. Thus, this model is especially useful in areas with limited computational and medical resources access. These benefits, viewed with the urgent perspective that the COVID-19 situation offers, definitely augment the practical usability of DeYOLO as an industry standard.

References

1. Aldughayfiq, B., Ashfaq, F., Jhanjhi, N., Humayun, M.: YOLO-based deep learning model for pressure ulcer detection and classification. In: Healthcare, vol. 11, p. 1222. MDPI (2023)
2. Alom, M.Z., Rahman, M., Nasrin, M.S., Taha, T.M., Asari, V.K.: COVID_MTNet: COVID-19 detection with multi-task deep learning approaches. arXiv preprint arXiv:2004.03747 (2020)
3. Anand, V., Gupta, S., Koundal, D., Singh, K.: Fusion of U-net and CNN model for segmentation and classification of skin lesion from dermoscopy images. Expert Syst. Appl. **213**, 119230 (2023)
4. Esteva, A., et al.: Dermatologist-level classification of skin cancer with deep neural networks. Nature **542**(7639), 115–118 (2017)
5. Felzenszwalb, P.F., Girshick, R.B., McAllester, D., Ramanan, D.: Object detection with discriminatively trained part-based models. IEEE Trans. Pattern Anal. Mach. Intell. **32**(9), 1627–1645 (2009)

6. Franquet, T.: Imaging of community-acquired pneumonia. J. Thorac. Imaging **33**(5), 282–294 (2018)
7. Girshick, R.: Fast R-CNN. In: Proceedings of the IEEE International Conference on Computer Vision, pp. 1440–1448 (2015)
8. He, K., Zhang, X., Ren, S., Sun, J.: Deep residual learning for image recognition. In: Proceedings of the IEEE Conference on Computer Vision and Pattern Recognition, pp. 770–778 (2016)
9. Huang, G., Liu, Z., Van Der Maaten, L., Weinberger, K.Q.: Densely connected convolutional networks. In: Proceedings of the IEEE Conference on Computer Vision and Pattern Recognition, pp. 4700–4708 (2017)
10. Kaggle: RSNA Pneumonia Detection Challenge (2018). https://www.kaggle.com/c/rsna-pneumonia-detection-challenge. Accessed 03 Dec 2022
11. Kaya, Y., Gürsoy, E.: A MobileNet-based CNN model with a novel fine-tuning mechanism for COVID-19 infection detection. Soft. Comput. **27**(9), 5521–5535 (2023)
12. Krizhevsky, A., Sutskever, I., Hinton, G.E.: ImageNet classification with deep convolutional neural networks. In: Advances in Neural Information Processing Systems, vol. 25 (2012)
13. LaCroix, A.Z., Lipson, S., Miles, T.P., White, L.: Prospective study of pneumonia hospitalizations and mortality of us older people: the role of chronic conditions, health behaviors, and nutritional status. Public Health Rep. **104**(4), 350 (1989)
14. Leng, B., Wang, C., Leng, M., Ge, M., Dong, W.: Deep learning detection network for peripheral blood leukocytes based on improved detection transformer. Biomed. Signal Process. Control **82**, 104518 (2023)
15. Merkow, J., Lufkin, R., Nguyen, K., Soatto, S., Tu, Z., Vedaldi, A.: DeepRadiologyNet: radiologist level pathology detection in CT head images. arXiv preprint arXiv:1711.09313 (2017)
16. Ozturk, T., Talo, M., Yildirim, E.A., Baloglu, U.B., Yildirim, O., Acharya, U.R.: Automated detection of COVID-19 cases using deep neural networks with x-ray images. Comput. Biol. Med. **121**, 103792 (2020)
17. Perumal, M., Nayak, A., Sree, R.P., Srinivas, M.: INASNET: automatic identification of coronavirus disease (COVID-19) based on chest X-ray using deep neural network. ISA Trans. **124**, 82–89 (2022)
18. Rajpurkar, P., et al.: CheXNet: radiologist-level pneumonia detection on chest X-rays with deep learning. arXiv preprint arXiv:1711.05225 (2017)
19. Rauf, Z., Sohail, A., Khan, S.H., Khan, A., Gwak, J., Maqbool, M.: Attention-guided multi-scale deep object detection framework for lymphocyte analysis in IHC histological images. Microscopy **72**(1), 27–42 (2023)
20. Redmon, J., Divvala, S., Girshick, R., Farhadi, A.: You only look once: unified, real-time object detection. In: Proceedings of the IEEE Conference on Computer Vision and Pattern Recognition, pp. 779–788 (2016)
21. Redmon, J., Farhadi, A.: YOLOv3: an incremental improvement. arXiv preprint arXiv:1804.02767 (2018)
22. Ren, S., He, K., Girshick, R., Sun, J.: Faster R-CNN: towards real-time object detection with region proposal networks. In: Advances in Neural Information Processing Systems, vol. 28 (2015)
23. Rui, P., Kang, K.: National ambulatory medical care survey: 2015 emergency department summary tables. Table 27 (2018)
24. Sermanet, P., Eigen, D., Zhang, X., Mathieu, M., Fergus, R., LeCun, Y.: OverFeat: integrated recognition, localization and detection using convolutional networks. arXiv preprint arXiv:1312.6229 (2013)

25. Szegedy, C., et al.: Going deeper with convolutions. In: Proceedings of the IEEE Conference on Computer Vision and Pattern Recognition, pp. 1–9 (2015)
26. Viola, P., Jones, M.: Rapid object detection using a boosted cascade of simple features. In: Proceedings of the 2001 IEEE Computer Society Conference on Computer Vision and Pattern Recognition, CVPR 2001. vol. 1, p. I. IEEE (2001)
27. Wang, X., Peng, Y., Lu, L., Lu, Z., Bagheri, M., Summers, R.M.: ChestX-ray8: hospital-scale chest X-ray database and benchmarks on weakly-supervised classification and localization of common thorax diseases. In: Proceedings of the IEEE Conference on Computer Vision and Pattern Recognition, pp. 2097–2106 (2017)
28. Xie, S., Girshick, R., Dollár, P., Tu, Z., He, K.: Aggregated residual transformations for deep neural networks. In: Proceedings of the IEEE Conference on Computer Vision and Pattern Recognition, pp. 1492–1500 (2017)
29. Yadav, M., Perumal, M., Srinivas, M.: Analysis on novel coronavirus (COVID-19) using machine learning methods. Chaos, Solitons Fractals **139**, 110050 (2020)
30. Zagoruyko, S., Komodakis, N.: Wide residual networks. arXiv preprint arXiv:1605.07146 (2016)

Fingerprint Anti-spoofing Analysis: From Minutiae to Transformers

Tushar Goyal[(✉)], Harshit Shakya, Aditya Khandelwal, Himanshu Patidar, and Tushar Sandhan

Perception and Intelligence Lab, Department of EE, IIT Kanpur, Kanpur, India
{tushg,harshit21,adityak21,patidar21,sandhan}@iitk.ac.in

Abstract. In the contemporary digital and interconnected world, the need for robust security measures is paramount. From personal devices to national security, biometric recognition has enhanced security, streamlined authentication processes, and improved overall efficiency. Fingerprint liveness detection plays a vital role in ensuring the security and reliability of biometric systems by differentiating between genuine fingerprints and presentation attacks. This work presents a detailed analysis on various computational algorithms for fingerprint liveness detection along with cross-sensor data evaluation. The study investigates the effectiveness of different feature extraction modules, including local binary pattern (LBP), histogram of oriented gradients (HOG), scale-invariant feature transform (SIFT), minutiae points, and deep feature extractors, including various convolutional neural architectures and transformers. Additionally, deep learning patch-based classification approaches with multiple weight initialization strategies and transfer learning from large-scale datasets are explored for liveness detection. The overall framework is achieving an outstanding average classification error (ACE) value of less than 0.5%. Moreover, the comparison of different architectures, evaluation on various large datasets, model complexity versus anti-spoofing robustness analysis and cross-sensor evaluations offer useful insights about fingerprint liveness detection.

Keywords: Fingerprint spoof detection · convolutional neural network · liveness detection · presentation attack detection

1 Introduction

Automatic access to services has become increasingly vital in this information age, leading to the development of biometric authentication [15]. Due to its uniqueness, cost-effectiveness, convenience, and a relatively high degree of accuracy, fingerprint recognition has been widely adopted in prevalent biometric technologies in various applications. And its presence is expected to continue growing with the recent push by technology companies.

However, the vulnerability of fingerprint-based systems to presentation attacks or spoofing and the widespread availability and ease of manufacturing presentation attack instruments (PAI) has emerged as a pressing security

H. Kaur et al. (Eds.): CVIP 2023, CCIS 2010, pp. 394–409, 2024.
https://doi.org/10.1007/978-3-031-58174-8_34

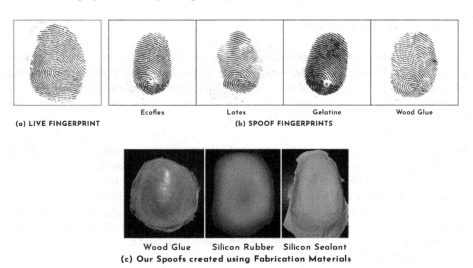

Ecoflex   Latex   Gelatine   Wood Glue
(a) LIVE FINGERPRINT   (b) SPOOF FINGERPRINTS

Wood Glue   Silicon Rubber   Silicon Sealant
(c) Our Spoofs created using Fabrication Materials

Fig. 1. (a) Live fingerprint vs (b) Spoof fingerprints made from Ecoflex, Latex, Gelatine and Wood Glue from LiveDet 2015 GreenBit sensor along with (c) Our spoofs created using various fabrication materials like wood glue, silicon rubber and silicon sealant.

concern [25]. A presentation attack (PA), as defined by the ISO standard IEC 30107-1:2016(E), is a "presentation to the biometric data capture subsystem to interfere with the operation of the biometric system" [35]. Artificially created fingerprint patterns, either by replication via mould and cast operations or by direct manufacturing via methods like 3D printing and surface etching, are called spoofed fingerprints. In the case of fingerprint authentication systems, these attacks typically involve presenting a spoofed fingerprint to the biometric device, mimicking the fingerprint of an authorized user. Deceiving a fingerprint biometric device requires minimal skill and resources. Common materials such as wood glue, gelatin, clay, and playdough (as shown in Fig. 1) can be easily used for making spoof fingerprints, with the required process readily available on the internet and accessible at everyone's fingertips.

The goal of presentation attack detection (PAD) is to identify and detect fraudulent attempts to deceive biometric systems through the presentation of spoofed fingerprints. Liveness detection is a subset of PAD focusing on determining the liveness of the biometric attribute captured, i.e., whether the biometric attribute presented is genuine and not a spoof or false representation.

Subsequently, the structure of the paper will be as follows: Sect. 2 presents a literature review, discussing previous studies and state-of-the-art methods related to fingerprint liveness detection; Sect. 3 describes the methods and techniques employed for the detailed problem investigation; and Sect. 4 presents the experimental results and our findings. Finally, Sect. 5 concludes the paper by summarizing the important insights.

2   Literature Review

Methods for detecting the fake fingerprints can be divided into hardware and software-based categories. Hardware-based approaches require the integration of additional sensors to assess characteristics like pulse oximetry [36], blood pressure [17], skin distortion [8], or other biometric traits [40] associated with fingerprints, such as odour [10]. Drahansky et al. [17] employed blood pressure to differentiate genuine and synthetic fingerprints. Blood pressure values outside the normal ranges indicated a spoof. However, their limitation arose from counterfeit prints with normal blood pressure, allowing potential exploitation by hypertensive individuals. Baldisserra et al. [10] investigated odour as a discriminator between real skin and synthetic materials (e.g., silicone, latex). Voltage shifts were observed by sensors, with actual skin and gelatin exhibiting a reduction and synthetic materials producing an increase in the sensor voltage. However, gelatin-based artificial fingers that imitated real finger sensor responses constrained the biometric system's accuracy.

Gomez-Barrero et al. [21] utilized laser speckle contrast imaging (LSCI) and short wave infrared (SWIR) spectrum images to analyze finger surface and interior structure. By combining features and classifiers, they achieved a notable BPCER (rate of misclassification of live fingerprints) of 0.1% and APCER (rate of misclassification of spoof fingerprints) of 3% on a dataset including unknown PA. This multi-modal approach shows potential for boosting the security of fingerprint recognition. Biometric systems can categorize fingerprints based on a variety of other physical characteristics. Hardware techniques are effective yet difficult, expensive, and vulnerable to presentation attacks. Hence to tackle these challenges effectively, software-based approaches are used.

Software-based PAD methods extract features from fingerprint samples captured by primary sensors, leveraging the inherent uniqueness of live fingerprints to detect presentation attacks. They are classified as dynamic or static methods. Dynamic methods rely on traits like skin deformation [8], perspiration [5] or sweat pores [31]. Due to temporal variations, dynamic methods require multiple images or video frames. Johnson and Schuckers et al. [28] conducted a study investigating the use of pores for liveness detection. Their research examined the feasibility of differentiating between real and counterfeit fingerprints by analyzing variations in skin pore properties. Antonelli et al. [8] contributed significantly in identifying synthetic fingerprints by analyzing skin distortions. Through careful dataset analysis, they achieved an accuracy of 98.5% and an equal error rate (EER) of 11.24%, using human skin's elasticity and deformation characteristics.

Static methods directly extract PAD features from fingerprint samples. They do not rely on dynamic behaviour but rather focus on the inherent properties of the fingerprint image. These properties include the ridge pattern [44], texture [19], quality [18], and other inherent features of the fingerprint image. Tan et al. [44], proposed a PAD method evaluating noise in fingerprint ridge-valley patterns. The technique achieved a high classification percentage (90.9% to 100%) on diverse genuine and artificial fingerprint datasets. Ghiani et al. (2013) [19]

used binarized statistical image features (BISFs) to utilize texture features from fingerprint images.

The progress in deep learning techniques, specifically in computer vision, has led to the emergence of robust architectures for detecting presentation attacks in fingerprints [32,38]. These approaches have demonstrated significant advancements compared to earlier techniques. Nogueira et al. [34] conducted a comprehensive evaluation of three established convolutional neural networks (CNN) for fingerprint presentation attack detection. Their proposed CNN model achieved the highest accuracy in the LivDet 2015 [33] competition, achieving an overall accuracy of 95.5%. However, a notable limitation of these methods lies in their reliance on learning specific features from the entire fingerprint image, assuming a fixed size. This approach faces challenges even when dealing with similar datasets like that of LivDet, but the region of interest (ROI) covers only a tiny portion of the entire image. As a result, the effectiveness of presentation attack detection is compromised.

DeFraudNet, developed by Anusha et al. [9], is a highly effective network for fingerprint spoof detection. It leverages LBP and Gabor filters for image preprocessing and extracting textural features. The network employs two DenseNets [27] for the simultaneous whole image and patch-based feature extraction. By combining patch features with the entire image and utilizing attention mechanism, they achieved accuracy as high as 99.77% when trained and tested on Crossmatch 2013 [20] dataset surpassing [34] method, which is also based on CNN.

Tarang et al. [13] introduced a formalized approach comprising offline training and an online testing stage for fingerprint spoof detection. In the offline training stage, minutiae detection was performed on the sensed fingerprint image, followed by the extraction of localized patches centred and aligned based on the minutiae location and orientation. A MobileNet model [26] was subsequently trained on these aligned patches to obtain a refined representation of the fingerprint image. The evaluation employed a spoofness score, wherein the individual scores corresponding to the local patches were averaged to derive a global score. On the LivDet dataset [33], the strategy produced great results that were superior to those of the best practices.

Thus it is evident from state-of-the-art approaches that various feature based as well as CNN based learned feature representations are capable of preventing presentation attacks. In the following subsequent sections, we give a detailed analysis incorporating feature engineering, CNN as well as transformer based feature representations for fingerprint anti-spoofing.

3 Methods

3.1 Feature Engineering

We explore the potential of various generalized feature extraction modules within a comprehensive classification pipeline, separating feature extraction from the

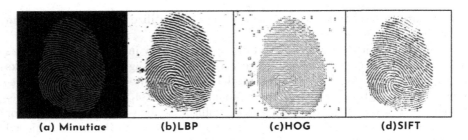

Fig. 2. Outputs of different texture analysis techniques used in feature engineering: a) Minutiae points [41] b) Local Binary Pattern [39] c) Histogram of Gradients [11] d) Scale-Invariant Feature Transform [46]

final classification task and employing various generalized classifiers. The different image preprocessing techniques used for feature extraction are (Fig. 2):

1. *Minutiae:* Minutiae points are the precise ridge characteristics, such as terminations and bifurcations, retrieved from pre-processed fingerprint pictures using binarization, thinning, and crossing number analysis methods [41]. We obtained a compact and representative image representation by quantizing these features into visual words using the bag-of-words (BOW) approach [47]. This enabled efficient comparison of visual word histograms for measuring image similarity, making the technique suitable for fingerprint anti-spoofing.
2. *Local Binary Pattern:* The local binary patterns (LBP) [39] are texture descriptors that compare the central pixel with its neighbours, generating a binary code that can represent different combinations. Considering two-bit transitions and reducing the feature vector length, we used the uniform or rotation-invariant LBP descriptor [6] in our study. We specifically take into account a radius of 24 pixels and eight neighbours around the core pixel. This configuration allowed us to capture and effectively represent local texture patterns in our analysis.
3. *Histogram of Gradients:* The histogram of oriented gradients (HOG) [11] is a feature descriptor that effectively characterizes visual material by quantifying gradient orientations within a detection frame. The gradient orientations used in our analysis were quantified using nine bins within a detection window. We divided the image into 8×8 pixel cells and then arranged them into blocks of 2×2 pixel cells. Using HOG with these settings successfully characterized the visual content of fingerprint images.
4. *Scale-Invariant Feature Transform (SIFT):* We used the bag-of-words method [47] with SIFT [46] for liveness detection due to its effectiveness and versatility. The SIFT methodology allowed us to extract robust and distinctive local features from the images, facilitating accurate description and identification by creating visual word histograms from the extracted key points (Fig. 3).

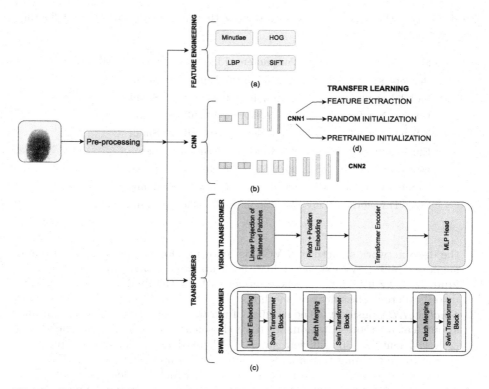

Fig. 3. Overview of the proposed comparative framework: (a) Handcrafted feature engineering methods used with different classifiers, (b) CNN1 (small architectures) and CNN2 (large architectures) are compared using same and cross-sensor evaluation, (c) Transformers (ViT and Swin Transformer), (d) Random initialization compared and contrasted with transfer learning.

The effectiveness of each of these important features is analyzed independently on 2 datasets in Table 3.

3.2 CNN and Transformer Based Analysis

Transfer learning efficiently utilises pre-trained models from source tasks to address data scarcity [42]. Rather than beginning from zero, transfer learning allows models to benefit from prior information and generalisations learnt from a different but related activity. We tested fine-tuning and feature extraction strategies, adapting models trained on the ImageNet dataset [14] for liveness detection.

1. *Deep Feature Extractor:* We employed DenseNet-121 [27] and VGG-19 [43], well-known pre-trained CNN models, as feature extractors. Densely connected convolutional blocks in densenet enable feature reuse and propagation, while

Table 1. Our classification of architectures with trainable parameters and floating point operations (FLOPs).

Model	Parameters	FLOPs	Our Classification
Resnet-18	12 Million	2 Billion	Small
MobileNet v3 Large	5 Million	0.22 Billion	Small
EfficientNet B0	5.3 Million	0.39 Billion	Small
EfficientNet B1	7.8 Million	0.70 Billion	Small
EfficientNet B7	66 Million	37 Billion	Large
Densenet 161	29 Million	8 Billion	Large
ViT-base 16 patches	86 Million	55.4 Billion	Transformer
Swin Transformer Tiny	29 Million	4.5 Billion	Transformer

the deep network structure of VGG is renowned for its simple structure and generalizability. We extracted high-level abstract representations from the input data by utilizing the whole model without the final classifier head and tested different classification methods.

2. *Small CNN:* Considering the number of parameters as well as generalizability about feature representation, we have chosen ResNet-18 [22], MobileNet v3 [26], EfficientNet B0, EfficientNet B1 [24] for liveness detection using fine-tuning by re-training the models initialized with imagenet weights. For evaluation, we employed tenCrop as given in [34], which divides the input image into ten overlapping patches, evaluates each patch separately, and finally combines the results. TenCrop improves the reliability of our classification task by collecting various spatial information from distinct parts of the fingerprint.

3. *Large CNN:* Large CNN (EfficientNet B7, DenseNet-161) have a better learning capacity as compared to small CNN and are better able to capture intricate and complex patterns in data. We tested Large CNN for liveness detection similarly to small CNN, by using the same training and evaluation scheme to test for the effectiveness of different architectures keeping other variables constant.

4. *Transformer:* The transformer design [45], which is built on the concept of self-attention mechanisms allows the network to balance the significance of various locations in the input sequence when processing each element. Vision Transformer (ViT) [16] applies the transformer architecture developed for language tasks to visual tasks such as image classification, object detection, and image segmentation by replacing the sequence of words with a grid of image patches. The Swin Transformer [29] modifies the original Transformer's [45] self-attention mechanism and provides a hierarchical structure that enables more efficient processing of large-scale pictures. This mechanism allows the model to capture local dependencies within each window while also considering global dependencies across different windows. We evaluate the effectiveness of ViT-base 16 patches version and Swin transformer tiny version for liveness detection.

4   Experiments

4.1   Dataset

The LivDet datasets [20, 30] are well known as a significant benchmark for evaluating the effectiveness of fingerprint liveness detection methods. The dataset used in this study is LivDet 2015 [33], a well-known and widely available source for research on fingerprint liveness detection. The dataset contains images from four optical scanners: Green Bit [4], Biometrika [1], Digital Persona [3], and Crossmatch [2]; over 4000 images on each device, including live images taken from numerous finger acquisitions in various conditions, including normal mode, wet and dry fingers, and high and low pressure. The spoof fingerprints present in an equal distribution in the dataset are gathered using cooperative techniques. A training set for algorithm configuration and a testing set for performance assessment are present in the dataset. We have followed the same settings for wide applicability of our study. We did not utilize the Biometrika dataset in this study due to its resolution of 1000 dpi, which exceeds the typical 500 dpi resolution used in real-world scenarios. We also rejected the Digital Persona dataset due to its small image size, which does not yield satisfactory results [33]; subsequently, choosing CrossMatch and GreenBit datasets for evaluating the proposed comparative framework (Table 2 and 4).

Table 2. Scanner specifications and materials used for fingerprint acquisition in training LivDet 2015 dataset [33]

Scanner	Model	DPI	Image Size	Samples	Materials Used
Digital Persona	U.are.U 5160	500	252×324	4500	Ecoflex, Gelatin, Latex, Wood Glue
Cross-Match	L Scan Guardian	500	640×480	5948	Body Double, EcoFlex, PlayDoh
GreenBit	Dacty-Scan 26	500	500×500	4500	Ecoflex, Gelatin, Latex, Wood Glue
Biometrika	HiScan-PRO	1000	1000×1000	4250	Gelatin, Latex, Wood Glue

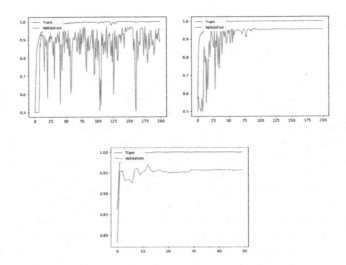

Fig. 4. Model accuracy at different epochs for different training schemes.

4.2 Performance Metrics

Standard evaluation metrics for liveness detection are accuracy, attack presentation error classification rate (APCER), bona fide presentation classification error rate (BPCER) and average classification error (ACE). Let, N_{live} = Total number of live fingerprint images,

N_{spoof} = Total number of spoof fingerprint images
$N_{spoof|live}$ = Number of live fingerprints misclassified as spoof,
$N_{live|spoof}$ = Number of spoof fingerprints misclassified as live
    Then,

$$APCER = \frac{N_{live|spoof}}{N_{spoof}}; \qquad BPCER = \frac{N_{spoof|live}}{N_{live}} \qquad (1)$$

$$ACE = \frac{APCER + BPCER}{2} \qquad (2)$$

Table 3. Average classification error (ACE) scores were obtained by evaluating different feature extractors (Minutiae, LBP, HOG, SIFT, VGG-19, Densenet-121) and classifiers (SVM-linear, RBF, polynomial; ANN; Random Forest; XG Boost; linear regression) on the Crossmatch and GreenBit datasets. The ACE scores provide insights into the effectiveness and performance of these combinations.

Dataset	Model	Minutiae	LBP	HOG	SIFT	VGG	Densenet
CrossMatch	SVM(linear)	43.01	18.70	35.70	10.36	19.37	14.70
	SVM(rbf)	34.77	**16.14**	33.71	10.68	15.72	14.59
	SVM(poly)	33.52	22.91	**33.56**	10.96	21.83	18.20
	ANN	37.23	16.92	34.67	**9.01**	15.64	**12.84**
	Random Forest	35.93	17.48	43.53	10.18	22.55	23.96
	XG Boost	**33.42**	16.99	36.47	9.63	19.37	18.68
	Logistic Regression	44.77	35.20	44.16	10.57	**15.38**	24.78
GreenBit	SVM(linear)	38.15	10.42	17.24	7.05	13.67	10.50
	SVM(rbf)	31.35	13.61	13.90	6.95	12.97	**7.94**
	SVM(poly)	31.9	12.92	17.75	7.9	13.55	11.42
	ANN	29.6	**9.44**	15.27	**6.75**	**12.06**	9.04
	Random Forest	**27.2**	10.62	13.86	11.65	13.70	12.08
	XG Boost	30.53	10.79	16.14	10.25	13.07	10.67
	Logistic Regression	37.8	19.76	**13.75**	11.7	15.65	9.94

4.3 Loss Function

The model weights for small, large CNN and transformer are updated by minimizing the binary cross entropy loss function.

$$L = -\frac{1}{N} \sum_{i=1}^{N} y_i \cdot log(p(y_i)) + (1 - y_i) \cdot log(1 - p(y_i)) \tag{3}$$

4.4 Evaluation and Results

We evaluated different feature extraction modules with different classifiers. We used the SVM classifier [23] through grid search cross-validation to optimize its cost and gamma parameters. Next, we used artificial neural network (ANN) classifier, employing a sequential model with dense layers, and trained using the Adam optimizer. Subsequently, random forest classifier [7], an ensemble classifier, was employed by initializing it with a set of 1000 decision trees. After that, we used the logistic regression classifier [37] with maximum iteration set to 500. Finally, XG Boost [12], an optimized gradient boosting algorithm, was employed for classification. The number of trees in the ensemble and the learning rate were set to 100 and 0.3, respectively. The ACE value from each of the above-mentioned classifiers along with each mentioned feature extractor are presented in Table 3.

Table 4. Our evaluation of various deep learning models on GreenBit and Crossmatch datasets. Models are re-trained for all layers while they are initialized with imagenet pretrained weights as a starting point. The models utilized include small CNNs, large CNNs and transformers as defined in Table 1. Training and testing times per epoch are reported for single GPU setup (Nvidia RTX 3060 12GB) for small CNNs and asterisk-marked (*) multi GPU setup (2xNvidia RTX 4080 16GB) for large CNNs and transformers. Testing time is greater than training time due to ten crop evaluation.

Model	Train	Test	Accuracy	ACE	Training Time(s)	Testing Time(s)
Resnet-18	CrossMatch	CrossMatch	99.11	0.98	6.19	16.67
		GreenBit	62	38		14.24
	GreenBit	CrossMatch	84.94	14.01	4.26	16.65
		GreenBit	97.25	2.75		14.47
Mobilenet v3 Large	CrossMatch	CrossMatch	99.32	0.81	6.04	15.33
		GreenBit	65.40	34.60		13.12
	GreenBit	CrossMatch	72.10	37.50	4.08	15.13
		GreenBit	97.15	2.85		12.91
EfficientNet B0	CrossMatch	CrossMatch	99.70	**0.36**	9.83	21.67
		GreenBit	63.10	36.90		18.54
	GreenBit	CrossMatch	87.15	6.58	6.73	22.08
		GreenBit	97.65	2.35		18.78
EfficientNet B1	CrossMatch	CrossMatch	99.06	1.29	15.70	54.24
		GreenBit	67.40	32.60		46.18
	GreenBit	CrossMatch	82.48	22.33	10.68	54.52
		GreenBit	97.45	2.55		46.64
EfficientNet B7	CrossMatch	CrossMatch	99.11	1.03	330.69*	643.07*
		GreenBit	55.25	44.75		546.26*
	GreenBit	CrossMatch	79.46	24.80	228.79*	646.80*
		GreenBit	98.05	1.95		548.71*
Densenet161	CrossMatch	CrossMatch	99.36	**0.75**	27.28*	95.20*
		GreenBit	61.35	38.65		80.68*
	GreenBit	CrossMatch	85.03	19.08	17.48*	94.02*
		GreenBit	96.10	3.90		78.89*
ViT-base 16 patches	CrossMatch	CrossMatch	96.00	4.55	29.09*	31.22*
		GreenBit	67.45	32.55		23.49*
	GreenBit	CrossMatch	55.65	34.89	18.88*	29.88*
		GreenBit	89.10	10.9		24.28*
Swin Transformer Tiny	CrossMatch	CrossMatch	96.85	3.81	23.50*	48.02*
		GreenBit	58.10	41.90		37.96*
	GreenBit	CrossMatch	48.26	40.62	13.39*	50.15*
		GreenBit	90.40	9.60		40.86*

CNN and Transformer Based Evaluation: Standard network architectures like Resnet [22], Mobilenet [26], Efficientnet [24], ViT [16] were used for classification, with the classifier head replaced by a 256-node penultimate layer and 2-nodes at final classifier head. A dropout layer with dropout probability of 0.4 was used for regularization. The models were initialized with imagenet weights [14] and standard data augmentation techniques like random cropping and horizontal flipping

Table 5. Comparison of pre-trained imagenet models [14] and models initialized with random weights. The pre-trained models were also used as feature extractors to assess the influence of imagenet weights on model accuracy. The models pre-trained on imagenet outperform those initialized with random weights even though the two domains are very different.

Model	Dataset	Feature Extractor	Random Weights	Imagenet Weights
Resnet-18	CrossMatch	96.26	98.68	99.10
	GreenBit	93.70	96.25	97.25
	Average Cross Sensor	71.17	66.50	73.46
Efficientnet B0	CrossMatch	95.32	98.85	99.70
	GreenBit	94.35	97.20	97.65
	Average Cross Sensor	68.34	66.96	75.12
Efficientnet B1	CrossMatch	96.68	98.97	99.06
	GreenBit	94.95	96.65	97.45
	Average Cross Sensor	71.9	67.23	74.94

of the images were used for increasing generalizability. The evaluation process involved cropping the original image into 10 patches (four from the corners, one from center and their horizontally flipped counterparts) and considering the average of the LogSoftmax of the model output for classification.

We performed cross-sensor testing to evaluate the model's capacity to adjust to new sensors. This involved assessing the models on a sensor other than the ones they were initially trained on. The results of different architectures, when trained and tested on CrossMatch and GreenBit 2015 dataset, are summarised in Table 4.

4.5   Effect of Transfer Learning

We tested the effects of transfer Learning on the model by using the model pre-trained on imagenet weights [14] as a feature extractor and training only the last 2 newly added layers. Initialization using random weights was also used to test the effect of those weights on the accuracy. As seen in Table 5, models pre-trained on imagenet perform better than random initialization on fingerprint liveness classification even though the domain of both differ significantly. The pre-trained models also generalize better as seen by the average cross sensor accuracy.

5   Conclusion

This provides the useful insights that feature representation learnt via imagenet training offers a very good initial starting point for optimization algorithms to find the optimal neural network weights. We presented a detailed comprehensive framework for accurate fingerprint liveness detection, focusing on feature engineering and classification techniques. Feature extraction methods, including texture analysis methods and deep feature extractors, were extensively evaluated on cross domain and cross-sensor datasets. The effectiveness of these techniques in capturing distinctive patterns and improving the precision of liveness detection in fingerprints was observed. Additionally, the efficacy of patch-based CNN classification algorithms to generalize to other sensors was examined. The effects of transfer learning on models was evaluated by initializing models with imagenet weights, using the pre-trained models as feature extractor and comparing them to random initialization. This research significantly advances fingerprint liveness detection by exploring feature engineering techniques, classification algorithms, CNN and transformer based approaches, examining accuracy and robustness.

Acknowledgement. This work is supported by the project C3IHUB/EE/2023221 C3i (cybersecurity and cybersecurity for Cyber-Physical Systems) Innovation Hub IIT Kanpur.

References

1. Biometrika HiScan-Pro Scanner. https://www.neurotechnology.com/fingerprint-scanner-biometrika-hiscan-pro.html
2. Cross-Match L Scan Guardian Scanner. http://www.itworks.co.th/L_Scan_Guardian/L_SCAN_Guardian.pdf
3. Digital Persona U.are.U 5160 Scanner. https://www.neurotechnology.com/fingerprint-scanner-digitalpersona-u-are-u-5100-5160.html
4. GreenBit Dacty-Scan 26 Scanner. https://www.neurotechnology.com/fingerprint-scanner-green-bit-dactyscan-26.html
5. Abhyankar, A.S., Schuckers, S.C.: A wavelet-based approach to detecting liveness in fingerprint scanners. In: Biometric Technology for Human Identification, vol. 5404. International Society for Optics and Photonics, SPIE (2004)
6. Ahonen, T., Matas, J., He, C., Pietikäinen, M.: Rotation invariant image description with local binary pattern histogram Fourier features. In: Salberg, A.-B., Hardeberg, J.Y., Jenssen, R. (eds.) SCIA 2009. LNCS, vol. 5575, pp. 61–70. Springer, Heidelberg (2009). https://doi.org/10.1007/978-3-642-02230-2_7
7. Ali, J., Khan, R., Ahmad, N., Maqsood, I.: Random forests and decision trees. Int. J. Comput. Sci. Issues (IJCSI) **9**, 272 (2012)
8. Antonelli, A., Cappelli, R., Maio, D., Maltoni, D.: Fake finger detection by skin distortion analysis. IEEE Trans. Inf. Forensics Secur. **1**, 360–373 (2006)
9. Anusha, B., Banerjee, S., Chaudhuri, S.: DeFraudNet: End2End fingerprint spoof detection using patch level attention. In: IEEE Winter Conference on Applications of Computer Vision (WACV) (2020)

10. Baldisserra, D., Franco, A., Maio, D., Maltoni, D.: Fake fingerprint detection by odor analysis. In: Zhang, D., Jain, A.K. (eds.) ICB 2006. LNCS, vol. 3832, pp. 265–272. Springer, Heidelberg (2005). https://doi.org/10.1007/11608288_36

11. Carcagní, P., Del Coco, M., Leo, M., Distante, C.: Facial expression recognition and histograms of oriented gradients: a comprehensive study. SpringerPlus **4**, 645 (2015)

12. Chen, T., Guestrin, C.: XGBoost: a scalable tree boosting system. In: Proceedings of the 22nd ACM SIGKDD International Conference on Knowledge Discovery and Data Mining. Association for Computing Machinery (2016)

13. Chugh, T., Cao, K., Jain, A.: Fingerprint spoof buster: use of minutiae-centered patches. IEEE Trans. Inf. Forensics Secur. **13**, 2190–2202 (2018)

14. Deng, J., Dong, W., Socher, R., Li, L.J., Li, K., Fei-Fei, L.: ImageNet: a large-scale hierarchical image database. In: 2009 IEEE Conference on Computer Vision and Pattern Recognition (2009)

15. Dharavath, K., Talukdar, F.A., Laskar, R.H.: Study on biometric authentication systems, challenges and future trends: a review. In: 2013 IEEE International Conference on Computational Intelligence and Computing Research (2013)

16. Dosovitskiy, A., et al.: An image is worth 16×16 words: transformers for image recognition at scale. In: International Conference on Learning Representations (2021)

17. Drahansky, M., Notzel, R., Funk, W.: Liveness detection based on fine movements of the fingertip surface. In: IEEE Information Assurance Workshop (2006)

18. Galbally, J., Alonso-Fernandez, F., Fierrez, J., Ortega-Garcia, J.: Fingerprint liveness detection based on quality measures. In: First IEEE International Conference on Biometrics, Identity and Security (BIdS) (2009)

19. Ghiani, L., Hadid, A., Marcialis, G.L., Roli, F.: Fingerprint liveness detection using binarized statistical image features. In: 2013 IEEE Sixth International Conference on Biometrics: Theory, Applications and Systems (BTAS) (2013)

20. Ghiani, L., Yambay, D., Mura, V., Tocco, S., Marcialis, G.L., Roli, F., Schuckers, S.: LivDet 2013 fingerprint liveness detection competition. In: 2013 International Conference on Biometrics (ICB) (2013)

21. Gomez-Barrero, M., Kolberg, J., Busch, C.: Multi-modal fingerprint presentation attack detection: analysing the surface and the inside. In: International Conference on Biometrics (ICB) (2019)

22. He, K., Zhang, X., Ren, S., Sun, J.: Deep residual learning for image recognition. In: IEEE Conference on Computer Vision and Pattern Recognition (CVPR) (2016)

23. Hearst, M., Dumais, S., Osuna, E., Platt, J., Scholkopf, B.: Support vector machines. IEEE Intell. Syst. Their Appl. (1998)

24. Hoang, V.T., Jo, K.H.: Practical analysis on architecture of EfficientNet. In: 14th International Conference on Human System Interaction (HSI) (2021)

25. Hosseini, S.: Fingerprint vulnerability: a survey. In: 2018 4th International Conference on Web Research (ICWR) (2018)

26. Howard, A., et al.: Searching for MobileNetv3. In: Proceedings of the IEEE/CVF International Conference on Computer Vision (ICCV) (2019)

27. Huang, G., Liu, Z., van der Maaten, L., Weinberger, K.: Densely connected convolutional networks (2017)
28. Johnson, P., Schuckers, S.: Fingerprint pore characteristics for liveness detection. In: 2014 International Conference of the Biometrics Special Interest Group (BIOSIG) (2014)
29. Liu, Z., et al.: Swin transformer: hierarchical vision transformer using shifted windows. In: Proceedings of the IEEE/CVF International Conference on Computer Vision (ICCV) (2021)
30. Marcialis, G.L., et al.: First international fingerprint liveness detection competition—LivDet 2009. In: Foggia, P., Sansone, C., Vento, M. (eds.) ICIAP 2009. LNCS, vol. 5716, pp. 12–23. Springer, Heidelberg (2009). https://doi.org/10.1007/978-3-642-04146-4_4
31. Marcialis, G.L., Roli, F., Tidu, A.: Analysis of fingerprint pores for vitality detection. In: 2010 20th International Conference on Pattern Recognition (2010)
32. Menotti, D., et al.: Deep representations for iris, face, and fingerprint spoofing detection. IEEE Trans. Inf. Forensics Secur. 10, 864–879 (2015)
33. Mura, V., Ghiani, L., Marcialis, G.L., Roli, F., Yambay, D.A., Schuckers, S.A.: LivDet fingerprint liveness detection competition. In: IEEE 7th International Conference on Biometrics Theory, Applications and Systems (BTAS) (2015)
34. Nogueira, R.F., de Alencar Lotufo, R., Campos Machado, R.: Fingerprint liveness detection using convolutional neural networks. IEEE Trans. Inf. Forensics Secur. 11, 1206–1213 (2016)
35. Organization, I.S.: ISO/IEC 30107-1: information technology - biometric presentation attack detection - part 1: framework (2016)
36. Osten, D.W., Carim, H.M., Blan, B.L., Arneson, M.R.: Biometric, personal authentication system (1995)
37. Peng, J., Lee, K., Ingersoll, G.: An introduction to logistic regression analysis and reporting. J. Educ. Res. 96, 3–14 (2002)
38. Pinto, A., Pedrini, H., Krumdick, M., Becker, B., Czajka, A., Bowyer, K., Rocha, A.: Counteracting presentation attacks in face, fingerprint, and iris recognition (2018)
39. Prakasa, E.: Texture feature extraction by using local binary pattern. INKOM J. 9, 45–48 (2016)
40. van der Putte, T., Keuning, J.: Biometrical fingerprint recognition: don't get your fingers burned. In: Domingo-Ferrer, J., Chan, D., Watson, A. (eds.) Smart Card Research and Advanced Applications. ITIFIP, vol. 52, pp. 289–303. Springer, Boston, MA (2000). https://doi.org/10.1007/978-0-387-35528-3_17
41. Ravi, J., Raja, K.B., Venugopal, K.R.: Fingerprint recognition using minutia score matching. CoRR (2010)
42. Ribani, R., Marengoni, M.: A survey of transfer learning for convolutional neural networks. In: 32nd SIBGRAPI Conference on Graphics, Patterns and Images Tutorials (SIBGRAPI-T) (2019)
43. Tammina, S.: Transfer learning using VGG-16 with deep convolutional neural network for classifying images (2019)
44. Tan, B., Schuckers, S.C.: New approach for liveness detection in fingerprint scanners based on valley noise analysis. J. Electron. Imaging (2008)

45. Vaswani, A., et al.: Attention is all you need. In: Advances in Neural Information Processing Systems (2017)
46. Wang, R., Jeon, J.W.: Design of real-time sift feature extraction. In: IECON - 43rd Annual Conference of the IEEE Industrial Electronics Society (2017)
47. Zhang, Y., Jin, R., Zhou, Z.H.: Understanding bag-of-words model: a statistical framework. Int. J. Mach. Learn. Cybern. **1**, 43–52 (2010)

Artificial Eye: Online Video Browsing Guide for Visually Impaired

Ratnabali Pal[1,2]([✉]), Samarjit Kar[1], and Arif Ahmed Sekh[3]

[1] National Institute of Technology Durgapur, Durgapur, India
pal.ratnabali@gmail.com, samarjit.kar@maths.nitdgp.ac.in
[2] Brainware University, Kolkata, India
[3] XIM University, Bhubaneswar, India

Abstract. Vision is essential for learning about the world around us. However, missing one's vision makes it challenging to lead a regular, everyday life. Either because of a lack of awareness or understanding or because of financial limitations, many visually impaired people may not have access to technology that could enable them to become independent. Our innovative research acts as a true companion, helping visually impaired (VI) people achieve online shopping independence in 2 major areas- category-specific Video Summarization and Visual Question-Answering (VQA). In this article, we propose a new dataset, namely PRVDVI (Product Review Video Dataset for the visually impaired). This dataset includes product review videos downloaded from YouTube for a variety of things, including everyday consumer goods, fashionable clothing, and technical gadgets. First, we used Whisper, a general-purpose speech recognition model developed by OpenAI to extract the text from the audio. Next, we employ a novel topic-guided summarization technique that allows VI people to navigate through the enormous video content of a product. We also keep a space for visual question answering in such large-volume videos. We make this dataset available to inspire the computer vision research community to develop more versatile algorithms that can help low-vision people (https://github.com/skarifahmed/ArificialEye).

Keywords: Visually Impaired · Assistive Technology · Product Review · Visual Question Answering (VQA)

1 Introduction

Recent research estimates that at least 2.2 billion people worldwide suffer from near- or distance vision impairment. Visually impaired people frequently experience complications during web contact. In recent years, numerous research projects have addressed these issues in an effort to boost intelligence, increase environmental comprehension, and facilitate digital shopping for VI individuals. With increased e-commerce websites to the internet's global reach, online shopping has gained appeal. In today's digital world, online product reviews

[1–4] play an important role in the product evaluation process for both a company and its customers. These also assist customers in making the right product selection with less time and effort. These reviews provide input for a company to improve product quality, strategy and observe the market value, and increase productivity and profit. As a result, it's been found that customers these days prefer to watch well-known online reviews of equipment like washing machines, refrigerators, smartphones, laptops, TVs, ACs, etc. on YouTube before making a purchase. The popularity of a video is determined by the vast majority of opinions expressed through comments, likes or dislikes, and replies. According to research, those who are visually impaired are 35% less likely to access the Internet than people without disabilities. The study included 100 popular product review videos of various technological gadgets, fashion garments, other consumer products, etc., with a total of 500 videos collected between January 2022 and June 2023. This article addressed a specific problem faced by visually impaired people and suggested a solution. The current solution is for VI people to search in social video media and listen individually to assess the product. Whereas, we provide an interactive solution to browse large volume of video data. The traditional and the proposed solution is depicted in Fig. 1.

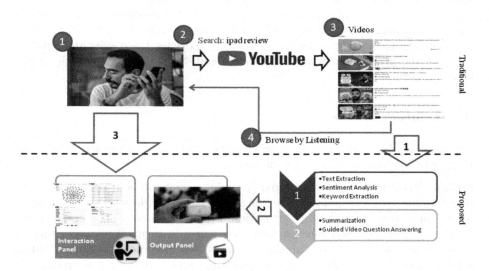

Fig. 1. Intelligent video analysis for visually impaired people. The top row represents a state-of-the-art video browsing mechanism for VI people, the bottom row is the proposed method. We propose to use a topic-guided interaction panel for a better video summary.

While research on online product review video analysis has recently received a lot of attention in the field of computer vision, there is still a limited video dataset for visually impaired people. We collect a new large video with no dataset available on product reviews from YouTube to considerably evaluate our methods.

Our aim is to generate a synopsis, that is composed of a selection of important audiovisual frames or video segments that have been consecutively merged to form a shorter video. Videos typically have audio components that correspond to the visual content exhibited on the screen; however, the audio explanation is more meaningful for a visually impaired individual. Videos typically include auditory components that correspond to the visual content exhibited on the screen, while audio explanation is especially important for visually challenged people. We suggested a methodology for the task and open up new challenges to the CV and NLP community. Firstly, we propose a video dataset from YouTube aimed specifically at visually challenged individuals. It contains user reviews of 100 products of different categories (technical products, fashion garments, and other consumer products). Secondly, we implemented Whisper [5,6], a pre-trained sequence-to-sequence model [1,7–9] for automatic speech recognition (ASR) [10–12] and speech translation [13,14]. Finally, we provide insight into a large video dataset to visually impaired people such that the person can listen to summarize the content and also be able to answer guided queries such as the 'battery life of a gadget.' Our work also provides the first dataset for enabling algorithm research on videos and queries submitted by the visually impaired, resulting in novel vision- and language-based challenges.

The rest of the article proceeds as follows: Sect. 2 describes recent works in the domain of product review and VQA for visually impaired people. Section 3 describes the proposed framework. In Sect. 4, we discuss the results and ablation study of the proposed methodology. In the end, Sect. 5 briefly highlights some concluding remarks.

2   Related Works

Our approach is influenced by earlier efforts on video and image accessibility for those with limited vision or sight impaired.

Online Product Review Videos: Nowadays, scientists and researchers have begun to pay special attention to online user-generated videos in order to capitalize on numerous marketing opportunities. Typically, customers report and give an idea of their personal consumption experiences in them. While searching for product information on YouTube, many times viewers come across such product review videos that include unboxing, utilizing, and maintaining a product. In this study [15] researchers focused to investigate the relationship between different emotions. This paper represented a four-factor model based on consumer engagement content found in online product videos to explore new insights for predicting the purchase goals of potential customers. Pfeuffer et al. [16] studied the theoretical framework of cue-based trust and signaling theory to examine content attributes in online consumer product review videos. That would act as trust cues and enable viewers to develop trust in the reviewer.

Visual Question-Answering from for Visually Impaired People: Assistance to visually impaired people is among the goals of several Visual-Question-

Answering applications [17] in recent history. This is mostly due to the ability of automatic VQA to answer daily questions, which may assist visually impaired persons in living without visual assistance barriers. Chen et al. [18] introduced visual questions originating by visually challenged people VizWiz-VQAGrounding dataset [19], who took both images and asked the questions about them in order to overcome actual visual challenges. Scientists implemented VQA and cover the emerging field of Scene Text VQA (ST-VQA) [20] and their accessibility for VIP assistants.

Online Product Review Videos for Low Vision People: Although these research concepts are encouraging, the accessibility of product review videos for the sight impaired has received less attention compared to other types of videos.

3   Proposed Method

Automatic speech recognition (ASR) [21], one of the key components of conversational AI, builds acoustic models that can convert voice to text using training corpora developed by researchers. We utilized one of the most specific neural-based ASR state-of-art frameworks to date Whisper [22] by openAI [23], which is trained using a fully supervised method. Chunk-wise, attention is more adaptable, even though it has a similar conceptual framework to block processing. Block processing is carried out at the level of the input features, which restricts the layers of the encoder to the context frame at the present chunk. Otherwise, in the convolution layers, chunk-wise attention is able to process contextual frames outside the current chunk. This model serves as an encoder-decoder Transformer [24,25] receives 80-channel log-Mel spectrograms [26,27] as input. This model is offered via Huggingface (https://huggingface.co/openai/whisper-large, accessed on 1 February 2023) [28,29]. We first extract the text from a given set of videos. Next, we employ state-of-the-art sentiment analysis [30] and text summarization methods [31] to produce a video summary. We have also explored topic models [32] to extract the keywords from the videos. These topics are then used as a guide for VI people to generate a meaningful summary of the video. Figure 2 shows the flow of the proposed pipeline. We have found that a topic-guided video summarization is more effective for VI people.

Dataset: Our proposed dataset includes things such as technical gadgets, clothing, and other consumer stuff. The dataset was obtained from the video network YouTube. The dataset provides video-rich data and highlights the limitations of various video analytics. As a result, we gather the top N category-specific videos for the search query as input to the suggested framework. Each video (V_i) is represented by a sequence of video segments, such as: $\{(V_i, S_1), (V_i, S_2), ..., (V_i, S_M)\}$. Each product item in our dataset is made up of $<V, Q, A>$, where V is the collection of videos for a product, Q is the set of questions for the video, and A is the ground truth response.

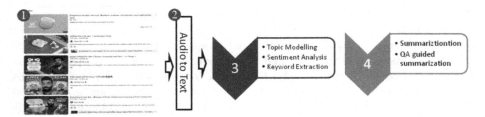

Fig. 2. Proposed pipeline for effective video browsing. We first take top-k videos by searching for product reviews on YouTube. Next, we extract audios that are converted into text. Finally, a state-of-the-art text summarization and a topic-guided summarization are proposed.

Fig. 3. Example of items in review dataset.

We evaluated several often asked questions such as, what is an extra battery backup feature for iPhone 14, will this vibrant color of clothing last, what is the book about as a whole, etc. Here in Table 1 we discuss some application-specific datasets used in Product review and VQA analysis.

Table 1. Popular Datasets used in various review and Visual Question Answering articles

Dataset	Online product review	Online product review videos for visually impaired	VQA for visually impaired
Yelp [33]	✓	✗	✗
Youtubean [34]	✓	✗	✗
VizWiz [35]	✗	✗	✓
Proposed PRVDVI	✓	✓	✓

Implementation and Training: The code is developed using state-of-the-art python library in a PC having 32 GB A5000 NVIDIA GPU. The dataset is split as 70% training and 30% validation. We have used default learning rates and other settings. In the case of unsupervised topic extraction, we have used topic ranges from 10 to 20 topics. We have not used any specific preprocessing. For the topic modeling, we limit the number of words to 50 and Word2Vec [36] as embedding (Fig. 3).

4   Results and Discussion

4.1   Metric

We introduced a requirement in the evaluation of the quality of the summarised video. We implemented a new method of measuring performance. In recent research articles, ROUGE scores [37] is used for text as a Unicode evaluation metric and precision-recall-based metrics [38] for multimodal video analysis. Precision evaluates positive prediction accuracy, whereas recall reflects the model's ability to detect positive samples. The video summarization technique together with generated video segments and segmented bunches are estimated using objective criteria. Precision and Recall are the two metrics that represent the entire framework of the video summarizing technique., which are calculated as:

$$Precision = \frac{matched\,frames}{Total\,frames\,in\,automatic\,summary} \in [0,1] \tag{1}$$

$$Recall = \frac{matched\,frames}{Total\,frames\,in\,user\,summary} \in [0,1] \tag{2}$$

Automated synopsis includes identified key-frames from various summarization techniques.

$$F - measure = \frac{2 * Precision * Recall}{Precision + Recall} \in [0,1] \tag{3}$$

F-measure [39] is the harmonic mean of both Precision and Recall, it generates the accuracy of the experiment. To determine whether the Automatic summary is better than the Ground truth summary for comparing segment similarity, the state-of-art algorithm uses Fidelity based on semi-hausdroff distance.

$$Fidelity = \frac{Sum\,Dist(F_i, AT_i)}{AT} \in [0,1] \tag{4}$$

In our article, none of these criteria are precise due to the fact that there is a lot of repetitive frames in different videos. Our goal is to provide summaries of information. For this reason, we suggest a simple question-answer F-measure metric for assessment.

Question-Answer F-Measure: We applied simple accuracy metrics where questions and answers can be asked to summarize video content. We have designed a list of topic-specific questions to product review for the task. For instance, "Is Adidas Duramo 10 comfortable as well as affordable to casual wear"? The F-measure will then be determined on the basis of the number of responses in the summary. The F-measure is calculated using Eq. 1.

In the case of topic-guided summarization, we also calculate the F1 score. The F1 score is calculated based on the answer available in the summary or not. For example, if the topic "battery life" is selected, whether the summary contains information about the battery is considered as the correctness of the summary.

4.2   Results

Here, we discuss the results of different state-of-the-art methods for the task. In Table 2, F-measure is presented using different methods. It is noted that the Text summarization [40] method gains a jump, comparatively to other state-of-the-art. Here, we proposed to use a text-based summarization for the task.

Table 2. Comparison of the summarization methods. It is observed that a text-based summarization is most suitable for VI people.

Method	Video-based	Text-based	F-measure
Sentiment-based [41]	✗	✓	0.21
Vision Fusion [42]	✓	✗	0.25
Scene-based [43]	✓	✗	0.41
Text summarization [40]	✗	✓	0.52

4.3   Case Study

Here, we present a case study of a product from our proposed dataset. We consider iPhone 13 for the study. We take the top 5 videos of different lengths. Different parameters of the data are:

Product: iPhone 13
No. of Videos: 5
Total Duration: 68 min

Figure 6 shows uni-gram and bi-gram topics extracted from the texts extracted from the dataset. It is observed that words like "camera", "video", "pro", etc., and bi-gram words such as "pro max", "dynamic range", "battery life", etc. popped up as topics. These topics are then used as a guide for summarization. Figure 5 depicts the word group of each topic.

We have conducted a topic-guided summarization experiment. First, the videos are analyzed and top-10 topics are prompted to a set of volunteers.

(a)  (b)

Fig. 4. (a) Extracted uni-gram keywords from the iPhone review videos. (b) Extracted bi-gram for the same.

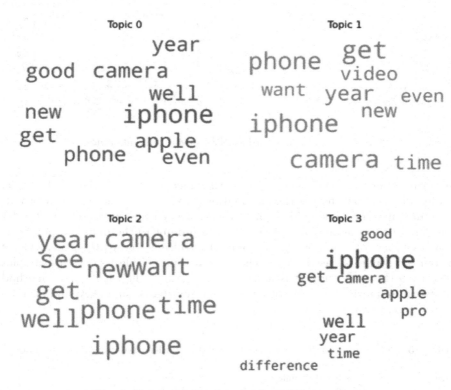

Fig. 5. Extracted top-4 topics from iPhone videos.

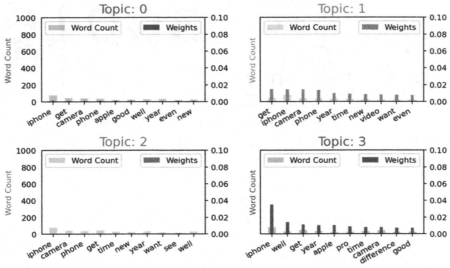

Fig. 6. Different keyword statistics over different topics.

Next, the summarization is generated on the video locations based on the topic. Finally, we examine whether the information is available in the summary or not. We found that the topic-guided summarization is correct up to 0.97 as the F1 measure. Due to the analyzed topic acts as a prompt to the impaired people, it becomes easier to browse using the topic. It also leads toward the generation of customized synopsis based on the choice of a topic. Table 3 shows 5 examples taken from the case study. It is noted that sometimes the topic-guided method generates summaries that are not present in a text-based summary, and also the length is comparatively low.

Table 3. Comparison of the text-based and topic-guided summarization methods.

Query	Text-based Summary		Topic-guided Summary	
	Duration (min)	Information Present	Duration (min)	Information present
Battery Life	8:30	Y	2:40	Y
Camera Quality	8:30	Y	3:20	Y
Pro Feature	8:30	N	3:10	Y
Video Quality	8:30	Y	5:60	Y
Price	8:30	Y	2:30	Y

5   Conclusion

This paper proposed a video dataset aimed at enabling visually impaired people to video browsing easier. We have chosen "product review videos" as the videos can help VI people in online shopping. Due to the small size of the data set employed in this experiment, the output was degraded. To determine the generalizability of the results for the visually impaired, more experimental analysis across other websites is required and benchmark the findings. This article considers user engagement content on online product review videos available only on one social media platform, the YouTube channel. Future research must be done separately on other video-sharing platforms for the sight impaired to compare how customers engage with them. In this study, we show how using topic-based features can enhance video synopsis. We aimed to explore more in this direction.

Funding Information. The Project funding including hardware resource (GPU) and other costs of the project is funded by the Science and Engineering Research Board (SERB), Govt. of India, Project No: SRG/2022/000122, executed in XIM University, Bhubaneswar, India, supervised by Arif Ahmed Sekh.

References

1. Pfeuffer, A., Li, X., Zhang, Y., Huh, J.: The effect of sponsorship disclosure in YouTube product reviews. J. Curr. Issues Res. Advert. **42**(4), 391–410 (2021)
2. Gupta, V., Aggarwal, A., Chakraborty, T.: Detecting and characterizing extremist reviewer groups in online product reviews. IEEE Trans. Comput. Soc. Syst. **7**(3), 741–750 (2020)
3. Li, X., Wu, C., Mai, F.: The effect of online reviews on product sales: a joint sentiment-topic analysis. Inf. Manage. **56**(2), 172–184 (2019)
4. Onan, A.: Sentiment analysis on product reviews based on weighted word embeddings and deep neural networks. Concurr. Comput.: Pract. Exp. **33**(23), e5909 (2021)
5. Mushtaq, M., et al.: Whisper: a tool for run-time detection of side-channel attacks. IEEE Access **8**, 83871–83900 (2020)
6. Jacoby, M., et al.: WHISPER: wireless home identification and sensing platform for energy reduction. J. Sens. Actuat. Netw. **10**(4), 71 (2021)
7. Nogueira, R., Jiang, Z., Lin, J.: Document ranking with a pretrained sequence-to-sequence model. arXiv preprint arXiv:2003.06713 (2020)
8. Pradeep, R., Nogueira, R., Lin, J.: The expando-mono-duo design pattern for text ranking with pretrained sequence-to-sequence models. arXiv preprint arXiv:2101.05667 (2021)
9. Lewis, M., et al.: BART: Denoising sequence-to-sequence pre-training for natural language generation, translation, and comprehension. arXiv preprint arXiv:1910.13461 (2019)
10. Bhardwaj, V., et al.: Automatic speech recognition (ASR) systems for children: a systematic literature review. Appl. Sci. **12**(9), 4419 (2022)
11. Alharbi, S., et al.: Automatic speech recognition: systematic literature review. IEEE Access **9**, 131858–131876 (2021)

12. Shahamiri, S.R.: Speech vision: an end-to-end deep learning-based dysarthric automatic speech recognition system. IEEE Trans. Neural Syst. Rehabil. Eng. **29**, 852–861 (2021)
13. Zhou, Z., et al.: Sign-to-speech translation using machine-learning-assisted stretchable sensor arrays. Nat. Electron. **3**(9), 571–578 (2020)
14. Inaguma, H., et al.: ESPnet-ST: all-in-one speech translation toolkit. arXiv preprint arXiv:2004.10234 (2020)
15. Agrawal, S.R., Mittal, D.: Optimizing customer engagement content strategy in retail and E-tail: available on online product review videos. J. Retail. Consum. Serv. **67**, 102966 (2022)
16. Pfeuffer, A., Phua, J.: Stranger danger? Cue-based trust in online consumer product review videos. Int. J. Consum. Stud. **46**(3), 964–983 (2022)
17. Antol, S., et al.: VQA: visual question answering. In Proceedings of the IEEE International Conference on Computer Vision, pp. 2425–2433 (2015)
18. Chen, C., Anjum, S., Gurari, D.: Grounding answers for visual questions asked by visually impaired people. In: Proceedings of the IEEE/CVF Conference on Computer Vision and Pattern Recognition, pp. 19098–19107 (2022)
19. Gurari, D., Zhao, Y., Zhang, M., Bhattacharya, N.: Captioning images taken by people who are blind. In: Vedaldi, A., Bischof, H., Brox, T., Frahm, J.-M. (eds.) ECCV 2020, Part XVII. LNCS, vol. 12362, pp. 417–434. Springer, Cham (2020). https://doi.org/10.1007/978-3-030-58520-4_25
20. Brick, E.R., et al.: Am i allergic to this? Assisting sight impaired people in the kitchen. In: Proceedings of the 2021 International Conference on Multimodal Interaction, pp. 92–102 (2021)
21. Koenecke, A., et al.: Racial disparities in automated speech recognition. Proc. Natl. Acad. Sci. **117**(14), 7684–7689 (2020)
22. Chen, Y., et al.: Devil's whisper: a general approach for physical adversarial attacks against commercial black-box speech recognition devices. In: USENIX Security Symposium, pp. 2667–2684 (2020)
23. Mhlanga, D.: Open AI in education, the responsible and ethical use of ChatGPT towards lifelong learning. Education, the Responsible and Ethical Use of ChatGPT Towards Lifelong Learning (2023)
24. Chefer, H., Gur, S., Wolf, L.: Generic attention-model explainability for interpreting bi-modal and encoder-decoder transformers. In: Proceedings of the IEEE/CVF International Conference on Computer Vision, pp. 397–406 (2021)
25. Zhou, X., Yılmaz, E., Long, Y., Li, Y., Li, H.: Multi-encoder-decoder transformer for code-switching speech recognition. arXiv preprint arXiv:2006.10414 (2020)
26. Rajaa, S.: Improving end-to-end SLU performance with prosodic attention and distillation. arXiv preprint arXiv:2305.08067 (2023)
27. Xu, M., Zhang, F., Khan, S.U.: Improve accuracy of speech emotion recognition with attention head fusion. In: 2020 10th Annual Computing and Communication Workshop and Conference (CCWC), pp. 1058–1064. IEEE (2020)
28. Hugging Face. Hugging face (2022)
29. Shen, Y., Song, K., Tan, X., Li, D., Lu, W., Zhuang, Y.: HuggingGPT: solving AI tasks with ChatGPT and its friends in HuggingFace. arXiv preprint arXiv:2303.17580 (2023)
30. Das, R., Singh, T.D.: Multimodal sentiment analysis: a survey of methods, trends, and challenges. ACM Comput. Surveys **55**(13s), 1–38 (2023)
31. Li, H., Yuan, P., Xu, S., Wu, Y., He, X., Zhou, B.: Aspect-aware multimodal summarization for chinese e-commerce products. In: Proceedings of the AAAI Conference on Artificial Intelligence, vol. 34, pp. 8188–8195 (2020)

32. Rani, R., Lobiyal, D.K.: An extractive text summarization approach using tagged-LDA based topic modeling. Multimed. Tools Appl. **80**, 3275–3305 (2021)

33. Hossain, M.S., Rahman, M.F.: Customer sentiment analysis and prediction of insurance products' reviews using machine learning approaches. FIIB Bus. Rev. 23197145221115793 (2022)

34. Marrese-Taylor, E., Balazs, J.A., Matsuo, Y.: Mining fine-grained opinions on closed captions of YouTube videos with an attention-RNN. arXiv preprint arXiv:1708.02420 (2017)

35. Gurari, D., et al.: VizWiz-Priv: a dataset for recognizing the presence and purpose of private visual information in images taken by blind people. In: Proceedings of the IEEE/CVF Conference on Computer Vision and Pattern Recognition, pp. 939–948 (2019)

36. Jang, B., Kim, I., Kim, J.W.: Word2vec convolutional neural networks for classification of news articles and tweets. PloS One **14**(8), e0220976 (2019)

37. Plummer, B.A., Brown, M., Lazebnik, S.: Enhancing video summarization via vision-language embedding. In: Proceedings of the IEEE Conference on Computer Vision and Pattern Recognition, pp. 5781–5789 (2017)

38. Khosla, A., Hamid, R., Lin, C.-J., Sundaresan, N.: Large-scale video summarization using web-image priors. In: Proceedings of the IEEE Conference on Computer Vision and Pattern Recognition, pp. 2698–2705 (2013)

39. Otani, M., Nakashima, Y., Rahtu, E., Heikkilä, J., Yokoya, N.: Video summarization using deep semantic features. In: Lai, S.-H., Lepetit, V., Nishino, K., Sato, Y. (eds.) ACCV 2016. LNCS, vol. 10115, pp. 361–377. Springer, Cham (2017). https://doi.org/10.1007/978-3-319-54193-8_23

40. Jiahua, D., Rong, J., Michalska, S., Wang, H., Zhang, Y.: Feature selection for helpfulness prediction of online product reviews: an empirical study. PLoS ONE **14**(12), e0226902 (2019)

41. Shah, J., Sagathiya, M., Redij, K., Hole, V.: Natural language processing based abstractive text summarization of reviews. In: 2020 International Conference on Electronics and Sustainable Communication Systems (ICESC), pp. 461–466. IEEE (2020)

42. Muhammad, K., Hussain, T., Tanveer, M., Sannino, G., de Albuquerque, V.H.C.: Cost-effective video summarization using deep CNN with hierarchical weighted fusion for IoT surveillance networks. IEEE Internet Things J. **7**(5), 4455–4463 (2019)

43. Rafiq, M., Rafiq, G., Agyeman, R., Choi, G.S., Jin, S.-I.: Scene classification for sports video summarization using transfer learning. Sensors **20**(6), 1702 (2020)

MediaPipe with LSTM Architecture for Real-Time Hand Gesture Recognization

Sougatamoy Biswas[1]([envelope])[ID], Anup Nandy[1][ID], Asim Kumar Naskar[2][ID], and Rahul Saw[1][ID]

[1] Computer Science and Engineering, National Institute of Technology Rourkela, Rourkela, Odisha, India
521CS6015@nirkl.ac.in, 222cs1484@nitrkl.ac.in
[2] Electrical Engineering, National Institute of Technology Rourkela, Rourkela, Odisha, India
naskara@nitrkl.ac.in

Abstract. Gesture recognition plays a vital role in the area of research for human-computer interaction (HCI). The integration of MediaPipe with Long Short Term Memory (LSTM) architecture holds tremendous potential for real-time hand gesture recognition. MediaPipe provides a robust and versatile framework for capturing and processing multimedia input, such as video streams from cameras or pre-recorded video files. The temporal modeling capabilities of LSTM captures the temporal dynamics of hand gestures. This research paper aims to present a novel method utilizing the MediaPipe with LSTM architecture for real-time hand gesture recognition. A test on real-time gesture recognition is performed to evaluate the performance of the suggested model. Our results demonstrate that the suggested method outperforms other state-of-the-art approaches on our custom made dataset with an accuracy of 98.99%.

Keywords: Gesture recognition · LSTM · MediaPipe · Human-computer interaction

1 Introduction

Gesture recognition is a way to read and understand a person's body language to communicate effectively. Based on computer vision technology, hand gesture recognition is getting great attention because of it's natural way of interaction between humans and computers. Different hand poses and their movements generally make a gesture [1]. Real time hand motion detection also depends on the image processing capability of the system and hand movements. In some cases, if the hand movements are too fast then it is a difficult task to capture the appropriate hand motions. So, figuring out the position of a hand in real time is still a

H. Kaur et al. (Eds.): CVIP 2023, CCIS 2010, pp. 422–431, 2024.
https://doi.org/10.1007/978-3-031-58174-8_36

difficult task that requires work from many different fields, such as pattern recognition, computer vision and image processing. A gesture is a sign for expressing one's behaviour or feelings physically. Humans and computers may communicate via the use of gestures. The intent of the user can be determined by analyzing the user's gestures and movements [2]. Multiple input images are collected to detect dynamic motion, but just a single image is needed to detect static gestures. The quality of the supplied image is improved using image enhancement techniques. Dynamic gesture recognition falls under the category of video classification since the data is predominantly presented in the form of video frames. Dynamic gesture detection is difficult because of factors such as inconsistent pixel quality, camera movement, and individual diversity in the execution of a particular action. It is difficult for an algorithm to accurately predict gestures due to the context dependent nature of gestures and the continuous movement of hands and arms. Overall, the integration of MediaPipe with LSTM architecture offers a powerful solution for real-time hand gesture recognition [3]. The subsequent sections of this paper are structured as follows: In Sect. 2, we discuss the deep learning techniques that other researchers have implemented for gesture recognition. The approach behind the MediaPipe based LSTM architecture for recognizing hand gestures in real-time is outlined in Sect. 3. Experiment results are described in Sect. 4. The last component of the paper serves as the final chapter.

2   Related Work

Hand gesture recognition is an essential aspect of HCI with significant implications for a wide range of applications, including virtual reality, robotics, sign language interpretation, and smart homes. Several methods are developed in this area including template matching, decision trees, and deep learning, to recognize hand gestures. Numerous approaches and techniques are proposed for hand gesture recognition. Throughout the years the system's accuracy and performance are improved in recognizing hand movements. In recent years, numerous studies are conducted utilizing MediaPipe and LSTM models for hand gesture recognition. Several research projects have used MediaPipe to analyze hand gestures. Javier et al. [4] proposed a framework for motion based head and eye gesture detection using egocentric visual input from an eyewear device. The approach is predicated on a LSTM for storing visual associations across time, and a homography estimation convolutional neural network (CNN) for representing motion between frames. In order to capture the temporal visual correlations the CNN output is fed into an LSTM network. The system operates with an accuracy of 90%. Between 20 and 30 frames per second MediaPipe posture is proposed in conjunction with convolutional neural network (CNN) models for LSTM based traffic gesture detection by Ong et al. [5]. In this method video data is analyzed using an LSTM classification model and a pose extraction tool MediaPipe. This allows for the detection and categorization of traffic movements. The Mediapipe posture recognition approach provides very accurate predictions of 3D body keypoint positions in real time. All kinds of gestures can be reliably classified by the model. A deep learning-based approach was introduced by Areeb et al. [6] to achieve precise prediction of Indian Sign Language (ISL). After the annotation of frames two models are created: one for object detection and another for categorization. One model combines traditional RNNs with a long short-term memory (RNN-LSTM) strategy, while another makes use of 3D convolutional neural networks (CNNs), VGG-16, and a LSTM network. The latest model was developed on top of the advanced YOLOv5 (You Only Look Once) object identification algorithm. The prediction accuracies of the two classification models are 82% and 98%, respectively with an average accuracy of 99.6%. The test results shows that the YOLO based model outperformed its competitors. Sundar et al. [7] suggested a technique for recognising ASL alphabets that is able to distinguish between static and dynamic motions in American Sign Language (ASL). Google's Mediapipe is used to acquire hand landmarks and a custom dataset is built for testing. Successful hand gesture recognition is achieved with the help of LSTM. The proposed approach is evaluated using 26 alphabets, and it achieves 98.99% accuracy. Recent research using MediaPipe and LSTM models for hand gesture recognition has shown promising results. Accurate and fast methods for hand identification and landmark estimation are provided by these approaches and also captures sequential relationship between hand motions.

3   Methodology

In this research, we provide a deep learning model for real-time gesture recognition using LSTM and the Mediapipe framework. Hand detection, landmark estimation, and gesture recognition [8] are the three basic pillars of the suggested technique. MediaPipe is used for hand detection and landmark estimation, while LSTM models are used for hand gesture recognition. The system can reliably recognize and follow the hand in real time due to MediaPipe's pretrained algorithms for hand identification and landmark estimation. The system uses a pretrained MediaPipe model to automatically extract the hand's landmark points [9] for successful hand detection and tracking. The landmark points are then used to train LSTM models to recognize gestures based on patterns of landmark points. The technique makes use of motion based signals, therefore the data received from video streams of signs should match the defined activities. In order to extract information from a moving sign, it is necessary to gather and combine data from each frame of the video in sequential sequence. Movement based signal data is significantly important to identify hands and body posture [10]. The human skeleton's joints serves as reference for these hand and body components. Each sign will exhibit a unique configuration of these core characteristics based on the behaviours it represents. An LSTM based deep learning strategy [11] is used to predict the sign from this pattern. The suggested hand gesture recognition system's flowchart is shown in Fig. 1.

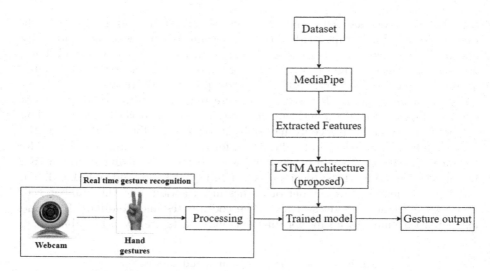

Fig. 1. Training and testing flow diagram of the proposed architecture

3.1 Dataset Description

In this research, a database of hand and facial gestures for five distinct activities ("Hello", "Help", "Thanks", "Go to" and "Bathroom") is compiled. For each gesture a total of 200 images are taken with face, hand and body motion. The lighting, and visibility factors while recording the face, hands, and body are maintained as natural environmental conditions. The performance of the Mediapipe model can degrade significantly for non-frontal faces, low-resolution images, and for hands in low-resolution scenarios. So, an average height of 5.7 feet human is considered for this experiment. The final data set is then separated into a 90% training set and a 10% testing set. All of the testing is done on a machine running Windows 10 and equipped with a 10th generation Intel processor and an NVIDIA GTX 1650TI graphics card with 4 GB of RAM. For the purpose of training networks, the popular PyTorch framework has been deployed. Python 3.10.9 and the Pytorch 1.13.1 framework were used in the experiment.

3.2 Data Preprocessing

The dataset is divided into its constituent activities during the data preparation phase, with 200 frames of images from each video that represents each individual activity. The MediaPipe library is used to identify the subject's keypoints like pose, face, left hand, and right hand in each image. From each frame, the most important characteristics with these four important keypoints are extracted. For each action, we compiled 200 data point sets with the accompanying keyframes. We used a total of 1000 data sets for model development and evaluation. This procedure of gathering data and determining its significance is repeated for each activity in the dataset. After that, landmark information is extracted from the images through MediaPipe to identify key anatomical features of the hand, body, and face. The MediaPipe holistic model [12] returns landmarks for hand, body, and face from each single frame. These are known as x, y, and z coordinates. Visibility is a further consideration in body posture. There are 21 individual controls for each hand. Identifying a posture requires a total of 33 identifiers. The human face has 468 identifiers that may be used to decode emotions. This implies that the number of coordinates obtained was 1662 for a single frame (21 * 3 for each hand on the left and right, 33 * 4 for the body position, and 468 * 3 for the face). A dataset of shapes (200,1662) was created by stacking a total of 1662 landmarks, including the subject's face, attitude, left hand, and right hand. The number 200 denotes the number of frames in an action, and the number 1662 denotes each landmark dataset size. The coordinates and landmark keypoints extracted through MediaPipe for different body parts are given in Table 1.

Table 1. The defined keypoints and coordinates

Body Parts	Coordinates	Keypoints
Right Hand	63	21
Left Hand	63	21
Face	1404	468
Body Pose	132	33
Total	1662	543

3.3 The Proposed LSTM Network Architecture

Training costs and error margin minimization in the output is the primary focus of LSTM model. The LSTM models [13] use the time-dependent relationships in hand movements by using the sequential information of the landmark points. The model is trained for 120 epochs on the training data, using a batch size of 13 for faster convergence during training and to lead better generalization. The LSTM models are trained using a collection of hand gesture videos that include both static images and dynamic images. LSTM models [7] are trained on the training set using the Adam optimizer with a learning rate of 0.001. The input video sequence to the LSTM is the MediaPipe extracted keypoints [5] with the shape of (200, 1662). The novel neural network architecture is designed with four layers of networks. The first two layers are LSTM layers and last two layers are dense layers. The model structure is shown in Fig. 2. To capture complex patterns in sequential data the Layer 1 of a Long Short-Term Memory (LSTM) network [14] is modified with 64 neurons and uses sigmoid activation with the parameter 'return_sequences' is set as 'True' for sending input to the Layer 2 of the LSTM layer from layer 1. If the "return_sequences" is not set as 'True' then the layer 2 will not receive input from layer 1. The LSTM layer 2 has 128 neurons and sigmoid as an activation function. This modified deep LSTM architecture can capture hierarchical features and dependencies in the data. The hierarchical network structure is created with the combination of two dense layers. This allows for a combination of temporal sequence modeling (LSTM) and feature extraction (dense). The first dense layer uses 64 neurons with the ReLU activation function. The last dense layer is the output layer uses softmax activation function and has number of neurons same as number of gesture [15] classes. The number of cells in the output layer is set as 5 the represents the number of classes. On the testing set, the models are evaluated by the evaluation measure [16]. The suggested model's success is measured by its accuracy [17].

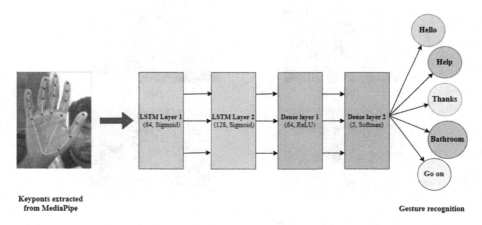

Fig. 2. The suggested LSTM model's network with pair of LSTM layer and Dense layer.

4   Result Analysis and Discussion

Models are trained and processed using our custom build dataset to perform precise gesture recognition. Figure 3 shows a variety of gestures that are recognized with our proposed model including "Hello", "Help", "Thank you", "Bathroom" and "GoTo". In the images, coloured dots stand in for landmarks and these points of interest are associated with coordinates (x, y, and z) and visibility levels. The most important x, y, and z positions are face, left hand, and right hand and with this the pose visibility value is also considered. In this research, we make use of the MediaPipe library to provide a framework for gesture recognition. The test results shows that the quality of MediaPipe's gesture recognition module creates a significant impact on the precision of recommended models. We also compared the suggested LSTM architecture of hand gestures to the state-of-the-art LSTM model after training the dataset on the proposed design. Model 1 describes the performance accuracy of the proposed LSTM architecture, whereas Model 2 describes the performance accuracy of the state-of-the-art LSTM design. The accuracy of Model 1 and Model 2 after training on our dataset is 98.99% and 95.15% respectively as shown in Fig. 4. The training of the LSTM model is done for 120 epochs, and the model accuracy starts a rise after just 10 epochs. However, the model's accuracy drops somewhat between epochs 21 and 23 and after that it continues to improve. Our research demonstrates the effectiveness of our proposed deep learning models in gesture recognition. The loss graph displayed in Fig. 5 depicts the variations in training and validation loss over time, providing insights into the performance of the LSTM model.

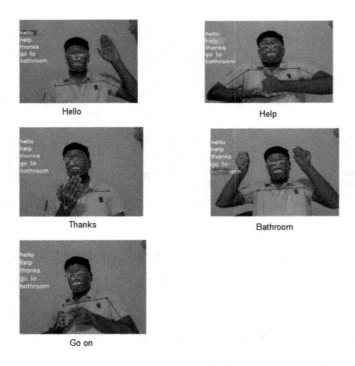

Fig. 3. Recognition of different hand gestures in real time

The loss function for both Model 1 and Model 2 gradually dropped during training, indicating that the models are learning and performing better. However, as it can be seen in the loss graphs that there are spikes in losses at specific times. The loss for Model 1 decreases steadily until epoch 84 and after that it spikes dramatically from 0.2620 to 1.0146 on the loss graph. After this initial increment in loss the model's performance improved, and the loss function subsequently decreased. The loss graph shows a fast surge followed by a steady decline and the loss reaches a minimum of 0.5060 towards the conclusion of training. The loss graph for Model 2 also gradually decreases before showing a little rise. The loss graph shows that after the first spike, the model's loss gradually goes down to a minimum of 0.1978 by the time training is complete. The confusion matrix used for comparing these models is shown in Fig. 6. The complete analysis of the two models results including loss, accuracy score and accuracy is shown in Table 2.

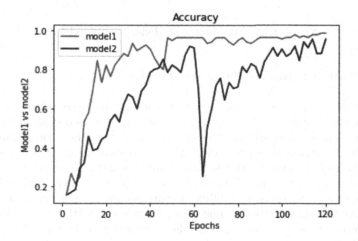

Fig. 4. Comparison of accuracy for Model 1 vs. Model 2.

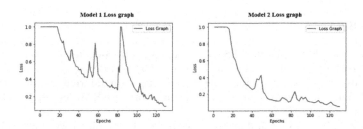

Fig. 5. Loss graph of Model 1 and Model 2.

Table 2. Result analysis of different models.

Model	Loss	Accuracy score	Accuracy (%)
Model 1	5.06%	1	98.99
Model 2	19.78%	0.933	95.15

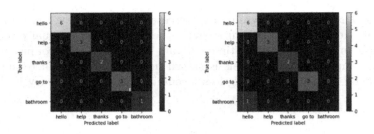

Fig. 6. Confusion matrix of Model 1 and Model 2.

5   Conclusion and Future Work

A methodology is proposed in this research work for recognizing hand motions by the use of MediaPipe with the LSTM network. Our results demonstrate that the suggested strategy outperforms the state-of-the-art method for gesture recognition. LSTM networks require a substantial amount of labeled training data to perform well. Gathering diverse and representative hand gesture data can be challenging, and the model's performance may suffer if the training dataset is limited in size or lacks variability. Future studies might use more realistic data set for the classification. Time series models like GRUs and Transformers may be necessary for interpreting complicated motions over extended periods of time. As human-computer interaction improves, it's possible that hand gesture recognition may find its way into more real-world applications.

References

1. Mittal, A., et al.: A modified LSTM model for continuous sign language recognition using leap motion. IEEE Sens. J. **19**(16), 7056–7063 (2019)
2. Aloysius, N., et al.: Incorporating relative position information in transformer-based sign language recognition and translation. IEEE Access **9**, 145929–145942 (2021)
3. Yang, Z., Zheng, X.: Hand gesture recognition based on trajectories features and computation-efficient reused LSTM network. IEEE Sens. J. **21**(15), 16945–16960 (2021)
4. Marina-Miranda, J., Traver, V.J.: Head and eye egocentric gesture recognition for human-robot interaction using eyewear cameras. IEEE Robot. Autom. Lett. **7**, 7067–7074 (2022)
5. Ong, A.J.S., Cabatuan, M., Tiberio, J.L.L., Jose, J.A.: LSTM-based traffic gesture recognition using MediaPipe pose. TENCON 2022 - 2022 IEEE Region 10 Conference (TENCON) (2022)
6. Areeb, Q.M., Maryam, Nadeem, M., Alroobaea, R., Anwer, F. Helping hearing-impaired in emergency situations: a deep learning-based approach. IEEE Access **10**, 8502–8517 (2022)
7. Sundar, B., Bagyammal, T.: American sign language recognition for alphabets using MediaPipe and LSTM. Procedia Comput. Sci. **215**, 642–651 (2022)

8. Xu, P.: A real-time hand gesture recognition and human-computer interaction system. ArXiv, abs/1704.07296 (2017). Accessed 6 July 2023.
9. Cheok, M.J., et al.: A review of hand gesture and sign language recognition techniques. Int. J. Mach. Learn. Cybernet. **10**(1), 131–153 (2017)
10. Iyer, V.H., Prakash, U.M., Vijay, A., Sathishkumar, P.: Sign language detection using action recognition. In: 2022 2nd International Conference on Advance Computing and Innovative Technologies in Engineering (ICACITE) (2022)
11. Ma, C., Wang, A., Chen, G., Xu, C.: Hand joints-based gesture recognition for noisy dataset using nested interval unscented Kalman filter with LSTM network. Vis. Comput. **34**, 1053–1063 (2018)
12. Olimov, B., et al.: AEDCN-Net: accurate and efficient deep convolutional neural network model for medical image segmentation. IEEE Access **9**, 154194–154203 (2021)
13. Choi, J.-W., Ryu, S.-J., Kim, J.-H.: Short-range radar based real-time hand gesture recognition using LSTM encoder. IEEE Access **7**, 33610–33618 (2019)
14. Wang, X., Garg, S., Tran, S.N., Bai, Q., Alty, J.: Hand tremor detection in videos with cluttered background using neural network based approaches. Health Inf. Sci. Syst. **9**, 1–14 (2021)
15. Herath, R.J., Ishanka, P.: An approach to Sri Lankan sign language recognition using deep learning with MediaPipe. In: Motahhir, S., Bossoufi, B. (eds.) ICDTA 2022. LNNS, vol. 454, pp. 449–459. Springer, Cham (2022). https://doi.org/10.1007/978-3-031-01942-5_45
16. Goel, P., Sharma, A., Goel, V., Jain, V.: Real-time sign language to text and speech translation and hand gesture recognition using the LSTM model. In: 2022 3rd International Conference on Issues and Challenges in Intelligent Computing Techniques (ICICT) (2022)
17. Chung, Y.-J., Shen, C.-H.: Research on deep learning with gesture recognition and LSTM in sign language. In: 2022 IEEE 5th International Conference on Knowledge Innovation and Invention (ICKII) (2022)

Channel Attention Network for Wireless Capsule Endoscopy Image Super-Resolution

Anjali Sarvaiya[1], Hiren Vaghela[1], Kishor Upla[1(✉)], Kiran Raja[2], and Marius Pedersen[2]

[1] Sardar Vallabhbhai National Institute of Technology (SVNIT), Surat, India
kishorupla@gmail.com
[2] Norwegian University of Science and Technology (NTNU), Gjøvik, Norway
{kiran.raja,marius.pedersen}@ntnu.no

Abstract. Wireless Capsule Endoscopy (WCE) is a technology used for examination of Gastrointestinal (GI) tract. WCE is comparatively pain-free process to examine the parts of GI tract including internal walls of small intestine, stomach and esophagus. WCE uses a capsule with camera installed on board to record video while traveling through GI tract. The acquired data is transmitted wirelessly to a device outside the body. Despite numerous benefits of WCE technology, the size and battery capacity limit the quality of acquired images. One such qualitative degradation of the spatial resolution of the images which is coarser depending on the frame rate of acquired video. An effective and economic way to enhance the spatial resolution of recorded samples is by employing software-driven algorithms referred to as "Super-Resolution (SR)". Recently, Deep learning-based approaches have been used in medical-domain due to their potential to obtain qualitative High-Resolution (HR) images without the cost of additional scans. This paper presents an approach for SR of WCE images with upscaling factor ×4 using deep neural network architecture which consists of a dense design of convolutional layers along with Channel Attention (CA) module to extract high-frequency details from Low-Resolution (LR) WCE images. The approach is validated on a derivative dataset of original Kvasir dataset consisting of 10, 000 samples and shows considerable improvement over the other state-of-the-art methods. Additionally, the perceptual quantitative assessment demonstrates the effectiveness of the proposed method over the others along with many distortion metrics.

Keywords: Wireless Capsule Endoscopy · Image Super-Resolution · Channel Attention

1 Introduction

The different medical imaging modalities such as Computerized Tomography (CT), Positron Emission Tomography (PET), Magnetic Resonance Imaging

H. Kaur et al. (Eds.): CVIP 2023, CCIS 2010, pp. 432–444, 2024.
https://doi.org/10.1007/978-3-031-58174-8_37

(MRI), Ultrasound Imaging, Endoscopy etc., have been well used to visualize the internal organs of the human body for clinical intervention. One of the promising and recent technologies is Wireless capsule endoscope (WCE) used for the screening and early diagnosis of diseases such as Crohn's disease, inflammatory bowel disease, colorectal cancer, etc. WCE is preferred over traditional endoscopy or colonoscopy as it is relatively easier for screening GI tract of a patient. With the decreased cost related to hospital stay along with other benefits (i.e., relatively painless), WCE can be conducted at a non-medical facility (e.g., residence of a patient). A pill-sized camera consisting of an optical dome, illuminator, imaging sensor, battery, and RF transmitter in a capsule-shaped structure with a length of 26 mm and a diameter of 11 mm is ingested by patients and the videos are transmitted to a processing unit for further diagnosis of abnormalities in GI tract [4]. However, the limitations of the pill camera used for WCE such as size and battery capacity constrains acquiring high quality images/videos. Limited optical ability (e.g., focus) of capsule camera and poor lighting conditions within GI tract limit the capture of High-Resolution (HR) images/videos.

Further, the transmission of HR images via a wireless transmission unit from pill-camera can consume high power and requires a high transmission bandwidth [3]. Image compression algorithms are therefore typically used in capsules to reduce power consumption and bandwidth, and this further degrades quality of acquired samples affecting both visual quality and diagnostic quality of the endoscopic recordings.

Despite the need for HR images, enhancing the resolution of images by increasing the size of the optics and sensor array is not always a feasible solution due to cost and space considerations. To circumvent this, software-driven methods known as "Super-Resolution (SR)", are generally employed in offline mode to enhance the spatial resolution of Low-Resolution (LR) images [17]. Super-resolved images can improve the accuracy of classification, segmentation and detection of abnormalities in medical data. A vast amount of work has been reported for performing SR of images from classical RGB cameras operating in visible spectrum. Motivated by such works, we super-resolve the WCE images in this work to improve visual and diagnostic quality of endoscopic recordings in this work. This paper aims to super-resolve WCE images with upscaling factor ×4 using a deep neural network architecture consisting of a dense design of convolutional layers along with a Channel Attention (CA) module to extract high-frequency details from Low-Resolution (LR) WCE images. Considering limited works in this direction and missing apt datasets, we make the following contributions in this work:

- A novel method super-resolving WCE images is proposed by employing Channel Attention Network (CAN) and a series of dense blocks in deep neural network architecture.
- The proposed model incorporates CAN module to dynamically rescale features, considering the inter-dependencies among various features such as edges, textures, color information, and other visual features. Additionally, the

utilization of short skip connections in convolution layers focuses on extracting high-level features to derive low-level features from the input LR image.
- Further, to address the unavailability of datasets suitable for SR tasks in WCE, a new derivative dataset sampled from original Kvasir Capsule Endoscopy [13]. Our new dataset comprises of 10,000 training samples that have been manually curated and pre-processed for the task of SR.
- The experiments validated with many state-of-the-art methods demonstrate the applicability of the proposed approach of SR. The results are further supplemented with a detailed analysis of distortion and perceptual metrics.

2 Related Work

Image super-resolution is a classical problem in the computer-vision community and based on the number of input images given to the algorithm, it can be divided into two categories: Multiple Image Super-Resolution (MISR) and Single Image Super-Resolution (SISR). The formal category takes multiple images instead of a single image in second category. Further, MISR demands additional task of image registration for appropriate SR output. Additionally, it also requires multiple LR images of same scene that may not be possible in many scenarios. Thus, comparatively, SISR is more practical and also very challenging which aims to reconstruct HR image from the single LR image [18].

The existing techniques for SISR can be categorized as traditional and learning-based methods. The traditional methods include interpolation-based and reconstruction based methods. The interpolation-based techniques are fast; however, they are inaccurate and often generate SR images with blur and ringing effects [14]. On the other side, the reconstruction based methods employ the statistical modeling along with prior term to reconstruct the HR image pausing it as an inverse function. These techniques are based on the types of priors to obtain qualitative SR image. Also, they fail to reconstruct spectral information with increasing upsampling factors. Contrarily, the learning-based methods use additional information from the database to learn the mapping function between low and high-resolution images. A variety of deep learning methods have been successfully applied to tackle SR task ranging from early Convolution Neural Network (CNN) to recent promising SR approaches using Generative Adversarial Nets (GANs). These techniques have greatly aided in obtaining better SR images for visible images. Adapting these techniques for medical data will also aid in offering easier detection facilities in the medical area.

The pioneering effort for image SR using CNN by Dong et al. [2] with shallow architecture consisting of one hidden layer only known as SRCNN provided better results than other state-of-the-art reconstruction-based methods. The success of SRCNN led to numerous SR works to achieve higher performance on PSNR/SSIM, such as using recursive convolutional network for feature extraction [9], stacking more convolutional filters [8], adding long and dense residual connections [15] and removing batch normalization layers to preserve range flexibility from networks [11]. Recently, Zhang et al. [19] designed a very deep CNN with stacked channel attention modules, referred as Residual Channel Attention Network (RCAN), and achieved state-of-the-art PSNR/SSIM. The aforementioned methods are considered as PSNR-oriented methods since they only take Mean Square Error (MSE) or Mean Absolute Error (MAE) as loss function during the network training, which is an intuitive idea to increase PSNR metric. Additionally, many works on image SR have been published where bicubic interpolation is used to pre-upsample input LR image and then apply a deep network for high-frequency reconstruction; however, this idea increases the computational costs. While other works are based on a post-upscaling strategy for increasing resolution of input LR observation. However, the generated images still become over-smoothed in many post-upscaling methods [10]. Since PSNR often disagrees with visual evaluation by human observers, such results are intolerable in medical imaging applications, which may hinder related clinical applications such as disease diagnosis and lesion detection.

To restore high-frequency details and obtain superior perceptual results in SISR, researchers train the CNN model with loss computed on feature level [7] instead on output images and employ GAN [5] to improve SR images as realistic as possible. Ledig et al. [10] made first attempt with GAN-based SR framework (SRGAN) which contains a generator network for high-resolution image generation. A discriminator network is employed in SRGAN for recognizing generated images from real-world images with perceptual and GAN loss functions. The SRGAN method obtained superior visual results than the PSNR-oriented methods though it compromised some PSNR/SSIM values. The success of CNN and GAN based models for SR of visible images was further extended for the medical images too. For instance, Mahapatra et al. in [12] use Progressive GAN (P-GAN) on MRI images for accurate detection of anatomical landmarks and pathology segmentation. Additionally, some SR techniques have also been utilized to increase the quality of images acquired by low-resolution endoscopic cameras. Recently, Yasin et al. [1] has proposed and quantitatively validate a novel framework to learn a mapping from low-to-high resolution conventional endoscopic images. They combine conditional adversarial networks with a spatial attention block to improve the resolution by up to factors of ×8, ×10, ×12 respectively. However, this approach is limited to conventional endoscopy images. With a detailed review of different SR methods, we summarize following research gap.

- There is a scarcity of specific SR techniques developed and applied to endoscopy images. The employability of SR is limited to different medical modalities such as MRI, CT, ultrasound, etc.
- Secondly, the current research on image super-resolution (SR) in the field of endoscopy is primarily focused on conventional endoscopy [17] and not on WCE.

3   Proposed Approach

The architecture of the proposed method is depicted in Fig. 1 for the task of SR of WCE images for upscaling factor ×4. It aims to learn mapping between

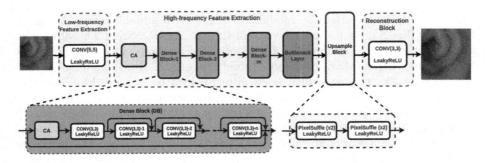

Fig. 1. The network architecture of the proposed model.

LR and HR WCE images. First, the given LR WCE image is pass through the different CNN modules to extract the rich features. Then, an upsampling nework is employed to accomplish upscling of feature maps to the desired factor and finally, an SR image is reconstructed through the reconstruction module. The proposed CNN network is divided in the following four modules as per its functionality:

- Low-frequency Feature Extractor (LFE)
- High-frequency Feature Extractor (HFE)
- Upsample Block
- Reconstruction Block

The detailed description related to each of above module is elaborated in the following subsections.

3.1   Low-Frequency Feature Extractor (LFE)

The given LR WCE image is first passed to the Low-frequency Feature Extractor (LFE) module. It includes single convolutional layer to extract features from LR observation. The kernel size, number of features, and stride value in this convolution layer are set to 5, 128, and 1, respectively. The larger receptive field is chosen in the first CNN layer to extract low-frequency details from the LR observation. A Leaky Rectified Linear Activation (LReLU) function is employed in the proposed architecture, which efficiently improves the learning performance at each layer. The parameters associated with LReLU activation at different layers are learned to make appropriate activation shapes to improve the SR performance.

3.2   High-Frequency Feature Extractor (HFE)

The different feature maps available at the output of LFE module are applied to High-frequency Feature Extractor (HFE) module (see Fig. 1). The design of HFE module is responsible for preserving the high-frequency details in the SR image. It consists of Channel Attention (CA) module followed by m number of

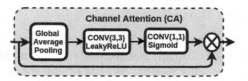

Fig. 2. The design of the Channel Attention (CA) used in the proposed model.

Dense Blocks (DBs) to improve the learning fidelity of the network. One skip connection is also added in the design of each DBs to overcome the problem of vanishing gradient. Finally, a bottleneck layer is added at the end of HFE module to control the number of feature maps. In wireless capsule, the acquired images do not contain high-frequency details due device limitations. In the proposed architecture, the novel design of Dense Block (DB) helps to reconstruct high-frequency details in the SR image. Its architectural design is depicted in Fig. 1 which comprises of one CA layer, one convolution layer with a kernel size of 3 followed by n number of convolutional blocks having kernel size 3. Additionally, one skip connection is also added in each convolutional layer to preserve meaningful features. Such design of DBs improves the performance of the network by extracting rich features from the LR observation.

Further, we employ CA module in each DB as well as at first block in HFE module to perform adaptive re-scaling of the channel-wise features. The architecture of CA network is displayed in Fig. 2. It consists of global average pooling followed by convolutional layer with kernel size of 3 with LReLU activation function. Then, it passes through convolutional neural network with kernel size 3 with sigmoid activation function and performs element wise multiplication with input. By dynamically recalibrating the channel-wise feature responses, CA encourages the model to focus on relevant features, leading to improved representation of the underlying structures and textures in the image. The incorporation of CA enables the model to selectively attend to informative channels, resulting in enhanced feature representation and preservation of fine details. Further, one can see from Fig. 1 that all feature maps in the network are concatenated, yielding more number of inputs for the subsequent Upscaling Block. Thus, if a large number of feature maps are directly fed into Upscaling Block, it will significantly increase the computational cost and size of the model. Hence, it is reasonable to reduce the number of input feature maps to keep model compact and to improve the computational efficiency. For this purpose, we utilize a bottleneck layer prior to upsample block. The bottleneck layer consists of a convolution layer having kernel size 1×1 with LReLU activation function.

3.3 Upsample Block

To upscale the feature maps to the desired scaling factor (i.e. ×4), the upsampling block is utilized. A series of two pixel-shuffle upsamplers with each of upsampling factor ×2 are employed. They are equipped with 64 feature maps and LReLU activation function.

3.4   Reconstruction Block

Finally, the output obtained from the Upsampling Block with the desired scaling factor (i.e. ×4) is passed through the Reconstruction module to generate the output WCE SR image. This module consists of one convolution layers with a kernel size of 3 and three channels of output (i.e., RGB image).

4   Experimental Analysis

The design of the proposed model is validated by conducting series of experiments. The SR results are benchmarked against state-of-the-art models such as SRDenseNet [15], RCAN [19], SRGAN [10] and ESRGAN [16] for visual and quantitative assessments. We employ quantitative evaluations performed by Peak Signal to Noise Ratio (PSNR) and Structural Similarity Index Metric (SSIM) in addition to perceptual metric i.e., Learned Perceptual Image Patch Similarity (LPIPS). In this section, we elaborate the different aspects of experimental results of the proposed method in details.

4.1   Dataset

This work introduces a noteworthy contribution by developing a novel derivative dataset from the existing Kvasir Capsule Endoscopy Dataset [13] which primarily consists of WCE images. In Kvasir dataset, each image is in RGB color space with size of 336 × 336 pixels. It contains a total of 47, 236 images, categorized according to different medical anomalies. As the dataset contained redundant images with border areas with black pixels, we have curated the dataset for the SR task by manually removing border pixels and redundant images from the Kvasir dataset. Thus, a new SR dataset, therefore, consists of 10, 000 training images, 550 validation images and 1000 testing images[1]. As mentioned earlier, the WCE images from the original Kvasir dataset containing non-informative part in the border area. Those regions are removed manually through cropping resulting images with 280 × 280 pixels. The proposed model along with all other models are experimented on the new dataset and SR results are obtained.

4.2   Training Details

The proposed SR algorithm is trained in a supervised manner. Hence, to prepare LR-HR pair of WCE images, we consider the original images as the HR image and apply bicubic down-sampling with factor ×4 to obtain LR image. These RGB LR-HR pairs are fed to the proposed model for training purpose. Further, the training process aimed to minimize the loss function, which was taken as the Mean Squared Error (MSE) Loss. To initialize the network parameters, we follow Kaiming initialization [6] and train it up to 300 epochs with a maximum batch size 32. Additionally, the Adam optimizer is used with β_1 and β_2 of 0.9 and

---

[1] The dataset will be made available to researchers working on SR task.

0.99, respectively. Here, we set a learning rate of 1×10^{-4} and decayed it by half at every 2×10^4 number of iterations. In the proposed network, we empirically choose the number of Dense Blocks (DBs) as eight (i.e., $m = 8$) and number of convolutional layer with skip connection used in Dense Blocks (DBs) is set to 8 (i.e., $n = 8$).

4.3   Comparison with State-of-the-Art Models

Qualitative Analysis: The qualitative comparison of various SR methods for scaling factor of ×4 is depicted in Fig. 3. Through a comprehensive qualitative analysis, we evaluate the performance of the proposed method by comparing it to various state-of-the-art methods such as SRDensenet, RCAN, SRGAN, and ESRGAN. It is apparent from Fig. 3 that the proposed method consistently demonstrates superior results in terms of enhancing the resolution and capturing fine details in WCE images. We observe that the proposed model successfully restores fine details such as blood vessels, mucosal patterns, and small lesions, which were previously indistinguishable in low-resolution images. This improvement enables medical professionals to perform a more accurate analysis, potentially leading to earlier detection of diseases and better patient outcomes. When compared to CNN-based methods like SRDensenet and RCAN, our proposed model excels in preserving high-frequency details (see Fig. 3). While the PSNR and SSIM metrics for RCAN are similar to our proposed model (see Table 1), the perceptual and visual quality of the proposed model surpasses that of RCAN. In contrast to GAN-based methods such as SRGAN and ESRGAN, the proposed model effectively recovers fine details. The SR results generated by ESRGAN exhibit block artifacts, which are absent in the outputs of our proposed method. Consequently, our method outperforms these SR methods by preserving texture and structural details.

The visual quality of images can be assisted by Structural Similarity Index (SSIM) maps, which provide insights into the perceptual similarity between the reference (original) and the reconstructed (super-resolved) images. Thus, it offers a visual representation of the structural and textural differences between the two images. For a better assessment of visual quality, we have generated SSIM maps of the proposed model and compared it with other SR methods which are depicted in Fig. 4. In SSIM map, regions with high similarity are typically depicted as brighter areas, indicating that the reconstructed image closely matches the reference image in terms of structure and texture. Conversely, darker regions indicate areas of lower similarity, suggesting discrepancies or distortions in the reconstructed image compared to the reference. It can be observed that the proposed model contains more brighter area compared to the other SR methods (See Fig. 4).

Quantitative Analysis. This section discusses the quantitative comparison in terms of distortion metrics such as PSNR and SSIM and perceptual metric such as LPIPS obtained using the proposed and recent existing supervised SR models. To validate the SR results quantitatively, the average SSIM and PSNR values for

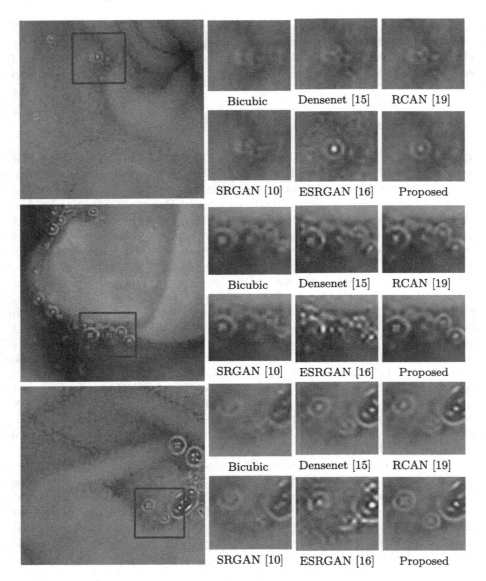

Fig. 3. The qualitative comparison of proposed SR model with other state-of-the-art models.

the testing images of each model are provided in Table 1. We calculated the average PSNR and SSIM on Y channel as well as the RGB channels. From the table, it can be observed that the proposed model has the highest PSNR in both Y and RGB channels. Additionally, the proposed model also demonstrates the highest SSIM values, implying better structural similarity. When considering LPIPS for

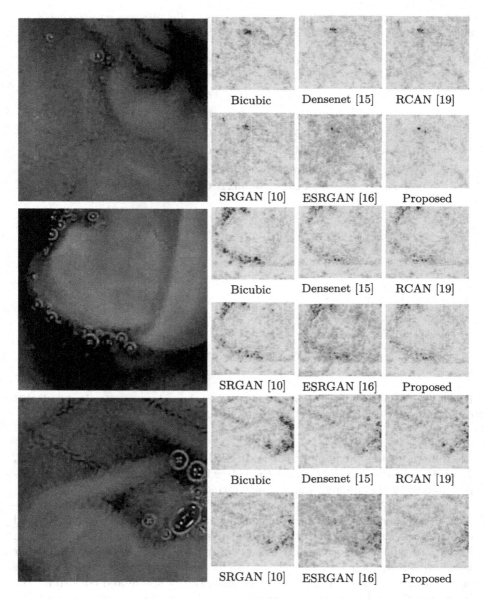

Fig. 4. The qualitative comparision of proposed and other existing models using SSIM maps. Here, yellow region shows similarity and blue region shows disimilarity. (Color figure online)

perceptual image comparison, lower LPIPS values emphasize the model's ability to capture perceptual similarity effectively. The LPIPS of the proposed model is slightly inferior when compared to SRDensenet and RCAN methods. However,

Table 1. The quantitative comparison of the proposed model over other models using different metrics such as PSNR, SSIM and LPIPS on RGB and Y-channels.

Model	PSNR ↑		SSIM ↑		LPIPS↓
	Y-channel	RGB	Y-channel	RGB	RGB
Bicubic	38.1069	37.2111	0.9296	0.9057	0.2310
SRGAN [10]	38.0377	37.0021	0.9291	0.9049	0.1972
ESRGAN [16]	33.4854	33.2381	0.8725	0.8334	0.2752
SRDenseNet [15]	39.6842	38.8596	0.9401	0.9369	0.1353
RCAN [19]	40.1438	39.4613	0.9427	0.9371	0.1359
Proposed	**40.2431**	**39.5521**	**0.9490**	**0.9386**	**0.1360**

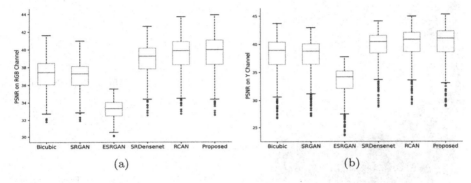

Fig. 5. The PSNR comparison of all models using box plots: (a) Box-Plot of PSNR comparison on RGB Channel (b) Box-Plot of PSNR comparison on Y Channel

these methods exhibit poor PSNR and SSIM values than the proposed model. Thus, the proposed model exhibits the better LPIPS along with distortions metrics among all the different models, suggesting superior perceptual similarity.

Additionally, to ensure the proposed model's performance consistency in comparison to other state-of-the-art models the statistical analysis is also conducted on the SR results. For this statistical analysis, the box-plots are depicted in Fig. 5 & 6 which demonstrate a box between 25% and 75% values and other values which are defined by circles known as outliers below the higher quartile of the boxplot. Thus, for a model to be statistically stable and consistent, the box's size should be as small as possible and also number of outliers should be low as well with high median value. We have conducted statistical analysis on PSNR and SSIM values for RGB and Y channel both as displayed in Fig. 5 and Fig. 6. It can be observed from these box-plots that the proposed model has the smallest size of the quartile box and lowest number of outliers with having high median among all the models indicating its stability and consistency over the other state-of-the-art methods.

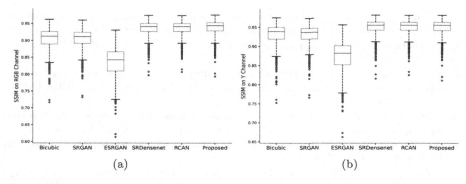

(a)   (b)

Fig. 6. The SSIM comparison of all models using box plots: (a) Box-Plot of SSIM comparison on RGB Channel (b) Box-Plot of SSIM comparison on Y Channel

5   Conclusion

Due to the hardware limitations of the WCE sensors, the captured samples results in coarser resolution which affects the visual quality and the diagnostic quality of images. We have presented a new SR approach using dense connections and channel attention modules to convert LR images to SR images. As the proposed network integrates Low Frequency Extractor (LFE), High Frequency Extractor (HFE) and Upsample Block, the proposed approach is able to effectively extract details and recover the structure details from LR observations. Experiments show that the proposed network not only performs better than other existing state-of-the-art SR models in terms of both quantitatively and qualitatively assessment, but also shows consistency over other methods. A future direction in this work is to focus on improving the perceptual quality and assessing it with medical practitioners.

Acknowledgment. Authors are thankful to Research Council of Norway (RCN) for International Network for Capsule Imaging in Endoscopy (CapsNetwork) project managed by Department of computer science, Norwegian University of Science and technology (NTNU), Norway for providing support for this research work.

References

1. Almalioglu, Y., et al.: EndoL2H: deep super-resolution for capsule endoscopy. IEEE Trans. Med. Imaging **39**(12), 4297–4309 (2020)
2. Dong, C., Loy, C.C., He, K., Tang, X.: Learning a deep convolutional network for image super-resolution. In: Fleet, D., Pajdla, T., Schiele, B., Tuytelaars, T. (eds.) ECCV 2014. LNCS, vol. 8692, pp. 184–199. Springer, Cham (2014). https://doi.org/10.1007/978-3-319-10593-2_13
3. Fante, K.A., Bhaumik, B., Chatterjee, S.: Design and implementation of computationally efficient image compressor for wireless capsule endoscopy. Circ. Syst. Signal Process. **35**, 1677–1703 (2016)

4. Iddan, G., Meron, G., Glukhovsky, A., Swain, P.: Wireless capsule endoscopy. Nature **405**(6785), 417 (2000). https://doi.org/10.1038/35013140
5. Goodfellow, I., et al.: Generative adversarial networks. Commun. ACM **63**(11), 139–144 (2020)
6. He, K., Zhang, X., Ren, S., Sun, J.: Delving deep into rectifiers: surpassing human-level performance on ImageNet classification. In: Proceedings of the IEEE-ICCV, pp. 1026–1034 (2015)
7. Johnson, J., Alahi, A., Fei-Fei, L.: Perceptual losses for real-time style transfer and super-resolution. In: Leibe, B., Matas, J., Sebe, N., Welling, M. (eds.) ECCV 2016. LNCS, vol. 9906, pp. 694–711. Springer, Cham (2016). https://doi.org/10.1007/978-3-319-46475-6_43
8. Kim, J., Lee, J.K., Lee, K.M.: Accurate image super-resolution using very deep convolutional networks. In: Proceedings of the IEEE Conference on CVPR, pp. 1646–1654 (2016)
9. Kim, J., Lee, J.K., Lee, K.M.: Deeply-recursive convolutional network for image super-resolution. In: Proceedings of the IEEE Conference on CVPR, pp. 1637–1645 (2016)
10. Ledig, C., et al.: Photo-realistic single image super-resolution using a generative adversarial network. In: Proceedings of the IEEE Conference on CVPR, pp. 4681–4690 (2017)
11. Lim, B., Son, S., Kim, H., Nah, S., Mu Lee, K.: Enhanced deep residual networks for single image super-resolution. In: Proceedings of the IEEE Conference on CVPR Workshops, pp. 136–144 (2017)
12. Mahapatra, D., Bozorgtabar, B., Garnavi, R.: Image super-resolution using progressive generative adversarial networks for medical image analysis. Comput. Med. Imaging Graph. **71**, 30–39 (2019)
13. Pogorelov, K., et al..: KVASIR: a multi-class image dataset for computer aided gastrointestinal disease detection. In: Proceedings of the 8th ACM on Multimedia Systems Conference, MMSys 2017, pp. 164–169. ACM, New York (2017)
14. Singh, A., Singh, J.: Super resolution applications in modern digital image processing. Int. J. Comput. Appl. **150**, 6–8 (2016)
15. Tong, T., Li, G., Liu, X., Gao, Q.: Image super-resolution using dense skip connections. In: 2017 IEEE-ICCV, pp. 4809–4817 (2017)
16. Wang, X., et al.: ESRGAN: enhanced super-resolution generative adversarial networks. In: Leal-Taixé, L., Roth, S. (eds.) ECCV 2018. LNCS, vol. 11133, pp. 63–79. Springer, Cham (2019). https://doi.org/10.1007/978-3-030-11021-5_5
17. Wang, Y., Cai, C., Zou, Y.X.: Single image super-resolution via adaptive dictionary pair learning for wireless capsule endoscopy image. In: 2015 IEEE International Conference on Digital Signal Processing (DSP), pp. 595–599 (2015). https://doi.org/10.1109/ICDSP.2015.7251943
18. Yang, W., Zhang, X., Tian, Y., Wang, W., Xue, J.H., Liao, Q.: Deep learning for single image super-resolution: a brief review. IEEE Trans. Multimed. **21**(12), 3106–3121 (2019)
19. Zhang, Y., Li, K., Li, K., Wang, L., Zhong, B., Fu, Y.: Image super-resolution using very deep residual channel attention networks. In: ECCV, pp. 286–301 (2018)

COMPUSR: Computationally Efficient Unsupervised Super-Resolution Approach for Wireless Capsule Endoscopy

Nirban Saha[1], Anjali Sarvaiya[1], Kishor Upla[1(✉)], Kiran Raja[2], and Marius Pedersen[2]

[1] Sardar Vallabhbhai National Institute of Technology (SVNIT), Surat, India
kishorupla@gmail.com
[2] Norwegian University of Science and Technology (NTNU), Gjøvik, Norway
{kiran.raja,marius.pedersen}@ntnu.no

Abstract. Wireless Capsule Endoscopy (WCE) is an imaging technology for diseases related to Gastrointestinal (GI) track. However, due to limited hardware, the spatial resolution of acquired images is usually coarser leading to poor diagnostic quality. To enhance high-frequency details associated to edges, object boundaries, corners, etc., which are required for detection and recognition tasks, High-Resolution (HR) images are usually constructed through software-driven Super-Resolution (SR) techniques. Deep learning-based SR approaches has been frequently explored in the computer-vision community recently to increase the SR picture's quality. However, the prime barrier associated with the presently available deep learning SR approaches is the usage of supervised training where, LR images are simulated by using known deterioration (for instance, bicubic downsampling) from the acquired HR images. It is apparent that the deep models trained on such LR-HR pair exhibits poor generalization on the real LR observation. On the other hand, it is challenging to collect large clinical datasets consisting of true LR-HR pair for supervised learning. To circumvent this problem, we propose a computationally efficient unsupervised approach for SR task using Generative Adversarial Network (GAN) for WCE images (referred as *COMPUSR*). The proposed model avoids LR-HR pair and is trained using unsupervised strategy to learn the degradation of LR observation. It is validated on a derivative dataset of the original Kvasir dataset consisting of $10,000$ training samples and reveals considerable improvement over the other state-of-the-art methods on subjective and quantitative evaluations. Remarkably, the proposed approach needs significantly less number of learnable parameters (i.e., 2.4M) and a number of GFLOPS (i.e., 91.56G) than that of other approaches.

Keywords: Super-Resolution · Wireless Capsule Endoscopy · Unsupervised Approach · GAN · Computational Efficient

© The Author(s), under exclusive license to Springer Nature Switzerland AG 2024
H. Kaur et al. (Eds.): CVIP 2023, CCIS 2010, pp. 445–460, 2024.
https://doi.org/10.1007/978-3-031-58174-8_38

1   Introduction

In recent years, medical domain has witnessed significant advancements, enabling healthcare professionals to obtain detailed visual information for the diagnosis and treatment for various diseases accurately. Among these, Wireless Capsule Endoscopy (WCE) is a non-invasive and patient-friendly imaging technique that is emerging as a powerful tool for investigating diseases related to the Gastrointestinal (GI) tract. It involves the ingestion of a small capsule pill equipped with a camera that acquires images while traveling through the digestive tract. There are numerous benefits of this technology as compared to traditional endoscopy or colonoscopy which is painful and also demands medical professionals for data collection. However, due to several inherent factors associated with the imaging process, the spatial resolution of WCE images is typically coarser. Size of capsule, battery life, transmission bandwidth and limitations of the imaging sensor within the capsule lead to practical limitations in WCE imaging. Thus, WCE images typically exhibit poor spatial resolution when compared to other advanced medical imaging modalities such as Computed Tomography (CT) or Magnetic Resonance Imaging (MRI). Consequently, the Low-Resolution (LR) of WCE images presents challenges to doctors for accurate diagnosis of disease, motivating the need of super-resolution techniques to enhance the image quality and enable more precise medical interpretations. Nevertheless, the feasibility of resolving the image resolution challenge by enlarging the optics and sensor array is hindered by factors such as cost and critical space limitations.

The field of computer-vision has witnessed significant progress in Super-Resolution (SR) techniques, which aim to enhance the spatial resolution and quality of LR images. While there have been significant advancements in SR algorithms, their application in the domain of WCE images remains relatively unexplored. Furthermore, recent super-resolution (SR) approaches predominantly utilize example-based training methods, learning to enhance image resolution through matched LR and HR image pairs. Nonetheless, due to a scarcity of HR endoscopy images, these pairings are not commonly found in this area. An option is to generate these pairs synthetically; however, obtaining this is only realistically possible if the acquisition procedure is highly well-defined. In most cases, only an approximate understanding of the acquisition process exists. By known downsampling (i.e., bicubic downsampling) and LR images are simulated. Thus, supervised training is performed on deep models by pair of LR-HR images in which LR is not acquired from true camera and hence, deep model is relatively able to learn degradation of simulated LR samples. Thus, it is apparent that when such supervised trained model encounters true LR observation, it exhibits poor generalization as they have been trained on simulated LR-HR pair. The idea to generate true pair of LR-HR imaging is worthless in medical domain as it needs camera settings to be varied accordingly. For these reasons, we propose a deep learning architecture trained unsupervisedly, without the need for the previously specified alignment of LR and HR on a one-to-one basis anymore. This research paper proposes a computationally efficient unsupervised approach for wireless capsule endoscopy image super-resolution. The main objective is to leverage the inherent structure and spatial information present in the low-resolution WCE images to generate high-resolution images without the need for explicit supervision. The primary benefits of the suggested network are outlined as follows,

- An unsupervised approach for SR of WCE images is proposed using Generative Adversarial Network (GAN) for upscaling factor ×4. To the best of our knowledge, this is first SR approach trained in unsupervised manner for WCE images. Without explicitly needing to estimate the degradation of the same, the proposed method has been trained end-to-end to infer SR results for WCE LR photos.
- The architectural aspects of the proposed model consists a new Basic Block (BB) which is incorporated to learn the rich characteristics from LR observation. As suggested in DUSGAN model [17], two discriminator networks have been employed where the first one is used to discriminate the features between the generated SR and unpaired HR images and the second discriminator uses to discriminate high-frequency features of SR and unpaired HR to make distinctions depending on the noise in a picture. Additionally, we add a texture loss to preserve the texture details of WCE images.
- Additionally, the proposed method is trained on the derivative dataset of original Kvasir dataset. The new dataset consists of 10,000 training images with manual cropping of unwanted border pixels. The experimental evaluation on the new dataset reveals considerable improvement in the SR images obtained using the proposed method both in terms of visual and quantitative assessments over the state-of-the-art unsupervised methods.
- Remarkably, the architecture of the proposed method needs considerably fewer trainable parameters and less Multi-Adds (i.e., FLOPS) than that of other methods which is beneficial for the implementation of the proposed model on the low computational devices in the future.

2 Related Works

The deep learning based SR methods aim to learn complex relationship between given LR and HR images. Dong et al. [3] introduced the pioneer SR network referred as Super-Resolution Convolutional Neural Network (SRCNN). The success of SRCNN lead to numerous SR works to achieve better SR performance based on distortion metrics such as PSNR/SSIM. Such networks are based on feature extraction using a recursive convolutional network [7], stacking more convolutional filters [6], adding long and dense residual connections [19] and deleting batch normalization layers to retain network range flexibility [8]. Subsequent to the favorable outcomes achieved in enhancing image resolution for natural RGB images, the utilization of these techniques in the domain of medical imaging emerged, recently. Rueda et al. in [1] apply HR and LR dictionaries learned from MRI images. This network performs well during training but it fails to show better accuracy for testing dataset. Progressive generative adversarial network (P-GAN) was proposed by Mahapatra et al. in [14] for accurate recognition of anatomical landmarks in medical images. In addition to above, many SR methods have been proposed to improve the quality of pictures taken by LR endoscopic cameras. For instance, Hafner et al. [13] proposed an SR algorithm that is based on the Projection onto Convex Sets (POCS) strategy. They seek to make visible subtleties such as mucosal structures that may not be seen under low-magnification HD endoscope conditions. This architecture is based on image restoration, registration, and fusion. Importantly, the common limitation in the aforementioned studies is the use of supervised training, which struggles to generalize effectively to real-world data that differs significantly from synthetically generated low-resolution observations [11].

In the supervised training, CNN models are trained in a supervised manner using known degraded LR images, including downsampling (i.e., bicubic), along with their corresponding HR images. However, due to differences in the distribution of synthetic LR images when compared to true LR observations in real-world scenarios, CNN models often show poor generalization on real-world LR images. One possible solution to address this challenge is to utilize real LR-HR pairs for training the network, which often is not feasible for all modalities and also limited to selected upscaling factors. On the other direction, Lugmayr et al. [11] presented the concept of unsupervised learning for training the CNN model for SR for visible images, overcome the LR-HR pair formation constraint. They used cycleGAN to understand how LR pictures in the real world are distributed. The SR network was trained in a supervised fashion using a dataset of LR pictures acquired using HR to LR. This idea was further explored by Fritsche et al. [12] in ESRGAN, which was the winning architecture in the AIM-2019 SR competition. This entails the capacity to conduct separate training of the low-resolution (LR) distribution for both low and high-frequency features, as described in [12], and it is integrated into the SRResCGAN framework [20] for the concurrent learning of degradation and super-resolution networks. It is trained with relativistic GAN, L1, Total-Variation (TV) and VGG losses. In the context of, in dSRVAE [9], the sequential implementation of de-noising followed by super-resolution is suggested. Here, an encoder-decoder architecture has been employed to eliminate noise from the low-resolution (LR) images. USISResNet [18], incorporates adversarial learning for unsupervised domain adaptation, enabling the conversion of noisy real LR images into clean SR images. However, Prajapati et al. [18] adopted more unpaired LR-HR dataset for direct learning and achieved better SR results for the unsupervised case. To enhance the SR solutions, the authors in [18] used the GAN-based technique with one generator and two discriminators and conducted training with various loss functions, including quality evaluation, total variation, content losses, and GAN. With a detailed review of different SR methods, we summarize the following research gap:

- In the medical domain, it is difficult to obtain large clinical datasets consisting of high and low resolution samples. Thus, the lack of such large training dataset often presents obstacles for supervised training of deep models.

– Further, the SR method in [2] is based on predicating learning from LR image directly. To obtain accurate SR findings, such technique requires known downsampling kernel, which is typically not accessible in real-world situations.
– Many techniques involve augmentation with a variety of degradations and make the deep network durable against such distortions, as opposed to learning the distribution of noisy LR pictures. However, these techniques fall short when the noise in augmented photos is different from the noise in true LR images.

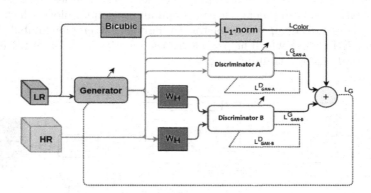

Fig. 1. The suggested method's block diagram i.e., *COMPUSR*. Here, W_H indicates kernel of High Pass Filter (HPF).

3   Proposed Method

To overcome the above listed limitations of the existing SR works, here we attempt to obtain SR of WCE images using unsupervised training for upscaling factor ×4 (referred as *COMPUSR*). The block diagram of the proposed method is depicted in Fig. 1. It is inspired from DUS-GAN model [17] which is intended for visible images. Thus, to become acquainted with straight domain transfer from LR to HR images, we employ generative adversarial learning which incorporate three networks: a generator (i.e., G), and two discriminators (i.e., D_A and D_B).

The true LR observation is first transmitted via the generator network G to get an SR images. The generated SR picture is subsequently differentiated from an unpaired HR picture using Discriminator-A (D_A). This discriminator operates on the SR space directly. As seen in Fig. 1, the second Discriminator-B (D_B) is utilized to enhance the quality of SR image by emphasizing high-frequency elements from both SR and unpaired HR images. Further, LSGAN loss is employed commonly in Discriminator-A and Discriminator-B to account for network stability. In order to integrate unsupervised learning, which alters the color information in the SR picture, a loss that corresponds to the color information in the SR version of the original LR image is sought in the suggested model. An L1 loss between SR and bicubically upsampled LR pictures is employed for this assignment in order to maintain the authenticity of color space in the SR image.

3.1 Generator Network (G)

The generator network architecture is depicted in Fig. 2. It consists one convolution block that extracts the low-frequency features, a series of Basic Blocks (BBs) to extract high-frequency features and an upsampler block which upsamples the LR features by upsample factor ×4. Further, we employ Global Residual Learning (GRL) block which helps to learn the identity function of LR image as well as to stabilize the training purpose.

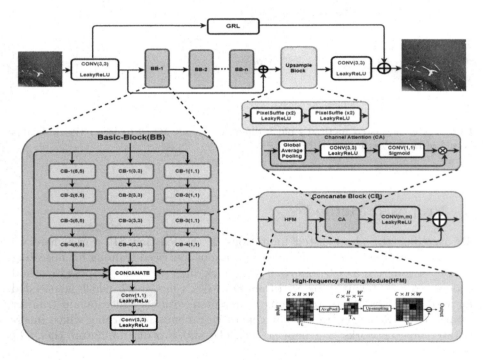

Fig. 2. The architecture of the Generator network used in the proposed method (i.e., *COMPUSR*).

Initially, an LR image is applied to a single convolution layer of 3 × 3 kernel size with LeakyReLU activation function, which extracts the low-frequency features such as shape, color, and texture from LR observation. To extract high-frequency details such as edges and structures, we pass the low-frequency features to n number of Basic Blocks (BB). Further, one skip connection is also added at the end of BBs to overcome the problem of vanishing gradient. In the proposed architecture, the novel design of BB helps to retain high-frequency details in the SR image. The architecture of BB is depicted in Fig. 2 which comprises of three parallel branches of Concanate Block (CB) with kernel size 5, 3 and 1, respectively. In each parallel branch, we deploy total 4 CBs in a series connection and one skip connection. Each parallel branch is concatenated and pass through two convolution layers which helps to maintain the same amount of channels after concatenation and thus reducing the amount of parameters that can be trained.

Moreover, each CB block consists a High-frequency Module (HFM) block, a Channel Attention (CA), and convolution layer of (m, m), where m is the kernel size in each parallel branch as depicted in Fig. 2. Such CB blocks help the network to learn high-frequency details. The channel-wise characteristics are adaptively rescaled using the CA module for improved generalization of the generator network. We have used convolution layers of different kernel sizes parallelly such that each channel can learn different features from each other and then finally all these channels are concatenated to preserve the learned features. Inspired from [10], the design of HFM block is used to estimate the high-frequency information from the LR space. The block diagram representation of HFM network is displayed in Fig. 2. Here, one can see that the input image dimension is $C \times H \times W$ and average pooling is applied to input feature map T_L. Here, k denotes the pooling layer's kernel size as well as the size of the intermediate feature map T_A is $C \times \frac{H}{k} \times \frac{W}{k}$. Each value in T_A might be thought of as the typical intensity of any particular little region of T_L. After that, T_A is upsampled in order to obtain a new tensor T_U of size $C \times H \times W$. Thus, T_U is viewed as an indication of the average smoothness information in comparison to the original T_L. Finally, T_U is removed element by element from T_L to collect the high-frequency data.

Finally, to upscale the feature maps to the desired scaling factor (i.e., $\times 4$), the up-sampling block is utilized. A series of two pixel-shuffle upsamplers with each of upsampling factor $\times 2$ are employed with LReLU activation function. In the last, an output obtained from the Upsampling Block with the desired scaling factor (i.e., $\times 4$) is passed through the convolution layer to generate the output WCE SR image. Additionally, we also employ the Global Residual Learning (GRL) block that consists a bicubic interpolation of upscale factor $\times 4$. The input LR image is pass through the GRL block and generates a bicubically upsample image that is added with the last convolutional layer to retain the low-frequency features in SR image and it also stabilizes the training process.

3.2 Discriminator Networks (i.e., Discriminator-A and Discriminator-B)

To improve SR performance, two networks of discriminators (Discriminator-A and Discriminator-B) are deployed. Both discriminators follow the same design as depicted in Fig. 3. Instead of attempting to determine if a picture is real or a hallucination, the proposed model's discriminator aims to discern $N \times N$ patches using the idea of PatchGAN [5]. As depicted in Fig. 3, convolutional layers make up the discriminator's several layers. The input images are sent via the first convolutional layer without batch normalisation; however, to increase the network's learning capacity, four convolutional layers with batch normalisation are used. To produce a single output image in the final layer, we employ a convolutional layer. With the exception of the last layer, which employs the sigmoid activation map the probability values function between 0 and 1 for various patches, LeakyReLU is used to activate all levels of the discriminator network. The sigmoid activation function has a bounded range between 0 and 1. This property helps in stabilizing the gradient during back-propagation. The gradients don't explode or vanish easily, which can improve the training process and convergence of the discriminator network. Further, in all layers where the feature size is reduced approximately half the size of the input, a kernel of size (4,4) with a stride of 2 is utilized for stride convolution. Additionally, except for the last two convolutional layers, where we have 512 feature maps, we double the quantity of feature maps (i.e., channels) in each succeeding convolutional layer.

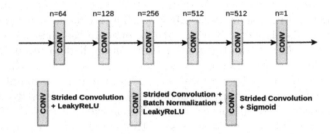

Fig. 3. The architecture of discriminators (D_A and D_B).

3.3 Loss Functions

In this section, we detail a variety of loss functions that are associated with different networks within the unsupervised super-resolution framework referred to as *"COMPUSR"*.

Generator: As depicted in Fig. 1, to enhance the performance of the generator network, the framework employs a weighted mixture of three distinct losses. Additionally, a texture loss is added to reconstruct the texture details. Mathematically, this loss (i.e., Loss$_G$) can be defined as,

$$\mathscr{L}_G = \beta_1 \mathscr{L}_{color} + \beta_2 \mathscr{L}_{GAN-A}^G + \beta_3 \mathscr{L}_{GAN-B}^G + \beta_4 \mathscr{L}_{Texture}, \tag{1}$$

where $\mathscr{L}_{color}$, $\mathscr{L}_G$, $\mathscr{L}_{GAN-A}$, $\mathscr{L}_{GAN-B}$, $\mathscr{L}_{Texture}$ reveal color loss, generator adversarial loss with discriminator-A, generator adversarial loss with discriminator-B and texture loss, respectively. The weights of each loss are noted with by β_i, $i = 1, \ldots, 4$.

In the proposed method, we use unpaired LR-HR images. Hence, the use of $L1$ or $L2$ loss between SR and HR photos does not maintain the LR observation's structure and color information in the final image. Thus, we employ color loss (see Eq. (2)) to determine the absolute difference between bicubically upsampled LR and generated SR images to solve such deficiency.

$$L_{color} = \frac{1}{N} \sum_{}^{N} |I_{SR} - B(I_{LR})| \tag{2}$$

Here, N stands for the size of the training batch, while $B(.)$ stands for the bicubic upsampling procedure. As mentioned earlier, we apply Least Square GAN (LSGAN) loss, to enhance training stability with both discriminators. The definition of the adversarial generator loss from discriminator-A is,

$$L_{GAN-A}^{G} = \frac{1}{N} \sum_{}^{N} |1 - D_A(I_{SR})|, \tag{3}$$

where $D_A(\cdot)$ indicates the function of discriminator-A. Similarly, the generator loss from discriminator-B can be represented as

$$L_{GAN-B}^{G} = \frac{1}{N} \sum_{}^{N} |1 - D_B(W_H(I_{SR}))|. \tag{4}$$

In the above equation, $D_B(\cdot)$ denotes the function of discriminator-B, and W_H specifies the kernel weights for a High-Pass Filter (HPF). We initially create a Gaussian LPF of kernel 9×9 with 0 mean and variance 0.8 before inverting it to acquire the weights of the HPF kernel (determined empirically). Along with all above losses, a texture loss is also added as stated in [4], the relationships between different feature maps of a layer that make up texture of an image, and characterize it as the Gramm matrix $J^{(n)} \in R^{(d*d)}$, where $J_{pj}^{(m)}$ is the inner product between the vectorized feature maps p and m on layer n. Using these as a basis, the texture loss is stated as:

$$L_{Texture}(I_{HR}, I_{SR}, n, \phi) = \frac{1}{d_n^2} \sqrt{\sum_{pm} (J_{i,j}^{(l)}(I_{HR}) - (I_{SR}))^2}. \tag{5}$$

Discriminator-A: Here, the discriminator-A is trained using a generator that discriminates produced SR picture from the original unpaired HR image in an adversarial way. The LSGAN [15] loss is used with discriminator-A to prevent instability of adversarial training which is represented as,

$$L_{GAN-A}^{D} = \frac{1}{N} \sum_{}^{N} \left(\frac{\| D_A(I_{SR}) + \| 1 - D_A(I_{HR}) \|}{2} \right), \tag{6}$$

where, $D_A(\cdot)$ denotes the function of Discriminator-A and I_{HR} is the unpaired HR image in the dataset.

Discriminator-B: To differentiate edge features between SR and HR pictures discriminator-B is deployed. Due to the fact that it tries to match the high-frequency elements of the SR picture with those of the up-paired HR image. The discriminator-B loss can be summarized as,

$$L_{GAN-B}^{D} = \frac{1}{N} \sum^{N} \left(\frac{\| D_B(W_H(I_{SR})) + \| 1 - D_B(W_H(I_{HR})) \|}{2} \right). \quad (7)$$

Here, $D_B(\cdot)$ represents operation of Discriminator-B.

4   Experimental Details

The design of the proposed model-$COMPUSR$ is validated by conducting qualitative and quantitative evaluations. The SR results are benchmarked against state-of-the-art models such as DUSGAN [17], dSRVAE [9], and DASR [22] for visual and quantitative assessments. These state-of-the-art models were proposed for natural images in unsupervised manner; however, for fair evaluation, we re-trained them on WCE images and generated the SR images. We empirically verify proposed model's effectiveness with above architectures qualitatively using non-reference metrics such as Blind/No-Reference Image Spatial Quality Evaluator (BRISQUE) and Perception based Image Quality Evaluator (PIQE). In addition to this, to prove the suggested method's effectiveness in terms of computing, we compare the number of learnable parameters and Multi-ADDs of the proposed method with that of all the above models.

4.1   Datasets and Training Details

We have trained the proposed model in an unsupervised manner in which unpaired LR-HR are used. Additionally, an another novel contribution of the work is the creation of new derivative dataset from the available Kvasir Capsule Endoscopy Dataset consisting of WCE images. In the original Kvasir dataset, each image is in RGB color space with size of 336×336 pixels. This dataset contains a total of $47,236$ images, which are categorized according to different medical anomalies. As the original dataset contained redundant images with many unwanted border pixels, we have curated the dataset for the SR task by manually removing redundant unwanted portions from the Kavasir dataset. The new SR dataset, therefore, consists of $10,000$ training images, 550 validation images and 1000 testing images. The size of each image in new dataset is 280×280 pixels. Additionally, the proposed model along with all other models are experimented on the new dataset and SR results are obtained. These images are employed as input in the LR block as depicted in Fig. 1. As the model is based on the unpaired LR-HR images, we used additional $10,000$ conventional endoscopy images of resolution 1024×1024 in HR block in Fig. 1. Thus, it is worth mentioning that the training dataset is not of true LR-HR pair; the LR images are of WCE images and HR dataset consists of images from conventional endoscopy images, making them truly unpaired in the training dataset.

4.2   Training Details

As stated earlier, all SR methods including the proposed trained on new dataset and SR results are obtained. Further, since LR dataset lacks high-frequency details and hence, to enhance those regions, the LR images are passed through High-boost filtering which is a classical image processing technique to enhance the high-frequency regions. In the suggested model, we use 32 features in Generator and Discriminator. Additionally, the weighted mixture of different loss functions depicted in Equation (1) as β_i, $i = 1, \ldots, 4$ are set empirically to 0.1, 0.5×10^{-10}, 0.2×10^{-5} and 10^{-3} values, respectively. During training, the LR pictures are supplemented by random rotation of 90°, random horizontal flipping and random cropping operations. The model attains Adam optimizer and it is trained upto $125K$ number of iterations with a batch size of 16. The number of BB used in the generator architecture is set to 5 (i.e., $n = 5$). The value k in the HFM architecture is kept to 2 and image resolution of datasets during training and testing must be divisible by the value of k. The learning rate is 1×10^{-4}, which decays by half to twenty percent, forty percent, sixty percentage and eighty percentage of the total number of iterations within this training set.

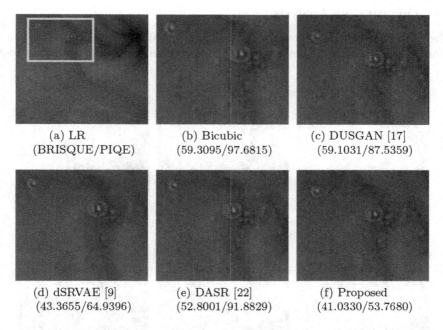

<table>
<tr><td>(a) LR
(BRISQUE/PIQE)</td><td>(b) Bicubic
(59.3095/97.6815)</td><td>(c) DUSGAN [17]
(59.1031/87.5359)</td></tr>
<tr><td>(d) dSRVAE [9]
(43.3655/64.9396)</td><td>(e) DASR [22]
(52.8001/91.8829)</td><td>(f) Proposed
(41.0330/53.7680)</td></tr>
</table>

Fig. 4. The qualitative comparison of proposed and other existing unsupervised SR methods for upsampling factor ×4. The values of BRISQUE and PIQE are also depicted below to each SR result.

4.3 Qualitative Analysis

The qualitative comparison of various SR methods for scaling factor of ×4 is depicted in Fig. 4, Fig. 5 and Fig. 6. Through a comprehensive qualitative analysis, we evaluate the performance of the proposed method by comparing it to various state-of-the-art methods such as DUSGAN, dSRVAE and DASR. One can observe that the SR results obtained by bicubic and dSRVAE method exhibit blurry results and do not reconstruct the high-frequency details. Further, the SR image obtained by DUSGAN method (see Fig. 5(c)) fails to retain structure properly while the proposed model performs better as it preserves the structure of the cell and the high-frequency details. Thus, it reveals that the proposed method consistently outperforms to other methods, exhibiting superior capabilities in enhancing image resolution and preserving fine details in Wireless Capsule Endoscopy (WCE) images. Notably, the proposed model effectively restores intricate features like blood vessels, mucosal patterns, and small lesions which were previously imperceptible in LR images. This advancement empowers medical professionals to conduct more accurate analyses, potentially leading to earlier disease detection and improved patient outcomes.

4.4 Quantitative Analysis

The proposed method is trained and tested in an unsupervised manner where true HR is unavailable. Thus, we employed no-reference quality assessment met-

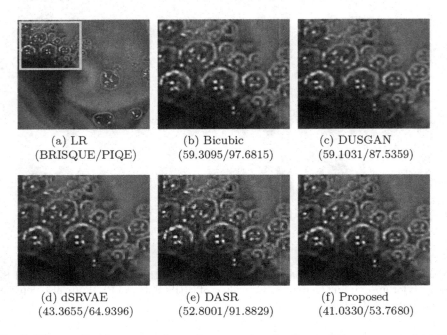

(a) LR	(b) Bicubic	(c) DUSGAN
(BRISQUE/PIQE)	(59.3095/97.6815)	(59.1031/87.5359)
(d) dSRVAE	(e) DASR	(f) Proposed
(43.3655/64.9396)	(52.8001/91.8829)	(41.0330/53.7680)

Fig. 5. The qualitative comparison of proposed and other existing unsupervised SR methods for upsampling factor ×4. The values of BRISQUE and PIQE are also depicted below to each SR result.

Table 1. The quantitative and computational analysis of proposed and other state-of-the-art methods.

Metrics	Bicubic	DUSGAN [17]	dSRVAE [9]	DASR [22]	Proposed
BRISQUE	59.3095	59.103	43.3655	52.8001	**41.0330**
PIQE	97.6815	87.5359	64.9396	91.8829	**53.7680**
Parameters (in millions)	–	5.86	7.96	11.2480	**2.4**
No. of Flops (in GIGA)	–	335.861	689.9515	470.831	**91.5546**

rics: BRISQUE [16] and PIQE [21] to evaluate the effectiveness of unsupervised SR methods. The quantitative analysis of the proposed model depicted in Table 1. Lower BRISQUE and PIQE scores correspond to higher perceived quality in the super-resolved (SR) observations. It can be observed that the proposed model has the lowest values of BRISQUE and PIQE. These lowest values suggest the SR image generated by the proposed model has superior perceptual quality when compared to other state-of-the-art models.

4.5   Computational Complexity

By prioritizing computational efficiency, models can achieve faster performance, seamlessly adapt to various environments and consume less power. The computational efficiency of a model can be quantified through metrics such as the

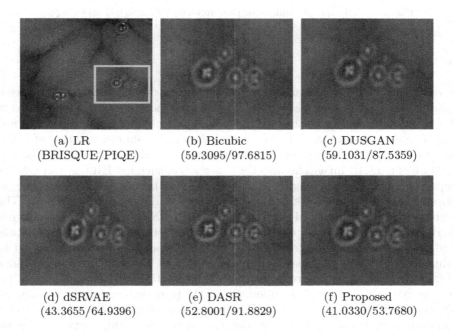

(a) LR
(BRISQUE/PIQE)

(b) Bicubic
(59.3095/97.6815)

(c) DUSGAN
(59.1031/87.5359)

(d) dSRVAE
(43.3655/64.9396)

(e) DASR
(52.8001/91.8829)

(f) Proposed
(41.0330/53.7680)

Fig. 6. The qualitative comparison of proposed and other existing unsupervised SR methods for upsampling factor ×4. The values of BRISQUE and PIQE are also depicted below to each SR result.

number of learnable parameters and the number of Floating Point Operations (FLOPs) involved in its architecture. Floating-point operations, such as addition, multiplication, subtraction, and division on floating-point integers, are explicitly referred by the term FLOPs. From Table 1, one can observe that the proposed model demonstrates computational efficiency as it possesses considerably less number of parameters and FLOPs when compared to state-of-the-art methods. In addition to that, Fig. 7 illustrates the computational comparison in terms of the BRISQUE vs number of parameters and PIQE vs number of parameters, respectively where once can observe that the proposed model has fewer number of parameters over the state of the art methods with better quantitative metrics.

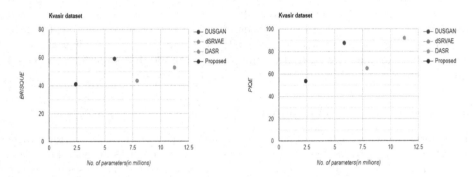

Fig. 7. The graph of number of parameters vs BRISQUE and PIQE.

5   Conclusion

Several aspects of medical image processing depends on an image's spatial resolution. The WCE images have a low spatial resolution due to the limitations of hardware and size. Due to the growing demand for high-quality images obtained with compact battery, camera, or limited sensor, the super-resolution of WCE images finds an emerging application in computer aided diagnostics. However, the lack of true HR images hinders the collection of such LR-HR pairs and makes supervised training challenging. To overcome this hurdle, we thus propose an unsupervised SR framework based on an adversarial deep neural network. The architecture of the proposed network (i.e., *COMPUSR*) incorporates a sequence of Basic Blocks (BBs) designed to effectively reconstruct high-frequency details and to preserve texture information. The model's architecture is optimized to minimize the number of learnable parameters and Floating Point Operations (FLOPs), resulting in computational efficiency. Both qualitative and quantitative analyses demonstrate the superiority of the proposed model when compared to other state-of-the-art methods. The model consistently achieves better performance in terms of capturing fine details and generating high-quality outputs, showcasing its efficacy and advancements over existing approaches.

Acknowledgment. Authors are thankful to Research Council of Norway (RCN) for International Network for Capsule Imaging in Endoscopy (CapsNetwork) project managed by Department of computer science, Norwegian University of Science and technology (NTNU), Norway for providing support for this research work.

References

1. Rueda, A., Malpica, N., Romero, E.: Single-image super-resolution of brain MR images using overcomplete dictionaries. Med. Image Anal. **17**, 43–63 (2013)
2. Ahn, N., Yoo, J., Sohn, K.A.: SimUSR: a simple but strong baseline for unsupervised image super-resolution. In: Proceedings of the IEEE/CVF Conference on CVPR Workshop, pp. 474–475 (2020)
3. Dong, C., Loy, C.C., Tang, X.: Accelerating the super-resolution convolutional neural network. In: Leibe, B., Matas, J., Sebe, N., Welling, M. (eds.) ECCV 2016. LNCS, vol. 9906, pp. 391–407. Springer, Cham (2016). https://doi.org/10.1007/978-3-319-46475-6_25
4. Gatys, L.A., Ecker, A.S., Bethge, M.: Texture synthesis and the controlled generation of natural stimuli using convolutional neural networks. CoRR abs/1505.07376 (2015). http://arxiv.org/abs/1505.07376
5. Isola, P., Zhu, J.Y., Zhou, T., Efros, A.A.: Image-to-image translation with conditional adversarial networks. In: Proceedings of the IEEE Conference on CVPR, pp. 1125–1134 (2017)
6. Kim, J., Lee, J.K., Lee, K.M.: Accurate image super-resolution using very deep convolutional networks. In: Proceedings of the IEEE Conference on CVPR, pp. 1646–1654 (2016)
7. Kim, J., Lee, J.K., Lee, K.M.: Deeply-recursive convolutional network for image super-resolution. In: Proceedings of the IEEE Conference on CVPR, pp. 1637–1645 (2016)
8. Lim, B., Son, S., Kim, H., Nah, S., Mu Lee, K.: Enhanced deep residual networks for single image super-resolution. In: Proceedings of the IEEE Conference on CVPR Workshops, pp. 136–144 (2017)
9. Liu, Z.S., Siu, W.C., Wang, L.W., Li, C.T., Cani, M.P.: Unsupervised real image super-resolution via generative variational autoencoder. In: Proceedings of the IEEE/CVF CVPR Workshops, pp. 442–443 (2020)
10. Lu, Z., Liu, H., Li, J., Zhang, L.: Efficient transformer for single image super-resolution. CoRR abs/2108.11084 (2021). https://arxiv.org/abs/2108.11084
11. Lugmayr, A., Danelljan, M., Timofte, R.: NTIRE 2020 challenge on real-world image super-resolution: methods and results. In: Proceedings of the IEEE/CVF Conference on CVPR Workshops, pp. 494–495 (2020)
12. Fritsche, M., Gu, S., Timofte, R.: Frequency separation for real-world super-resolution. In: Proceedings of the IEEE/CVF ICCVW, vol. 14, pp. 3599–3608 (2019)
13. Häfner, M., M.L., Uhl, A.: POCS-based super-resolution for HD endoscopy video frames. In: Proceedings of the 26th IEEE International Symposium on Computer-Based Medical Systems (2013). IEEE
14. Mahapatra, D., Bozorgtabar, B.: Image super-resolution using progressive generative adversarial networks for medical image analysis. Comput. Med. Imaging Graph. **71** (2018)
15. Mao, X., Li, Q., Xie, H., Lau, R.Y., Wang, Z., Smolley, S.P.: Least squares generative adversarial networks. In: 2017 IEEE-ICCV, pp. 2813–2821 (2017)

16. Mittal, A., Moorthy, A.K., Bovik, A.C.: Blind/referenceless image spatial quality evaluator. In: 2011 Conference Record of the Forty Fifth ASILOMAR, pp. 723–727 (2011)

17. Prajapati, K., et al.: Direct unsupervised super-resolution using generative adversarial network (DUS-GAN) for real-world data. IEEE TIP **30**, 8251–8264 (2021)

18. Prajapati, K., et al.: Unsupervised single image super-resolution network (USIS-ResNet) for real-world data using generative adversarial network. In: Proceedings of the IEEE/CVF Conference on CVPR Workshops, pp. 464–465 (2020)

19. Tong, T., Li, G., Liu, X., Gao, Q.: Image super-resolution using dense skip connections. In: 2017 IEEE International Conference on Computer Vision (ICCV), pp. 4809–4817 (2017). https://doi.org/10.1109/ICCV.2017.514

20. Umer, R.M., Foresti, G.L., Micheloni, C.: Deep generative adversarial residual convolutional networks for real-world super-resolution. In: Proceedings of the IEEE/CVF Conference on CVPR Workshops, pp. 438–439 (2020)

21. Venkatanath, N., Praneeth, D., Bh, M.C., Channappayya, S.S., Medasani, S.S.: Blind image quality evaluation using perception based features. In: 2015 Twenty First NCC. pp. 1–6 (2015)

22. Wang, L., Wang, Y., Dong, X., Xu, Q., Yang, J., An, W., Guo, Y.: Unsupervised degradation representation learning for blind super-resolution. In: Proceedings of the IEEE/CVF Conference on CVPR. pp. 10581–10590 (2021)

A Novel Real-Time Helmet Wearing Detection Technique of Motorcyclists Using Fine-Tuned YOLOv8 Model for Indian Urban Road Traffic

Sambit Prusty[✉] iD, Swayam Ranjan Nayak iD, and Ram Chandra Barik iD

Department of Computer Science and Engineering, C.V. Raman Global University,
Bhubaneswar 752054, Odisha, India
sambitprusty0111@gmail.com, swayamranjannayak@gmail.com,
ram.chandra@cgu-odisha.ac.in

Abstract. Motorcycle is a rapidly growing industry. But it has maximum fatal rate of accidents than heavy vehicles. Above 37 million of people in India use motorcycle for transportation. Out of all the road accidents happening in India approximately 45% of accidents are caused by motorcycles and among them 32% of accidents are caused due to not wearing helmets. With the heavy traffic condition, the road transport authority essentially require automation model to detect wearing helmet of two wheelers and penalize if any violation of laws. This paper addresses such problem of heavy Indian urban road traffic conditions and proposed a fine-tuned deep learning based YOLOv8-SS2 helmet wearing detection technique. This model classifies helmet and non-helmet riders. The proposed model outperforms while comparing with existing literature having high accuracy of 95% and Mean Average Precision (m-AP) of 99%.

Keywords: Helmet Detection · Person Detection · Bike Detection · You Only Look Once (YOLOv8) · Open-cv · Mean Average Precision (m-AP)

1 Introduction

In this growing world transportation is the major development field of any country or region. So there are exit so many mediums of transportation. As India is the one of the busiest country of the world people always try to find easy and convenient ways to work out things. As a result 70% of the Indian population like to ride motorbikes as it is the most convenient ride to ride on Indian busy roads [1]. During the year 2021, the maximum road accidents of two wheelers have accounted as nearly 70000 which is a wholesome of 44.5% of total road accidental deaths. Around 32% of the total road accident deaths are due to non-wearing of helmets which is approximately 47000 persons [14].

WHO states that the risk of sustaining fatal injuries in the event of a crash can be reduced to 42 percent and head injuries to 69 percent if and only if people use and correctly wear certified quality helmet. Adhering to the law and wearing securely attached ISI-marked good quality helmets significantly reduces the chances of injuries for crash victims. [15]. The Indian government has given laws about multiple and different penalties. Like wearing helmets of at least weighing 1.2 kg. 1000 rupees amount is fined to the person who doesn't wear helmet and driving license can be disqualified and in several states they can be punished upto 3 months in jail. Although there are these rules still people do break the rules and tries to escape from the crime they committed. Therefore the traffic system should be automated with the help of deep learning models like CNN, YOLO to reduce both crimes and accidents. These models can be used for object detection, image segmentation, computer vision. Now a days CNN is being used to develop in the sectors like semantic segmentation and pixel-level vision task. The developed system aims in minimising the count of accidents and many deaths. Helmets are very beneficial during driving the motorbikes. It also minimises risk of injuries upto 45% and nearly 70% of head injuries.

2 Related Works

Bhaskar, P. K., and Yong, S.-P. et al. [2] concentrate on vehicle detection using image processing techniques applied to video frames. Their approach combines algorithms for vehicle recognition and tracking, incorporating Gaussian mixture models and blob detection methods. By differentiating between the background and foreground elements in a selected frame, they utilize a foreground detector to identify objects and enclose them within rectangular areas using binary computation. They got an impressive detection accuracy of 91%.

Rattapoom et al. [3] explores the utilization of a moving object detection mechanism for the purpose of head classification. Their approach primarily involves two techniques: extraction of head image and classification. Head extraction is achieved through profiling methods and classification relies on extracted features from the head regions. The experimental results of their tests exhibited an accurate discrimination of helmet wearers, achieving a success rate of 74% for both lanes. They also propose the implementation of an automatic number plate extraction system which extracts text from the number plates which will help the government law system. Dharma et al. [4] developed a system that employs image processing and convolutional neural network (CNN) to detect violation of helmet laws. The system consists of motorcycle detection, helmet no-helmet classification, and license plate recognition of motorcycle. CNN models were created for each classifier. One challenge encountered was distinguishing between cases where a motorcyclist wears hat and while the front rider wears a helmet, but the second person does not. To address this, the authors suggest increasing the training data for these scenarios, including more samples of individuals wearing hats and instances where the first rider wears a helmet while the second rider does not. By expanding the dataset in this way, they aim to improve the system's accuracy.

N. Boonsirisumpun et al. [5] propose an alternative system that implies Single-Shot Detection (SSD) for object detection and a Binary Classifier for classification purposes. In the classifier the classes were divided into bikers wearing helmets and without helmets. Both bike and the rider included in the class image, focusing specifically on the rider's head region. The binary classifier employed various models like VGG16,VGG19, Inception V3 and MobileNet, which achieved respective accuracies of

78%, 79%, 84.5%, and 85%. This approach enables accurate differentiation between helmeted and non-helmeted bikers, providing an effective solution for enforcing helmet laws.

H. Lin et al.[6] developed a model using a pre-trained model called RetinaNet and with suitable fine-tuning techniques. They detected motorcycles from frame of the video and they were able to achieve an accuracy of 80.6%.

B. Yogameena et al. [7] [IET Intell. Transp. Syst., 2019, Vol. 13 Iss. 7, pp. 1190–1198] propose a model based on Faster R-CNN for the detection of helmets and non-helmets on vehicles. The model utilizes pre-trained sample data for detection and employs character-sequence encoding and ST techniques for recognizing license plate numbers of motorbikes without helmets. Using a character-sequence encoding CNN model, the researchers achieved a detection accuracy of 92%.

Vishnu et al. [8] presented a system for automatically detecting motorcyclists without helmets in surveillance videos. Their approach involved background subtraction on video edges to identify moving objects. By utilizing CNN, they achieved an impressive detection rate of 92.87% for violators, while maintaining a low false alarm rate of 0.5% on average. This highlights the efficiency and effectiveness of their proposed methodology in enforcing helmet regulations and enhancing road safety.

Rohith C A et al. [9] presented a model for motorbike and person detection. They cropped overlapping bounding boxes from the frame and used an classifier to classify images as either helmet or no-helmet. The model employed a modified InceptionV3 model trained on a new dataset to achieve accurate results. Caffe model was used for detection and extraction. Their model achieved an accuracy of around 86%, demonstrating its effectiveness in detecting helmets.

3 Proposed Methodology

The roads of a country-like India with a vast population, consists of huge traffic which includes 2-wheeler, 3-wheeler,4-wheeler and even 6 or 8-wheeler on national highways. As it consists such busy and congested traffic, it becomes very difficult to detect any helmetless driver and helmet-driven drivers. Their have been multiple approaches which are described in literature reviews which detects and classifies them accurately. But in every model they processed the frames of the video for detection, which results in time consumption. To solve this the author has proposed a model which crops out the images from the video without processing all the frames and YOLO version 8 deep learning model as it is the latest updated version for live and accurate helmet detection.

It consists of five steps (see Fig. 1). The first step is motorbike detection model which includes motorbike and rider. Initially, the processed image is to be detected from an input video using the improved YOLOv8 algorithm, namely YOLOv8-SS, as saved in a.pt file. It predicts the motorbike from the video, which consists of at least one rider. In this step the tracker function creates diagonal points for bounding box. In the second step area function creates a focused area inside the video and when motorbike crosses that area it crops out the image. The third step is upon person detection, which uses the cropped image as the input, and then continues to use predict persons. Then the fourth step is Helmet And Non-Helmet Detection using improved YOLOv8 algorithm, namely

YOLOv8-SS2 as a.pt file. In the fifth step the connector code evaluates whether there more than 2 riders or any non-helmet riders.

The pseudo code of the proposed methodology is given below:

Algorithm 1 Fine Tuned DNN based Helmet Detection Algorithm

```
1:    Procedure DNN-Per-Hel Detection (Traffic Video Dataset)
2:            Convert 500 × (Img Dataset)₂₀₀×₂₀₀×₃ ←Traffic Video Dataset
3:            Annotate Label_{i=1...500} ← (Img Dataset)₂₀₀×₂₀₀×₃
4:            Train ←_{DNN(YOLOv8)₁₆×₁₆} (Img Dataset)₂₀₀×₂₀₀×₃
5:            for test_images do check
6:                    if  test_image == Motorbike then
7:                            if  test_image == person then
8:                                    if  Count_person > 2 then
9:                                            return Faulty file ← test_image
10:                           else if  test_image != helmet then
11:                                    return Faulty file ← test_image
12:                           else if  Count_helmet < Count_person then
13:                                    return Faulty file ← test_image
14:                           end if
15:                   end if
16:           end if
17:           end for
18:   End Procedure
```

As the creation of motorbike detection, person detection and helmet detection are quite different, the has proposed models for each stage, that is, YOLOv8-SS, YOLOv8m and YOLOv8-SS2 respectively to improve the detection performances. Section 3.1 introduces the proposed network, Sect. 3.2 describes the dataset used Sect. 3.3 introduces the motorbike detection method, Sect. 3.4 introduces the person detection method 3.5 introduces the helmet detection method and 3.6 introduces the connector code and faulty file.

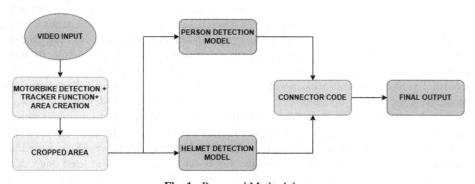

Fig. 1. Proposed Methodology

3.1 Proposed YOLOv8 Network

YOLO is a one-stage object detection algorithm that transforms the detection problem into regression. It directly generates bounding box coordinates and class probabilities, eliminating the need for Region of Interest (RoI) extraction. This approach significantly improves detection speed compared to faster R-CNN. YOLOv5, introduced in 2020, and YOLOv8, released in 2022, are advanced versions that enhance the success of previous YOLO models. YOLOv8 is a cutting-edge, state-of-the-art (SOTA) model with new features and improvements. It excels in speed, accuracy, and usability, making it suitable for object detection, tracking, instance segmentation, image classification, and pose estimation tasks. Its streamlined design makes it suitable for various applications and easily adaptable to different hardware platforms, from edge devices to cloud APIs [10].

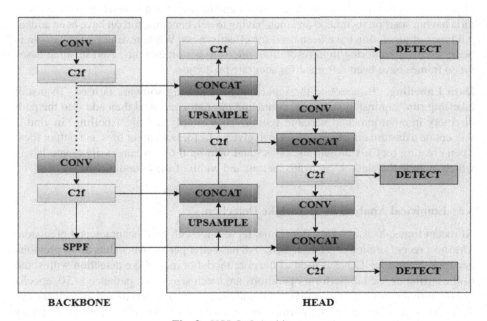

Fig. 2. YOLOv8 Architecture

There are a series of updates and new convolutions in the YOLOv8 architecture (see Fig. 2). The updates are as follows:-

1. The backbone of the system underwent changes with the introduction of C2f, replacing C3. The first 6x6 convolution in the stem was switched to a 3 × 3 convolution.
2. In the C2f architecture, the outputs from the Bottleneck, which consists of two 3x3 convolutions with residual connections, are combined. On the other hand, in the C3 architecture, only the output from the last Bottleneck is utilized. This difference in combining the outputs of the Bottleneck layers distinguishes the two architectures.

3. Backbone contains 5 convolution(conv) layers, 3 C2f layers and Head contains 4 C2f, 2 upsample, 2 conv, 4 concatenation(concat) layers.
4. In YOLOv8, the Bottleneck structure remains the same as YOLOv5, except for a change in the first convolution's kernel size from 1×1 to 3×3. This modification aligns YOLOv8 with the ResNet block introduced in 2015 [11], indicating a potential benefit in object detection.

3.2 Dataset Description

Data Overview. The data used for this proposed detection model is collected from different google sources. To increase the diversity in the training part different types of datasets have been collected like for motorbike detection model more than 1000 images have been collected that consist of traffic containing motorbikes, their back view, side view, front view and for helmet detection 1100 images have been collected that consist of person containing helmet, without helmet and to keep the distinctiveness, images of girls having scarf on their head and men having towel, bandana, turban have been added. All types of resolution have been used for effectiveness. While testing phone camera is being used for capturing high resolution videos to get predictions. And in some cases video frames have been reframed for accurate prediction.

Data Labelling. To annotate the input images labelImg software is used. To install labelImg run 'pip install labelImg' command through cmd. And then add it to the path directory in environmental variable setting. Then simply calling 'labelImg' in cmd it will create a dashboard where you have to give paths for both input files and output files. Then creating rectBox around the object and naming those, it can easily create labels which include the classes, centroids, height and width of the bounding box.

3.3 Empirical Analysis of Motorbike Detection

At recent times, YOLO series algorithms represents with high accuracy and precision. The most recent version of YOLO, YOLOv8 has better performance than all its previous versions. Hence, YOLOv8 is used as the core model of motorbike detection with some of the attributes used to perform operations are batch size $= 32$, patience $= 50$, epochs $= 100$, momentum $= 0.937$, worker $= 8$ and the image size as 640 and also customise YOLOv8 with modified bbox, normalised and data augmentation on cropped images which is explained in section Data Labeling of 3.2. And named it as YOLOv8-SS. Patience value helps to determine the number of epochs (training iterations) that the model will tolerate without any improvement in its performance on a validation set before stopping the training process. The primary purpose of using patience in YOLO models is to prevent overfitting.

The dataset includes the images of local busy traffic includes vehicles such as tri-cycles, motorbikes, cars and even trucks. And mainly the accuracy of this model is to detect the motorbikes precisely among the 2000 images of motorbikes. This model's dataset images consist of multiple operations such as image flipping, rotating and noise eliminated images. The detection includes both motorbike and its rider as a total image.

All the data images of this stage has a high resolution, and also has the following challenges:

1. The motorbikes have various scale of size. This create a challenge for the model to detect accurately the different scaled images.
2. The images also consists of different angles such as front-view, back-view and different view-angles of the images.
3. Majorly a challenge in a crowded traffic, is some motorbike rider blocks some other motorbike riders behind on them.

The images get predicted by YOLOv8-SS model and gives the result as result.boxes which contains the centroid points of the bounding box, width, height, confidence, and class.

Proposed Tracker Function. The author has developed a tracker function which takes the centroid point (xc, yc), width and height (nw, nh) as inputs and uses it to evaluate top-left and bottom-right corner points (see Fig. 3). It also uses a counter to give a special or unique ids to each object. This motorbike detection lastly gives output as cropped images of every object having unique ids.

```
xc *= w
yc *= h
nw *= w
nh *= h
top_left = (int(xc - nw/2) , int(yc - nh/2))
bottom_right = (int(xc + nw/2) , int(yc + nh/2))
```

Fig. 3. Sample Code of Tracker Function

In the above code snippet it evaluates the corners, situated at the top left and at the bottom right by subtracting the half of the width (nw) and half of the height (nh) from the mid-point(xc, yc), and adding half of the width (nw) and half of the height (nh) to the mid-point (xc, yc) respectively.

Focused Area Function and Data Preprocessing. Video are of different types according to their fps values. As an example, if a video is of 15fps and length of 30 s then it will get 15 * 30 or 450 frames. As like that, if the models is going to work on real-life videos, it will get huge amount of frames and it will take larger amount of processing time to process those frames. In addition to that, an object in that video will have a minimum of 6–7 frames. This will lead to data duplicacy of that object. Hence, it will lead to huge storage consumption.

To solve this problem, the author has proposed a new data processing method. It includes 2 steps. First, it will create a specific or focus area (this can be a single line or a polygon) inside the video as specified with variable name as 'area' with 4 coordinates (x, y). In the second step, pointpolygon test function of opencv is implemented. The function takes area as array input, (x4, y4) coordinate. The function describes that when the detected image (having its bounding box) touches or crosses the focus area, the image of the object is cropped according to its bounding box size. This is calculated using the output of result variable. If the results value as 0 or greater than 0, the frame is cropped. Figure 4 conveys a way how these two steps work.

```
area=[(x1,y1),(x2,y2),(x3,y3),(x4,y4)]
result = cv2.pointPolygonTest(np.array(area,np.int32),((x4,y4)),False)
if results>=0:
    crop=frame[y3:y4,x3:x4]
```

Fig. 4. Sample Code of Area Function

This proposed method solves the data duplicacy problem directly and it also uses skip_frame function to reduce some frames of the video.

3.4 Empirical Analysis of Person Detection

The cropped images are further processed for person detection. The author has used the YOLOv8 model to detect person. YOLOv8 has multiple sub-models such as YOLOv8n, YOLOv8s, YOLOv8m, YOLOv8l and YOLOv8x. These models vary in terms of the accuracy and CPU speed on ONNX. YOLOv8m model is used for detection of person. This model is trained under custom dataset of about 1000 images with epochs number of 100 and batch size of 16. This dataset consists of multiple classes classification in the images. In the custom dataset, person varies in terms of multiple features such as appearance, pose, different angles, scale size, and uncleared images. It also includes the pictures of multiple time stamp of a whole day. The code has been customized to retrieve only the person class from the vast images.

The person detection is performed on motorbike cropped images using the predict function of YOLOv8. The predicted image is saved and used for counting of total number of persons. If the count is greater than 2, then the image is saved into the faulty folder. Faulty folder is the folder of faulty images which disobeys some laws of traffic rules.

3.5 Empirical Analysis of Helmet Detection

The task of this stage is to detect whether the motorbike riders are wearing a helmet or not. It crops the helmet or no-helmet of a person. This dataset consists of nearly 1000 images with nearly 1100 instances in total. The motorbike cropped images is used to perform helmet detection on them. The author has used YOLOv8 as the core model of motorbike detection and made major improvements using modified bbox, image normalisation and data augmentation of cropped images named as YOLOv8-SS2. There are two classes in this stage: helmet and no-helmet. The main challenges at this stage are as follows:

1. The foremost problem lies on the similarity between black hair drivers an black helmet riders.
2. A hat wearing rider might be detected as helmet-wearable rider.
3. When multiple riders occupy a motorbike, the presence of additional individuals obstructs the view of the passenger positioned in the rear.

These challenges are solved by training a large amount of images of people driving the vehicles with precision of multiple variation of appearance, angles, scale and even in background environments. The datasets are generally trained upon multiple parameters as mentioned in Table 1 to produce an optimised and sustainable model with minimal errors.

Table 1. Parameters of proposed YOLOv8-SS2 model

Parameters	Values
batch size	32
patience	50
epochs	100
momentum	0.937
worker	8
image size	640

The detected images are further classified and saves the cropped objects of helmet and no-helmet. If a no-helmet is detected, the image is saved in a faulty folder. Or else, the number of helmets are counted for future reference.

Figure 5 depicts all the steps that have been covered till now. Its Sect. 1 shows the input frame of video, in Sect. 2 area creation is demonstrated, in Sect. 3 bike images with persons have been cropped out, in Sect. 4 persons have been cropped out and lastly in Sect. 5 helmet and non-helmet images are demonstrated and classified(in this input video there are no non-helmet classes detected).

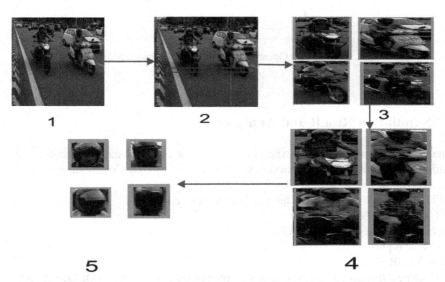

Fig. 5. Operational Flowchart of the Proposed Methodology

3.6   Connector Module and Faulty Log File

This connector module connects motorbike detection, person detection, helmet detection models by considering a loop of the output labels. It contains all the law breaking possibilities while driving a bike like Tripple sitting and Biking without helmet. Then after counting out the person classes no if more than 2 people get noticed then the image file of the same label file get saved in Faulty Folder. If all is okay like person count is 2 then it compares with the no of helmets containing in that helmet label folder and if it results not equal then that same name file get saved inside the Faulty Log Folder file. Further that faulty folder file which contains all the bike riders which disobeyed the law, can be used to detect their HSRP number plates and notice fine against them.

Figure 6 shows all these steps of the proposed methodology in flowchart format.

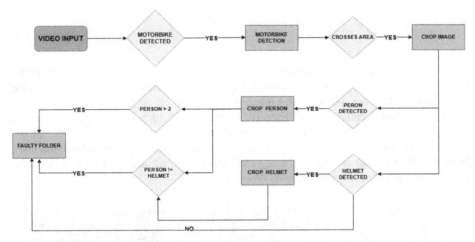

Fig. 6. Step by step Operational Flow of the Proposed Methodology

4   Simulation Result and Analysis

The proposed model has been experimented with the collected dataset where the author initially trained and tested the models with the help of Google Collaboratory. The specs used as follows.

GPU-Tesla K80, compute 3.7, having 2496 CUDA cores.

VRAM-12 GB GDDR5

CPU- Xeon Processors @ 2.3 Ghz

RAM-12.6 gb

Disk-33 GB

The best fine tuned model has been employed using the recent YOLOv8 deep learning anchor free model. Anchor-free model doesn't predicts the offset of an object instead it predicts the center of the object. It reduces number of the bounding box predictions, which accelerate NMS, i.e., Non-Maximum Suppression which is a complex processing phase that shifts from person detections after inference [12]. Yolov8 includes C-IoU which is the intersection of aggregation of overlap area(S), normalized distance(D) and aspect ratio(V).By considering these additional factors, CIOU offers a more comprehensive measure of bounding box similarity compared to traditional IoU. The equation of C-Iou,

$$\lambda = S\left(B, B^{gt}\right) + D\left(B, B^{gt}\right) + V\left(B, B^{gt}\right) \tag{1}$$

where S, V, and D are constant to regression scale and are values lie between 0 and 1. CIoU loss makes regression very fast with extreme aspect ratios [13].

4.1 Prominent Classification Parameters

After completion of the process of training of the custom models using the custom datasets, models have initiated detecting or predicting the desired classes. In this paper, the author has proposed the detection of 3 classes i.e., motorbike (as person_bike), person and helmet or no-helmet. The author has measured the performance of the models using multiple performance metrics such as accuracy, precision, F1-score and recall. These are some of the most fundamental metrics for a machine learning model. The metrics defined as follows:

$$Accuracy = \frac{TP + TN}{TP + FN + TN + FP} \tag{2}$$

$$Recall = \frac{TP}{TP + FN} \tag{3}$$

$$Precision = \frac{TP}{TP + FP} \tag{4}$$

$$F1 = \frac{2 \times Precision \times Recall}{Precision + Recall} \tag{5}$$

$$mAP = \frac{1}{N} \sum_{i=1}^{N} AP_i \tag{6}$$

The proposed fine-tuned YOLOv8 model also provides some of the loss functions to classify the particular area of loss of the model. The various types of loss functions are:-

1. box_loss- The box loss is responsible for calculating the accuracy of the predicted bounding boxes. It quantifies the discrepancy between the predicted box coordinates and the ground truth box coordinates. One commonly used loss function for box regression is the smooth L1 loss (also known as Huber loss).
2. cls_loss- The class loss is used to evaluate the accuracy of the predicted class probabilities. It calculates the difference between the predicted class probabilities and the true class labels for each object in the image. Typically, the cross-entropy loss is employed for multi-class classification tasks.

3. dfl_loss- DFL loss is a machine learning technique that considers the problem of
   class imbalance while training a neural network. Class imbalance occurs when there
   is one class which occurs too frequently and another which occurs less. DFL treats
   the detections better when boundaries of the ground truth are blurred.

This performance metrics and various losses contributes in optimising the overall
model performance.

4.2 Comparative Result Analysis of Motorbike Detection

First, the motorbike detection is performed over the input video. The motorbikes are
labelled as 'person_bike'. As per the labelled images, motorbike detection detects and
crops the bounding box of motorbike which includes both person and motorbike of the
specified detection. So far the author got a F1-Score of 93% and mAP-50 of 97%, recall
of 99%, precision of 1.00 at 0.892, which is an optimum result, which is shown in the
Table 2.

The author has compared with different models trained with different methods and
got a result that YOLOv8-SS model has done comparatively better than any other models,
which is shown in the Table 3. Only CNN and Gaussian Mixture models have reached
near proposed model's near accuracy point. And YOLOv8-SS model's F1-Score and
mAP performances are shown in Figs. 7 and 8 respectively.

Table 2. Performance Metrics Of Motorbike Detection

Metrics	MOTORBIKE DETECTION
Precision	1.0 at 0.892
Recall	99%
MAP-50	97%
F1-Score	93%

4.3 Comparative Result Analysis of Person Detection

Then, the cropped and saved images of motorbikes are treated as an input for person
detection. Person detection model is the version of YOLOv8 model. The author has
trained, tested and compared all the 5 models of YOLO v8 i.e. YOLOv8n, YOLOv8s,
YOLOv8m, YOLOv8l and YOLOv8x which is shown in Table 4. To make a fair comparision, author has used same dataset and parameter values such as epoch, and batch
size. All the models have been trained on customed person dataset.

After this comparison, it is cleared that YOLOv8s and YOLOv8m are best person
detection models which had mAP as 99% and F1-score as 0.97. But, YOLOv8s model
doesn't perform better than YOLOv8m for real-time data. YOLOv8m is a balanced
model so, the author has used this model for person detection. And its mAP and F1-
Score performances are shown in Figs. 9 and 10 respectively. This model crops person

Table 3. Comparative Study of Performance of Motorbike Detection

METHODS	Model	ACCURACY	MAP50
P. K. Bhaskar [2]	Gaussian Mixture	91.26%	–
Boonsirisumpun et al. [5]	Inception V3	84.38%	–
Boonsirisumpun et al. [5]	MobileNet	85.40%	–
Balasubramanian et al. [7]	CNN-Y	–	76%
Balasubramanian et al. [7]	Fast R-CNN	–	79%
Balasubramanian et al. [7]	Faster R-CNN	–	76%
Balasubramanian et al. [7]	YOLO	–	–
C. Vishnu et al. [8]	CNN	92.87%	70%
C. A. Rohith et al. [9]	Caffe & Inception V3	76%	–
Proposed Model	YOLOv8-SS	95%	97%

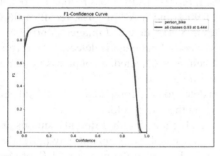 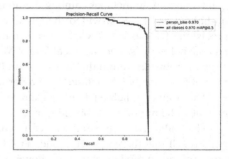

Fig. 7. F1-Score Confidence Curve of Motorbike Detection

Fig. 8. Precision-Recall Curve with mAP value of Motorbike Detection

Table 4. Performance Comparison of different Models of YOLOv8 for Person Detection

Metrics	YOLOv8n	YOLOv8s	YOLOv8m	YOLOv8l	YOLOv8x
Precision	1.00 at 0.067	1.00 at 0.78	1.00 at 0.78	0.95 at 0.78	0.86 at 0.78
Recall	1.00 at 0.00	1.0 at 0.00	1.00 at 0.00	1.00 at 0.00	1.00 at 0.00
MAP-50	99%	99%	99%	99%	95.8%
F1-Score	0.92 at 0.05	0.97 at 0.438	0.97 at 0.440	0.80 at 0.43	0.82 at 0.453

object images and saved it in a local folder to use a counter to count the number of persons sitting in that particular motorbike.

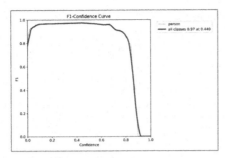
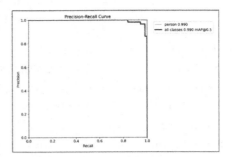

Fig. 9. Precision-Recall Curve with mAP value of Person Detection

Fig. 10. F1-Score Confidence Curve of Person Detection

4.4 Comparative Result Analysis of Helmet Detection

At last, helmet detection is performed on motorbike cropped images to detect and classify helmet and no-helmet class among the images. It represents the class helmet as "0" and no-helmet as "1". It provided the F1-Score of 90% and mAP of 93%, recall of 96%, precision of 1.0 at 0.931 which is shown in Table 5. The detected images of no-helmet and the helmet is stored in a local folder. When a no-helmet class is detected, motorbike image is transferred into the faulty folder. If a helmet is detected, a counter is evaluated to count the number of helmets of the particular motorbike.

The counter of helmet detection and person detection are compared and if the doesn't matches, the motorbike cropped image is saved in the faulty folder.

The author has compared with different models trained with different methods and got a result that the proposed model YOLOv8-SS2 has done comparatively better than other reference models, which is shown in the Table 6. And the model's F1-Score and mAP performances are shown in Figs. 11 and 12 respectively.

Table 5. Performance Metrics Of Helmet Detection

Metrics	HELMET DETECTION
Precision	1.0 at 0.931
Recall	96%
MAP-50	92.6%
F1-Score	90%

Table 6. Comparative Study Of Performance of Helmet Detection

METHODS	ACCURACY	MAP50
VGG16 [5]	78.19%	–
VGG19 [5]	79.11%	–
Inception V3 [5]	84.58%	–
MobileNet [5]	85.19%	–
KNN [6]	74%	–
RetinaNet [6]	80.6%	–
Caffe & InceptionV3 [9]	86%	–
YOLOv8-SS2	92%	92.6%

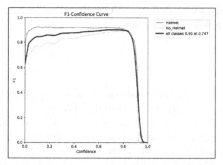

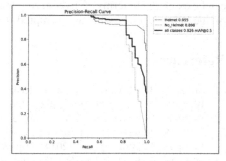

Fig. 11. F1-Score Confidence Curve of Helmet Detection

Fig. 12. Precision-Recall Curve with mAP value of Helmet Detection

5   Conclusion

This paper proposes a fully connected and networked model for trial of undisciplined motorbike riders who violates the traffic rules. Those riders increases the accidents in a traffic or highway. So this model provides a small contribution on saving their lives and also others lives. The model is able to detect those rider's image which can be further passed to the assigned charge personnels to the legalized authority. This can be used to reduce and share the personnel officers duty on catching those lawbreakers. This model is made up of 3 sub-models of motorbike detection, person detection and helmet detection. Proposed motorbike detection model YOLOv8-SS is able to detect the motorbike with the person as a whole and able to achieve an high accuracy of 95% with mAP of 97%. The person detection is predicting the person with a high accuracy of nearly 95% with an mAP value of 99%. And the helmet detection is detecting the helmets and no-helmets classes with an accuracy of 92% with mAP value of 92.6%. After that all the law breakers are saved to a particular file. The proposed model outperforms over many existing models and also solves the automated detection of helmet in heavy traffic under Indian urban roads.

6 Future Scope

In future, the ongoing research can be improved into a vast extent. It can be developed by training with much more dataset images with distinct variations and extending the analysis for further problematic conditions such as night vision, and rainy weather conditions. Another method of advancement would be on the technologies such as Optical Character Recognition (OCR), which enables the extraction of text from images with high accuracy. OCR had been used in multiple real-life applications such as real-time text recognition from videos, handwriting recognition, fraud and security detections. This technology can be used in License Plate Detection with a better accuracy. It can enhance the safety and enforce stricter rules and regulations for riders. Research Paper can be extended in terms of diversifying more by calculating exclusively for the children of age below 4 years who are exempted from helmet violation.

References

1. Sumit, K., Ross, V., Brijs, K., et al.: Risky motorcycle riding behaviour among young riders. BMC Public Health **21**, 1954 (2021). https://doi.org/10.1186/s12889-021-11899-y
2. Bhaskar, P.K., Yong, S.-P.: Image processing based vehicle detection and tracking method. In: 2014 International Conference on Computer and Information Sciences (ICCOINS), Kuala Lumpur, Malaysia, pp. 1–5 (2014). https://doi.org/10.1109/ICCOINS.2014.6868357
3. Waranusast, R., Bundon, N., Timtong, V., Tangnoi, C.: Machine vision techniques for motorcycle safety helmet detection. In: 28th International Conference on Image and Vision Computing, New Zealand (2013)
4. Raj, K.C.D., Chairat, A., Timtong, V., Dailey, M.N., Ekpanyapong, M.: Helmet violation processing using deep learning. Asian Institute of Technology Khlong Luang, Pathum Thani, 12120, Thailand (2018)
5. Boonsirisumpun,- N., Puarungroj,- W., Wairotchanaphuttha, P.: Automatic detector for bikers with no helmet using deep learning. In: 2018 22nd International Computer Science and Engineering Conference (ICSEC), Chiang Mai, Thailand, pp. 1–4 (2018). https://doi.org/10.1109/ICSEC.2018.8712778
6. Lin, H., Deng, J.D., Albers, D., Siebert, F.: Helmet use detection of tracked motorcycles using CNN-based multi-task learning. IEEE Access (2020). https://doi.org/10.1109/ACCESS.2020.3021357
7. Yogameena, B., Menaka, K., Perumaal, S.S.: Deep learning-based helmet wear analysis of a motorcycle rider for intelligent surveillance system. IET Intell. Transp. Syst. (2019)
8. Vishnu, C., Singh, D., Chalavati, K.M., Babu, S.: Detection of motorcyclists without helmet in videos using convolutional neural network. In: 2017 International Joint Conference on Neural Networks (IJCNN), Anchorage, AK, USA, pp. 3036–3041 (2017). https://doi.org/10.1109/IJCNN.2017.7966233
9. Rohith, C.A., Nair, S.A., Nair, P.S., Alphonsa, S., John, N.: An efficient helmet detection for MVD using deep learning. In: 3rd International Conference on Trends in Electronics and Informatics (ICOEI), India (2019)
10. Ultralytics. https://docs.ultralytics.com/

11. Encode. https://encord.com/blog/yolo-object-detection-guide/
12. Roboflow. https://roboflow.com/
13. Analytics-Vidhya. https://medium.com/analytics-vidhya/different-iou-losses-for-faster-and-accurate-object-detection
14. The Hindu. https://www.thehindu.com/news/national/two-wheelers-claimed-highest-number-of-lives-in-accidents-in-2021-ncrb-report/article65829329.ece
15. WHO. https://www.who.int/news-room/fact-sheets/detail/road-traffic-injuries

Automatic Signboard Recognition in Low Quality Night Images

Manas Kagde[1], Priyanka Choudhary[1(✉)] ⓘ, Rishi Joshi[2], and Somnath Dey[1] ⓘ

[1] Indian Institute of Technology Indore, Indore, Madhya Pradesh, India
{ms2004101012,phd2201101006,somnathd}@iiti.ac.in
[2] Shri Vaishnav Vidyapeeth Vishwavidyalaya, Indore, Madhya Pradesh, India

Abstract. An essential requirement for driver assistance systems and autonomous driving technology is implementing a robust system for detecting and recognizing traffic signs. This system enables the vehicle to autonomously analyze the environment and make appropriate decisions regarding its movement, even when operating at higher frame rates. However, traffic sign images captured in inadequate lighting and adverse weather conditions are poorly visible, blurred, faded, and damaged. Consequently, the recognition of traffic signs in such circumstances becomes inherently difficult. This paper addresses the challenges of recognizing traffic signs from images captured in low light, noise, and blurriness. To achieve this goal, a two-step methodology is employed. The first step involves enhancing traffic sign images by applying a modified MIRNet model. In the second step, the YOLOv4 model recognizes traffic signs from enhanced images. The proposed method has achieved a 5.40% increment in mAP@0.5 for low-quality images on YOLOv4. The overall mAP@0.5 of 96.75% has been achieved on the GTSRB dataset. It has also attained mAP@0.5 of 100% on the GTSDB dataset for the broad categories, comparable with the state-of-the-art work.

Keywords: Traffic Sign Recognition · Traffic Sign Detection · YOLOv4 · Modified MIRNet · GTSRB · GTSDB

1 Introduction

Traffic sign recognition is a technology by which intelligent systems like Advanced Driver Assistance Systems (ADAS) [6] can recognize the traffic sign boards on the roads. ADAS are intelligent machines that increase the vehicle's safety by guiding the driver about front road conditions and providing better driving instructions. ADAS and vehicular automation rely on traffic sign recognition algorithms for roadway decision-making processes. Traffic sign detection encompasses the tasks of generating bounding boxes and classifying the content within those bounding boxes. Figure 1 shows the predicted bounding box for the 'Keep right' traffic sign. Traffic sign recognition can be done on both broader and fine-grained categories. In the fine-grained category, each traffic sign acts as a single class, whereas in the case of broader categories, all similar kinds of traffic signs are grouped into

H. Kaur et al. (Eds.): CVIP 2023, CCIS 2010, pp. 478–490, 2024.
https://doi.org/10.1007/978-3-031-58174-8_40

one class. For example, in Fig. 2, all circular traffic signs having background color white and red color border can be grouped under 'Prohibitory' signs, and all the triangular traffic signs with a red border are grouped as 'Danger' signs. Traffic sign recognition becomes even more challenging for fine-grained classes with unfavorable environmental and weather conditions (Fig. 3) [20] such as low contrast, noise, blur, faded, damaged, and occluded signs due to trees, persons or objects.

Fig. 1. Keep Right sign-board with bounding box

Fig. 2. Sample GTSRB Traffic Sign Images (Color figure online)

Fig. 3. Unfavorable environmental road conditions (Color figure online)

The traffic sign recognition methods mainly employ traditional and modern state-of-the-art approaches. Conventional methods like color segmentation [17], color-shape change [19], and Histogram of Oriented Gradients (HOG) [5,24] leverages color, shape, and gradient features to extract the information from images. However, these approaches face challenges due to noise and illumination changes. Modern state-of-the-art algorithms apply Convolutional Neural Network (CNN)-based models [3,16,23] with different data preprocessing methods to reduce the noise in an image. Current state-of-the-art models like Faster R-CNN [8,14], Single Shot Detector (SSD) [10,22], and YOLOv3 [11,13] have recently gained popularity due to notable advancements in performance on object detection and remarkable speed capabilities. Nevertheless, they exhibit computational complexity and encounter issues related to over-fitting as the network size expands. Additionally, their predictive accuracy diminishes when dealing with fine-grained categories in adverse environmental and weather conditions.

Our proposed work adopts a two-step methodology for traffic sign recognition under these challenges. Initially, low-contrast, noisy, and blurry images of traffic signs are enhanced by a modified MIRNet [25] model. The modification is focused on the spatial attention layer and replaced Global Average Pooling + Global Max Pooling with Median Pooling. Then, the enhanced images are passed further to YOLOv4 [1] for traffic sign detection and recognition. The significant contribution of the proposed approach is that it can produce better results on the fine-grained traffic sign categories, mainly when dealing with low-quality images.

The rest of this article is structured as follows: Sect. 2 presents the related work. Section 3 presents our proposed approach. Subsequently, the experimental evaluation and its results are shown in Sect. 4, and Sect. 5 offers our conclusions.

2   Related Work

Extensive research is being conducted in the field of traffic sign recognition, encompassing two primary approaches: traditional methodologies and modern

Deep Learning-based techniques. Sun et al. [16] utilized hough transform and image segmentation to localize traffic signs in the German Traffic Sign Recognition Benchmark (GTSRB) [15] dataset for circular-shaped signs. They used deep learning to detect traffic signs and achieved an accuracy of 98.2%. The authors simplified the problem by condensing the two broader groups from 43 original traffic sign classes. Han et al. [3] proposed a traffic sign recognition method based on LeNet architecture, incorporating shape and color segmentation for Region of Interest (ROI) extraction. The proposed methodology demonstrated 96.2% of accuracy on the GTSRB [15].

Khnissi et al. [7] upgraded a new YOLOv4-tiny-based compact classifier. The model could recognize all 43 GTSRB [15] traffic signs with an average accuracy of 95.44%. At the same time, they tried to save computational power and processing time by squeezing the network. Novak et al. [11] proposed a model for road object detection into five broad classes. The method achieved a classification accuracy of 99.2% for detected traffic signs in different weather conditions for their independently created dataset. Jianjun et al. [22] used SSD [10], which integrates the Path Aggregation Network (PAN) with the Receptive Field (RF) module, resulting in improved accuracy. The authors also claimed that as compared with the common object detection algorithms such as Faster R-CNN [2], RetinaNet, and YOLOv3 [12], the SSD-RP could achieve a better balance between detection time and detection precision.

3   Proposed Method

This paper introduces a novel two-step methodology for traffic sign recognition for various challenging conditions. In the initial step, a Modified MIRNet [25] is employed to enhance the quality of low-quality test images. Subsequently, the YOLOv4 [1] model is utilized in the second step to predict the improved output results in terms of mean Average Precision (mAP) and accuracy. The spatial attention layer of the MIRNet [25] model has been modified and trained the model to generate better-enhanced test image results.

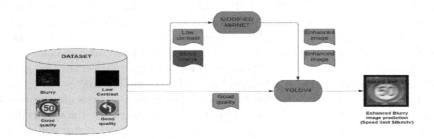

Fig. 4. Flow diagram of the proposed architecture

Figure 4 illustrates the flow diagram of the proposed architecture. The proposed approach mentions the two-step process, wherein the first step, the low-quality images, are passed to the Modified MIRNet model. Subsequently, in the second step, the enhanced images obtained from the Modified MIRNet model are fed into the YOLOv4 model for prediction. Moreover, the good-quality images are provided directly to the YOLOv4 model for prediction.

3.1 Original Architecture of YOLOv4

The YOLOv4 model has been used as our base model for prediction. Regarding optimal speed and accuracy, YOLOv4 [1] performs much better at a higher frame rate. It comes in a one-stage detector category, where detection and recognition happen in a single shot during training. There are the following building blocks of YOLOv4:

1. **Backbone** generates a feature map with the help of CSPDarknet53 [18]. It is like a DenseNet architecture, which concatenates the previous inputs with the current input.
2. **Neck** aggregates features from different backbone stages with several top-down and bottom-up paths to segregate the useful contextual features using Spatial Pyramid Pooling (SPP) [4] and Path Aggregation Network (PAN) [9].
3. **Head** is responsible for the classification and the bounding box generation. Despite these, YOLOv4 introduces new features, Bag of Freebies (BoF) and Bag of Specials (BoS), to leverage a combination of cost-effective modifications in training strategy and deliver significant accuracy improvements, respectively.

3.2 Modified MIRNet

Image enhancement is a sophisticated methodology to generate a refined and superior-quality image by utilizing low-quality source images. To accomplish this task, the most suitable approach involves an MIRNet [25] model, which is based on CNN. It has proven to be highly effective in generating solutions for this purpose. This study has modified the architecture of MIRNet, shown in Fig. 5. The different resolution low contrast, noisy, and blurred images are passed through the modified MIRNet model. The feature maps of each image with the different resolutions are then inputted into the modified Dual Attention layer for feature extraction as shown in Fig. 5b. These are then passed to the Selective Kernel Feature Fusion (SKFF) for feature aggregation. The Dual Attention Unit and SKFF are applied again to produce the final results.

Multi-scale Residual Block (MRB). The primary component of MRB encompasses the Selective Kernel Feature Fusion, a modified Dual Attention block, and an upsampling-downsampling module. Figure 5a shows the MRB's structure in MIRNet [25]. MRB facilitates the sharing of valuable information among interconnected layers operating in parallel. This process leads to the generation of improved-quality features from initially low-quality images.

Selective Kernel Feature Fusion (SKFF). This feature aggregation network employs a self-attention mechanism to integrate features obtained from various resolutions. It is responsible for the effective fusion and representation of information. Figure 5a shows the SKFF structure in MIRNet [25].

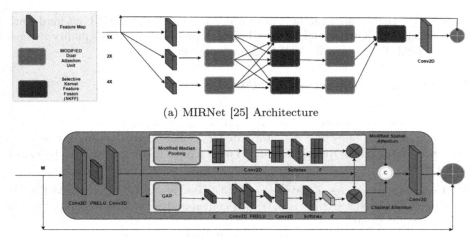

(a) MIRNet [25] Architecture

(b) Modified dual attention unit of MIRNet Architecture

Fig. 5. Proposed Modified MIRNet Architecture Diagram

Dual Attention Unit (DAU). The network incorporates a feature extraction mechanism that effectively suppresses irrelevant features and selectively allows only highly relevant features to be retained. Figure 5a shows the dual attention mechanism in MIRNet [25]. The term "dual" refers to utilizing both spatial and channel attention to capture valuable features. The spatial channel combines Global Average Pooling (GAP) and Global Max Pooling (GMP) techniques to capture the inter-spatial dependencies in the convolutional features. On the other hand, channel attention focuses on extracting connections between different channels within the feature maps. This is achieved through GAP to encode global context across spatial dimensions and two convolutional layers with a sigmoid activation function.

Modified Spatial Attention. Figure 5b shows the modified dual attention mechanism in the MIRNet [25] model. The GAP+GMP combination in the Spatial Attention layer has been substituted with Median Pooling. Average pooling is a technique that disperses noise across all blocks within a given context. In contrast, median pooling is employed to eliminate noise from the data. It further helps in elucidating edges and extracting some useful spatial feature maps. It also helps to integrate two different operations performed individually on each feature map.

4   Experimental Results and Analysis

This section encompasses the dataset, data preparation, training, results, and comparisons of our proposed approach with existing approaches. We have used

Python programming language within the Anaconda environment, incorporating libraries such as OpenCV, TensorFlow, and Keras for MIRNet and the darknet framework for YOLOv4. All the experiments have been conducted on NVIDIA GeForce RTX 3090 GPU equipped with 24 GB of RAM and 10496 cores.

4.1 Datasets and Preprocessing

The GTSDB [5] and GTSRB [15] datasets have been utilized for our experiment since they contain a wide variety of traffic signs, which help to make a fine-grained classification. Table 1 shows the categorization of the GTSDB and GTSRB datasets, respectively. The training images of the GTSDB contain full-size images of the traffic sign on roads, whereas GTSRB contains cropped smaller-size traffic sign images. The GTSDB dataset has four major classes: Prohibitory, Mandatory, Danger, and Other. In contrast, the GTSRB dataset encompasses a more detailed classification framework with 43 fine-grained classes. To effectively train the network, it is necessary to preprocess and convert the images and annotations into the desired format. Specifically, the conversion of images from ppm and png formats to jpg format. Additionally, each image's annotation files in CSV format are separated in both the GTSDB and GTSRB datasets, resulting in the input being in YOLO format.

Table 1. Details of GTSDB [5] and GTSRB [15] dataset.

Dataset	Total Images	Training Images	Test Images	Classes	Categories
GTSDB [5]	900	600	300	4	4
GTSRB [15]	51838	39209	12629	43	43

4.2 Training and Validation on Modified MIRNet

The main objective of the proposed approach is to enhance the low-quality traffic images using the modified MIRNet [25] model. The training of the Modified MIRNet model requires both low and high-quality images of the same training image. However, GTSRB and GTSDB datasets do not contain a pair of low and high-quality images of the same input image. So, the modified MIRNet model is trained with the Low Light (LOL) [21] benchmark dataset, which contains low and high-quality general-purpose image pairs. Specifically, 300 pairs for training and 185 pairs for validation have been utilized in our study.

The parameters used for training are *max-batches* as 4, *image-size* of 600 × 400, *random-crops* of 128 × 128. The parameters for checking the performance of the Modified MIRNet model are: *Loss* and *PSNR* (Peak Signal Noise Ratio). *Loss* tells how close our predicted image is to the actual image, and *PSNR* gives the ratio of the image signal to that of the noise present in it. So, the lower the noise, the higher the *PSNR*, leading to better prediction results.

The *Epochs* vs. *Loss* curve for the training and validation is shown in Fig. 6. It has been observed that the validation loss is within the range of 0.10 to 0.12 after

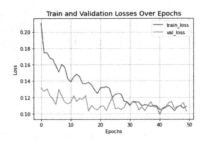

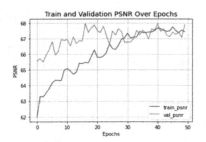

Fig. 6. Epochs vs Loss curve with Modified MIRNet [25]

Fig. 7. Epochs vs PSNR curve with Modified MIRNet [25]

20th iteration and reaches the lowest at 0.10 at the 40th iteration. The *Epochs* vs. *PSNR* curve, as shown in Fig. 7 indicates that the validation *PSNR* is always in the ratio of 67% to 68% after 30th iteration and reached the maximum at the 40th iteration.

4.3 Training and Validation on YOLOv4 Model

The YOLOv4 model is trained on both GTSRB [15] and GTSDB [5] datasets to test the performance of traffic sign recognition on broad categories and fine categories, respectively. The training parameters used in the model for the GTSRB dataset are: *batch* = 64, *subdivisions* = 32, *saturation* = 1.5, *exposure* = 1.5, *hue* = 0.1, *learning-rate* = 0.01, *max-batches* = 86000, *steps* = [68800, 77400], *scales* = [0.1, 0.1] and *classes* = 43.

On the other hand, the training parameters used in the GTSDB dataset are *max-batches* = 8000, *steps* = [6400, 7200], *exposure* = 1.5 and *hue* = 0.1. Here, classes are modified to 4 and each of its preceding convolutional filters to 27. Model training takes around 5,000 iterations to get better results.

The model overfitting is risky due to insufficient training images. Consequently, it is essential to incorporate data augmentation techniques. We have employed the Mosaic data augmentation technique built with YOLOv4. This includes random rotation, crop, saturation, exposure, and hue changes.

The performance of the YOLOv4 model is usually measured with the help of Precision, recall, *f1−score* and Mean Average Precision *(mAP)*. *Precision* can be defined as the correctness of the model prediction compared to all the model predictions. *Recall* can be defined as the correctness of the model predictions compared to the actual. *f1−score* is the harmonic mean of the *Precision* and the *recall* values, and *mAP* is the mean of the average Precision of each class.

4.4 Results of Proposed Model

Our proposed approach passes low-quality images like blurry, noisy, and low contrast through the modified MIRNet [25] model as mentioned in Fig. 4. In

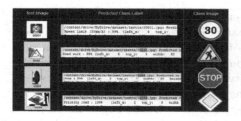 

Fig. 8. Prediction results on the good quality GTSRB [15] test images

contrast, the good-quality images are directly fed to the YOLOv4 [1] model for prediction.

Results on Good-Quality Images. The good-quality images in the GTSRB [15] test set are passed to the YOLOv4 model for the prediction. Figure 8 shows that the proposed model correctly predicts the traffic sign in good quality test images with a probability of more than 99% for the GTSRB dataset. Hence, the proposed model performs well on good-quality test images.

Results on Low-Quality Images in Unconstrained Environment. In an unconstrained environment, it is challenging to predict traffic signs due to partial occlusion, faded or damaged signboards, partial or complete illumination, snow-

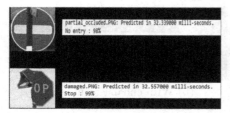 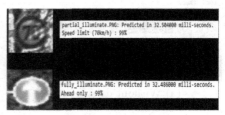

(a) Traffic sign recognition on partially occluded and damaged images.

(b) Traffic sign recognition on partially and fully illuminated images.

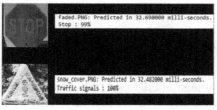 

(c) Traffic sign recognition on faded and snow-covered images.

(d) Traffic sign recognition on multiple sign images.

Fig. 9. Traffic sign recognition for low-quality test images.

covered, multiple signs in a single image, etc. The proposed approach is tested for low-quality images caused by the above issues. Figure 9a shows that the proposed model correctly predicts the traffic sign from partially occluded and damaged images. In partial or over-illuminated conditions, the proposed model correctly predicts traffic signs with high probability, as shown in Fig. 9b. Figure 9c shows the correct prediction of the model if signs are faded or covered by snow with the probability of 99%. With multiple traffic signs in a single image, the proposed model can predict 'Yield' and 'Priority Road' traffic signs with high probability, as shown in Fig. 9d. YOLOv4 effectively identifies multiple signs in the image, but it erroneously predicts the 'Speed limit 50 kmph' sign, identifying it as '20 kmph'. It is worth noting that the confidence level for this misclassification is relatively low. From Fig. 9, it is evident that the proposed model performs well for low-quality images.

Results on the Modified MIRNet Enhanced Images. One thousand six hundred low-quality images are manually chosen and provided to the modified MIRNet [25] model. The resultant enhanced quality images from the modified MIRNet model are passed through the YOLOv4 [1] model. Figure 10 shows the predicted class on the original low-quality images (Fig. 10a) and enhanced images (Fig. 10b). It has been observed that the predictions made by the YOLOv4 model on the enhanced images are correct and uniquely localized.

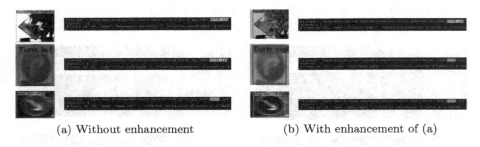

(a) Without enhancement   (b) With enhancement of (a)

Fig. 10. YOLOv4 [1] prediction results with and without modified MIRNet enhancement

4.5   Results on GTSDB with YOLOv4

With the broader categories of GTSDB [5] dataset as shown in Table 2, the YOLOv4 [1] model is trained with a lesser number of full-sized traffic sign images, which are suitable for the real-time scenarios. An average precision of 99.99% with Prohibitory traffic signs, 100% with Mandatory class, 100% with Danger signs, and 100% with other classes has been achieved. The overall Precision of 99%, Recall of 99%, and the **mAP@0.5** of 100% have been achieved for four broad categories.

Table 2. Testing results of GTSDB [5] dataset: **mAP**: 99.99% **(or 100%), precision = 99%, recall% and F1-score=** 99.99%.

Class	AP	TP	FP
Prohibitory	99.99%	122	1
Mandatory	100%	39	0
Danger	100%	38	1
Other	100%	39	0

4.6 Comparison of YOLOv4 and YOLOv4 + Modified MIRNet Results

The following subsections provide a comprehensive evaluation of the performance of the YOLOv4 model, both before and after the image enhancement.

Comparison with Low Quality Images. One thousand six hundred low-quality images are manually selected and enhanced using a modified version of MIRNet. The enhanced images are then passed through YOLOv4 for prediction. When GTSRB [15] low-quality images are passed through YOLOv4, the **mAP** of 84.78% is achieved. However, when the same images are enhanced through modified MIRNet [25] and passed through YOLOv4, the **mAP** is increased to 90.18%. The YOLOv4 [1] has demonstrated superior performance when combined with the modified MIRNet [25] model (Fig. 4).

Comparison with Full Dataset. The model is trained initially with the GTSRB [15] dataset. The model's performance is first checked without applying any enhancement to the test images of the full GTSRB [15] dataset. The low-quality images are then enhanced and replaced with the 1600 modified MIRNet-enhanced images in the GTSRB [15] test set. In both cases, the Precision (accuracy) is improved by 1%, and the overall mAP@0.5 has been increased from 96.65% to 96.75%. Thus, the modified MIRNet model is able to achieve an overall improvement in mAP.

4.7 Comparison with the Existing Work

This subsection covers the comparative analysis of results achieved by our model on accuracy and mAP values with other existing models.

Comparison Between Different Techniques on GTSRB Dataset. Table 3 shows the comparisons of results of the proposed approach with different CNN-based techniques in terms of accuracy and with earlier YOLO versions in terms of mAP. The proposed method is able to generate an mAP of 96.75%, which is better than earlier YOLO versions. On the low contrast, noisy, and blurry test set images, the accuracy is increased by 5%, and the overall mAP is increased from 84.78% to 90.18% on our model. After image enhancement on Modified MIRNet, the overall GTSRB [15] test-set accuracy is increased by 1%, and the mAP increased from 96.65% to 96.75%. The accuracy achieved by our model is comparable to the CNN technique used in [16]. In terms of mAP@0.5 score, our approach easily beats YOLOv3 [7,13], YOLOv3 Tiny [7,13], and Compact Squeezed YOLOv4 [7].

Table 3. Results Comparison of Different Models with GTSRB

Algorithm	mAP % @ 0.50	Av. IOU	Accuracy
CNN [16]	–	–	98.2%
CNN (NVIDIA Jetson Embedded TX1) [3]	–	–	96.2%
YOLOv3 [7,13]	94.05	75.63	–
YOLOv3 Tiny [7,13]	90.04	75.26	–
YOLOv4 Tiny [1,7]	97.06	74.15	–
Compact New Squeezed YOLO [7]	95.44	71.68	-
YOLOv4 without enhancement	**96.65**	**78.24**	**95%**
modified MIRNet+YOLOv4 (proposed)	**96.75**	**78.92**	**96%**

Comparison Between Different Techniques Trained on GTSDB Dataset. The YOLOv4 model is trained with the GTSDB dataset for the four broad categories. A precision of 99%, recall of 99%, and mAP of 100% have been achieved on the YOLOv4 [1] model. Table 4 shows the comparisons of the different traffic sign detector results with YOLOv4 [1]. As mentioned in Table 4, mAP achieved by Faster R-CNN [8,22] is 97.9% using ResNet50 backbone, SSD [10,22] is 93.2% using VGG16 backbone, YOLOv3 [13,22] is 93.8% using Darknet53 backbone, SSD-RP [22] is 95.4% using ResNet50 backbone, and RetinaNet [22] is 96.7%. All the mAP percentages are lesser than YOLOv4 [1] using CSPDarknet53 [18] as a backbone.

Table 4. Results comparison of different models with GTSDB

Detection algorithms	Backbone networks in algorithms	mAP (%)
Faster R-CNN [14,22]	ResNet50	97.9
SSD [10,22]	VGG16	93.2
YOLOv3 [13,22]	DarkNet53	93.8
SSD-RP [22]	VGG16	95.4
RetinaNet [22]	ResNet50	96.7
YOLOv4 [1]	**CSPDarknet53 [18]**	**99.99**

5 Conclusion

We have proposed a two-step approach for traffic sign recognition. In the first step, a Modified MIRNet is used for low-quality image enhancement, and in the second step, the YOLOv4 model is employed to produce better output results in terms of mAP and accuracy. The experiments have been performed on the GTSDB and GTSRB datasets. Through experiments, the proposed approach has achieved higher mAP and accuracy values with both broader categories (4 categories) and fine-grained classes (43). The modified MIRNet model has also attained a higher mAP value on low-quality images. In future works, more changes can be made to the proposed architecture using other enhancement techniques. The changes can be made to the PAN in the Neck part of YOLOv4. Also, different state-of-the-art algorithms can be tested with the GTSRB dataset to check the model performance.

References

1. Bochkovskiy, A., Wang, C.Y., Liao, H.Y.M.: YOLOv4: optimal speed and accuracy of object detection. arXiv preprint arXiv:2004.10934 (2020)
2. Girshick, R.: Fast R-CNN. In: 2015 IEEE International Conference on Computer Vision (ICCV), pp. 1440–1448 (2015)
3. Han, Y., Oruklu, E.: Traffic sign recognition based on the NVIDIA Jetson TX1 embedded system using convolutional neural networks. In: 2017 IEEE 60th International Midwest Symposium on Circuits and Systems (MWSCAS), pp. 184–187 (2017)
4. He, K., Zhang, X., Ren, S., Sun, J.: Spatial pyramid pooling in deep convolutional networks for visual recognition. IEEE Trans. Pattern Anal. Mach. Intell. **37**(9), 1904–1916 (2015)
5. Houben, S., Stallkamp, J., Salmen, J., Schlipsing, M., Igel, C.: Detection of traffic signs in real-world images: the German traffic sign detection benchmark. In: The 2013 International Joint Conference on Neural Networks (IJCNN), pp. 1–8 (2013)
6. Karthika, R., Parameswaran, L.: A novel convolutional neural network based architecture for object detection and recognition with an application to traffic sign recognition from road scenes. Pattern Recognit. Image Anal. **32**(2), 351–362 (2022)
7. Khnissi, K., Jabeur, C.B., Seddik, H.: Implementation of a compact traffic signs recognition system using a new squeezed YOLO. Int. J. Intell. Transp. Syst. Res. **20**(2), 466–482 (2022)
8. Lin, T.Y., Dollar, P., Girshick, R., He, K., Hariharan, B., Belongie, S.: Feature pyramid networks for object detection. In: IEEE Conference on Computer Vision and Pattern Recognition (CVPR), pp. 936–944 (2017)
9. Liu, S., Qi, L., Qin, H., Shi, J., Jia, J.: Path aggregation network for instance segmentation. In: 2018 IEEE/CVF Conference on Computer Vision and Pattern Recognition, pp. 8759–8768 (2018)
10. Liu, W., et al.: SSD: single shot multibox detector. In: Leibe, B., Matas, J., Sebe, N., Welling, M. (eds.) ECCV 2016. LNCS, vol. 9905, pp. 21–37. Springer, Cham (2016). https://doi.org/10.1007/978-3-319-46448-0_2
11. Novak, B., Ili?, V., Pavkovi?, B.: YOLOv3 Algorithm with additional convolutional neural network trained for traffic sign recognition. In: 2020 Zooming Innovation in Consumer Technologies Conference (ZINC), pp. 165–168 (2020)

12. Redmon, J., Divvala, S., Girshick, R., Farhadi, A.: You only look once: unified, real-time object detection. In: 2016 IEEE Conference on Computer Vision and Pattern Recognition (CVPR), pp. 779–788 (2016)

13. Redmon, J., Farhadi, A.: YOLOv3: an incremental improvement. arXiv preprint arXiv:1804.02767 (2018)

14. Ren, S., He, K., Girshick, R., Sun, J.: Faster R-CNN: towards real-time object detection with region proposal networks. IEEE Trans. Pattern Anal. Mach. Intell. **39**(6), 1137–1149 (2017)

15. Stallkamp, J., Schlipsing, M., Salmen, J., Igel, C.: Man vs. computer: benchmarking machine learning algorithms for traffic sign recognition. Neural Netw. **32**, 323–332 (2012)

16. Sun, Y., Ge, P., Liu, D.: Traffic sign detection and recognition based on convolutional neural network. In: 2019 Chinese Automation Congress (CAC), pp. 2851–2854 (2019)

17. Tai, Y.W., Jia, J., Tang, C.K.: Soft color segmentation and its applications. IEEE Trans. Pattern Anal. Mach. Intell. **29**(9), 1520–1537 (2007)

18. Wang, C.Y., Mark Liao, H.Y., Wu, Y.H., Chen, P.Y., Hsieh, J.W., Yeh, I.H.: CSPNet: a new backbone that can enhance learning capability of CNN. In: 2020 IEEE/CVF Conference on Computer Vision and Pattern Recognition Workshops (CVPRW), pp. 1571–1580 (2020)

19. Wang, Q., Liu, X.: Traffic sign segmentation in natural scenes based on color and shape features. In: 2014 IEEE Workshop on Advanced Research and Technology in Industry Applications (WARTIA), pp. 374–377 (2014)

20. Wang, Z., Wang, J., Li, Y., Wang, S.: Traffic sign recognition with lightweight two-stage model in complex scenes. IEEE Trans. Intell. Transp. Syst. **23**(2), 1121–1131 (2022)

21. Wei, C., Wang, W., Yang, W., Liu, J.: Deep retinex decomposition for low-light enhancement. arXiv preprint arXiv:1808.04560 (2018)

22. Wu, J., Liao, S.: Traffic sign detection based on SSD combined with receptive field module and path aggregation network. Comput. Intell. Neurosci. **2022** (2022)

23. Yang, Y., Luo, H., Xu, H., Wu, F.: Towards real-time traffic sign detection and classification. IEEE Trans. Intell. Transp. Syst. **17**(7), 2022–2031 (2016)

24. Yao, C., Wu, F., Chen, H.J., Hao, X.L., Shen, Y.: Traffic sign recognition using HOG-SVM and grid search. In: 2014 12th International Conference on Signal Processing (ICSP), pp. 962–965 (2014)

25. Zamir, S.W., et al.: Learning enriched features for real image restoration and enhancement. In: Vedaldi, A., Bischof, H., Brox, T., Frahm, J.-M. (eds.) ECCV 2020. LNCS, vol. 12370, pp. 492–511. Springer, Cham (2020). https://doi.org/10.1007/978-3-030-58595-2_30

An Effective CNN-Based Approach for Synthetic Face Image Detection in Pre-social and Post-social Media Context

Protyay Dey$^{(\boxtimes)}$ ⓘ, Abhilasha S. Jadhav ⓘ, and Kapil Rana ⓘ

Indian Institute of Technology Ropar, Rupnagar, Punjab, India
`2022aim1009@iitrpr.ac.in`

Abstract. The proliferation of image manipulation techniques, including DeepFake technology, has posed significant threats to the authenticity and credibility of images. Accurately classifying real and fake images has become crucial in fields such as forensics, security, and media authentication. However, detecting fake images during downloading and uploading from social networks is even more challenging. In this paper, we present an approach based on the EfficientNet model to learn discriminative features for classifying real and synthetic face images shared on social networks. We conducted extensive experiments using the TrueFace dataset, which comprises real and synthetic facial images shared on three major social media platforms. We employed the EfficientNet-B2 model trained on a combination of pre-social and post-social images from the TrueFace dataset. The presented approach outperforms all other methods, achieving accuracies of 99.98%, 100%, and 100% for images shared on Facebook, Telegram, and Twitter. This approach demonstrates exceptional performance when evaluated on a distinct dataset of images shared on social media platforms, separate from the images used for training.

Keywords: EfficientNetB2 · TrueFace dataset · DeepFakes · Image Forensics · Fake face identification

1 Introduction

With recent advances in mobile technology and the Internet, social media platforms have become an important channel for sharing photos and videos publicly. It is also a major source of information because a person pays more attention and is more actively engaged with visual content, substantially improving the probability of sharing such content. Digitally created deep fake images have caused great public concern. Advanced image processing tools based on generative adversarial networks (GAN) are available to everyone. These GANs can create very realistic fakes, especially for images. Recent studies have shown that even experts have difficulty distinguishing between real faces and synthetic faces generated by GANs, which are incredibly realistic [1]. This has led to the emergence

H. Kaur et al. (Eds.): CVIP 2023, CCIS 2010, pp. 491–502, 2024.
https://doi.org/10.1007/978-3-031-58174-8_41

of deep fakes that threaten the credibility of visual content online, especially on social media platforms. Fake profiles on social networks have already caused damage and attempts have been made to manipulate information about events such as the Russian-Ukrainian war [2]. This is an alarming trend of image manipulation that is causing the spread of misinformation and fake information [3].

Therefore, it is crucial to prioritize the development of methods that ensure trust in images shared on social media platforms. Several works in image forensics have focused on detecting image manipulation and identifying digital sources [4, 5]. These studies have shown promising results in controlled environments [6]. Recently, research communities have attempted to apply forensic methods to real-world applications, including social media platforms where digital media are shared online [7]. In the context of deep forgeries, researchers have demonstrated their ability to distinguish synthetic images from real images by training data models to detect traces of [8,9] generators.

Creating synthetic images involves different generation methods, and data-driven detectors often face challenges when the test and training generators are distinct. Fake content tends to gain popularity on social media before forensic analysis can be performed. Post-processing used by sharing platforms can mask and weaken detection methods [10]. Post-processing functions of social networks (compression, resizing) can change the statistics specific to the image and affect the evaluation. It is crucial to develop a method to distinguish between real images posted on popular sharing sites and content created artificially using sophisticated methods. In this work, we present a CNN method based on EfficientNet [11] for real and synthetic image face recognition. Importantly, the presented method can distinguish between real and synthetic facial images shared on three major social media sites.

The main contributions of this paper are as follows:

- We present a CNN-based EfficientNet-B2 model specifically designed for classifying real and synthetic facial images shared on social networks. This model includes compound scaling, which allows us to balance accuracy and computational efficiency.
- Extensive experiments were conducted on the TrueFace dataset containing real and synthetic facial images shared on popular social media platforms such as Facebook, Twitter, and Telegram.
- The robustness of our approach was evaluated in a cross-dataset environment, demonstrating that it could generalize and accurately classify real and synthetic images shared across different social media platforms.
- We performed a comprehensive evaluation of the proposed method by comparing it with alternative CNN-based approaches such as VGG19, ResNet50, DenseNet121, and MnasNet.

The rest of the paper is organized as follows. Section 2 summarizes the related work. Section 3 explains the EfficientNet-B2 model for real and synthetic facial image classification. Experiments and results including the comparison with comparative models are presented in Sect. 4. Finally, we conclude the paper in Sect. 5.

2 Related Works

Researchers have focused on media forensics to address the challenges of maintaining the authenticity of manipulated visual media and shared images and videos. However, if the test generator is different from the training generator, it becomes difficult to detect fake content as it spreads quickly on social networks and evades forensic analysis. Benchmark datasets containing synthetic and real images are essential for evaluating forensic detectors in real-world scenarios.

Related works on DeepFake image classification have emerged as an important research area in recent years. The goal of deepfake image classification is to develop algorithms and models capable of distinguishing between authentic and manipulated images. The survey of [3] provides a comprehensive overview of various face manipulation techniques like Extensive Face Synthesis, Identity Swap, Attribute Manipulation, and Expression Swap, also includes deepfake generation methods, and presents an extensive review of deepfake detection methods. The study described in [12] utilized the ResNet50 model as the primary architecture to achieve their results. Initially, the researchers fine-tuned the baseline model using pre-social data. Subsequently, the fine-tuned model was further adjusted to handle datasets from Facebook, Twitter, Telegram, and a combined dataset. This multi-step fine-tuning process enabled the model to adapt and improve its performance on each specific dataset. In addition, the researchers conducted cross-testing across different datasets to thoroughly analyze and evaluate the obtained results.

The works on StyleGAN and StyleGAN2 by Karras et al. [13] have significantly contributed to the field of generative adversarial networks (GANs) and image synthesis. This work introduced StyleGAN, which incorporates a style-based generator architecture that separates the high-level and low-level structure information of images. This enables control over different aspects of the generated images, such as their style, pose, and content. In this study [14], the authors perform an in-depth analysis of the image quality produced by StyleGAN. They propose improvements to the model, including modifications to the generator's architecture and loss functions, resulting in higher-fidelity generated images.

In recent years, the field of convolutional neural networks (CNNs) has witnessed significant advancements in model scaling techniques. The conventional approach involves independently scaling the depth, width, or resolution of CNNs, but this often results in sub-optimal performance or excessive computational requirements. To address these limitations [11] presents a novel compound scaling method that uniformly scales the network width, depth, and resolution while maintaining a constant resource constraint. The authors propose a scaling formula, referred to as compound scaling, which involves finding optimal scaling coefficients for each dimension. These coefficients are determined using a grid search technique, with the constraint being a specific resource metric such as the number of floating-point operations (FLOPs). To further enhance computational efficiency, EfficientNet introduces a new scaling technique, inspired by the MobileNetV2 [15]. This method focuses on reducing the number of parameters without compromising performance. It achieves this by employing a combination of depth-wise separable convolutions and inverted residual blocks.

The EfficientNet models are trained using standard data augmentation techniques, including image scaling and random cropping, and are evaluated on various benchmark datasets such as ImageNet [16]. The results demonstrate that EfficientNet achieves state-of-the-art performance while being more computationally efficient compared to previous scaling approaches. The authors achieve superior performance with fewer computational resources. The proposed methodology represents a significant contribution to the field of model scaling for CNNs and paves the way for future advancements in efficient neural network architectures.

3   Proposed Methodology

This section describes the approach for the detection of real and synthetic images, given an input face image. In the presented approach an RGB image is passed as an input to the EfficientNet-B2 model for feature extraction and further classification. EfficientNet-B2 is a deep CNN model from the EfficientNet class of CNN models. It is specifically designed to achieve a balance between model size and computational efficiency while delivering high performance in image classification problems. The architecture of EfficientNet-B2 is built upon a combination of key components, including convolutional layers, skip connections, and efficient network scaling techniques. The architecture of the EfficientNet-B2 model is shown in Fig. 2 and the building block of the model is shown in Fig. 1.

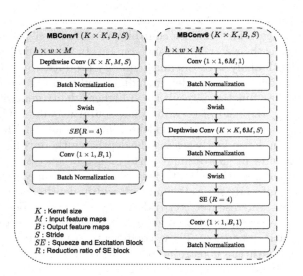

Fig. 1. The architecture of building blocks of EfficientNet.

The model consists of multiple blocks, each containing a sequence of convolutional layers, batch normalization layers, and non-linear activation functions. EfficientNet-B2 adopts compound scaling, a technique that uniformly scales the network's width, depth, and resolution while adhering to a consistent resource constraint. This scaling method enables the model to efficiently capture and represent the complex features and patterns inherent in the dataset. By employing a depth-wise separable convolution strategy, EfficientNet-B2 decomposes the traditional convolution operation into two distinct operations: a depth-wise convolution and a point-wise convolution. This approach effectively decreases the number of parameters and computational complexity, resulting in enhanced efficiency. These architectural choices highlight EfficientNet-B2's ability to trade off between model performance and computational requirements, making it well-suited for image classification problems. EfficientNet-B2 has a similar architecture to other different CNN models in the EfficientNet family (EfficientNet-(B0, B1, B2, B3, B4, B5, B6, and B7)) but with specific scaling factors determined based on the B2 configuration. The input image is then passed to the EfficientNet-B2 model. The model extracts low-level and high-level features related to real and synthetic facial images for classification.

Stage i	Operator $\hat{\mathcal{F}}_i$	Resolution $\hat{H}_i \times \hat{W}_i$	#Channels $\hat{C}_i$	#Layers $\hat{L}_i$
1	Conv3x3	224×224	32	1
2	MBConv1, k3x3	112×112	16	1
3	MBConv6, k3x3	112×112	24	2
4	MBConv6, k5x5	56×56	48	2
5	MBConv6, k3x3	28×28	88	3
6	MBConv6, k5x5	14×14	120	3
7	MBConv6, k5x5	14×14	208	4
8	MBConv6, k3x3	7×7	352	1
9	Conv1x1 & Pooling	7×7	1408	1
10	FC	1408	2	1

Fig. 2. Architecture and parameters of EfficientNet-B2 model [11].

4   Experiments and Results

In this section, we first present information about the datasets and settings used for our experiments. Then, we share the results obtained from our proposed approach and compare them with other comparative methods. In the subsequent subsections, we provide detailed insights into our experimental settings, describing the specific models utilized, the preprocessing techniques applied, and any data augmentation methods employed. Additionally, we outline the experiments conducted, present the evaluation metrics used, and discuss the obtained results in terms of model performance and classification accuracy.

Additionally, we conducted an ablation study to ensure optimal model selection for our image classification task in a post-social media context. In particular, we investigate the performance of three different versions of EfficientNet: B0,

B1, and B2. Through a comprehensive and systematic evaluation of these models within our experimental setup, we aim to discern the most effective model among the various variations.

4.1   Dataset

We evaluate our proposed approach on the TrueFace dataset [12]. To the best of our knowledge, the TrueFace dataset is currently the only publicly available dataset that includes both real and synthetic facial images shared on social media platforms. It provides images to perform experiments to determine the difference between real and synthetic images. It consists of 210,000 face images divided into two sets: pre-social and post-social. The pre-social set consists of 70,000 real and 80,000 synthetic images. All the images in the pre-social set are of size $1024 \times 1024 \times 3$. The synthetic images were created using two popular generator models called StyleGAN and StyleGAN2. Each GAN model generated 40,000 synthetic images. The real images present in the TrueFace dataset are included from the FFHQ dataset [13]. The FFHQ Dataset was originally designed as a benchmark for Generative Adversarial Networks (GANs) [17], as a reliable source of authentic facial images. The sample images of the pre-social set are shown in Fig. 3. The post-social dataset contains 60,000 images shared on three popular social media platforms: Facebook, Twitter, and Telegram where each social media platform has 20000 images: 10000 real images and 10000 synthetic images. The reason there are three different versions of a single image is that each social media platform applies different post-processing to the uploaded images while storing them on their servers. Analyzing all three variants provides us with useful insights into a model's behavior when provided with images having different post-processing applied to them.

Fig. 3. Illustration of sample images from the pre-social set of TrueFace dataset.

4.2 Experimental Setting

The experiments were conducted on a system consisting of an A100 Tensor Core GPU of 40 GB memory and a 3.39 GHz AMD-EPYC-7742 CPU with 64 GB RAM. The TrueFace dataset has been divided into two sets: the training set and the testing set in a proportion of 70% and 30%, respectively. We employed a seed-based random splitting technique to distribute the images evenly across both sets to ensure reproducibility and integrity. This approach ensured that our models were trained and evaluated consistently on a predetermined set of images throughout our experiments. The purpose of implementing this strategy was to mitigate potential biases or inconsistencies that may arise from using different subsets of images for training and testing. All images were resized to a dimension of $224 \times 224 \times 3$. The models aimed to perform binary classification, distinguishing between real and synthetic input images. The experiments were conducted using the PyTorch 2.0.1 framework and CUDA version 11.7 for GPU acceleration. A mini-batch size of 64 was used across all experiments. The models were trained for a maximum of 100 epochs, employing an early stopper with a patience factor of 10. The early stopper monitored the loss to determine when to stop training. We picked the model with maximum testing accuracy. We utilized the AdamW optimizer with an initial learning rate of 3×10^{-4}, benefiting from its regularization capabilities by separating weight decay from exponential moving averages compared to traditional Adam. Additionally, a learning rate scheduler was applied, with a minimum learning rate set to 10^{-6} and a patience of 10.

4.3 Results and Analysis

We thoroughly evaluate our approach through three experiments using different combinations of the TrueFace dataset to assess its effectiveness. In the first experiment, models were trained on the pre-social set of the TrueFace dataset. The second experiment involved training on a combined variant of the True-Face dataset, which included both pre-social and post-social set images. Lastly, cross-dataset testing was conducted, where models were trained exclusively on each social media platform image and evaluated on the same and other social media platform images. We conduct a set of experiments to evaluate the performance of the proposed approach along with a comparative analysis with different CNN-based approaches including VGG19 [18], ResNet50 [19], DenseNet12 [20], MnasNet [21].

Table 1. Comparative analysis of different CNN based methods on pre-social set of TrueFace dataset.

Models	# Parameters	Accuracy	F1-score
VGG19	144M	99.95	99.95
ResNet50	26M	99.71	99.71
DenseNet121	7.97M	99.82	99.83
MnasNet	4M	99.88	99.88
EfficientNet-B2	9.2M	**99.97**	**99.97**

Results on Pre-social Dataset. In this experiment, the proposed approach is evaluated on the pre-social set of the TrueFace dataset. The main focus of the performed experiment is to achieve optimal results by leveraging lightweight models with fewer parameters. The proposed method utilizing EfficientNet-B2 [11] provides the maximum accuracy of 99.97% and F1-score of 99.97% on the pre-social set as shown in Table 1. This can be attributed to its advanced architecture, parameter efficiency transfer learning capabilities, and effective optimization techniques. The architectural design of EfficientNet B2 incorporating depth, width, and resolution scaling allows for accurate capturing and representation of crucial image features. With a smaller number of parameters, EfficientNet-B2 achieves better generalization and effectively mitigates overfitting issues resulting in improved classification accuracy. Enhancing its adaptability for tasks like real vs synthetic image classification. Furthermore, the utilization of the AdamW optimizer significantly enhances regularization and generalization by decoupling weight decay from exponential moving averages.

Table 2. Accuracy of various models when trained over the combined dataset and cross-tested across different splits of TrueFace dataset.

Models	Pre-Social	Telegram	Twitter	Facebook	Combined
VGG19	99.09	99.90	99.92	99.87	99.73
ResNet50	97.90	99.82	99.82	99.78	99.39
DenseNet121	98.94	99.90	99.92	99.93	99.73
MnasNet	99.40	99.93	99.93	99.92	99.79
EfficientNet-B2	**99.85**	**100**	**100**	**99.98**	**99.96**

Results on Combined Dataset. In this experiment, we combined the pre-social and post-social sets, each containing an equal number of images. The post-social dataset consisted of 20,000 images from each social media platform (Facebook, Twitter, and Telegram), resulting in a total of 60,000 images. Additionally, we included 20,000 images from the pre-social dataset. Our aim is to propose and evaluate a robust approach that can perform real vs synthetic image classification even if an image is post-processed using social media platforms. We conducted tests on both the pre-social and post-social test datasets to perform a comparative analysis. This approach allowed us to assess how well the models performed on images from different sources and gain a better understanding of their ability to generalize across diverse datasets. Table 2 shows the accuracy of comparative approaches when tested on different splits of the TrueFace dataset. From the Table 2, it can be that the proposed approach consistently achieves high accuracy across all splits of the TrueFace dataset. Specifically, it demonstrates remarkable performance in classifying real and synthetic images, with accuracy ranging from 99.85% to 100% on the different splits of the TrueFace dataset. This indicates its ability to accurately differentiate between real and synthetic images shared across diverse social media platforms.

Results on Post-social Dataset. In this experiment, we evaluate the robustness of the proposed approach. All the comparative methods are trained on each social media platform individually and evaluated on different social media platforms (cross-dataset). The presence of unknown post-processing operations with varying parameters across different social media platforms can introduce uncertainty and potentially impact the performance of a naively trained CNN model. Furthermore, This experiment holds significance as it demonstrates the effectiveness of our proposed approach in capturing intrinsic features associated with both real and synthetic images. Table 3 shows that the proposed approach utilizing EfficientNet-B2 has performed significantly better than all other comparative methods across all the cross datasets settings. Considering different social media platforms, the proposed approach performs better in the case of Telegram. The proposed approach demonstrates exceptional accuracy of 99.05%, 99.15%, 99.55%, and 99.67% on pre-social, Telegram, Twitter, and Facebook images, respectively, when trained on Telegram images. EfficientNet ability to adapt to different resolutions and compression techniques through compound scaling enables it to effectively learn and extract meaningful features from images with varying quality. This adaptability, combined with its optimized use of computational resources, contributes to its superior performance in classifying images from diverse sources, making it a reliable choice for handling images with different resolutions and JPEG compression levels.

Table 3. Accuracy of various models trained on different datasets and tested on different social media platforms.

Training dataset	Models	Pre-Social	Telegram	Twitter	Facebook	Overall
Telegram	VGG19	96.84	96.78	93.80	97.10	96.15
	ResNet50	96.68	96.43	98.65	98.75	97.65
	DenseNet121	98.40	98.18	99.17	99.25	98.75
	MnasNet	95.80	95.58	97.73	98.67	96.85
	EfficientNet-B2	**99.05**	**99.15**	**99.55**	**99.67**	**99.38**
Twitter	VGG19	93.11	97.03	97.22	97.55	96.28
	ResNet50	93.59	97.93	97.23	98.27	96.74
	DenseNet121	96.18	98.83	98.20	99.18	98.11
	MnasNet	95.49	97.93	94.82	96.38	96.09
	EfficientNet-B2	**97.97**	**99.57**	**99.17**	**99.52**	**99.10**
Facebook	VGG19	93.75	98.22	97.63	93.67	95.97
	ResNet50	95.46	98.72	98.72	95.22	97.03
	DenseNet121	98.00	99.38	99.32	97.93	98.73
	MnasNet	97.20	99.20	98.87	97.25	98.14
	EfficientNet-B2	**98.65**	**99.68**	**99.67**	**98.87**	**99.25**

4.4   Ablation Study

In our study, we performed an ablation study on the TrueFace dataset to evaluate the performance of different variants (B0, B1, and B2) of the EfficientNet models in a post-social scenario. This study aimed to identify the most effective model for classifying synthetic and real images in the context of post-social media images, especially on the subset of telegram images because it keeps the images as close as possible to their original form and uses the smallest amount of JPEG compression [12]. We trained and evaluated three variants of the EfficientNet models, namely B0, B1, and B2, using the post-social image data. Each model was trained using the above-mentioned experimental setup.

Table 4. Accuracy of EfficientNet models when trained over the Telegram dataset and cross-tested across different sets of TrueFace dataset.

Models	Pre-Social	Telegram	Twitter	Facebook	Combined	Average
EfficientNet-B0	99.09	98.98	98.85	99.63	99.14	99.14
EfficientNet-B1	99.41	99.38	97.50	99.55	98.93	98.95
EfficientNet-B2	99.05	99.15	99.55	99.67	99.38	**99.36**

Based on the results presented in Table 4, it is clear that the performance of the three EfficientNet variants (B0, B1, and B2) was at par with each other but among these variants, EfficientNet B2 proved to be a superior performer, showing significant improvements when compared to B0 and B1.

The superiority of EfficientNet B2 demonstrates its suitability to effectively distinguish between synthetic and real images in post-social media. The model's exceptional performance demonstrates its robustness in capturing complex patterns and features in images shared on various social media platforms such as Twitter, Facebook, and Telegram.

5   Conclusion

This paper presents an approach based on the EfficientNet model for the classification of real and synthetic images shared on various social media networks. This approach is evaluated using the comprehensive TrueFace dataset, which encompasses a wide range of real and synthetic face images shared on popular platforms such as Facebook, Telegram, and Twitter. Through extensive experiments and evaluations, our proposed approach outperforms existing methods in the field, achieving remarkable accuracy rates across different social media platforms. Specifically, we achieved outstanding accuracy of 99.98%, 100%, and 100% on images shared through Facebook, Telegram, and Twitter respectively.

The results demonstrate the effectiveness and robustness of our approach in accurately classifying synthetic and real images shared on social media. Furthermore, our approach showcases its superior performance in a cross-social media platform setting, where it successfully classifies images shared on social media platforms that differ from the ones used for training. This capability highlights the adaptability and generalizability of our presented approach, making it suitable for real-world applications where images originate from diverse sources. We conducted a series of comprehensive experiments on the TrueFace dataset. We believe that our work opens up new possibilities for addressing the challenges posed by image manipulation and deepfake proliferation on social media platforms. In the future, potential areas of focus may include conducting real-time image validation studies, development of an application for image classification, expanding the dataset with more diverse social media platform images and real-world data, and by considering the challenges posed by sharing of images across multiple social media networks and adversarial attacks.

References

1. Lago, F., Pasquini, C., Böhme, R., Dumont, H., Goffaux, V., Boato, G.: More real than real: a study on human visual perception of synthetic faces [applications corner]. IEEE Signal Process. Mag. **39**(1), 109–116 (2021)
2. Kshetri, N., DeFranco, J.F., Voas, J.: Is it live, or is it deepfake? Computer **56**(07), 14–16 (2023)
3. Tolosana, R., Vera-Rodriguez, R., Fierrez, J., Morales, A., Ortega-Garcia, J.: Deepfakes and beyond: a survey of face manipulation and fake detection. Inf. Fusion **64**, 131–148 (2020)
4. Rana, K., Singh, G., Goyal, P.: MSRD-CNN: multi-scale residual deep CNN for general-purpose image manipulation detection. IEEE Access **10**, 41267–41275 (2022)
5. Singh, G., Goyal, P.: SDCN2: a shallow densely connected CNN for multi-purpose image manipulation detection. ACM Trans. Multimed. Comput. Commun. Appl. **18**(3s), 1–22 (2022)
6. Verdoliva, L.: Media forensics and deepfakes: an overview. IEEE J. Sel. Top. Signal Process. **14**(5), 910–932 (2020)
7. Rana, K., Singh, G., Goyal, P.: SNRCN2: steganalysis noise residuals based CNN for source social network identification of digital images. Pattern Recogn. Lett. **171**, 124–130 (2023)
8. Marra, F., Saltori, C., Boato, G., Verdoliva, L.: Incremental learning for the detection and classification of GAN-generated images. In: 2019 IEEE International Workshop on Information Forensics and Security (WIFS), pp. 1–6. IEEE (2019)
9. Nguyen, T.T., et al.: Deep learning for deepfakes creation and detection: a survey. Comput. Vis. Image Underst. **223**, 103525 (2022)
10. Pasquini, C., Brunetta, C., Vinci, A.F., Conotter, V., Boato, G.: Towards the verification of image integrity in online news. In: 2015 IEEE International Conference on Multimedia & Expo Workshops (ICMEW), pp. 1–6. IEEE (2015)
11. Tan, M., Le, Q.: EfficientNet: rethinking model scaling for convolutional neural networks. In: International Conference on Machine Learning, pp. 6105–6114. PMLR (2019)
12. Boato, G., Pasquini, C., Stefani, A.L., Verde, S., Miorandi, D.: TrueFace: a dataset for the detection of synthetic face images from social networks. In: 2022 IEEE International Joint Conference on Biometrics (IJCB), pp. 1–7. IEEE (2022)
13. Karras, T., Laine, S., Aila, T.: A style-based generator architecture for generative adversarial networks. In: Proceedings of the IEEE/CVF Conference on Computer Vision and Pattern Recognition, pp. 4401–4410 (2019)

14. Karras, T., Laine, S., Aittala, M., Hellsten, J., Lehtinen, J., Aila, T.: Analyzing and improving the image quality of StyleGAN. In: Proceedings of the IEEE/CVF Conference on Computer Vision and Pattern Recognition, pp. 8110–8119 (2020)
15. Howard, A.G., et al.: MobileNets: efficient convolutional neural networks for mobile vision applications. arXiv preprint arXiv:1704.04861 (2017)
16. Deng, J., Dong, W., Socher, R., Li, L.J., Li, K., Fei-Fei, L.: ImageNet: a large-scale hierarchical image database. In: 2009 IEEE Conference on Computer Vision and Pattern Recognition, pp. 248–255. IEEE (2009)
17. Goodfellow, I., et al.: Generative adversarial networks. Commun. ACM **63**(11), 139–144 (2020)
18. Simonyan, K., Zisserman, A.: Very deep convolutional networks for large-scale image recognition. arXiv preprint arXiv:1409.1556 (2014)
19. He, K., Zhang, X., Ren, S., Sun, J.: Deep residual learning for image recognition. In: Proceedings of the IEEE Conference on Computer Vision and Pattern Recognition, pp. 770–778 (2016)
20. Huang, G., Liu, Z., Van Der Maaten, L., Weinberger, K.Q.: Densely connected convolutional networks. In: Proceedings of the IEEE Conference on Computer Vision and Pattern Recognition, pp. 4700–4708 (2017)
21. Tan, M., et al.: MnasNet: platform-aware neural architecture search for mobile. In: Proceedings of the IEEE/CVF Conference on Computer Vision and Pattern Recognition, pp. 2820–2828 (2019)

Anomaly Detection Across Multiple Farms Through Remote Sensing

Hrishikesh Bodkhe$^{(\boxtimes)}$, Harsh Raj , Deepak Kumar ,
Nitesh Wadhavinde , Neeraj Goel , and Mukesh Saini

Department of Computer Science and Engineering, Indian Institute of Technology
Ropar, Bara Phool, India
{2022csm1006,2022csm1004,2022csm1002,2022aim1006,
neeraj,mukesh}@iitrpr.ac.in

Abstract. In effective agricultural management, monitoring crop
growth is crucial. Various factors, including climate, pests, diseases, and
soil variations, can lead to abnormal yields. Detecting anomalies, where
one farm's growth deviates from its neighbors with similar crops and
sowing dates, can help identify early signs of crop diseases. Remote sensing technologies, like satellites and drones, provide real-time crop growth
information, enabling informed decisions for farmers. This paper presents
a satellite-based anomaly detection technique. We extract NDVI values,
sowing dates, and current dates for each farm, normalize the data, and
employ the DBSCAN algorithm to detect anomalies. Our results demonstrate that DBSCAN outperforms other models with a silhouette score
of 0.5369, improving crop yield prediction.

Keywords: Anomaly · Remote-Sensing · Vegetation Index · NDVI ·
DBSCAN · ARIMA · Precision Agriculture

1 Introduction

Agricultural production is one of the most basic and important activities in
human society and is the basic condition for human survival and development. Growth monitoring of crops is a vital aspect of modern agriculture, providing valuable insights into the development and health of cultivated plants.
By carefully observing and measuring various growth parameters, farmers and
researchers can make informed decisions regarding crop management practices,
optimize resource allocation, and maximize yield potential.

1.1 Growth Monitoring

One of the primary reasons for monitoring crop growth is to assess plant health
and identify potential issues at an early stage. By regularly observing crop growth
patterns, farmers can detect signs of stress, nutrient deficiencies, diseases, pests,

H. Kaur et al. (Eds.): CVIP 2023, CCIS 2010, pp. 503–514, 2024.
https://doi.org/10.1007/978-3-031-58174-8_42

or adverse environmental conditions. Early detection allows for prompt intervention, reducing the risk of crop failure or yield loss. Crop management decisions heavily rely on growth monitoring data. Farmers can utilize growth observations to determine the timing and intensity of various practices, such as irrigation, pest control, and pruning. By monitoring growth rates, farmers can make informed decisions regarding harvest logistics, storage capacities, and marketing strategies, optimizing overall farm profitability.

1.2 Remote Sensing

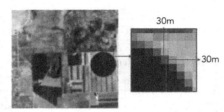

Each Landsat-8 pixel is 30m*30m area on the ground!

Fig. 1. Example of Landsat 8 [8]

In the field of sustainable agriculture, technologies like Remote Sensing and Satellite imagery play a vital role. They help monitor crops comprehensively and collect timely yield data [1], revolutionizing modern agriculture. Recent advances in Remote Sensing (RS) technology, including high-resolution and hyperspectral RS images, bring both opportunities and challenges. These images facilitate rapid data collection and analysis over large areas, supported by satellites like MODIS, LANDSAT, DOVE, SuperDove, and Dove-R (Fig. 1).

Table 1. Different Satellites and their Spatial Resolutions

Satellite	Spatial Resolution
MODIS	250–1000 m
Landsat MSS	60 m
Landsat TM, ETM+, OLI	30 m
Sentinel-2	10–60 m
ASTER	15 m
Digital Globe	0.3 m (30 cm)

Spatial Resolution represents the smallest detectable element in images. It is represented as the length of one side of a square (e.g., $10\,m \times 10\,m$ for 10 m spatial resolution) on the ground. Generally, a higher spatial resolution is desirable, but it is expensive to capture, process, and distribute. Table 1 shows different satellites and their Spatial Resolutions. Temporal Resolution, defining the time between area acquisitions or image frequency (typically in days), varies among satellites. Some offer on-demand imaging. Table 2 provides temporal resolutions for these satellites. Various platforms provide satellite images. Some of them are - PlanetScope, United States Geological Survey (USGS), EOS Data Analytics (EOSDA), etc. For our studies, the images are taken from PlanetScope and EOSDA.

Table 2. Different Satellites and their Acquisition Frequency (Days)

Satellite	Acquisition Frequency (Days)
MODIS	1
Landsat 8	16
TrippleSat	1
Quickbird	1
Spot 7	1

1.3   Vegetation Indices

Vegetation indices play a crucial role in monitoring and detecting changes in vegetation over time. These indices are numerical measures derived from remote sensing data that capture various aspects of vegetation health, density, and vigour. They provide valuable insights into the overall condition and changes occurring in plant cover across different landscapes. One commonly used vegetation index is the Normalized Difference Vegetation Index (NDVI), which compares the reflectance of near-infrared (NIR) and red light wavelengths. Equation 1 shows the mathematical formula for NDVI calculation of an image [2] (Fig. 2).

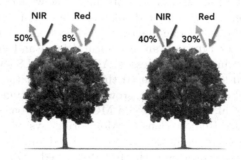

Fig. 2. Healthy Plants Usually Have Higher NDVI

$$\text{NDVI} = \frac{\text{NIR} - \text{RED}}{\text{NIR} + \text{RED}} \tag{1}$$

where NIR is the near-infrared reflectance and Red is the red reflectance. The NDVI values range from 0 to 1. High NDVI values indicate dense and healthy vegetation, while low values suggest sparse or stressed vegetation. By comparing NDVI values from different periods, scientists and environmental researchers can identify changes in vegetation cover and assess the impact of factors such as climate change, deforestation, or land use practices. In our study, we use NDVI to gauge farm health, noting sowing dates and NDVI estimation days per farm. These data are fed into a clustering model like DBSCAN to group similar points. Farms showing poor growth on estimation day stand out as anomalies, highlighting areas of concern effectively.

2   Related Works

Anomaly detection involves identifying patterns in data that deviate from the expected behaviour. Anomalies and outliers are the terms most commonly used interchangeably in the context of anomaly detection. Anomaly detection finds extensive use in a wide variety of applications. In [5], Chen et al. introduced an anomaly detection method for agricultural sensor data. They applied linear regression to various sensor metrics (soil temperature, humidity, etc.). Unusual sensor data in agricultural settings may signal unfavorable crop conditions. The method calculated regression line slopes to assess data trends over time. An interquartile range (IQR) approach established outlier thresholds. Slopes exceeding these bounds were identified as anomalies. Deep-learning techniques were applied in agriculture with DeepAnomaly being proposed in [6]. The method combines background subtraction and deep learning to detect obstacles and anomalies in agricultural fields. The primary objective is to identify objects that are distant and heavily obscured, as well as unknown object categories. Obstacles such as people, barrels, wells, and a distant house were detected. Meanwhile, Mustafa Abdallah et al. [7] explored anomaly detection using transfer learning in both agricultural and manufacturing IoT systems. Their study involved data from seven sensor types on an agricultural farm and vibration sensors in advanced manufacturing. They assessed ARIMA and LSTM models for time series prediction and subsequently used the predicted data for anomaly detection. Several studies emphasize farm growth monitoring via vegetation indices like NDVI. Huang et al. [3] introduced a MODIS-NDVI-based approach within the China Agriculture Remote Sensing Monitoring System (CHARMS). They adapted the model's parameters using meteorological and field observation data, enabling crop growth monitoring with MODIS-derived NDVI data from satellite imagery.

Several studies have used machine learning techniques for detecting different types of anomalies in agricultural data [4]. As far as there are not many studies that talk about the detection of anomalous farms among multiple farms. In this paper, we present a technique for anomaly detection across multiple farms using satellite images and the DBSCAN algorithm.

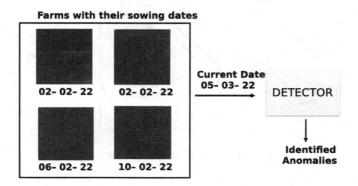

Fig. 3. Outline of the system

3 Problem Definition

An anomaly across multiple farms can be defined as a farm whose growth is not the same as its neighbouring farms, with nearby sowing dates and growing the same crops. Detecting anomalies across multiple farms presents a significant challenge in agricultural monitoring and management. Anomalies in agricultural growth, such as uneven crop development or poor health, can be indicative of underlying issues such as diseases, pests, nutrient deficiencies, or sub-optimal cultivation practices. Addressing this problem requires the development of an effective anomaly detection system that utilizes remote sensing data to identify and differentiate farms exhibiting abnormal growth patterns within a homogeneous region.

4 Methodology

In this research paper, we propose a methodology for anomaly detection in crop age and average NDVI (Normalized Difference Vegetation Index) values using the DBSCAN (Density-Based Spatial Clustering of Applications with Noise) algorithm. The following sections outline our approach.

4.1 Data Collection

The dataset used in this study is obtained from EOS Data Analytics, which provides NDVI (Normalized Difference Vegetation Index) data for selected farms over a period using the SENTINEL-2 satellite with a 10m spatial resolution. The

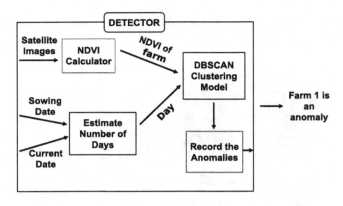

Fig. 4. Working of Detector

data collection is done manually by visiting the nearby farms of the IIT Ropar region and noting the location coordinates and the sowing dates. The dataset contains NDVI statistical data for 13 farms, recorded 2–3 times a month for the past 3 years. For our study, we have chosen wheat farms.

4.2 Data Preprocessing

The dataset is preprocessed to create a training dataset for the anomaly detection model. For each farm, the sowing date and the date at which the NDVI is calculated are noted (Acquisition Date). The training dataset is normalized using the Min-Max Scaler method. To balance out the data for training we have used sowing date as a baseline for measuring the growth stages of wheat for individual farms. The "Day" column is added to calculate the gap between the farm's sowing date and acquisition date. Table 3 shows a snapshot of the data frame.

Table 3. Sample Farm Data

Farm name	Sowing date	Acquisition Date	NDVI	Day
farm1	2020-11-20	2020-11-20	0.1942	0
farm1	2020-11-20	2020-12-15	0.4961	25
farm1	2020-11-20	2021-01-27	0.7439	68
farm13	2022-11-18	2023-02-13	0.7753	87
farm13	2022-11-18	2023-02-26	0.6886	100

Fig. 5. Visual Wheat growth timeline seen from satellite

4.3 Observing NDVI Changes

Figure 5 shows different images of the same wheat farms near IIT Ropar, taken from the Sentinel-2 satellite. Growth changes can be observed over the whole period from sowing to harvesting. Sowing dates of farms can be different. In Punjab, generally, the wheat is sown in November and harvested in April. From Fig. 6 it can be observed that the NDVI values start to rise from November because wheat is in its vegetative state. Once wheat reaches maturity, the leaves turn yellow and the plant begins to dry out, known as the ripening or senescence stage then the NDVI values start to fall from March to April. This rise and fall in NDVI values can be used to measure the growth stages of wheat for farms. The same growth pattern and NDVI variations are observed each year from the period of November to April. The period from May to September is for different crops but shows the same variation.

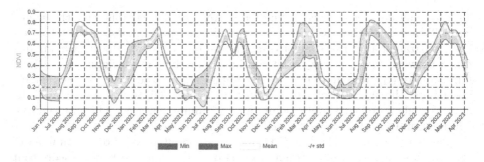

Fig. 6. Wheat NDVI timeline of a farm over 3 years. Taken from EOS Data Analytics [11].

4.4 DBSCAN Clustering

The DBSCAN (Density-Based Spatial Clustering of Applications with Noise) algorithm performs both clustering and anomaly detection by grouping data points in close proximity based on a specified distance threshold. Anomalies, or noise points, are unassigned data points. DBSCAN's strength lies in its ability to identify clusters of various shapes, which is crucial in our study where crop growth patterns among multiple farms may exhibit diverse and complex shapes. In crop growth analysis, anomalies may represent farms significantly differing from neighboring farms with similar sowing dates. DBSCAN not only identifies clusters but also automatically detects outlier noise points, aiding in the identification of farms with unusual growth patterns among the considered set.

Algorithm 1. Anomaly Detection using DBSCAN

Require: DataFrame *df* containing NDVI data for multiple farms
Ensure: Anomaly predictions for each farm
1: **Preprocessing:** Convert dates in the dataset to datetime objects
2: Calculate the number of days since sowing for each farm
3: **Visualization:** Create a heatmap of the NDVI values for all farms
4: Plot the NDVI values over time for each farm
5: **Data Splitting:** Split the dataset into training and testing sets
6: **Data Scaling:** Apply data scaling using MinMaxScaler to normalize the features
7: **DBSCAN Algorithm:** Apply the DBSCAN algorithm to detect anomalies in the data
8: **Hyperparameter Tuning:** Perform grid search to determine the optimal hyperparameters for DBSCAN
9: **Anomaly Prediction:** Predict anomalies for each farm using the trained model

---

4.5   Model Training

The training dataset is fitted to the DBSCAN model, available with the scikit-learn library in Python to build our anomaly detection model. We set the following parameters for the algorithm: [1)] 1) eps (epsilon, the maximum distance between two samples to be considered in the same neighbourhood), 2) min_samples (the minimum number of samples required to form a dense region). We record the number of clusters created by the DBSCAN model and the assigned labels for each data point in the training dataset. This information will be useful for identifying anomalies later in the process.

The performance of the DBSCAN model is evaluated based on the number of clusters formed, the number of noise points detected, and a silhouette score that measures the quality of the clustering in the sense of how well-defined clusters are created by the model.

4.6   Anomaly Detection

To detect anomalies in new data, the input data is first normalized using the Min-Max Scaler and then passed to the DBSCAN model's prediction function. The predict function determines the minimum Euclidean distance from any of the core points determined by the DBSCAN model. If the distance is less than the epsilon distance used in training, the input data is considered normal; otherwise, it is classified as an anomaly. Figure 3 and Fig. 4 show the outline of the system and the working of the detector. By following this methodology, we aim to achieve early identification of irregularities or potential issues in agricultural systems.

5   Experimental Results

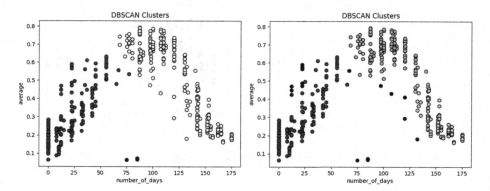

Fig. 7. DBSCAN Clustering analysis for respective hyper-parameter values 1) eps: 0.1 and min_sample: 7, 2) eps: 0.07 and min_sample: 7

The experimental results of the anomaly detection across multiple farms using remote sensing are as follows.

1. **DBSCAN Clustering Results:** The DBSCAN model [10] is fine-tuned by varying epsilon distances and minimum sample values. Smaller epsilons create more clusters, focusing on nearby data points sharing similar "Number of days" values. The minimum sample setting influences data points forming core points, with fewer samples resulting in more data points. Optimal parameters are determined by assessing cluster count, noise points and domain knowledge of healthy wheat crops. In our observations, an epsilon of 0.07 and a minimum sample of 5 produced an optimal configuration, yielding 3 clusters representing crop growth stages. The clustering results are visualized by plotting data points with colours representing the assigned cluster labels in Fig. 8. The core points are represented using different colors while anomalies or noise points are represented in black. Figure 7 illustrates the clusters formed under various parameter configurations.

2. **Anomaly Detection on New Data:** After training the DBSCAN model, it is used to detect anomalies in new unseen NDVI data for the crop along with its age. The input data is normalized using the same normalization method as the training data and passed to the predicted function of the DBSCAN model. If the distance of unseen NDVI data from the core point exceeds the threshold distance the New unseen data point is labelled as an anomaly else, not an anomaly.

3. **Time Series Forecasting:** As an additional analysis, a time series forecasting model, such as ARIMA (AutoRegressive Integrated Moving Average) [9], is trained using the NDVI values of a specific farm. The ARIMA model has

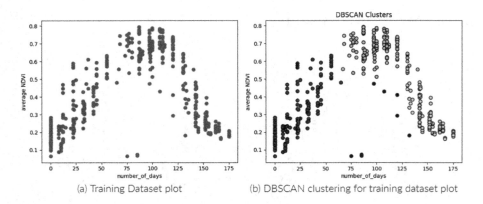

(a) Training Dataset plot   (b) DBSCAN clustering for training dataset plot

Fig. 8. DBSCAN Clustering Results Plot(eps: 0.07 and min_sample: 5)

the salient feature of learning the seasonality in the given training data thus it can predict the target value for the unseen data which in turn, helps determine whether the recorded NDVI value is anomalous or not. The predicted to actual NDVI values are shown in Fig. 9.

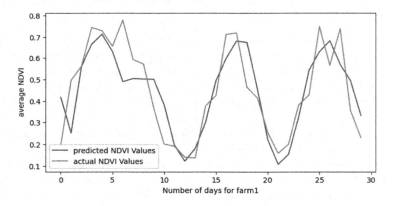

Fig. 9. ARIMA model's Prediction

In comparison with DBSCAN Algorithm against the ARIMA model, we observed the following differences:

DBSCAN excels in scalability and efficiency, handling large datasets and high dimensionality. It's distribution-agnostic and robust to irregular structures and noise. In contrast, ARIMA assumes stationary data, limiting its effectiveness with complex datasets. DBSCAN offers intuitive interpretability through clusters, while ARIMA is more oriented towards time series forecasting and may struggle with non-temporal anomalies.

6   Discussion and Future Works

Various platforms provide satellite images. The better the spatial resolution, the better will be the performance of the algorithm. Platforms like PlanetScope provides images with approximately 3 m per pixel resolution. The PlanetScope satellite constellation consists of multiple launches ("flocks") of Dove satellites. Our work doesn't discuss the automatic extraction of a particular farm from a group of farms. For application, the farmer will need to provide the location coordinates of his or her farm and the nearby farms. Detecting the farm image and feeding it to the detector can be achieved in future. For anomaly detection, we have assumed that all farms are sharing the same likelihood conditions. But this need not be true. The dataset collected is for limited farms in the Punjab region. An extensive collection of different farms can be good research work for the future. Further in addition to NDVI, other factors like temperature, soil pH, humidity, rainfall, etc. can also be considered to increase the accuracy of anomaly detection.

7   Conclusion

In conclusion, this research paper presents a technique for detecting anomalies across multiple farms using satellite images. By extracting NDVI values from multiple band images and using the DBSCAN algorithm, the proposed method can identify farms with abnormal growth patterns. The results show that this approach is favourable compared to other alternatives and thus, outperforms other models such as the ARIMA model, with a silhouette score of 0.5369. By detecting early signs of crop diseases, farmers can take corrective actions before the disease spreads, leading to improved crop yields, increased profits, and more sustainable agriculture. This demonstrates the potential of remote sensing technologies in effective agricultural management.

Acknowledgment. This work is supported by the grant received from DST, Govt. of India for the Technology Innovation Hub at the IIT Ropar in the framework of the National Mission on Interdisciplinary Cyber-Physical Systems.

References

1. Xiong, D.: Crop growth remote sensing monitoring and its application. Sens. Transducers **169**, 174–178 (2014)
2. Gandhi, G.M., Parthiban, S., Thummalu, N., Christy, A.: NDVI: vegetation change detection using remote sensing and GIS - a case study of Vellore District (2015)
3. Huang, Q., Wu, W., Zhang, L., Li, D.: MODIS-NDVI-based crop growth monitoring in China agriculture remote sensing monitoring system. In: 2010 Second IITA International Conference on Geoscience and Remote Sensing, Qingdao, China, pp. 287–290 (2010). https://doi.org/10.1109/IITA-GRS.2010.5603948
4. Chandola, V., Banerjee, A., Kumar, V.: Anomaly detection: a survey. ACM Comput. Surv. **41**(3), 58, Article no. 15 (2009). https://doi.org/10.1145/1541880.1541882

5. Ou, C.-H., Chen, Y.-A., Huang, T.-W., Huang, N.-F.: Design and implementation of anomaly condition detection in agricultural IoT platform system. In: 2020 International Conference on Information Networking (ICOIN), Barcelona, Spain, pp. 184–189 (2020). https://doi.org/10.1109/ICOIN48656.2020.9016618
6. Christiansen, P., Nielsen, L., Steen, K., Jørgensen, R., Karstoft, H.: DeepAnomaly: combining background subtraction and deep learning for detecting obstacles and anomalies in an agricultural field. Sensors **16**, 1904 (2016). https://doi.org/10.3390/s16111904
7. Abdallah, M., Lee, W.J., Raghunathan, N., Mousoulis, C., Sutherland, J.W., Bagchi, S.: Anomaly Detection through Transfer Learning in Agriculture and Manufacturing IoT Systems (2021)
8. Geospatial Online. https://gsp.humboldt.edu/OLM/Courses/GSP_216_Online/lesson3-1/resolution.html
9. Fattah, J., Ezzine, L., Aman, Z., Moussami, H., Lachhab, A.: Forecasting of demand using ARIMA model. Int. J. Eng. Bus. Manag. (2018). https://doi.org/10.1177/1847979018808673
10. Jain, D.: Design and Implementation of DBSCAN Algorithm for Generating Clusters in Dense Region of Complex Datasets (2017)
11. EOS Data Analytics: Space solutions for Earth problems. https://eos.com/

Free-Throw Prediction in Basketball Sport Using Object Detection and Computer Vision

Mayur S. Gowda[1], S. Dhruv Shindhe[2], and S. N. Omkar[3(✉)] [iD]

[1] Center for Imaging Technologies, Ramaiah Institute of Technology, Bangalore, India
[2] ARTPARK, Indian Institute of Science, Bangalore, India
dhruv@artpark.in
[3] Department of Aerospace, Indian Institute of Science, Bangalore, India
omkar@iisc.ac.in

Abstract. The most important things that must be taken care of in a basketball game include teamwork, perfect team coordination, and execution of the skills of the players at the right point of time, without which it will be difficult to win a game. So, a player must realize these things while he is playing, but in order to do that, he must analyze his posture and the way he plays the game. In order to help the players, a system is developed using computer vision techniques which provides better insights into improving games using deep learning algorithms such that the insights can be used in improving the player performance and strategies in individual or team games. This paper provides a deeper knowledge of the kinematic and physiological markers that might better capture athletic performance by looking at the present state-of-the-art AI approaches by analyzing how AI methods and techniques are applied in basketball play. This work mainly concentrates on the Basketball sport, in which different features such as the release angle of the basketball, and the shot predictions are analyzed and tested in real-time. The object detection is performed using the YOLOv5 algorithm and we have obtained a mean average precision of 96.8%. Further, the release angle is calculated using the combination of pose landmarks and object detection and has resulted in the optimal angle for a perfect free throw, which is to be within the range of 45 to 60°. Based on the combination of object detection, release angle, and the polynomial regression, shot prediction is performed and has resulted in accurate results for real-time experimental analysis.

Keywords: Basketball Analysis · Computer Vision · (You Only Look Once) YOLOv5 · Pose estimation · Polynomial Regression

1 Introduction

AI has been used in sports to provide better insights and formulate plans based on the athlete's performance [1, 2]. The conventional training approach develops a training plan based on the ideas, philosophy, and expertise of the coach, as well as the skill level of the basketball player. Precision and efficiency are at the heart of contemporary sports training, and enhancing the scientific rigor of the training plan and boosting the

© The Author(s), under exclusive license to Springer Nature Switzerland AG 2024
H. Kaur et al. (Eds.): CVIP 2023, CCIS 2010, pp. 515–528, 2024.
https://doi.org/10.1007/978-3-031-58174-8_43

player's effectiveness [3] can be done by collecting and evaluating data on basketball player's posture and precisely identifying the player's posture [4, 5]. AI is also used in sports to boost health and performance through predictive modeling, creating strategies, executing plans of action, and playing to strengths.

The objective of this project is to perform object detection and object tracking of the basketball and the basket for a video feed. The YOLO model is one of the suitable algorithms that can be extensively used for object detection. Transfer learning, a feature of deep learning that trains the convolutional neural network algorithm using a small quantity of training data, [6] is one example of how the Convolutional Neural Network (CNN) based approach YOLOv5 reuses a classifier model to identify new goals. The object detection results can be used for the analysis of the specific features of the basketball to improve the player's performance and skill set.

Basketball players must possess the skill to make free throws, and the release angle should be in the range of 49–60 ° [7] to make a successful shot. The ball should be released at the maximum angle possible to make a perfect shot. The positional landmarks of the index finger and the position of the basketball in the particular frame are utilized to calculate the release angle of the free throw made. The other feature that is being analyzed in the work is the prediction of the basketball shot. The concept of polynomial regression is extensively used in this part of the work. In polynomial regression, the relationship between the independent variable x and the dependent variable y is modeled by an nth-degree polynomial in x. Polynomial regression can be used to fit a nonlinear relationship between the value of x and the associated mean value of y, denoted E(y |x). Thus, the free throw made can be analyzed to predict whether the shot is made even before it reaches the basket or the hoop. This can be achieved using object detection combined with the concept of polynomial regression which helps predict the ball's position through the frames in a given video. Thus, the analysis of features in basketball can help players improve their skillset and performance, resulting in higher chances of winning games.

Further, the paper is organized as follows: Section 2 discusses the Literature Survey, Section 3 discusses how the dataset was built and how it was pre-processed. Section 4 provides information on the methodology that has been used to carry out the work for object detection, release angle calculation, and shot prediction. Section 5 shows the results that were obtained during the experimental work and the pseudo real-time analysis of the data captured during the practice session. Section 6 provides the Conclusion and gives an overview of the Future Scope.

2 Literature Survey

Computer vision is used to acquire visual data comparable to the naked eye and interpret it before relaying it to people. Basketball player's postural data is collected using an image feature extraction technique and [8] Gaussian hidden variables to accurately categorize and -recognize shooting patterns.

A system for automatically analyzing long-range basketball shots from video sequences is developed [9] to identify and follow the ball during a sequence of shots. The ball's throwing angle and speed have a significant impact on how accurately a long shot is made, and the height, speed, and release angle [10, 11] of the ball and the trajectory in which the basketball goes in the presence of wind are the key variables impacting the shooting rate. To determine the release angle, height, and speed of the shot, a forecast analysis in conjunction with mechanical theory and motion trajectories is applied, and MATLAB is used to convert the video images into static images. To create a trajectory map, basic kinematics theory from one-hand shoulder shot technology is used to analyze and calculate the link between shot angles and shot speed. The trajectory prediction method and shooting rate reference are produced, using which the shot prediction is made. Sensing technology can be integrated into sporting equipment to measure performance, develop athletes, and promote participation. [12] measures the 94Fifty's sensor accuracy on release angle and dribbling concerning the DartfishTM software.

By analyzing factors such as shooting form, release angle, release height, and shooting kinematics [13], the study identifies individual-specific optimal release strategies. Using motion capture technology and data analysis, the research demonstrates that each player has a unique set of optimal techniques that align with their shooting mechanics. The findings emphasize the importance of tailored training programs to improve shooting accuracy and highlight the need to consider individual shooting styles for optimizing team strategies. Computer vision techniques and Kalman filter have been used to track player movement and provide real-time feedback on position, angle, and projectile trajectory [14]. By considering factors such as gravity, initial velocity, and distance to the rim, the algorithm determines the optimal shooting angle. It also takes into account parameters like drag coefficient, basketball mass, and ball radius. The algorithm provides additional statistics such as total travel time, maximum distance, maximum height, and time to reach the peak.

The most important feature of basketball is the prediction of free throws made by the players. Convolutional neural networks are developed to use deep learning techniques in CNNs, and a camera-based basketball scoring detection (BSD) [15] is used for shot detection. Semantic-based shot identification [16] is performed using Dynamic Bayesian Networks (DBN). Kalman filter is used to pinpoint the shot events in this case.

An experiment was set up, in which 10 players (age: around 22 years) were made to play (particularly focusing on free throws) and the videos collected were analyzed to provide accurate results for the release angle calculation and the shot prediction. It uses object detection combined with polynomial regression to track the basketball in each frame based on the starting position of the basketball and provides the count of the number of perfect basketball shots made.

3 Dataset Preparation

The main goal of this work is to analyze the features of the basketball sport, such as recognition of the ball and hoop. A custom dataset is used for object detection, release angle, and shot prediction. The custom dataset built consists of 29,789 images with two classes (Basketball and Hoop). The preparation of the dataset includes the collection of images from the videos recorded during a live basketball match and similar videos downloaded from YouTube and a few images from internet sources.

The tools that have been utilized in data preparation include Visual Object Tagging Tool (VoTT) and ROBOFLOW.

VoTT: VoTT is used for tagging the images and exporting them in the required annotation format. The process of annotation includes collecting the images either in ".jpeg" or ".png" format and tagging the objects using a bounding box in the image with a particular class label (in our case BasketBall and Basket). And finally exporting the annotated information in ".JSON" format.

ROBOFLOW: Roboflow is used to convert the JSON type annotations to COCO format for the training of the custom dataset.

Figure 1, depicts the image that has been annotated using the VoTT tool. Once the images are annotated, the annotations and the images together are exported either in VoTT-JSON format or Pascal VOC format.

Fig. 1. Example of an annotated image using the VoTT tool

The exported annotated images and labels are fed into the ROBOFLOW online tool for further processing and splitting, and the fully processed dataset is downloaded from the tool and used in the training process for object detection.

4   Proposed Approach

This section discusses the system design and its implementation, and the flow of the design from the training phase to the testing phase of the model that has been developed. The things that have been implemented in the work include object detection using YOLOv5, followed by the release angle estimation, and finally the shot prediction.

The YOLOv5 architectures provide different models that are used based on the variation in the parameter size. The different models that are available under the YOLOv5 model are nano, small, large, and extra-large models. In this work, the YOLOv5l model is used because the custom dataset used consists of an image size (640×640) with a total of 29,789 images.

The next phase is training the model for the custom dataset that is built. Several parameters are present during the training process that must be addressed, such as batch size, number of epochs, image size, etc. The batch size was set to 16 (A batch size of 16 strikes a balance between computational efficiency and model convergence. It allows for parallel processing on GPUs, which can speed up training. Additionally, smaller batch sizes may lead to more stochastic updates, allowing the model to explore a wider range of examples and potentially generalize better. Also, Constraints on the computational resources led to the selection of the batch size as 16), the image size as 640 (640 is the maximum image size supported by yolov5l), and the model is trained for 100 epochs (The model's improvement stabilized around 100 epochs and was observed that additional training beyond this point did not yield significant improvements in the results obtained by the model). Once the model is trained, the next step is to test it on an unseen video or image, the test dataset resulted in an accuracy of 96.8%.

The bounding box coordinates of the object along with the center coordinates of the object were obtained and these position coordinates were loaded onto a list. This list of coordinate points is further used in the calculation of the release angle of the basketball and the prediction of the basketball shots.

Release Angle Estimation

The release angle calculation of the basketball is based on the pose estimation concept which is provided by the media-pipe framework. Machine learning pipelines are built using Media-Pipe to handle time-series data, including audio and video. Human position estimate from the video is essential in numerous applications, such as tracking physical activity, deciphering sign language, and directing full-body movements. Figure 2, shows the pose landmarks that can be utilized for Hand position detection.

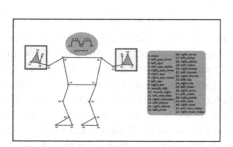

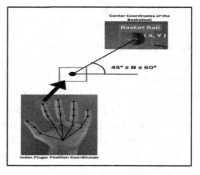

Fig. 2. Hand pose landmarks used for release angle calculation

Fig. 3. Release angle requirement for perfect basketball shot

Based on the survey conducted and the performance evaluated in basketball practice matches. It was seen that the release angle (Θ), must be within the range of $+ 45°$ to $+ 60°$ i.e. $\{\Theta \in Z \mid 45 \leq \Theta \leq 60\}$. Figure 3, shows the release angle calculated using the positional landmarks.

Figure 4, depicts the flow of the procedure carried out for the calculation of the release angle of the basketball. After obtaining the list of center coordinates of the bounding box for the basketball that has been detected in each frame, the mediapipe framework is used for posture analysis and implements the landmarks points that are present in each frame. Using the available pose landmarks the index finger of both left and right hands are extracted for each frame and these points are collected in a list. So, the center coordinates of the basketball and the index finger coordinates that are present in each frame are analyzed and the difference between these points in both the x and y directions are calculated.

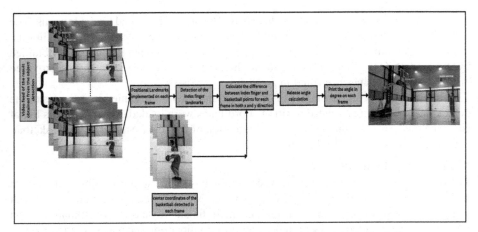

Fig. 4. Flow chart for the release angle calculation of the basketball

Using these difference values in both the x and y directions the angle between them is calculated in degrees. The angle is then printed on the corresponding frame and the resulting video is displayed.

Free-Throw Shot Prediction

During the practice session, the players tend to make mistakes either in their stance or the velocity with which the player is making a basketball shot, and even sometimes the alignment of the basketball in the hand matters to make a perfect basketball shot. These are some of the factors which play a greater part in making a free throw, all these skill sets can be improved by the detailed analysis obtained from both the release angle calculation and the shot prediction that is made in advance. The importance of shot prediction also includes the following usage: Basketball games require the use of scoring boards or judges to maintain scores. Setting up these things for each basketball game becomes difficult. Therefore, automatic shot detection along with the count of the number of perfect basketball shots can be used in basketball courts.

The basketball shot detection performed in the work is a combined result of both the object detection performed through YOLOv5 and the polynomial regression concept. Polynomial regression (Typically, any projectile that is released with an initial non-zero velocity follows a parabolic trajectory in the absence of external disturbance. Thus, we are using Polynomial regression for shot prediction) is used to generate a polynomial equation or provide the trajectory to fit the model based on the previous points of the basketball in the previous frames. The list of center coordinates of the ball in the first few frames is collected in a list and then based on the center points the equation is generated to fit the points, such that the future trajectory of the ball is predicted. Also to detect, if the ball goes inside the basket or not is performed by collecting the basket or hoop's coordinates, based on the center coordinates of the ball that is predicted, such that if the x value of the basketball lies within the range of the x values of the basket's boundary and only if the ball is at the height of the y value of the basket, then it is indicated as a shot made or else it is indicated as shot missed. A count variable is used in the algorithm, which indicates the number of perfect basketball shots made for a given video feed. And if the shot has been missed then there is no increment in the count variable and the previous count value is displayed. Figure 5, depicts the flowchart of the proposed approach for the basketball shot prediction.

For shot prediction, during the first few frames, the position coordinates for the basket or the hoop from the object detection are obtained, in which the variation in the x direction is taken (x-min to x-max), and the upper limit (y-max) are used as the boundaries to determine if the basketball passes through those mentioned coordinates. The center position coordinates of the basketball i.e. ((x, y) of the basketball) are taken and the quadratic equation is set up to fit a curve along the path in which the ball travels. Only the first few center points of the basketball positions are used to estimate the trajectory of the basketball.

After the first few points the prediction is done in such a way that the polynomial curve passes through the given position coordinates i.e. (between x-min and x-max and passes through the y-max).

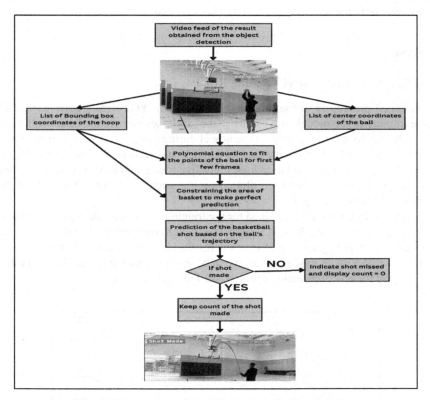

Fig. 5. Flow chart depicting the basketball shot prediction

The quadratic equation to fit the trajectory of the basketball:

$$y = Ax^2 + Bx + C \tag{1}$$

The polynomial coefficients a, b, and c used in the equations will be:

A = x positional coordinates of the basketball.

B = y positional coordinates of the basketball.

C = 2 (since it is a 2nd order equation).

To see if the ball passes through the given position. The predicted x value should be between the fixed x-min and x-max coordinates of the hoop/basket detected. The x value is estimated using the equation:

$$x = (-b - sqrt(b**2 - 4*a*c))/(2*a) \tag{2}$$

where a = A, b = b and c = (C - ymax).

So, if the quadratic equation value passes through the given points then it is indicated as a shot made which in turn means that the basketball passes through the hoop.

In the case of perfect prediction, the algorithm also keeps track of the shots and prints them along with the shot prediction. So, if a shot is predicted then a count variable is incremented by one. And kept constant until a new basketball shot is made. In case the shot is missed then it will be indicated as a shot missed.

5   Results

5.1   Object Detection Model Training Results

As explained previously in the proposed approach the YOLOv5l algorithm was used for the training of the model which consisted of 2 classes namely the basketball and the hoop. 100 epochs were used to train the model during which it attained a mean average precision (mAP) of 0.968 during the 85th epoch and remained constant till the final epoch. The training loss, validation loss, precision, recall, and mAP values are recorded for each epoch and the points are plotted on the graph. The curve for each of these parameters is shown in Fig. 6.

As seen in Fig. 6 the plot obtained for the training box loss, training object loss, and the training class loss i.e., the first 3 plots. It is clear that during the training process, the losses have decreased gradually. As per the results obtained and based on the testing of the trained model on an unseen video, it can be inferred that the model that is trained is good enough for object detection of the basketball and the hoop.

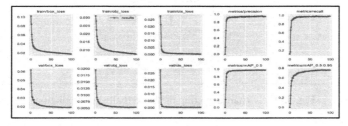

Fig. 6. Plot of different loss values and the mAP values recorded during the training process

The trained model was tested on several videos and images that were not used in the training and validation process. And the results obtained were good enough for the recognition of both the basketball and the hoop. Figure 7, shows the object detection result that was obtained after testing the trained model.

Fig. 7. Object detection results after testing the trained model

5.2 Release Angle Results

The theoretical possibilities of the free throw trajectories at different release angles when a free throw is made from the proper position (Charity Stripe) is shown in Fig. 8. The horizontal distance (4.19 m) is the distance between the player's position (Default position for making a free throw) to the center of the basket ring and the vertical height (3 m) refers to the height at which the basket ring is placed from the ground. So, it can be seen that when a release angle between 45 to 60° is achieved in a free throw, the chances of getting a perfect shot are higher when compared to other release angles.

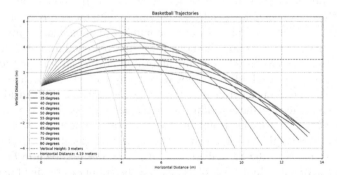

Fig. 8. Theoretical possibilities of free throw trajectories at different release angles.

The major work that has been carried out is concentrated on the analysis of release angle and shot prediction that is based on the object detection results. The video feed obtained as output from the object detection is fed to the algorithm that is developed for the calculation of the release angle of the basketball. Figure 9 and 10, shows the release angle of the ball for different videos.

The results of two videos that were passed through the algorithm are presented in this section, one in which there is a perfect basketball shot made and the other one in which the shot has been missed. Video-1 in Fig. 9 consisted of a player making a basketball shot perfectly and as per the results, the release angle was calculated to be around 50.671728 °. And in video-2 shown in Fig. 10, consisted of a player missing the basketball shot, and hence the result was accurate enough to show that the release angle was around 25.3245 °. From this, it can be understood that for a perfect basketball shot the release angle to be within the range of 45 to 60 ° as per the literature survey done and as per the results obtained from the algorithm that has been developed.

Fig. 9. Release angle calculation during free throw (shot made)

Fig. 10. Release angle calculation during free throw (shot missed)

5.3 Basketball Shot Detection Results

The other feature of the basketball on which the work is carried on is the shot detection of the ball. The object detection results are combined with the polynomial regression to detect the shots properly and the count of the number of shots made is displayed each time a shot is made. Figure 11 and 12, shows the results obtained from the shot detection.

Multiple videos were tested using the algorithm developed for shot detection and the results obtained for each of the videos were up to mark. Video-1 shown in Fig. 11, consists of a player making a perfect free throw in which the ball lands inside the basket. The video-1 was tested and the algorithm provided the output stating as "Shot Made" and even the number of Shots Made is obtained as 1, which was accurate because the video consisted only of a single basketball shot. The algorithm was also tested on video-2 in which the player misses the basketball shot, and a similar is shown in Fig. 12, which shows the prediction as "Shot Missed". Thus, the algorithm can predict the shot in both scenarios and also provides the count of how many perfect basketball shots were made.

Fig. 11. Shot Detection results (shot made)

Fig. 12. Shot Detection results (shot missed)

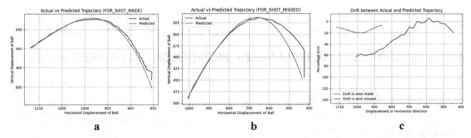

a   b   c

Fig. 13. a) Actual vs. Predicted Trajectory for a shot made; **b)** Actual vs. Predicted Trajectory for a shot missed; **c)** Drift between actual and predicted trajectories in both cases.

The predictions of the ball trajectory, are not always in the same path as that of the actual trajectory. Hence, a plot of actual vs. predicted trajectories for both shot made and shot missed is shown in Figs. 13a, and b, and c shows the Percentage Error between the actual and the predicted trajectory in both cases. The average percentage error for the shot made is 14.14% and the average percentage error for the shot missed is 36.15%. For a free throw to land perfectly in the basket ring, several external conditions influence the shot, such as the release angle, the initial velocity, the wind conditions, etc. In our experimental setup, we have tried to analyze the release angle to predict the shots. For real-time analysis of the shot prediction, we should consider all the parameters so that we can predict the shots and signal the same to the players. The experimental setup consisted of a total of 278 shots. In which, there were 2 sets: 130 shots made and 148 shots missed, in which 117 were perfectly detected out of 130 and 122 perfectly detected out of 148 and the same is shown in Fig. 14. A comparison between different datasets and the experimental analysis is done and the results have been tabulated in Table 1.

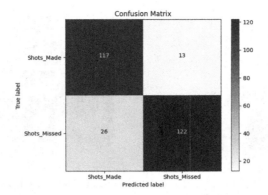

Fig. 14. Confusion matrix for the Shot prediction (y-axis: True Label and x-axis: Predicted label)

Table 1. Comparison between the proposed approach and existing methods

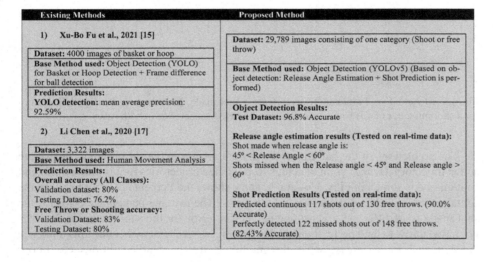

Existing Methods	Proposed Method
1) Xu-Bo Fu et al., 2021 [15]	**Dataset:** 29,789 images consisting of one category (Shoot or free throw)
Dataset: 4000 images of basket or hoop	
Base Method used: Object Detection (YOLO) for Basket or Hoop Detection + Frame difference for ball detection	**Base Method used:** Object Detection (YOLOv5) (Based on object detection: Release Angle Estimation + Shot Prediction is performed)
Prediction Results: **YOLO detection:** mean average precision: 92.59%	**Object Detection Results:** **Test Dataset:** 96.8% Accurate
2) Li Chen et al., 2020 [17]	**Release angle estimation results (Tested on real-time data):** Shot made when release angle is:
Dataset: 3,322 images	45° < Release Angle < 60°
Base Method used: Human Movement Analysis	Shots missed when the Release angle < 45° and Release angle > 60°
Prediction Results: **Overall accuracy (All Classes):** Validation dataset: 80% Testing Dataset: 76.2% **Free Throw or Shooting accuracy:** Validation Dataset: 83% Testing Dataset: 80%	**Shot Prediction Results (Tested on real-time data):** Predicted continuous 117 shots out of 130 free throws. (90.0% Accurate) Perfectly detected 122 missed shots out of 148 free throws. (82.43% Accurate)

6   Conclusion

In this paper, a novel method is proposed for the analysis of different features of the sport basketball based on an object detection algorithm i.e., the YOLOv5l model. The results obtained from the object detection were combined with the pose estimation framework and an algorithm was developed to calculate the release angle of the basketball, which is necessary to analyze if the ball correctly goes inside the hoop or not based on the player's free throw. Finally, shot prediction is one of the main features of the work which provides information if a shot is going to be made, based on the trajectory that the ball takes when a free throw is made. The object detection results were combined with the polynomial regression and an algorithm was developed that made an accurate prediction of the shots in advance and also provides the count for the number of perfect basketball shots that are made. We have also analyzed the drift between the actual and the predicted trajectory and have obtained the average percentage error for both: shots made (Average Percentage Error: 14.14%) and shots missed (Average Percentage Error: 36.15%). In ideal conditions, the release angle in the range of 45 to 60 ° provides an accurate prediction for the shots (which has been seen in the analysis done through the experimental setup).

The algorithm developed only looks at a single parameter (release angle), which is not the only thing that influences a perfect basketball shot (Free throw). Multiple features that come into play during a free throw include the initial velocity at which the ball is released, alignment of the ball with respect to the basket ring, shooting distance, height of the player, etc. And also, the external disturbance plays an important role in the perfect shot. So, analysis of all these factors can improve the chances of making a perfect shot. Long short-term memory networks (LSTMs) can be employed to take into account the sequential nature of the shot process. They can be trained on a dataset that includes various features like release angle, initial velocity, ball alignment, shooting distance, player height, and external disturbances, along with the corresponding outcomes of the shots (e.g., made or missed). The LSTM can learn to capture the relationships between these different features and their impact on the shot outcome over time. By considering the temporal dynamics of the shot process, the LSTM can potentially identify complex patterns and dependencies that a simple analysis of individual factors might miss.

Acknowledgments. The work was supported by ARTPARK, Indian Institute of Science, Bangalore, India.

References

1. Verhoeven, F.M., Newell, K.: Coordination and control of posture and ball release in basketball free-throw shooting. Hum. Mov. Sci. **49**, 216–224 (2016). https://doi.org/10.1016/j.humov. 2016.07.007
2. Delextrat, A., Martinez, A.: Small-sided game training improves aerobic capacity and technical skills in basketball players. Int. J. Sports Med. **35**2013).https://doi.org/10.1055/s-0033-1349107
3. Wei, Y., Jiao, L., Wang, S., Bie, R., Yinfeng, C., Liu, D.: Sports motion recognition using MCMR features based on interclass symbolic distance. Int. J. Distrib. Sens. Netw. **2016**, 1–15 (2016). https://doi.org/10.1155/2016/7483536
4. Li, G., Zhang, C.: Automatic detection technology of sports athletes based on image recognition technology. EURASIP J. Image Video Process. **2019**2019)https://doi.org/10.1186/s13 640-019-0415-x
5. Abian-Vicen, J., et al.: A caffeinated energy drink improves jump performance in adolescent basketball players. Amino Acids **46**(5), 1333–1341 (2014). https://doi.org/10.1007/s00726-014-1702-6
6. Pingel, J.: Introduction to Deep Learning: Machine Learning vs. Deep Learning. MathWorks (2017)
7. Khlifa, R., Aouadi, R., Hermassi, S., Chelly, M.S., Jlid, M., Gabbett, T.: Kinematic adjustments in the basketball free throw performed with a reduced hoop diameter rim. Int. J. Sports Sci. Coach. **7**, 371–382 (2012). https://doi.org/10.1260/1747-9541.7.2.371

8. Ji, R.: Research on basketball shooting action based on image feature extraction and machine learning. IEEE Access. **8**, 1 (2020). https://doi.org/10.1109/ACCESS.2020.3012456

9. Chakraborty, B., Meher, S.: A trajectory-based ball detection and tracking system with applications to shooting angle and velocity estimation in basketball videos. In: 2013 Annual IEEE India Conference, INDICON 2013 (2013). https://doi.org/10.1109/INDCON.2013.6725963

10. Zhiwen, W., Pengtao, W., Lianyuan, J., Bowen, T., Canlong, Z., Zhenghuan, H.: Analysis of influencing factors of shooting rate based on trajectory prediction of the basketball. In: 2017 14th Web Information Systems and Applications Conference (WISA), Liuzhou, China, pp. 176–180 (2017).https://doi.org/10.1109/WISA.2017.18

11. Cabarkapa, D., Fry, A.C., Carlson, K.M., Poggio, J.P., Deane, M.A.: Key kinematic components for optimal basketball free throw shooting performance. Central Eur. J. Sport Sci. Med. **36**, 5–15 (2021). https://doi.org/10.18276/cej.2021.4-01

12. Abdelrasoul, E., Mahmoud, I., Stergiou, P., Katz, L.: The accuracy of a real time sensor in an instrumented basketball. Procedia Eng. **112** (2015)https://doi.org/10.1016/j.proeng.2015.07.200

13. Slegers, N.: Basketball shooting performance is maximized by individual-specific optimal release strategies. Int. J. Perform. Anal. Sport **22**, 1–14 (2022). https://doi.org/10.1080/24748668.2022.2069937

14. Egi, Y.: Basketball self-training shooting posture recognition and trajectory estimation using computer vision and Kalman filter. J. Electr. Eng. **73**, 19–27 (2022). https://doi.org/10.2478/jee-2022-0003

15. Fu, X.-B., Yue, S.-L., Pan, D.-Y.: Camera-based basketball scoring detection using convolutional neural network. Int. J. Autom. Comput. **18**(2), 266–276 (2020). https://doi.org/10.1007/s11633-020-1259-7

16. Liu, Y., Liu, X., Huang, C.: A new method for shot identification in basketball video. JSW **6**, 1468–1475 (2011). https://doi.org/10.4304/jsw.6.8.1468-1475

17. Chen, L., Wang, W.: Analysis of technical features in basketball video based on deep learning algorithm. Sign. Process. Image Commun. **83**, 115786 (2020). https://doi.org/10.1016/j.image.2020.115786

Hierarchical CNN and Ensemble Learning for Efficient Eye-Gaze Detection

G. R. Karthik Kumar$^{(\boxtimes)}$ and Tushar Sandhan

Perception and Intelligence Lab, Department of Electrical Engineering,
Indian Institute of Technology, Kanpur, U.P., India
{karthikgr22,sandhan}@iitk.ac.in

Abstract. An eye, as a sensory organ, not only captures visual information but also provides critical cues about human attention and intentions. It is also possible to infer focus, interest, and even truthfulness from where one's gaze is directed. Gaze also helps in influencing social interactions and human behavior. Our gaze can reveal our engagement, attraction, and subconscious reactions, contributing to nonverbal communication and shaping interpersonal dynamics. Eye gaze direction estimation is a crucial task in many real-world applications, such as driver drowsiness detection, human-computer interaction, and assistive technologies. Traditional single-stage CNN classifiers may not be so useful in such applications due to less representation of data for particular classes. Data augmentation can help up-to some extent, but we need multiple novel ideas to be employed to overcome these limitations. In this work, we proposed a hierarchical CNN architecture for eye gaze direction classification, that integrates predictions of three distinct stages to create an ensemble learning based classifier. The proposed model is trained on a dataset of eye images with ground-truth class labels for each gaze direction. Experimental results demonstrate that our proposed method achieved improved classification results on the eye gaze dataset, indicating its potential for real-world applications.

Keywords: Eye gaze · Convolutional Neural Networks · Human intentions and focus · Ensemble Learning · Transfer Learning

1 Introduction

Eye gaze classification is a fundamental task in computer vision that plays an important role in human-computer interaction, allowing machines to interpret human intentions and actions. Eye gaze classification has numerous applications in the fields of human-computer interaction and assistive technologies [1–3]. In human-computer interaction, eye gaze can serve as a non-intrusive input modality to control the computer, enabling users to perform various tasks, such as selecting items on a screen, scrolling through content [4], and even typing [5]. In assistive technologies, eye gaze can be used to improve the quality of life for individuals with disabilities, such as those with motor impairments [6], by enabling

H. Kaur et al. (Eds.): CVIP 2023, CCIS 2010, pp. 529–541, 2024.
https://doi.org/10.1007/978-3-031-58174-8_44

them to control their environment, communicate with others, and perform daily activities independently. Overall, eye gaze classification has the potential to revolutionize the way humans interact with technology and each other. Eye gaze classification is the task of categorizing the gaze direction of a person's eye into predefined classes. Unlike eye gaze estimation, which aims to estimate the exact point where a person is looking, eye gaze classification focuses on predicting which general direction a person is looking in. This task is useful in applications such as driver safety systems, where detecting whether a driver is looking in a certain direction can help prevent accidents. Due to their ability to learn complex patterns and features from data, Convolutional neural networks (CNN) have become a popular choice for image classification tasks. In recent years, several studies have explored the use of CNN for eye gaze classification, achieving promising results for binary and ternary gaze classification tasks [7–9]. However, less attention has been given to the more challenging task of multi-class gaze classification. Multi-class gaze classification involves classifying an image into one of several gaze directions. This task is particularly challenging due to the high degree of similarity between some gaze classes, as well as the variability in gaze direction across different individuals and contexts. Despite these challenges, several recent studies have explored the use of CNN for multi-class gaze classification tasks, with promising results [12–14]. While deep learning approaches have shown superior performance over traditional methods, they often require large amounts of labeled data and computational resources for training. As a result, traditional methods still play a crucial role for gaze detection, where limited data and computing resources are available. Model-based methods [19, 20] typically involve the use of geometric models to estimate gaze direction based on the position of the pupil and the corneal reflection. Appearance-based methods [21, 22], on the other hand, rely on extracting features from the eye region, such as edges, corners, and texture, and using them to train a regression model to estimate gaze direction. In addition to CNN, a group of machine learning algorithms have been found effective for classifying eye gaze. Support vector machines (SVM), for instance, have been successfully used for this task [23]. SVM divide classes using a linear boundary in a high-dimensional feature space where the input data is mapped. The amount and complexity of the dataset, as well as the computing power available for model training and testing, all have a role in the decision of which machine learning method to choose (Fig. 1).

In this paper, we propose a novel multi-level CNN model, along with selective data-augmentation and transfer learning methods for multi-class eye gaze classification using a dataset of four classes: *close look, forward look, left look, and right look*. We further divided this dataset into 10 classes: *close, up, forward, down, left, right, left-up, left-down, right-up, right-down*. Due to the limitations like less variability among few classes, under-representation of data in few classes, a single architecture fails to produce promising results for our 10-class eye-gaze classification problem. Hence, we adopt ensemble learning technique i.e., combining multiple models to build a single, efficient gaze classifier model. The proposed hierarchical CNN model consists of three sequential stages for eye

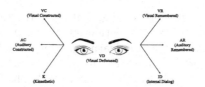

(a) Inferences made from eye gaze directions in Neuro-Linguistics programming [33].

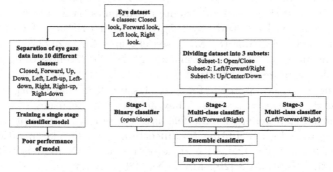

(b) Schematic of our proposed methods.

Fig. 1. An overview of our proposed method for eye-gaze classification.

state classification. In Stage-1, the model predicts whether an eye is in an open or closed state. In Stage-2, it further refines the classification by determining whether the eye is looking to the left, forward, or right. Finally, in Stage-3, the model adds another layer of granularity by identifying whether the eye gaze is directed upward, centered, or downward. To enhance the model's accuracy and robustness, ensemble learning is employed. The outputs of all three stages are combined using an ensemble approach. This ensemble classifier integrates the individual predictions from each stage, providing a comprehensive assessment of the eye's state. Consequently, the ensemble classifier's collective predictions offer a more nuanced and accurate characterization of the eye's condition.

2 Related Works

Eye is the most interactive and sensitive organ. Eye gaze classification and direction estimation has gained a lot of importance in research domain in the recent past. Gaze classification system detects and processes the eye region from an image and extracts relevant information and patterns, like person's attention and focus. Eye is a good indicator of a person's emotional state as well [24]. Eye gaze detection plays an important role in many applications including eye movement-based assistive & interactive communication systems for people with disability in terms of muscle control [34]. Several approaches and methods have been adopted to address pre processing, feature extraction and efficient training to develop efficient eye gaze detection solutions. Another approach to eye gaze classification is using ensemble learning, which combines multiple models to improve the overall performance. For instance, in [23], an ensemble of three different models was used: a CNN, RNN, and a SVM. The CNN and RNN models were trained using raw images, while the SVM model used hand-crafted features. The final classification was based on a weighted combination of the outputs of the three models, achieving an accuracy of 94.5% on a dataset of 1,500 images. A third approach involves using feature extraction techniques such as Local Binary Patterns (LBP) and Histogram of Oriented Gradients (HOG) to extract features from the eye images. In a study by [17], they used LBP and HOG features to train support vector machine (SVM) based classifier for gaze classification. They achieved an accuracy of 84.4%, demonstrating the effectiveness of feature extraction techniques for gaze classification. In a study by [18], the authors proposed a generative model-based approach for gaze classification that incorporates uncertainty in the classification process. They achieved an accuracy of 85% on their test set, showing that generative models have the potential to improve gaze classification accuracy by accounting for uncertainty in the classification process. In our work, we initially trained 4 state-of-the-art CNN models (VGG16 [27], ResNet50 [28], InceptionV3 [29], MobileNet [30]). After comparing the results, we used the best performing model for training the 10-class gaze direction estimation dataset (the subset created from our main dataset). In the subsequent phase, we implemented a selective data augmentation approach. Specifically, we developed an image augmentation pipeline that generates multiple augmented images for each individual image belonging to a particular class. This process took into account the size of that specific class and compared it to the sizes of other classes. Though this method improved the accuracy of model to an extent, it was still not satisfactory. Hence, in the final stage, we employed a hierarchical ensemble learning approach to capitalize on the limited variability of our data. Each of these methods and their progressive effect on efficiency of our classifier are discussed in detail in further sections.

3   Experimental Works

3.1   Eye Gaze Classification: 4 Classes

In the first stage, we trained several state-of-the-art CNN models for classification of eye gaze into 4 classes: Eye closed, Forward look, Right look, Left look. For this training, we used eye dataset created by Kavyan shah [26]. This dataset is a subset of MRL Eye Dataset by Fusek [25]. Few samples from the dataset and the dataset distribution are shown in the Fig. 2. The dataset contains a total of 14544 images across 4 classes. The dataset exhibits a nearly even distribution among the classes, with small imbalances observed across the classes. The transfer learning models are efficient to overcome these minor class imbalances and achieve robust classification across all classes. With its relatively balanced composition, this dataset provides a favorable composition for training our 4-class eye-gaze direction classifier. The detailed distribution of data among classes is shown in the histogram Fig. 2(b). Our initial work involves training four state-of-the-art CNN models: VGG16, ResNet50, InceptionV3, and MobileNet, for our 4-class eye gaze direction classification. The subsequent sections provide a comprehensive analysis and discussion of the results obtained from each individual model, evaluating their performance and choose the best model for further classification tasks.

VGG16: It is a 16 layers CNN architecture, proposed by Visual Geometry Group [27], also called VGGNet. It is familiar for it's depth of 16 layers (13 convolutional and 3 fully connected). What sets VGG16 apart is its use of small 3×3 filters throughout the network, which helps capture detailed features in images. This design choice allows VGG16 to effectively recognize complex patterns and distinguish different objects in tasks like image classification and object recognition.

ResNet50: Residual network, also known as ResNet [28] is known for its depth, with 50 layers including convolutional and fully connected layers. Uniqueness of ResNet50 lies in its incorporation of residual connections, allowing for more efficient training and mitigating the vanishing gradient problem, which effectively addresses gradient flow. This enables ResNet50 to capture complex features from images, thereby achieving exceptional performance in image classification and object recognition.

InceptionNetV3: Inception networks [29] are a class of deep neural networks with an architectural design that consists of repeating blocks, also known as

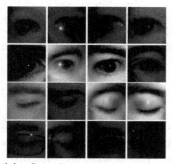

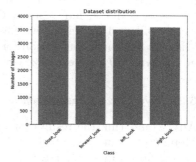

(a) Sample images from dataset.

(b) Dataset distribution among classes.

Fig. 2. Dataset description. Dataset was assembled from Kavyan shah [26]. This dataset is a subset of MRL Eye Dataset by Fusek [25]. The dataset is having a total of 14544 images distributed among 4-classes: 'close look': 3828 images, 'forward look': 3641, 'left look': 3498, 'right look': 3577.

Inception modules. It is a renowned CNN architecture known for its depth and sophisticated design. With multiple layers and intricate module structures, InceptionV3 can capture intricate image features and extract meaningful representations. Its inception modules employ various filter sizes, allowing it to efficiently learn both local and global features. It has demonstrated remarkable performance in image classification and object recognition tasks, making it a valuable asset in the field of computer vision.

MobileNet: MobileNet [30] is a class of convolutional neural networks (CNN) and widely recognized for its efficiency and compactness. Its streamlined design enables high-performance image recognition and classification on resource-constrained devices. By leveraging depth-wise separable convolutions, MobileNet achieves a balance between accuracy and computational efficiency. MobileNet's lightweight architecture makes it ideal for mobile and embedded applications, where it demonstrates remarkable performance while minimizing computational overhead (Fig. 3).

The observations made after training demonstrate that VGG16 and ResNet50 are the best performing models for this task. The respective training patterns Fig. 4(a) & 4(b), prove that these models followed ideal training progress. The results from InceptionNetV3 were not satisfactory, with a best reported accuracy of 66.85%, with the training pattern in Fig. 4(c) shows that the accuracy is further

Model	Accuracy (%)
VGG16	**98.71**
ResNet50	98.26
InceptionV3	66.85
MobileNet	81.79

Fig. 3. Comparison of CNN Models for 4-class gaze direction classification

deteriorating. Although Mobilenet, by it's nature, has demonstrated a faster training progress (in terms of time taken for training), the results were unsatisfactory Fig. 4(d), with a best test accuracy of 81.79%. On comparing the above results, we conclude that VGG16 is the best performing model for our task, closely followed by ResNet50. The results obtained from the comparative analysis acts as proper foundation for future dataset expansion and training aimed at achieving 10-class eye gaze classification.

3.2 Eye Gaze Classification: 10 Classes

After comparing the results for all 4 models (VGG16, ResNet50, InceptionV3, MobileNet), our next stage of work involves creating a dataset of 10 classes: closed, down, forward, left, left-down, left-up, right, right-down, right-up, up.

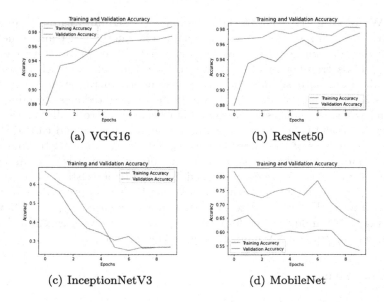

(a) VGG16   (b) ResNet50

(c) InceptionNetV3   (d) MobileNet

Fig. 4. Performance analysis of standard CNN architectures for our task.

The state of eyes under each gaze direction are shown in the Fig. 5. Next stage of our work involves determining the state of eyes from images. For this task, we trained a VGG16 based CNN model. With best test accuracy of 38.97%, the results were not satisfactory. Hence, we adopted methods like "image augmentation", "weighted-class training" and "hierarchical training".

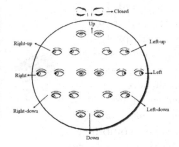

Fig. 5. Eye gaze directions.

Image Augmentation: Image augmentation is a technique that can improve the robustness of a deep learning model. It is helpful in cases where the available data is of less size or imbalanced. It refers to the process of creating variations of data from existing limited dataset, through various image processing techniques. The process aims at increasing the number of images for each class, which can be helpful in situations where the original dataset has a disproportionate number of images among the classes in a dataset. In our work, we implemented a selective augmentation pipeline which reads the size of each class of the dataset, and adjusts the number of output images to be generated per each image of the class.

Class Weighting: It refers to the technique of assigning weights to images of each class according to the size of each class. This method of training help balance out the data and reduce the bias associated with a disproportionate dataset. Weighted class training in CNN seems to be favourable for such cases which include datasets with significant class imbalances, where certain classes have limited samples compared to others. Additionally, weighted class training proves beneficial when the goal is to achieve high accuracy across all classes, ensuring that the model is not biased towards the majority class and can adequately capture the nuances of the minority classes. After incorporating techniques like augmentation and weighted class training, we observed improved accuracy (test accuracy obtained is 58.59%) compared to the previous stage. However, the attained results were still not satisfactory. For further improvement in performance of the model, we need to explore a more advanced approach beyond a single-stage CNN model. Therefore, we employed multi-stage ensemble learning i.e., stacking multiple CNN models for gaze classification.

Ensemble Learning: It is a process where multiple base models are combined or stacked in a meaningful order and trained to solve our base problem. This method is employed in the conditions where a weak learner alone performs task poorly but when combined with other weak learners, they form a strong learner and these ensemble models produce better results. Given the

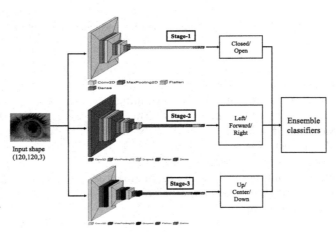

Fig. 6. Architecture of our 3-stage hierarchical eye-gaze classification model

high degree of similarity between classes such as left, left-up, and left-down, as well as right, right-up, and right-down, our case necessitates the application of ensemble learning techniques. By leveraging the collective knowledge and diverse perspectives of the ensemble network, we can build an effective classifier that can address the challenge of accurately distinguishing between these visually similar classes. Functionality of our ensemble architecture, and the prediction flow are shown in Fig. 6 and Table 1 respectively.

Stage-1 of our hierarchical model predicts whether the state of the eye open/closed. Hence we need to employ a binary classifier network with sigmoid

Table 1. Final predictions of hierarchical model as a combined decision of all stages.

Final prediction	Stage-1	Stage-2	Stage-3
Close	Close	–	–
Forward	Open	Forward	Center
Up	Open	Forward	Up
Down	Open	Forward	Down
Left	Open	Left	Center
Left-up	Open	Left	Up
Left-down	Open	Left	Down
Right	Open	Right	Center
Right-up	Open	Right	Up
Right-down	Open	Right	Down

activation function at the last fully connected layer, and binary cross-entropy [31] as loss function. Stage-2 is a multi-class classifier network that predicts the direction of eye Left/Forward/Right. Here, we use categorical cross-entropy [32] as the loss function, and softmax as the activation function in the last fully connected layer. This will return an array of class-probabilities. The class corresponding to the maximum probability is the output prediction of the network. Stage-3 is again a 3-class classifier network, which predicts the direction of eye as up/center/down. Since the number of classes are same as that of stage-2, and for generalizability, the network architecture of stage-2 is retained for stage-3.

Loss Functions: Binary cross-entropy (BCE) is a loss function commonly used in CNN models for binary classification tasks. It works on the principle of quantifying the dissimilarity between the class labels and predicted class-probabilities, thereby providing an effective measure for optimizing the binary classifier model parameters. Categorical cross-entropy (CCE) is a loss function widely employed in CNN models for multi-class image classification tasks. It works on quantification of the discrepancy between class labels and predicted class probabilities, enabling the model to learn the optimal parameters for accurate multi-class classification.

$$BCE(y,p) = -(y\log(p) + (1-y)\log(1-p)),$$
(1)

$$CCE(y,p) = -\sum_{c=1}^{M} y_{o,c}\log(p_{o,c}),$$
(2)

where,

- M - number of classes,
- log - natural logarithm,

- y - binary indicator (0 or 1). It indicates if predicted class label c is the correct classification for observed data o,
- p - predicted probability (observation o belongs to class c).

Classification Metrics:

- **Accuracy** is defined as the proportion of correct predictions to the total predictions. It measures the overall correctness of the model's predictions.
- **Precision** is the proportion of correct positive predictions (true positives) out of all positive predictions (true positives + false positives). It quantifies the ability of a model to correctly classify all the positive data.
- **Recall** is the proportion of true positives to the total of true positives and false negatives. In other words, it measures the ability of a model to predict correct positive predictions.

$$\text{Accuracy} = \frac{TP + TN}{TP + TN + FP + FN}, \text{Precision} = \frac{TP}{TP + FP}, \text{Recall} = \frac{TP}{TP + FN},$$

TP-True Positives, TN-True Negatives, FP-False Positives, FN-False Negatives.

4   Results

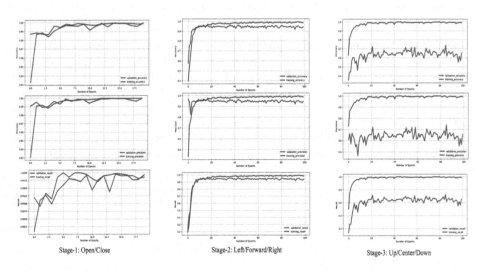

Stage-1: Open/Close   Stage-2: Left/Forward/Right   Stage-3: Up/Center/Down

Fig. 7. Training history and performance of stage-1,2 and 3 on respective train and test datasets. The training pattern indicates that the models corresponding to stage-1 & 2 are efficient in all aspects, while stage-3 model require larger data for training.

Following the workflow from Fig. 1, our stage-1 network is a binary classifier network that predicts the state of eye open/closed. This network has shown promising results on our data (because of sufficient data for these classes in our original 4-class dataset), with faster convergence and best test accuracy of 99.75%. Our stage-2 is a 3-class (Left-Forward-Right) classifier. The results after training this network were satisfactory, as expected, with a best test accuracy obtain is 96.22%. Stage-3 is also a 3-class network, with Up-Center-Down as our 3 classes. This particular subset of the dataset contains less data representation, we had to adopt methods like manual data-labelling, data augmentation, model fine-tuning and other training techniques like save best weights i.e., saving model weights corresponding to best test accuracy (73.65%) achieved. These metrics indicate the need of expansion of dataset for the classes corresponding to stage-3 network (Fig. 7 and Table 2).

Table 2. Best performance achieved by each stage on their respective test datasets.

Stage/Model	Accuracy (%)	Precision (%)	Recall(%)
Stage-1	99.75	99.62	100
Stage-2	96.22	96.30	96.03
Stage-3	73.65	74.08	72.46

5 Conclusion

In this work, we introduced a novel approach to eye-gaze direction estimation through the development of a multi-stage network. Considering the challenges posed by limited data availability and less variability among certain classes, we employed ensemble learning. By leveraging the collective performance of multiple models, we aimed to enhance the robustness and accuracy of our predictions, ultimately achieving more satisfactory results. Once our model consistently demonstrates success on larger data set, we will proceed with its deployment in our future research works. This dependable foundation for eye-gaze analysis in embedded systems has the potential to catalyze advancements in virtual reality related fields, ultimately enhancing our understanding of human-computer interaction and enabling innovative applications in areas such as assistive technology and human behavior analysis. Furthermore, to advance the state of our research, we advocate for the adoption of the latest iterations of CNN architectures. Specifically, it is suggested to use a larger and diverse dataset, and advanced versions of state-of-the-art models such as VGG19, advanced versions of inception networks, and deep ResNet architectures. Also, the study underscores the need for future work to focus on increasing the dataset size, addressing the under-representation of data, particularly for the third stage, where data limitations posed challenges to achieving higher accuracy.

Acknowledgement. This work is supported by the project C3IHUB/EE/2023221 C3i (Cyber Security and Cyber Security of Cyber-Physical Systems) Innovation Hub IIT Kanpur.

References

1. Miah, P., Gulshan, M.R., Jahan, N.: Mouse cursor movement and control using eye gaze - a human computer interaction. In: ICAIoT (2022)
2. De Gaudenzi, E., Porta, M.: Towards effective eye pointing for gaze-enhanced human-computer interaction. In: Science and Information Conference (2013)
3. Chandra, S., Sharma, G., Malhotra, S., Jha, D., Mittal, A.P.: Eye tracking based human computer interaction: applications and their uses. In: MAMI (2015)
4. Neogi, D., Das, N., Deb, S.: Blink-con: a hands free mouse pointer control with eye gaze trackingG. In: IEEE MysuruCon (2021)
5. Sengupta, K., Sun, J., Menges, R., Kumar, C., Staab, S.: Analyzing the impact of cognitive load in evaluating gaze-based typing. In: IEEE 30th CBMS (2017)
6. Hyder, R., Chowdhury, S.S., Fattah, S.A.: Real-time non-intrusive eye-gaze tracking based wheelchair control for the physically challenged. In: IECBES (2016)
7. Cui, Z., Zhang, Y., Meng, D.: Eye gaze tracking using convolutional neural networks. In: ICVRV (2018)
8. Fan, X., He, Z., Zhang, J., Zhu, X.: Multi-view convolutional neural networks for eye gaze estimation. IEEE Trans. Cybern. (2017)
9. Hsiao, Y.L., Chuang, C.F., Lien, J.J.: Eye gaze tracking with deep neural networks. In: Proceedings of the CSAI (2018)
10. Fan, W., Wang, H., Zhu, L., Jiang, T.: Person-independent 3D gaze estimation using face frontalization. In: ICCV (2017)
11. Hsiao, Y., Chang, Y.J., Lu, H.C., Chen, K.H.: Eye gaze estimation based on convolutional neural networks using RGB-D sensors. IEEE Trans. Multimed. (2018)
12. Agrawal, P., Stent, A., Tetreault, J.: Towards modeling eye gaze in multi-party conversations: data collection and annotation. LREC (2016)
13. Duan, Y., Yin, X., Zhang, Z., Wei, S.: Efficient gaze tracking using multi-scale convolutional neural networks. IEEE Trans. Instrum. Measur. (2020)
14. Zhang, T., Liu, W., Wu, W., Wu, X., Jiang, T.: Gaze estimation using dual deep networks with unsupervised pre-training. In: CVPR (2019)
15. Jiang, C., Bai, X., Liu, W., Wang, C., Tu, Z.: Learning gaze biases with conditional generative adversarial networks. In: ICCV (2019)
16. Smith, P.J., Gatica-Perez, D.: Combining first-and third-person video for egocentric gaze estimation in natural everyday activities. IEEE Trans. Pattern Anal. Mach. Intell. (2020)
17. Cazzato, D., Leo, M., Distante, C.: Gaze classification from eye features using Local Binary Patterns and Histogram of Oriented Gradients (2012)
18. Agarwal, R., Alahi, A., Ramanathan, V.: Learning to estimate gaze from synthetic data. In: CVPR (2016)
19. Krafka, K., et al.: Eye tracking for everyone. In: CVPR (2016)
20. Park, J., Yun, S., Choi, J., Park, H., Yoo, C.D., Lee, S.: Learning to estimate gaze direction for human-robot interaction using transfer learning (2018)
21. Recasens, A., Khosla, A., Vondrick, C., Torralba, A.: Where are they looking? In: CVPR (2015)
22. Wang, C., Ma, C., Yang, X., Zhang, X., Yang, J., Zhang, Z.: Learning adaptive appearance features for gaze estimation. In: CVPR (2019)

23. Chae, W., Kim, D., Kim, D.W., Kim, J., Ko, H.: Ensemble-based eye gaze estimation using multi-task convolutional neural networks (2019)
24. Beymer, D., Flickner, M.: Eye gaze tracking using an active stereo head. In: CVPR (2003)
25. Fusek, R.: Pupil localization using geodesic distance. In: Bebis, G., et al. (eds.) ISVC 2018. LNCS, vol. 11241, pp. 433–444. Springer, Cham (2018). https://doi.org/10.1007/978-3-030-03801-4_38
26. Shah, K.: Eye-dataset. Kaggle (2020). https://doi.org/10.34740/KAGGLE/DSV/1093317
27. Liu, S., Deng, W.: Very deep convolutional neural network based image classification using small training sample size. In: ACPR (2015)
28. He, K., Zhang, X., Ren, S., Sun, J.: Deep residual learning for image recognition. In: CVPR (2016)
29. Szegedy, C., et al.: Going deeper with convolutions. In: CVPR (2015)
30. Howard, A.G., et al.: MobileNets: efficient convolutional neural networks for mobile vision applications (2017)
31. Shannon, C.E.: A mathematical theory of communication (1948)
32. Bishop, C.M.: Pattern Recognition and Machine Learning. Springer, Cham (2006)
33. George, A., Routray, A.: Real-time eye gaze direction classification using convolutional neural network. In: SPCOM (2016)
34. Pradeep Raj, K.B., Lahiri, U.: Design of eyegaze-sensitive virtual reality based social communication platform for individuals with autism. In: ISMS (2016)

Learnable GAN Regularization for Improving Training Stability in Limited Data Paradigm

Nakul Singh[✉] and Tushar Sandhan

Perception and Intelligence Lab, Electrical Engineering,
Indian Institute of Technology Kanpur, Kanpur, India
nakul692k@gmail.com

Abstract. Generative adversarial networks (GAN) are generative models that require large amounts of training data to ensure a stable learning trajectory during the training phase. In the absence of sufficient data, GAN suffers from unstable training dynamics that adversely affect the quality of generated data. This behavior is attributed to the adversarial learning process and the classifier-like functioning of the discriminator. In data-deficient cases, the adversarial learning procedure leads to the discriminator memorizing the data instead of generalizing. Due to their wide applicability in several generative tasks, improving the GAN performance in the limited data paradigm will further advance their usage in data-scarce fields. Therefore to circumvent this issue, we propose a loss-regularized GAN, which improves the performance by forcing a strong regularization on the discriminator. We conduct several experiments using limited data from the CIFAR-10 and CIFAR-100 datasets to investigate the effectiveness of the proposed model in overcoming discriminator overfitting in the lack of abundant data. We observe consistent performance improvement across all the experiments compared to state-of-the-art models.

Keywords: GAN · Generator · Discriminator · Regularization · Overfitting · Limited data

1 Introduction

Generative adversarial networks (GAN) have come a long way since their invention in 2014 by Goodfellow et al., and nowadays, GAN are used for various tasks like face generation, texture synthesis, object detection, resolution enhancement, etc. Models like Super-resolution (SRGAN) [17] are used to produce photo-realistic natural images, Markovian GAN [18] and Spatial GAN [11] are used for texture synthesis, and methods like Segan [5], perpetual GAN [19] are used

Supplementary Information The online version contains supplementary material available at https://doi.org/10.1007/978-3-031-58174-8_45.

for object detection. Apart from computer vision-specific tasks, GAN have been applied successfully in other diverse fields like medicine and natural language processing. Conditional GAN have been used for denoising medical low-dose CT scans [33], organ segmentation, and skin legion synthesis for malignant and benign tumor analysis are some of the medicine-specific applications of GAN [34].

The extensive use of GAN in generative tasks is due to their ability to generate high-quality and diverse data. For example, the BigGAN model trained on the ImageNet dataset [4] can generate high-fidelity natural images. This unparalleled advantage, however, comes with several caveats due to the training framework of GAN. It uses an adversarial training method that requires a large model and infinite training data to achieve the Nash equilibrium [6]. With increasing computational power training large models has become possible. For instance, the StyleGAN [13] model used for style transfer has nearly 26.2 million parameters that can be trained using GPU to accelerate computations. However, several areas still do not have enough data to supply a large training set for GAN. GAN are prone to drawbacks like discriminator overfitting, mode collapse, and unstable training dynamics in data-insufficient scenarios.

Mode collapse, also known as the Helvetica scenario, is a phenomenon that occurs when the generator produces only a certain kind of output. When a GAN suffers from mode collapse, the generated data may have high fidelity but lack variety. Although mode collapse can occur even with a large amount of training data, conditional GAN are more susceptible to it in case of limited data [27]. Figure 1 demonstrates mode collapse in images generated by a conditional StyleGAN trained on limited image data from the ImageNet carnivore class. We can observe that the images are of good quality, but there are no intra-class variations. In this work, we use a conditional BigGAN for our experiments and show qualitatively that our proposed regularization scheme helps mitigate mode collapse in the limited data paradigm.

The rest of the paper is organized into four sections. Section 2 briefly reviews the existing literature on GAN stabilization in a limited data paradigm. In Sect. 3, we explain the GAN training functions, the regularization used by Tseng et al. [30], and our extension over their work. Next, Sect. 4 explains the experimental setup and provides a comparative analysis between the proposed algorithm and the baseline. Section 5 is the concluding section summarizing our contribution. Throughout this paper, we use the terms fake data and generated data interchangeably to denote the data created by the generator.

2   Related Work

Generative adversarial networks are implicit density generative models that, given large data sets, can generate high-quality, diverse samples. This prerequisite of a high-quality large dataset impedes the use of GAN in fields that are data scarce [34]. The discriminator of the GAN inherently uses a supervised learning framework, so GAN suffers from failures of supervised learning like overfitting and underfitting [6]. Therefore, the discriminator tends to memorize

Fig. 1. Mode collapse. Images generated by a conditional StyleGAN on training with limited images from the ImageNet Carnivores class. (Reused from [27]).

the labels in tasks with smaller datasets instead of generalizing. This overfitting severely degrades the feedback provided to the generator causing the training to diverge [35].

Over the past few years, several approaches have been proposed to improve the GAN training stability in case of limited data. Encouraged by the success of data augmentation as a regularization method in deep learning, several researchers adopted this method for stabilizing GAN training. Zhao et al. [37] proposed using a differentiable augmentation operator $\mathcal{T}$, which can augment both the real and fake samples. They use simple augmentation techniques like translation and cutout to implement $\mathcal{T}$ and show the effectiveness of differentiable data augmentation in improving the training dynamics. Karras et al. [12] take on a similar perspective and impose additional constraints of invertibility on the augmentation operator. An invertible augmentation ensures that the augmentation does not leak into the generated samples and is also called a non-leaking augmentation operator.

GAN training can also be stabilized by normalization techniques like batch normalization [10], spectral normalization [24], layer normalization [2], and weight normalization [26]. Normalization balances the GAN training by providing a more stable gradient flow and enhancing the representational richness of the neural network layers [16]. In batch normalization, each node in a neural network layer is normalized to a learned mean and standard deviation value before applying the activation. Batch normalization is done separately for each node in the layers for a given batch [10]. In layer normalization, the nodes in a particular layer share the same normalization parameters. In contrast to batch normalization, layer normalization is done at a sample level instead of a batch level, due to which each sample is normalized differently [2]. Spectral normalization is a kind of weight normalization method that improves the stability of

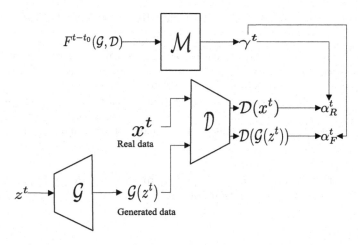

Fig. 2. Overview of the feed-forward step at the tth iteration for the proposed GAN model

discriminator training by controlling the Lipschitz constant of the discriminator function [24].

Transfer learning is another machine learning paradigm that has shown promising results when applied to generative models in scenarios having limited training data [32]. Wang et al. [31] use transfer learning and a mining-based GAN structure to improve GAN performance with a few training images. They use a miner network (implemented as a trainable MLP) that shifts the latent distribution to regions that can generate target images. They finetune the pretrained GAN and miner networks to reduce the source and target distribution distance.

Another well-studied option is adding a regularization term to the objective function to stabilize the GAN training. Liu et al. [20] apply self-supervised learning to regularize the discriminator by adding a reconstruction loss term to the discriminator loss, ensuring that the discriminator extracts a more comprehensive representation from the inputs. Consistency regularization is used by Zhang et al. [36] to make the discriminator invariant to valid domain-specific data augmentation. Zero-centered Gradient penalty [22], adding noise [28], and using stable objective functions like in LS-GAN [21], WGAN [1] are some other prominent methods for stabilizing GAN.

Different adversarial losses proposed for GAN tend to minimize distance based on different metrics between the source and target distribution. The original GAN loss presented by Goodfellow et al. [7] minimizes the Jensen-Shannon divergence between the two probability distributions, and the adversarial loss in LSGAN minimizes the Chi-squared ($\mathcal{X}^2$) divergence [21] and WGAN minimize the Wasserstein distance [1]. Inspired by this, Tseng et al. [30] proposed a regularization term which, when added to the objective function in WGAN, minimized a type of f-divergence called the LeCam-divergence. In this work, we

Table 1. FID($\downarrow$) for 10%, 20% CIFAR-10 and CIFAR-100 datasets. Best performance in bold.

Model	CIFAR10(10%)	CIFAR10(20%)	CIFAR100(10%)	CIFAR100(20%)
Non-saturated GAN [7]	41.99 ± 0.18	18.59 ± 0.15	70.50 ± 0.38	32.64 ± 0.19
LS-GAN [21]	41.68 ± 0.18	21.60 ± 0.11	54.69 ± 0.12	27.09 ± 0.09
BigGAN [3]	48.08 ± 0.10	21.86 ± 0.29	66.71 ± 0.01	32.99 ± 0.24
BigGAN+R_{LC}(baseline)	35.19 ± 0.28	17.17 ± 0.21	50.60 ± 0.27	25.44 ± 0.09
BigGAN+R_{LG}(ours)	$\mathbf{28.22 \pm 0.29}$	$\mathbf{13.97 \pm 0.05}$	$\mathbf{42.77 \pm 0.03}$	$\mathbf{23.80 \pm 0.17}$

further investigate the LeCam GAN [30] by making the decay hyperparameters used in the regularization function learnable.

3   Method

A GAN consists of a generator ($\mathcal{G}$) and discriminator ($\mathcal{D}$) block, which are functions modeled as neural networks. A generator maps a latent variable (z) to samples in the generated data and a discriminator acts as a classifier taking generated and real data as input and a prediction value as the output.

$$V(\mathcal{G}, \mathcal{D}) = \mathbb{E}_{x \sim p_{data}}[\mathcal{F}_{\mathcal{D}}(\mathcal{D}(x))] + \mathbb{E}_{z \sim p_z}[\mathcal{F}_{\mathcal{G}}(\mathcal{D}(\mathcal{G}(z)))] \tag{1}$$

$$\max_{\theta_{\mathcal{D}}} \min_{\theta_{\mathcal{G}}} V(\mathcal{G}, \mathcal{D}) \tag{2}$$

In Eq. (1), $\mathcal{F}_{\mathcal{D}}$, $\mathcal{F}_{\mathcal{G}}$ are loss functions for the discriminator and the generator respectively. Goodfellow et al. [8] used a cross-entropy loss function; However, several other loss variants are possible that apply a different transformation to the discriminator prediction [14, 21]. Equation (2) describes the objective for the GAN at each training iteration.

Using appropriate loss functions, the minimax optimization problem in Eq. (2) amounts to the discriminator ($\mathcal{D}$) trying to distinguish generated data $\mathcal{G}(z)$ from the samples from true distribution p_{data}; while the generator ($\mathcal{G}$) attempts to generate data close to the training data.

This work extends the discriminator-based loss regularization proposed by Tseng et al. [30] for GAN training under the limited data regime. The discriminator objective is regularized using exponential moving average variables called anchors. These anchors improve the stability of GAN training by minimizing

Table 2. IS($\uparrow$) for 10%, 20% CIFAR-10 and CIFAR-100 datasets. Best performance in bold.

Model	CIFAR10(10%)	CIFAR10(20%)	CIFAR100(10%)	CIFAR100(20%)
BigGAN+R_{LC}(baseline)	8.16 ± 0.17	8.52 ± 0.24	7.71 ± 0.17	9.73 ± 0.42
BigGAN+R_{LG}(ours)	$\mathbf{8.18 \pm 0.10}$	$\mathbf{8.91 \pm 0.20}$	$\mathbf{7.95 \pm 0.20}$	$\mathbf{10.06 \pm 0.21}$

Table 3. FID($\downarrow$) for 10%, 20% CIFAR-10 and CIFAR-100 datasets with differentiable augmentation. Best performance in bold.

Model	CIFAR10(10%)	CIFAR10(20%)	CIFAR100(10%)	CIFAR100(20%)
BigGAN+DA+R_{LC}(baseline)	16.97 ± 0.22	12.60 ± 0.25	28.24 ± 0.20	20.08 ± 0.30
BigGAN+DA+R_{LG}(ours)	$\mathbf{16.50 \pm 0.19}$	$\mathbf{12.28 \pm 0.14}$	$\mathbf{24.89 \pm 0.27}$	$\mathbf{19.87 \pm 0.40}$

the LeCam divergence between the distributions of training data and generated data.

$$L_{\mathcal{D}} = \min_{\theta_{\mathcal{D}}} -V(\mathcal{G}, \mathcal{D}) + \lambda R_{LC}(\mathcal{D}) \tag{3}$$

$$R_{LC}(\mathcal{D}) = \mathbb{E}_{x \sim p_{data}}[||\mathcal{D}(x) - \alpha_F||^2] + \mathbb{E}_{z \sim p_z}[||\mathcal{D}(\mathcal{G}(z)) - \alpha_R||^2] \tag{4}$$

$$\alpha^t = \gamma \alpha^{t-1} + (1 - \gamma)v^t \tag{5}$$

Equation (3) defines the regularized discriminator loss function, Eq. (4) is the regularization term where α_R and α_F are the anchors updated at each iteration according to Eq. (5). In Eq. (5), v^t is the average value of the discriminator output for real and generated images at the tth iteration. For the anchor α_R, $v^t = \mathbb{E}(\mathcal{D}(x^t))$ and for α_F, $v^t = \mathbb{E}(\mathcal{D}(\mathcal{G}(z^t)))$. While training, v^t is implemented as an empirical average for both the anchors α_R and α_F.

Tseng et al. [30] kept the decay factor γ in Eq. (5) constant at a value of 0.99 throughout all the iterations. This causes the update rule for the anchors to be skewed towards the past values of the anchors (α^{t-1}). To overcome this and allow a more dynamic update of anchors, we make the decay factor γ a trainable parameter as

$$\alpha^t = \gamma(\boldsymbol{\theta}_{\mathcal{M}})\alpha^{t-1} + (1 - \gamma(\boldsymbol{\theta}_{\mathcal{M}}))v^t \tag{6}$$

In the above equation, $\boldsymbol{\theta}_{\mathcal{M}}$ represents the parameters of the Multilayer perceptron model (MLP), $\mathcal{M}$ that we add to the existing network to learn the decay factor. Thus at each iteration, the updates of the anchors α are made based on a learned decay factor γ. The input features of the MLP are based on the GAN metrics over a specific window of past iterations; the output is the decay factor to be used at the current step. The MLP is implemented as an auxiliary network to the discriminator network, allowing weight updates during the backpropagation step for the discriminator. Figure 2 provides an overview of the GAN training at the tth iteration. The block $\mathcal{M}$ represents the MLP used to train the decay factor, $F^{t-t_0}(\mathcal{G}, \mathcal{D})$ represents the feature input for the MLP based on the metrics of the GAN in the previous t_0 iterations.

4   Experimental Results

We perform several experiments with limited data constraints to validate our hyperparameter augmentation. We use the conditional BigGAN architecture

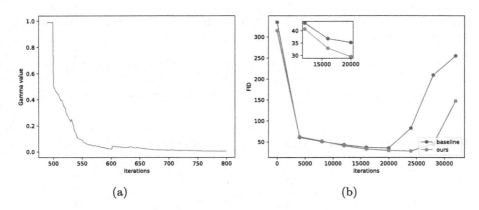

(a)   (b)

Fig. 3. (a) **Variation of decay factor** γ. It is plotted from iteration number 490 to 800, we observe that γ tends to zero as the iterations increase, (b) FID variation with training iterations for 10% CIFAR-10 dataset.

with a hinge-loss for the generator and discriminator as our basic GAN model. Therewithal, we add the LeCam regularizer [30] with an adaptable decay factor.

Model. The MLP for the decay factor has an input feature size of 10 units and a hidden layer of 6 units. Rectified linear unit (Relu) function introduces non-linearity between the input layer and hidden layer, and softmax is used as the function for the output layer. The GAN metrics applied as input features for MLP are generator loss, discriminator loss, discriminator predictions for real and fake data, and gamma value in previous iterations. These metrics' mean values and standard deviations are averaged over a window size of 500 iterations before feeding into the network.

Dataset. We work with CIFAR-10 and CIFAR-100 datasets for our experiments. The CIFAR10 dataset contains 60000 32 × 32 colored images divided into ten classes. CIFAR100 also has 60000 32 × 32 images, but the class division is into 100 classes with coarse and fine labels for further grouping [15]. The training is done with only a subset of the datasets to simulate the limited data conditions. We train with 10% and 20% of both datasets in our work for experimentation.

Metrics. We evaluate sample-based metrics like Frechet inception distance (FID) and inception score (IS) to compare our algorithm with the baseline quantitatively. For calculating the IS, the images generated by the generator are passed through an inception model [29]. A score is assigned based on the quality and diversity of generated images [25]. A GAN generating a high-quality, diverse set of images will have a high inception score and vice-versa.

IS calculation doesn't consider real images, thus discounting any insights into the generator's performance against the training images. FID overcomes this drawback by allowing for a statistical comparison between the distributions of the generated and training images [9]. For calculating FID, generated and real images are fed into an inception model, and the Frechet distance is measured

Fig. 4. Images generated by the proposed model after every 2k training iterations on 10% CIFAR-10.

between the intermediate coding layer of the model for both inputs. A low FID implies high quality and variety in the generated images.

Baseline. The regularized GAN implemented in LeCam paper [30] is used as baseline. Two NVIDIA GTX 1650 GPU are used for training. FID and IS are computed every 4000 iterations of the training, and the generator weights are saved if FID improves over the previous one. We use a generator having the least FID during training for the testing phase, which involves averaging the FID score over three evaluation cycles [37].

We perform two kinds of experiments to compare our implementation and the baseline model. In the first experiment, we use only the discriminator regularization versions of both the algorithms on 10%, 20% CIFAR-10 and CIFAR-100 datasets. The results of this experiment are tabulated in Tables 1 and 2. In the second experiment, we supplement the discriminator regularization with a data augmentation technique called differentiable augmentation [37]. The corresponding results are presented in Table 3. From the FID and IS scores in Tables 1, 2 and 3, we can see that our algorithm outperforms the baseline both as an independent regularization method and also when appended to other regularization approaches.

In the next section, we analyze the performance improvement the proposed algorithm offers over the baseline. We draw inferences based on quantitative metrics such as loss and FID scores and provide a qualitative analysis using the images generated by the trained generator.

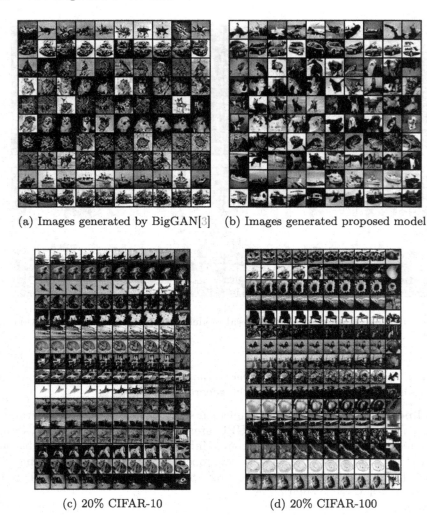

(a) Images generated by BigGAN[3]   (b) Images generated proposed model

(c) 20% CIFAR-10   (d) 20% CIFAR-100

Fig. 5. Qualitative analysis. (a), (b) include images generated by best FID generators after training on 10% CIFAR-10 dataset, (c), (d) provides the results of latent space interpolation for the proposed model on 20% CIFAR-10, CIFAR-100 datasets respectively.

4.1   Analysis

We fix the value of the decay factor, γ, to 0.99 for the first 500 iterations and vary it according to a trainable MLP for subsequent iterations. Figure 3a shows that the value of the decay factor tends to zero as the iterations increase. According to Eq. (5), this implies that in updates of anchors at later iterations, more weight is given to the anchor values at the current step. This leads to a more robust regularization, reducing discriminator overfit. Once the discriminator starts memo-

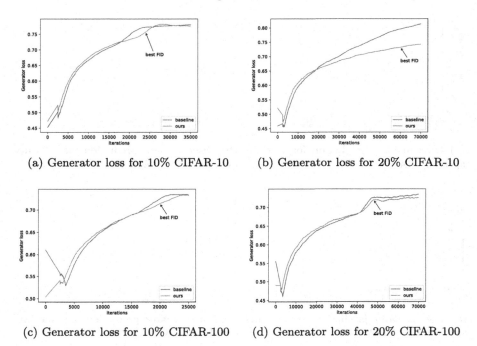

(a) Generator loss for 10% CIFAR-10   (b) Generator loss for 20% CIFAR-10

(c) Generator loss for 10% CIFAR-100   (d) Generator loss for 20% CIFAR-100

Fig. 6. Generator loss. In the neighborhood with the best FID score, we observe a lower generator loss than the baseline.

rizing instead of generalizing, the quality of generated images degrades, causing the FID to increase. From Fig. 3b, we can observe that the FID increase is steeper for the baseline than the proposed model suggesting a stronger regularization when using an adjustable decay factor.

Figure 5 provides a qualitative analysis of the proposed model. In Fig. 5b, we can see that the images generated by our model are more diversified and of finer quality than those generated by an un-regularized BigGAN (Fig. 5a). For latent space interpolation, we generate images corresponding to the latent variables obtained by linear interpolation between two points in the latent space. In Figs. 5c, 5d, we see a gradual transition in the images generated by latent space interpolation, demonstrating the generalization power of our model [23]. Images generated after every 2000 training iterations are grouped in Fig. 4. We can see a drastic improvement in the image quality in the first 2000 iterations, which is quantitatively represented by the sudden drop in FID in Fig. 3b.

A regularized discriminator allows the propagation of useful gradients to the generator, thus improving its performance. Figure 6 plots the generator loss for the limited data experiments. Our model has lower generator loss than the baseline in the neighborhood of best FID because of the improved generator performance. The refinement in the generator is also visible from the discriminator predictions for fake images in Fig. 7. Discriminator predictions for fake images

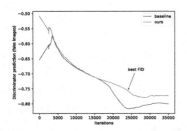
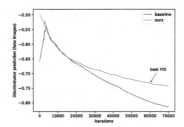

(a) Discriminator prediction for fake images for 10% CIFAR-10

(b) Discriminator prediction for fake images for 20% CIFAR-10

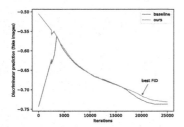
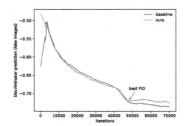

(c) Discriminator prediction for fake images for 10% CIFAR-100

(d) Discriminator prediction for fake images for 20% CIFAR-100

Fig. 7. Discriminator prediction for fake images. In the neighborhood with the best FID score, we observe a higher discriminator prediction than the baseline. A higher prediction value implies lower confidence of the discriminator in the image being fake.

are higher for our model because of better-quality (and closer to the training set) images generated by the generator.

5   Conclusion

This paper presents a regularization-based algorithm for stabilizing GAN training under limited data. The proposed algorithm extends the state-of-the-art work done by Tseng et al. [30] previously. Our augmentation makes the GAN training more stable by improving the generator performance and delaying the overfitting of the discriminator. The experiments show that the proposed model performs better on FID and IS metrics as a stand-alone regularizer and when supplemented with differentiable augmentation.

Acknowledgement. This work is partially supported by the TCS/EE/2019156 project at IIT Kanpur.

References

1. Arjovsky, M., Chintala, S., Bottou, L.: Wasserstein generative adversarial networks. In: International Conference on Machine Learning, pp. 214–223. PMLR (2017)

2. Ba, J.L., Kiros, J.R., Hinton, G.E.: Layer normalization. arXiv preprint arXiv:1607.06450 (2016)
3. Brock, A., Donahue, J., Simonyan, K.: Large scale GAN training for high fidelity natural image synthesis. arXiv preprint arXiv:1809.11096 (2018)
4. Deng, J., Dong, W., Socher, R., Li, L.J., Li, K., Fei-Fei, L.: ImageNet: a large-scale hierarchical image database. IEEE (2009)
5. Ehsani, K., Mottaghi, R., Farhadi, A.: SEGAN: segmenting and generating the invisible. In: Proceedings of the IEEE Conference on Computer Vision and Pattern Recognition, pp. 6144–6153 (2018)
6. Goodfellow, I.: NIPS 2016 tutorial: generative adversarial networks. arXiv preprint arXiv:1701.00160 (2016)
7. Goodfellow, I., et al.: Generative adversarial networks. Commun. ACM 139–144 (2020)
8. Goodfellow, I.J., et al.: Generative adversarial networks (2014)
9. Heusel, M., Ramsauer, H., Unterthiner, T., Nessler, B., Hochreiter, S.: GANs trained by a two time-scale update rule converge to a local Nash equilibrium (2018)
10. Ioffe, S., Szegedy, C.: Batch normalization: accelerating deep network training by reducing internal covariate shift. In: International Conference on Machine Learning, pp. 448–456. PMLR (2015)
11. Jetchev, N., Bergmann, U., Vollgraf, R.: Texture synthesis with spatial generative adversarial networks. arXiv preprint arXiv:1611.08207 (2016)
12. Karras, T., Aittala, M., Hellsten, J., Laine, S., Lehtinen, J., Aila, T.: Training generative adversarial networks with limited data (2020)
13. Karras, T., Laine, S., Aila, T.: A style-based generator architecture for generative adversarial networks. In: Proceedings of the IEEE/CVF Conference on Computer Vision and Pattern Recognition, pp. 4401–4410 (2019)
14. Kavalerov, I., Czaja, W., Chellappa, R.: A multi-class hinge loss for conditional GANs. In: Proceedings of the IEEE/CVF Winter Conference on Applications of Computer Vision (WACV), pp. 1290–1299 (2021)
15. Krizhevsky, A., Hinton, G., et al.: Learning multiple layers of features from tiny images (2009)
16. Kurach, K., Lucic, M., Zhai, X., Michalski, M., Gelly, S.: A large-scale study on regularization and normalization in GANs (2019)
17. Ledig, C., et al.: Photo-realistic single image super-resolution using a generative adversarial network. In: Proceedings of the IEEE Conference on Computer Vision and Pattern Recognition, pp. 4681–4690 (2017)
18. Li, C., Wand, M.: Precomputed real-time texture synthesis with Markovian generative adversarial networks. In: Leibe, B., Matas, J., Sebe, N., Welling, M. (eds.) ECCV 2016. LNCS, vol. 9907, pp. 702–716. Springer, Cham (2016). https://doi.org/10.1007/978-3-319-46487-9_43
19. Li, J., Liang, X., Wei, Y., Xu, T., Feng, J., Yan, S.: Perceptual generative adversarial networks for small object detection. In: Proceedings of the IEEE Conference on Computer Vision and Pattern Recognition, pp. 1222–1230 (2017)
20. Liu, B., Zhu, Y., Song, K., Elgammal, A.: Towards faster and stabilized GAN training for high-fidelity few-shot image synthesis (2021)
21. Mao, X., Li, Q., Xie, H., Lau, R.Y., Wang, Z., Paul Smolley, S.: Least squares generative adversarial networks. In: Proceedings of the IEEE International Conference on Computer Vision, pp. 2794–2802 (2017)
22. Mescheder, L., Geiger, A., Nowozin, S.: Which training methods for GANs do actually converge? In: International Conference on Machine Learning, pp. 3481–3490. PMLR (2018)

23. Mi, L., He, T., Park, C.F., Wang, H., Wang, Y., Shavit, N.: Revisiting latent-space interpolation via a quantitative evaluation framework (2021)
24. Miyato, T., Kataoka, T., Koyama, M., Yoshida, Y.: Spectral normalization for generative adversarial networks. arXiv preprint arXiv:1802.05957 (2018)
25. Salimans, T., Goodfellow, I., Zaremba, W., Cheung, V., Radford, A., Chen, X.: Improved techniques for training GANs (2016)
26. Salimans, T., Kingma, D.P.: Weight normalization: a simple reparameterization to accelerate training of deep neural networks. In: Advances in Neural Information Processing Systems (2016)
27. Shahbazi, M., Danelljan, M., Paudel, D.P., Gool, L.V.: Collapse by conditioning: training class-conditional GANs with limited data (2022)
28. Sønderby, C.K., Caballero, J., Theis, L., Shi, W., Huszár, F.: Amortised map inference for image super-resolution. arXiv preprint arXiv:1610.04490 (2016)
29. Szegedy, C., Vanhoucke, V., Ioffe, S., Shlens, J., Wojna, Z.: Rethinking the inception architecture for computer vision (2015)
30. Tseng, H.Y., Jiang, L., Liu, C., Yang, M.H., Yang, W.: Regularizing generative adversarial networks under limited data. In: Proceedings of the IEEE/CVF Conference on Computer Vision and Pattern Recognition, pp. 7921–7931 (2021)
31. Wang, Y., Gonzalez-Garcia, A., Berga, D., Herranz, L., Khan, F.S., van de Weijer, J.: MineGAN: effective knowledge transfer from GANs to target domains with few images (2019)
32. Weiss, K., Khoshgoftaar, T.M., Wang, D.: A survey of transfer learning. J. Big Data 1–40 (2016)
33. Yi, X., Babyn, P.: Sharpness-aware low-dose CT denoising using conditional generative adversarial network. J. Digit. Imaging 655–669 (2018)
34. Yi, X., Walia, E., Babyn, P.: Generative adversarial network in medical imaging: a review. Med. Image Anal. 101552 (2019)
35. Zhang, D., Khoreva, A.: Progressive augmentation of GANs (2019)
36. Zhang, H., Zhang, Z., Odena, A., Lee, H.: Consistency regularization for generative adversarial networks. arXiv preprint arXiv:1910.12027 (2019)
37. Zhao, S., Liu, Z., Lin, J., Zhu, J.Y., Han, S.: Differentiable augmentation for data-efficient GAN training (2020)

Real Time Video Stitching Using Fixed Camera Configuration

Bhavesh Singhal(✉)[iD], Saquib Mazhar[iD], and M. K. Bhuyan[iD]

Indian Institute of Technology, Guwahati, Guwahati, Assam, India
bhavesh.singhal89@gmail.com, {saquibmazhar,mkb}@iitg.ac.in

Abstract. Video stitching is crucial in multi-camera-based systems that provide 360-degree surveillance and monitoring applications. Homography estimation is the most important step in video/image stitching. All the existing methods mainly focus on homography estimation through traditional keypoint detection or a more recent deep learning approach. These estimation methods are primarily based on multiple homography calculations and fail for featureless images, which lack keypoints, such as the plain sky. To overcome these limitations, we propose a novel real-time video stitching method based on homography estimation through camera calibration using fixed camera configuration. As the proposed method is based on the relative position of two cameras, the overall image/video stitching process is independent of the world scene. In addition, our method calculates the homography matrix only once during the video stitching process. Thus reducing the per-frame stitching time by about 30% compared to multiple homography estimations. As camera calibration information is unavailable with the existing datasets, we record a novel dataset for benchmarking our method.

Keywords: Video stitching · Object detection · Homography estimation

1 Introduction

Real-time Video Stitching is equivalent to performing image stitching to a sequence of frames, such that the stitching time per frame is comparable to the real-time scenario. It is used in virtual reality, autonomous driving, generating panoramic images/videos, and live video surveillance. Consider a scenario where a military camp is to be protected against drone attacks. For this purpose, the user needs 24 × 7 360-degree surveillance of the airspace above the military campus and must be notified when any drone is detected approaching from any direction. To achieve this, we need a model capable of providing continuous real-time stitched video from a featureless background, covering the airspace.

The image stitching network has two main components - Homography Estimation and Blending techniques. Homography is the transformation matrix relating the correspondence points in an image pair. It aligns the two images

© The Author(s), under exclusive license to Springer Nature Switzerland AG 2024
H. Kaur et al. (Eds.): CVIP 2023, CCIS 2010, pp. 555–566, 2024.
https://doi.org/10.1007/978-3-031-58174-8_46

captured from two camera views in the same coordinate system. Traditionally, homography is estimated based on keypoint detection and matching [1,4,5,10,12]. However, several deep learning-based methods have evolved with recent advancements [2,9,11]. In a general image stitching pipeline, initially, homography is estimated between two images; then, both images are warped in the same coordinate system. Once the images are aligned, several blending techniques and gain compensation techniques are applied to achieve a seamless result. The keypoint-based methods use point-based feature descriptors for feature matching. However, all these methods depend upon the image's content and hence fail when image contents are featureless, like the plain sky. In this work, we attempt to develop a novel real-time video stitching model for fixed camera configuration independent of the world scene. The significant advantage of a fixed camera configuration is that we need to calculate the homography once, which can be reused for all frame stitching. This reduces the stitching time, a prime requirement for real-time methods.

A novel dataset has also been recorded for video stitching in challenging featureless backgrounds like the plain sky, as in existing datasets, the camera configuration is unknown.

2   Related Works

Image Stitching methods can be broadly categorized into keypoint-based and deep learning-based. Both these methods are dependent on feature detection and matching. While keypoint-based image stitching utilizes various algorithms for feature detection, deep-learning models detect these features automatically. First, we discuss the keypoint-based methods in the following paragraph. Next, we discuss deep learning-based methods.

[1] proposed the most widely used method for fully automatic panorama stitching using Scale Invariant Image stitching Feature Transform (SIFT) and Multi-Band Blending. Initially, features are extracted and matched, and then Random Sample Consensus (RANSAC) is used to identify valid correspondence pairs between two images. The homography matrix is calculated using these pairs; then, this matrix is used to warp the images in the same coordinate system. The images are blended using Multi-Band Blending (MBB) and stitched to obtain the output. [12] considered moving cameras for real-time video Stitching. The proposed pipeline involved feature extraction using Speeded Up Robust Features (SURF), feature matching using KNN and then RANSAC implementation for Homography estimation. [10] compared SIFT, SURF and FAST algorithms for feature detection and matching purposes. [5] introduced a hybrid feature descriptor based on SIFT and DAISY to improve the feature matching accuracy in case images with similar textures. [4] prepared a novel dataset of indoor and outdoor scenarios using static camera configuration. SIFT is used for feature extraction, and Root-SIFT is used for feature description. They proposed a novel hybrid matcher using Brute Force (BF) and Fast Linear Approximate Nearest Neighbour (FLANN) to improve the matching accuracy and calculate

one-time homography using RANSAC. [8] brought out that the SIFT algorithm is computationally expensive and has low matching efficiency. As a solution, the authors proposed an improvised SIFT method and compared the results with traditional SIFT and SURF methods. [7] offered a hardware accelerator to enhance the speed of SIFT feature extraction for High frame rate video stitching applications.

[2] proposed a supervised deep learning model for homography estimation based on VGG. They proposed a novel way of creating ground truth for model training purposes on the MS-COCO [6] dataset. Two model variants were proposed: the classification model and the regression model. Mean Corner Error (MCE) is considered a metric to compare the results of the proposed method with the ORB + RANSAC method. [9] proposed a novel unsupervised model for homography estimation based on the VGG model and used the same approach mentioned in [2] to create the dataset for training. [11] proposed an end-to-end stitching network based on an encoder, regressor, and decoder. Car Learning to Act (CARLA) [3] simulator was used to create a virtual dataset for model training. The encoder extracts features from the input image pairs in the proposed network, and the regressor estimates multiple homographies. Further, the decoder generates depth maps and displacement maps to obtain the final stitched result.

However, the methods discussed above either require repeated homography calculation or depend upon the availability of features in the input image pair. Thus failing on images with featureless backgrounds. In the next section, we discuss the proposed method.

3   Proposed Method

In this section, we first propose a novel Homography estimation method based on camera calibration for fixed camera configuration and then propose a novel real-time video stitching method. As already explained, homography matrix estimation between an input image pair for image stitching is the first and most critical part of the image stitching process.

In the proposed method of homography estimation, we have tried to make homography estimation independent of the world scene, which can be implementable for the case of images with plain backgrounds. Consider a fixed configuration of two cameras in a stereo vision manner as shown in Fig. 1, such that the field of view of given cameras overlaps by 20–30%. Given cameras are being used for real-time video surveillance and provide two frames as per the frame rate, which acts as an input image pair. The algorithm is given below:

3.1   Proposed Algorithm for Homography Estimation

- **Step 1.** Position a two-camera configuration at position A, as shown in Fig. 1. At position A, cameras are facing a world scene that has a sufficient number of keypoints. Carry out the Camera Calibration of both cameras to obtain respective intrinsic matrices and distortion coefficients.

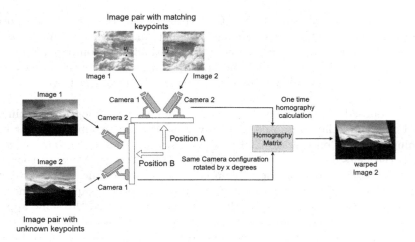

Fig. 1. Proposed homography estimation method.

- **Step 2**. Using the obtained intrinsic parameters and distortion coefficients of the individual cameras, perform individual camera image rectification on the images of the scene at Position A so that we have the rectified images in the image plane of the respective cameras.
- **Step 3**. Detect matching keypoints in the left and right undistorted images of the scene at Position A by using any one of the keypoint detection and matching algorithms. We have implemented SIFT and ORB.
- **Step 3**. Estimate the homography matrix for the scene at Position A using RANSAC and DLT.
- **Step 4**. Shift/rotate the complete camera configuration to the unknown scene at position B, such that the relative position of the two cameras with respect to each other does not change. As our cameras are calibrated, and we have already obtained the homography matrix for the given configuration of cameras at position A, we need not find the homography matrix from images of the scene at position B.
- **Step 5**. Apply the homography matrix of the scene at Position A to the scene at Position B.

The proposed method is based on the traditional uncalibrated stereo problem, discussed next.

3.2 Relation Between Uncalibrated Stereo Problem and Proposed Homography Estimation Method

To show that the proposed fixed camera approach can be used for homography estimation, we model it as an uncalibrated stereo problem. We address the two cameras used in this configuration as the left and right. Suppose Intrinsic Matrices of two cameras in a fixed configuration are known. In that case, we

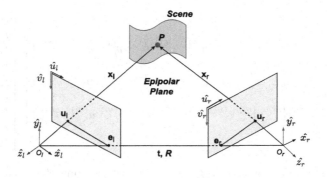

Fig. 2. Uncalibrated stereo system.

can easily compute the relative position of one camera with respect to another, i.e. t: Position of Right Camera in Left Camera's frame, R: Orientation of Left Camera in Right Camera's frame, using epipolar geometry, refer Fig. 2.

To calculate the relative position parameters t and R, some correspondence points between images/video frames obtained from camera 1 and camera 2 are required. These points can be calculated using keypoint detection and matching techniques. From the uncalibrated stereo problem, we already know that correspondence points in the image plane of the left camera and right camera are related by the fundamental matrix, as shown in Eq. (1), where $(u_l^{(i)}, u_r^{(i)})$ and $(v_l^{(i)}, v_r^{(i)})$ are corresponding pixel coordinates of ith matching pair between the left image and right image. Equation (1) is also known as epipolar constraint.

$$\begin{bmatrix} u_l^{(i)} & v_l^{(i)} & 1 \end{bmatrix} \begin{bmatrix} f_{11} & f_{12} & f_{13} \\ f_{21} & f_{22} & f_{23} \\ f_{31} & f_{32} & f_{33} \end{bmatrix} \begin{bmatrix} u_r^{(i)} \\ v_r^{(i)} \\ 1 \end{bmatrix} = 0 \tag{1}$$

where fundamental matrix, F is given by

$$F = \begin{bmatrix} f_{11} & f_{12} & f_{13} \\ f_{21} & f_{22} & f_{23} \\ f_{31} & f_{32} & f_{33} \end{bmatrix} \tag{2}$$

Using all the correspondence points between the left and right images, we can write Eq. (1) for each of the pair and then obtain the matrix shown below:

$$
\begin{bmatrix}
u_l^{(1)}u_r^{(1)} & u_l^{(1)}v_r^{(1)} & u_l^{(1)} & v_l^{(1)}u_r^{(1)} & v_l^{(1)}v_r^{(1)} & v_l^{(1)} & u_r^{(1)} & v_r^{(1)} & 1 \\
\vdots & \vdots & \vdots & \vdots & \vdots & \vdots & \vdots & \vdots & \vdots \\
u_l^{(i)}u_r^{(i)} & u_l^{(i)}v_r^{(i)} & u_l^{(i)} & v_l^{(i)}u_r^{(i)} & v_l^{(i)}v_r^{(i)} & v_l^{(i)} & u_r^{(i)} & v_r^{(i)} & 1 \\
\vdots & \vdots & \vdots & \vdots & \vdots & \vdots & \vdots & \vdots & \vdots \\
u_l^{(m)}u_r^{(m)} & u_l^{(m)}v_r^{(m)} & u_l^{(m)} & v_l^{(m)}u_r^{(m)} & v_l^{(m)}v_r^{(m)} & v_l^{(m)} & u_r^{(m)} & v_r^{(m)} & 1
\end{bmatrix}
\begin{bmatrix}
f_{11} \\ f_{12} \\ f_{13} \\ f_{21} \\ f_{22} \\ f_{23} \\ f_{31} \\ f_{32} \\ f_{33}
\end{bmatrix}
=
\begin{bmatrix}
0 \\ \vdots \\ 0 \\ \vdots \\ 0
\end{bmatrix}
\tag{3}
$$

Equation (3) is of the form $Af = 0$, which can be converted to a constrained least square problem,

$$
\min_f ||Af||^2 \tag{4}
$$
$$
\text{s.t.} ||f||^2 = 1
$$

Once F, the fundamental matrix is estimated, we can use another two important equations of uncalibrated stereo system to find the relative position of two cameras, Eq. (5) and Eq. (6), where E is (3×3) matrix called the essential matrix.

$$
E = K_l^T F K_r \tag{5}
$$

$$
E = T_X R \tag{6}
$$

K_l and K_r are the calibration matrices of the left camera and right camera; E can be written in an expanded form of T_X and R as shown in Eq. (7).

$$
E = \begin{bmatrix} 0 & -t_z & t_y \\ t_z & 0 & -t_x \\ -t_y & t_x & 0 \end{bmatrix} \begin{bmatrix} r_{11} & r_{12} & r_{13} \\ r_{21} & r_{22} & r_{33} \\ r_{31} & r_{32} & r_{33} \end{bmatrix} \tag{7}
$$

Hence, once both the cameras are calibrated, we can obtain the rectified images in the image plane of both cameras and subsequently, we can find the relative position of one camera with respect to the other camera.

3.3 Relation Between Fundamental Matrix and Homography Matrix

During the process, we can observe that the E and F matrix calculation is based on the relative position of two cameras, which are the external parameters. If we keep the relative positions of two calibrated cameras unchanged and rotate the complete stereo camera system to another world scene, in that case, the fundamental matrix should still be the same because it depends upon E, which is dependent upon t and R.

Also, we know from Eq. (1) that two correspondence points of a matching pair of the left image and right image are related by the fundamental matrix, so if F remain unchanged after the rotation, then the pixel coordinates of correspondence matching pairs between left and right camera should also remain unchanged after the rotation. Therefore, if $(\mathbf{u}_l, \mathbf{u}_r)$ (refer Fig. 1) is a matching pair at Position A, then it should still be the matching pair at Position B. Therefore, if we calculate a homography matrix using the matching pair coordinates between two video frames/images from a fixed camera configuration at Position A, that homography matrix should still be the same at Position B because the relative position of two cameras with respect to each other is same at Position A and Position B and hence, the matching pair image coordinates are not changing for this particular stereo camera system after moving this system from Position A to Position B. This means we can apply H, calculated from these correspondence points at Position A to Position B.

Earlier works estimate homography for each video frame and fail at the first step of 'Feature Extraction' when features are unavailable due to plain background. The novelty of the proposed method is in its approach toward estimating the homography matrix without extracting features from the scene. As the proposed method does not require feature extraction from every new scene, it is independent of the world scene if the cameras are calibrated.

3.4 Proposed Real-Time Video Stitching Method

Once the homography matrix between image pair/video frames from two cameras in fixed configuration is estimated using the proposed method, we go for the video stitching. The complete pipeline can be seen in Fig. 3. An estimated homography matrix is used to align the images from the left and right camera in the same coordinate system; they are pre-stitched using a linear blending technique and passed through a deep learning-based autoencoder for denoising. As we are talking about real-time video stitching and considering the application of 360-degree real-time video surveillance to detect drones in the plain sky, we want the stitched output free from various noises due to poor weather and other environmental reasons like rain, dust storms, etc. Considering this, we have introduced a denoising autoencoder in the pipeline. The autoencoder takes patches of size 128×128 pixels as input. Hence, the pre-stitched image is converted to patches for autoencoder processing. After denoising, the patches are joined to form the original size image.

To achieve real-time video stitching, each recorded frame from the two cameras is passed through this model, and stitched output is obtained. Another advantage of considering fixed camera configuration is in reducing the average image stitching time per frame; as we have seen in Sect. 3.2, if cameras are fixed with respect to each other, we need to calculate the homography only once and use it for subsequent frames. This reduces the time needed to re-calculate the homography, thus further reducing the inference time.

4 Experiments

In this section, we validate the existing keypoint-based and deep learning-based methods on our novel dataset with featureless background and known camera

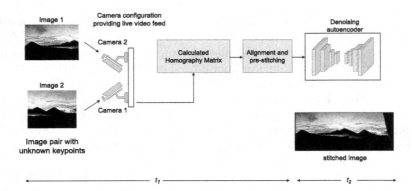

Fig. 3. Proposed video stitching model.

configuration. Then, we report the performance of our proposed algorithm on the recorded dataset. First, we give details about the recorded dataset in the following sub-section, followed by the training details of the auto-encoder for denoising.

4.1 Dataset Collection

As there is no open source image dataset or video dataset available for image stitching analysis of images with plain backgrounds captured with fixed camera configuration. We designed and fabricated a customized platform to fulfil our requirements, as shown in Fig. 4. We recorded 14 different video streams from the left camera, right camera and ground truth camera at a resolution of 640 × 480 at 30 frames per second using simple webcams. The designed platform has a round-shaped top with adjustable camera mountings, and the platform top can spin about its axis. The recorded dataset mainly comprises images with plain backgrounds. We recorded videos for two cases, where in case 1, both the cameras were mounted in a horizontal line, and in case 2, both the cameras were mounted on different mountings, which can be adjusted from the base such that the overlap between the vision of the two cameras may be adjusted. This platform allows us to record the datasets with varied overlap percentages between two cameras.

4.2 Training Details for Autoencoder

We train the autoencoder on the custom dataset for 70 epochs, using Adam optimizer. The initial learning rate was 0.001 with a mean square error loss function. Initially, 3600 patches of size (128 × 128) were created, and then the noise was added to the original patches to form the training model input data. Noisy patches were used as input and original patches as ground truth. The trained autoencoder is used to obtain the final denoised stitched image.

Fig. 4. Customized platform for dataset recording.

4.3 Qualitative Results for Existing Methods of Image Stitching

First, we show the stitched panorama results on images with featured backgrounds for the ORB-based method. Figure 5 shows the input images with sufficient background features. In Fig. 6, the ORB-based stitching method performs well on the input images.

Fig. 5. Input images with featured backgrounds. Image 1–4 (left to right).

Figure 7 shows the result of ORB based method on our novel recorded dataset. However, we can observe that using the existing method, the keypoints are matched wrongly in the image pair, leading to a false stitching result. In Fig. 8, we see the homography estimation results of the deep learning method [2] on the MS-COCO dataset. The warped images have a low Mean Corner Error (MCE) due to the feature-rich background. However, Fig. 9 shows a very high value of MCE for our custom dataset, which has resulted in the failure of this method to stitch images with plain backgrounds.

4.4 Qualitative Results for Proposed Method

Figure 10 and 11 show the results of the proposed stitching method for fixed camera configuration on the recorded dataset. While both keypoint-based and deep learning methods have failed on similar images, our method perfectly aligns and stitches the images with a plain background. We calculate the homography matrix from feature-rich scene 1 video frames and use it for stitching in scene 2.

Fig. 6. Stitched panorama images; ORB based keypoint matching (left); stitched image (right).

Fig. 7. Failed result of ORB-based method on frames from our novel dataset with plain background; matched keypoints after RANSAC (left); stitched image (right).

Fig. 8. Deep learning homography estimation on some images from MS-COCO dataset. The calculated homography shows low MCE.

Fig. 9. Homography estimation and stitching results on our dataset using the deep learning-based method. Image 1–5 (left to right). Image pairs (1,2) and (3,4) have high MCE. The stitched image 5 shows the failure of the method.

Fig. 10. Result of the proposed method on our dataset 1. Image 1–5 (left to right). Image 1,2: Input image pair 1; Image 3,4: Warped images; Image 5: Stitched image.

Fig. 11. Result of the proposed method on our dataset 2. Image 1–5 (left to right). Image 1,2: Input image pair 2; Image 3,4: Warped images; Image 5: Stitched image.

4.5 Average Image Stitching Time per Frame

We select two video streams from the custom dataset for average Image Stitching time per frame analysis of the proposed method. The first stream has 237 frames, and the second has 227 frames. The total inference time comprises the time required for homography estimation, alignment and pre-stitching (t_1) and the time required for denoising using autoencoder ($N \times t_2$, where N is the number of patches at the input of encoder), refer Fig. 3. [11] and [12] propose an image stitching method that estimates the homography matrix multiple times. The results for estimating the homography matrix for each video frame are compared with the proposed methods in Table 1. We see a time saving of 20.09% and 17.07% for video 1 and 36.04% and 27.63% for video 2, which is significant for a real-time method. This saving is due to one-time homography calculation in our method compared to repeated homography calculation in other methods.

Table 1. Inference time results for the proposed method on our dataset.

Video	No. of frames	Proposed Method	Method [11]	Reduction	Method [12]	Reduction
1	237	0.34 s	0.43 s	20.09%	0.41 s	17.07%
2	227	0.55 s	0.86 s	36.04%	0.76 s	27.63%

5 Conclusion

We have proposed a novel method for real-time video stitching for fixed camera configuration. Our method proposes a novel homography estimation method using intrinsic camera parameters and stereo vision without the need for feature detection and extraction. We also prepared a challenging novel dataset with a plain background to test the proposed method in challenging backgrounds. Our method provides a substantial speedup in average image stitching time per frame compared to the existing methods using one-time homography estimation.

References

1. Brown, M., Lowe, D.G.: Automatic panoramic image stitching using invariant features. Int. J. Comput. Vis. **74**(1), 59–73 (2007)

2. DeTone, D., Malisiewicz, T., Rabinovich, A.: Deep image homography estimation (2016). http://arxiv.org/abs/1606.03798

3. Dosovitskiy, A., Ros, G., Codevilla, F., Lopez, A., Koltun, V.: CARLA: an open urban driving simulator. In: Proceedings of the 1st Annual Conference on Robot Learning. Proceedings of Machine Learning Research, vol. 78, pp. 1–16. PMLR (2017)

4. Imran Hosen, M., Baharul Islam, M., Sadeghzadeh, A.: An effective multi-camera dataset and hybrid feature matcher for real-time video stitching. In: 2021 36th International Conference on Image and Vision Computing New Zealand (IVCNZ), pp. 1–6 (2021)

5. Li, Y., Huang, J., Deng, F., Lu, R., Yao, M.: An image stitching algorithm based on sift and daisy descriptor. In: 2020 4th Annual International Conference on Data Science and Business Analytics (ICDSBA), pp. 271–274 (2020)

6. Lin, T.Y., et al.: Microsoft COCO: common objects in context (2014). http://arxiv.org/abs/1405.0312

7. Liu, B., et al.: An energy-efficient SIFT based feature extraction accelerator for high frame-rate video applications. IEEE Trans. Circuits Syst. I Regul. Pap. **69**(12), 4930–4943 (2022)

8. Liu, Y., He, M., Wang, Y., Sun, Y., Gao, X.: Farmland aerial images fast-stitching method and application based on improved sift algorithm. IEEE Access **10**, 95411–95424 (2022)

9. Nguyen, T., Chen, S.W., Shivakumar, S.S., Taylor, C.J., Kumar, V.: Unsupervised deep homography: a fast and robust homography estimation model. IEEE Robot. Autom. Lett. **3**(3), 2346–2353 (2018)

10. Ravi, C., Gowda, R.M.: Development of image stitching using feature detection and feature matching techniques. In: 2020 IEEE International Conference for Innovation in Technology (INOCON), pp. 1–7 (2020)

11. Song, D.Y., Um, G.M., Lee, H.K., Cho, D.: End-to-end image stitching network via multi-homography estimation. IEEE Signal Process. Lett. **28**, 763–767 (2021)

12. Yeh, S.H., Lai, S.H.: Real-time video stitching. In: 2017 IEEE International Conference on Image Processing (ICIP), pp. 1482–1486 (2017)

Joint-YODNet: A Light-Weight Object Detector for UAVs to Achieve Above 100fps

Vipin Gautam, Shitala Prasad[✉], and Sharad Sinha

School of Mathematics and Computer Science, Indian Institute of Technology Goa,
Farmagudi, Ponda, India
{vipin2113106,shitala,sharad}@iitgoa.ac.in

Abstract. Small object detection *via* UAV (Unmanned Aerial Vehicle) images captured from drones and radar is a complex task. This domain encompasses numerous complexities, including size and scale variations, image resolution constraints, and occlusion issues, all of which impede the accurate detection and localization of small objects. To address these challenges, we propose a novel method called Joint-YODNet for UAVs to detect small objects, leveraging a joint loss function specifically designed for this task. Our method revolves around the development of a joint loss function tailored to enhance the detection performance of small objects. Through extensive experimentation on a diverse dataset of UAV images captured under varying environmental conditions, we evaluated different variations of the loss function and determined the most effective formulation. The results demonstrate that our proposed joint loss function outperforms existing methods in accurately localizing small objects. Specifically, Joint-YODNet achieves a recall of 0.971 and a F1Score of 0.975, surpassing state-of-the-art (SOTA) techniques. Additionally, our method achieves a mAP@.5(%) of 98.6, indicating it's robustness in detecting small objects across varying scales.

Keywords: Object Detection · SAR Ship Detection · SAR · Small Object Detection · Unmanned Aerial Vehicle · Deep Neural Networks

1 Introduction

Unmanned aerial vehicles (UAVs) have garnered significant popularity across various domains, encompassing surveillance, search and rescue operations, and environmental monitoring [2, 23, 29]. The detection of small objects, such as vehicles or pedestrians, within UAV images and radar scans holds the utmost importance for numerous applications [1, 21]. However, accomplishing this task is inherently challenging due to a multitude of factors including limitations in resolution, object occlusion, background clutter, low contrast, motion blur, complexities in data annotation, and real-time processing requirements.

V. Gautam and S. Prasad—These authors contributed equally to this work.

H. Kaur et al. (Eds.): CVIP 2023, CCIS 2010, pp. 567–578, 2024.
https://doi.org/10.1007/978-3-031-58174-8_47

Despite of these challenges, there has been significant progress in small object detection algorithms for UAV/aerial imaging [13,25]. These algorithms typically use a mix of techniques, such as image segmentation, feature extraction, and machine learning, to identify and classify small objects. Some of the most promising approaches include deep learning methods, which have been shown to be very effective at extracting features from aerial images. Advancements in deep learning (DL) have improved object detection methods used in various applications, including aerial imaging [8,10]. However, these methods face challenges in detecting small objects in high spatial resolution aerial images. Detecting objects in aerial images presents several challenges due to the high spatial resolution and presence of small objects. Challenges include information loss from rescaling, Limited tolerance for shifts in bounding box (BBox), and perturbated feature representations [4]. In the existing literature, various object detection methods have been proposed with different strategies to improve system performance. These strategies include enhancing deep network architectures [22], introducing new loss functions [17], and proposing innovative learning approaches [18]. Among these, the use of dedicated loss functions has shown significant improvements in overall performance, motivating the focus of this paper on introducing a new loss function.

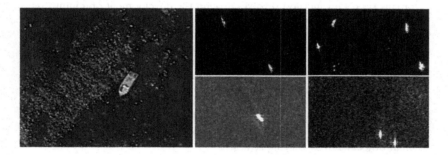

Fig. 1. Demonstration of Detection challenges in images obtained through UAV.

Specifically, we propose a joint loss function tailored for small object detection in aerial views. This joint loss is integrated into a deep model, enhancing the learning capability of the network compared to conventional training methods. The optimization of gradients and convergence leads to higher detection accuracy. To further improve feature representation, we incorporate the Omnidimensional dynamic convolution (ODConv) [11], which enhances overall performance. Furthermore, we explore the training process using a smaller dataset, making our system more practical and easier to deploy in real-world scenarios.

In this study, we focus on detecting ships and vessels using drone imagery, see Fig. 1. These objects play crucial roles in maritime surveillance, security, and navigation applications. However, detecting these relatively small objects in UAV images and radar scans can be challenging due to varying scales, occlusion, and cluttered backgrounds [26,28].

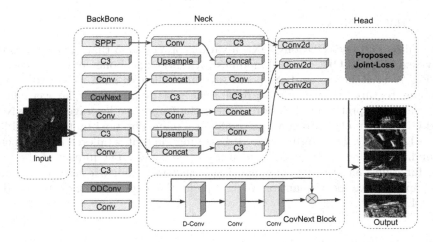

Fig. 2. Joint-YODNet Structure

2 Methodology

This section presents a comprehensive overview of our proposed light-weight small object detector called Joint-YODNet (Joint-loss based YOLO Omni Dimensional Dynamic Convolution Network) and discusses its various modules in detail.

2.1 You Only Look Once (YOLO)

YOLO version 5 (YOLOv5), a lightweight CNN-based object detection model, is widely recognized for its efficiency [9]. The model comprises three main components: the Backbone, the Neck, and the Head. The Backbone utilizes a convolutional neural network (CNN) to capture high-quality feature maps from the input image. Notably, it incorporates the CSP (C3) module, inspired by the CSPNet design [24]. The Neck consists of additional convolutional layers that capture intricate details and spatial information in the feature maps. The Detection Head utilizes the processed feature maps to perform the final steps of object detection, including BBox prediction and class probability estimation.

The loss function comprises three components: objectness loss, localization loss, and classification loss. These components are combined using weights to optimize the model for accurate object detection, precise BBox prediction, and correct classification during training. The complete loss function can be formulated as:

$$L_{loss} = \lambda_1 L_{cls} + \lambda_2 L_{obj} + \lambda_3 L_{loc} \tag{1}$$

Binary cross-entropy (BCE) loss is employed as the classification loss L_{cls} and object loss L_{obj} while for localization loss L_{loc} CIoU loss is used. Detailed discussion is done in Sect. 2.3 which demonstrates the loss functions used for BBox regression.

2.2   ODConvNeXt

We utilize YOLOv5-ODConvNeXt, a variant of YOLOv5 that incorporates the CovNext [16] and ODConv [11] modules within the backbone network, as shown in Fig. 2. SAR image analysis poses several challenges such as speckle noise, complex texture, limited training data, scale variations, shadow/layover effects, and data interpretation. To address these challenges, we leverage the CovNext and ODConv modules to enhance the feature maps obtained by this model [3].

Additionally, we introduce a *Joint Loss* function that is tailored for enhancing bounding box localization and expediting convergence. The impact of the joint loss function's effectiveness in enhancing localization ability is assessed through a comprehensive set of quantitative and qualitative experiments, as discussed in Sect. 4.

2.3   Loss Functions for BBox

BBox regression is a key technique in object detection that predicts the location of target objects using rectangular BBoxes. It aims to enhance the precision of the predicted BBox.

To achieve this, the regression process uses loss functions that are derived from Intersection over Union (IoU), which quantifies the overlap between the predicted (PD) BBox and the ground truth (GT) BBox. IoU is computed as the proportion of the shared area between the GT and PD BBoxes to their combined area:

$$IoU = \frac{|GT \cap PD|}{|GT \cup PD|} \tag{2}$$

The IoU loss function is effective when there is an intersection between the PD and GT BBoxes. However, it struggles to produce meaningful gradients and slow convergence when there is no overlap between the BBoxes.

Generalized Intersection over Union (GIoU) [20] loss maximizes the overlap between the PD and GT BBoxes by gradually adjusting the size of the PD Bbox. It is particularly effective when the BBoxes initially do not intersect. The GIoU formula is defined as follows:

$$GIoU = IoU - \frac{|C - (GT \cup PD)|}{|C|} \tag{3}$$

where, C denotes the smallest BBox that contains both the PD and GT BBoxes. It acts as a penalty term, guiding the PD BBox towards the target GT BBox. The $GIoU$ loss outperforms the Mean Squared Error (MSE) loss and IoU loss in terms of precision. While it addresses the issue of vanishing gradients in non-overlapping scenarios, it may have slower convergence and less accurate regression for boxes with extreme aspect ratios.

Distance IoU ($DIoU$) [33] is a measure of the normalized distance between the center points of the PD and GT BBoxes. By incorporating distance information, it enables faster convergence and more precise regression.

$$DIoU = IoU - \frac{d^2}{c^2} \tag{4}$$

In this formula, d represents the Euclidean distance between the center points of the PD and GT BBoxes, while c denotes the diagonal length of the smallest enclosing box that covers both BBoxes. The inclusion of distance information in the loss function enhances optimization by enabling faster convergence. It also improves the accuracy of regression, resulting in better localization of objects in object detection tasks.

Complete Intersection over Union ($CIoU$) [34] loss incorporates three essential geometric factors: overlap area, distance, and aspect ratio. $CIoU$ loss is a versatile approach to BBox regression, surpassing both $GIoU$ and $DIoU$. However, when the aspect ratio of the GT BBox matches that of the PD BBox, $CIoU$ degenerates to $DIoU$.

Efficient IoU [31] addresses limitations of traditional IoU loss by incorporating additional components to reflect the closeness between BBoxes and improve convergence. The Efficient IoU loss comprises three terms: IoU loss (L_{iou}), distance loss (L_{dis}), and aspect ratio loss (L_{asp}). By combining these terms, the Efficient IoU loss enhances the training efficiency and improves performance. Retaining the positive effects of CIoU loss, Efficient IoU demonstrates the potential for further improvement in neural network training, defined as:

$$L_{eiou} = 1 - IoU + \frac{\rho^2(b, b^{GT})}{(w^c)^2 + (h^c)^2} + \frac{\rho^2(w, w^{GT})}{(w^c)^2} + \frac{\rho^2(h, h^{GT})}{(h^c)^2} \tag{5}$$

where h^w and h^c are the width and height of the smallest enclosing box covering the two boxes. Variables b and b^{GT} are the center of the PD and GT BBox.

Proposed Joint Loss. We propose the *Joint Loss*, an enhanced approach that combines multiple loss components to address existing limitations. The Joint Loss is computed using a formula involving coefficients α, β, γ, and η, determined through empirical tests: $\alpha = 0.1$, $\beta = 0.1$, $\gamma = 0.1$, $\eta = 0.7$.

$$L_{\text{joint}} = \alpha L_{\text{ciou}} + \beta L_{\text{diou}} + \gamma L_{\text{giou}} + \eta L_{\text{eiou}} \tag{6}$$

Compared to a single loss, a joint loss function combines multiple components, enabling the model to optimize for multiple objectives simultaneously. It improves overall performance, captures different aspects of the problem, and addresses challenges through specific loss components. The joint loss helps overcome the gradient vanishing problem and facilitates generalization to unseen data. It allows customization and fine-tuning, incorporating domain-specific knowledge for better results. Mathematically, the joint loss is denoted as L_{joint}

and consists of individual loss components L_{ciou}, L_{diou}, L_{giou}, L_{eiou}. The gradients of the joint loss are computed by summing the gradients of the individual components, as shown in Eq. (7). Binary cross entropy (BCE) is used for classification. In the following section, we present the experimental setup and evaluation of the proposed loss function.

$$\Delta L_{joint} = \alpha \Delta L_{ciou} + \beta \Delta L_{diou} + \gamma \Delta L_{giou} + \eta \Delta L_{eiou} \tag{7}$$

3 Implementation and Datasets

The hardware setup consists of 2 x Intel Xeon Gold 6248 processors, each with 20 cores running at a clock speed of 2.5 GHz, and an NVIDIA DGX A100 GPU. All experiments are conducted using the PyTorch framework. The proposed Joint-YODNet is optimized using Stochastic Gradient Descent (SGD) with an initial learning rate of 0.01, a momentum factor of 0.937, and weight decay set to 0.0005. During training, a batch size of 32 is used, and the training process is carried out for a total of 500 epochs. The network input size used in this work is 640 × 640. Additionally, the experiments use an IoU threshold of 0.5.

3.1 Evaluation Criterion

To evaluate the proposed Joint-YODNet, we used standard performance metrics, including precision (P), recall (R), F1 measure (F1), and mean average precision (mAP). The mAP is calculated as the average of the average precision (AP) values for each category, which are obtained from the Precision-Recall (PR) curve. Precision and recall are computed using the formulas:

$$P = \frac{TP}{TP + FP}, \quad R = \frac{TP}{TP + FN}, \quad F1 = 2 \cdot \frac{P \cdot R}{P + R} \tag{8}$$

where TP represents true positives, FP represents false positives, and FN represents false negatives. Frames per second (FPS) have been used to evaluate the real-time application of the proposed method. We base the FPS calculation on the formula provided by the official repository created by Ultralytics [9]. The formula used for FPS calculation can be defined as.

$$FPS = \frac{1000}{P + I + NMS} \tag{9}$$

where P, I, and NMS are preprocessing, inference, and non max suppression time, respectively.

3.2 Datasets Description

For evaluating the proposed Joint-YODNet, we utilized two well-known benchmark datasets for Aerial Image Detection: SAR Ship Detection and Aerial Ship Detection datasets. These datasets are widely recognized and present significant challenges in the field of aerial images for small object detection.

SAR Ship Detection Dataset. For the SAR Ship Detection (SAR-SD) dataset, we utilized the publicly available SSDD dataset [12]. This dataset contains 1160 SAR images with 2540 ship instances of varying resolutions (1 to 15 m). The ships in this dataset are small, with some being only tens of pixels in size. We divided the SAR-SD dataset into a training set of 641 images, 271 for the validation set, and a separate test set of 232 images. Our focus was to assess the generalization capability of the proposed method using this dataset.

Aerial Ship Detection Dataset. The Aerial Ship Detection (ASD) dataset, sourced from Roboflow [6], comprises 1395 JPEG aerial images. The images have a spatial resolution of 600 pixels in width and 400 pixels in height. We used an official split of a training set of 1224, a validation set of 113, and a test set of size 58 images. To ensure uniformity, the images underwent preprocessing steps including auto-orientation and resizing to 640×640 pixels. Data augmentation techniques were applied, including a noise augmentation called salt and pepper, which introduced up to 5% noise through pixel manipulation within the BBox. These augmentations were implemented to enhance the robustness and generalizability of Joint-YODNet.

4   Experimental Results

This section presents the experimental analysis conducted on the aforementioned public datasets. The results are comprehensively examined, encompassing both qualitative and quantitative aspects. We compare our method with existing state-of-the-art (SOTA) approaches, followed by conducting ablation studies to evaluate the impact of different components in our proposed method. Additionally, we assess the computational speed of our method to gauge its efficiency.

4.1   Comparison with SOTA Methods

Joint-YODNet is evaluated and compared to several SOTA networks on SAR-SD dataset, as summarized in Table 1. The results indicate that the Joint-YODNet achieves competitive performance compared to existing networks. YOLOv5-ODConvNeXt [3] achieves remarkable results, with a precision of 0.971, recall of 0.96, and F1Score of 0.965. It also achieves an mAP@.5(%) of 98.10 and an mAP@.5:.95(%) of 72.70. However, FIERNet [26] and CR2A-Net [28] achieve the highest precision scores of 0.98. Our proposed Joint-YODNet achieves a precision of 0.979, demonstrating excellent performance comparable to FIERNet and CR2A-Net. In terms of recall, F1Score, and mAP@.5(%), Joint-YODNet achieves a recall of 0.971, an F1Score of 0.975, and a mAP@.5(%) of 98.6, outperforming YOLOv5-ODConvNeXt and other compared methods. SOTA methods, including SSD [15], Faster R-CNN [19], YOLOv5 [9], RetinaNet [14], DDNet [32], Quad-FPN [30], SAR-ShipNet [5], and HA-SARSD [27], exhibit varying levels of performance in terms of precision, recall, F1Score, mAP@.5(%), and mAP@.5:.95(%).

Table 1. State-of-the-art comparison with existing networks on SAR-SD.

Networks	P	R	F1	mAP@.5(%)	mAP@.5:.95(%)
SSD [15]	0.846	0.811	0.828	–	–
Faster R-CNN [19]	0.871	0.856	0.863	–	–
YOLOv5 [9]	0.964	0.897	0.929	95.2	–
RetinaNet [14]	0.901	0.891	0.896	–	–
DDNet [32]	0.931	0.912	0.921	–	–
Quad-FPN [30]	0.90	0.957	0.925	95.20	–
SAR-ShipNet [5]	0.95	0.763	0.847	89.08	–
FIERNet [26]	**0.98**	0.879	0.927	94.14	–
CR2A-Net [28]	**0.98**	0.878	0.927	89.8	–
HA-SARSD [27]	0.97	0.920	0.944	97.0	–
YOLOv5-ODConvNeXt [3]	0.971	<u>0.96</u>	<u>0.965</u>	<u>98.10</u>	**72.70**
Joint-YODNet	<u>0.979</u>	**0.971**	**0.975**	98.6	<u>72.6</u>

Bold: best; <u>Underlined</u>: second-best results. The dash represents results not found.

In summary, our proposed method shows competitive performance compared to existing state-of-the-art networks. It achieves high precision comparable to FIERNet and CR2A-Net, while surpassing YOLOv5-ODConvNeXt and other methods in terms of recall and F1Score.

4.2 Ablation Study

Evaluation on SAR-SD. The Table 2 compares different loss variations for small object detection on the SAR-SD dataset. The baseline method, YOLOv5-ODConvNeXt, achieved a precision of 0.971, recall of 0.96, F1Score of 0.965, mAP@.5(%) of 98.10, and mAP@.5:.95(%) of 72.70. The EIoU [31] method improved precision (0.984) and F1Score (0.976), achieving the highest values in these metrics. The SIoU [7] method also performed well, achieving a precision of 0.979 and an F1-score of 0.974. The combination of EIoU and SIoU, denoted as EIoU + SIoU, resulted in a precision of 0.975, recall of 0.969, F1Score of 0.972, mAP@.5(%) of 98.50, and mAP@.5:.95(%) of 72.70.

Our Joint-YODNet achieved a precision of 0.979, recall of 0.974, F1Score of 0.976, mAP@.5(%) of 98.60, and mAP@.5:.95(%) of 72.60. These results show that our method outperforms the baseline YOLOv5-ODConvNeXt method and performs at par with the EIoU and SIoU methods.

Overall, the results in Table 2 show that our proposed method is a promising approach for small object detection in SAR images. It achieves superior performance compared to the baseline method and performs at par with the SOTA methods. Additionally, our method is computationally efficient and has a lightweight architecture, making it well-suited for real-time applications and deployment on resource-constrained edge devices (discussed in 4.4).

Table 2. Comparison of various BBox regression losses on SAR-SD.

Loss Variations	P	R	F1	mAP@.5(%)	mAP@.5:.95(%)
YOLOv5-ODConvNeXt [3]	0.971	0.96	0.965	98.10	<u>72.70</u>
EIoU [31]	**0.984**	0.968	**0.976**	**98.60**	**72.80**
SIoU [7]	0.979	0.969	<u>0.974</u>	98.40	72.10
EIoU + SIoU	0.975	<u>0.969</u>	0.972	<u>98.50</u>	72.70
Joint-YODNet	<u>0.979</u>	**0.974**	**0.976**	**98.60**	72.60

Bold: best; <u>Underlined</u>: second-best results. Reported best of three runs.

Table 3. Comparison of various BBox regression losses on ASD dataset.

Loss Variations	P	R	F1	mAP@.5(%)	mAP@.5:.95(%)
YOLOv5-ODConvNeXt [3]	<u>0.85</u>	0.61	0.705	<u>68.90</u>	**31.40**
EIoU [31]	0.81	<u>0.62</u>	0.699	66.60	31.10
SIoU [7]	0.83	0.62	0.707	68.10	29.10
EIoU + SIoU- Combined	**0.88**	0.60	<u>0.716</u>	68.20	29.90
Joint-YODNet	0.84	**0.63**	**0.720**	**70.30**	<u>31.20</u>

Bold: best; <u>Underlined</u>: second-best results.

Evaluation on ASD Dataset. The Table 3 illustrates the performance comparison of different loss variations on the ASD dataset. Notably, our proposed method exhibits promising results, showcasing competitive performance across various metrics. Our method achieves a precision of 0.84, outperforming other loss variations, including YOLOv5-ODConvNeXt (0.61), EIoU (0.62), and SIoU (0.62). Furthermore, our approach achieves a recall of 0.63, surpassing all other variations.

In terms of F1-score, our method achieves a value of 0.720, indicating a balanced trade-off between precision and recall. This outperforms other loss variations, including YOLOv5-ODConvNeXt (0.705), EIoU (0.699) and SIoU (0.707). Moreover, our method demonstrates superior performance in terms of mAP-@.5(%), and mAP@.5:.95(%) metrics. Our method achieves a mAP@.5(%) of 70.30, surpassing other variations, including YOLOv5-ODConvNeXt (68.90), EIoU (66.60), and SIoU (68.10). Similarly, our method achieves a mAP@.5:.95(%) of 31.20, showcasing competitive performance compared to other loss variations, such as YOLOv5-ODConvNeXt (31.40), EIoU (31.10), and SIoU (29.10).

4.3 Qualitative Study

A qualitative analysis was undertaken to compare the detection performance of the proposed Joint-YODNet with that of YOLOv5-ODConvNeXt, as depicted in Fig. 3. The analysis involved examining visual results derived from images showcasing both the ground truth ship instances and the detection results generated by the two methods. Specifically, (a) denotes the ground truth BBoxes,

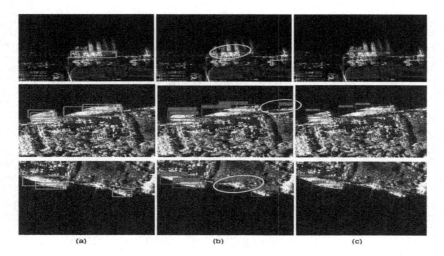

Fig. 3. Comparing object detection performance on the SAR-SD Dataset: (a) Ground truth labels, (b) Detection by YOLOv5-ODConvNeXt, and (c) Detection achieved through Joint-YODNet.

(b) represents the detection results obtained from YOLOv5-ODConvNeXt, and (c) corresponds to the BBox detections obtained through the proposed method. The visual comparison demonstrates the superior performance of our proposed method in accurately localizing and recognizing ship instances despite their varying small sizes. Conversely, the detections generated by YOLOv5-ODConvNeXt (a) exhibit certain limitations. Some instances are either missed or incorrectly identified, resulting in lower precision and recall, as evidenced in Fig. 3. These disparities in detection quality further emphasize the advantages of our proposed method in real-life scenarios.

4.4   Computational Analysis

Joint-YODNet not only achieves superior performance but also demonstrates remarkable computational efficiency, with a high frame rate (FPS) of 136 (used Eq. 9). This makes it ideal for real-time applications that require timely and accurate ship detection. Additionally, our method features a lightweight architecture, making it compatible with resource-constrained edge devices. This enhances its versatility for deployment in various practical scenarios. Joint-YODNet has a parameter size of 6.99M and a memory size of 14.4 MB.

5   Conclusion

In this study, we proposed a novel method for small object detection in UAV imagery, utilizing a tailored joint loss function. Joint-YODNet outperforms existing methods, achieving superior precision, recall, F1Score, and mAP@.5 scores, demonstrating its robustness across object scales. The qualitative analysis further validates the effectiveness of our method in real-life scenarios. Our research contributes to the field by addressing the challenges of small object detection in UAV imagery and enabling accurate localization and recognition. The results highlight its potential in surveillance, object tracking, and environmental monitoring in UAV-based systems.

Acknowledgement. This work is supported by MeitY, Govt. of India under the Capacity Building for Human Resource Development in Unmanned Aircraft System (Drone and related technology) project with grant no. L-14011/29/2021-HRD.

References

1. Abraham, A., Nagavarapu, S.C., Prasad, S., Vyas, P., Mathew, L.K.: Recent trends in autonomous vehicle validation ensuring road safety with emphasis on learning algorithms. In: 17th ICARCV, pp. 397–404. IEEE (2022)
2. Chaoying, T., Xianghui, W., Biao, W., Prasad, S.: A cross-border detection algorithm for agricultural spraying UAV. Appl. Eng. Agric. **35**(2), 163–174 (2019)
3. Chengshuxiao: Yolov5-odconvnext for ship detection on drone-captured images. https://github.com/chengshuxiao/YOLOv5-ODConvNeXt (2022)
4. Deng, S., et al.: A global-local self-adaptive network for drone-view object detection. IEEE TIP **30**, 1556–1569 (2020)
5. Deng, Y., Guan, D., Chen, Y., Yuan, W., Ji, J., Wei, M.: Sar-shipnet: sar-ship detection neural network via bidirectional coordinate attention and multi-resolution feature fusion. In: ICASSP, pp. 3973–3977. IEEE (2022)
6. Dwyer, B., Nelson, J., Solawetz, J., et al.: Roboflow (version 1.0) [software] (2022). https://universe.roboflow.com/yolo-ht89e/yolo-pd6w1/dataset/1
7. Gevorgyan, Z.: SIoU loss: more powerful learning for bounding box regression. arXiv preprint arXiv:2205.12740 (2022)
8. Han, J., Ding, J., Xue, N., Xia, G.S.: Redet: a rotation-equivariant detector for aerial object detection. In: CVPR, pp. 2786–2795 (2021)
9. Jocher, G., Chaurasia, A., Stoken, A., Borovec, J., NanoCode012, Yonghye Kwon, E.A.: ultralytics/yolov5: v7.0 - YOLOv5 SOTA Realtime Instance Segmentation (2022). https://doi.org/10.5281/zenodo.7347926
10. Lacoste, A., et al.: Toward foundation models for earth monitoring: proposal for a climate change benchmark. arXiv preprint arXiv:2112.00570 (2021)
11. Li, C., Zhou, A., Yao, A.: Omni-dimensional dynamic convolution. arXiv preprint arXiv:2209.07947 (2022)
12. Li, J., Qu, C., Shao, J.: Ship detection in SAR images based on an improved faster R-CNN. In: IEEE SAR in Big Data Era: Models, Methods and Applications, pp. 1–6 (2017)
13. Li, S., Yang, X., Lin, X., Zhang, Y., Wu, J.: Real-time vehicle detection from UAV aerial images based on improved yolov5. Sensors **23**(12), 5634 (2023)
14. Lin, T.Y., Goyal, P., Girshick, R., He, K., Dollár, P.: Focal loss for dense object detection. In: ICCV, pp. 2980–2988 (2017)
15. Liu, W., et al.: SSD: single shot multibox detector. In: Leibe, B., Matas, J., Sebe, N., Welling, M. (eds.) ECCV 2016. LNCS, vol. 9905, pp. 21–37. Springer, Cham (2016). https://doi.org/10.1007/978-3-319-46448-0_2

16. Liu, Z., Mao, H., Wu, C., Feichtenhofer, C., Darrell, T., Xie, S.: Convnet for the 2020s. arxiv. arXiv preprint arXiv:2201.03545 (2022)
17. Prasad, S., Chai, T., Li, J., Zhang, Z.: Cr loss: Improving biometric using classroom learning approach. Comput. J. bxac134 (2022)
18. Prasad, S., Kong, A.W.K.: Using object information for spotting text. In: ECCV, pp. 540–557 (2018)
19. Ren, S., He, K.: Faster r-cnn: towards real-time object detection with region proposal networks. In: Advances in Neural Information Processing Systems, vol. 28 (2015)
20. Rezatofighi, H., Tsoi, N., Gwak, J., Sadeghian, A., Reid, I., Savarese, S.: Generalized intersection over union: a metric and a loss for bounding box regression. In: CVPR, pp. 658–666 (2019)
21. Singh, P.P., Ramchiary, P., Bora, J.I., Bhuyan, R., Prasad, S.: An ensemble approach for moving vehicle detection and tracking by using NI vision module. In: Gupta, D., Bhurchandi, K., Murala, S., Raman, B., Kumar, S. (eds.) CVIP 2022. CCIS, vol. 1777, pp. 712–721. Springer, Cham (2022). https://doi.org/10.1007/978-3-031-31417-9_54
22. Tan, M., Pang, R., Le, Q.V.: Efficientdet: scalable and efficient object detection. In: CVPR, pp. 10781–10790 (2020)
23. Tran, T.M., Vu, T.N., Nguyen, T.V., Nguyen, K.: UIT-ADrone: a novel drone dataset for traffic anomaly detection. J. Sel. Top. Appl. Earth Obs. Remote Sens. (2023)
24. Wang, C.Y., Liao, H.Y.M., Wu, Y.H., Chen, P.Y., Hsieh, J.W., Yeh, I.H.: CSP-Net: a new backbone that can enhance learning capability of CNN. In: CVPR Workshops, pp. 390–391 (2020)
25. Wang, X., He, N., Hong, C., Wang, Q., Chen, M.: Improved YOLOX-X based UAV aerial photography object detection algorithm. Image Vis. Comput. **135**, 104697 (2023)
26. Yu, J., Wu, T., Zhou, S., Pan, H., Zhang, X., Zhang, W.: An SAR ship object detection algorithm based on feature information efficient representation network. Remote Sens. **14**(14), 3489 (2022)
27. Yu, N., Ren, H., Deng, T., Fan, X.: HA-SARSD: An effective SAR ship detector via the hybrid attention residual module. In: Radar Conference (RadarConf23), pp. 1–6. IEEE (2023)
28. Yu, Y., Yang, X., Li, J., Gao, X.: A cascade rotated anchor-aided detector for ship detection in remote sensing images. TGRS **60**, 1–14 (2020)
29. Zhang, M., Li, X.: Drone-enabled internet-of-things relay for environmental monitoring in remote areas without public networks. Internet Things J. **7**(8), 7648–7662 (2020)
30. Zhang, T., Zhang, X., Ke, X.: Quad-FPN: a novel quad feature pyramid network for SAR ship detection. Remote Sens. **13**(14), 2771 (2021)
31. Zhang, Y.F., Ren, W., Zhang, Z., Jia, Z., Wang, L., Tan, T.: Focal and efficient IOU loss for accurate bounding box regression. Neurocomputing **506**, 146–157 (2022)
32. Zhao, K., Zhou, Y., Chen, X.: A dense connection based SAR ship detection network. In: 9th Joint ITAIC, vol. 9, pp. 669–673. IEEE (2020)
33. Zheng, Z., Wang, P., Liu, W., Li, J., Ye, R., Ren, D.: Distance-IOU loss: faster and better learning for bounding box regression. In: AAAI, vol. 34, pp. 12993–13000 (2020)
34. Zheng, Z., et al.: Enhancing geometric factors in model learning and inference for object detection and instance segmentation. IEEE Trans. on Cybern. **52**(8), 8574–8586 (2021)

Automated Deep Learning Technique for Accurate Detection of Regional Wall Motion Abnormality in Echocardiographic Videos

A. Shamla Beevi[1]($\boxtimes$) , K. Mohammed Hashim[1] , Abbad Maliyekkal[1] ,
K. V. Hamraz[1] , Saidalavi Kalady[1] , and Jenu James Chackola[2]

[1] National Institute of Technology Calicut, Kozhikode, Kerala, India
shamlabeevia@gmail.com
[2] Aster MIMS Hospital, Kottakkal, Malappuram, Kerala, India

Abstract. Regional wall motion abnormality (RWMA) is a significant diagnostic indicator for diagnosing heart problems, especially in cardiac imaging such as echocardiography. RWMA is a sign of reduced regional wall motion, mainly caused by myocardial infarction (MI), the world's leading cause of death. Automated identification of RWMA improves efficiency, consistency, early detection, objective quantification, and personalised techniques in cardiovascular diagnostics. The proposed study develops a powerful and automated deep learning technique based on convolutional neural network for accurately detecting RWMA in echocardiographic videos. Our approach consists of a pipeline that first preprocesses the data by segmenting the LV chamber from the apical four-chamber (A4C) image using U-net architecture, followed by a 3D CNN detects RWMA binary classification. The pipeline was developed and evaluated using data from the HMC-QU dataset of 162 echocardiography and data from a hospital of 178 echocardiography. The RWMA detection model obtained 98.1% accuracy, 96.5% precision, 100% recall, and a 98.2% F1 score, while the unet achieved 97.18% accuracy on LV segmentation. This study shows that developing a completely automated system for LV segmentation and RWMA identification can be effective and beneficial.

Keywords: Echocardiographic images · deep learning · Medical image analysis · Regional wall motion abnormality · LV Segmentation

1 Introduction

Cardiovascular disease (CVD; 19.1 million deaths) is one of the leading causes of death globally [1]. Coronary heart disease(CHD) or coronary artery disease(CAD) is the cause of more than half of CVD deaths. Blockage of coronary arteries is the main reason for CVD. Reduced blood flow to the heart muscle damages the contractility or movement of the area of the heart muscle supplied by the clogged artery, called ischemia. The main causes of Cardiovascular disease include smoking/tobacco use, physical inactivity, nutritional problems, overweight, obesity, high blood pressure, diabetes mellitus, and kidney diseases [2]. A myocardial infarction (heart attack) frequently leads in restricted blood flow to a particular section of the heart wall, which in turn causes damage to that portion of the heart muscle. This condition is known as regional wall motion abnormality(RWMA) and refers to the impaired movement of that particular region of the heart wall. The three most popular techniques for diagnosing CVD are cardiac magnetic resonance imaging (MRI), echocardiogram (echo) and cardiac computer tomography (CT). The first and most effective method for detecting RWMA is an echo which is a non-invasive and cost-effective ultrasound imaging modality, which severely suffers from intra-observer and inter-observer variability, making it prone to human error and judgments.

In clinical settings, the primary method for evaluating RWMA is a visual inspection of echocardiographic images. One of the most important skills in the evaluation of cardiac function is the ability of echocardiographers to identify patterns of endocardial and epicardial motion, thickness in each segment of the left ventricle (LV) and to quantitatively evaluate them using a four-point scale (1: normal, 2: hypokinetic, 3: akinetic, and 4: dyskinetic). These abilities are essential for properly recognising and assessing the severity of regional wall motion impairment, which provides important information for diagnosing and keeping track of heart problems. [3]. The treatment decision-making process is facilitated and optimized by this procedure, which is typically referred to as visual RWMA scoring. One of the main disadvantages of visual assessment is its heavy reliance on qualified and experienced echocardiographers. Significant interobserver and intraobserver variability also plagues this approach. Automatic echo image analysis would be time-saving and cost-effective technique, even in low-resource settings.

The goal of automated detection of Regional Wall Motion Abnormalities (RWMA) is to improve early detection of cardiac conditions such as myocardial infarction and cardiomyopathy by providing healthcare professionals with accurate, efficient, and standardised tools for identifying and quantifying RWMA in medical imaging, thereby improving patient care, reducing human error, increasing diagnostic efficiency, enabling research, supporting telemedicine, and lowering costs.

The primary contributions of this paper are:

- We created our own dataset for LV segmentation and RWMA detection
- Created an automated echocardiography LV segmentation system followed by RWMA detection that achieved 98.1% accuracy on the HMC-QU benchmark dataset
- Developed a method for the early diagnosis of RWMA in echocardiography that obtained 91.41% accuracy, 87% precision, and 99.22% recall on the Aster dataset

The paper's outline is structured as follows. Section 2 focuses on the most recent techniques for identifying RWMA. Section 3 provides an explanation of the methodology employed in the study. Moving on to Sect. 4, it showcases the experimental results obtained and includes a comprehensive discussion of those results. Finally, Sect. 5 serves as the conclusion, summarizing the overall work and its key findings.

2   Related Works

There have been numerous previous studies aimed at developing an automatic detection of regional wall motion abnormality. Recently, tremendous progress has been made in Deep learning models for RWMA detection. Kusunose et al. [4] investigated whether a deep convolutional neural network (DCNN) could distinguish between groups of coronary infarction areas from conventional two-dimensional echocardiographic images and detect regional wall motion abnormalities (RWMAs) more accurately than sonographers, cardiologists, etc. Huang et.al. [5] suggested a more effective method to interpret RWMA from transthoracic echocardiography using deep neural networks. They have used echocardiogram videos for their study. A 3D Convolutional neural network was first built using data from transthoracic echocardiography. Second, a U-net model was constructed to illustrate the location of the LV wall. Finally, a 3D convolutional neural network model is used to assess an echocardiographic video from four standard perspectives (both before and after segmentation). They collected raw data from a hospital and the labels were processed for binary classification (RWMA present or absent). Limitations of their study were the small dataset to train the model and were confined to only standard views. Detection of RWMA using non-rigid image registration is also used in this area.

3   Methodology

The proposed technique is divided into three steps, which include proprocessing, Left ventricle(LV) segmentation, and RWMA detection as shown in Fig. 1. In this section, we first describe a brief overview of the datasets that are used in the experiments. Next, outline the three steps employed in this work in detail. The first stage involves several preprocessing techniques, including video cropping to isolate relevant regions, spatial windowing to focus on specific areas of interest, and denoising to reduce image noise. Subsequently, a U-Net architecture is employed in the second stage for Left Ventricle (LV) segmentation, enabling precise identification of the LV boundaries. Finally, leveraging the segmented data, a 3D Convolutional Neural Network (3DCNN) is utilized for RWMA detection. This multi-stage approach enhances the reliability and effectiveness of RWMA detection, providing valuable insights into cardiac function and aiding in the diagnosis and treatment of cardiovascular diseases.

3.1   Dataset

In our work, we used two distinct datasets: the first dataset, HMC-QU [6] benchmark dataset, which is a publicly available dataset that allows for a fair comparison with existing methods, sample image is shown Fig. 2a. The dataset

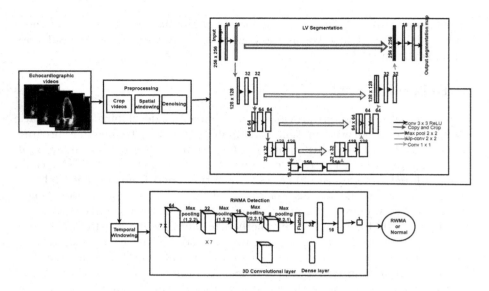

Fig. 1. Proposed work flow of RWMA Detection

contains a collection of apical 4-chamber (A4C) and apical 2-chamber (A2C) view 2D echocardiography recordings from 2018 and 2019. The echocardiogram recordings are made using ultrasound machines from Phillips and GE Vivid (GE-Health-USA). The echocardiogram recordings have a temporal resolution of 25 frames per second. Pixel sizes range from 422×636 to 768×1024 pixels. The information can be used to diagnose myocardial infarction (heart attack) as well as segment the left ventricular wall. The second dataset called Aster dataset, was collected with the consent of the Scientific Research Committee (SRC) and the institutional ethics committee (EC/13/2021, dated March 25, 2021) at Aster MIMS Hospital Kottakkal, Kerala, India. The dataset was created with the Philips Epiq 7C cardiology US System, and the echocardiography videos were saved in the DICOM format, which is widely used for medical imaging data. The dataset comprises Apical four-chamber (A4C) images, their corresponding LV segmentation mask, and their labels, whether it contains RWMA or not.

The temporal resolution of the echocardiogram recordings is 25 fps(frames per second), and the spatial resolution is 600×800. We obtained 178 patient data from the hospital and sonographers manually segmented seven segments of A4C in the left ventricle. The masks are color labeled to segment the LV region into seven parts shown in Fig. 2b. The seven segments include Basal inferoseptal, Mid inferoseptal, Apical septal, Apex, Apical lateral, Mid anterolateral, and Basal anterolateral marked in different colors blue, green red, white, magenta, yellow, and cyan respectively. We have collected 2 to 6 masks per echo video.

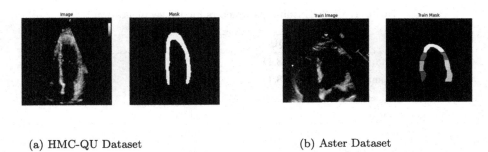

(a) HMC-QU Dataset   (b) Aster Dataset

Fig. 2. Sample images from two datasets

3.2 Preprocessing

In this stage,the first step involves cropping the videos to remove patient-specific information, ensuring confidentiality and compliance with privacy regulations. The second step in the preprocessing pipeline is spatial windowing, which involves extracting individual image frames from the echo videos. This process allows for the isolation and analysis of specific frames that contain relevant cardiac information. Furthermore, denoising using the Speckle Reducing Anisotropic Diffusion (SRAD) [7] technique is employed to improve the quality of the video frames. Cardiac videos often suffer from noise artifacts, such as speckle noise, which can obscure important anatomical details and hinder subsequent analysis tasks. By applying SRAD, the noise is effectively reduced while preserving the essential structural information, resulting in cleaner and clearer video frames that facilitate more reliable and precise cardiac video analysis.

3.3 LV Segmentation

Assessing the left ventricle during the diagnosis of cardiac illness provides essential information about cardiac function, anatomical abnormalities, and prognostic indicators. The left ventricle (LV) is segmented using the U-Net architecture, which is a prominent method for accurately delineating the LV region in cardiac imaging. The U-Net model has a U-shaped design and consists of an encoder and a decoder. The encoder captures spatial information at many scales by extracting hierarchical features via a sequence of convolutional and pooling layers. Transpose convolutions are used by the decoder to upsample the encoded information and regain the spatial resolution. Skip connections are used to connect low-level and high-level characteristics, allowing for exact localisation and the preservation of small details. The U-Net model learns to detect and segment the LV area in fresh unseen pictures by training it on a collection of cardiac images with accompanying LV segmentation masks. The simplicity and efficacy of the U-Net architecture make it a popular choice for LV segmentation, which aids in heart function analysis and cardiovascular disease diagnostics. Table 1 provides the different parameters used in Unet model for LV segmentation. We created

Table 1. Unet Training parameters for LV segmentation

	HMC-QU	Aster
Input shape	(128,128,1)	(256,256,3)
Output shape	(128,128,1)	(256,256,8)
Batch Size	128	16
Learning rate	0.001	0.001
Optimizer	Adam	Adam
Number of epochs	50	100
Loss function	Binary cross entropy	Categorical cross entropy

the UNET model with five blocks in the contracting path and four blocks in the expansive path, with the number of filters increasing as the network gets deeper. Each block in the contracting path consists of two 3×3 convolutions with ReLU activation, followed by batch normalization and a 2×2 max pooling operation. Each block in the expansive path consists of an upsampling operation followed by concatenation with the corresponding block from the contracting path and then two 3×3 convolutions with ReLU activation and batch normalization. The final convolutional layer in the network has a sigmoid activation function to output probability maps. The network also includes dropout layers with different probabilities of dropping out of some activations to prevent overfitting. The weights of the convolutional layers are initialized using the He normal initialization method. Also, we used the Adam optimizer and binary/categorical cross entropy for the model. Finally, we trained our model and calculated important evaluation metrics.

3.4 RWMA Detection

Detecting Regional wall motion abnormalities (RWMA) in 2D echocardiography can be accomplished using a 3D Convolutional Neural Network (3DCNN) designed to process sequential 2D echocardiographic images. By analyzing the temporal sequence of 2D echocardiographic images, a 3DCNN can effectively identify and localize regions with abnormal wall motion. Table 2 shows the training parameters of 3D CNN architecture for RWMA detection. Experiments were conducted with different window size on HMC-QU dataset. Convolutional layers are used to extract features in the 3DCNN architecture for RWMA detection, along with pooling layers for downsampling and fully connected layers for classification. By training the 3DCNN on a dataset of sequential 2D echocardiographic images with corresponding RWMA annotations, the model learns to recognize patterns and changes in wall motion over time that are indicative of regional abnormalities. Table 2 shows different parameters used to train the RWMA detection model. The model trained on different window sizes to get the accurate result on RWMA detection.

Table 2. 3DCNN training parameters for RWMA detection

Parameters	Window size		
	5	7	9
Input samples	5015	4794	4573
Input shape	(5,128,128,2)	(7,128,128,2)	(9,128,128,2)
Loss function	Binary cross entropy		
Optimizer	Adam		
Epochs	50		
Batch size	128		
Learning rate	0.001		

4   Experimental Results and Discussion

This section discusses implementation details, such as the experimental setup, evaluation metrics used for the study and results of LV segmentation and RWMA detection.

4.1   Experimental Setup

The model was trained on a Google Colab Pro platform with NVIDIA Tesla P100 GPU server and 27.3 GB of RAM. Python was used as the programming language, and the TensorFlow and Keras libraries were utilized for building and training the deep learning model.

4.2   Evaluation Metrics

The following metrics are considered while evaluating performance and LV segmentation model effectiveness.

- **Dice coefficient (DC)**: It determines the areas where the predicted segment (P) and the actual segment (GT) overlap.
- **Intersection over union (IoU or Jaccard Index)**:It is a measurement metric that compares the segmentation performed by experts (GT) compared to the segmentation predicted by the model (P) for each individual image.

The following evaluation metrics are commonly used to assess an algorithm's effectiveness in detecting Regional Wall Motion Abnormality (RWMA):

- **Recall**: It measures the proportion of actual positive cases (RWMA) correctly identified by the algorithm.
- **Accuracy**: It represents the overall correctness of the algorithm's predictions by measuring the proportion of correctly classified cases (both RWMA and normal wall motion).

– **Precision**: It calculates the percentage of real positive cases (RWMA) out of all positive predictions generated by the method.
– **F1 Score**: F1 score is a precision and recall-based accuracy measurement function.

4.3   Results of LV Segmentation Using UNET

We trained our model on both datasets and calculated important evaluation metrics like dice coefficient and IoU score.

Experiment 1: Using HMC-QU Dataset. The initial stage is to create a labelled dataset, with each input as an echocardiogram video frame and each output as a segmentation mask. The LV wall from the A4C is covered by the segmentation masks that are part of the dataset. Each video consists of at least one cardiac cycle, or one systole (when the heart pumps blood) and one diastole (when the heart fills with blood).

Fig. 3. Qualitative analysis of LV segmentation on HMC-QU Dataset

Figure 3 shows the results of LV segmentation on HMC-QU dataset.The input echocardiographic image is displayed in the first image, followed by the corresponding true mark and the predicted mask using the Unet LV segmentation model in the final image.

Experiment 2: Using Aster Dataset. In this experiment, we used selected frames and corresponding masks. Both images and masks were cropped to avoid unnecessary regions. Eight different classes of a mask were color mapped to create an 8-channel final mask where each layer contains a particular part of the LV region. Color ranges were adjusted to get the correct shape of segments.

Figure 4 illustrates the test image used for LV segmentation, along with the associated actual and predicted masks and seven distinct segments in each image. Figure 5 shows the LV segmentation result on Aster dataset after combining seven segments. Table 3 shows the quantitative analysis of LV segmentation on two datasets. IoU and dice coeffient are the evaluation metrics used for quantitatively assessing the performance and accuracy of the segmentation method.

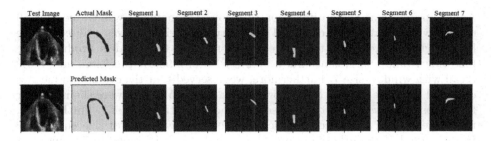

Fig. 4. The predicted seven segments on Aster Dataset

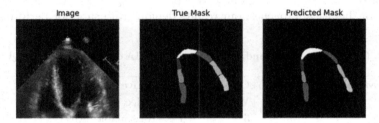

Fig. 5. Qualitative analysis of LV segmentation on Aster Dataset after combining seven segments

Table 3. Quantitative analysis of LV segmentation on different datasets

Dataset	IoU	Dice Coefficient
HMC-QU	0.9610 ± 0.0152	0.9800 ± 0.9980
Aster	0.9351 ± 0.0228	0.9663 ± 0.0121

4.4 Results for RWMA Detection

The newly created segment concatenated videos are used for 3DCNN. To achieve a consistent number of frames, we used the sliding window approach on the videos. Videos are divided into smaller temporal windows with a set number of frames using this technique. With overlaps of 4, 6, and 8 frames, we extracted temporal windows with sizes of 5, 7, and 9 frames using the sliding window method. Our 3DCNN model consists of four 3D convolutional layers, four 3D max-pooling layers, and three dense layers. The Relu activation function is used for all the layers except the output layer, which uses the sigmoid activation function.

Experiment 1: Using HMC-QU Dataset. We created three separate models for each window size. The model dataset was separated into two parts: training and testing: 80:20 The training set was divided 80:20 between training and validation. For the last layer, we used the sigmoid activation function and the

Adam optimizer as the optimisation function. The network was trained for 50 epochs with a batch size of 128. The binary cross-entropy was utilised as the loss function to evaluate the model's performance. Our models produced the following results: 98.17% accuracy, 98.2% F1 score, 96.5% precision, and 100% recall with window size 7. Furthermore, we observed that the evaluation metrics obtained from the dataset of windows with a size of 5 frames were slightly lower than those obtained from the dataset of windows with a size of 7. Furthermore, the values of the evaluation metrics received over windows of size equal to 9 frames were less than those obtained over windows of size equal to 7 frames but greater than those obtained over windows of size equal to 5. Table 4 shows the qunatitative analysis of RWMA detection on HMC-QU dataset. When compared to state-of-the-art approaches, our results demonstrate superior performance.

Table 4. Quantitive analysis and comparison of RWMA detection on HMC-QU dataset

Evaluation metrics (%)	Ours			Active Polynomials [8]	
	Window size			Video quality	
	5	7	9	Reasonable	All
Accuracy	**95.8**	98.1	97.2	87.9	83.1
F1 score	**95.9**	98.2	97.2	90.1	85.7
Precision	92.7	96.5	94.5	87.6	82.6
Recall	**99.3**	100	100	92.8	89.0

Evaluation metrics (%)	3DCNN [9]			E-D CNN [6]			
	Window size			5 segment features			
	5	7	9	LDA	DT	RF	SVM
Accuracy	90.3	90.9	90.0	78.5	72.6	76.6	80.2
F1 score	94.8	97.2	92.3	83.2	80.0	82.6	84.8
Precision	**94.7**	100	94.7	86.6	81.7	84.9	86.8
Recall	95.0	94.7	90.0	81.3	79.0	82.2	83.0

Experiment 2: Using Aster Dataset. We created only one model for window size 7. The model dataset was divided into training and testing as follows: 80:20 Again, the training set was split 80:20 across training and validation. With an 8-batch size, we trained the network for 50 epochs. Our model produced the following results: 91.4% accuracy, 90.8% F1 score, 83.7% precision, and 99.2% sensitivity. Our RWMA detection on Aster dataset results are presented in Table 5.

Table 5. Quantitative analysis of RWMA detection on Aster dataset

Window size	Accuracy	Recall	F1 score	Precision
7	0.9141	0.9922	0.9080	0.870

The above results of RWMA detection models show that we can accurately detect RWMA either using HMC-QU or MIMS dataset. By using the HMC-QU dataset we can only determine whether the patient has RWMA or not inspecting the entire LV region as one large segment. Using the Aster dataset we can further predict which portion of the LV region have RWMA. We can conclude that increasing LV segmentation accuracy must increase the RWMA detection accuracy.

5   Conclusion

Automatic detection of RWMA using echocardiographic images will assist medical experts. In this study, we have implemented two different models for the segmentation of LV region and detection of RWMA using two different datasets. Using the HMC-QU dataset, we have created the UNET model, which segments the entire LV region, and the 3D CNN model, which detects RWMA in segment-concatenated temporal windows. A similar approach was followed for the Aster dataset, except the LV region was again split into seven different regions. Our task was to detect RWMA in all seven segments. Our results show that RWMA detection using the HMC-QU dataset outperformed existing models in predicting RWMA. The UNET model created using the Aster dataset was satisfactory, giving good results even after using seven segments. Further, RWMA detection performance was comparable to existing methods. In future studies, we can integrate attention modules that perform feature fine-tuning at the spatial and channel levels to boost local features while suppressing irrelevant information.

Data Availibility Statement. Due to privacy and security considerations, the Aster datasets produced during this study are not publically available, but are available from the corresponding author upon reasonable request.

References

1. Tsao, C.W., et al.: Heart disease and stroke statistics-2022 update: a report from the American heart association. Circulation **145**(8), e153–e639 (2022)
2. Golubnitschaja, O., et al.: Ischemic stroke of unclear aetiology: a case-by-case analysis and call for a multi-professional predictive, preventive and personalised approach. EPMA J. 1–11 (2022)
3. American Heart Association Writing Group on Myocardial Segmentation, Registration for Cardiac Imaging:, Manuel D Cerqueira, Weissman, et al. Standardized

myocardial segmentation and nomenclature for tomographic imaging of the heart: a statement for healthcare professionals from the cardiac imaging committee of the council on clinical cardiology of the american heart association. Circulation, 105(4), 539–542 (2002)

4. Kusunose, K., et al.: A deep learning approach for assessment of regional wall motion abnormality from echocardiographic images. Cardiovasc. Imaging, 13(2_Part_1), 374–381 (2020)

5. Huang, M.-S., Wang, C.-S., Chiang, J.-H., Liu, P.-Y., Tsai, W.-C.: Automated recognition of regional wall motion abnormalities through deep neural network interpretation of transthoracic echocardiography. Circulation **142**(16), 1510–1520 (2020)

6. Degerli, A., et al.: Early detection of myocardial infarction in low-quality echocardiography. IEEE Access **9**, 34442–34453 (2021)

7. Yu, Y., Acton, S.T.: Speckle reducing anisotropic diffusion. IEEE Trans. Image Process. **11**(11), 1260–1270 (2002)

8. Kiranyaz, S., et al.: Left ventricular wall motion estimation by active polynomials for acute myocardial infarction detection. IEEE Access **8**, 210301–210317 (2020)

9. Hamila, O., et al.: Fully automated 2D and 3D convolutional neural networks pipeline for video segmentation and myocardial infarction detection in echocardiography. Multimedia Tools Appl. **81**(26), 37417–37439 (2022)

10. Moghaddasi, H., Nourian, S.: Automatic assessment of mitral regurgitation severity based on extensive textural features on 2d echocardiography videos. Comput. Biol. Med. **73**, 47–55 (2016)

11. Lin, X., et al.: Echocardiography-based AI detection of regional wall motion abnormalities and quantification of cardiac function in myocardial infarction. Front. Cardiovas. Med. **9**, 903660 (2022)

Enhancing Computer Vision Performance: A Hybrid Deep Learning Approach with CNNs and Vision Transformers

Abha Singh Sardar[✉] and Vivek Ranjan

Department of Computer Science and Engineering, Maulana Azad National Institute
of Technology, Bhopal, Madhya Pradesh, India
abha.pratiti27@gmail.com

Abstract. This article explores the growing prominence of deep learning algorithms in computer vision tasks, focusing on the strengths and weaknesses of Convolutional Neural Networks and Vision Transformers (ViTs). Convolutional Neural Network (CNNs) have dominated computer vision tasks since their inception due to their ability to identify features irrespective of their location, scale, or orientation. However, their efficiency is limited, particularly in managing long-range dependencies. Conversely, Vision Transformers (ViTs), while high performing, are "data-hungry" and require substantial training data to reach their full potential, posing a significant obstacle in areas with limited data availability such as healthcare and plant pathology. To address these limitations, we propose a hybrid approach that integrates the strengths of both CNNs and ViTs, aiming to create a robust model that is efficient with a range of data sizes. Testing on the Plant Disease and Tomato Leaf Disease Classification datasets demonstrates the efficacy of our model, with a marked improvement in F1 score, accuracy, and a significant reduction in loss compared to the base CNN. These findings demonstrate the potential of the suggested method in identifying plant diseases, making a significant contribution to advancements in agricultural technology. This research initiates a crucial discussion on balancing performance and practical data constraints in the fast-evolving field of deep learning.

Keywords: Convolutional Neural Networks (CNNs) · Vision Transformers (ViTs) · Image classification · Plant Disease · Limited data

1 Introduction

The field of deep learning is witnessing a rapid rise in demand and continuous advancements with new algorithms emerging each year. These algorithms often outperform their predecessors in accuracy and learning speed. Deep learning is especially well-known for its effectiveness in tasks related to computer vision, such as object detection and classifying images. CNNs are a specific type

© The Author(s), under exclusive license to Springer Nature Switzerland AG 2024
H. Kaur et al. (Eds.): CVIP 2023, CCIS 2010, pp. 591–602, 2024.
https://doi.org/10.1007/978-3-031-58174-8_49

of neural network extensively applied in these tasks and generally outperform other deep learning techniques, including Recurrent Neural Networks (RNNs), Long Short-Term Memory (LSTM) networks, and traditional Artificial Neural Networks (ANNs) [1].

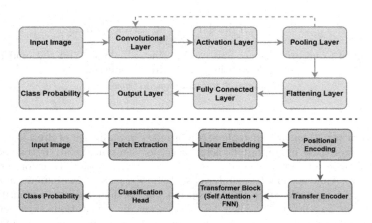

Fig. 1. Comparative workflow Analysis of CNN and Vision Transformer Approaches.

Since the introduction of AlexNet [2], CNNs have become a cornerstone in computer vision due to their effective convolutional layers and inbuilt spatial invariance. The efficiency of CNNs is attributed to sparse interactions, weight sharing, and equivariant representations. These features, along with pooling layers, allow CNNs to detect features and objects regardless of their location, scale, or orientation in the image [3].

CNNs have shown superior performance on smaller datasets and efficiency over transformer models due to their lower training time, data requirements, and fewer needed parameters. However, they have limitations in handling long-range dependencies compared to attention mechanisms. However, CNNs continue to play a crucial role within the realm of computer vision.

The world of deep learning has recently shifted its attention towards transformers due to their sharp rise in popularity. This wave of interest was triggered following the publication of a pioneering paper titled "Attention Is All You Need" [4]. Despite the paper's primary focus being natural language processing, the concepts introduced have stirred up a whirlwind of research around transformer and attention-based models, extending its reach even into the domain of computer vision.

Dosovitskiy et al. [5] introduced the Vision Transformer (ViT), which utilizes raw image patches as inputs for visual categorization tasks. Though ViTs have good performance, they require significantly more training data compared to traditional CNNs. When both ViTs and Residual Networks (ResNets, a type of CNN) are trained on a similar data set like ImageNet [6], ResNets generally perform better. This can be attributed to CNNs' intrinsic qualities such as locality, translation invariance, and hierarchical organization, which are lacking in the ViT model. Due to the absence of these features, ViTs require a substantial amount of training data to reach their full potential, making them more "data-hungry" than CNNs. This highlights the need for a balance between performance and practical constraints like data availability in deep learning.

The "data-hungry" nature of transformer models poses significant challenges in areas with limited data availability, such as healthcare research and plant pathology. These fields often don't have access to large datasets like ImageNet, making it harder for them to take advantage of these models. This issue hampers research progress and limits the applicability of these models due to the high computational resources they require.

In healthcare, for instance, acquiring enough image samples of a rare disease for training can be difficult. Furthermore, pre-training models on similar data might not be effective, as medical problems often differ substantially from the domains of available pre-trained models. It's also observed that a model's performance on a dataset like ImageNet doesn't necessarily translate to success in other domains. While self-attention mechanisms provided by transformers could potentially benefit fields with limited data, they can't be overly "data-hungry." Therefore, there is an increasing demand to create effective methods that can perform well with smaller datasets, particularly for fields that are different from typical data-rich domains like computer vision and natural language processing.

ViTs and CNNs each have their unique strengths that make them well-suited for statistical inference and prediction, but they also come with their own set of challenges. In our work, we aim to integrate the beneficial features of both ViT and CNN architectures, formulating a framework that can extract significant characteristics from images while also preserving spatial invariance. This would enable the network to facilitate sparse interactions and weight sharing, traits that are central to efficient computational processing.

While CNNs have proven to be effective for small datasets, transformers, on the other hand, have a notorious reputation for being "data-hungry" and often underperform when dealing with smaller datasets. To navigate around these limitations, our approach entails developing a combined framework that harnesses the strengths of both CNNs and ViTs. This methodology aims to create a more robust and flexible model that performs well across a range of different data sizes.

Additionally, we will be diverging from conventional practices by not applying our model on standard benchmarked datasets. The rationale behind this decision is that pre-trained models already exist for these datasets, thus offering limited potential for innovation or improvement. Instead, we have chosen to implement our model on the datasets of plant diseases [8] and Tomato Leaf Disease Classification images [7]. These datasets not only provide a more unique testing ground but also offer opportunities to make substantial contributions to areas of significant societal and scientific relevance.

1. The research article analyzes the advantages and limitations of ViTs and CNNs, highlighting the necessity for techniques that perform effectively with limited data.
2. The proposed method presents an innovative approach that combines ViTs and CNNs, aiming to build a model that can accurately interpret both smaller and larger datasets by leveraging the strengths of these two architectures.
3. The proposed model is evaluated on datasets of plant diseases and Tomato Leaf Disease Classification images, demonstrating a commitment towards impactful and relevant applications in areas with data scarcity.

The rest of this article is arranged in this way: In Sect. 2, we discuss about past work that has been done on CNN and Vision Transformer. Section 3 is about the new method we are suggesting, which is a hybrid of CNN and Vision Transformer. Then, in Sect. 4, we show the results we got from testing our new method on different data sets. Finally, Sect. 5 wraps up the research article with a conclusion and a look at what we plan to do in the future.

2   Related Work

The application of CNNs in image classification, an essential task in the domain of computer vision, has led to significant advancements. Image classification involves assigning an image to one of several predefined categories. In this task, a CNN takes an input image, processes it, and classifies it under a certain category.

CNNs approach this task by learning image features automatically during the training process, without any need for manual feature extraction. The architecture typically starts with a sequence of convolutional and pooling layers to generate feature maps from the image. These layers work hierarchically, capturing low-level features like edges and textures in the initial layers, then composing them into more complex, high-level features in the deeper layers.

The last layers of a CNN consist of fully connected layers, which merge the extracted high-level features to generate the final classification. In Fig. 1 layers interpret the content of the image based on the feature analysis performed by the preceding convolutional layers.

A well-known instance of a CNN being used for image classification is AlexNet, which was developed by Krizhevsky et al. [2]. This deep CNN notably won the 2012 ImageNet competition, significantly reducing the error rates previously seen and revolutionizing the field of image classification. Since then, more advanced CNN architectures, such as VGG, GoogLeNet, and ResNet, have been developed, each bringing further enhancements and efficiencies to the task of image classification.

2.1   Convolutional Neural Network

The Convolutional Neural Network (CNN) is a cornerstone technology in the field of deep learning, particularly when it comes to computer vision tasks. Since its inception, it has consistently proven its worth through outstanding performances across a variety of applications, prompting extensive research and review of its principles, capabilities, and limitations. CNNs, at their most basic level, are multilayer neural networks designed to process data with a grid-like topology, most commonly an image [9]. The origin of CNNs can be traced back to the 1980 s, but it wasn't until the development of more powerful computational resources and larger datasets that CNNs became a popular choice for machine learning practitioners. The groundbreaking research of Krizhevsky et al., [2] that introduced AlexNet, a deep CNN, marked a turning point in the field. By a significant margin, the architecture emerged as the winner of the 2012 ImageNet competition, igniting a revolution in the field of computer vision and reaffirming the potential of CNNs. AlexNet demonstrated how the convolutional layers could effectively address visual tasks owing to their in-built invariance to spatial translations. Convolutional layers, the distinguishing feature of CNNs, allow these networks to automatically and adaptively learn spatial hierarchies of features [10]. These layers implement a convolution operation that recognizes patterns of varying complexities in images, irrespective of their position. Convolutional layers achieve this capability through three critical properties: local receptive fields, shared weights, and pooling [3]. Local receptive fields facilitate sparse interactions by reducing the number of connections and parameters, allowing the network to scale to larger inputs. Shared weights in CNNs lead to the detection of the same feature at different spatial locations, providing the model with translational invariance. The pooling mechanism helps to achieve a level of translational invariance and reduces the spatial size of the representation, thereby controlling the computational load [9]. CNNs have evolved and grown complex over the years, with architectures like VGG [11], GoogLeNet [12], and ResNet [6] demonstrating increasingly effective performance on complex computer vision tasks. However, despite their success, CNNs are not without limitations. One of the primary challenges is the handling of long-range dependencies, a feature that Transformer models have shown a superior capacity to handle [4]. Furthermore, the training of deep CNNs can often be difficult and unstable, leading to the problem of vanishing or exploding gradients [13]. As machine learning and computer vision progress, there is a growing trend of combining CNNs with other models, such as transformers, to take advantage of their respective strengths and address their limitations. This fusion of architectures opens the door to novel approaches and further research into the exciting field of computer vision.

2.2   Vision Transformer

Vision Transformers have recently become a focal point of attention in the realm of computer vision, particularly for image classification tasks. Introduced by Dosovitskiy et al., [4], the ViT model deviates from the conventional CNNs and utilizes the transformer architecture, which was initially designed for natural language processing tasks, for image classification. This groundbreaking approach marked a significant shift from the traditional reliance on convolution-based methods in image processing. ViTs operate by treating an image as a sequence of patches, [15] where each patch is treated as a token similar to how transformers process a sentence in natural language processing tasks. These patches are then linearly embedded and forwarded into a standard transformer encoder. A noteworthy distinction is that Vision Transformers (ViTs) can capture long-range dependencies between pixels in an image, without relying on max-pooling or other downsampling techniques commonly used in CNNs. This is achieved through the use of self-attention mechanisms in transformers, which consider the relationship between all pixels regardless of their distance from each other. Despite these promising characteristics, ViTs are also known for their data-hungry nature. The original ViT model was trained on a very large dataset (ImageNet-21k), which contained around 14 million high-resolution images. When trained on smaller datasets, ViTs often underperform in comparison to their CNN counterparts, as indicated by Dosovitskiy et al., [4]. Moreover, recent studies such as Touvron et al., [14] have proposed adaptations to the ViT model to make it more data-efficient. For instance, the DeiT (Data-efficient Image Transformer) model leverages a distillation technique where a smaller student network is trained to mimic a larger teacher network, reducing the amount of data needed. Overall, while ViTs represent a promising avenue for image classification, further research is necessary to fully unlock their potential, especially in terms of data efficiency and performance across different datasets.

The article [16] presents a deep learning approach for image quality assessment by combining CNN with transformers. Leveraging a vision transformer backbone for feature extraction and a CNN decoder for quality estimation, this hybrid framework, tested on various IQA datasets, demonstrates superior performance in both Full Reference and No Reference settings.

This study introduces a hybrid image classification model that combines the feature extraction capabilities of CNNs with the long-range, pixel-level interaction modeling of ViTs. The method employs various layers, including convolutional, pooling, and transformer encoding, to process images into categorized outputs, providing a versatile tool for multiple computer vision tasks.

3   Methodology

Let's delve into this ingenious method that leverages the power of CNNs and ViTs for image classification.

Imagine we start with an image that we want to classify or process. This image first passes through a phase called convolution, which essentially picks out the most prominent features in the image, giving us what we call 'feature maps'. This step can be summarized with the equation Eq. 1:

$$f_j = g(b_j + \sum_{i=1}^{N} w_{ij} * I) \tag{1}$$

where I is the input image, $*$ denotes the convolution operation, w_{ij} are the weights, b_j is the bias term, g is the Rectified Linear Unit (ReLU) activation function, and f_j is the resulting feature map.

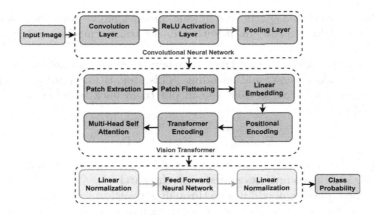

Fig. 2. Illustration of the Hybrid Approach for Image Classification, integrating Convolutional Neural Network (CNN) and Vision Transformer (ViT) models.

The ReLU function then weaves its magic by introducing non-linearity, allowing the model to pick complex patterns. The function is represented by $g(z) = \max(0, z)$. where $g(z)$ represents the output of the ReLU function. The variable z represents the input to the function. The ReLU function takes the input z and returns the maximum value between 0 and z. In other words, if z is positive or zero, the function outputs z itself. However, if z is negative, the function outputs 0.

To control the complexity and avoid overfitting, a pooling layer is applied. This layer essentially simplifies our feature maps without losing the important information. This is represented by $f_{\text{pool}} = \max /\text{avg}(f_{ij})$. where the variable f_{ij} represents the feature map and the indices i and j refer to the row and column positions in the feature map. An average of f_{ij} values is taken.

Following this, the image is divided into small, equal-sized patches. Subsequently, these patches are flattened into one-dimensional vectors, resembling the transformation of three-dimensional objects into flat, two-dimensional drawings. The operation is represented as Eq. 2:

$$\text{Patch}_i = \text{flatten}(f_i) \tag{2}$$

where f_i represents a small, equal-sized patch of the image upon which flatten operation is employed.

These one-dimensional vectors, or 'patches', are then transformed into higher-dimensional vectors using a linear transformation. It's like turning our simple, flat drawings into complex, multi-dimensional objects that can store more information. This transformation is represented by Eq. 3

$$\text{Embed}_i = W_{\text{lin}} * \text{Patch}_i \tag{3}$$

where $Patch_i$ refers to a specific patch (one-dimensional vector), the transformation is achieved by multiplying it with a linear transformation matrix denoted as W_{lin}.

But we don't want to lose track of where each patch was in the original image, so we add a positional encoding. This step is like marking each piece with its original location so that we can put them back together accurately as represented in Eq. 4

$$\text{Embed}_{\text{pos},i} = \text{Embed}_i + \text{Pos}_i \tag{4}$$

where $Embed_i$ is a higher-dimensional vector for a specific patch and Pos_i refers to the positional encoding associated with the patch.

Next, these patch embeddings go through a Transformer encoder, which consists of two sub-layers: a multi-head self-attention mechanism and a position-wise fully connected feed-forward network. Layer normalization is applied to make sure all the patch embeddings are on the same level as given in Eq. 5

$$\text{LN}(x) = \frac{x - \mu_x}{\sigma_x} \tag{5}$$

where $LN(x)$ represents the layer-normalized version and μ_x and σ_x represent the mean and standard deviation of the elements in the input vector respectively.

Finally, we arrive at the output layer that produces class probabilities, which is the model's prediction for the image's classification. This can be represented by Eq. 6

$$P(y = j|x) = \frac{\exp(x_j)}{\sum_{k=1}^{K} \exp(x_k)} \tag{6}$$

where $P(y = j|x)$ represents the output, which corresponds to the probability of the image belonging to class j given the input vector x.

The beauty of this method lies in its unique blend of CNNs and ViTs. The approach deftly merges the CNNs' capacity for local feature extraction with the ViTs' proficiency in capturing long-range pixel-level relationships. Consequently, it proves effective across a range of computer vision tasks, from image classification to object detection and semantic segmentation.

To summarize, this method starts with an image, Fig. 2 identifies important features using convolution and pooling, breaks the image into manageable patches, and transforms these patches into higher-dimensional vectors. Positional encoding preserves the original context of each patch. These enriched patches then go through a Transformer encoder where they interact and share information. After layer normalization, the model predicts the image's class, completing the journey from an image to a classification. This proposed method is a versatile tool for many computer vision tasks, owing to its unique combination of CNNs and ViTs.

4   Result and Analysis

Dataset Used: The proposed model is evaluated using two distinct image classification datasets: the Tomato Leaf Disease Classification dataset and the Plant Disease Recognition dataset (Fig. 3).

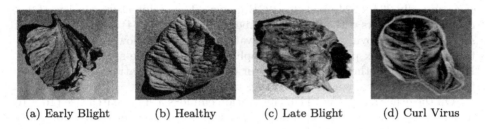

   (a) Early Blight   (b) Healthy   (c) Late Blight   (d) Curl Virus

Fig. 3. Tomato Leaf Disease Classification dataset's classes

The Tomato Leaf Disease Classification dataset [7], sourced primarily from the PlantVillage dataset, encompasses over 20,000 images of tomato leaves categorized into 10 disease classes and one healthy class, forming a multi-class classification task. The images were collected under both lab conditions and in-the-wild scenes. To enhance the dataset, various advanced augmentation techniques were employed, including Gamma correction, PCA color augmentation, image flipping, noise injection, rotation, and scaling. Additionally, certain images were generated offline using Generative Adversarial Networks (GANs). To ensure fairness and consistency in assessment, the dataset was divided into 70% for training, 10% for validation, and 20% for testing, following standard practices. The evaluation covers three metrics: Accuracy, F1 score, and Loss (Fig. 4).

    (a) Healthy   (b) Powdery   (c) Rust

Fig. 4. Plant Disease Recognition dataset's classes

The Plant Disease Recognition dataset [8] comprises a total of 1,530 images divided into three classes: "Healthy", "Powdery", and "Rust", making it a multi-class classification task. Just like the Tomato Leaf Disease Classification dataset, this dataset is also partitioned into 70% for training, 10% for validation, and 20%

for testing. The evaluation metrics used for this dataset are identical to those of the Tomato Leaf Disease Classification dataset, ensuring a uniform basis of comparison across datasets.

Experimental Setup: The experiment employs a hybrid model combining a Convolutional Neural Network (CNN) and a Vision Transformer (ViT) Fig. 2. For the CNN configuration, the input layer accommodates images of a consistent size, typically 224×224 pixels for RGB images. The architecture consists of 2–3 convolutional layers with a limited number of filters (32 or 64) and a small kernel size (3×3), employing the ReLU activation function. Following each convolutional layer, a max pooling layer is applied to decrease the spatial dimensions. Regularization methods such as dropout or batch normalization are added after the pooling layers to control overfitting.

On the other hand, the ViT configuration employs a small patch size (16×16 or 32×32), allowing detailed information capture despite increased computational complexity. The model consists of a small number of layers (12 layers) for efficiency, with a moderate number of heads (8 heads) in the multi-head self-attention mechanism. The hidden size, referring to the dimension of the input tokens and the output layer, is set to 768, while the hidden layer size in the feed-forward network is 3072. Regularization in the transformer is achieved through dropout or layer normalization. Finally, the model's output layer consists of a dense layer with a number of units equal to the class count, which is 11 and 3 in this scenario. The activation function used is softmax. All experiments were performed on a 16 GB NVIDIA Tesla T4 GPU, utilizing PyTorch.

Results: The evaluation of the proposed approach's performance compared to the base Convolutional Neural Network (CNN) reveals significant improvements in both the Plant Disease Dataset and the Tomato Disease Dataset, as shown in Tables 1 and 2. In the Plant Disease Dataset (Table 1), the proposed approach outperformed the base CNN across all metrics in both training and validation phases. Specifically, the F1 score increased from 0.8711 to 0.9522 and the accuracy increased from 0.8835 to 0.9646 in the training phase. The loss was reduced significantly from 0.4154 to 0.0439. Similarly, in the validation phase, the proposed approach also yielded better results with an F1 score of 0.9138, an accuracy of 0.9084, and a reduced loss of 0.1734, compared to the base CNN's F1 score of 0.7978, accuracy of 0.8254, and loss of 0.4611.

Table 1. Comparison of CNN and Proposed Method on the Plant Disease Dataset

	Base CNN			Proposed Approach		
	F1 Score	Accuracy	Loss	F1 Score	Accuracy	Loss
Train	0.8711	0.8835	0.4154	0.9522	0.9646	0.0439
Validation	0.7978	0.8254	0.4611	0.9138	0.9084	0.1734
Test	0.8842	0.9068	0.3182	0.9819	0.9263	0.0956

Table 2. Comparison of CNN and Proposed Method on the Tomato Disease Dataset

	Base CNN			Proposed Approach		
	F1 Score	Accuracy	Loss	F1 Score	Accuracy	Loss
Train	0.9505	0.9565	0.2261	0.9829	0.9856	0.0503
Validation	0.9404	0.9476	0.2632	0.9636	0.9750	0.1043
Test	0.9608	0.9724	0.2108	0.9947	0.9823	0.0343

The comparison between the proposed approach and the base CNN on the Tomato Disease Dataset (Table 2) also exhibited improved performance metrics with the proposed approach. In the training phase, the proposed approach achieved an F1 score of 0.9829, an accuracy of 0.9856, and a significantly reduced loss of 0.0503. In contrast, the base CNN had an F1 score of 0.9505, an accuracy of 0.9565, and a loss of 0.7261. In the validation phase, the proposed approach continued to outperform the base CNN, achieving an F1 score of 0.9636, an accuracy of 0.9750, and a loss of 0.1043, compared to the base CNN's respective values of 0.9404, 0.9476, and 0.7632 respectively.

In summary, the proposed approach demonstrates a significant enhancement compared to the base CNN on both datasets. This demonstrates the potential efficacy of the proposed approach in recognizing plant diseases, which is of critical importance in advancing agricultural technology.

5   Conclusion and Future Work

This study highlights the potential of a hybrid model, blending the strengths of CNNs and Vision Transformers for computer vision tasks. This novel model efficiently deals with data limitations, an issue prevalent in various domains, such as healthcare and plant pathology. Significant improvements were observed in the Plant Disease and Tomato Leaf Disease Classification datasets, where the hybrid model outperformed the basic CNN across multiple parameters, contributing notably to the progress of agricultural technology by enhancing plant disease recognition accuracy.

Nevertheless, the journey doesn't stop here. Future work could focus on refining the model for specific tasks or different fields with scarce data, to explore its adaptability. As the deep learning arena evolves, incorporating emerging techniques into our model could keep our approach at the forefront of advancements. Furthermore, while our model addresses ViTs' "data-hungry" aspect to a degree, further exploration is needed to devise strategies for reducing data requirements without compromising performance, extending the usability of such models to even more data-scarce scenarios.

Conclusively, this study emphasizes the necessity of harmonizing performance and practical data constraints in deep learning, a perspective that we anticipate will stimulate future innovation and widen the application spectrum of deep learning across various domains.

References

1. Teuwen, J., Moriakov, N.: Convolutional neural networks. In: Handbook of Medical Image Computing and Computer Assisted Intervention, pp. 481–501. Academic Press, 1 January 2020
2. Krizhevsky, A., Sutskever, I., Hinton, G.E.: ImageNet classification with deep convolutional neural networks. In: Advances in Neural Information Processing Systems, vol. 25 (2012)
3. Heaton, J.: Ian Goodfellow, Yoshua Bengio, and Aaron Courville: deep learning. Genetic Program. Evolvable Mach. 19(1-2), 305–307 (2018). The MIT Press, 2016, 800 pp, ISBN: 0262035618
4. Vaswani, A., et al. Attention is all you need. In: Advances in Neural Information Processing Systems, vol. 30 (2017)
5. Dosovitskiy, A., et al.: An image is worth 16×16 words: transformers for image recognition at scale. arXiv preprint arXiv:2010.11929, 22 Oct 2020
6. He, K., Zhang, X., Ren, S., Sun, J.: Deep residual learning for image recognition. In: Proceedings of the IEEE Conference on Computer Vision and Pattern Recognition, pp. 770–778 (2016)
7. Arjun Pandian, J., Gopal, G., Huang, M.-L., Chang, Y.-H.: Tomato disease multiple sources [Data set]. Kaggle (2022). https://doi.org/10.34740/KAGGLE/DSV/4270691
8. Plant disease recognition dataset. https://www.kaggle.com/datasets/rashikrahmanpritom/plant-disease-recognition-dataset. Accessed 1 July 2023
9. LeCun, Y., Bottou, L., Bengio, Y., Haffner, P.: Gradient-based learning applied to document recognition. Proc. IEEE 86(11), 2278–324 (1998)
10. Zeiler, M.D., Fergus, R.: Visualizing and understanding convolutional networks. In: Fleet, D., Pajdla, T., Schiele, B., Tuytelaars, T. (eds.) ECCV 2014. LNCS, vol. 8689, pp. 818–833. Springer, Cham (2014). https://doi.org/10.1007/978-3-319-10590-1_53
11. Simonyan, K., Zisserman, A.: Very deep convolutional networks for large-scale image recognition. arXiv preprint arXiv:1409.1556, 4 September 2014
12. Szegedy C., et al.: Going deeper with convolutions. In: Proceedings of the IEEE Conference on Computer Vision and Pattern Recognition, pp. 1–9 (2015)
13. Hochreiter, S., Bengio, Y., Frasconi, P., Schmidhuber, J.: Gradient flow in recurrent nets: the difficulty of learning long-term dependencies (2001)
14. Touvron, H., Cord, M., Douze, M., Massa, F., Sablayrolles, A., Jégou, H.: Training data-efficient image transformers & distillation through attention. In: International Conference on Machine Learning, pp. 10347–10357. PMLR, 1 July 2021
15. Baffour, A.A., Qin, Z., Wang, Y., Qin, Z., Choo, K.K.: Spatial self-attention network with self-attention distillation for fine-grained image recognition. J. Vis. Commun. Image Represent. 1(81), 103368 (2021)
16. Zeng, C., Kwong, S.: Combining CNN and transformers for full-reference and no-reference image quality assessment. Neurocomputing 13, 126437 (2023)

CED-Net: A Generalized Deep Wide Model for Covid Detection

Shivani Manoj Toshniwal[1], P. Pranav[1], M. N. Toshniwal[2], M. Srinivas[1], and P. Radha Krishna[1(✉)]

[1] National Institute of Technology Warangal, Warangal, India
{stcs21109,pp22csm1s02}@student.nitw.ac.in, {msv,prkrishna}@nitw.ac.in
[2] Public Health Division, Akola, Maharashtra, India

Abstract. Attention-based deep learning models in medical imaging have demonstrated appreciable results, with wide models focusing on memorization and deep models on generalization. COVID detection involves different types of CT scan and X-ray images of varying severity, demands a generalized model with high sensitivity. However, the generalization of deep learning models with selective specialization for specific data is still challenging. We introduce a deep-wide structured block architecture (called CED-Net), involving a *convolution-attention* mechanism that combines the strengths of both wide linear and deep neural network models. The dimension scaling of the proposed model by EfficientNet with pre-trained knowledge of DenseNet complements the multi-headed self-attention of CNNs meet Vision Transformers model to effectively generalize the model for varying lesions on X-ray and CT-scan images. By leveraging feature retention and impedance avoidance, our proposed model has demonstrated good performance on COVID datasets.

Keywords: Covid detection · attention · convolution · transformers · neural networks

1 Introduction

COVID Detection has been a significant problem in the past three years. The low sensitivity of the Reverse Transcription-Polymerase Chain Reaction Test (RTPCR) led to the development of machine learning models for covid detection. The use of CT-scan and X-ray images as diagnostic measures to detect covid boosted research in deep learning models, specifically Convolutional Neural Networks (CNNs) as they serve as the state-of-the-art architecture for vision tasks.

Recent developments in attention models such as *Vision Transformers* (ViT) [1] and *CNNs meet Vision Transformers* (CMT) [2] have revealed the merits of attention models for vision tasks, specifically anomaly detection. Medical imaging, involving certain lesions significant for diagnosing a disease, needs attention

H. Kaur et al. (Eds.): CVIP 2023, CCIS 2010, pp. 603–611, 2024.
https://doi.org/10.1007/978-3-031-58174-8_50

mechanism to attain high sensitivity. Covid Detection involving CT-scan and X-ray datasets needs a generalized model architecture for capturing lesions. Challenges such as overfitting, the inability to capture complex features, and learning false lesions prove to be open problems for deep learning models. These problems can be solved by an integrated model involving robust models, resulting in selective feature learning and greater generalizability.

Figure 1 demonstrates medical images of the chest highlighting Ground Glass Opacities (GGOs), also called *lesions*. Figure 1 (a) shows CT-scan covid positive and negative images. Discussions with medical experts reveal that the lesions in these images prove significant in detecting a patient as covid *positive* or *negative*. Similarly, Fig. 1 (b) shows covid *positive* and *negative* X-ray images. Efficient capture of lesions needs an attention mechanism. In addition, intra-patch knowledge involving feature learning from neighborhood patches is equally significant for detecting covid. A deep learning model involving both attention and convolution mechanism serves both purposes simultaneously. We use CMTs in our proposed method, which is a combination of convolution and attention mechanisms.

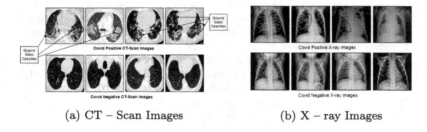

(a) CT – Scan Images   (b) X – ray Images

Fig. 1. Medical Images showing Ground Glass Opacities (Lesions)

Deep Learning models often scale in either of the three dimensions: *depth*, *width*, and *resolution* [3]. Wider models capture more fine-grained features and are easy to train. But high-level features such as low-resolution lesions present in X-ray images are hard to get captured by *highly wide* and shallow networks. Deeper models capture more complex features in medical images and are also more generalizable. However, they are hard to train due to the *vanishing gradient* problem. *Resolution* scaling can significantly capture crisp lesions. EfficientNet [3] is one such parameter-efficient model that uses the compound scaling method to scale all three dimensions simultaneously. We use the EfficientNet model as part of our proposed model to achieve dimension scaling.

In this paper, we propose a generalized deep wide model that integrates CMT, EfficientNet, and DenseNet (CED-Net) models for covid detection. Concatenating the outputs of CMT, EfficientNet, and DenseNet models can be an effective way to determine the lesions in CT scan and X-ray images because it allows the models to leverage their unique strengths and compensate for each other's weaknesses. By concatenating the outputs of these models, the resulting model can benefit from the specialized capabilities of CMT for lesion detection, the dimension scaling of EfficientNet, and the dense connectivity and feature reuse of DenseNet to learn features at multiple levels of abstraction. This can result in a more comprehensive and accurate detection of lesions in CT scan and X-ray images, especially for covid detection. Furthermore, by using multiple models, the concatenated model can be less prone to overfitting and can have a better ability to generalize to new and unseen data. This can result in a more robust and reliable lesion detection in medical imaging analysis.

The rest of the paper is organized as follows: Section 2 describes related work. Section 3 gives a detailed description of the proposed model. Following it, Section 4 presents the experimental results. We finally conclude the paper in Section 5.

2   Related Work

Advancements in deep learning led to new developments in medical imaging. Covid detection using deep learning models gained momentum with the spread of coronaviruses and their acute consequences. In [4], the transmission and recovery rates of the coronavirus were illustrated using Support Vector Regression (SVR). Fan et al. [5] proposed a transfer learning-based method where MobileNetv2 with the Adam optimizer performed superior to other CNN architectures. Ensemble Deep Learning models [6] use the sensitivity-specific weighted averaging ensemble method to detect covid from chest X-ray images. Hemdan et al. [7] proposed COVIDX-Net, a combination of VGG16 and Google MobileNet architectures.

Covid detection was not limited to CNNs. Attention-based models such as COVID-Transformer were used in [8], forming a ViT-based deep learning pipeline for covid detection. A dense attention mechanism-based network (DAM-Net) for COVID-19 detection in CXR was described in [9], which is composed of dense layers, channel attention layers, an adaptive downsampling layer, and a label smoothing regularization loss function. The Residual Attention Network [10] involves a combination of residual connections and attention mechanisms, resulting in appreciable results. An attention-based VGG-16 [11] model was used for covid X-ray image classification.

Various CNN architectures such as ResNets [12], SqueezeNet [13], Xception, and VGG are fine-tuned to detect covid. Some of the existing architectures related to covid detection are COVID-CAPS [14], COVID-Net [15], Coro-Net [16], and DarkCovid Net [17]. A YOLOv5 network-based model using CT-scan images was proposed in [18]. In [19], Fractal Dimension Texture Analysis (FDTA) and Gray Level Co-occurrence Matrix (GLCM) were compared. Their results show better performance with the texture feature extraction method FDTA for 3-class classification. Many models use depth-wise convolutions [20] for optimizing computations. CMT uses depthwise convolutions to decrease key and value matrix sizes to reduce computations. CMT is one of the components in our proposed model.

CT-scan and X-ray image lesions vary in nature. There exists a need for a model that can handle lesions in both CT-scan and X-ray images, generalizing the model. Existing methods face difficulty in generalization due to reasons such as single-dimension scaling and overfitting. The types of features captured by wide models do not get captured by deep models, and vice versa. Challenges such as detecting lesions lying within crisp class boundaries, differential learning of lesions following type of image, and spatial and structural feature extraction remain open problems. We integrate three robust models, namely CMT, EfficientNet, and DenseNet, for feature retention and impedance avoidance.

3   Proposed Method

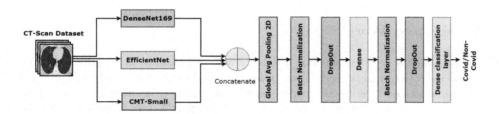

Fig. 2. Block Diagram of CED-Net

Figure 2 represents the block diagram of the proposed model, CED-Net. We combine the multiheaded self-attention of CMT with pre-trained EfficientNet and DenseNet CNN architectures through concatenation. EfficientNet performs efficient compound scaling in three dimensions: width (w), depth (d), and resolution (r). It balances the tradeoff of dimension scaling (see equation (1)).

$$
\begin{aligned}
&depth: d = \alpha^{\phi} \\
&width: w = \beta^{\phi} \\
&resolution: r = \gamma^{\phi} \\
&s.t. \quad \alpha \cdot \beta^2 \cdot \gamma^2 \equiv 2 \\
&\alpha \geq 1, \beta \geq 1, \gamma \geq 1
\end{aligned}
\tag{1}
$$

where, ϕ is a coefficient that manages available resources for model scaling, while α, β, and γ indicate how to assign these resources to network width, depth, and resolution respectively. Let input image X be passed through the EfficientNet B1 model. In this work, we use a pre-trained model as given below:

$$
effNet = EfficientNet(X, pretrained = imagenet, include\_top = False)
\tag{2}
$$

The depth of the model network captures high-level complex lesions lying at the crisp boundary of two classes, while the width captures the fine-grained features.

The input image X is passed parallelly to the CMT model. CMT is performing the convolution operation on the input image. CMT is a staged architecture involving four stages. Each stage has multiple CMT blocks. Each block has three components: the Local Perception Unit (LPU), the Lightweight Multi-headed Self-attention Unit (LWMHSA), and the Inverted Residual Feed Forward Neural Network (IRFFN). Mathematically, these inputs for the ith block can be represented as:

$$Y_i = LPU(X_{i-1}) \tag{3}$$

$$Z_i = LMHSA(LN(Y_i)) + Y_i \tag{4}$$

$$X_i = IRFFN(LN(Z_i)) + Z_i \tag{5}$$

Here, Y_i represents the output feature of LPU, and Z_i represents the output of LWMHSA. X_i is the final output from CMT for the ith block. LN refers to Layer Normalization. Let X_i correspond to the output of the ith (last) block of the last stage. The final output of CMT together can be represented as :

$$cmt = CMTSmall(X, num\_classes = 0, num\_blocks = [1, 1, 1, 1]) \tag{6}$$

Here, we modify hyperparameters - the number of blocks in CMT stages to $[1, 1, 1, 1]$ to reduce the parameters of the overall model. CMT's multi-headed self-attention focuses on the lesions, and LPU extracts features from the neighborhood patches. In short, CMT takes care of intra-patch as well as inter-patch knowledge.

The input X is also passed parallelly through the DenseNet Model. The sparse nature of covid datasets requires pre-trained knowledge for better feature extraction. So, we use a robust, pre-trained DenseNet model. The dense connectivity of DenseNet can be represented as:

$$X_l = H_l([x_0, x_1, \ldots, x_{l-1}]) \tag{7}$$

$H_l(.)$ is a composite function of batch normalization (BN), Rectified Linear Unit (ReLU), and a 3*3 convolution, and the output of the lth layer is represented by X_l. The DenseNet output can be represented as:

$$densenet = DenseNet(X, pretrained = imagenet, include\_top = False) \tag{8}$$

Finally outputs from Eqs. (2), (6) and (8) are concatenated as

$$X' = Concatenate(effnet, cmt, densenet) \tag{9}$$

Features learned by the three models are concatenated, and the output is passed to the Global Average Pooling Layer. It is a layer that performs a channel-wise average of all feature maps.

$$X'' = GlobalAvgPooling(X')$$ (10)

X'' is further passed to Batch Normalization and then to Dropout Layer to avoid overfitting.

$$P = Dropout(BN(X''), dropoutRate = 0.5))$$ (11)

P is further passed to Dense Layer. Here, the dense layer is the fully-connected layer in which neurons of one layer are connected with all neurons of the preceding layer.

$$P' = Dense(P, numberofNeuronUnits = 256, activation = relu)$$ (12)

Again, the output P' is passed through BN, DropOut and Dense classification layer with activation function as softmax.

$$Q = Dropout(BN(P'), dropoutRate = 0.5)$$ (13)

$$Q' = Dense(Q, numberofNeuronUnits = 2, activation = softmax)$$ (14)

Here, Q' is the final output probability giving Covid or non-covid class. Depending on the value of Q', the model predicts whether the input CT scan or X-ray image is covid positive or not.

Using feature retention, impedance avoidance, pre-trained knowledge, dimension scaling, and a self-attention mechanism with multiple heads, CED-Net makes it easier to find lesions. The spatial attention gained by local feature learning units and their structural orientations captured by global attention-based units in CMTs work well with the pre-trained knowledge of DenseNet to find lesions that are hard for base models to find. Our proposed model is general, and the hyperparameters can be tuned further for other medical image classification tasks.

4   Experimental Results

We perform experiments using two datasets : (1) SARS-CoV-2 CT [21] - scan Dataset, and (2) X-Ray covid Dataset [22]. To overcome the sparse nature of the datasets, we perform data augmentations such as shift, zoom, and flip for better feature learning. In our experimental setup, we allocate 70% of the data for training purposes, reserve 10% of the data for validation, and utilise the remaining 20% of the data for testing the performance of our model. We have performed five-fold cross-validation on the training dataset. The model is trained for a total of 80 epochs. Our proposed model CED-Net (EfficientNetB1 + DenseNet121 + CMTS1111), demonstrated superior performance compared to other individual models for both the CT Dataset (97.99%) and the X-ray dataset (97.53%) (refer to Table 1).

Table 1. Results of Various Models on CT-scan and X-ray datasets

Dataset	Model	Loss	Accuracy	Precision	Recall	F1-score	Sensitivity	Specificity
CT	DenseNet121	0.1675	0.9398	0.9454	0.9398	0.9396	0.8845	0.996
	DenseNet169	0.1351	0.9557	0.956	0.9557	0.9557	0.9442	0.9675
	CMTSmall	0.2826	0.9215	0.9246	0.9215	0.9214	0.8805	0.9634
	DenseNet121 + EffNetb1	0.1493	0.9658	0.9662	0.9658	0.9658	0.9522	0.9797
	DenseNet169 + EffNetb1	0.6018	0.8169	0.8616	0.8169	0.8115	0.6454	0.9919
	CED-Net (169_b1_cmts)	0.3361	0.8833	0.8833	0.8833	0.8833	0.8805	0.8862
	CED-Net (121_b1_cmts)	**0.0765**	**0.9799**	**0.98**	**0.9799**	**0.9799**	**0.9721**	**0.9878**
X-Ray	DenseNet121	0.1531	0.9483	0.9533	0.9483	0.9486	0.9134	0.9962
	DenseNet169	0.1165	0.9645	0.9646	0.9645	0.9644	0.9804	0.9425
	CMTSmall	0.2635	0.895	0.9104	0.895	0.8956	0.8324	0.9808
	CED-Net (169_b1_cmts)	0.0857	0.9693	0.9701	0.9693	0.9694	0.9581	0.9847
	CED-Net (121_b1_cmts)	**0.0902**	**0.9753**	**0.9758**	**0.9758**	**0.9757**	**0.9832**	**0.9655**

Confusion matrices of the CED-Net model for both datasets are given in Fig. 3 (a) and (b) respectively. The number of misclassified examples in both cases are 10 and 15 respectively resulting in high sensitivity and specificity of the models in both cases. The model's ability to accurately detect lesions in unseen test images is justified by its lower incidence of false positives and false negatives. The graphs depicted in Fig. 4 (a) and (b) illustrate the relationship between training accuracy and epoch for the CT-scan and X-ray datasets, respectively. In the case of the CT-scan dataset (as shown in Fig. 4 (a)), the CED-Net model achieves a higher level of training accuracy compared to the CMT-Small model. On the other hand, for the X-ray dataset (as depicted in Fig. 4 (b)), the CED-Net model outperforms both the CMT-Small and DenseNet121 models in terms of training accuracy. The model's high accuracy during training provides justification for its ability to perform well regardless of the distribution of data in both the training and test sets, as it encompasses a substantial amount of data.

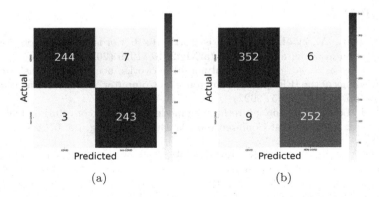

(a)   (b)

Fig. 3. Confusion Matrices of CED-Net (a) CT-scan and (b) X-ray datasets

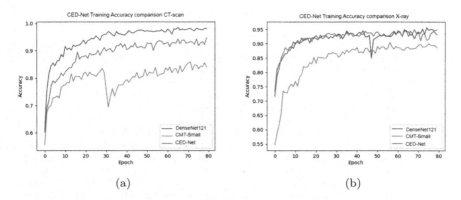

Fig. 4. Training Accuracy versus epochs of CED-Net on (a) CT-scan and (b) X-ray datasets

5 Conclusion

CED-Net attempts to generalize feature learning by scaling the width and depth of the network involving attention and convolution mechanisms. The generalized model architecture resulting in appreciable accuracies of 97.99% and 97.53% on CT-scan and X-ray datasets respectively can be used as a prototype model for other medical imaging tasks as well. Combining the advantages of three robust models - CMT, EfficientNet, and DenseNet into an integrated model - CED-Net, we scale the model in three dimensions capturing lesions that remain uncaptured by individual models. The width and depth dimensional tradeoff gets handled. The pretrained knowledge of DenseNet with multi-headed self-attention of CMT helps to generalize the model efficiently.

References

1. Dosovitskiy, A., et al.: An image is worth 16x16 words: transformers for image recognition at scale, *arXiv preprint*arXiv:2010.11929 (2020)
2. Guo, J., et al.: Cmt: convolutional neural networks meet vision transformers. In: Proceedings of the IEEE/CVF Conference on Computer Vision and Pattern Recognition, pp. 12175–12185 (2022)
3. Tan, M., Le, Q.: EfficientNet: rethinking model scaling for convolutional neural networks. In: International Conference on Machine Learning, pp. 6105–6114. PMLR (2019)
4. Yadav, M., Perumal, M., Srinivas, M.: Analysis on novel coronavirus (covid-19) using machine learning methods. Chaos, Solitons Fractals **139**, 110050 (2020)
5. Fan, Z., Jamil, M., Sadiq, M.T., Huang, X., Yu, X.: Exploiting multiple optimizers with transfer learning techniques for the identification of covid-19 patients. J. Healthcare Eng. **2020**, 13 (2020)
6. Tang, S., et al.: EDL-covid: Ensemble deep learning for covid-19 case detection from chest x-ray images. IEEE Trans. Industr. Inf. **17**(9), 6539–6549 (2021)

7. Hemdan, E.E.D., Shouman, M.A.,Karar, M.E.: Covidx-net: a framework of deep learning classifiers to diagnose covid-19 in x-ray images,' *arXiv preprint*arXiv:2003.11055 (2020)
8. Shome, D., et al.: Covid-transformer: interpretable covid-19 detection using vision transformer for healthcare. Int. J. Environ. Res. Public Health **18**(21), 11086 (2021)
9. Ullah, Z., Usman, M., Latif, S., Gwak, J.: Densely attention mechanism based network for covid-19 detection in chest x-rays. Sci. Rep. **13**(1), 1–14 (2023)
10. Sharma, V., Dyreson, C.: Covid-19 screening using residual attention network an artificial intelligence approach. In: 2020 19th IEEE International Conference on Machine Learning and Applications (ICMLA), pp. 1354–1361 (2020)
11. Sitaula, C., Hossain, M.B.: Attention-based VGG-16 model for covid-19 chest x-ray image classification. Appl. Intell. **51**(5), 2850–2863 (2021)
12. He, K., Zhang, X., Ren, S., Sun, J.: Deep residual learning for image recognition. In: Proceedings of the IEEE Conference on Computer Vision and Pattern Recognition, pp. 770–778 (2016)
13. Ucar, F., Korkmaz, D.: Covidiagnosis-net: Deep bayes-squeezenet based diagnosis of the coronavirus disease 2019 (covid-19) from x-ray images. Med. Hypotheses **140**, 109761 (2020)
14. Afshar, P., Heidarian, S., Naderkhani, F., Oikonomou, A., Plataniotis, K.N., Mohammadi, A.: Covid-caps: A capsule network-based framework for identification of covid-19 cases from x-ray images. Pattern Recogn. Lett. **138**, 638–643 (2020)
15. Wang, L., Lin, Z.Q., Wong, A.: Covid-net: a tailored deep convolutional neural network design for detection of covid-19 cases from chest x-ray images. Sci. Rep. **10**(1), 1–12 (2020)
16. Khan, A.I., Shah, J.L., Bhat, M.M.: Coronet: a deep neural network for detection and diagnosis of covid-19 from chest x-ray images. Comput. Methods Programs Biomed. **196**, 105581 (2020)
17. Anila Glory, H., Meghana, S., Kesav Kumar, J.S., Shankar Sriram, V.S.: Stacked dark covid-net: a multi-class multi-label classification approach for diagnosing COVID-19 using chest x-ray images. In: Santosh, K., Hegadi, R., Pal, U. (eds.) Recent Trends in Image Processing and Pattern Recognition, RTIP2R 2021, CCIS, vol. 1576, pp. 61–75. Springer, Cham (2022). https://doi.org/10.1007/978-3-031-07005-1_7
18. Qu, R., Yang, Y., Wang, Y.: Covid-19 detection using CT image based on yolov5 network. In: 2021 3rd International Academic Exchange Conference on Science and Technology Innovation (IAECST), pp. 622–625. IEEE (2021)
19. Nugraha, D.A.T., Nasution, A.M.: Comparison of texture feature extraction method for covid-19 detection with deep learning. In: 2022 IEEE International Conference on Cybernetics and Computational Intelligence (CyberneticsCom), pp. 393–397 (2022)
20. Chollet, F., et al.: Xception: Deep learning with depthwise separable convolutions. In: Proceedings of the IEEE Conference on Computer Vision and Pattern Recognition, pp. 1251–1258 (2017)
21. Soares, E., Angelov, P., Biaso, S., Froes, M.H., Abe, D.K.: Sars-cov-2 CT-scan dataset: a large dataset of real patients CT scans for sars-cov-2 identification, *MedRxiv* (2020)
22. Ahemateja, K.: Covid x-ray dataset (2021). https://www.kaggle.com/datasets/ahemateja19bec1025/covid-xray-dataset

Author Index

Printed in the United States
by Baker & Taylor Publisher Services